KT-166-003

MONTY PYTHON
ENCYCLOPEDIA

Robert Ross

B.T. Batsford Ltd · London

introduction

Is this the right room for an argument???... well, if you are about to question the fact that a little television comedy series by the name of *Monty Python's Flying Circus* remains one the most influential and inventive examples of British humour, then you're damn right it is!! From the moment that Michael Palin's It's Man first ushered in the pomp and circumstance of the stirring, flag-waving refrain of John Phillip Sousa's *The Liberty Bell March* which heralded a huge bear foot crashing down somewhere around bar 32 on 5 October 1969 a new, outlandish comic genre caught hold of the British public's imagination, shocked the establishment and formed the perfect coda to the swinging sixties decade of revolutionary change in the arts. Almost 30 years later, *Monty Python* has come to sum up a particularly surreal, bizarre and challenging source of comic expression, two words which immediately bring to mind sadly departed tropical birds, copious amounts of a brand name tinned meat and rather dubiously attired woodcutters. Above all, it made lasting star players in the film and television market of its five British writer performers and one off-kilter American animator.

Within the pages that follow, I will carefully and affectionately lay before the patient reader every single *Python* member effort, together and apart, before, during and beyond the halcyon days of the BBC series, tracing the origins of their intellectually driven strains of social awareness and, hopefully, far more importantly than that, preserve the timeless laughter of six truly original comedy talents. Packed full of priceless bits of trivia, full credit listings and great swathes of opinion, this is the ultimate celebration of those wild, wacky, inventive and influential lads of *Monty Python's Flying Circus*.

My first real problem with this project was the format the information would take. It is by no means the first volume to tackle the *Monty Python* legacy, although I believe it is the first to tackle so many aspects of the genre in a single go. However, unlike the *Carry On*s, chronological order wouldn't work, for in between seasons and, indeed, episodes of say, *Fawlty Towers*, came work from the other five members. One could, alternately, study all the *Monty Python* group efforts together and individually tackle the six solo careers, but even this solution is scuppered by the continual semi-reunion of team members on other projects. Like the Beatles, the *Monty Python* team worked so well together that even when the team disbanded, two, three or even four members would join forces on one of their number's pet projects. So, where would *Yellowbeard*

go, under Chapman, Cleese or Idle? Therefore, the most accessible and satisfactory system for me came down to strict alphabetical order for everything, allowing one mention for all projects regardless of who is involved, keeping all *Monty Python*, *Fawlty*, *Ripping Yarns* et al episodes together and building up into a fact-packed tribute. For a year-by-year, blow-by-blow breakdown of key events, there's also the *Monty Python* chronology round-up at the end.

Between that and this, settle down, relax, drop out, tune in and turn on to a generation-enhancing collection of comic nonsense, social comment, nightmarish danger and inspired strangeness. Put down that copy of *A Tale of Two Cities* by Charles Dickkens (with two Ks, the well-known Swiss author), direct all your hard-earned pay on this little beauty and prepare yourself for a journey into the uncharted and unknown world of *Monty Python*...

I'M OFF TO JOIN THE CIRCUS
or Six Authors in Search of a Format

On 5th October 1969 the calm and collected portals of BBC television were shocked by the explosion of a new and radical form of comedy - in the universally acclaimed shape of *Monty Python's Flying Circus*. In retrospect it is almost impossible to imagine a time without The Dead Parrot Sketch being endlessly repeated through drunken stupors in a university bar, but through just under 50 BBC half hours and five feature films the *Monty Python* team restructured the face of British comedy forever.

But then again, was *Monty Python* really challenging codes and conventions or simply following the lead of other, more established comedians? Certainly, like the *Carry On* films before it, *Monty Python's Flying Circus* was the epitome of a growing trend of absurdist comedy which spans back to at least the benchmark jottings of William Shakespeare - the manic pricking of Malvolio's pomposity in *Twelfth Night*/the magical ass-headed antics of Bottom in *A Midsummer Night's Dream* et al. The thread of Carnivalesque, normality twisting, has been the very essence of comic expression since the first gag was cracked, but it is worthwhile documenting in some detail the ever growing anarchic link through British comedy dating back to 1939 (when the oldest Python – John Cleese – was born) and influences were beginning to seep into the *Monty* subconscious, allowing comic variations and fantasies to brighten their cosy, middle-class, middle-England, post-war blues, National Service threatening, stifling existences. For them comedy was an escape route and a chance to pinpoint the absurdity of authority through well meaning but faceless figures of the law, religion and medicine. The major immediate pre-war ground breakers have to be The Crazy Gang (a jumble of three double acts in a British variation on Marx Brothers madness) reigning supreme at The Victoria Palace and addressing the audiences of blue collar, gentry and even royalty, crackling surrealist riffs of nonsensical, spiralling dialogues, deconstructing the art of performance and latching onto pre-*Hellzapoppin'*-like film studio antics for *O-Kay For Sound* – indeed, across the Atlantic, Ole Olsen and Chic Johnson were breaking just about every stage/cinematic convention known to man.

On radio, Tommy Handley, an underestimated founding figure in renewed social comment, insane surrealism and unforgettable characterisations was making the blueprint for Ted Ray, Kenneth Horne and other anchor men surrounded by vocal grotesques with *ITMA*, a show, huge before the war but absolutely all-conquering post September 1939. This was awash with familiar, stock types with unorthodox slants, oft-repeated catchphrases and a fresh, quick-witted string of jokes which, heard even today, sound funny, relevant and very familiar from the back catalogue of everyone, be it Milligan or Ronnie Barker. Although the authority figures are idiots, the British chaps, only naturally in light of the country's community embrace, also outshine the comic enemy. *ITMA* planted a seed (flourishing, albeit with less clout, until Handley's death in 1949) that cross-fertilised with military smut and a dark sense of impending death for those heroes emerging as a clutch of talented comic forces fresh from fighting in World War II.

Although each tackled the system in different ways, they all questioned and reshaped the standard delivery and regimented punchline style of mainstream, music hall delivery. Tony Hancock, really taking his initial leave from Sid Field's flights of fancy, honed in on the absurdities of reality and added a war-weary sense of embitterment, observing the frailty of life with resigned disinterest. Alfred Marks played straight deadpan mournfulness with elements of the droll, while Kenneth Connor and Jon Pertwee injected subversion into character grotesques. Peter Ustinov did a minor league Orson Welles with his 1947 film *Vice Versa* which took an old Victorian-styled chestnut atmosphere and retold the attitude via bizarre authority figures and surreal undertones – later injected into the 1952/53 Ustinov/Peter Jones radio series *In All Directions*. Peter Butterworth, happily tossing in bizarre surreal humour with such nonsensical notions as playing records of complete silence on the radio, quickly uprooted himself from surrealism for film support status and Jimmy Edwards enjoyed introducing inspired madness in a similar through the back-door manner via uncontrolled musical recital.

However, without question the most influential figures at this time were Those Crazy People – The Goons, enlivened by the Windmill-routined rasping and gasping of Harry Secombe, the mind-blowing acting brilliance of Peter Sellers and his galaxy of outlandish characters, the off-kilter energy of Michael Bentine and, above all, the writing and sheer performing genius of Terence Milligan. Although many more performers were on his manic wavelength, none symbolised this era of anarchic change more than Spike. Through innuendo, satire, surrealism and funny voices *The Goon Show* revolutionised British humour, becoming one of the first and most vibrant comedy cults of all time. With the collective fear of battle, the desire to change British wartime austerity and biting comic attacks on class, authority and society, The Goons' influence continues to echo to this day. Back in the late 1950s, when a whole new generation of futile comic minds were tuning into the BBC radio waves for a regular fix of Goonish delights, one young man by the name of Peter Cook would feign illness and listen intently in his room; another such devotee was a certain John Cleese. A decade later, the *Python* team would create a visual response to Goon humour, rebelling in a typically mild and British fashion against the post-war boredom of home life and youthful experiences in various tedious provincial towns across the country. The Goons emerged from war, the Pythons from conforming, middle-class normality, but the result was the same – a safe, anarchic but potent comedy fusion which challenged convention, tackled the introspective satire of broadcasting itself, mocked authority and resulted in total undiluted pleasure for the central team members involved. Even as late as 1980 Peter Sellers was explaining that his Goon days were the most enjoyable of his whole career and the energetic pleasures of the *Python* team at full throttle also literally burst off the screen. However, that vital decade between intent listening to Milligan and inspired flying sheep requires closer study.

On television, Milligan, Sellers and Kenneth Connor reshaped the surreal genius of The Goons for *A Show Called Fred* and *Son of Fred*, puncturing sketch offerings with manic musical numbers and BBC baiting. Michael Bentine's *It's A Square World* based much of its humour around sending up television convention, utilising both the spinning globe and the TV centre into the humour. Anthony Newley's Granada series *The Strange World of Gurney Slade* created its own universe with our hapless hero playing outside of performance convention, enjoying conversations with trees, animals and inanimate objects, reacting against the system of television and, most importantly of all, setting off one of the greatest title sequences ever, starting the catchy theme tune by fingering the notes in mid-air. This edge of surrealism leaked into Newley's recording career with not only a hit coming from the *Slade* theme, but his comic number, *That Noise*, featuring such mind-bending observations as "Have you ever tried to push a wise man through twice his normal fee?" A young Liverpudlian lad by the name of Kenny Everett was already reinventing Goonish ideas on radio long before taking on television. The speeded-up, anti-authority, surrealistic cinematic treatment of the Beatles in *A Hard Day's Night* saw Richard Lester combine Milligan's vision from *The Running, Jumping and Standing Still Film* with sixties rebellion, while very *Python*esque elements crop up in 1965's *Help!* Even the physical comedy of children's favourite *Crackerjack* with roots in slapstick, music hall and pantomime incorporated a disrespectful attitude to official presenters and authority, latching onto the growing anarchic way of humour and, perhaps most interestingly, actually getting away with it within the confines of middle-of-the-road family fun. But that opens up a whole new can of worms.

While the Goon performers were radically challenging ideas, family entertainers were quietly doing the exact same thing within light entertainment. Tommy Cooper, building on the bumbling magician idea with bucket loads of corny gags, contrasted his mainstream act with outrageous twists of insanity which, Trojan horse-like, slipped into the public consciousness. Frankie Howerd's no-nonsense innuendo, delivered with apologetic embarrassment and full-on audience pleading, accepted his place as the desperate jester and so doing, subverted the tradition to become the greatest stand-up of his generation. Morecambe & Wise, the Kings of mainstream, perverted normality by injecting the absurdist invisible ball and bag routine into familiar patter, spinning lyrical tales of lost youth and poverty-stricken times, twisting dramatic seriousness with loutish misbehaviour and forging a shared bed friendship, while borrowed from Laurel & Hardy, remained totally asexual and acceptable in a much more permissively sensitive era.

All of these and more were performing in the *Monty Python*-type field well before 1969, and even the remnants of The Crazy Gang (who even pre-war had stepped well beyond convention) would have been more justified than Spike Milligan in providing their act. But this is taking ideas to extremes and placing far too much responsibility on the Pythons themselves. As Aristotle wrote, all comedy is like a buckled wheel, exploring the normal and looking at it from an abnormal angle. Every comic who's cracked a joke or performed a sketch is turning our world slightly and pinpointing the absurdity. What *Monty Python* did was follow a distinguished trend, inject Oxbridge education and sixties understanding to produce something fresh rather than totally new. Indeed, it could be argued that before *Monty Python* hit home in 1969 comedy greats Spike Milligan and Marty Feldman had been there, done that and buried the T-shirt. Certainly, the genius of Milligan and Feldman were the epitome of this linear pattern of absurdist, off-centre television comedy, but in the end, who really led to whom? Certainly Milligan had been on the scene for a much longer period of time but it was only after *Marty* had scored that he found his perfect small-screen format with the various *Q* shows.

Behind the rise of Marty Feldman the performer (in the ATV series *At Last the 1948 Show*) were the co-founders of *Python*, John Cleese and Graham Chapman. Indeed, the two were joined by Idle, Jones and Palin as writers for *Marty*, while even Gilliam was roped aboard for animation work. Besides this, the early combinations of *Python* folk had already more than left their mark, notably Idle, Jones, Palin and Gilliam with *Do Not Adjust Your Set,* Jones and Palin reinventing history for the television age in *The Complete and Utter History of Britain* and Cleese, Chapman and Idle creating ground-breaking ideals from groan-worthy smut via *I'm Sorry I'll Read That Again*. While the power of Spike Milligan was the driving force behind everybody that followed, his greatest television success came slow on the trail of *Twice A Fortnight, The Frost Report, No, That's Me Over There, Broaden Your Mind, Not Only... But Also* and many other pointers which took his unique vision of the world and perfected it for the small screen. Of course, when the Pythons saw Milligan's *Q* series it was clear that both he and they had arrived at virtually the same comic plain within months of each other. However, Spike was still Spike, the unique genius who, whether dressed as vicar, waiter, Admiral or Adolf Hitler, was always Milligan the star of the show surrounded by experienced actor stooges including Peter Jones, David Lodge and John Bluthal. Whatever he did, nothing could overshadow memories of *The Goon Show*. The Pythons had served a high-profile apprenticeship in front of the camera, but were joining forces on equal terms with a shared vision of the world. Thus, in its simplest, broken-down form, the animation of Gilliam fused with the twisting of television conventions from Idle, the historical elements of Palin and Jones and the overall silliness within everyday situations from Cleese and Chapman. Naturally, these dividing lines blurred and mutated out of recognition, but the strands from *Do Not Adjust Your Set, The Complete and Utter History of Britain* and *At Last the 1948 Show* created *Monty Python's Flying Circus*. With Idle, Jones and Palin aboard Jeremy Issacs of Thames guaranteed a television spot but his continual putting-off of firm plans disillusioned Idle. Besides, with the Cambridge/Oxford meeting being forged when Palin worked with Cleese on *How To Irritate People*, the various tied links (Cleese–Chapman, Palin–Jones, who in turn roped in Idle, who in turn roped in Gilliam) dictated the team's expansion. Cleese, a BBC favourite, was continually turning down offers of his own series in favour of developing the BBC's *Frost Report* format for the ITV network show *At Last the 1948 Show*. Roving producer Barry Took, Feldman's old co-writer, *The Frost Report* pen-pusher and important figure at the BBC felt that combining the obvious potential of the Chapman/Cleese team with the Jones/Palin team would work. (Indeed, an early title was *Baron Von Took's Flying Circus*.) Idle and Gilliam really came along as part of the *Adjust* crowd and certainly allows speculation that both David Jason and Tim Brooke-Taylor were potential Pythons as well. Jason was outside of the university clan; Brooke-Taylor's humour was similar to the urban insanity of Chapman, but despite Palin and Cleese having made the connection before, it was on 11 May 1969 that the Pythons first met after Chapman and Cleese had watched a recording of *Do Not Adjust Your Set*.

Of the six prospective Pythons, the BBC knew the work of all but Terry Gilliam but the corporation trusted the judgement of chief champions Idle and Jones. Cleese and Chapman didn't really give a hoot how the sketches were linked or the edges smoothed, they just loved the idea of total freedom. Peter Cook had told Cleese that if he couldn't think of a decent punchline for some *Not Only... But Also* piece he would just finish flat rather than lose the material altogether. With Gilliam, Cleese and Chapman could take Cook's ideal further with the essence to link these non-punchline gems together. The basic idea was to do a similar-style sketch format to *The Frost Report* but with more challenging, bizarre comedy moving away from the official BBC censoring phrase of 'They won't understand that in Bradford' with an attitude of 'How the hell do you know if you don't let them see it!' Following the first BBC meeting of Cleese, Chapman, Idle, Jones, Palin and Gilliam on that ultra historic day of 23 May 1969, under the guidance of Took, the BBC commissioned a 13-show series with no pilot episode required. Frost excused Cleese from his contract and the life of *Python* could begin, although, at least not before a suitable name could umbrella the diverse talents of the six comic forces. Scores of ideas were thrown into the pot, notably *Bunn, Wackett, Buzzard, Stubble & Boot* the football forward line-up from a John Cleese monologue and some use of the name Gwen Dibley which Michael Palin had spotted in a Woman's Institute magazine and loved. The team were already causing general confusion and raised eyebrows at the BBC. Director General Hugh Carlton-Greene, whose vision and bravery saw the Pythons get a chance to see their series commissioned purely on past reputation, had left the corporation on 1 April 1969 and with him much of the freedom vanished. Allegedly, reputed bigwig Michael Mills, at the time Head of BBC Comedy, dubbed the whole farce a 'Flying Circus' – a term for annoying nuisance since Baron Von Richthofen's antics in the First World War and, indeed, a source for popular culture labelling as contemporary to the Pythons as the 1968 Warner Brothers cartoon *Flying Circus,* while Cleese and Chapman had already served in *Cambridge Circus*. So the lads liked Flying Circus; it was just a case of whose Flying Circus it could be. Palin certainly fancied the idea of giving the honour to his Gwen Dibley and loved the idea of an unsuspecting member of the public opening her *Radio Times* only to find her own series on television. Although it is believed Cleese contributed the all-important 'Python' and Eric Idle knew a chap at his local pub who answered to the handle of Monty, the actual inspiration has been lost in the mists of time but somehow between the six of them, *Monty Python's Flying Circus* was chosen.

In a mixture of title justification and Milliganesque madness, the BBC press material provided a fictional history of the team, embracing RAF wartime memories and military mocking – with the exploits of Terry 'Pud' Jones, Mike 'Smudger' Palin et al. The viewing population probably didn't know what to expect when they tuned in to BBC1 at 10.55pm on that fateful day in October. The Pythons, replacing a familiar Sunday evening religious programme, immediately attracted scores of complaints about decency, while the proceeding BBC selection, an *Omnibus* on photo journalism, a detective drama starring Hannah Gordon and Malcolm Muggeridge pontificating on theological thought, was hardly a prelude to television history in the making, while the *Radio Times* struck completely the wrong note by billing *Python* as a "satire show".

But whatever the drawbacks, *Python* touched a nerve and it's almost impossible to think that in terms of media history those six creative powerhouses burst on the scene an age ago. Other television favourites making their debuts were *Stars On Sunday, Mr. & Mrs* and *The Wombles,* Patrick Troughton faced his own people and handed over the TARDIS key, the Beatles gave their swansong in the shape of the monumental *Abbey Road* and Jim Dale left the *Carry On*s before returning to discover America. Neil Armstrong became the first man to walk on the moon, it was the Investiture of the Prince of Wales, Judy Garland went somewhere over the rainbow and the Vietnam war engulfed a generation. *Monty Python* wasn't a huge ratings success at first, indeed, for the first BBC screenings between 1969 and 1974 the figures hardly got above two million (compared to the mainstream 18 million fans of Dick Emery or Morecambe & Wise), but as I said, it touched a nerve. Many of its young followers didn't understand everything the show was trying to say, but the core of viewers immediately realised that this was gleefully bypassing adult concessions of taste, dissecting sacred cows and making authority a laughing stock. *Python* challenged the way television makers saw the media and certainly saw a new generation of performers tune in a new generation of viewers to the absurdities of small screen convention. It was the complete, dysfunctional nemesis of BBC1's cosy variety show comic format. *Python* never embraced guest stars for effect (a staple and indeed vital part of the Eric and Ernie legacy) and even when Cleese departed and the energies flagged those easy, supportive, spice things up a bit, phone calls to Milligan, Cook and Feldman were never made.

Although the familiar stock company (Cleveland, Innes, Davidson, Booth) filled in the gaps, only twice did outsiders venture into *Python* – the mega huge Ringo Starr (with Lulu in tow) included to abuse/question the importance of celebrity via a throwaway gag appearance and the totally ground-breaking crossover appearance from ITN newsreader Reginald Bosanquet (repeated later with David Hamilton). Thus, the guest star idea was used to smash television's unwritten law and bashed home a powerful message rather than simply using the clout of familiarity. Today the television audience has fragmented for good and the shared watching experience which saw Tony Hancock empty pubs and everybody talking about the Rover's Return fire at work is over. In these days of multi-channel, sky TV, video playback choice, it is almost impossible to imagine the massive war-lines drawn up between BBC and ITV – this was a definitive merging of cultural divides, between the cheap and cheerful entertainment of commercialism and the booming, experienced, educational voice of the Beeb. John Cleese always maintained that the best place to satirize television was on television itself, and via *Python* the notion of well spoken, impeccably dressed announcers, Live from Golders Green broadcasts, high-brow discussion programmes, sports coverage, historical drama, children's television, Party Political Broadcasts and even the sainted BBC spinning globe itself were mocked without mercy. Beyond 5 October 1969 no serious small screen show could ever be taken quite seriously again.

* * * *

This was a hugely important revue staged by the Oxford Theatre Group and providing Terry Jones with his first major break into comedy. The original line-up featured Jane Brayshaw, Ian Davidson, Douglas Fisher, Robin Grove-White and Paul McDowell, with a slant towards the fast-fading satirical style of *Beyond the Fringe*. Having performed the revue with great success at the 1962 festival, it was decided to give it another airing, although there would be one crucial alteration. Paul McDowell had recently hit the big time by providing the clipped 1930s-style lead vocal for The Temperance Seven's classic number one hit, *You're Driving Me Crazy*. Although it was hardly the wisest career move, this knee-jerk popularity kept McDowell away from the Edinburgh Festival and Davidson recruited Jones as replacement. A major turning point by anybody's reckoning. The press praised the cast as superb mimics, although rather too much copy was concerned with their scruffy appearance, while the material was priceless.

Looking at the creator of the tattoo, an anti-peerage Labour MP, a Peter Cookian stab at the Prime Minister and tennis score gamesmanship, the hour-long show was a feast of comedy, music and song. Naturally, it was decidedly *Python*esque in parts, calling on the cast to don women's clothes for some anarchic Tory voters, including a documentary-styled piece on the Modern English Civil War and, most interestingly of all, featuring a "You too can be the life of the party" skit. Jones and the team also tackled the concept of the joke about joke-making, including the Eric Idle-like concept of two joke salesmen desperately trying to enliven the life of some sad punter and the vital, all-powerful Evolution of Comedy routine.

Originally written for *Loitering Within Tent*, not only was this the first ever sketch from the Terry Jones/Michael Palin partnership, it survived beyond Oxford, cropped up in the Cleese/Chapman revue *Cambridge Circus* and even strolled on into *Python* myth with various stage show performances, seen in definitive terms in *Monty Python Live at the Hollywood Bowl*. **** proved so successful that the cast enjoyed a brief run at London's Phoenix Theatre in 1964.

THE ADVENTURES OF BARON MUNCHAUSEN

The final part of Terry Gilliam's growth of fantasy trilogy is, by common consent, the least effective – not as much fun as *Time Bandits* and never as profound as *Brazil*, the *Baron* is still more fun and profound than most movies of its time. The basic structure reworks *Bandits* to a major extent, with a collection of fascinating, magical encounters throughout the Universe, linked with the Baron's gift for attracting danger and his ramshackle group of travelling companions. There are references to other classic fantasy productions of the past, not least the several earlier film versions of the Baron (Gilliam's movie ends with a coda disassociating itself with the 1940s film – a cover due to threatened legal action over allegedly ripping off the previous filmmaker), although other references are more subtle – the great sea monster community, with skeleton-like sunken ships captured in its belly, stems from *Pinocchio* and the whale Monstro; the Baron's escape plan is even the same: making the beast sneeze. There's a subtle nod to Hitchcock with the initial *Pyscho*-like detail of the exact day events took place, and is this the first Hitch homage, Gilliam cameo appearance since *Jabberwocky* with accordion performance within the stomach-incarcerated ship? Back to classic fantasy and the entire project has the feel of Korda's *The Thief of Baghdad* (even allowing the Baron a catchy tune à la Sabu's *I Want to be a Sailor*),

but the major influence is clearly *The Wizard of Oz*, and this is illustrated via the dual role performances from Idle, Thurman and the like. Most of the *Baron*'s fantasy figures have a more solid, down-to-earth counterpart in the 18th-century setting of the Age of Reason. Indeed, his four companions with amazing skills are playing their alter egos in the grand dramatised version of the Baron's life which first causes his outraged opinionating.

This very notion of beginning with a performance within a performance film taps into Laurence Olivier's *Henry V*, which opens out from a traditional stage-bound experience at The Globe to the wide landscapes of England's green and pleasant land. Here, Neville's taking of the stage leads directly into the reality of the Sultan's anger – or at least, the reality of Gilliam's fantasy. Scriptwriters Gilliam and Charles McKeown looked over the book, written by Rudolph Erich Raspe in 1785, and based the film on the exaggerated tales of a German cavalry officer. Although finding the various tall tales perfect for cinema, they decided that the project needed a narrative base. That became the Turkish siege and the *Oz*-like collection of fantasy-distrusting folk whom the Baron regales with his magic.

The basic thread of the film is whether this flamboyant figure is a great hero or a great liar, the Gilliam-minded would fall firmly on the former, of course, while Neville's energised performance is a stunning piece of work, unforgettably making his first appearance wheezing with fury at the theatre poster plugging his story and bringing a touch of William Hartnell's *Who* irascibility, sending swathes of testiness towards his young female companion sugar-coated with grudging affection. The contrast is quite charming (especially with his unnecessary shielding of the Moon Queen's supposed sexual pleasures) while his troupe of friends – boasting lovely character work from Dennis, Purvis and McKeown himself – is completely dominated by a breakneck-speed, cockney mega-turn from Eric Idle.

Both as the Baron's trusted, fast of

foot pal and his actor doppleganger, Idle steals the film with the only totally comical role, throwing in delicious *Python*esque disdain ('Listen cocky!'/'You Swine!'), unappreciated one-liners ('Is there a doctor in the fish?') and merrily following his over-confident master and making the very special effects look all the better with a rounded, solid gold piece of acting. From his first 'Oh! bugger' as his actor persona misses the cue, this is pure, vintage Idle, reinforced with the Baron's initial tale, complete with youthful Idle averting his eyes from the scantily clad harem girls and literally breaking up the floor as he's unshackled to let rip fully with the Billy the Whizz-like action. His bullet chasing madness is beautifully directed, the initial fantasy dash for wager-winning refreshment is wonderfully 'tortoise and the hare' and the distracting jig performed to amuse Oliver Reed's petulant Vulcan is a major treasure.

Reed, in fact, shines brightest of the impressive (to be expected) galaxy of names in a Gilliam film, effectively awash with red in his hellish underworld, rolling his eyes, snarling and generally playing the epitome of evil as a loud-mouthed Northern businessman, injecting Charles Laughton elements from *The Old Dark House* and bellowing with riotously over-the-top emotion, furiously trying to control his temper as he presents the lush Waterfall ballroom. It's only a very small role but he gives a vicious delivery, charmingly fluttering his eyelids, his evil touching the earthbound working community with a stirring rendition of *Men of Herlick* and, best of all, his spellbinding explanation that his button-pushing will lead to total family (plus livestock) destruction. Uma Thurman, breathtakingly gorgeous as his wife, makes her entrance in one of Gilliam's most powerful images: the opening shell with Venus, naked and lovingly wrapped in silk by handmaidens. It's also a nice link to the dead parrot introducing *Python* Venus animation, a link reinforced with the exact image depicted on one of Neville's playing cards.

Robin Williams, a surprise unrevealed guest star does his usual, almost non-scripted comic assault on the senses, embracing two separate personalities – with head attached and unattached – with lustful bodily function pleasure in contrast to his freedom-loving, silver-painted, flowing attitude. It's a manic tour de force which certainly gives the film a jolt of vigour and Gilliam introduces him with a fine shock appearance from behind a cardboard façade of buildings while the final Moon escape, complete with Atlas-like view of the world and astrological map details all around, is peerlessly done. Jonathan Pryce, taking on the slimy, officious quality of his *Brazil* enemy, injects Palin-like accountancy tendencies into his childish war by negotiation, Peter Jeffrey is wonderfully larger than life as the torture loving, black-hearted Sultan, and even Sting pops in for a few granite-jawed comments of bravery before heading off for execution at Pryce's orders because his selflessness may distress the home team. Everything looks wonderful and the acting is top notch, but the characters seem to lack either the heart or the inclination to really grab the story and run with it. The writers string the yarns together effectively and the top and tail battle sequences are well orchestrated, although the continual use of thoughts of war-torn home being voiced by Neville and visually vindicated by Gilliam tends to become a rather lazy tool of irony. However, the various set pieces like the upside-down images in the ocean, the *Bandits*-like cage hanging over dark nothing-ness and, best of all, the *Around the World in 80 Days* homage balloon made out of ladies knickers, work brilliantly, but again, it's Idle's sex-crazed observations that really make this scene kick in. It's only natural that the major on-screen *Python* link should be the hilarious one and Idle works superbly with Gilliam's fantastic, dark directorial touch. For indeed, if the laughs come from Idle, then it's Gilliam's vision that drives this adventure forward, embracing his usual love of macabre

elements, notably the Sultan's delicious musical interlude (co-written by Idle) and played on an organ which tortures captives as the notes are hit, the shock theatrical moment as Neville cuts off Paterson's false nose, and most forbidding of all, the continual motif of death's avenging angel on the trail of the Baron. This overshadows Polley from the very first scene (when the horrors of war are all around and the little girl scribbles out 'Son' on the theatre poster – a deliberately double-edged, feminist blow which is making a point rather than heralding a dead member of the group). This very *Thunderbirds*-like image pops up everywhere, a cross between Bela Lugosi's *Fantasia* influence and John Cleese's *Meaning of Life* figure, thwarted by the bearded hero and ultimately embodying his oft-mentioned fear of doctors. It's sublime stuff and arguably Gilliam's most powerful thread in the movie – brilliantly allowing him to address the difference between real fantasy and theatrical fantasy with a memorable fireball attack on the real evil, cross-fading to a burning backcloth picture of the creature, contrasting the Baron's couldn't care less attitude to dying (asked what his last words are he replies 'Not yet!') with his *Who*/Vampire-like weariness at all this reality in life and finally, embracing the earthbound image of evil (Pryce) as he shoots the Baron from behind the stone statue of the winged threat – thus beginning and ending this story within a story from the same high angle.

A real rip-roaring adventure which doesn't quite get under your skin as much as Gilliam's earlier work; nevertheless it's a stunning example of his flights of surreal imagination. It allows Oliver Reed to stake his claim as the wonderful, scene-stealing actor we all know he is, includes a priceless turn from Eric Idle and, importantly, sees the final cutting of ties with Gilliam's *Python* past as he headed off into Hollywood's inner-circle.

Did You Know? The idea for this film originally came about because Gilliam liked the 1962

Czechoslovakian movie and felt the old man as dreamer ideal was perfect for him. While in the middle of his *Brazil* hassles he struck a deal with 20th Century-Fox and producer Arnon Milchan. The deal folded and Gilliam/Milchan went their separate ways while the reigns of the *Baron* were grabbed by Columbia and a $45 million budget was on the cards. A myriad of problems, documented in both the book, *Losing the Light*, and the film, *Hot Air and Fantasy*, saw the Rome filming schedule hit rock bottom, disasters mounting, the threatened sacking of Gilliam as director and the departure of David Puttnam from Columbia Studios. Throughout, Gilliam clung to his old *Python* buddy, Eric Idle, for moral support. Ultimately, with the problematic but pivotal balloon sequence the project was very close to complete abandonment. Finally, Gilliam saw his film as bargaining power and revenge scoring with Columbia winning the studio war, effectively dropping the movie in order to give a final dig in the sides of Puttnam and seeing Gilliam himself fuel the negative publicity with interview after interview documenting the trials and tribulations of the film's production rather than plugging the film itself. Columbia made just 115 prints of the film and coughed up $2 million for publicity.

Artistically Gilliam's film is a huge success of courage over ordeal, although the right casting proved elusive. As The Great Liar, the Baron himself, Gilliam wanted a great actor who had sort of got lost in the shuffle, receiving no knighthood and no big movie parts but having became a respected giant of the stage. John Neville was the perfect choice, having almost vanished from the public consciousness but standing as director of Stratford Ontario Shakespeare Festival and eventually, enjoying mystic cachet in *The X-Files*. However, Neville had said he had no time for movies, but a makeup lady on the film had grown up with his daughter, phoned him, plugged the movie and discovered Neville was a huge *Python* fan – Click! Several

other actors had been on the cards, but the most likely Baron before Neville's acceptance was Jon Pertwee – would that have been the best ever casting, or what? In keeping with *The Wizard of Oz* homage Eric Idle felt the moon sequence needed a real show-stopping song, à la *Somewhere Over the Rainbow*, to make it perfect. The director disagreed. Sean Connery was originally up for The King of the Moon, but time and money problems saw the filming date put back and Gilliam's plan of a populous of 2,000 floating heads cut to just two. The alteration was smoothed via several dramatic scenes being cut and a lot of more anarchic comedy injected; thus Eric Idle's friend Robin Williams was offered the part as special guest star. In fact Williams had already been approached to play Vulcan, but couldn't oblige at the time as he was needed for *Good Morning Vietnam* publicity. Wary of ominous news from the troubled production and conscious of Williams being in the running for an Oscar, his people would only play ball if Gilliam allowed the star to take an uncredited part in the film. Gilliam wanted regular player Katherine Helmond to play The Queen of the Moon, while Vulcan was originally written with *Brazil* actor Bob Hoskins in mind. Hoskins was filming *Who Framed Roger Rabbit* and third choice, the peerless Oliver Reed, jumped aboard. Gilliam now admits that nobody could have played it better.

Prominent Features/Allied Filmmakers
Columbia Pictures
Baron Munchausen **JOHN NEVILLE**
Berthold/Desmond **ERIC IDLE**
Sally Salt **SARAH POLLEY**
Vulcan **OLIVER REED**
Adolphus/Rupert **CHARLES McKEOWN**
Bill/Albrecht **WINSTON DENNIS**
Gustavus/Jeremy **JACK PURVIS**
Queen Ariadne of the Moon/Violet **VALENTINA CORTESE**
Horatio Jackson **JONATHAN PRYCE**
Henry Salt **BILL PATERSON**
Sultan **PETER JEFFREY**
Venus/Rose **UMA THURMAN**
Daisy **ALISON STEADMAN**
Functionary **RAY COOPER**

Commander **DON HENDERSON**
Heroic Officer **STING**
Colonel **ANDREW MACLACHLAN**
Dr. Death **JOSE LIFANTE**
Executioner **MOHAMED BADRSALEM**
King of the Moon **RAY D. TUTTO (ROBIN WILLIAMS)**
Executioner's Assistant **KIRAN SHAH**
Treasurer **FRANCO ADDUCCI**
Generals **ETTORE MARTINI & ANTONIO PISTILLO**
Gunners **MICHAEL POLLEY & TONY SMART**
Screenplay by **Terry Gilliam & Charles McKeown**
Music **Michael Kamen**
The Torturer's Apprentice music & lyrics by **Michael Kamen & Eric Idle**
Photography **Giuseppe Rotunno**
Production designer **Dante Ferretti**
Editor **Peter Hollywood**
Costume **Gabriella Pescucci**
Make-up & hair design **Maggie Weston**
Make-up **Fabrizio Sforza**
Special effects **Richard Conway**
Supervising art director **Massimo Razzi**
Art director **Teresa Barbasso**
First assistant directors **John Cozzo & Lee Cleary**
Model unit: photography **Roger Pratt**
Script supervisor **Nikki Clapp**
Camera operator **Franco Bruni**
Line producer **David Tomblin**
Supervising producer **Stratton Leopold**
Co-producer **Ray Cooper**
Executive producer **Jake Eberts**
Producer **Thomas Schuhly**
Director **Terry Gilliam**
This film is for MAGGIE, AMY and HOLLY... and now, HARRY
Filmed at Cinecittà Studios SpA (Rome), Pinewood Studios and on location in Italy & Spain
126 mins, 1988

THE ALBUM OF THE SOUNDTRACK OF THE TRAILER OF THE FILM OF MONTY PYTHON AND THE HOLY GRAIL

Although basically developed as a soundtrack album of the *Holy Grail*, almost half of the material was recorded especially for the project, while the rest consists of edited favourite soundbites from the film. With a grandiose Gilliam cover hiding the makeshift wrapping paper

quality of the reverse, the Pythons (with a very active contribution from Cleese) create reams of new material when they could have easily got away with a simple transcript of classic film sequences. Side One – There's no Black Knight or Swallows dialogue; instead, this plays as a 3.10pm screening of *Grail* at The Classic, Silbury Hill, kick-starting with Chapman's enthused congratulatory introduction of this Executive Version (despite the cover's warning that 'This record can only be played ONCE!'), quality graded with only the mouthful of smut incorporated into the initial diatribe. Slimy host, Eric Idle, gives the listener a welcoming tour round the cinema, opened by Gary Cooper, name-dropping a plethora of uninteresting audience members before sharing edited highlights of the star-studded West End premiere with Steve McQueen et al in car crashes.
A mind-numbing Cleese sets the scene for *Grail,* explaining the visual Coconuts opening gag, pinpointing the audience's overdone roar of hilarity and happily delivering a running commentary over the first sequence of dialogue in the film. Ultimately some of the film is actually presented intact, with Idle's 'Bring Out Your Dead!'/old man – Dennis/Witch burning, linking into Cleese's new monologue as a frantic Professor obsessed with logical thinking, 'pure bullshit', a dead Alma Cogan, getting his supper and bedding his shamelessly unfaithful wife. Camelot and the Voice of God setting the quest makes way for Palin's fascinating inspection of the Silbury Hill car park, a bit more of the film (Frenchmen's Castle), a bomb scare in the cinema with Jones desperately flogging filmic treats before the big bang and Chapman's smooth executive announcement of nothingness.
Side Two begins with Palin's impassioned 'Do not play this side!' order before calm Chapman steps in to apologise to us executive record buyers for that 'predatory' beginning. The story so far goes into manic irrelevance with Idle's narrator, before Palin's real story so far is

The lads on location for *Monty Python and the Holy Grail*

quickly usurped by Idle's Bondian adventure, complete with suitable mood music, reappearing policemen and firecracker action. But back to the film for the Ballad of Sir Robin, a very brief snippet of the three-headed Knight (complete with over-played Jones voice-over), the Ni Knights and the impossible herring test hardly getting started before the projectionist has a problem, the wrong film reel is put on and Chapman's laid-back director, Carl French, is interviewed about his new movie starring the late Marilyn Monroe in various states of decomposition/urn interment. Palin's disgruntled interviewer, distressed at the film's leading lady appearing in various ashtrays, finally breaks into homo baiting with barbed comments about Chapman being a 'raving queen' who is into activity with little boys. Not even the promise of James Dean can save the interview before Jones shifts things back to the film with the Swamp Castle/thicko guards/Tim the Enchanter and more new stuff with Shakespearean football matches, Gielgud banging them in and the crowd going beserk. The killer rabbit has his moment, the holy hand grenade sketch is intact and our host returns. He explains

that the cheapskate's version has already finished while we, the people who had forked out more, have another three minutes with some bloke, allegedly Sir Kenneth Clark, saying 'Hello' and what a 'very nice record' this is (it's actually Palin with a nerdy, Goonish voice – swiz!). Chapman defends his word by explaining to a telephone complaint that this was Clark, but with a cold, before Jones rounds up the story, sheepishly mutters that this is it, the ending's mainly visual and whistling, walks out of the studio. Essential stuff, and if you think just owning the film is more than enough, you ain't heard nothing yet.

The Album of the Soundtrack of the Trailer of the Film of *Monty Python and the Holy Grail* – Charisma (CAS 1103) 1975.
Recorded and produced at Sunrise Music and Recording Ltd. by **Andre Jacquemin, Dave Howman, Michael Palin, Terry Jones and Terry Gilliam** Additional music **DeWolfe**

ALICE IN WONDERLAND

Jonathan Miller's celebrated retelling of Carroll's classic tale headlined with a starry cast of performers and retold in dark, mournful tones with a contrasting smattering of comedians playing the bizarre surrealism with haunting intensity. Its swinging sixties, hip cachet was reinforced by Ravi Shankar's sitar score and among its lesser known cast at the time was Eric Idle as part of the Caucus Race, wearing a top hat and drowning in Alice's pool of tears.

Alice **ANN MARIE MALLIK**
Dormouse **ALAN BENNETT**
Frog Footman **JOHN BIRD**
Mad Hatter **PETER COOK**
JOHN GIELGUD
The White Rabbit **WILFRID BRAMBELL**
MALCOLM MUGGERIDGE
MICHAEL REDGRAVE
The King of Hearts **PETER SELLERS**
The Queen of Hearts **ALISON LEGGATT**
The Knave of Hearts **PETER EYRE**
Caucus racer **ERIC IDLE**
Written, produced & directed by
Jonathan Miller
BBC1, 80 mins, Ealing Studios,
28 November 1966

Trini Alvarado, Connie Booth and Michael Palin in a sedate publicity pose for *American Friends*

AMERICAN FRIENDS

If you are looking for the Michael Palin of *Python* or *Wanda* then this will probably not be for you. If, on the other hand, you fancy a beautifully filmed gentle romantic tale, then give this a try. Following on from Palin's autobiographical play *East of Ipswich*, reunited here with the director and producer from that BBC Screen One presentation, this film traces the diary of Edward Palin, the author's great grandfather, who, in 1866 sacrificed his academic career to marry an Irish-American girl he had met on holiday in Switzerland. An untypical venture for Michael Palin, it took him four years to gain the backing and support he needed, while friends like Eric Idle continually told him that a great film lay in the story. All through *A Fish Called Wanda*, *Around the World in 80 Days* and other high-profile assignments this was Palin's pet project. Eventually, with the *Ipswich* venture successfully under his belt, the BBC co-produced this enchanting gem.

It isn't a comedy in any way, although there are moments of subtle humour included, notably via Bryan Pringle's wonderful jobsworth performance and an aged bit of eccentric banter from Jimmy Jewel, energetically cracking his croquet balls. Palin's performance is a model of restraint and respectability, tapping into the stiff upper-lipped, play the game attitude of his *Ripping Yarns* persona while removing the dash of *Python*esque vision which reflected the repressed laughter. There is certainly comment on the lack of sexual freedom of the British male but this notion is never mocked, merely quietly questioned by nagging emotion. The no-wife policy of educational superiors is simply accepted rather than torn apart and even American Connie Booth's condemnation of the English attitude is highlighted as a human trait shared across the Atlantic when both Palin and Booth can't bring themselves to express their love in letter form – his to Elinor and hers to him both remain unposted and rejected. While

the overtly American style of the ladies is instrumental in dismissal from the college, when compounded by Booth's comment this is the sort of subtle, unmalicious but truthful Anglo-American contrast which *A Fish Called Wanda* failed to achieve. Palin's acting part is straight-laced, unsmiling and unyielding, although the first sight his future lady love gets of him is one of singing hymns stark-naked in a mountain stream while her companion (Connie Booth) contrasts the sight with a long-winded, unintentionally humorous travelogue. The beaming smile at the close when Palin finally finds out about this moment is the only sign that the cold shutter of repressed Britishness is completely removed to reveal the old Palin we know and love. It's a stunning performance, played at a sedate pace, with a tangible obsession for his Oxford college.
Both fledging film director and writer/actor are Oxford old boys, with the film's cluttered, rustic atmosphere capturing life at the college, with the quad, the leather-

bound, reverently treated books and shadowy corridors. Apart from his early bath, his stern exterior is only broken with a semi-attempt at a silly walk, although orchestrated by a damaged ankle rather than any government grant. This is an independent, contented, self-satisfied man, whose world of books, public education and male domination is shattered, bumbling through a classic faux pas concerning Booth's father and his work on philosophy, expressing lack of fantasy when dismissing Swiss religious customs as ignorance and finally embracing the fairytale beauty of the location with a dodgy, injury-conscious dance. A multi-faceted piece of work, Palin's biting, corrective dismissal of John Weeks' application to college contrasts with the tender understanding of Elinor's Irish origins, the powerful dinner sequence with Booth – a quite breathtaking piece of acting work from both and, perhaps, most memorably of all, Palin's speech protesting too much about his lady friends, continually interrupting the president's trembling wine pouring and bringing a look of understanding from his chief rival in love/work, add to the delight.
The film is awash with familiar *Python*-geared faces, with Booth joined by *Ipswich*'s John Nettleton and the almost ever-present Charles McKoewn (his rain-sodden fool in *King Lear* is a farcical high point), while Alfred Molina mixes Terry-Thomas-like caddishness with playful, anti-academia behaviour and the wonderful Alun Armstrong creeps about on the sidelines with grinning, Uriah Heep-like sincerity. There's even a touching chance for *Whacko!* veteran Arthur Howard to show some classic school-based comedy with brief support during the college elections.
But it's an awe-inspiring contribution from Trini Alvarado that really brings out the maturing best in Palin, both as writer and actor, with fiery elaborations on Booth's distinguished charity work, touching outbursts of open heartache and wide-eyed, uncomplicated love for the kind and gentle soul of Palin's authority figure.

Tinged with glorious British eccentricity, this is a powerful story of restrained desire unleashed and a shining example for Palin's brave attempt at changing direction.

Millennium Films/Mayday/Prominent Features presented by British Screen in association with the BBC
Francis Ashby **MICHAEL PALIN**
Elinor Hartley **TRINI ALVARADO**
Caroline Hartley **CONNIE BOOTH**
Oliver Syme **ALFRED MOLINA**
Haskell **BRYAN PRINGLE**
Hapgood **FRED PEARSON**
Mrs. Cantrell **SUSAN DENAKER**
Cable **JONATHAN FIRTH**
Gowers **IAN DUNN**
William **GRANGER RUSHDEN**
College President **ROBERT EDDISON**
Pollitt **DAVID CALDER**
Anderson **SIMON JONES**
Maynard **CHARLES McKEOWN**
Dr. Butler **ROGER LLOYD PACK**
Groves **JOHN NETTLETON**
Dr. Victor Weeks **ALUN ARMSTRONG**
Mrs. Weeks **SHEILA REED**
John Weeks **EDWARD RAWLE-HICKS**
Swiss Guide **MARKUS GEHRIG**
Undergraduate 'King Lear' **JO STONE-FEWINGS**
Ashby Senior **JIMMY JEWEL**
Cave **WENSLEY PITHEY**
Voe **ARTHUR HOWARD**
Canon Harper **CHARLES SIMON**
Screenplay by **Michael Palin & Tristram Powell**
Story by **Michael Palin**
Camera operator **Philip Sindall**
Editor **George Akers**
Photography **Philip Bonham-Carter**
Music **Georges Delerue**
Art director **Chris Townsend**
Production designer **Andrew McAlpine**
Production supervisor **Linda Bruce**
Producion co-ordinator **Lucinda Sturgis**
Production manager **Sandor Von Orosz**
Producers **Patrick Cassavetti & Steve Abbott**
Director **Tristram Powell**
1991
95 mins

AN AMERICAN TAIL: FIEVEL GOES WEST

A spirited follow-up to the Disney-esque mouse travelogue/adventure across the States, this may pale in comparison to even the most recent favourites from Uncle Walt's dream factory in terms of animation, but it's a fun battle of good and evil. There are a few sentimental ditties thrown in (although the Linda Ronstadt tune which ended the original picture is cheerfully mocked), a dutifully 'for the right reasons' ending and bucketloads of *Roger Rabbit*-like cartoon convention signposting. Where the film really scores is its glittering cast of vocal artistes, notably the celebration of cinematic Western values from a rasping Jimmy Stewart, brilliantly cast as a weary old dog Sheriff. A disappointing hero to the hapless central mouse character, animated with all the John Wayne iconology firmly in place and delighting in outrageous, obvious dog-related gags in a spiralling twist on Western philosophy. Stewart's last film role, affectionately embodying all his vintage Western figures, is a touching, priceless addition to this cartoon film and if all the references pass over the head of the intended audience it's still a treat for buffs everywhere. Of equal interest here is John Cleese as the black-hearted, villainous cat, tapping into the deliciously rounded nasties like J. Worthington Foulfellow, with injections of refined sophistication, heartless promises (he advises the mouse family from the first film to go West where cats and mice live in harmony). His evil plans (his cor-ruption is highlighted by his mouse-abusing bar and ideas on slavery) are curtailed with typically Disneyesque irony by finding himself cursed to be the pampered moggie of some local dignitary.

Did You Know? John Cleese received a very small fee for his voiceover work as the villainous Cat R. Wall. Asked by Spielberg's people to do promotions for the film he told them rather curtly that he didn't advertise his charity work!

Universal/Amblin Entertainment
Fievel **PHILLIP GLASSER**
Wylie Burp **JAMES STEWART**
Mama **ERICA YOHN**
Tanya **CATHY CAVADINI**

Papa **NEHEMAH PERSOFF**
Tiger **DOM DELUISE**
Miss Kitty **AMY IRVING**
Cat R. Waul **JOHN CLEESE**
Chula **JON LOVITZ**
with **JACK ANGEL**
MICKIE McGOWAN
FAUSTO BARA
LARRY MOSS
VANNA BONTA
NIGEL PERAM
PHILIP CLARKE
PATRICK PINNEY
JENNIFER DARLING
LISA RAGGIO
ANNIE HOLLIDY
LAWRENCE STEFFAN
SHERRY LYNN
DAVID TATE
LEV MAILER
ROBERT WATTS
Screenplay by **Flint Dille**
Story **Charles Swenson**
Art director **Neil Ross**
Music **James Horner**
Executive producers **Frank Marshall,
Kathleen Kennedy & David Kirschner**
Associate producer **Stephen Hickner**
Production executive **Deborah
Newmyer**
Production co-ordinator **Colin J.
Alexander**
Production manager **Cynthia
Woodbyrne**
Producers **Steven Spielberg & Robert
Watts**
Directors **Phil Nibbelink & Simon
Wells**
1991, 75 mins

AMNESTY'S BIG 30

To mark the 30th anniversary of the foundation of Amnesty International, Central Television gave over its Nottingham Studios for a two-hour fundraising telethon on 28 December 1991. The culmination of seven live concert galas which had begun with 1976's *A Poke In The Eye (With A Sharp Stick)*, all of which bar 1991's *The Famous Compere's Police Dog* saw Python involvement. This special includes just a brief case history of Amnesty's work from John Cleese. Hosted by Alexei Sayle, Jonathan Ross, Paula Yates and Cathy MacGowan, the wealth of talent

involved in this show included Julian Clary, Steve Coogan, Dave Gilmour, Steve Punt & Hugh Dennis, Kim Wilde, Frank Skinner, Ian Hislop, Paul Merton, Angus Deayton, Lisa Stansfield, Gregory Fisher, Morrissey, Hale & Pace, Smith & Jones, Reeves & Mortimer, French & Saunders and Tom Jones.

AND NOW FOR SOMETHING COMPLETELY DIFFERENT

The oft used phrase, delivered by John Cleese in dapper BBC black suit and tie while remaining unfazed in outlandish locations, was chosen for the title of this 1971 'best of' feature film version of classic *Monty Python's Flying Circus* television sketches – akin to Hammer's use of Bernard Bresslaw's famous catchphrase, I Only Arsked!, for their film presentation of *The Army Game*. The team's first big screen venture together, importantly the material is not just a compilation of old television successes but newly filmed remakes for a hard-nosed cinema audience. The notion of punters actually coughing up their hard-earned dough to see something which they had already seen in the comfort of their own home was an intriguing one. From its maniacally violent beginnings with super-restrained John Cleese getting increasingly surreal as he happily blows up various Brits in dreadful attempts at concealment, to the mammoth resurrection of The Upper Class Twit of the Year, this anthology of *Python* gold is the perfect 90-minute filler for anyone starved of this unique brand of comedy.
All the film is culled from seasons one and two for the obvious reason that the team hadn't made season three as yet, but there's still enough old favourites to amuse. Indeed, with the benefit of a second chance and with the knowledge of popularity, some of the performances are even better. For me, this is Eric Idle's most energetic and eye-popping run through Nudge, Nudge, while John Cleese frantically struts through the Banana Defence Class with gusto.

Terry Gilliam's linking dub between the aforementioned sketches is a masterpiece, while the pick of his cartoon contributions includes the cancer-ridden Prince, the pram that eats elderly ladies and the grouchy caterpillar transforming into the showbiz-styled butterfly. Graham Chapman gives his military pride the full treatment, shocked by the somewhat suspect camp-it-up soldiers and clearly enjoying the tongue-in-cheek, 'got to finish with a punchline' routine of the dirty fork sketch. Film debutees Terry Jones and Michael Palin do their stuff brilliantly, feeding Idle's Nudge nightmare with constrained displeasure and personifying the boring ethos of accountancy for all time. Palin even has the chance to showcase both his chief *Python* traits – dull dependability and crass sparkle, side by side, as dear old Arthur Putey transmogrifies into the glittering host of *Blackmail* with the merest causal removal of his moustache.
There are very slight alterations to some sketches – the Arthur Putey conflict ends with Cleese's voice of God advising Palin rather than the black-cloaked Westerner, but the end result is the same and any change is simply detail rather than restructuring. Besides any change that allows Carol Cleveland to reveal more than before can't be condemned. In the end, this was a safe bet for the Pythons which didn't quite work. Although they developed their BBC satire from television to encompass cinema satire in *And Now For Something Completely Different* – the film ends immediately after the Gilliam title sequence and Jones as the cinema manager calms the audience and introduces some sepia material of Chapman's tape recorder up the nose routine – this is quickly bypassed in order to present the Pythons in all their old television glory. Seen today this is the ultimate package, and besides, there is the unmissable opportunity to enjoy The Dead Parrot sketch followed directly by Palin's *Lumberjack Song*, complete with Cleese, bemused and distressed, screaming from off camera; Whatabout my bloody parrot!'. Class in a glass...

Did You Know? *And Now For Something Completely Different* was made over a five-week shoot in Totteridge during the November/December of 1970 with most of the interior filming being recorded in a former milk depot in North London – oh, the glamour! The budget was a mere £80,000 and the idea originally came about due to a suggestion from major *Python* fan Victor Lownes of London's Playboy Club, who wanted a compilation movie to promote *Monty Python* for the American student market. In fact it would be another four years before the US began appreciating everything *Python,* but the compilation proved popular enough to make its production costs back fairly quickly in the home market and now remains an oft screened favourite on American television. Akin to *The Best of Benny Hill*, this classic slice of reheated television material surprisingly scored well at the cinema. Lownes, with a tight grip over the production, angered some of the team when he insisted Palin's gloriously grotesque Ken Shabby be edited from the film and instructed Terry Gilliam to give his name the same grandiose, Cecil B. De Mille-style credit design as the film's title. In the end, the Pythons found unfathomable reactions from test screenings, with Jones in particular sorting out re-edit after re-edit. The result proved that people's *Python* threshold was about 50 minutes, for no matter what order the sketches appeared laughs tended to trail off about halfway through. Thus, the film was left as it was and released, put down as a cinematic experiment and chance to perfect arguably their most impressive material.

A Kettledrum/Python Productions Film
Columbia/G.S.F. Organisation
Written & performed by **GRAHAM CHAPMAN, JOHN CLEESE, TERRY GILLIAM, ERIC IDLE, TERRY JONES & MICHAEL PALIN**
With **CAROL CLEVELAND
CONNIE BOOTH
LESLEY JUDD**
Assistant Director **Doug Hermes**
Animation Photography **Bob Godfrey**

Editor **Thom Noble**
Special Effects **John Horton**
Art Director **Colin Grimes**
Sound Recordist **John Brommage**
Production Manager **Kevin Francis**
Producer **Patricia Casey**
Director **Ian MacNaughton**
Opened 28 September 1971, 88 mins
Cert AA

ANIMATIONS OF MORTALITY

Terry Gilliam's ingenious guide to the world of animation, presented by the endearing host Brian the Badger and featuring extensive material from his work on *Monty Python*, *The Marty Feldman Comedy Machine* and *The British Gas Board*. Gilliam discovered that the quality of some of his early animations dictated that he redo them for the book with his *Python* animations revealing flaws when captured as still images. Also, as if to justify the whole venture, he added some completely new pieces. Brian acted as the perfect multi-faceted guide, obsessed by good business practice and greedily spinning out the financial gain behind the beauty of art. Although ostensibly a record of Gilliam's animation, this is far more than a coffee table picture book. The narrative has a flowing continuity, Brian makes an interesting anti-hero and there's even a cameo from the notorious Black Spot from *Python*'s second series at the end. As such, Gilliam's publishers had a field day publicising the work, adapting their plug to suit the publication and pinpointing certain aspects, whether serious art book pretensions, knockabout comedy or a document detailing successful business ideas within the industry.

Lesson 1: Creating Nothing Out of Somethings
Lesson 2: How To Ruin the Pleasure of a Painting Forever
Lesson 3: Discovering the Secret of Cut-Out Animation
Lesson 4: Where Ideas Come From
Lesson 5: Looking the Part
Lesson 6: Meaningless Political Statements
Animations of Mortality by **Terry Gilliam**

with **Lucinda Cowell**
Methuen 1978

ANOTHER MONTY PYTHON RECORD

While Eric Idle became the major Python voice for the book projects and Terry Jones orchestrated the films, it was Michael Palin who took strongest control on the records – here with Jones in tow. Packaged as Beethoven's *Symphony No. 2 in D Major* with a huge black crayon crossing out the classical and proclaiming the Python (with the spine even continuing the gag), later pressings of the record removed the Be A Great Actor, Sgt. Pepper-like extras of instructions, effects sheet and two printed mini plays. This first venture with Charisma was exactly what the Pythons wanted. Although, as with the BBC effort, it's mostly television material, this record is re-recorded and reworked for the vinyl medium (with the studio guys high on dope according to Jones), altering elements of the sketches and adding new items and links for the record. As usual for Python records, the tracks were not listed on the album and no differentiation of sides made the playing order interchangeable but the recognised sequence is as follows. Although the Gilliam cover (complete with hastily inserted, poorly typed cover note by Stanley Baldwin) promises Beethoven, Palin's sheepish announcer begins the record with an apology, explaining that this is nothing to do with the television series *Monty Python's Flying Circus* (despite the hurriedly written cover title) but, in fact, *Pleasures of the Dance*, a collection of Norwegian carpenters' songs. Cleese, quickly corrects this correction with his own apology, injecting a forced laugh into his voice as he explains that this is *Monty Python* after all, quickly illustrated with a burst of Norwegian dance music. Cleese returns to fully reassure the listener, the *Liberty Bell* springs into action and effortlessly merges with the Jarrow bell for the initial madness of Spanish Inquisition. The hosted critic tones of

Eric Idle introduces Gumby Theatre with the brain-hurting, handkerchiefed ones performing Chekhov's *The Cherry Orchard*, Cleese/Jones perform the contradictory interview and there's another fleeting extract from *Pleasures of the Dance* before Cleese goes into insanity overdrive for The Architect sketch. There's another burst of Spanish Inquisition (with Chapman's petulant 'What about fear?') while Palin presents a clumsy classical rendition from The Festival Hall which ends in mass musical warfare. The conclusion of side one is a faithful resurrection of Ethel the Frog: Piranha Brothers. Palin throws himself into the gangland ethos and it's his hired hood that breaks into Cleese's TV links with a few sweet words from Doug, asking quietly for this part of the record to end. With BBC authority Cleese disagrees, prompting Palin's priceless 'He don't want a debate about it!', a rowdy shuffle and, finally a 'Sorry Squire!' as insincere apologies of 'I've scratched the record!' repeat into infinity. A brilliant use of the recorded medium lost, to a large extent, on anything other than the original vinyl version.

Side two kicks off with The Death of Mary Queen of Scots, Pepperpots on Penguins, a few itemised oddities, more Spanish fun with the comfy chair and Palin's embrace of comic convention with a comment on everyone saying 'comfy chair' as an intro to his *Sound Quiz* – guessing the identity of the famous personality getting up in the morning (I won't spoilt it for you. It's quite easy really). Terry Jones presents the Be A Great Actor section, propelling you into the Olivier/Guinness/Harvey league with, following a false start (with coppers Chapman and Cleese reliving *Frost* memories with the 'Super'/'Wonderful' exchange), gaps in dialogue for you to perform the part of Charles opposite a breathless Carol Cleveland. Cleese's Theatre Critic goes ballistic over Neville Shunt's railway time-table plays, Palin repeats the Royal Festival Hall Concert nightmare to the letter, he joins Idle in being a couple of camp

judges and hands over to Cleese's insistent host of *Stake Your Claim*. And there's Spam.

This wealth of Series Two gems is virtually over with the television conclusion of cannibal sailors (with an additional, phoned-in ranting complaint from Palin in a white wine sauce) and the Undertaker, with no compromising ending, before those loveable Spaniards finish this record obsessed with its own non-identity as a *Python* venture with a spot of folk singing – a gloriously Goonish presentation of *Knees Up, Mother Brown*.

A promotional single (Charisma CAS 192) featured an edited version of Spam (utilising just the song section) and the Royal Festival Hall Concert sketch.

The American issue (Buddah CAS 1049) included track listings and also boasted extra items (World Forum) as well as longer versions of Spanish Inquisition, Gumby Theatre and some different linking material.

Written and performed by **GRAHAM CHAPMAN, JOHN CLEESE, TERRY GILLIAM, ERIC IDLE, TERRY JONES & MICHAEL PALIN.**
Charisma (CAS 1049), 1971

AROUND THE WORLD IN EIGHTY DAYS

With Michael Palin just setting of on his more celebrated journey, NBC dished out this version of Jules Verne's classic novel, swamping the screen with guest stars, outrunning Mike Todd's far superior 1956 film and embracing *Python* familiarity with an excellent lead performance from Eric Idle as the faithful, bumbling, passionate and comic-edged Passepartout. Pierce Brosnan, somewhere between Steel and James Bond, seems a tad earnest and certainly lacks the casual, superior charm of David Niven, but this is an enjoyable, faithful retelling of the tale and Idle was given a stunning central chance to wow the States with his own sitcom, *Nearly Departed*, on the strength of its success.

Did You Know? Both the 1956 film and this 1989 TV special attracted tons of guest stars but only one actor appeared in both – Sir John Mills.

Phileas Fogg **PIERCE BROSNAN**
Passepartout **ERIC IDLE**
Princess **JULIA NICKSON**
Detective Fix **PETER USTINOV**
with **JACK KLUGMAN, RODDY McDOWALL, DARREN McGAVIN, ROBERT MORLEY, STEPHEN NICHOLS, LEE REMICK, JILL ST. JOHN, ROBERT WAGNER, HENRY GIBSON, JOHN HILLERMAN, CHRISTOPHER LEE, PATRICK MACNEE, JOHN MILLS, PAMELLA ROBERTS**
Screenplay by **John Gay**
Based on the novel by **Jules Verne**
Producers **Renee Valente & Paul Baerwald**
Director **Buzz Kulik**
Filmed on location in London, Macau, Hong Kong, Thailand and Yugoslavia
NBC TV, 300 mins
Broadcast 16, 17, 18 April 1989

AROUND THE WORLD IN 80 DAYS

Mammoth travelogue, following in the footsteps of the Jules Verne character Phileas Fogg, who set off from London's reform club on 2 October 1872. This retrodden journey undertaken some 116 years later saw Michael Palin become everybody's ideal travelling companion.
Part I – The Challenge. A tongue-in-cheek smoke screen of unavailability begins with Palin's script reading, phone ringing and towering excuses involving movies with Marlon Brando and Nobel prizes. But once that stirring theme tune starts up and the pastel images of Palin blowing up his mini globe hit you, the journey has begun and it's a major television experience. Palin brings his warm sincerity to the project, continually dipping into comic expression and twisting film technique – initially injecting a *Python*esque reference to Proust as regards his heavy reading matter and entertaining his wife Helen with an impromptu Tommy Cooper impersonation. Beginning his

own journey from the Reform Club and travelling in luxury on the Orient Express, a huge chunk of the first episode backtracks and details copious planning for this epic journey across the globe. A few choice words of advice from favourite *Python* figure of fun, Alan Whicker, an impressive nod from the Coutts and Co bank chappie who suggests Palin's film *Jabberwocky* as his international code-word – although the film was released in 1977 and not 1979 as he believes! – and Palin in training, jogging around the place with a T-shirt bearing the unforgettable names of those valiant 11 from the *Ripping Yarns* classic *Golden Gordon*, all tap into comedy heritage past. There's much pride at being considered an explorer, some wonderful innuendo humour about getting his globe down every night and a betting shop visit running a book on Palin's chances, illustrated with a computer graphic *Python* foot crashing down on the odds.

However, this trend reaches its peak with Palin's choice of judges to verify his feat. In Fogg's case it was a couple of bankers; for Palin it's a couple of Pythons – Terry Jones and Terry Gilliam – who join other friends for a meal with some priceless anti-BBC barbs from Jones and the perfect summary of the whole enterprise as to 'celebrate travel', before they say their farewells at Victoria Station and the journey proper begins.

It's a cross-fade into luxury, with a little nap, fine wine and conversation with pipeline buffs. The first stop, Italy, highlights the style of the native man with Palin's consideration that everybody looks like Worzel Gummidge besides them, while our *Python* hero goes one step further by becoming an honorary Venetian rubbish collector, discovering a pseudo-Sheffield Wednesday cup and injecting an inspired bit of comedy with an off-screen splash into the canal. A trend continued with the woman's scream as Palin searches for his cabin, a muttered 'swine!' as the camera catches him sleeping and a warm radio conversation with Helen eagerly devouring the latest football results. An extra stop-off in Athens,

not included in the Verne book, presents shades of his past life with an American fan's obsession cries of *Python*ology and begging for Palin to do his *Wanda* stutter, while happily away from the limelight he twists travelogue conventions by allowing us, the viewers, to enjoy shots of the sea before curtailing the image with 'enough of that!'

Part II – Arabian Frights, takes Palin on the road to Cairo, struggling through an awkward conversation with the owner of Larry the horse and finally introducing himself as Michael Caine, suffering the discomfort of no milk or hot water on the train in stark contrast to the Orient Express and finally satisfying his thirst for football with a manic match in a foreign language. A stumble upon a director of photography allows Palin the film writer and actor to envy the huge production roster in comparison with the British industry and eventually find his way into an Egyptian movie, playing bemused man coming out of lift in a Safeway store, or something. Check it out for your complete, definitive Palin filmography! The theme music, eagerly endorsing and embracing sound-bites to heighten the exotic feel of the locale, incorporates a snatch of the *Lawrence of Arabia* theme as the three wise Michaels, Palin, guide and camel, slowly cross the desert as the 80-day clock is ticking. Stuck in Suez and with Fogg three days ahead of him, Palin's concerned 'Oh God!' at the sheer size of his project is the first sign of pessimism, although his Liverpool-obsessed Captain, Palin's own helpful introduction of a couple of Yorkshiremen and some wacky art monuments enliven this moment of bleakness. However, with the schedule falling behind and no option but to drive cross country, Palin abandons his BBC Passepartout of five technicians and heads off on his own, with a bundle of snapshots to document his journey.

If things were beginning to look bad, Part III – Ancient Mariners, really kicked in with hardship. For the first time, Palin's BBC comfort is seriously removed and the real, sincere, world-

weary traveller is exposed. Palin's honesty shines through from the very beginning, but here he admirably refuses to put on a brave face, opting for admittance that he's feeling pain, illness and exhaustion, while keeping that British pride intact by accepting things as they are and damn well getting on with it. This was the episode that once and for all highlighted Palin as the perfect man for the job, sailing on a dhow, one week late and suffering six days on the high seas with absolutely no radio contact. With makeshift bedding, perilous journeys to the loo and feeling as though he were testing fairground equipment because of the precarious conditions, this is the strong British character coming through with endearing charm. With his refined bathing techniques mocked by the crew, a lovely shared moment of Bruce Springsteen on his Walkman with the dhow's elder statesman, explaining that a bizarre treatment for indigestion is not fit for prime time viewing, *Ancient Mariner* quotations and enchanting images of spending quality time with birds and dolphins, this is quite a powerful television experience. Recalled with affection by Palin, the final warm hug from his Springsteen-loving cohort is a very moving moment.

But Part IV – A Close Shave, breaks away from primitive community into a Wormwood Scrubs-like hotel and a beautiful young Indian girl begging. It's an explosion of poverty and noise with our Mr. Palin joyfully wandering through as the archetypal chap abroad. He's endearingly playful with the kids and desperately tries some Brit small talk banter with the blind barber who shaves him in the open air, wielding a sharp knife and a vacant stare. But the highlight comes when some shady Sid James-like Indian offers him any amount of joints, women and other illegal niceties. With an awkward comical 'You're a naughty man!' Palin sails through with ease, bless 'im! This episode also features a touching, last-post salute to those who died in defence of the British residency and a more personal homage to Palin's late father, adopting his 1923 rowing cap worn on the Punah. A visit to an astrologist resident at a posh hotel reveals that, correctly, this will be the first of several epic trips and Palin's Madras train journey reservation seems to have been filled by two other Michael Palins – one of whom is a woman!

Enhanced by Indian-style theme music, Palin is accepted as temporary sound man and the journey moves on into Part V – Oriental Express, with his Geordie Captain docking his 'little bit of Britain' four miles off shore and ushering in an 8.45am chauffeur-driven, champagne-fuelled luxury introduction to China. Believing he's stumbled into the bar rather than his hotel room, receiving an invitation to a swish cocktail reception and rediscovering civilisation, Palin latches onto a favourite phrase which perfectly sums up his emotions – century deprivation. A makeshift tailor, whose work and clients speak volumes, skilfully kits out Palin for his swell affair as Our Man in the Orient looks over photos of such notable suit buyers as *Python* favourite Henry Kissinger, David Bowie, Harold Wilson and even Derek Nimmo, prompting Palin's celebrated impression of the man. I just hope that little, select tailor now boasts a shot of Michael Palin, 'presenter, third class', hero and comic genius.

The illusion of past glories continues via an impromptu meeting with a very much alive parrot, addressed by Palin with 'I've been in a sketch with you!' and culminating with the enquiry, 'Do you know John Cleese?' Pure gold dust. Waxing lyrical about the resurrected Glaswegian trams in the orient, enjoying a day at the races, giggling over his vast winnings, our host calls on friends Basil and Pat, whose newly born babe came into the world at about the exact time Palin was leaving Victoria Station. With Basil as comforting guide, the money-obsessed reception is endured, a gaggle of staff insures quick entry over the border and the series' most controversial moment concerns a rather off putting meal of snake. But, this is real life and despite comic

reaction to the concept of 'snake balls!' Palin's reaction mirrors the attitude of any Westerner, feeling uneasy watching his meal killed and prepared before him, finding the wriggling death throws rather unpleasant and dismissing the main course in order to avoid killing three creatures. It's a stomach-churning piece of film, capturing a culture we cannot comprehend, reflected in the discerning eye of Palin. In the end, shredded cobra looks no more forbidding than chicken and chips and both meals cause suffering to a living thing; it's simply that the primitive ideal of facing slaughter does not do much for our sensibilities.

A further train journey in Edwardian luxury provides an encounter with a vintage steam engine, enables Palin to pick up a genuine Chinese roof tile as the requested gift for Terry Gilliam, features the relaxing refrains of Mozart on a train radio request programme and introduces a delightful young lady yuppie-type whose burning Brit-based question concerns the continual carrying of umbrellas. As always Palin is the perfect, charming British ambassador. Part VI – Far East and Farther East starts with Palin enjoying what looks like some glorious English country house relaxation, but no; this is not back projection (despite his tongue-in-cheek claims that the whole journey has been faked). This is a oasis of Britishness in the orient, contrasting greatly with the train feast of 'distilled woodland' herbal remedies endured and the Westernisation of the land via BBC worshipping followers, American jazz fanatics playing Benny Goodman and Harry James, washed down with the sublime location where Noel Coward penned *Private Lives*. Very civilised. There's a breathtaking moment of departure as Palin takes to the water once more, complete with lush sunset and priceless bit of comic irritation. The luxurious surroundings seem deserted, however, with sea-bound fun unused, and a lone, charming but slightly unsure stewardess serving the main man some sustenance. It's purely by chance that the music

welcoming the ship is a blast of Sousa, while there's something certainly *Python*esque in Palin's embrace of the craze Karoake, almost unknown over here in 1989. Struggling through a rendition of *You Are My Sunshine*, Palin's performance includes Tom Jones-like mike swinging and a bit of comic mugging to mask his embarrassment – the copious supplies of whiskey certainly can't do it! The 'luxury morgue' of the capsule hotel, an ingenious solution to drunken folk wandering the streets, ushers in a private television screen whose scantily clad dollies are prized as highly instructional by Palin before it's time to embark on an 11-day sea voyage, rushing through a 15-year supply of books, chucking in a genuine but *Python*esque handkerchief/wind direction test, a manic stab at charades as a Yugslovakian deck-hand and a prime bit of Bruce-like Aussie banter explaining that there's nothing poofy about ironing his own shirt. With a coy reference to the old Gumby flower-arranging sketch, the crossing of the International Date Line and a wonderfully straight-faced tannoy announcement explaining that the day will be repeated again, it's onto the final leg of the journey with Part VII – Dateline to Deadline. Arriving in America two days behind Fogg, Palin is treated to the eerie regal splendour of the *Queen Mary*, retaining its distinguished heritage via huge photographs of past travellers like Spencer Tracy and Laurel and Hardy, while now it no longer moves. The massive train journey, according to Palin somewhere between a mobile holiday camp and the Titfield Thunderbolt, presents the chance to chat to a delightfully nutty rent-a-clown, allows a few hours off for a hot springwater bath, complete with mock news reporter attacked by marine creatures, a condemnation of Mike Todd's filmic inclusion of a hot air balloon which is not in the book, hastily endorsed by a Palin trip and a joyous dog sleigh ride across country. Straight-faced Palin listens to the perils of obesity on the train as an employee relates the tale of a traveller getting sucked into the toilet bowl, while finally the hassle of travel catches up on Palin's charm and he dismisses a passer-by's words of cinematic recognition before unBritishness takes over and he guiltily jumps a queue. This is the last hurdle, panicking about a mysterious message and finally wishing for a quiet life in an old folks' home with just the delight of a Maidenhead-to-London train journey. Again discovering a common import today, the Chippendales, and finding some feel-good Christmas cheer for the Sally Army, Palin suffers the only untalkative cabby in New York, makes a swift trip across the Atlantic and arrives in the undeniably unimpressive Felixstowe on the 79th day, with flagging energy and a relaxed afternoon tea with enchanting countryside view to reintroduce him to the old country. Desperate to share his experiences, denied the correct tube stop, badly treated by an ironically 'charming and jolly' newspaper vendor and finally unable to film in the Reform Club, this is a rather downbeat ending for him. However, the good old BBC is always there, playing host to Gilliam and friends for a final burst of tired comic invention and warm companionship. This is peerless television and, like the Jules Verne book, worth several revisits.

Did You Know? *Around the World in 80 Days* was a project turned down by many of the Beeb's fave chaps, including Noel Edmonds. The offer fell to Palin due to his excellent presenting on his first *Great Railway Journey* in 1980.

Written & presented by **Michael Palin**
Music **Paddy Kingsland**
Graphic design **Liz Friedman & Iain Macdonald**
Production co-ordination **Brian Hall & Kitty Anderson**
Location manager, Italy **Heidi Wenyon**
Location manager, Egypt **Romany Helmy**
Location manager, India **Shernaz Italia**
Location manager, Japan **Naeko Funakoshi**

Camera **Nigel Meakin, Julian Charrington, Nigel Walters, Jim Peirson & Simon Maggs**
Sound **Ron Brown, David Jewitt & Morton Hardaker with John Hale, Michael Narduzzo, Aad Wirtz & Peter Smith**
Film editors **David Thomas, Howard Billingham, Jonathan Rowdon & Andy Metcalf**
Production assistants **Ann Holland & Angela Elbourne**
Travel research **Angela Elbourne**
Series producer **Clem Vallance**
Directed by **Roger Mills & Clem Vallance**
A BBC TV production in association with The Arts and Entertainment Network, 7x 50 mins, 11 October–29 November 1989

THE ART OF TRAVEL

By this stage, Michael Palin really had become *Monty Python*'s answer to Alan Whicker with a series of four themed half-hour journeys with an emphasis on his beloved train travel

1. LMS An interaction with posters from the 1920s/1930s (director John Metherall)
2. Southern Railways A trip to Paris on the Golden Arrow (director Denise Winterburn)
3. LNER A golfing trip to St. Andrew's via the East coast of Britain (director John Metherell)
4. GWR (director Denise Winterburn)
Series producer Trevor Hearing
7–15 November 1989
Repeat season – 6–20 October 1990

AT LAST THE 1948 SHOW

This classic and ground-breaking show stemmed from David Frost's desire to showcase his merry band of clowns from *The Frost Report* in their own television vehicles. His two prized discoveries, John Cleese and Tim Brooke-Taylor, were to be given their own shows and this was to be Cleese's centrepiece utilising writing talents from *I'm Sorry I'll Read That Again* and *Round the Horne* – Brooke-Taylor, Oddie, Garden,

Feldman and Took – for television. However, both Cleese and Brooke-Taylor agreed that it would be best to join forces for the venture. It was via Cleese that Chapman became part of the team and, again, it was Cleese himself who asked for Feldman to be part of the performing team.
Up to that point Feldman had been known solely as a comedy writer but within a year his popularity saw him win his own BBC series. The writing/performing team of Brooke-Taylor, Chapman, Cleese and Feldman are caught at their fledgling best and many of the show's sketches remain classic examples of British comedy, more than able to hold their own alongside the best of official *Python*. The overriding feeling of the cast was that they could be as silly and off-the-wall as they wanted, resurrecting rejected *Frost Report* skits that had been abandoned because the performer had feared for their public reputation in dishing out a load of infantile material.
Aimi MacDonald, bless her, does little but flash her legs like an embryonic Carol Cleveland, highlighting the clear fact that the lads couldn't write young female parts outside of the stereotyped and blinkered world of showgirl types. At times poor old Aimi was reduced to just smiling sweetly and saying 'And now...', linking sketches and, importantly, getting near that rather immortal linking phrase of Cleese for *Python*. However, she does it stunningly and, Feldman particularly, latched onto the satirical treatment of Aimi's glam girl parody with the 'Make the lovely Aimi McDonald a rich lady' appeal, twisting her character from showgirl cuteness to knowing bimboesque delivery. Subtle but potent.
Python is clearly in early development and, indeed, Eric Idle cropped up frequently, playing fillers like dead bodies and reduced dialogue defence counsellors. There's the stunning trailer for the film that couldn't be made, featuring the official, bowler-hatted figure of John Cleese in outlandish situations like a foaming bath, and the medic authority figure of Graham Chapman playing his

stuff like television drama and latching onto the dramatic classical soundtrack music from within the narrative. The parody of television conventions starts with outrageous variety-style introductions of Aimi and the glam girls, embracing everything from casting couch sexual favours with the director to an abridged opera sung by a string of chorus girlies. This was a Cleese/Chapman trick of including one more glam girl for each show in the series – thus the fourth show would have Aimi joined by three nubile young things – although some regions like ATV's Midlands ran the programmes in the wrong order and destroyed this subtle touch.

The irritating British chaps on holiday are here, clones from Peter Cook's *Interesting Facts* characterization, all talking in the same whining voices and clad in flowery shirts. The *Python* similarities extend to their shared name, Sydney Lotterby (a real television producer, later of *Porridge* fame, and played à la the clan of Aussie Bruces), ironically celebrating the spirit of individuality (as with *Life of Brian*) and even sharing the same wife, a totally *Python*esque concept. Material like Speak-a English has that magical touch of surrealism within the commonplace, with Cleese, Brooke-Taylor and Chapman, bowler-hatted and robotic, all repeating 'I am a chartered accountant!' before Feldman bursts the bubble of sanity with 'I am a gorilla.' Again, Brooke-Taylor's robotic hospital visitor, disturbing the bedridden patient (an early filmed collaboration with Bill Oddie, resurrecting a magical *Cambridge Circus* moment – others included Jo Kendall/Cleese in the first John & Mary skit and a version of the monumental *Judge Not*) tackles the one step beyond nonsense of everyday life, contrasting Cleese's straight role as the doctor with his wind-up action, jostling round the room with flowers and a continuous stream of cheer-up clichés, including a bit of sexual knowingness about the nurses and a suggestion of touching the nose, nudge-nudging two years before

Idle immortalised it for *Python*. Total surrealism was embraced with the notion of a dentist being swallowed by his patient only to discover Welsh miners in the stomach. And the Cleese/Chapman psychiatrist sketch with Brooke-Taylor's weedy Mr. Gibbon posture (the actor was advised by Feldman to stamp on Cleese's foot during recording to really get the angry abuse flowing). Chapman's legendary self-wrestling and the Cookian park bench discussion between Cleese and Feldman about the various cries of ants pointed the *Python* way. Written by all four team members during a late night session, it remains one of the masterpieces of post-war comedy. As with Python, the Cleese/Chapman partnership was prolific, but other combinations were commonplace including the Cleese/Feldman penned gem *Lucky Gypsy*. Stuff like Feldman's appeal for sleep, contrasted with his continual dozing off and lapsing into déjà vu, directly walks the line between vintage Ronnie Barker and Graham Chapman, layering the joke with a bit of next week's appeal concerning imaginative bat attacks (right!) slotted in. Feldman could embrace black humour with relish, memorably doing his goggle-eyed, suspiciously pleased with himself Jack the Ripper, announced and performed like a Music Hall show with a classic rendition of *Give Me the Moonlight*, while Chapman's farmer with a killer sheepdog, interviewed by Brooke-Taylor's sheepish reporter and the non-communicative diatribe in the Chinese restaurant reek of vintage *Python*. Television formats are mercilessly sent up, notably via John Cleese's outrageous parody of Michael Miles and *Take Your Pick* with the immortal *Nosmo Claphanger Quiz Show*, terrorising nice old Feldman and Brooke-Taylor with oceans of biting satire, cruel comments and twisted variations on the usual game show pleasantries ('Who cares what you think!'/laughing at contestants' stupid names and stupid answers). Treating the studio audience like the ultimate

inferior, Cleese roars with venom, mocking the working classes, ordering spontaneous laughter and delighting in total character assassination. Like a Jeremy Paxman on humiliation overload, Cleese rips into his contestants ('Even I know that!'), contrasting the whole picture of demonic progress with moments of ingratiating smiles and over-friendly hospitality. Resurrected for both the *1948 Show* spin-off *How to Irritate People* and, indeed, *Monty Python* with Terry Jones taking over from Tim's drag act; this was a stable area for the fledging *Python* generation to tear apart – the final intercut of Nazi archive footage clearly points the way forward. And above all, like *Python*, the *At Last the 1948 Show* team clearly had great fun putting the shows together. No surviving sketch highlights this more endearingly than the undercover policemen. *Python*esque beyond words, it stars Feldman, Chapman and Cleese as coppers in drag with a uniformed Brooke-Taylor trying to keep order. Chapman, complete with give-away pipe, starts the corpsing going with an impromptu adoption of the name Phyllis, much to Tim's amusement and surprise. The others, sensing Brooke-Taylor losing control, twist the knife Peter Cook-like with Cleese suppressing giggles and giving knowing looks and Feldman grabbing the bull by the horn, delighting in his surreal cockney roughness while imparting his thoughts about his 'English rose complexion!' But it's Chapman, having a whale of a time and using his authority-like vocals to add extra weight to the absurd goings on, who really steals the scene, cracking up all over the shop and scoring a masterpiece of timing with his 'cheeky face' comment. Brooke-Taylor, losing his grip and trying to control the team with screams of 'Gentlemen!' finally gets through the sketch and exits stage left. It's hilariously written comedy performed with a delightful sense of naughty students having a good time. A show of immeasurable importance.

Did You Know? *The Rhubarb Tart Song* performed by John Cleese ends series two to the tune of Sousa's *Washington Post* – *Python* is certainly on the way. The series was plagued by television politics dictating that only the London area would receive all shows and the complete heritage was destroyed when David Frost's own company, Paradine Productions, wiped the original tapes – only three complete shows survive, as well as five 'best of' editions retained by Swedish television. As a result, the classic skits were fair game for revival. Corbett and Barker performed a version of Grublian Holidays in 1973 for series three of *The Two Ronnies* alongside interpretations of Spiv Doctor, Psychiatrist & Choral Repetition. Popular in America, skits appeared on *The Dean Martin Show*, with Marty Feldman appearing in dinner jacket and, alongside Martin, performing *1948*'s Door-to-door Undertaker sketch.

The 1968 comedy special *How to Irritate People*, resurrected Topic Discusses Freedom of Speech as well as the airplane cockpit sketch later used on *Marty*. Feldman reused *1948* material for *Marty Amok* – Bookshop with John Junkin and *Marty Back Together Again* – Door-to-door Undertaker with James Villiers. The Pythons would plunder the rich *1948* vaults with the Drury Lane album boasting Secret Service, Wrestling and Four Yorkshiremen. Chapman would reuse sketches for *The Big Show* and performed Wrestling in the second German *Python* show and *Live at the Hollywood Bowl*. Sound and Sight Impaired would get the Python treatment in the German show; *Contractual Obligation Album* included the definitive version of Bookshop with Cleese and Chapman. Unfamiliar, easy to do, fresh and, above all, still hilarious, *1948* material was ripe for the Amnesty concerts with *Mermaid Frolics* presenting Cleese and Connie Booth performing Bookshop, *The Secret Policeman's Ball* featuring Four Yorkshiremen, while *The Secret Policeman's Other Ball* wallowed in reunion when Cleese, Chapman and Brooke-Taylor resurrected Clothes

Off!, Beekeeping and Top of the Form. In the following episode listing all italicized sketches survive, although a complete sound-only version of episode one and other segments are around, while a pristine audio record of Bookshop, Sheepdog Trials, Where Were You?, The Wonderful World Ant, Gentleman Farmer, Witch, Doctor and Man with Skinny Legs, Job Description and Vox Pop are available on the *At Last The 1948 Show* album released by Pye.

Series 1. 15 February – 22 March 1967
1. Doctor and Man with Skinny Legs, Witch, One Man Wrestling, Secret Service Chief, Treasure Trove, Vox Pop.
2. *Four Sydney Lotterbys*, Lucky Gypsy, Judge Not.
3. *Vistors For the Use Of, Sleep Starvation, Mice Laugh Softly, Charlotte*, Sheepdog Trials, Bookshop, Job Description.
4. *Someone Has Stolen the News, Grublian Holidays, Memory Training, One-Man Battalion, Ministerial Breakdown, Engine Driver, Undercover Policemen.*
5. *Top Of the Form*, Gentleman Farmer, The Wonderful World of the Ant, John and Mary in Malaya.
6. *Let's Speak-a English, Headmaster, The Siege in the Frock, Choral Repetition*, Chinese Restaurant, Beekeeping, Ferret Song.
Series 2. 26 September – 7 November 1967
1. *Spiv Doctor, Reptile Keeper, Thief in Library, Come Dancing*, Joke Shop
2. *Shirt Shop, Nosmo Claphanger Game Show*, Clothes Off!, Insurance For Accident Prone Man, *Thuggish Ballet Supporters*.
3. *Pessimistic Customer, Meek Bouncer, Men's Club, Neurotic Scientist, Sydney Lotterby Craves the Test Score, Shop for the Sight and Sound Impaired.*
4. Discussion on Pornography, Door-to-door Undertaker, *Uncooperative Burglars, Topic Discusses Freedom of Speech, Programme Announcement, Studio Tour.*
5. *Reluctant Choir, Psychiatrist, Secret Service Cleaner,* Reprimanded Soccer Player, *Deadly Architectural Model.*
6. Sydney Lotterby's Renewed Acquaintance, *Chartered Accountants*

Dance, Dangers of Dentistry, *Four Yorkshiremen.*
7. TV Current Affairs, *Railway Carriage,* Pet Shop, The Rhubarb Tart Song.

Written and performed by **TIM BROOKE-TAYLOR, GRAHAM CHAPMAN, JOHN CLEESE & MARTY FELDMAN**
also starring **AIMI MacDONALD**
With **MARY MAUDE, CHRISTINE RODGERS, JACQUELINE ROCHELLE, FRANCIS DEAN, BILL ODDIE, JO KENDALL, DICK VOSBURGH, BARRY CRYER & ERIC IDLE**
Programme editors **John Cleese & Tim Brooke-Taylor**
Designer **John Clarke**
Executive producer **David Frost**
Director **Ian Fordyce**
Rediffusion London Production

THE AVENGERS: Look – (Stop Me If You've Heard This One) But There Were These Two Fellers...

From the last in the original series of this surreal, psychedelic, bizarre and totally groovy crime adventure series comes this particularly surreal, psychedelic, bizarre and totally groovy tale of death via comedy traditions. Chief protagonist is a stunning old timer performance from Jimmy Jewel, adopting clown make-up and big shoes for his acts of vengeance. Akin to Vincent Price and his Shakespearean dispatches in *Theatre of Blood*, Jewel's comedy-obsessed clown is bumping off a wealthy business franchise which bought up and closed down his beloved Vaudevillian theatre. Revealing the chilling aspect in humour, Jewel adapts the custard pie, mock pistol and various tricks of his trade for dark deeds, tossing in sly, bottom-of-the-bill comments about first house on Mondays, while ably assisted by bumbling, white-faced mime artist Julian Chagrin who latches onto Harpo Marx horn-blowing and takes up Bud Flanagan's leftover fur coat and battered boater for a fine touch of homage. The delicious, champagne-fuelled banter between the ever present Macnee and

Thorson (oft overlooked stunning successor to Honor Blackman and Diana Rigg) is crisp and amusing. Indeed, Thorson's sexually charged, awkwardly delivered act of body guarding with Kendall is a high point of the series, while the theatrical juices of Macnee flow like fine wine. The origins of the clown red nose prompts some knowing vocal jostling and there's some good fun Music Hall energy during the *Batman*-like finale.

However, the show's major stroke lies in its casting of a crop of distinguished comedy talents from various eras of great British humour. Notably, Tony Hancock's old television cohort John Vyvan, familiar character man Bill Shine and the ultimate scowling figure of bombastic big-headedness for everyone from George Formby to Arthur Lucan, Gerry Marsh, disinterestedly dismissing any threats from a clown before being unceremoniously blown sky high. Bernard Cribbins, in a major guest starring spot, is perfect as the ever wisecracking joke merchant, desperately trying to hide Macnee's subtle sense of humour and ultimately ending up swamped in a mound of his own discarded funnies. More importantly for our purposes, the new breed of satire is handsomely represented by John Cleese as a nervous, super-efficient, straightlaced authority figure acting as make-up registrar. His characterisation could have stepped out of a *Frost Report* skit, retaining that clipped delivery in the face of his obsessive and absurdist profession, painting unique clown masks on delicate egg shells. With his office door emblazoned with text like Music Hall billing and a tangible horror as his life's work is put to the sword, Cleese's comedy comes from his gently manoeuvred tiptoeing past his prized collection of comedy while projecting a persona of humourlessness. It's a quite stunning supporting turn, sadly short-lived but eye-catching in his shattered eggshell exit. This is weird television for the connoisseur, perfecting the essence of sixties ideology while remaining strangely timeless and unmatched. Class stuff.

John Steed **PATRICK MACNEE**
Tara King **LINDA THORSON**
Merry Maxie Martin **JIMMY JEWEL**
Bradley Marler **BERNARD CRIBBINS**
Marcus Pugman **JOHN CLEESE**
Seagrave **JOHN WOODVINE**
Jennings **JULIAN CHAGRIN**
Lord Dessington **WILLIAM KENDALL**
Brigadier Whitshire **GERRY MARSH**
Miss Charles **GABY VARGAS**
Cleghorn **BILL SHINE**
Sir Jeremy Broadfoot **RICHARD YOUNG**
Merlin **ROBERT JAMES**
Firey Frederick **TALFRYN THOMAS**
Tenor **JAN DENYER**
Escapologist **JOHN VYVAN**
Ventriloquist **LEE BELMONT**
Written by **Dennis Spooner**
Production controller **Jack Greenwood**
Production designer **Robert Jones**
Photography **Gilbert Taylor**
Production manager **Ron Fry**
Thorson's costumes **Alun Hughes**
Set dresser **Kenneth Tait**
Assistant director **Ron Appleton**
Camera operator **Brian Elvin**
Editor **Lionel Selwyn**
Producers **Albert Fennell & Brian Clemens**
Director **James Hill**
Associated British, Elstree 1968
50 mins

AWAY FROM IT ALL

At about the same time as masquerading as Norman Fearless for *To Norway, Home Of Giants*, John Cleese took on the mantle of Nigel Farquar-Bennet for this classic mock travelogue which utilises footage from several old Rank *Look at Life* shorts with Cleese's commentary getting more and more unconventional as the thing goes on. It was released in cinemas as the short subject complementing *Monty Python's Life of Brian* and remains one of Cleese's proudest achievements, with the outrageous final burst of manic comedy slowly building from mocking believable begins.
Taylor-Hyde International/Python

Pictures
Written by **John Cleese & Clare Taylor**
Narrated by **John Cleese**
13 mins, 1979

BEHIND THE CREASE

Brilliant and unfairly overlooked Eric Idle musical comedy for radio, tackling the major potential in gutter journalism, royal scandal and the English cricket tour of the West Indies island St. Jonus. As composer, writer and star, Idle does a sublime job, suitably keeping all the best laugh lines for his seedy *Sun*-type journo – relishing the cheapest, most common denominator gag and perfectly capturing the flavour of the piece; 'This is Sexy Sandy. She has a lovely pair of bouncers and wants to open for England'.

Throughout, it's the easy comic style of Idle which lifts this show, masquerading as a pink rabbit at the regal bash (while injecting the rabbi reference following another *Brian*-like mention of Jehovah), mocking the less than impressive cricketing prowess of the visitors ('"You don't look very athletic'/'No, I'm with the English Team'), finding himself hoist by his own petard in a compromising position with the Princess, preening upper-class sex bait/local glam girl and memorably justifying the barrel-scraping ethos of newspaper reporters with the brilliant blues song *The Public Has a Right to Know* (introduced with a cheery 'listen!' and covering every possibility strolling down the street of shame). Gary Wilmott is perfectly unrestrained and devious as the hotel owner, aware of his audience and narrating the events as he strolls in and out of them. There's an effective, classy, music hall

double act between the intellectual Captain and the worker Vice-Captain; the Gracie Fields-like girlfriend lament, *North of England*, with the classic wedding line 'Paul McCartney will lead the choir'; a patriotic, tongue-in-cheek xenophobic cricketing song which is joyfully curtailed suddenly when, in *Python* terms, things have got too silly; and the rock 'n' roll *Don't Hold the Back Page* (on the heals of Idle's throwaway 'Can you confirm Elvis has been approached to Captain England?' – bliss).
There's some really clever lyrics ('E=MCC'), biting legal jibes, television sponsorship references ('Thanks for the cheque from Sky TV' in the gospel rock *Oh Lord's*) and a comic milestone with Idle's head-throbbing performance of *I'm Never Going To Drink Again*, but the show's highlight is a deliciously *Python*esque ('Well, that's what they say!') duet between Idle and Wilmott, *I Like Dinosaurs*. Most of the threads have been tied up, the story is almost told and Idle can be funny for funny's sake – chucking in Darwin's theory, South China sources and occasional character flows, culminating in Wilmott's pinpointing the song as irrelevant, highlighting that this is merely musical entertainment and embracing the notion of aware performance in perfect *Python* style. This is a landmark Idle achievement certainly with television, if not cinematic, potential. As it is, Radio 2's gain was most people's loss, but check this little beauty out; I maintain it's the best thing Idle's written in the 1990s.

Boyle **ERIC IDLE**
Nelson **GARY WILMOTT**
Brian Steam **ROBERT BROADBENT**
Martin Hope **JULIAN LITTMAN**
Princess Joan **ANN HOWARD**
Cindy **VICKY LICORISH**
Nikki **FLAMINIA CINQUE**
Helen **CHARLIE DOVE**
Alf **BRIAN BOWLES**
Music & script by **Eric Idle & John Du Prez**
Producer **Harry Thompson**
Radio 2, 6pm–7.15pm, 28 July 1990

BERT FEGG'S NASTY BOOK FOR BOYS AND GIRLS

This book followed the style of *Do Not Adjust Your Set* in that while it was aimed at children it was never childish or condescending. Bridging the gap between *Python* and *Ripping Yarns* for its writers Terry Jones and Michael Palin, many of these stories were conceived during the *Python* shows but discarded, while one of the highlights – Aladdin and his Terrible Problem by George Bernard Fegg – was a throwback to their panto writing days for Watford's Civic Theatre. In the glorious grotesque tradition of Roald Dahl, this book proved a huge success, with its unpleasant host, Dr. Fegg, taking children's imaginations through an A-Z journey of strange characters and delightfully macabre tales, injecting elements from *Roy of the Rovers* (Soccer – My Way by the Supremes), *Marvel Comics* (Captain Fegg) and *Hop-A-Long Cassidy* (A Cowboy Story). Originally a character drawn by Terry Jones to relieve boredom during maths lessons, this was simply written as a pleasant burst of comic invention in the immediate aftermath of *Python*'s television demise. In the same way as *Do Not Adjust Your Set* was children's television with an eye on the adult market, thus Bert Fegg was directed at the younger reader with a clear attempt to appeal across the range. In other words, like the great writers of children's fiction, Jones and Palin addressed their target audience on a higher, more intelligent level. Even so, Jones was furious when he saw the book often on shelves in the humour section rather than the children's section. Anything that includes pieces dedicated to Alcoholic Dogs, Make Your Own 747, the Turkish Wall Goat, Magic by The Great Feggo, Learn to Speak French in Four Minutes and Zero-Rated, I Was Hitler's Double deserves to be in any self-respecting *Python* fan's library. An advert for Fegg's Permanent Head Restorer, a one-page history of the world and, best of all, The Famous Five Go Pillaging, are my personal favourites, while there's even a very

brief sneak preview of the *Ripping Yarn* to be, Across the Andes by Frog. Class stuff, just don't restrict it to your kids!

Written by **Terry Jones & Michael Palin**
Published by Eyre Methuen, 1974

THE BEST HOUSE IN LONDON

Relentless cheap laughs and scantily clad dolly birds is the name of the game for this costume comic romp headlining sixties kid David Hemmings as two sides of the same coin. Apart from establishing the trend for knicker-dropping sex farce which would rollercoaster into the seventies, this is a feeble, long drawn-out effort, utilising a crop of new satirists – Rushton, Bird – some old stand-bys – Fraser, Denham – and chugging along with its best source of laughs coming from an over-used technique of incorporating well known historical and fictional figures into the narrative (everybody from Charles Dickens to Sherlock Holmes). Even the appearance of John Cleese, in his first movie role, can't save the day, although he does crop up in the best realised sequence. Typical of his cameos in *Frost* and *Python*, Cleese is the official, officious type, fighting for dignity and sophistication in the face of adversity. Here, in surprising Indian guise complete with darkened skin and outrageous whiskers, Cleese adopts the dinner jacket and manners of English aristocracy alongside the film's major plus, George Sanders, barking and ranting with patriotic energy. In a scene nicked from the climactic masterpiece of *Carry On... Up the Khyber*, Sanders dogmatically enjoys his meal as the natives revolt, with Cleese fumbling and mumbling with his wine in a muted Peter Butterworth fashion. Cleese needs only to react to the mayhem around him and, in a glorious moment, his steely expression breaks into a smile as glass from the table is smashed. Sanders, holding aloft the Union Jack, dies for his principles and the stirring refrains of the National Anthem fusing with his death knell is the film's most effective moment. Cleese, like most of the class performers present, is left floundering. For those *Python* fans in a hurry, his scene comes 45 minutes into the film...

MGM/Bridge/Carlo Ponti
Walter Leybourn & Benjamin Oakes **DAVID HEMMINGS**
Sir Francis Leybourn **GEORGE SANDERS**
Josephine Pacefoot **JOANNA PETTET**
Count Pandolfo **WARREN MITCHELL**
Babette **DANY ROBIN**
Sylvester Wall **WILLIAM RUSHTON**
Inspector MacPherson **BILL FRASER**
Editor of *The Times* **MAURICE DENHAM**
Headmistress **MARTITA HUNT**
Lord Tennyson **HUGH BURDEN**
Mr Fortnum **ARTHUR HOWARD**
Mr Mason **CLEMENT FREUD**
Girl **VERONICA CARLSON**
with CHARLIE DICKENS, ARNOLD DIAMOND, OSCAR WLDE, JOHN DE MARCO, **JOHN CLEESE**
Written by **Denis Norden**
Photography **Alex Thompson**
Music **Mischa Spoliansky**
Production designer **Wilfrid Shingleton**
Producers **Philip Breen & Kurt Unger**
Director **Philip Saville**
96 mins, Eastmancolor, 1969

THE BIG PICTURE

An unfairly forgotten movie about movies from Christopher Guest, this is a more subtle comic slant on the celebrated Robert Altman film *The Player* which appeared four years later with more street-cred and tons of cameos from Hollywood's mega-star brigade. At its epicentre is Kevin Bacon's film-mad student who, having won a young film-makers' competition with his avant garde piece, is eagerly sucked into the corrupt and uncaring world of Hollywood where his social comment is gradually stripped away in favour of teenage romping and box office conventions.
It's a sort of *The Bad and the Beautiful* for *This Is Spinal Tap* fans, with Bacon's naive and passionate performance complemented by movie

buff touches (his walls are dotted with Astaire/Rogers/Garland images, Eddie Albert presents his prize following a quote from the legendary Frank Capra), with his life continually dropping into black-and-white movie mode. Along the way there are manic producers, effeminate agents, youthful wannabes and a stunning bimbo starlet from a pre-*Lois & Clark* Teri Hatcher. Need I say more!
Mind you, it's a very, very long wait for John Cleese, cropping up well over a hour into the picture during one of Bacon's movie-inspired daydreams. Bacon, unshaven and quietly drunk, sits inside a bar at Christmas time; the snow is cascading down outside with decorations filling the window. In an extension of the Capra link this is *It's A Wonderful Life* country (with elements of Billy Wilder's *The Lost Weekend* thrown in for good measure) with Cleese as Frankie the bar tender (thus a performance gathering huge swathes of Sheldon Leonard mixed with a dash of Henry DeSilva), initially refusing Bacon another drink, being painfully reminded of the long gone good old days when the drunken bum before him was the king of the block and finally pouring him another shot. There's real emotion in Cleese's eyes, trying to save this guy from himself but relenting in order to soothe his inner turmoil. It's a marvellous few minutes, but what follows is even better. The dream disappears and we cut to Bacon sat in a contemporary bar with the Capra classic *It's A Wonderful Life* playing on the television. Just as James Stewart is giving it his all in a mass of twisted emotions, Cleese, the rather more unemotional bartender, gives the television a hefty whack and the screen bursts into the shameless colour version of the 1946 masterpiece. Without regard for cinema history Cleese mutters 'That's better!' as Bacon looks on dumbfounded. It's a wonderful comment on the disrespect paid to Hollywood's masters and Cleese's unconcerned delivery makes this the prize vignette in a very under-rated film.

Did You Know? Cleese did *The Big Picture* as a favour to his *Wanda* co-star Jamie Lee Curtis whose husband, Christopher Guest, was writer-director. Despite working on *Silverado* and *Cheers* Cleese had to join the US Equity, having been allowed a couple of jobs without joining but now requested to do so – unfortunately, the office staff didn't know him and took great pity on this 50-year-old beginner!

Columbia Pictures An Aspen Film Society Production
Nick Chapman **KEVIN BACON**
Susan Rawlings **EMILY LONGSTRETH**
Allen Habel **J.T. WALSH**
Lydia Johnson **JENNIFER JASON LEIGH**
Emmet Sumner **MICHAEL McKEAN**
Jenny Sumner **KIM MIYORI**
Gretchen **TERI HATCHER**
Jonathan Tristan-Bennet **DAN SCHNEIDER**
Carl Manknik **JASON GOULD**
Lori Pressman **TRACY BROOKS SWOPE**
Todd Marvin **DON FRANKLIN**
Mark **GARY KROEGER**
Mr. & Mrs. Chapman **ALICE HIRSON & GRANT OWENS**
Special appearances by M.C. **EDDIE ALBERT, Sr.**
Video show host **RICHARD BELZER**
Bartender **JOHN CLEESE**
Attorney **STEPHEN COLLINS**
Polo Habel **FRAN DRESCHER**
Janet Kingsley **JUNE LOCKHART**
Judge **RODDY McDOWALL**
Story & screenplay by **Michael Varhol, Christopher Guest & Michael McKean**
Script supervisor **Judith Saunders**
Music **David Nichtern**
Editor **Martin Nicholson**
Photography **Jeff Jur**
Casting **Nina Axelrod**
Production designer **Joseph T. Garrity**
Camera operator **Don Devine**
Associate producers **Valen Watson & Richard Luke Rothschild**
Executive producers **William E. McEuen & Richard Gilbert Abramson**
Producer **R Michael Varhol**
Director **Christopher Guest**
15 cert. Deluxe 101 mins, 1988

THE BIG SHOW

A failed attempt by NBC television to revive the variety show format saw Graham Chapman, during his residency in Hollywood, roped in as part of the regular sketch comedy team – which also included the ex-partner of Jack Douglas, Joe Baker. A couple of fresh hosts would orchestrate the plethora of song, dance, laughs, ice-skating and chat while Chapman eagerly tried to enliven the tepid material with revivals of *1948* and *Python* pieces but to little effect. The show lasted less than three months and remained a frustrating if enlightening experience for the Brit guest star.
4 March 1980 – Steve Allen and Gary Coleman present Chapman as a General in a disaster movie clip, an airplane pilot and a chap involved in an aggression clinic.
11 March 1980 – Gavin McLeod and Marie Osmond present Chapman as a theatre critic.
18 March 1980 – Dean Martin and Mariette Hartley present Chapman in *At Last the 1948 Show*'s Bookshop sketch.
25 March 1980 – Tony Randall and Herve Villechaize present Chapman hosting a genetics lecture and in a chemist sketch.
8 April 1980 – Steve Lawrence and Don Rickles present Chapman in *At Last the 1948 Show*'s Beekeeping sketch.
29 April 1980 – Barbara Eden and Dennis Weaver present Chapman as a gloriously pompous British actor who disrupts his minor contribution to Weaver's directorial effort and a *Python*esque dentist who falls into a patient's mouth à la *1948 Show*!
6 May 1980 – Gene Kelly and Nancy Walker appear in a Chapman sketch while the Python crops up as an aircraft designer and a frustrated guest desperately trying to check out of his hotel.
13 May 1980 – Steve Allen and Shirley Jones present Chapman as an airplane pilot.

The series also featured **MIMI KENNEDY, JOE BAKER, PAUL GRIMM, CHARLIE HILL, EDIE**

McCLURG & SHABBO-DOO
Producer **Nick Vanoff**
Directed by **Steve Binder, Tony Charmoli & Walter C. Miller**

THE BLISS OF MRS. BLOSSOM

Weak, would-be hip sixties comedy, with a surprisingly naive narrative attitude with Shirley MacLaine keeping her second husband (James Booth) hidden in the attic. In this post Summer of Love euphoria, coy sexuality must have seemed like vintage Noel Coward, although the film remains interesting today for desperately trying to contrast its backward outlook with the flotsam and jetsam of swinging counter culture, with supporting work from Freddie Jones, Willy Rushton (as a couple of detectives on the case of Booth's disappearance over several years) and John Cleese, in another typical Denis Norden-related film cameo, working opposite the sublime Freddie Jones for half a day's shoot as a bemused shopkeeper.

Paramount
Harriet Blossom **SHIRLEY MacLAINE**
Robert Blossom **RICHARD ATTENBOROUGH**
Ambrose Tuttle **JAMES BOOTH**
Sergeant Dylan **FREDDIE JONES**
Assistant **WILLIAM RUSHTON**
Dr Taylor **BOB MONKHOUSE**
Miss Reece **PATRICIA ROUTLEDGE**
Clerk **JOHN CLEESE**
Judge **JOHN BLUTHAL**
Doctor **HARRY TOWB**
Dealer **BARRY HUMPHRIES**
Jan **CLIVE DUNN**
Assistant **SANDRA CARON**
Written by **Alec Coppell & Denis Norden**
Production designer **Assheton Gorton**
Music **Riz Ortolani**
Producer **Josef Shaftel**
Director **Joe McGrath**
Technicolor, 93 mins, 1968

CONNIE BOOTH

Born into a farming community in Indianapolis in the Mid-West of America, Connie Booth moved with her family to New Rochelle, New York at the age of four. By the time she was 14 a desire for an acting career was being fuelled with junior high school experience, playing Mary in *The Children's Hour*, the witch in *Hansel & Gretel* and the Devil in *Everyman*. As she had studied in the American Theater Wing in New York, appeared in a Shakespearean festival, performed the Bard in San Diego and even made a few brief film appearances, several American critics considered the young actress meeting John Cleese as the end to a promising career. She was working as a waitress in a Second Avenue cafe called The Living Room when she met the British comedian during his run with the Establishment. Subsequently Connie sobbed opposite Palin's lumberjack, was knocked for six by Cleese's boxer and played a princess with wooden teeth for *Python* immortality. Of course, she went on to co-write and star in the sublime *Fawlty Towers*, Cleese's *Romance with a Double Bass* and, much later, Michael Palin's *American Friends*. As she had emerged to become famous playing a waitress, the British public were forever reluctant to forget Polly and even 20 years later, with prestigious BBC drama credits like *Little Lord Fauntleroy*, *Caring* and *The Story of Ruth* to her name, she is still, subconsciously, stuck in our minds somewhere in Torquay.

BRAZIL

'Walter Mitty meets Franz Kafka' is a phrase that Terry Gilliam endorses but five words could never fully sum up this nightmarish, off-the-wall, cinematic milestone. From the moment force-fed television advertising is blown to bits with the ominous backing of *Night On Bare Mountain*, this is a disturbing and powerfully constructed piece of work. The title may be irrelevant, although the 1930s song is a continual motif, contrasting the regimented office block duties and enhancing the first moment of passion between Pryce and Griest, while, like *The Third Man*'s Harry Lime Theme, giving the entire bleak project an upbeat quality. Released in the year after George Orwell's grand vision of things to come had become a reality and had itself been turned into a film, this Gilliam journey of discovery latches onto *1984* terminology (the whole idea of the individual against the state, Michael Palin's mysterious office being Room 5001 (as opposed to Orwell's sinister *Room 101*), while Jonathan Pryce's priceless leading performance takes on elements of Winston Smith as well as, indeed, Danny Kaye's flights of dream fantasy and Kafka's surreal minion lost in bureaucracy.

Gilliam succeeds in creating a chilling air of the future by setting his story within a not too distant timescale, thus, these are not the manic sub-human creatures of H.G. Wells some centuries away but a recognisably mechanised, slightly off-centre reworking of 1980s work ethos. The 'sometime in the 20th century' label brings home the immediacy shrouded in uncertainty, while his Hitchcockian trick of pinpointing the precise time sets up the manic obsession with working to the clock while pulling the audience into Sam Lowry's situation. As with *Twelve Monkeys,* Gilliam creates a future surrounded by outmoded, wheezing devices and redundant modernity, struggling to incorporate old-fashioned, 1930s-styled filing systems into the next millennium, allowing the surviving remnants of the past to take on a spooky air of failed ghosts battling the corruption and violence of the new age.

The icing on the cake of this nightmarish situation is its setting around the festive season, with shades of Charles Dickens and Father Christmas twisted into irrelevant fairy stories and bloodthirsty insincerity – one of the film's most powerful moments has wickedly grinning Peter Vaughan in Santa Claus garb. As a backcloth to whispered intrigue, mindless torture and self-centred commercialism, the film has poignant snatches of Christmas carols and children bemoaning their special day with no chimney for Santa to come down.

The deconstruction of civilised society reveals public fresh air points like telephones, pinball-based escaping turncoats, madly shrieking telegram girls and a dark obsession for correct behaviour at all times, even in the face of cold-hearted, misunderstanding decay. Forbidden pleasures are grabbed and enjoyed in quiet – Kim Griest perfectly capturing the desire for freedom while relaxing in a steaming bath and laughing uncontrollably at a Marx Brothers movie.

Old films are very important to *Brazil*'s sub-text, standing tall as the ultimate invasion into the work ethic and continually distracting white-collar employees from their mindless office duties. Ian Holm's Peter Lorresque boss, deepens his voice for intercom instructions, whining and trembling, earnestly trying to catch his men tuning into black and white images, protecting self-esteem behind Jonathan Pryce's intelligence and endearingly fighting the system by half-heartedly upholding its teachings. Holm sums up the dangers of vintage Hollywood by muttering about his screens 'picking up old films' as though it is an anti-authority signal from the past, a secret passion embraced by the men who eagerly devour some old Western and wait with bated breath for the start of *Casablanca*. A blast from their past, old movies do in fact shape the very way this community of law-obsessed people live, shuffling paper in huge stone monuments to repression, dressing in Bogart-geared sharp suits and trilbys and Pryce endorsing the struggle for self-expression via copious movie pin-ups of Greta Garbo and Marlene Dietrich. Pryce's elongated dream sequences place him firmly in the angelic position of John Phillip Law in Roger Vadim's *Barbarella* while, most potently of all, the final battle of wits between the good guys and the bad guys is highlighted by a machine careering down a flight of steps followed by relentless marching soldiers, in homage to the loss of innocence with the descending pram in Eisenstein's Odessa Steps sequence from *Battleship Potemkin*. Haunting,

confused, angry, adventurous and plain scared, Pryce covers the whole gamut of human expression, giving a peerless performance surrounded by surreal, beautifully etched cameos from a class cast of players. Paramount in terms of billing and marketing is, of course, Robert De Niro, almost covered from head to foot in a boiler-suit, crusading round the city on wires righting wrongs and illegally fixing faulty equipment, desperately staying one step ahead of the authorities and latching onto the forbidden spirit of Errol Flynn-like action values as he whizzes through Gilliam's bizarre imagination. It's a small part with the stamp of a great film actor, happily whistling *Brazil* as he works, playing cinema hero convention with straight-faced relish and ultimately, pseudo-saving the day for our hero, bemoaning 'bloody paperwork' and, in Pryce's vision of things, finally and fatally succumbing to it. Crashing through the red tape like a computer game character, De Niro's characterization has an air of Super Mario Brother about him just before the real thing, in the shape of Bob Hoskins, wanders into the picture with manic grins and job satisfaction.

Kim Griest, questioning the rules, barking out streetwise observations and fighting for her individuality takes on the Sigourney Weaver attitude of leading lady, typed as blonde sex object through Pryce's male gaze while incorporating this desirability into her own toughness for the climactic sex scene before ultimate prosecution. Away from Griest, the female characters are either mindlessly caught up in the system (Palin's secretary touch-typing the depraved dialogue from a recording of a violent attack) or mindlessly caught up in their struggle for beautification. Pryce's mother, a skin-crawling grotesque from Katherine Helmond, has her own obsession with plastic surgery technique (graphically depicted in slackened skin tugging from Jim Broadbent), while her associate, Barbara Hicks, gradually melts away into a pile of slime via her acid, youth treatment from Time Bandit

Jack Purvis. The contrast between the enforced social niceties of Kathryn Pogson's bimbo-like, automatic, repeated utterances concerning salt at the meal and the corpse-like, heartfelt, repeated utterances concerning her dead husband's body from Sheila Reid are powerful indeed. They haunt Pryce's mind like Oppenheimer's bomb victims, personifying the destructive system he created and adding an even darker edge to Gilliam's catastrophic, mentally unhinged universe. Ian Richardson's uncontrolled, manic, strolling boss, barking orders and dealing with everything at once turns in a stunning contribution, Peter Vaughan's wheelchair-bound *Wizard of Oz*-like figure, dictating events safe within his ivory citadel, pompously uses cricket terminology against the mysterious forces of violence. Bryan Pringle, adopting Cleese-like cynical restraint as the waiter, angrily insisting on the food being delivered in numerical format, is a wonderfully grotesque caricature of modern efficiency, and regular *Python* players Simon Jones and Charles McKeown play the official authority game on its own terms with enthusiastic acceptance of their lot. This is not a faceless band of madmen though, for despite the initial destruction of Christmas cheer by masked hoodlums, later purveyors of terror are humanised via chatty cameos from Don Henderson and Howard Lew Lewis, firmly but with pleasant manners restraining Pryce's law-breaking actions.

However, the plum performance comes from Michael Palin, bringing with him his *Python* and Gilliam baggage, playing up to his nice guy image and sailing through Pryce's predicaments with an understanding shake of the head. Written especially with Palin in mind, Gilliam was initially worried when De Niro expressed interest in playing the part of Jack Lint. Wisely though, Gilliam allowed the gentle charm of Palin to set up the multi-faceted madness of Lint while effortlessly watching De Niro turn a fairly minor character on paper into a major film performance. After all, Tuttle is the key to the destruction of the system and is the escapee originally causing the clerical misunderstanding.

Thus a major name was needed to carry off the importance of the role, as with Orson Welles injecting sheer magnetism into Harry Lime for *The Third Man*. On the other hand, Jack Lint is a slow burning character, developing from chatty friend offering a swift shoulder to cry on into a spine-tingling nutter desperately trying to defend his position while dismissing old companionship in favour of necessary political torture. Stylish, superior and quietly insane, Palin bootlicks for Britain, addressing his wife as Barbara just because boss Peter Vaughan has mistakenly called her that, enjoying Goonish vocal play with one of his triplets, continually forgetting her name, and standing at the very heart of information retrieval, adopting a calm, good-natured attitude to his grisly work. Still charming and upbeat while washing bloodstains from his hands, this journey from nice bloke to total slave to the cause is wonderfully captured in his sinister white-coated and baby-face masked appearance opposite a bound and gagged Pryce. It is testament to Palin's fine acting that this raving authority-abuser is one of the most effective pictures of pure evil on screen, thanks totally to the mind-bending contrast with his own, well-liked, well-defined persona. The face of pure terror is that of a trusted friend, perverted. A major epic in terms of length and imagination, *Brazil*'s final, broken-down happy ending which allows the twisted power of Palin and Vaughan to go on, leaves Pryce quietly to create a stunning closing moment. In the end, while the body cannot beat the system, nothing can tie down the human imagination, and with breathtaking use of the song *Brazil*, this remains an unforgettable film sequence – without doubt, this is Gilliam's masterpiece.

Universal
Sam Lowry **JONATHAN PRYCE**
Harry Tuttle **ROBERT DE NIRO**
Mrs. Ida Lowry **KATHERINE**

HELMOND
Mr. Kurtzmann **IAN HOLM**
Spoor **BOB HOSKINS**
Jack Lint **MICHAEL PALIN**
Mr. Warrenn **IAN RICHARDSON**
Mr. Helpmann **PETER VAUGHAN**
Jill Layton **KIM GREIST**
Dr. Joffe **JIM BROADBENT**
Mrs. Terroin **BARBARA HICKS**
Lime **CHARLES McKEOWN**
Dowser **DERRICK O'CONNOR**
Shirley **KATHRYN POGSON**
Spiro **BRYAN PRINGLE**
Mrs. Buttle **SHEILA REID**
TV Interviewer & Salesman **JOHN FLANAGAN**
Technician **RAY COOPER**
Mr. Buttle **BRIAN MILLER**
Boy Buttle **SIMON NASH**
Girl Buttle **PRUDENCE OLIVER**
Arrest Official **SIMON JONES**
Bill – Dept. of Works **DEREK DEADMAN**
Charles – Dept. of Works **NIGEL PLANER**
TV Commercial Presenter **TERENCE BAYLER**
M.O.I. Lobby Porter **GORDEN KAYE**
Neighbour in Clerk's Pool **TONY PORTACIO**
Bespectacled Lurker **BILL WALLIS**
Samorai Warrior **WINSTON DENNIS**
Small Sam Double **TOBY CLARK**
Telegram Girl **DIANA MARTIN**
Dr. Chapman **JACK PURVIS**
Alison 'Barbara' Lint **ELIZABETH SPENDER**
Porter – Information Retrieval **ANTONY BROWN**
Typist in Jack's Office **MYRTLE DEVENISH**
Holly **HOLLY GILLIAM**
Basement Guard **JOHN PIERCE JONES**
Old Lady with Dog **ANN WAY**
Black Mario Guards **DON HENDERSON & HOWARD LEW LEWIS**
Interview Officials **OSCAR QUITAK HAROLD INNOCENT JOHN GRILLO RALH NOSSEK DAVID GANT & JAMES COYLE**
Cell Guard **PATRICK CONNOR**
Priest **ROGER ASHTON-GRIFFITHS**
Young Gallant at Funeral **RUSSEL KEITH GRANT**
Co-Screenplay by **Terry Gilliam, Tom**

Stoppard & Charles McKeown
Photography **Roger Pratt**
Editor & 2nd Unit Director **Julian Doyle**
Original music **Michael Kamen**
Brazil music by **Ary Barroso** English
lyrics **S.K. Russell**
Performed by **Oeoff & Maria Muldaur**
Forces of Darkness arranged &
perfomed by **Mark Holmes**
Stunt arranger **Bill Weston**
Assistant director **Guy Travers**
Camera operator **David Garfath**
Sound recordist **Bob Doyle**
Unit manager **Linda Bruce**
Script supervisor **Penny Eyles**
Production designer **Norman Garwood**
Special effects supervisor **George Gibbs**
Model effects supervisor **Richard Conway**
Costume designer **James Acheson**
Hair & make-up **Maggie Weston**
Art directors **John Beard & Keith Pain**
Production manager **Graham Ford**
Casting director **Irene Lamb**
Producer **Patrick Cassavetti**
Producer **Arnon Milchan**
Director **Terry Gilliam**
Lee International Film Studios and on
location in London and Cumbria, England
and France
Technicolor, 138 mins, 1985

THE BRAND NEW MONTY PYTHON BOK

The cover is emblazoned with the promise of Tits 'n' Bums – A Weekly Look at Church Architecture – hidden under a black and white cover jacket with dirty fingerprints all over it. Gilliam was distressed at Methuen's obvious fake efforts and eagerly redesigned the look with convincing brown stains for total confusion and intriguing repulsion! It contains loads of new material, lavish cut-out pages and inserts. Biggles is Extremely Silly (1938), Notice of the Availability of Film Rights to Page Six, The Bigot (a newsletter), The London Casebook of Detective Rene Descartes, The Adventures of Walter Wallabee (comic strip), Film Review with Philip Jackson, Rat Recipes and Chez Rat (menu), The British Apathy League, Let's Talk About Bottoms, Page 71, Ferndean School Report for God, Cheeseshop (The Word Game),

The Official Medallic Commemoration of the History of Mankind, The Anagrams Gape (4) and the Anagram-Haters Page, Teach Yourself Surger. *The Brand New Monty Python Papperbok* appeared in 1974 – the same except for the Tits 'n' Bum cover.

Written by **GRAHAM CHAPMAN, JOHN CLEESE, TERRY GILLIAM, ERIC IDLE, TERRY JONES & MICHAEL PALIN**
Methuen, 1973

BROADEN YOUR MIND – AN ENCYCLOPAEDIA OF THE AIR

Comedy series desperately trying to repeat the enthusiastic audience involvement of *I'm Sorry I'll Read That Again* for television. The first series, starring Tim Brooke-Taylor and Graeme Garden, ran for six weeks from 28 October 1968. Guest appearances came from Chapman, Palin and Jones under the production eye of Sydney Lotterby – rubbed up so wonderfully by the *At Last the 1948 Show* team. *I'm Sorry I'll Read That Again* gags were resurrected with alarming regularity as well as veteran *Cambridge Circus* moments like the Elizabethan Music Hall double act. Chapman and Cleese wrote very little for the programmes although they contributed a brilliant reworking of the almighty ant skit from *1948 Show* as a discussion of birds dropping stones – pointing the way towards *Monty Python and the Holy Grail*. Cambridge player Bill Oddie joined his future *Goodies* pals for one episode of the first series, but when the second series enjoyed a seven-week run from 17 November 1969, Oddie's hard-nosed comic genius was a permanent performing and writing force. Oddie's pessimistic barbs were the perfect contrast to the joyful optimism of Brooke-Taylor and Garden and the Beeb were keen to secure a third series. But by then, *Monty Python* was beating the reheated antics with ease and Oddie realised that he, Brooke-Taylor and Garden needed to create another format for themselves. The result

appeared the following year in the shape of *The Goodies*...

TIM BROOKE-TAYLOR
GRAEME GARDEN
BILL ODDIE
GRAHAM CHAPMAN
TERRY JONES
MICHAEL PALIN
Written by **Oddie/Garden, Brooke-Taylor, Cleese/Chapman, Jones/Palin & Idle**
Editor **Jim Franklin**
Producer **Sydney Lotterby**
1st Series 28 October–2 December 1968
2nd Series 17 November–29 December 1969
BBC2

BULLSEYE!

Two blokes stagger round England in hot pursuit of two other blokes who look exactly like them and there, my friends, is where the similarities between William Shakespeare and this film come to an end. Produced and directed by Michael Winner, the film came about simply because good mates Michael Caine and Roger Moore had never worked together and longed to do comedy. Here the dream team come together, overact blindly and create one of the most boring thrillers in history. There's no doubting that our two heroes seem to be having a good time and, besides, this is Moore and Caine, two icons of British cinema, so it's not all doom and gloom. But, really the storyline is so confusing it would take Raymond Chandler to work it out, and Michael Caine's commentary just adds to the confusion – even though it's only due to this voice-over that the audience can tell which Caine and Moore is which during the Scottish finale. There's some good physical business with Caine getting beaten about the head, but with everything from Buster Keaton sight gags (the broken home visual) and a bonking Rotweiller, the only way for this film is down. Somehow, into all this mess, Winner persuaded John Cleese to make a gag appearance. Sadly, although Winner was a huge admirer of *A Fish Called*

Wanda, Cleese does not cameo as Archie Leach here – a nice touch to see the lawyer enjoying his ill-gotten gains in Barbados – no, in *Bullseye!* Cleese plays a bloke who looks like John Cleese, pinching Caine's idea for a movie of the wacky adventures and supposedly doing a runner with the money. Looking totally bemused, muttering a few words about the number for the bank vault and sharing the scene with a glam girl, Caine and the Barbados scenery, Cleese is totally wasted. The in-joke isn't that funny either and it might as well have been either you or I playing the scene, apart from the fact that it would have had a lot less street cred... and we don't look anything like John Cleese.

21st Century Film/Castle Premier
Gerald Bradley-Smith & Sir John
Bavistock **ROGER MOORE**
Sidney Lipton & Dr Daniel wicklar
MICHAEL CAINE
Willie Metcalfe **SALLY KIRKLAND**
Inspector Grosse **DERREN NESBITT**
Sir Hugh **NICHOLAS COURTNEY**
With guests **PATSY KENSIT,
ALEXANDRA PIGG, JENNY
SEAGROVE** and
appearing without permission from his
mother – **JOHN CLEESE**, as the man
on the beach who looks like John Cleese
Screenplay by **Leslie Bricusse,
Laurence Marks & Maurice Gran**
Associate Producer **Stephen Barker**
Executive Producer **Menaham Golan &
Ami Artzi**
Director **Michael Winner**
1990, 92 mins

CAMBRIDGE CIRCUS

From its inception in 1883, the Footlights had played an important part at Cambridge University. Flirting with West End success with Jack Hulbert's Footlights Club in the 1930s, it was not until 1960 and the explosion of *Beyond the Fringe* that the group was really put on the map. Within a few short months, Peter Cook, Dudley Moore, Jonathan Miller and Alan Bennett became the four most famous Englishmen until the Beatles came along. Their success, combined with a mutual obsession with Spike Milligan's work, formed the comic ideals of the fledgling Pythons with, importantly, Chapman, Cleese and Idle moving to Cambridge in the footsteps of the Footlighters. With Chapman returning to medicine, Cleese alone of the pre-*Python*s was involved in the Summer of 1963 revue *A Clump of Plinths*. The title, deriving from the word Clump, which amused Brooke-Taylor, and Plinth, which took the fancy of Cleese, replaced the original random suggestion You Can't Call a Show 'Cornflakes', although cast members subsequently believed Humphrey Barclay had fiddled the ballot. Whatever the case, the 34 skits included in the revue proved a huge success (five were written by Cleese, who appeared in 13), theatrical impresario Michael White rustled up equity cards for the members while Barclay's persistence eventually led to a crack at the West End stage and a title change to *Cambridge Circus*. The Edinburgh festival was completely bypassed as the original line-up of Tim Brooke-Taylor, Tony Buffery, John Cleese, David Hatch, Jo Kendall, Chris Stuart-Clark and Bill Oddie, with music by Oddie and Hugh MacDonald tuned the performance for one week at the Robin Hood Theatre, Averham, and a week at the York festival, before beginning a three-week run at the New Arts on 10 July (which was extended to five weeks due to popular demand) and transferring to the Lyric Theatre on 16 August 1963. Slightly elongated and amended for the West End, Graham Chapman, putting down his trainee stereoscope at St. Barts, jumped aboard the show when Tony Buffery opted out soon after the West End opening to continue his psychology research. Show highlights included David Hatch, Chris Stuart-Clark, Tim Brooke-Taylor and John

Cleese in the Oscar Wilde sketch, Patients for the Use Of with Brooke-Taylor and Oddie (later resurfacing for *At Last the 1948 Show*); the debut for Cleese and Kendall as John & Mary – later a regular feature of *I'm Sorry I'll Read That Again*; the Elizabethan frolic Swap A Jest with Shakespearean comedy delivered as a contemporary double act performed by Brooke-Taylor and Stuart-Clark; Buffery's farmyard impressions; and, perhaps most interestingly of all, the rare Oddie/Cleese collaboration on a Somerset Maugham parody It Can't End Like This.

But, by common consent, the finest part of the show was John Cleese's Judge Not courtroom sketch with Cleese in sparkling form explaining every obvious detail to Hatch's Judge, bantering with Brooke-Taylor's music hall comedian in the dock, Percy Molar (tapping into traditional gags via the 'Jamaica' hook and objecting before the expected punchline), milking Bill Oddie's dwarf defendant Sidney Bottle by allowing brief, pointed glimpses of hand (later extended to include a third and then a fourth hand – which was black to boot!) and giving the close of the show over to Brooke-Taylor's doddering old usher, towards the end of the run literally taking up minutes to shuffle across the stage. In this 80th anniversary year of The Footlights, it was a definitive return to music hall tradition, tugging a forelock to the ground-breaking but out-of-style satire boom and following the same road of fame opened up by Cook and co. by doing their own thing. During the Lyric run Chris Stuart-Clark left the revue and, indeed, show business altogether, to tackle a career in teaching. However, David Hatch, with an offered teaching post in Basingstoke and John Cleese, set for a career in law, resisted the temptation of solid employment and stayed with the show. After five months *Cambridge Circus* was laid to rest on 9 November 1963, but not before all the cast had enjoyed invaluable, much celebrated experience and Cleese's student debts of £600 had been wiped clean.

In December producer Humphrey Barclay put together a BBC radio presentation of *Cambridge Circus*, which eventually transmogrified into the legendary radio series *I'm Sorry I'll Read That Again*. During Cleese's early days at the BBC it was suggested that the *Cambridge Circus* should be resurrected for a new audience; thus it was that the team journeyed to face the bemused stage-hands and confused waiters of New Zealand and perform the show for six weeks. For both Cleese and Barclay it was goodbye to stable BBC posts, while for Chapman it was far more permanent, turning his back on a medical career. Among a group of medical students chosen to meet the Queen Mother for a tea party opening of a new biochemistry building at St. Barts Hospital, Chapman mentioned his chance to go to New Zealand, received positive feedback and broke the news to his parents, explaining it was practically by Royal command! Chris Stuart-Clark having left during the Lyric run, saw his prime pieces taken over by post-*Cambridge Circus* Footlighter Jonathan Lynn (a student contemporary of Eric Idle). New material featured Brooke-Taylor, Oddie and Lynn performing the classic custard pie education skit from Terry Jones and Michael Palin, which had originally appeared in Oxford Mafia revues. Dubbed Humour Without Tears for the Cambridge folk, the piece was brilliantly injected with the comedy of pain typical of the group, pinpointing that slapstick humour hurts and is unpleasant for those taking part, perversely making it even more funny for those merely watching. Touring the country for six weeks and billed as Masters of Mirth, thanks to their university training, the team met some audiences who expected a film presentation and even a few who complained that this was the only circus they had been to which didn't have any elephants!
New Zealand also offered the chance to resurrect a load of old material for four radio specials with absurd names like *The Cardinal Richelieu Show*,

The Peter Titheridge Show and *The Mrs. Muir Show*, named in honour of some old dear who thought the arrival of the team was an invasion by cinematic Zulus – the Michael Caine film due in town shortly afterward. The revue was successful enough to warrant a stab at the American market, settling in New York and playing Broadway for 23 performances at the Plymouth Theater from 6 to 24 October 1964 under the guidance of respected impresario Sol Hawk – celebrated for bringing Russian ballet and opera to America. Prize items like Brooke-Taylor's outlandish Dame Edith Evans in the Oscar Wilde sketch hit the cutting room floor, while Cleese's Cloak and Dagger was refashioned. Fresh material for this major assignment included Chapman's parody of Marc Antony's death scene, Cleese's Slightly Less Silly Than the Other Court Skit Court Skit and the company, with its finger firmly on the pulse, presenting a Hallelujah Chorus à la Beatles – a pre-*Rutles* Eric Idle item brought along by Jonathan Lynn – which was a major hit. Indeed the fab lads from Cambridge followed the Fab Four from Liverpool onto *The Ed Sullivan Show* performing two sketches, followed by a one-off gig *In Pursuit of Excellence* – An Afternoon for the John F. Kennedy Library on 15 November 1964, decamped in Connecticut and fully transferred off Broadway to Greenwich Village, 'Square East' 15 West 4th Street until February 1965 when, akin to *Beyond the Fringe*, an American cast took over the performances. All but Cleese returned home immediately, but, thankfully, a record of this unique comedy event captures the spirit and imagination of the piece. The original soundtrack of the show features Cleese in five sketches. The major highlights are his weather forecast in terms of BBC style during the Old Testament era in *B.B.C.B.C.* and his typically officious prosecuting council in the courtroom sketch *Judge Not*. Cleese also crops up in *Great Moments in British Theatre* (*How Green Was My Buttonhole?*), *Sing Sing and O.H.M.S.* – other

tracks being *Green Line Bus, Patients For The Use Of, Boring Sexy Song, Pride and Joy, Boring Straight Song, Swap A Jest, Those Were the Days.*

Odeon PPMC 1208 (1963)/Odeon PCS 3046 (1965)
original presentation
Music by **Bill Oddie & Hugh MacDonald**
Designer **Stephen Mullin**
Costumes **Judy Birdwood**
Lighting **Tim Fell**
Director **Humphrey Barclay**
Presented by **Michael White**

CASPER

Stunning ghost effects, frantic over-acting and loads of ranting from almost everybody involved, this is an enjoyable family movie from the ultra-productive Spielberg stable, taking the essence of 1950s *Casper* cartoons and comics, injecting some heartfelt super cool teenage lust elements and creating a three-dimensional spectre universal courtesy of George Lucas and co. Starting with a classic inclusion of the Universal logo into the opening sequence, the modern-day Cinderella parable is charming enough, although the signposted reference towards the Halloween ball and the time limit to the duration of the wish makes the whole thing a tad obvious. However, the voice of Casper could melt the coldest heart, coupled with the endearingly bulbous head and watery eyes filled with emotion as he remembers his past life via wondrous toys and parental regrets, while Bill Pullman, in Jimmy Stewart terrain, reasons with the spooks and fights to get over the loss of his wife, total fear and fatherly angst.
The major earth-bound attraction is Christina Ricca's sexual awakening and longing for friendship (aptly enough, having just grown out of the cinematic Addams Family), with eyes almost as wide as Casper's, a delightful little girl lost in paradise attitude coupled with 90s street-cred. Certainly, she takes no nonsense from the trio of repulsive Uncle ghosts ('Drop dead!' 'Too Late!' like

Feldman in *Young Frankenstein*), who work poor Casper like Cinders, enjoying life with quickly digested food, copious amounts of alcohol and some impromptu singing of the pop classics – notably *It's My Party and I'll Die If I Want To* – (well, it tickled me) and a classic rendition of *Harvest Moon* with Casp as an accordion! There's a snatch from my favourite Frank Sinatra song, *That's Life*, and Bill Pullman even bonds with the trio of ectoplasmic scumbags via a touching lads night out with Elvis karaoke – giving the King a mention like every recent fantasy movie worth its salt. The sub-plot – focusing on the blonde snobbish girl, her dippy boyfriend, tricks to break Ricca's heart and also her party – are dealt with rather half-heartedly. Mind you, Pullman's brilliantly animated ghost, the life and death machines, break-ins and hidden treasure are all being resolved at the same time so the petty backbiting of teenage romance can hardly stand the pace.

For film nuts, movie references are superb, ranging from the obvious name check for Steven King to the rather more interesting seven dwarf-like beds for the three manic ghosts and Ricca's apt throwaway comment. Obvious and hidden references come together during Pullman's wash and brush up after being infiltrated by spirits; he peers into the mirror reminiscent of *Poltergeist* – pumped up and decorated by the mega-bucks guest star turns of Rodney Dangerfield (good company), Clint Eastwood (brilliantly self-parodying) and Mel Gibson (spot-on with just a look of appreciation for the new face) before reverting to horror and a rather splendid ghoul. The key to the whole game of life is hidden within a leather-bound, cut-out copy of Frankenstein – seemingly left over from Colin Clive's last experiment, the trio of ghosts fool Pullman into thinking sunlight kills them by doing the old 'I'm Melting!' act from *The Wizard of Oz* and best film gag of all, an early guest appearance from Dan Aykroyd in Ghostbuster gear, totally beaten and muttering – 'Who you gonna call? – Someone else!'

Total class.

However, naturally the best laughs come from Eric Idle's cowardly bad luck plagued baddie, enlivening a rather minor supporting turn with touches of visual comic business and his usual ineffectual, bumbling British niceties. Greed is the name of the game and if Idle's evil is doubled by Cathy Moriarty's performance (an apt name for an apt master criminal) then the continual reliance on his intellectual knowledge and foolhardy actions creates some nifty comic moments. Like a refugee from the Walt Disney School of Villainy, Idle sits by during the reading of the will, with animals across the globe getting millions and his female associate getting – yep, you guessed it – the haunted house, complete with clichéd cryptic message to a treasure. Idle's great at acting petrified in front of a computer animator's imagination; the spaced-out exorcist sequence is cleverly off the wall, and Idle, gingerly looking over the top of his car, gives Moriarty more than a lesson or two in comic scene stealing. Sure, Idle's the put-upon Brit, ordered about by his American female ogress companion, suffering burnt hand, bashed bandages and chaotic ride on Casper's father's mad machine, but in the end he lets rip with a short-lived but glorious fight back – although his character is just booted into touch rather than given a proper farewell. His screen time may be limited but there are some treasurable moments, notably his karate chops into thin air, complete with slicked hair and charming foam moustache, and best of all, his early repeated instructions to the dismembered voice of Casper before shouting 'I am armed!' and whipping out his mobile phone. Timed to perfection. It may not be great art but the actors all throw themselves into the nightmarish fun, the effects are amazing and there's a nice glow of family community and back to ghostly basics at the close. It's really for kids, but hey, if that's the case I 'aint growing up... and check out the superb and gob-smacking beyond words Little Richard riff through *Casper the Friendly Ghost* – if you walk out on

those credits you are no longer my friend!

Amblin Entertainment Universal
Dr James Harvey **BILL PULLMAN**
Kat Harvey **CHRISTINA RICCI**
Carrigan Crittenden **CATHY MORIARTY**
Dibs **ERIC IDLE**
Voice of Casper **MALACHI PEARSON**
The Ghostly Trio **JOE NIPOTE, JOE ALASKEY & BRAD GARRETT**
reenplay by **Sheeri Stoner & Deanna Oliver**
Editor **Michael Kahn**
Music **James Horner**
Producer **Colin Wilson**
Director **Brad Silberling**
Photography **Dean Cundey**
Executive producers **Steven Spielberg, Gerald R Molen & Jeffrey A Montgomery**
1995 110 mins

GRAHAM CHAPMAN

If one image was chosen to epitomise *Monty Python* it would have to be Graham Chapman wandering around as if nothing is wrong while sporting a pair of antlers on his head. It sums up the intelligent, sophisticated, repressed British character brought starkly into contrast with total absurdity while both sides work in perfect harmony.

Graham Chapman was born 8 January 1941 in Leicester, Midlands to his policeman father, Walter, and mother, Edith. Educated at Melton Mowbray Grammar School, from the age of seven Chapman was obsessed with listening to radio comedy, importantly nursing an interest in the writing and, predictably, finding himself on the exact same wavelength as Spike Milligan and *The Goon Show*. Of the Cambridge-based Pythons, Chapman was the first to arrive, continuing his medical studies at Emmanuel College (Graham's elder brother John, born 1937, was a qualified doctor – having shared a wartime experience of witnessing bits of human body after an air-raid both were fascinated with all matters medical) and desperately trying to get into the Footlights. He was initially turned down by the club secretary,

David Frost, being informed that members were asked for auditions by appointment only. The place to be seen was in Smoking concerts, put on for other students at the college and events folk with Footlight clout frequently checked out for new talent. Thus, with a fellow student, Chapman mounted his own smoker fuelled by plenty of claret and involving a simple drama teacher parody which allowed for the inclusion of Graham's love of silly mime. In his second year he became a prized member of Footlights with early genius spotted in his act concerning the growth of a giant magnetic hand. Teaming up with John Cleese, the two wrote and appeared in the 1962 revue *Double Take* alongside Tim Brooke-Taylor, Humphrey Barclay, Alan George, Nigel Brown, Miriam Margolyes, Robert Atkins and Tony Hendra. Directed by none other than Trevor Nunn, this ramshackle but vitally important show included items like I Buffoon, Duello and the subsequently cringe-making musical number We're Most Important Cavemen featuring the cast in fur skins. Items like Don't Touch the Duke, Meek Week and several of Bill Oddie's songs warranted resurrection later for *I'm Sorry I'll Read That Again* while the Chapman/Cleese/Brooke-Taylor karate sketch was reworked for *At Last the 1948 Show*. *Double Take* was the culmination of Chapman's university career, leaving a year before Cleese, to further his medical studies at St. Bart's Hospital. During the evenings, however, Chapman continued performing cabaret with future *National Lampoon* editor and co-creator of *Spitting Image*, Tony Hendra – an old pal from *Double Take* days.

A belated addition to *Cambridge Circus*, Chapman stayed with the show until the close on Broadway, returned to England and successfully finished his studies to become a qualified doctor. As he couldn't afford to pay his back tax if he returned to medicine, Chapman, returned to the lucrative and productive world of comedy – although qualified in medicine throughout his life he would have needed a year's experience in hospital before being allowed into general practice. However, even before fully ditching his career in medicine Chapman continued to keep his comic eye in by writing some solo material for *The Illustrated Weekly Hudd* with Roy Hudd before reuniting with Cleese for *The Frost Report*, *At Last the 1948 Show*, *Broaden Your Mind*, *Marty* and *Doctor in the House*. Cleese and Chapman were commissioned to write eight scripts for *Marty* – although six were returned as unsuitable (written for group comedy rather than Feldman's required one funny character surrounded by stooges). The work though was certainly up to scratch as five of the rejected items were later used in *Python* – including the classic Mouse Problem (already once removed from *The Magic Christian*). Chapman wrote filler gags for *The Petula Clark Show*, while alongside regular *Frost* writer Barry Cryer, he contributed scripts to Ronnie Corbett's sitcom *No – That's Me Over There*, penned several *Doctor in the House* episodes and wrote the Canadian series, *Look Here Now*, starring Ronnie Corbett – some days would see him writing *Python* in the morning, Corbett in the afternoon and *Doctor* at night! In the meantime, Chapman and Cleese had been embraced by cinema with several screenplays and additional material credits, including *Rent a Dick* and the legendary Peter Sellers comedy *The Magic Christian*. One unfulfilled project, commissioned by director Carlo Ponti and destined to reunite his wife, Sophia Loren, and *Millionairess* co-star, Peter Sellers, was entitled *Ditto*. Based on a short story concerning a man who duplicates his wife and creates a sexy, younger model. Graham Chapman and John Cleese constructed an elongated, more manic variation on the possibilities, creating scores of Sellers and Loren clones. However, due to a run of unsuccessful pictures, Ponti's power faded, the scriptwriters were not contacted again and despite retaining a copy of the script, the director controlled all rights to the film. By now, of course, Chapman was fully in swing with *Monty Python*, accepting outside offers such as appearing in *Doctor in Trouble* and writing *Doctor On the Go*, when team assignments permitted. His fame saw him embraced by the music fraternity MCing a gig performed by The Who, with his close friend Keith Moon. Although failing to enthuse the audience, Chapman called for two minutes of abuse and they loved it – following which Moon broke into a hotel to get Chapman a bottle of gin! Perhaps the abuse technique explains why Chapman didn't MC Paul McCartney's Wings gig at the Hard Rock Cafe.

However, he was always the most self-conscious Python, with nervous mannerisms, pipe-smoking, mad comedy and plenty of drink; his performance was often affected. Over Christmas 1977 he gave up the booze for good but still retained that off-kilter *Python* edge. He received a *Sun* award from Lord Mountbatten by leaping in the air, squawking and crawling off with the prize in his mouth. Earlier, in the mid-1970s, he had returned to Cambridge to give a speech, terrified, dressed as a carrot (a costume run up for him by *Python* designer Hazel Pethig) and saying absolutely nothing as his comment on the whole thing! Initially greeted with interest, he quietly walked off the stage to the bemusement of his audience and while this disturbing surrealism remained Chapman eventually found stability in his private life with a 20-year relationship with David Sherlock with whom he became guardian to an adopted son, John Tomiczek, a Liverpudlian teenage runaway whom Graham met in London in 1971. John died in 1992. However, professionally, nothing gave him more pleasure than reforming with the Pythons for *Life of Brian*. Following the completion of the film, publicity and making gaining far more time than Chapman's solo cinematic attempt with *The Odd Job*, he lived in Los Angeles for part of 1979/1980 appearing on *Hollywood Squares* and *The Big Show* while still maintaining his English obsession of

His finest hour: Graham Chapman as the man they call Brian

devouring *The Times* crossword. He wrote his brilliant *A Liar's Autobiography Vol. VI* in 1980 and the successfully wacky retelling of key events in his life led to Chapman's revolutionary series of campus lectures and stand-up presentations across American and Australia through the 1980s. These initially came about thanks to concentrated publicity for the book and arriving at a Film Society meeting held at Facets Multimedia, Chicago. The appearance, plugging the book and introducing a screening of a Python film meant Chapman had to say a few words to the audience and answer questions. The introspective performer loved the experience and, on returning home and listening to a tape of his triumph, devised a comic lecture which he toured over 23 US college campuses. Trying to fit in at least one tour a year, Chapman slightly changed the emphasis for comedy club audiences, re-enacting his legendary one-man wrestling act, performing his musical masterpiece, Medical Love Song and even digging

up the old *Matching Tie* album material Elephantoplasty. His reminiscences always embraced his days with the *Monty Python* team (often illustrated with clips of 'Sam Peckinpah's Salad Days' and the notorious but perfectly Chapmanesque Cannibal close to series two), comments on his fellow Pythons' solo ventures, memories of his pal Keith Moon, candid but above all hilarious observations about his drink problem and comments on homosexuality. He even demonstrated the legendary practice of 'Shitties' taught to him by Moon. Beginning with a resurrection of The Who's two minutes of abuse, Terry Jones caught his performance and was astonished at his confident manner with the audience. Kenneth Williams-like, Chapman enthused about retreading old glories for an audience while his current assignments were forever on the starting blocks. While his lectures wowed the crowds he struggled to float his pet project of a pirate romp, named *Yellowbeard*. Roping in a barrel-load of old pals like John Cleese, Eric Idle, Marty Feldman and

Peter Cook, Chapman starred, produced and co-wrote the film. Despite the film's half-baked quality, rumours abounded that a sequel was on the cards although Chapman, distressed at losing directorial and editorial control of the film and weeding over old ground, decided against it. However, the characters did, he felt, lend themselves to further adventures, and he initially mused on the thought of basing a movie round the characters of Clement and Mansell – played by Eric Idle and Nigel Planer – whom he felt stole the show in *Yellowbeard*.

In the mid-1980s Chapman became involved with the Dangerous Sports Club – reflected in his hosting of the movie compilation show *The Dangerous Film Club* – a group which pioneered bungee jumping and celebrated adrenaline junkies and thrill-inducing excitement. Eventually footage from the club's ventures replaced the *Python* pieces in his lectures. As part of his obsession Chapman once tobogganed down a St. Moritz slope and raised money for Bob Geldof's Sports Aid by being catapulted through Hyde Park. In 1988 Chapman was working on a film exploring the exploits of the Dangerous Sports Club while still hard at work plugging for the American television time-travelling comedy *Jake's Journey* which he wrote and starred in. He served as executive producer on *Love Potion*, directed by *Python* film editor, Julian Doyle and towards the end of his life dug up his old script for the aborted Peter Sellers film *Ditto*. Despite Ponti's control over the piece, Chapman contacted Cleese with a view to rewriting it. Although Cleese willingly supported Chapman's resurrection of the idea, he declined to get involved and thus Graham freshened up the screenplay with David Sherlock for a production based in Canada in which Chapman would star and also direct. Chapman changed certain elements of the film and vastly reduced the special effects budget in order to get this cloning comedy made. Sherlock has vowed to get Chapman's last written piece filmed even now. Although Chapman had never found his post-*Python Fawlty Towers* or *Ripping Yarns*, he was at his happiest and busiest in 1988 with several promising film and television projects on the boil. Tragically he was diagnosed as suffering from cancer of the tonsils in November 1988. The disease spread to his spine and for a year he was in and out of hospital. Chapman was still working, contributing filmed material for *The Movie Life of George* and *Parrot Sketch Not Included*, signing a new deal with Imagine Entertainment and promising to attend *Python* celebrations at the Chicago Museum of Broadcasting in the first week of October. However, in September 1989, home from hospital, it was a mere three days before the pain became unbearable. He was rushed back to hospital and told that cancer had spread irretrievably. His son, John Tomiczek, flew in from the US, David Sherlock was with him till the end and his old *Python* cohorts rallied round. Indeed, the enthusiastic ideas of a filmic reunion kept Chapman buoyant, but sadly death intervened while the project was still very much a lifeline of hope. Terry Jones was with Chapman the day of his death and at his bedside when he died was old partner John Cleese and Michael Palin. Chapman passed away on 4 October 1989, just a day short of the 20th anniversary of the first broadcast of *Monty Python's Flying Circus*. The slightly skew-whiff timing of a comic genius seemed strangely apt right up to the end. Terry Jones called it 'the worst case of party-pooping I've ever seen!' while Eric Idle, holding back his tears, explained that he always thought Palin talked too much and Chapman had died rather than take any more. A small family funeral was held which none of the Pythons attended, preferring to sent a large floral wreath in the shape of a giant foot with the words – 'To Graham from the other Pythons. Stop us if we're getting too silly.' The Rolling Stones sent flowers and two months later the Pythons gathered for Chapman's memorial service.

CHAUCER'S KNIGHT: THE PORTRAIT OF A MEDIEVAL MERCENARY

Terry Jones returned to his historian roots for this controversial retelling of 30 lines from the prologue of Chaucer's *Canterbury Tales*. Jones feels Chaucer was a dangerous influence, writing the truth in English under the cover of comedy – indeed much like Pythons centuries after him. The work of Terry Jones was, at first, humoured by his historian peers but embraced by enthused, academic outsiders. Jones had never lost his love of history and owns an expensive library of Chaucer scholarly works – suitably that library now contains a book written by Jones himself. Far from the gallant chap he was always interpreted as being, Jones revealed the knight to be a cunning, despicable figure who, via Chaucer's inspired use of satire, was painted as a hero while in fact perpetrating vicious acts of violence. Over 300 pages of addressing a 600-year-old joke, this was hardly the Terry Jones *Python* followers loved, but his contemporary, uncluttered approach allows the reader to enter the world of Chaucer without academic hang-ups. An idea for this stemmed from his university days when he wrote a thesis on Chaucer's Knight at Alexandria. This was far more than just a comic talent using his name to publish a book; this was challenging, ground-breaking stuff which questioned accepted learned theories. Literary historians celebrate this piece of prose as Chaucer's telling of a victory while in historical truth the battle was a complete disaster. Jones the historian firmly believed this discrepancy was there for a purpose and decided to track down the truth. Writing during *Python*, grabbing time at the British Museum for research over a period of ten years and finally finishing the piece post *Python*, Jones considers the historian never stops learning and rewrote the vast sections concerning Prussia when the book came out in paperback. With a focused and well-informed mind, Jones paints a convincing, interesting and exciting piece of history.

Chaucer's Knight: The Portrait of a Medieval Mercenary by **Terry Jones** Published by Weidenfeld & Nicolson, 1985

CHEERS: Simon Says

Beloved American sitcom which gathered a Damon Runyon-like bunch of social misfits, drunken eccentricities and fractured romantics in a cosy bar where all human frailties/desires are played out. The heart and soul of the well-rounded characters made the jokes gell and the playing was universally excellent. The series won an Emmy in 1983 and it continued to reform and adjust to keep the freshness flowing. By 1987, award-laden and hugely popular, the show was injected with British sophistication when John Cleese took five days to film a guest-starring turn in *Simon Says*. Playing the old school friend of perennially stressed Frasier, Cleese embraced the superiority of his marriage guidance counsellor part, as a man in town to collect an honorary degree. He sang a duet from their old school, and gave the benefit of his intellectual, cold reasoning to the series regulars. As an outsider, Cleese doesn't get to be endearing, faces a myriad of anti-Brit jibes and throws a hated spanner in the romance of Sam/Diane by claiming they are incompatible for marriage. The show's comedy comes from the frantic attempts to convince Cleese to say the opposite, allowing the British prime ranter to get frustrated, anxious and wild-eyed, dragged from his meal, shower and bed until the final moment of typically overheated angst. James Burrows was inspired to write *Cheers* with such care having become an admirer of *Fawlty Towers* and to get Cleese involved was a dream come true. Indeed, there is an awful lot of Fawlty in Cleese's role here.

Did You Know? This was Cleese's first appearance on an American sitcom and it won him an Emmy. So popular was his performance that Burrows arranged for Cleese to reprise his role for a show scheduled

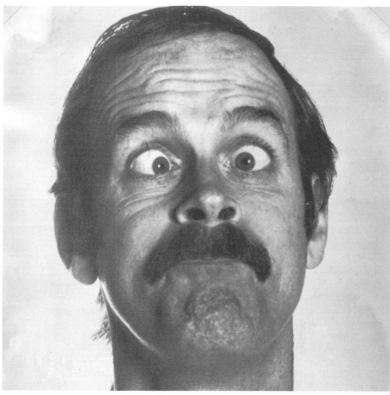

Classic John Cleese pose from 1979

on 13 April 1989. The story would see Cleese returning to collect the money for his previous marriage consultation but, sadly, Cleese couldn't free himself from other commitments.

TED DANSON, SHELLEY LONG, RHEA PERLMAN, JOHN RATZENBERGER, WOODY HARRELSON, KELSEY GRAMMER, GEORGE WENDT
Dr. Simon Finch-Royce **JOHN CLEESE**
Screenplay by **Peter Casey & David Lee**
Producer **David Angell**
Director **James Burrows**
Paramount/Charles Burrows Charles
Broadcast 5 March 1987, NBC TV

JOHN CLEESE

One of the main men in the history of British comedy and as I write, arguably the funniest human being in the country. His entry in *The International Film & TV Year Book*

includes references to four fictitious movies, one added every year until Cleese got so frustrated that nobody had noticed so he stopped doing it. The unmade classics are *The Bonar Law Story*, *Abbott & Costello Meet Sir Michael Swann*, *The Young Anthony Barber* and *Confessions of a Programme Planner*. Such is the nature of the man – second only to Peter Cook in flamboyant unflagging comic genius – that in the same vein his most cherished possession is recorded as 'four nasal hairs from Alexander the Great' and his favourite memory 'scoring England's winning goal in the 1966 World Cup Final'.
John Marwood Cleese was born 27 October 1939 in Western-Super-Mare, his father changed the family name from Cheese to Cleese in order to avoid ridicule when he enlisted for WWI. Plagued by over-protective parents in relatively old age when Cleese was born (Dad, Reginald Francis, 46, Mum, Muriel Cross, 40 – John's middle name came from his

grandfather, Marwood Joseph Cross) led to a sheltered if comfortable childhood. His major complaint was that he was never allowed to own a bike in case he hurt himself and Tim Brooke-Taylor remembers Cleese always going on about it even at Cambridge. However, comedy (in the shape of favourites George Burns, Amos 'n' Andy, Frankie Howerd and The Marx Brothers) soon usurped the perilous pleasures of the Raleigh. At the age of ten, sick in bed, Cleese wrote a few pages of comic dialogue in his school exercise book in the cross-talking style of Jimmy Jewel and Ben Warris – at the time sparring with Jon Pertwee in the radio show *Up the Pole*. Six foot tall at the age of 12, Cleese, as with everyone from Hattie Jacques to Harry Enfield, started making people laugh as a defence mechanism. Educated at St. Peter's Preparatory School, Weston-super-Mare during the early 1950s he half-heartedly got involved in acting, with a role in *A Cure for Colds* and the title part in *Scenes from Twelfth Night: The Tricking of Malvolio*, winning the Christmas 1951 award for 'The Twelve and over writing competition'. He later attended Clifton College, from 1953 to 1958 gaining A levels in physics, maths and chemistry, and where as well as playing for the football team he contributed to the house entertainments appearing in Molière's *Tartuffe* and lifting Flanders & Swann material for a revue. Like Chapman, Cleese was also spellbound by *The Goon Show* at the same time as John Lennon was allowing his Rock 'n' Roll obsession to embrace bizarre comic language and Peter Cook was faking illness to stay in his university bed, all tuning into Milligan and the gang.
Cleese's other chief love was cricket, eventually reaching the 1st XI and playing at Lord's for several public school matches. In a 1958 Clifton college v. M.C.C. match Cleese got Denis Compton out (caught Whitty, bowled Cleese 22).
An early interest in biology and the B.F. Skinner tests on rats gave way to an interest in the legal system and Cleese was set for Cambridge and a

career in law. He passed the entrance exams for Downing College – although he would have preferred Pembroke. Although eventually working under two grand law tutors he couldn't enrol for another two years thanks to the 1957 abolition of National Service resulting in many more applications than normal. Thus, Cleese returned to his old prep school to teach.

Once at Cambridge he was encouraged to try for the Footlights, although his half-hearted introduction echoes the infamous Fred Astaire audition. Admitting incompetence in both song (he had been forced to take extra Greek at school to compensate) and dance, when asked what he actually could contribute to the group, he meekly suggested that, 'I suppose I try to make people laugh!' Rejected, Cleese found his way in via the back door, co-writing and performing a sketch with his friend Alan Hutchinson, whom he had met on his second day at Cambridge. Besides, Hutchinson had a semblance of influence thanks to a friendship with the Footlights treasurer and Cleese saw one of his sketches feature in the 1961 Revue *I Thought I Saw It Move*. Performed between 6 and 17 June, it headlined David Frost during his mega Peter Cook-fixation period, plus Humphrey Barclay, Mike Burrell and John Wood who would find fame following a name change to John Fortune. The Cleese/Hutchinson contribution was a typically black BBC news-type report delivered by Barclay and detailing a dog stuck down a mineshaft which leads to the deaths of its owners.

Having moved to digs less than 100 yards from the Footlights and 300 yards from the law school, Cleese began hanging out with Tim Brooke-Taylor, Bill Oddie and Chris Stuart-Clark, furnishing his comedy with elements lifted from Flanders & Swann while finding his niche with biting comic barbs – one aimed at his housemaster caused another member of staff to fall off a chair with laughter. Soon after, Cleese met Graham Chapman for the first time and, despite initially finding him

rather distant company, began penning material with him, completing a dozen top-notch pieces at university, including a mountaineering skit for the revue. The two gained quite a reputation together. If he was disturbed in his room with paper, pens and an open Bible, fellow students would automatically know he had been working with Chapman! The two would perform together for the first time in 1962's *Double Take* (later performed in Edinburgh hand in hand with Ibsen and Cocteau's *Intimate Relations*), while Cleese would ultimately head straight into *Cambridge Circus*, the Footlights' second most celebrated production. It was during these progressive days that two grey suits from the BBC, Peter Titheradge and Ted Taylor, collared Cleese at the Footlights Club and suggested he should attempt a career as a BBC radio comedy writer for £15,000 per year. The stability of the Beeb reassured his parents, who were naturally hoping for great legal things for their son, and his first assignment was for a Christmas show entitled *Yule Be Surprised* starring Terry Scott and Brian Rix. The script was written by Eddie McGuire and Cleese's instruction was to edit some of the jokes out! Soon he was called upon to put some jokes into *The Dick Emery Show*, *Emery At Large* (moulding Cookian bus stop discussion between Emery and Deryck Guyler) and *Not to Worry*, with Ronnie Barker and Cyril Fletcher. A scant four months since leaving Cambridge he was hard at work behind his BBC desk.

Despite a minor problem concerning his antipathy towards wearing a collar and tie, at the age of just 24 Cleese was a successful West End comedy player and writer with the main firm. But comedy performance was the future, and basing his style on Peter Cook's immortal *Interesting Facts*, Cleese opted out of his BBC desk job in the middle of 1964 when a return to *Cambridge Circus* beckoned. Following the successful appearances in New Zealand and New York, Cleese stayed in America for the off-Broadway version of

Cambridge Circus and a second, slightly reheated, rearranged production at the same venue. Its off-Broadway exposure was caught by Tommy Steele who liked what Cleese was doing and suggested him for a part in his Broadway show *Half A Sixpence*. Cleese auditioned for a laugh and got the part of the straight-laced, English twit, Young Walsingham with a smattering of dialogue (about 30 lines) including some embezzling comic business with Steele. Although the part was mostly in the singing chorus, Cleese, happy to admit to being the least musically geared chap in Europe, impressed the director Gene Sachs to such an extent that he was allowed to mouth the songs just to keep his acting performance within the production. Indeed, he is credited on the original Broadway recording. Following its opening at The O'Keefe Center Toronto in February 1965 it was performed in Boston up until April when it transferred to The Broadhurst Theater, Broadway from April to July 1965. It gave Cleese further experience in stage acting and remains an extremely impressive feather in his cap. As does employment by the International Affairs Department of *Newsweek* magazine which saw Cleese published, albeit heavily edited, on such news items as a major oil spill. Although a concentrated break away from entertainment, Cleese injected sardonic humour into his contributions, and was eventually reduced to writing obituaries for living celebs on the edge. However, after six weeks he felt the pressure and resigned, eagerly walking straight into another job touring with the John Morris production of the old Establishment material from Peter Cook and co in *American Establishment Review*.

Beginning in Chicago in September 1965, Cleese journeyed with the production to Washington a few weeks later and as he planned to return home, received a call from David Frost concerning a new show with Ronnie Barker and Ronnie Corbett. Cleese would perform and write for *The Frost Report* and later make contributions to *Frost* spin-off ventures like *The Two Ronnies*, *Broaden Your Mind* and *Marty*, as well as, of course, create the finest pre-*Python* comedy material for *At Last the 1948 Show* and kickstart the hugely successful *Doctor in the House* for LWT in 1969. Cleese had married the American actress Connie Booth the year before on 20 February 1968. Together with Chapman, Cleese was writing for such films as *The Magic Christian*, *The Rise and Rise of Michael Rimmer*, *Rentadick* and the aborted *Ditto*, while at the same time gaining quite a reputation as a useful character actor in films like *The Statue*, *The Best House in London* and *Interlude*. In performance Cleese used his imposing height and superiority to give weight to his comedy but as the *Sunday Telegraph* observed in a 1967 review of the *1948 Show* he was setting a trend for the comedian not to appear physically funny – 'he looks like an accountant who in his spare time is a bit fierce on the tennis court.' By 1969 Cleese was very big news indeed, receiving frequent offers from the BBC for his own headlining comedy series. Eventually this turned into the six-way grouping of *Monty Python*, while during the show's success Cleese appeared in *I'm Sorry I'll Read That Again* and *Sez Les*. The first to leave *Python*, although he always returned for the film reunions, Cleese enjoyed the biggest solo success of the team with the seminal situation comedy *Fawlty Towers*. The Cleese/Booth scripts remain untarnished by time and receiving just £1,000 per episode with a six weeks writing time for each, Cleese supplemented his earnings via copious adverts and Video Arts training films. The key figure behind the Amnesty International concerts, Cleese enjoyed Shakespearean performance, a guest starring turn with the Muppets and even a cameo in *Doctor Who*. A key figure also in various advertising campaigns and a major shareholder in the *Python* fortune, Cleese can afford to avoid work he dislikes, turning down a planned collaboration with ABBA, mega-bucks from American television

for a five-year, 39-show-a-year series based around a bumbling private eye and the central part of the British journalist in *The Bonfire of the Vanities* ultimately played by Bruce Willis. Divorced from Connie Booth in 1976 (the couple had one daughter, Cynthia Caylor, born in February 1971), Cleese married American actress Barbara Trentham in 1981, having met during the Hollywood Bowl *Python* shows – their daughter Camilla was born in 1984, but the marriage ended in divorce in 1990. He was eager to preserve his own legacy of comedy in a tongue-in-cheek irreverent way. After years of giving Frank Muir *Python* material for his regular *Frank Muir Christmas Sketch Book* Cleese finally published his own anthology under the title of *The Golden Skits of Wing Commander Murial Volestrangler FRHS and Bar*.
In 1984 with the final *Python* movie in the can, Cleese began working with Ealing and Video Arts director Charles Crichton on a film called *Corruption* (as well as coming up with the title for another movie *The Last Prawn* – as yet unrealised!) which eventually became *A Fish Called Wanda*, the most commercially successful film of any post-*Python*. It certainly knocked the pseudo-*Fawlty Clockwise* into a cocked hat and flushed with *Wanda* success, Cleese began work on a follow-up film project reuniting with Michael Palin, Jamie Lee Curtis and Kevin Kline. The proposed title, *Death Fish II*, revolved round a story involving a murderous electric eel, but this plot was abandoned and the notion gradually resolved into the almost ten-year gap before the final appearance of *Fierce Creatures*. Comic demons under control Cleese married Freudian/Kleinian/Jungian psychoanalytical psychotherapist Alyce Faye Eichelberger in Barbados in December 1992. The couple live in a Holland Park house once belonging to Brian Ferry, while Cleese owns several other homes in London and an apartment in New York. Looking back over his long career in comedy, Cleese notes that he has been a lot less prolific than many of his

cohorts, but with someone who stands at the epicentre of both *Monty Python* and *Fawlty Towers* the heights could never get higher. One of the great English men.

CAROL CLEVELAND

Born in 1943, East Sheen, London, Carol Cleveland is dubbed by many as 'the seventh Python' and if it's really a toss-up between her and Neil Innes, Carol would get my vote every time. Her parents met on a film set during the war and married ten days later, (mother Pat was a model and film extra who often cropped up in *Python* – once as a hospital patient with an axe in her head). Carol's father left home when she was three. Carol showed an early interest in dance, taking ballet lessons from the age of five, spending her teenage years in amateur dramatics and eventually playing the title role in *Cinderella*. Her mother married an American airforce guy, Cleve and the family moved to America – first Texas, then California (where Carol appeared in *Swan Lake*). On a television show at the age of 12 Carol confidently predicted she would be a movie star and in 1961 she returned to London to attend RADA. Carol soon became a popular and familiar face on sixties British television with appearances in *The Saint*, *The Avengers* and *Doctor At Large*. She appeared with Spike Milligan, Peter Sellers, Ronnie Barker and Ronnie Corbett before being put forward for *Monty Python*. She was hired by director/producer John Howard Davies for just the first five shows, but her brilliant self-parodying delivery, manic understanding of the *Python* scripts and popularity with the team saw her feature almost every week, perform in various live shows (including the Hollywood spectaculars) and feature in all the films. Nicknamed Carol Cleavage by the Pythons, she was the definitive blonde stereotype for deconstruction and eventually enjoyed character parts along the way although she was often unhappy at her range of unchanging blonde bimbos, longing

The *Clockwise* team on location – still overshadowed by time

to grab the more meaty female roles usually bagged by Terry Jones or Graham Chapman. Her wedding to Peter Breet in the 1970s was a real *Python* affair, with Cleese and the lads in attendance, but the union was brief and Carol now lives in Brighton, enthralling fans with the comic story of her life as The Royal Pavilion for the Brighton Festival. Although restricted to very little save looking stunning in tight skirts, Carol remains a major part of the *Python* legacy.

CLOCKWISE

The first major feature film role for John Cleese in the wake of his *Fawlty Towers* persona was this rambling Michael Frayn script, a rare occasion when a posted script appealed to the actor, coupled with admiration for the writer's other work, *Noises Off*, and an agreement was made. However, in the event *Clockwise* became the blueprint for every mistake Cleese corrected in *A Fish Called Wanda*, painstakingly mulling over the ending, injecting feelgood factors into as much as possible, embracing the American ethos and building up his own characterisation in order to fall from dignity all the

more powerfully.

Despite becoming a moderate hit in Australia and at home, *Clockwise* failed in the States and, on retrospect, it fails in creating ideal comic situations for Cleese to shine fully. Although there is a lip-smacking cast of distinguished thespians to back up the madcap journey to Norwich (notably Benjamin Whitrow's delightfully charming, angst-masking delivery and Joan Hickson's blue rinsed, continually talking old dear), the entire film boils down to carefully structured set pieces for Cleese's time-frustrated headmaster. But from the initial opening credits based on the railway timetable and Cleese's first concentration camp commandant appearance, there is an overriding sense of hidden likeability in the character. Whereas Fawlty was always in the audience's affections and he was a complete bastard to most of the people he met, Cleese's Brian Stimpson is obsessed with manners and time-keeping but builds a basically endearing relationship with his pupils, openly mocking his regime in order to create a bridge between his powerful authority and those pupils in his charge. Throughout the film, Frayn creates disastrous happenings, eccentric annoyances and faulty equipment and indeed, the

occupied/broken telephone booth sequence and the mud-stuck car with well-timed Cleese boot could have come from a *Fawlty* film. Unfortunately, these flashes of visual comic greatness are swamped by acres of mistimed pathos and elongated situations. The manic trek across the countryside with Penelope Wilton, driving through fields and passing cows with no comic or locational direction at all sags well before Farmer Tony Haygath's brilliant cameo opposite an ever-more angst-ridden Cleese (singularly the best piece of comic dialogue in the film and rich in Fawlty anger). The continual cutaway to lovelorn, pupil seducer Stephen Moore, Cleese's misunderstanding wife Alison Steadman and the Shakespearean defence of a young girl's honour from the pupil's parents all sap far too much screen time and weaken the focal thread of the comedy, ie. Cleese's mad dash to the headmaster's conference set at the fictitious University of Norwich. From the outset, Cleese is proud and privileged to represent his school and, more importantly, infiltrate the upper echelons of posh school education from his comprehensive situation. His fastidious attitude to everything sets him out as a pompous bore but, immediately, we see an endearing persona who merely keeps his life in order because he knows the problems that await him if he doesn't. Indeed, the shared tongue-in-cheek observations used as reprimands are seen as 'executions' and link the pupil/teacher situation with self-aware parody. Even the single, fatal error of right/left with his train platform stems from addressing punk-oriented pupils and upholding his educational trust. One feels that if Cleese had written the script there would have been much needed injections of nasty streaks to contrast the situations and develop the comedy; however, Cleese himself, does a wonderful job as actor, toning down his Fawlty mannerisms, treating the written word with respect and interacting spiritedly with a feast of fine actors.

Apart from the obvious Fawlty-like

moments, there are several moments of gloriously subtle acting from Cleese which reward patient viewers, notably the entire monastery sequence with an almost silent Michael Aldridge. He reacts with restraint to all Cleese's bizarre, introspective observations; the one moment of relaxed pleasure as the bath is invaded by slim possibilities of the mission being accomplished; and, best of all, the touching, pathos-dipped exchange between disgraced, law-breaking headmaster and confused, endearing pupil as Cleese explains his political goals and pride in achievement in heartfelt manner. There is an earlier concern for Sharon Maiden's parents and an eager offer to pay for the petrol (with Cleese's first break in good citizenship coming with his accepting to drive to Norwich with his pupil) and, later acceptance of his lot, calmness in the light of surreal behaviour and beautifully collected assurances to his pupils with 'we can't eat now because we're in the middle of a field!' Despite Cleese's fine performance, there is something which continually disappoints in Clockwise, never fully grabbing the manic comic mettle and seeming to justify the comedy of confusion and bad time-keeping with self-aware reassurances. The totally bizarre three-way strip in the woods goes beyond this sort of comic structure; the climactic combination of Benny Hillesque music and The Italian Job-like car antics don't gell and the final scene completely deflates the comic tension surrounding the rest of the film. Throughout the film, Cleese and Maiden have shared the suggestion of monks' sexuality, reunions of old friends, muddy fields, relations misunderstanding them and criminal activities, arriving from a journey of self-discovery and maturing situations to face the greatest moment of Cleese's school career. The film needed an upbeat ending to release the comic tension of the journey and with Benjamin Whitrow's nervous beginnings of apology as the clock clicks to 17:00 it almost gets there. For director Morahan builds up the sequence with a momentary pause

(heightened throughout the film with clock ticking), a stirring horn-based burst of music and Cleese's ill-clothed, imposing, confident figure strolling up the aisle to delivery his speech. The journey is at an end, the comedy vindicated, our anti-hero has beaten the odds and made it. But no, the speech trails into disaster, all the loose threads of martial, senile and policing problems break into this moment of glory as the bleakest of bleak endings sees arrest, inability to deliver the goods, an ironic recurrence of the left/right misunderstanding and even more ironic performance of This Is My Lovely Day. The spiral into childish treatment of his distinguished group of listeners is misplaced and untruthful, having not even treated his pupils in such a way and reaching the climax of his comic journey of mind game madness with a lapse into totally insanity. The film taught Cleese lessons in time for Wanda but at the end of the day, Clockwise showcases an interesting, pure performance from Cleese in between brushing the memories of Basil Fawlty from his shoes and embracing pin-up status for American housewives.

Clockwise
Moment Films/Lumiere Pictures/Universal Pictures/Cannon-Thorn EMI Screen Entertainment
Brian Stimpson **JOHN CLEESE**
Laura Wisely **SHARON MAIDEN**
Gwenda Stimpton **ALISON STEADMAN**
Mr. Jolly **STEPHEN MOORE**
Pat **PENELOPE WILTON**
Paul Stimpson **CHIP SWEENEY**
Mrs. Wheel **CONSTANCE CHAPMAN**
Mrs. Trellis **JOAN HICKSON**
Mrs. Way **ANN WAY**
Mrs. Wisely **PAT KEEN**
Mr. Wisely **GEOFFREY HUTCHINGS**
Prior **MICHAEL ALDRIDGE**
Ivan with the Tractor **TONY HAYGRATH**
Headmasters **BENJAMIN WHITROW, GEOFFREY PALMER, NICHOLAS LE PREVOST, PETER CELLIER, DAVID CONVILLE, PATRICK GODFREY, RUPERT MASSEY, JOHN ROWE, PHILIP VOSS & JEFFRY WICKHAM**
Ted **HOWARD LLOYD-LEWIS**
Clint **JONATHAN BOWWATER**

Glen Scully **MARK BURDIS**
Woman Teacher **PENNY LEATHERBARROW**
Mandy Kostakis **NADIA CARINA**
Man at Station **DICKIE ARNOLD**
1st Class Passenger **ANGUS MacKAY**
Porter **PETER NEEDHAM**
Taxi Driver **PETER LORENZELLI**
Petrol Station Cashier **ANN-MARIE GWATKIN**
Manager **MOHAMMED ASHIQ**
Policeman with Mrs. Wheel **GEOFFREY GREENHILL**
Policemen at Crash **RICHARD RIDINGS & GEOFFREY DAVION**
Man in Telephone Box **CHARLES BARTHOLOMEW**
Pat's Mother **SHEILA KEITH**
Pat's son **CHRISTIAN REGAN**
Policeman at Telephone Box **ALAN PARNABY**
Monks **RONALD SOWTON & ALAN GRANTON**
Woman in Lane **SUSAN FIELD**
Policeman arresting Pat **LESLIE SCOFIELD**
Policeman with Black Eye **MIKE GLYNN**
Det. Sgt. Rice **NICK STRINGER**
Dectective Constables **GRAEME GREEN & BRIAN PORTSMOUTH**
Porsche Driver **SIDNEY LIVINGSTONE**
Man in Wood **MICHAEL PERCIVAL**
Det. Insp. Laundryman **PETER JONFIELD**
Studious Boy **MARK BURTING**
Streaker **ROBERT WILKINSON**
Ticket Collector **JOHN BARDON**
Screenplay by **Michael Frayn**
Music **George Fenton**
Production designer **Roger Murray-Leach**
Editor **Peter Boyle**
Camera operator **Malcolm Vinson**
Photography **John Coquillon**
Production executive **Graham Easton**
Production associate **Bob Mercer**
Associate producer **Gregory Dark**
Executive producers **Verity Lambert & Nat Cohen**
Producer **Michael Codron**
Director **Christopher Morahan**
96 mins, 1986

THE COMPLETE AND UTTER HISTORY OF BRITAIN

Still trying to find his feet with LWT, producer Humphrey Barclay commissioned a series of seven comedy shows written and performed by *Do Not Adjust Your Set* favourites Terry Jones and Michael Palin. Headman Frank Muir was keen to see what the duo could do and the duo themselves were very keen to prove themselves without David Jason and the rest of the *Do Not Adjust* team. In the end, these scripts were edited down to a series of six shows, featuring the writer/performers, surrounded by a cast of stolid character actors of the old school under the direction of Australian Maurice Murphy, whom Barclay would later recruit for *Doctor in the House*. Colin Gordon, distinguished character actor, was cast as the straight-laced narrator figure; Roddy Maude-Roxby was called upon to enliven the batty linking discussions of absent-minded Professor Weaver and Diana Quick, an old pal of Palin's from Oxford, brought life to some of the more powerful female creations. However, both Palin and Jones considered some of the cast unsatisfactory and that their traditional acting mentality would be unable to grasp the total nature of the work with, of course, only themselves and Quick able to understand the essence of the comedy fully.

Even in 1969, so close to the full freedom of *Python*, Jones and Palin were impossibly restricted in their writing. The two history graduates savoured the chance to turn historical study on its head and examine the subject through the eyes of contemporary broadcasting. Indeed, the basic idea of retelling great moments of British history as though television cameras were capturing the moment is an inspired one and something which often cropped up in *Monty Python* just a few short months later. *Complete and Utter* was actually broadcast just before the second series of *Do Not Adjust Your Set* and while that show highlights the surreal elements of Jones, Palin and Idle, this programme clearly points the way forward to their favourite *Python* contributions and *Ripping Yarns*. Giving history that contemporary edge, with moments like the Battle of Hastings victors

interviewed in the communal baths after their win, discussions between Samuel Pepys and a David Frost-like Oliver Cromwell caught up in a chat show format, are clearly very *Python*esque. Other notable sketches included Palin's estate agent trying to sell Stonehenge to Jones and Maye, the non-event of the 1065 scrapbook, Palin's red tape obsessed Knight F.R. Lancelot, making damsel in distress Quick sign before rescue (covering copyright on ballads resulting from the adventure), the 1558 Battle of Calais with a French victory coming via garlic and the joyous spectre of four William Shakespeares all reciting at once. Worthy ideas which were cut when the one episode was culled included Britons copying down Latin after the Roman Invasion, words pouring out in the wrong order when introduced to Christianity and a nice idea concerning a caveman trying to patent the chair. Sadly, all the material bar the brief on-film inserts is missing, believed wiped from the archives, and it's thanks only to Terry Jones that even the few remaining filmed remnants are around for future *Python* historians to savour. Recently Columbia television tentatively suggested a plan to refilm the scripts, but this, as yet, has gone unfulfilled.

1. From the Dawn of History to the Norman Conquest
2. Richard the Lionheart to Robin the Hood
3. Edward the First to Richard the Last
4. Perkin Warbeck to Bloody Mary
5. The Great and Glorious Age of Elizabeth
6. James the McFirst to Oliver Cromwell

Written & performed by **TERRY JONES & MICHAEL PALIN**
With **WALLACE EATON, COLIN GORDON, RODDY MAUDE-ROXBY, DIANA QUICK & MELINDA MAYE**
Producer **Humphrey Barclay**
Director **Maurice Murphy**
12 January–16 February 1969
London Weekend Television

CONSUMING PASSIONS

Although this was almost universally

snubbed by critics, this is a classic return to the character-based, British comedies of the immediate post-war years. Although Michael Palin and Terry Jones were commissioned to write the film for Sam Goldwyn Jr, disagreements led to their mutual suggestion of *King of Comedy* writer Paul Zimmerman and, subsequently, Goldwyn himself brought in other people to rewrite the material. Thus this finished product is very much an elongation from *Secrets*, the original television play by Palin and Jones. However, *Consuming Passions* is a superb sort of Joe Orton re-evaluation of *I'm Alright Jack* with an amalgam of *Python*, Carry On and Norman Wisdom tossed in for flavour. Although receiving third billing, Tyler Butterworth is the real star of the piece, transformed from put-upon bumbler incorporating elements of Wisdom (notably during the climactic chocolate vat battle), Ian Carmichael and Tyler's father, Peter Butterworth. It's a wonderful comic performance, full of sexual nervousness, half-hearted business prowess and bucketfuls of prat-falling incompetence.

The basic thread of *Consuming Passions* is the old, old fight between the traditional face of British industry and the corporate sparkle of modernity – highlighted by the contrast between the two forms of advertising, with factory images and cosy British stability against Linda Lusardi's plunging neckline and erotic French groaning. As the old face of British industry, the film is blessed with great character actor Freddie Jones gibbering and foaming at the slow destruction of his family heritage of Chumley's chocolates, condescending and sending up the brash figure of the future, Jonathan Pryce's sharp-suited, paranoid wide-boy. Continually flipping his head back with a casual reaction scarcely disguising his practised technique and conscious attempt to project an air of carelessness, this money-oriented picture of market trends, disregard for the populace's taste buds and anxious attempts to corrupt, destroy and cheapen everything in sight is the towering element of dark, humorous aggression throughout the film. His throwaway line following less than impressive trial comments – 'We could even put a bit of chocolate in...' is the very essence of the comedy. Vanessa Redgrave's top billing performance includes a flamboyantly sex mad torrent of dubious vocal excesses, hamming with carefree abandon and teaching the novice young Butterworth the glories of wild sexual pleasure. Ooer!! There are dozens of fine, under-played comic moments (Jones banging his fist with anger and not suppressing his pain, Pringle's gateman continuing to raise and lower the barrier despite Butterworth's destruction of virtually everything), coach loads of under-employed film comedy players (Prunella Scales, Timothy West, Andrew Sachs) and a sense of good old, Brits-on-top values. Primarily, there is a rich vein of macabre, *Python*esque humour running through the film: Butterworth's desperate softening-up gift of chocolates slipped onto a coffin, Butterworth covered in chocolate as he is announced as Chocolate Man of the Year, his final suspicious measuring-up of the delectable Northern sweetie from Sammi Davis and the nub of the whole production – human meat causing chocolate to become delicious and thus turning the nation into cannibals. The final fight between Butterworth and Pryce is a masterpiece, taking place on a raised platform above a vat of chocolate; the colour signifiers of good and evil are reversed, with Pryce's white jacket and Butterworth's black one, while the whole thing resolves into a sort of comic variation on the big wheel discussion between Orson Welles and Joseph Cotten in *The Third Man*. The thread of dark humour is lightened by Pryce's unbreakable champagne bottle and, when it does final shatter, his familiar cocky flick of the hair is screen acting perfection. This is not your average British comedy film but the basic inspiration from the Palin and Jones original creates a unique and totally enjoyable experience.

Euston Films Limited & The Samuel Goldwyn Company present *Consuming Passions*
Mrs. Garza **VANESSA REDGRAVE**
Mr. Farris **JONATHAN PRYCE**
Ian Littleton **TYLER BUTTERWORTH**
Mr. Graham Chumley **FREDDIE JONES**
Ethel **PRUNELLA SCALES**
Felicity Stubbs **SAMMI DAVIS**
Mrs. Gordon **THORA HIRD**
Dr. Rees **TIMOTHY WEST**
Mrs. Eggleston **MARY HEALEY**
Big Teddy **WILLIAM RUSHTON**
Gateman **BRYAN PRINGLE**
Jason Eggleston **ANDREW SACHS**
Dr. Forrester **JOHN WELLS**
French beauty **LINDA LUSARDI**
Frenchman **GERALD DIMIGLIO**
Rastafarian **ARCHIE POOL**
Ambulancemen **MARC BOYLE & PAUL DALTON**
Supermarket Assistant **HELEN PEARSON**
Thin lady **GERALDINE GRIFFITHS**
Fat lady **JO WARNE**
Piano Player **JULIAN RONNIE**
Furniture Store Assistant **DAVID NEVILLE**
Butcher **DICK BRANNICK**
Mrs. Coot **DEDDIE DAVIES**
Porter **DONALD PELMEAR**
Josiah **PRESTON LOCKWOOD**
Josiah's son **ANGUS BARNETT**
T.V. Presenter **WINCEY WILLIS**
Trevor **ADAM STOCKER**
Ladies on Television **SUSAN FIELD & VICKY IRELAND**
Old lady on Television **JULIE MAY**
Tramp **PADDY WARD**
Wooster **ROBERT BRIDGES**
Lester **PATRICK NEWELL**
Mayor **LEONARD TROLLEY**
Screenplay by **Paul D. Zimmerman & Andrew Davies**
Based on the play *Secrets* by **Michael Palin & Terry Jones**
Music **Richard Hartley**
Production designer **Peter Lamont**
Production manager **Patricia Carr**
Casting **Sue Whatmough**
Assistant director **Roger Simons**
Camera operator **David Worley**
Art director **Terry Ackland-Snow**
Costumes **Barbara Kidd**
Specials effects supervisor **Ian Wingrove**
Photography **Roger Pratt**
Editor **John Grover**
Producer **William P. Cartlidge**
Director **Giles Foster**

Pinewood Studios, Technicolor, 98 mins, 1988

THE CRIMSON PERMANENT ASSURANCE

A short film subject that served as the support picture for *Monty Python's The Meaning of Life*, this tackles the major issues of corporate insensitivity and faceless business later developed in Terry Gilliam's *Brazil*. The clever comparison between slavery over a desk and slavery rowing an ancient galleon is brought together when a crop of aged-old employees turn their oppressive office building into a pirate ship sailing the accountant sea (accountancy, get it...). It's the old favourite bug bear of modern values against traditional affection, brilliantly brought to life by some valued old-timers, happily mixing bloodthirsty cut-throat action with preparations for plenty of tea. All pirate convention is embraced and reworked, notably the progress chart-cum-skull 'n' crossbones and the filing cabinets as firing cabinets, with the entire film having a lavish and impressive feel, particularly as the old-styled British symbol of international finance sails into the glittering world of commerce. After a while the idea may pale a wee bit and the pretentious elements outweigh the swashbuckling fun, but as an appetiser for the final major Python collaboration this is perfectly acceptable.
Actually, despite the obvious thematics, the only on-screen link with *Python* are wordless cameos from bewildered window-cleaners Michael Palin and Terry Gilliam. It's a classic touch and Gilliam's window-cleaner whip of his eyes is a priceless moment. To cap it all there's a wonderfully bleak conclusion backed by the optimistic Eric Idle chanting of the song *Accountancy Shanty*, which originally stemmed from *Rutland Weekend Television* and became available on the *Monty Python's The Meaning of Life* soundtrack album.

Did You Know? Terry Gilliam's over-

41

ambitious sets for this mini masterpiece makes this the only Python film to go over budget.
The Crimson Permanent Assurance
Universal/The Monty Python Partnership
Starring **SYDNEY ARNOLD, GUY BERTRAND, ANDREW BICKNELL, ROSS DAVIDSON, MYRTLE DEVENISH, TIM DOUGLAS, ERIC FRANCIS, MATT FREWER, BILLY JOHN, RUSSELL KILMISTER, PETER MANTLE, LEN MARTEN, PETER MERRILL, CAMERON MILLER, GARETH MILNE, LARRY NOBLE, PADDY RYAN, LESLIE SARONY, JOHN SCOTT MARTIN, ERIC STOVELL & WALLY THOMAS**
Featuring **JACK ARMSTRONG, ROBERT CARRICK, DOUGLAS COOPER, GEORGE DALY, CHICK FOWLES, TERRY GRANT, ROBIN HEWLETT, TOMMY ISLEY, JUBA KENNERLEY, TONY LANG, JOHN MURPHY, TERRY RENDELL, RONALD SHILLING & ALBERT WELCH**
With **MICHAEL PALIN & TERRY GILLIAM**
Photography **Roger Pratt**
Art director **John Beard**
Music **John Du Prez**
Performed by **The Philharmonia Orchestra**
Assistant director **Gary White & Jonathan Benson**
Production assistant **Patricia Carr**
Continuity **Maggie Jones**
Fight arranger **William Hobbs**
Sound **Debbie Kaplan**
Director **Terry Gilliam**
EMI Elstree Studios, Borehamwood, Technicolor, 1983, 16 mins

CRUSADES

Terry Jones grabbed the chance to mix *Monty Python* convention with his historian passion for this memorable four-part lecture, tackling the significant direct orders from the Holy Roman Emperor Gregory to the Pope, deflating the heroic myth of Richard the Lionheart, serious threats to the ordinary foot soldier to fight or go to hell and the exploits of these 11th/12th-century vandals. Jones enthuses on the subject with passion, throws in useful sound-bites from animated mosaics and delivers the deeply researched material with energetic fun – travelling to Asia Minor, the Mediterranean, Tel Aviv & Venice (recreating the Fourth Crusade for the Venice Carnival) and demonstrating the difficulty of stepping from a boat while dressed in full armour. Thus he puts crucial points across with laughter, often contrasting the piece of comic-edged information with a dramatic shift to a totally serious historian which drives the point home even further. Detailing the 1,000-mile trek from Bosphorus to the Holy City where four out of five died on the road, examining the cannibalistic behaviour of the fanatical survivors – the slaughter of defenceless people, children impaled on sticks then eaten... grilled – and the first Palestinian refugees calling for holy war, this is gory, fascinating history delivered with tangible glee. Jones crosses Syria and Jordan and discusses the Arab counter-crusade to win back Jerusalem; we see the rise of the young Kurd, Saladin, destroying the Christian Kingdom in the space of a day while battling the murderous ideals of Richard the Lionheart and King Philip II of France. In his eagerness to rise to power to capture Jerusalem, Richard made his infamous comment about selling London if he could find a buyer.

Crusades Part 1. Pilgrims in Arms
Part 2. Jerusalem Part 3. Jihad
Part 4. Destruction
Executive producer **Laurence Rees**
Producers **Alan Ereira & David Wallace**
4 x 50 mins. Tuesday 9.30pm-10.20pm BBC2, 10 January–31 January 1995

CRY OF THE BANSHEE

Anyone who doubts the sinister quality of Terry Gilliam's animation should check out the stunning credits for this AIP Vincent Price horror film classic. A return to the sadistic realism frights of *Witch-Finder General*, Gilliam's title sequence complements an Edgar Allan Poe quote with a primitive etching design, incorporating Albrecht Dürer's engravings, before bursting into blood red colour and a haunting musical score. A cut-out picture of Price emerges like a rising sun from behind the hills, splits in two and shoots out *Night on Bare Mountain*-like ghoulish demons. Sweeping across the scene against a backdrop of red, these hideous creatures include the typical Gilliam technique of playfully mobile eyes, amusing in *Python* but simply chilling here. The final fade to black and the moon's incorporation into nightmarish horror is a powerful effect, perfectly setting the scene for Vincent Price's crusade through heretic activity and witchcraft. The last of his historical terror fests, Price delivers his self-righteous dialogue with malevolent pleasure.

Did You Know? Contrary to the book *Monty Python: The Complete and Utter Theory of the Absurd*, Gilliam does not make an uncredited guest appearance in the film.

Cry of the Banshee
American International Pictures
Starring **VINCENT PRICE** as Lord Edward Whitman
With **ESSY PERSSON, HILARY DWYER, CARL RIGG, STEPHEN CHASE, MARSHALL JONES, MICHAEL ELPHICK, PATRICK MOWER, PAMELA FAIRBROTHER, HUGH GRIFFITH, SALLY GEESON, GERTAN KLAUBER & ELISABETH BERGNER** as Oona
Screenplay by **Tim Kelly & Christopher Wickling**
Art director **George Provis**
Music **Les Baxter**
Editor **Oswald Hafenrichter**
Titles **Terry Gilliam**
Executive producer **Louis Heyward**
Associate producer **Clifford Parkes**
Produced & directed by **Gordon Hessler**
22 July 1970, 87 mins

THE CURSE OF THE VAMPIRE'S SOCKS

A collection of children's poetry by Terry Jones typified by 'If dead leaves were money I'd never be broke and if troubles were funny we'd all share the joke.'

Written by **Terry Jones**
Illustrated by **Michael Foreman**
Published by Pavilion Books, 1988

CYRIL AND THE DINNER PARTY

Three-year-old Cyril discovers he has the ability to turn people into grotesque objects, ranging from an ostrich to an awful smell. Palin followed this success with *Cyril and the House of Commons*, with the little boy with manic powers turning politicians into sheepdogs and balloons.

Both books by **Michael Palin**
Illustrations by **Caroline Holden**
Published by Pavilion Books, 1986

THE DANGEROUS FILM CLUB

Taking inspiration from his involvement with The Dangerous Sports Club, Graham Chapman hosted this series of tongue-in-cheek celebrations of wacky home movies, bizarre film clips and animation, linking the material in a variety of *Python*esque costumes. Slipping past police lines to discover a film projector in the first show, broadcast August 1987, highlights include a very *Python*-like guide in how to recognise dangerous films and a screening of part 1 of *A Trip Through the Brooks Home*. In the guise of Police Sergeant Willie Dawkins (ret.) Chapman reveals a two-minute extract of the 13-hour epic *That's Not How It Seems*, screens *Service*, interacts with a teenager and his father from the 1950s cult classic *Leisure Time* and presents a clip from *The Trouble*

With Fred. Adopting a Pith helmet, Chapman introduces *Dog Baseball* and *Jean-Jean and the Evil Cat*, lapsing into French painter mode, wearing clothes in bed and ordering viewers to send in their tapes for the next show as *School Safety Patrol* runs over the credits.

Show 2 – September 1987 featured Snack of the Dead and Hold the Mayo
Show 3 – October 1987 dished up Spontaneous Combustion and Doggie Doo Check
Show 4 – November 1987 delighted in Brides and Croutons and You
Show 5 – December 1987, presented Julie Brown's The Homecoming Queen's Got A Gun and Pervasive Percussion.

DEAD PARROT SKETCH

Without doubt *Monty Python*'s all-time greatest contribution to popular culture, it is the comic answer to *Pyscho*'s shower scene in the cascade of spin-offs, influences and homages paid. Written by Graham Chapman and John Cleese, performed by Cleese, Michael Palin with a little help from Terry Jones, its first appearance in series one episode eight was under-played and, naturally, unheralded. Cleese's beloved Mr. Praline figure, with slightly creepy, British air of oppressed madness, stands as a comic figure to rank with Dickens. The logical thought behind a rapid run-through of colloquialisms for death and the British character acting against tradition to complain about a defective purchase strips bare the finest piece of sketch comedy this century. The bulk came from Cleese, but Chapman's twisted genius injected acidic touches and, most importantly of all, changed the original faulty item from a broken toaster to the legendary deceased Norwegian Blue.

The official seed of inspiration came from a real-life story told to Cleese by Palin concerning a garage struggling with a clapped-out motor car – a Chapman/Cleese sketch written around this premise appeared in the 1968 special *How To Irritate People* and was considered strong

enough for reworking in *Python*. However, for me the idea spans beyond the time when *Python* players had set foot in the BBC, set up via the mainstream genius of Tony Hancock in the 1959 radio masterpiece *Sid's Mystery Tours*. Galton & Simpson, delighted in mild touches of surrealism throughout *Hancock's Half Hour* and in this classic episode the embodiment of cool deceit Sidney James, has to fend off a petulant vocal attack from Hancock having just bought a rather lifeless tortoise from the twister. In the end, the animal's total lack of movement is explained by the fact that what Sid sold Tub was merely a shell with nothing else included. For a few minutes *Hancock's Half Hour* walks the same line as the parrot sketch, a shared radio favourite for all the Python members and a subconscious comic memory that was strapped to the *Monty Python* rocket and fired into comedy orbit – check out the television Hancock, *Spanish Interlude*, for *Python* 'funny' walks and *Fawlty* Hitler impersonations. The Dead Parrot became the most requested and familiar sign of Python comedy, cropping up in *And Now For Something Completely Different* and various stage performances. Indeed, the item became so familiar that Cleese & Chapman could happily twist and turn the sketch, elongating it for Amnesty, beginning the oft-uttered beginning (surely 'I wish to register a complaint!' remain *Python*'s five most quoted words) only to curtail the sketch immediately and even consciously removing it from their collective history, *Parrot Sketch – Not Included*. Repeated in book form, audio version and original filmic glory, the sketch always seems to have been with us and as long as two or more people shall gather they shall quote the Parrot sketch – 'it has ceased to be!' Classic beyond the dreams of Avarice.

DO NOT ADJUST YOUR SET

On a crest of a wave following *Cambridge Circus* and the radio hybrid *I'm Sorry I'll Read That*

Again, producer Humphrey Barclay received a letter from Rediffusion Television's Jeremy Isaacs. Barclay thought at first that he wanted to rework some of his Cambridge material for another show (possibly *At Last the 1948 Show*). In fact, what Isaacs wanted was a children's comedy show – a sort of less smutty variation on *I'm Sorry I'll Read That Again* capturing the audience's imagination and developing their involvement in the programme – later he tried an adult televised attempt at this with the less successful *Twice A Fortnight*. The *Do Not Adjust Your Set* programmes saw Terry Jones recruited from **** and Michael Palin coming via Jones, although Barclay didn't know his work. The key reason for the show was to promote the Cambridge comic talents of Eric Idle. Although active in the writing of *I'm Sorry I'll Read That Again* and brief appearances in *At Last the 1948 Show*, Barclay wanted to build up his under-valued talents while also feeling it useful to balance the university clan with knockabout comic force David Jason (although Jones maintained he was a perfectly good slapstick comedian) and the diminutive joker Denise Coffey, whose height formed a gallery of good-natured japes – both would later join Idle, Jones and Palin as the show's writing team. The brief was for a funny children's programme, but it was only a matter of weeks before the programme became a cult favourite with adult viewers and television critics praising it as the funniest thing on the screen – even knocking the spots off adult-oriented successes such as *At Last the 1948 Show*.

From the moment the title appeared shaking on a living room television set it was clear that the three fledgling Pythons were going to flex their anti-media muscles, continuing to embrace the breakdown of convention for the title with the commercial break card reading Do Not Adjust Your Set Yet. There's a smattering of one-liners and quickie sketches, including the rather obvious maternity ward scenario with the baby looking like its father cliché – Terry Jones appearing in nappy and

gurgling – or the more darkly *Python* moment when an approaching figure is questioned 'Friend or foe?' by Jones' sentry. Palin's concealed Officer shouts 'Foe!', gets shot and congratulates his man before dying. Inspired elements like these rest alongside more childish forms of comic expression like the classical quartet (delightfully silly titters from their Germanic name boiling down to one, two, three, four) whose instruments make the wrong sounds in a Goonish variation.

More interestingly, Idle takes the conventions of television his young audience are used to and does his comic version, appearing in iconographic mortar board, sending up those patronising lecture programmes for schools with a stern discussion on gravity via his detailed description on dropping a pencil. Television and film convention is continually questioned, notably in Eric Idle's *Scotland Yard*-like narration of the plainclothes policeman working undercover. Michael Palin's painfully obvious bumbler with 'hello, hello' introductions and 'evening all' muttered all over the place clearly resembles the later, more polished *Python* sketches of thick copper on the beat. The quickly snatched idea that there is such a thing as a Gang College where crooks can learn their trade is also near fruition, with familiar names like Sgt. Pepper (bit of youth culture) and Raymond Francis (television culture – star of groundbreaking police drama *No Hiding Place*), leading to a final realisation that all present are on the side of right and eagerly embrace the criminal code to make the system work. It's very primitive stuff but the seed of *Python* is very much apparent, as in Palin's supercilious salesman desperately trying to sell an awful and incomplete suit with ingratiating lies and pleading manners. Complete craziness was successfully incorporated with Palin's manic chef cooking a selection of silly things while the Stocking skit on army training films showing wannabe Santas receiving a chimney-pot drill from regimental gnomes could and

should have been resurrected for *Python*. Ideas like the suicide, hanging from a cliff, being cautioned by some passer-by who recognises him from the telly and bores him with his impressive credits work brilliantly, as does the magical fairy grotto conversation with a militant, self-aware gnome debunking and dismissing magical curses and desperately trying to convince his pals that human beings really do exist with throwaway lines like 'If there aren't people, who makes Frank Sinatra records?' and the classic sardonic comment 'What trod on Basil – the magic stoat!' David Jason and Denise Coffey benefited from the writing prowess of fledgling *Python* mongers with Jason's James Watt inventing the steam kettle and imagining all the possible developments, mirroring the advance of railway technology, before this idol's tongue-in-cheek dream is punctured by a tongue-in-cheek Idle dreamily explaining that his tardy entrance was due to his train running late! Other material like the Tartan thistle Club, full of 'ooh ays' and Robbie Burns impersonations plays like bad *Two Ronnies* and is aimed for folksy giggles which probably left even the most undemanding children cold. With elements of later *Two Ronnies* surrealism and, naturally, chunks of *Python*esque madness, early *Do Not Adjust Your Set* sketches like the David Jason/Michael Palin grocers sequence are clearly on the right road. After Jason's mounting frustration at his lengthy order being rewarded with only a tin of shoe polish, Terry Jones wanders in with an order of shoe polish and receives Jason's lengthy order. You can see the punchline coming a mile off but it works nevertheless. Later, the players would admit that that's as far as the sketch could go and would cross-fade into something else, here it's rather left in limbo, but this was early days folks and those three hubs of *Python* comedy were finding their feet with skill and speed. Indeed, the Jones and Palin idea of treating businessmen as children, knocking for their mate to play, is pure *Python*. A regular part of the show reflected a throwback to *I'm Sorry I'll Read That Again* days with a structured story format with David Jason's slapstick serial as Captain Fantastic mixing Marty Feldman and Peter Cook mannerisms with some pretty desperate comic scenarios all done in a cold, silent movie serial format. Rather risqué, it's introduced by Eric Idle in the buff. This was very much in the tongue-in-cheek Saturday matinee style, with Jason's inept, shabby worker facing exploding lunch boxes, perilous duck pond antics, Mrs. Black and her evil Blint Men and various escapades through normality. Amazingly, this thread of the show proved popular enough to warrant its own spin-off series. The Bonzo Dog Doo-Dah Band (Vivian Stanshall, Neil Innes, 'Legs' Larry Smith, Rod Slater, Dennis Cowan, Roger Rushkin Spear) were manic guest-star rock icons doing their bits here just before shooting off to *Top of the Pops* or *Beat Club* but happily throwing themselves into the madness of it all. In the first show they performed a campy, ghoulish version of *Monster Mash*, continuing the comedy rather than being a musical break from it, with Neil Innes holding up a pic of Liberace on the 'Dracula and his son' line. Innes would, of course, become a firm fixture in later *Python* milestones while Vivian Stanshall, an eccentric among eccentrics, with spooky fake eyeballs, cut-out Mona Lisas, six-foot extension arms and a delight in ripping through any pomp and circumstance, pushed aside images to reveal other elements of the show and, in a way, worked like a musical variation on Gilliam's *Python* cartoons, breaking into the ends of sketches and smoothing out the edges. Of course, the real thing was not far in coming, with Gilliam's arrival in England, a contact with producer Humphrey Barclay via Cleese, a blank month of desperate attempts to make a breakthrough and finally getting to impress the amateur cartoonist Barclay with some written bits and animation ideas. Much to the initial chagrin of Jones and Palin, a couple of Gilliam's script suggestions were included in the show, but although going against their little scheme of

promoting their own writing and performance, it was clear that Gilliam gave the show a biting edge. From the middle of the first series Gilliam was involved on a subdued level but come the explosive second series, by which time Ian Davidson had taken over as producer, he was fully geared up with ideas and even Jones and Palin saw the amazing advantage of having his work bridge and smooth the gaps between their flights of comic fancy. Gilliam's Christmas card montage, featuring clichéd images of season's greetings getting involved in a frantic chase, was singled out for praise in reviews for the special broadcast, *Do Not Adjust Your Stocking*. But it was the truly revolutionary Elephants which really made the other fledgling Pythons sit up and take notice. Utilising a dismembered head used as a ball, a soap flake ad with Enoch Powell and a cowboy hold-up squashed by a giant hand, this was delicious, disturbing and wondrous stuff. When the second series came to a close in early 1969, London Weekend Television (in the massive telly franchise shake-up, Rediffusion was now defunct) were very keen to reunite the principal team members for another programme and, indeed, at this stage Eric Idle was close to drafting a *Python*-like, adult version of *Adjust* for the network. This would have presented the old firm, David Jason, Eric Idle, Michael Palin, Terry Jones, Terry Gilliam and the like in a 45-minute variation on the comedy style, probably developing those adult bits that were rejected for the children-oriented *Do Not Adjust Your Set*. Chapman and Cleese certainly would not have been involved. However, with Palin drifting into the Cleese/Chapman camp for *How To Irritate People*, the Cleese phone call suggesting a team effort following *The Complete and Utter History of Britain* and the ultimate realisation of a union between *Do Not Adjust Your Set* and *At Last the 1948 Show* (both ITV shows) *Monty Python* was born and, thanks to Cleese's strong BBC connections, the other side got it.

Did You Know? The first broadcast of *Do Not Adjust Your Set*, 5.25pm 4 January 1968, saw the wrong episode screened. The incorrect programme, with no commercial break time, overran by a few minutes before being cut abruptly to fit into schedules – the mistake made the national newspapers and gave *Do Not Adjust Your Set* the biggest media impact it could have hoped for! The fourth episode won first prize in Youth Programming for 12-15 years: Plays and Entertainment, Prix Jeunesse International TV Festival, Munich 1968.
In 1976 Denise Coffey later joined Chris Emmett, Fred Harris and Nigel Rees in Radio 4's *Python*esque sketch show *The Burkiss Way* (scripted by Andrew Marshall and David Renwick). She was replaced after the first series by none other than *I'm Sorry I'll Read That Again*'s Jo Kendall until the close in 1980.

Do Not Adjust Your Set
Starring **DENISE COFFEY, ERIC IDLE, DAVID JASON, TERRY JONES & MICHAEL PALIN**
With **THE BONZO DOG DOO DAH BAND**
Written by **Eric Idle, Terry Jones & Michael Palin**
Additional material **Peter Goodwin, Robert Hewison, Michael Rose & Terry Gilliam**
Script editor **Ian Davidson**
Signature tune **Dave Lee**
Animations **Terry Gilliam**
Animation cameraman **Peter Goodwin**
Film editor **Stuart Hall**
Designer **Sylva Nadolny**
Series 1 Producer **Humphrey Barclay**
Series 2 Producer **Ian Davidson**
Series 1 Director **Daphne Shadwell**
Series 2 Director **Adrian Cooper**
Series 1 Rediffusion London Production
4 January–28 March 1968
Do Not Adjust Your Stocking Thames TV
26 December 1968
Series 2 Thames TV 19 February–14 May 1969
Broadcast Wednesday, 5.20pm

THE DOCTOR SERIES

Richard Gordon's best selling comic novel concerning his trials and tribulations as a medical student, *Doctor in the House*, effortlessly passed into our collective heritage via the classic 1954 Betty Box/Ralph Thomas Rank film starring Dirk Bogarde, Kenneth More and Donald Sinden. Helped along by the British nation's healthy obsession with unhealthy people, the *Doctor* books and films became a hugely lucrative phenomenon, moulded for the big screen by Nicholas Phipps. The films allowed matinee idol Bogarde to stutter and stammer in front of glam girls in various states of undress through priceless adventures, in *Doctor at Sea* with the delectable French import Brigitte Bardot in her first English-speaking picture, *Doctor At Large*, a gag appearance as Dr. Sparrow in *We Joined the Navy* and, finally, *Doctor in Distress*. In between Bogarde's last two official medical flings for Betty Box, Leslie Phillips and Michael Craig had wandered through some mild smut with Liz Fraser in *Doctor in Love* and following the full-time departure of Bogarde, Phillips headlined in 1965's *Doctor in Clover* and, five years later, saw the close of the film series with *Doctor in Trouble*, with supports from Geoffrey Davies and Graham Chapman.

A year earlier, as actor and writer respectively, the two had helped launch the *Doctor* series on television. In 1969, Frank Muir was secured as the Head of Light Entertainment of the newly formed London Weekend Television and commissioned three hugely successful, 'beans on toast' audience-geared comedy shows. *On the Buses, Please Sir!* and *Doctor In the House*, grabbing, for the later, the fledging writing talents of four Cambridge Footlighters, Graeme Garden, Bill Oddie, John Cleese and Graham Chapman. Marking the social changes since Dirk Bogarde's coy 1950s adventures, this television spin-off starred Barry Evans, fresh from swinging sixties excess in *Here we Go Round the Mulberry Bush*, and surrounded him with the likes of George Layton, Robin Nedwell, Geoffrey Davies and, in the Lancelot Spratt-like creation of Loftus, the *Doctor* film character player Ernest Clark.

The all-important first episode, *Why Do You Want To Be A Doctor?* established this trend for new faces and new attitude, immediately set the scene with the familiar location of St. Swithins and launched a comedy that would last, through various transformations, for a run of 150 shows. It also remains of vital interest for being the only *Doctor* episode that Chapman and Cleese wrote together, just a few months before taking the BBC by storm with *Monty Python's Flying Circus*. Leaving an indelible mark on the series, leading character, Michael Upton (as played by Evans) was in fact, the name of a great friend of Cleese and Chapman's, while Dick Stuart-Clark was a nod to old *Cambridge Circus* cohort Chris Stuart-Clark. Broadcast at 7.35pm with full approval from Richard Gordon, the majority of the two series episodes of *Doctor In the House* were left in the hands of the pre-Goodies, but Chapman co-writing and Cleese working on his own fleshed out many of the *Doctor At Large* episodes which took our hapless hero Barry Evans out in to the real world of practice with Geoffrey Davies' private patients and the homely comforts of country medical life with Arthur Lowe. With the departure of Evans, *Doctor In Charge* saw Robin Nedwell's character take centre stage, with an all-out celebration of the madcap fun of Davies and Layton, while in 1974 Nedwell, Davies and Clark (as Captain Norman Loftus) took to the high seas with *Doctor At Sea*. Thirteen episodes of that were enough before a return to St. Swithins and *Doctor On the Go* which chugged on until 1977. But that wasn't quite the end. Nedwell and Davies had successfully toured Australia in *Doctor in the House*, strangely taking on the mantle of Bogarde's Simon Sparrow and More's Tony Grimsdyke, but the popularity of the LWT shows prompted Australia's Seven Network to recruit the two actors for their own variation – *Doctor Down Under* – several of which were written by Chapman's old partner Bernard McKenna. Two

series were made, the last being broadcast in May 1980 and 11 years later, the BBC belatedly jumped on the band-wagon with seven episodes of *Doctor At the Top*. Scripted by George Layton and Bill Oddie these recruited Layton, back for the first time since *Doctor In Charge*, Nedwell, struggling with a mortgage and general practice, Geoffrey Davies, now the head of surgery at St. Swithins, and Ernest Clark, injecting some aged rants at his old co-stars. Despite initial curiosity value the shows proved unsuccessful but formed a charming coda to an impressive run of medical comedy.

DOCTOR AT LARGE

Now, Dr. Upton...
For the first episode of this second batch of *Doctor* shows Chapman again (with McKenna in tow) initiated the format with our hapless hero Evans stuck in Eye, Nose and Throat, Davies caught up in the supposed glamour of Harley Street and Layton struggling with general practice. As before, this is a fairly standard introduction to the new situation, as a whole, the series seemed rather disjointed and the only real innovation was presenting about a minute of dialogue before the title appeared, although the playing is a marked improvement on *Doctor in the House*, notably with Evans being far more relaxed and streetwise. Clive Morton's rugger-loving head is a familiar stock type from before, while Richard O'Sullivan creeps around the place, but there's no space for Clark or Nedwell here and the writing is simply a string of old hat medical sketches. Still, there's an effective string of cases for Evans' first day, the 'them and us' of fun-loving medics and boot-licking swines is once again promoted and there's at least one gloriously typical Chapman creation in the bogus singing vicar with a long list of hospital visits. Totally mad.

Written by **Graham Chapman & Bernard McKenna**
Broadcast 28 February 1971

You're Really Landed Me In It This Time

Perhaps the best episode of the entire series, this is a glorious mini farce built round the interchanging local doctor figures of Layton and Evans. The scenario is very old hat and the jokes aren't that original, but the beautiful manic playing of the leads is peerless. Evans, fresh-faced and nervous, turns in a stunning piece of work frantically defending his honour, mugging with deep-voice and light sensitive eyes to fool Layton's patient and enjoying a classic exchange with the naive new recruit, memorably contrasted with a grand bit of character playing as the simpleton. Layton, cool dude on the loose, does the drunk act brilliantly, muddles up the names in a low-key Shakespearean romp and energetically gets involved in the final door-slamming chase around the house. Best of all though are a couple of glorious performances from man-hungry Patsy Rowlands, slinking round the place with gusto, and James Hayter in Andrew Cruickshank mood, bellowing orders and guzzling malt whiskey. This standard comic situation is effortlessly made into pure gold dust.
Written by **Graham Chapman & Bernard McKenna**
Broadcast 7 March 1971

Lock, Stock And Beryl

After a glorious run with Arthur Lowe in residence of some cracking Garden/Oddie scripts, the return of Chapman here was quite a let-down. Basically it's back to wacky student activities with Richard O'Sullivan's slimeball talking dissection at breakfast, Davies picking up drunken women and in-fighting about jobs between Evans and Layton juxtaposed with huge swathes of medical banter. Relief is at hand with a wonderfully constructed game of medical-jargon dominated scrabble resulting in childish bickering. The flamboyant first appearance of Geoffrey Davies almost single-handedly saves the whole show – his case of leather-based equipment and books on bondage cause raised eyebrows, while there's a typically Chapmanesque moment with one dubious publication shrouded by the cover of a Biggles classic!
Written by **Graham Chapman & Bernard McKenna**
Broadcast 25 April 1971

Saturday Matinee

It wasn't really in John Cleese's career plan to return to the *Doctor* series but an unsuccessful business venture in a gym, which collapsed when his partner died, resulted in the need for some quick cash. The solution was a string of hastily constructed episodes for *Doctor At Large* beginning with this embarrassing farce of bedside manners. Evans, left in charge of a high class medical practice, has to deal with Geoffrey Davies's over-sexed, cold-shouldered girlfriend (a rather disconcerting dolly bird with attitude from Maureen Lipman), a scantily clad cabinet minister, various confused females mistaken for a dignified charity contact concerning teddy bears for under-privileged children and Ivor Dean's under-rehearsed and sardonic butler. It's all pretty standard fare and you can see Cleese's heart is never in it but there are some delicious moments along the way, including the bizarre one-way conversation with the aged buffer in the waiting room, Geoffrey's biting observation that landed gentry get on with horses/dogs because of the easy conversation, and the questioning of authority/awareness of political power. But more often than not, this is just an excuse for sexual stereotyping with dripping lushpots unseen since *Adventures of a Private Eye*, trouser-dropping farce and comedy of misunderstanding. But at least Cleese made a few quid and, more importantly, found the seed of something priceless in the following episode.
Written by **John Cleese**
Broadcast 9 May 1971

No Ill Feeling

In terms of later comic development, this is the most important episode, if not the funniest (that's surely the following programme). However, this is the script from John Cleese from which producer Humphrey Barclay famously thought a series could spring. That series appeared four years later under the title of *Fawlty Towers*. Although there are, obviously, many differences between this *Doctor* show and the Cleese masterpiece, the basic premise is clearly fixed, with the similar dining room angst-dialogues, hassles with the wife figure and temperamental treatment of unaware guests. Timothy Bateson is far more restrained than Cleese in ranting mood but brilliantly channels the furious sense of comic frustration, contrasting the weak as dishwater Evans with a fine line in powerless bemusement.
Written by **John Cleese**
Broadcast 30 May 1971

Let's Start At the Beginning

Cracking episode with Chapman's medical madness tuned to perfection, this benefits from a couple of stunning comic eccentrics in the shape of jittering David Jason (with a touching conclusion of flowery gift) and a barn-storming performance from Freddie Jones running the psychiatrist centre with a brain full of angst. His office, a cross between a *Doctor Who* despot and *The Wizard of Oz*, is the setting for a hilariously confused conversation with Barry Evans while Geoffrey Davies oozes self-assured charm all over the place. Noel Coleman gives a memorable, straight-laced, height of normality military-type rant before lapsing into *Python*esque obsession with the size of his nose and, for a change, Evans isn't confined to sympathetic shaking of the head but revels in dumbstuck reactions, funny pay off lines and wide-eyed amazement.
Written by **Graham Chapman & Bernard McKenna**
Broadcast 6 June 1971

It's All in the Mind
The usual medic goings-on plus some hilarious occult comedy with Evans and Layton at a cocktail party allegedly hosted by witches!.
Written by **John Cleese**
Broadcast 13 June 1971

Cynthia Darling
Evans pampers a young girl and her overpowering mother.
Written by **John Cleese**
Broadcast 20 June 1971

Operation Loftus
A make-shift collection of Loftus' old students performs an urgent operation.
Written by **Graham Chapman & Bernard McKenna**
Broadcast 11 July 1971

Mother And Father Doing Well
Written by **John Cleese**
Broadcast 18 July 1971

A Joke's A Joke
Evans and Layton act as anatomy demonstrators.
Written by **Graham Chapman & Bernard McKenna**
Broadcast 25 July 1971

It's The Rich Wot Gets The Pleasure
Davies comes into a fortune.
Written by **Graham Chapman & Bernard McKenna**
8 August 1971

Things That Go Mump In The Night
Evans gets the mumps and faces familiar student incompetence.
Written by **Graham Chapman & Bernard McKenna**
Broadcast 15 August 1971

Mr. Moon
Evans is trapped in a health farm.
Written by **John Cleese**
Broadcast 22 August 1971

The Viva
Written by **Bernard McKenna & Graham Chapman**
Broadcast 29 August 1971

DOCTOR IN THE HOUSE

Series One
Why Do You Want To Be A Doctor?
The first ever episode of the classic small screen retellings of Richard Gordon's medical books sees the only series contribution from the all-powerful Cleese/Chapman collaboration just months before embarking on *Monty Python's Flying Circus*. Suitably as the starting point for a major television institution, this episode does little bar establish the main characters and inject a bit of medical mugging – it's certainly very subdued when compared with the non-stop innuendo fests of, say,

Doctor In Charge, but retains a quiet, naive charm with Barry Evans' fresh-faced student bumbling through lofty expectations and Loftus's threats with a timid smile, happily resigned to life on campus as he sinks a pint with pals Nedwell and Davies.
The starting point is clearly the 1954 film, with Evans in the Dirk Bogarde mould, Davies smoking with sophistication in Kenneth More's shoes, Layton as an under-used (here) Donald Sinden and Nedwell as a sort of Bogarde/More reflection to calm Evans and endorse the hard-drinking, womanising ideals of the others – boyish but quickly latching onto the medical fun ethos. The first half is all Evans, apart from a very brief, downtrodden word from Nedwell, and relates our central hero's enlistment into St. Swithins, with heart-stopping interviews, over-advisor father and wideboy doorman. The initial parental chat is brilliantly timed, while Evans, complete with stock answers, bumbled responses and sheepish grin, is endearingly ineffectual, gaining good comic mileage from his ballet dancing brother and expressing shocked surprise at Clark's knowing request about his marital status. There's ghoulish fun with a dismembered arm bound for dissection but ending up causing panic both in the maternity wing and outside with an inquisitive copper. There's a warm endorsement of the 1954 movie with a gorilla mascot and some delicious put-downs from Ernest Clark, but the finest moment belongs to Dean Ralph Michael, rambling through his tried, tested and oft-delivered welcoming speech, pinpointing the dos and don'ts of medical life, driving home the importance of English law and quite stunningly shifting gear to intense interest while plugging his beloved but floundering rugby team. Apart from an easy laugh from the notion of founding the hospital after venereal disease there is nothing much of Chapman's wonderful use of gruesome medical nonsense, but as the beginning of a long-running success this episode couldn't have been in two safer pairs of hands.

Written by **John Cleese & Graham Chapman** Broadcast 12 July 1969
The War Of The Mascots
This was Chapman's belated return to the series with new writing partner in tow and a reliance on fairly standard medical student antics. The scripts were still far too respectful of the 1954 film, allowing the cast to inject their own sixties slant on a very fifties formula. Here, there is rape of the ape fun with St. Swithins' chimp mascot (it was a gorilla in both the film and the first episode of the television series but a chimp is easier to hoist away!), while the majority of comedy comes from youthful lusting with rugger songs (the Virgin Sturgeon et al), copious amounts of alcohol (Layton going for the yard of ale twice!) and healthy, aggressive rivalry. Evans is his usual 'not me Sir!' self, although he and Nedwell get into hot water during the midnight raid on Highcroft, while the stereotypical mucking about with our heroes disguised in nurses' uniforms is more panto than radical. Besides, everyone but Geoffrey Davies (giving a particularly smooth account of college tradition with an air of sophisticated superiority) seems to have picked up the script two minutes before the director shouted action and has barely learnt a line. Ralph Michael's bumbling performance, akin to William Hartnell's Doctor Who, injects great pauses for eccentric dramatic effect while certainly trying to cover the fact that he hasn't got a clue what he's talking about! Anyway, the lavatorial, lowbrow drinking, pride in your school mugging of the cast gets the juices flowing and there's a splendid few minutes of reasoning and counter-reasoning between Evans and Nedwell before the onslaught with the Dean – skilfully set up via his enforced policy of making folk wait and sweat. The serious handshake between the two first-term pals taps into the military camaraderie of mascot pinching and adds an endearing edge to this typically slow-motion *Doctor in the House* episode.
Written by **Graham Chapman & Barry Cryer**
Broadcast 30 August 1969

Getting The Bird

Abysmal episode clearly put together for Graham's beer money which, despite injecting a feel for swinging sixties taboo-breaking with a heart-to-heart talk about losing virginity and the perils of Brewer's droop, really succumbs to reusing old formulae from the movies. Evans here is in the Dirk Bogarde innocent mould, getting lumbered with the hospital madwoman Rigor Mortis – played by Joan Sims in the film but fleshed out by Helen Fraser here (later to marry Richard O'Sullivan in a different guise in *Doctor in Charge*). She sups her gin, rips off her tights seductively and clears off just as Evans prepares himself. There's the regular sweetener of seeing Yutte Stensgaard wandering round in various states of undress, but this really is a poorly constructed, unoriginal and cheesily acted piece of comedy. The sheer exuberance of Robin Nedwell and Geoffrey Davies (brilliantly putting across the obvious but hilarious innuendo) carries the thing through, but a drunken Martin Shaw babbles on about nothing, Layton drinks himself into unsuccessful action and Evans seemingly sleepwalks through his big sexual awakening moment. The multi-proposal ploy is pinched from *Doctor in Clover* and even the usually glam Angharad Rees looks a bit miffed.

Written by **Graham Chapman & Barry Cryer**

Broadcast 6 September 1969

Pass Or Fail

Good clean fun at St. Swithins with the students cramming for final exams and rushing round the place like beer-fuelled nutters – so what's new! A tightly written and amusing episode, there's plenty of typical medical pontificating, a choice opportunity for Ernest Clark to be unwelcome and even a pre-Hinge & Brackett appearance from Patrick Fyffe. He enjoys a hilarious nightclub scene at the outset, rebuffing knowing comments with well-worn but perfectly delivered one-liners, tapping into the innuendo sense of humour of the series and going through his number. Barry Evans, amid fear and

panic about the impending study, uncharacteristically throws in the towel for some more bar activity while Layton gleefully holds court with everybody displaying an equally uncharacteristic knowledge of medicine. Evans enjoys a grand scene opposite Clark's officious examiner, embracing gore with the dropped tongue item and sheepishly grinning his way to a pass via the saucy probing phrases of Geoffrey Davies. Martin Shaw wanders around wrenching, drinking and standing as the spirit of rugger – ditto Relph's Dean, apart from the wrenching and drinking of course – and Yutte Stensgaard looks the embodiment of sexiness, even while reduced to making the lads some coffee – keeping the ladies in their place, very radical and sixties 'right on'. Robin Nedwell shines as ever, with some cheeky exam technique, an explosive practical experiment and bucketloads of fresh-faced enthusiasm, with the whole show finishing on some spontaneous beer chucking antics in the bar. This episode, closing the first series of *Doctor In The House*, was LWT's get-out policy. Unhappy with everything save the huge ratings figures, the men in grey suits decided to pull the plug on the good docs but, of course, people power won the day and a second series was gleefully rushed into production while the first series was still airing. However, with the lads all passing the exams, theoretically the closing of the student doctor storyline could also close the series – spin-offs would happily spin off into the 1990s and this final booze-up of pleasure and relief allows Davies to almost get his trousers ripped, Evans to have pint after pint poured over him and a group of fine young actors to really let their hair down.

Written by **Graham Chapman & Barry Cryer**

Broadcast 3 October 1969

DOCTOR IN TROUBLE

The seventh and last of the big screen *Doctor* adventures from producer Betty Box and director Ralph

Thomas starred the bumbling charmer Leslie Phillips, by now desperately trying to retain the old girl magnet personality in the face of younger competition, and featured a very brief cameo from James Robertson Justice, in his last film. By now, the series that had started in 1954 had pretty much given up its individuality and happily latched onto the commercial sure-thing of *Carry On* innuendo. Indeed, apart from Phillips, a decade away from the *Carry On*s but still the king of cool dudes, there's an unusual support from Joan Sims here as a lusty Russian captain, bucketloads of *Carry On* glam girls (Angela Grant/Janet Mahoney/Yutte Stensgaard) and one glance at the credits will reveal the influx of *Carry On* back-room boys. None more imposing than Eric Rogers, penning a typically *Carry On*esque score and injecting copious amounts of his trade-mark rasping horn section, making the audience expect a priceless Sid James swagger that never comes.

The setting and style make *Doctor in Trouble* a sort of cross between *Doctor at Sea* and *Carry On Cruising,* the climactic deck party certainly nudges memories of Sid and the gang, and even Mahoney's strip-tease at the close uses the same theme that Jenny Cox would undress to in *Carry On Behind* five years later. Sadly though, the scripting here is fairly lacklustre, putting out the same old clichés for a very impressive cast to sleep walk through. Harry Secombe is a joy as a flamboyant, conceited pools winner, slobbering all over the dolly birds and even chucking in a Goonish raspberry to authority for good measure. Irene Handl plays the cockney old dear to perfection and Robert Morley, setting up the similar plot for television's *Doctor at Sea* when Ernest Clark plays his own Professor Loftus's brother, stands in for the ailing Robertson Justice as the barking figure of power aboard ship. There's cracking support from Graham Stark, Freddie Jones, John Le Mesurier and Joan Benham (later to play Ernest Clark's long suffering wife on TV), but it's clear that the medics had run their course in cinema and Leslie Phillips seems quite ill at ease throughout, particularly during the toe-curling drag scene which simply doesn't come off. There's the novelty of watching Phillips chase, adore and charm his wife, Angela Scoular, but even that doesn't conclude in a happy ending on screen, finishing with Jacki Piper and the family from hell. However, the chief interest from our *Python* viewpoint is the presence of two pioneers of *Doctor in the House* on television.

This seventh film is a real case of handing the baton over, for a year earlier the television spin-off had proved hugely popular. Although he is uncredited, Geoffrey Davies, one of the small screen stars, clearly recreates his role of Dick Stuart-Clark for an early scene opposite Leslie Phillips in the film. Importantly, it is a meeting between the two icons of cool caddishness from the small and big screen series, merging the two together and allowing the new boys in white to take over fully. Of even more interest is a supporting performance from Graham Chapman who, along with John Cleese, had moulded the scenario for television via the first ever episode. Although always welcome and continually popping up throughout the seafaring misadventures, Chapman is restricted to a standard camp glamour photographer persona, eyeing up the likes of Simon Dee with flowery 'darlings' and 'loves' all over the place, skipping through the slapstick, flashing his bare midriff, panicking about losing his camera, fighting to be the first to the lifeboats, pratfalling through the party with a trifle in the face and eagerly taking up any offer of being chased by the hunks aboard. In line with the *Carry On* flavour of the entire project, Chapman is tossed into Hawtrey and Williams cameoland (indeed his reaction to the striptease is pure Williams and resurrected by the man himself in *Carry On Behind*), even though he injects a touch of acidic angst about the part, spitting out 'Bitch!' when his sexuality is questioned. A typical persona of camp in the face of glam 'ruddy

girls', he happily fops and fusses around the place, although in his first scene, taking pics from his swimming pool vantage point, he delights in feminine fashion and the female form. Clearly, his idea of characterisation shifted to total Hawtrey overload along the way. In hardly the most taxing of film roles, Chapman had, by now, already launched into immortality with *Python* and quickly escaped playing other peoples' stereotypes in favour of playing his own twisted ones.

LESLIE PHILLIPS Dr. Tony Burke
**HARRY SECOMBE, JAMES ROBERTSON JUSTICE, ANGELA SCOULAR, IRENE HANDL, SIMON DEE, ROBERT MORLEY ,FREDDIE JONES, JOAN SIMS, JOHN LE MESURIER, GRAHAM STARK, JANET MAHONEY.
JACKI PIPER, FRED EMNEY, YURI BORIENKO, GERALD SIM YUTTE STENSGAARD, JIMMY THOMPSON, SYLVANNA HENRIQUES, MARCIA FOX, TOM KEMPINSKI, ANTHONY SHARP MARIANNE STONE, JOHN BLUTHAL, & ANGELA GRANT, GEOFFREY DAVIES**
Roddy **GRAHAM CHAPMAN**
Screenplay by **Jack Davies**
Based on the novel *Doctor On Toast* by **Richard Gordon**
Music **Eric Rogers**
Photography **Ernest Steward**
Editor **Peter Boita**
Art director **Lionel Couch**
Assistant director **Bert Batt**
Camera operator **James Bawden**
Producer **Betty E. Box**
Director **Ralph Thomas**
90 mins, Technicolor, Pinewood 1970

DOCTOR IN CHARGE

Series One
The Devil You Know
Duncan Waring returns to his old haunting ground of St. Swithins hospital only to be greeted by a jolly jape orchestrated by Paul Collier – that all his old chums pretend not to remember him. Cracking wheeze, what!! This is a classic episode of *Doctor in Charge*, blessed with a

particularly spot-on comic performance from the ever reliable Robin Nedwell and some clever medical innuendo from Chapman and McKenna.

By this stage of the game, of course, *Python* on BBC television had pretty much run its course, but Chapman was still able to restrain his surreal sense of humour and effortlessly deliver the required burst of family-oriented situation comedy. However, as always, there are traces of *Python*esque tomfoolery within the structure of the piece, of especial note, the wonderfully written, American-styled operation, with Nedwell's insistent on first names only, deliciously taking his time with the knife and cheekily leading Davies in a stirring rendition of *Oklahoma!* The finest moment comes as Davies goes a bit far with friendly names and addresses Nedwell as 'Duncie!', only to be castigated and changes his mind to 'Sweetie!' – a direct use of the Sir Edward Ross interview between Chapman and Cleese in *Python* episode one series one. Outside of this particular injection of *Python* comedy there are some lovely touches from Mollie Sugden's hypochrondria and medically distressed Mrs. Waring, showering her son with a brand new stethoscope, in the wake of every man and his dog doing the selfsame thing. There is a hilarious over-reaction from stuffy Professor Loftus, with Ernest Clark going into semi-Cleese overdrive with elongated delivery and outraged facial expressions (warranting Nedwell kisses and cuddles as the only old face to recognise him) Arthur English's underplayed, cockney wide-boy of a caretaker and Harold Goodwin's dumbstruck barman. The final reunion of the doctors, Stuart-Clark and Collier and some rib-tickling ignoring of Waring, results in boyish pats on the back and suggested hard drinking only to collapse into Hancockian passages of silence and realisation that boredom and lack of similar interest defuses the heartfelt gathering of old medical pranksters. Every funny story from the intervening years falls flat since

Waring knows them all via letters he received, and his newly found interest in medicine and the American way of things allows Geoffrey Davies one priceless moment of absolute disgust at his freshly dedicated pal. Chapman's medical knowledge again helps lend some reality to the corny gags and friendly banter, while Nedwell's professional and clever checking of medical tests adds a sense of humility and strength to his usual smart alec characterisation, with the respect of his superior and colleagues adding weight to his position of authority. As always with Chapman's work, the doctors could be girl-chasing, drinking nutters, but behind all the naughty boy behaviour there were always highly qualified and caring medics.

Written by **Graham Chapman & Bernard McKenna**
Broadcast 9 April 1972

The Research Unit
Loftus is up for a knighthood (which subsequently came in the Layton/Lynn script *Long Day's Journey Into Knighthood*) and tries to promote his hospital and himself via a revolutionary new medical discovery. Cue Waring and the lads involved in a top priority bit of research. Chapman's great strength in writing these shows, outside of his obvious ability and understanding in the serious subject of medicine, was his delight in building up the pomposities of Clark's benighted authority figure as the hapless young medics fight over dolly birds and rounds of booze. Here, with the ultimate status symbol dangled in front of his nose, Loftus almost drools throughout the episode with projected glee and mini dream sequences taking the form of black and white snapshots of his brush with nobility. Importantly this authority figure is never really highlighted as a bad cornerstone of the establishment, simply keeping a watchful eye over his flock of randy, drunkard doctors and bellowing with sugar-coated kindness. As a result, all the manic elements are kept firmly in place and this episode ends on a

happy note for St. Swithins' king bee. O'Sullivan, for one of the only times in his life, constrained as a weak and irritating nobody (away from his dashing, streetwise rogue of, say, *Man About the House*) panics, tells tales and flusters about the place like a pregnant mother hen, and his fate is sealed totally as not only do the fun-loving docs hate him but Loftus as well. This episode is interesting for a particularly surreal beginning with Nedwell abandoned in his superior's house following a party, clad in nothing but a pair of woollen gloves and wellington boots. Later this, as always, turns out to be a practical joke orchestrated by those clever wags Davies and Layton. Outside of this piece of bizarre content, the medical gags flow pretty much in average quantities, punctuated by two notable homosexual assertions. Firstly, and of most interest, Sammie Winmill's comment concerning the stripped naked exploits of the party prank pinpoints that the woman-hungry lads were boring not to have let anything else happen after Nedwell was exposed and sozzled. Davies, with a rather dubious reaction, as Winmill's meaning dawns on him, effortlessly steers our red-blooded boys away from the thought but Chapman's script cleverly allows the notion to develop, remain perfectly acceptable and, through Winmill's girlie charms, be the obvious option. Latterly, this situation is tackled in more conventional British comedy terms as a courting couple disturb Nedwell and O'Sullivan in a comprising (but totally innocent) clinch. The gag is repeated with a throwaway suggestive comment from Layton to Nedwell as the same heterosexual couple wander in, but the humour comes totally from the absolute absurdity of the docs getting down to anything outside of the latest blonde glam girl. Winmill's example remains the most potent and, importantly, her sexual drive is highlighted by a pretty obvious but still powerful innuendo concerning her feeling much better when she has something inside her. The line may mean the omelettes she is preparing for the men (the nurse,

whether qualified or not, is still the caring, slave-like figure to the male community, later the other side of the coin is firing on all cylinders as Winmill appears in black undies and suspenders as Davies saucy pic companion), although her cheeky grin and pause before the next scene allows the gag to seep through and hit home. Despite remaining the archetypal bimbo figure, with nothing to do save cook and look decorative, Winmill was a regular character and her observations held more weight than the usual leggy bits from something like *On the Buses*. There's also a clever look at gutter journalism and the ill-used funds of the National Health Service, abused by Layton and his home-made wine scam, with Davies delighting in the secret sexual activities of his patients and colleagues, while the press find bickering, corrupted and disgruntled intervention from O'Sullivan. All adds up to a successful research project and smiles all round.

Written by **Graham Chapman & Bernard McKenna**
Broadcast 16 April 1972.

The Minister's Health
The major thread of comedy here comes from the standard Shakespearean and farcical ploy of mistaken identity between two similarly named people – here the high ranking Minister of Health and a bemused, softly spoken Minister of the Church. The normal hilarious mishaps take place with the wrong food and over-indulgence being showered on the vicar while the VIP suffers but appreciates the unfussy and unembellished medical treatment of St. Swithins. In light of the opening credits, this episode was penned by McKenna with Graham Chapman, the latter injecting minor pieces of dialogue and standing as a constant link with material harking back to themes explored in *The Research Unit* (Loftus and his knighthood/Collier's home-made wine). The episode remains important thanks to the addition of some underlying social comment, with the hierarchy of the hospital

desperately trying to ingratiate
themselves, serve the supposed
Minister with sumptuous restaurant
grub, provide sickly smiles and overdone niceties, while O'Sullivan slimes
in for some top notch restructuring of
the NHS chat. The trio of fun-loving
medics act as stooges to the madness
going on around them although
Davies is in particularly fine form,
happily researching his medical book
based around sexual experience and
reeling goggle-eyed from the aged
one's public transport memoirs. All in
all this is a brilliantly played
comment on the corruption of power
but again, as in so many of these
Doctor shows, the authority figure is
highlighted as a regular sort of chap.
Despite his rather over-superior
entrance, the VIP's wish to be treated
as a normal patient seems to ring true
and, although he gets his wish by
mistake (Loftus almost bursting a
blood vessel in his effort to instil the
man's importance on Waring), the
Minister sees the system as it really is
and appreciates it. Political comment
or cold feet... I leave it to you.

Written by **Bernard McKenna &
Graham Chapman**
Broadcast 23 April 1972

Mum's the Word
A similar script-writing arrangement
as *The Minister's Health* and, indeed,
tackling very similar comedy ideas.
Basically, in order to impress the
chairman and help get Waring on the
hospital board, the other two lads let
it be known that the good doctor's
mother is a wealthy Countess with a
love of donating money to medical
courses. Bingham is delighted when
Waring's real mother (in the
endearing cockney form of Mollie
Sugden) arrives with a twisted ankle
and a charade between the real thing
and Stuart-Clark's hilarious dignified
drag act takes up a huge chunk of the
laugh quota. This is a fairly standard
entry in the good fun canon of St.
Swithins comedy, but as usual, there's
an underlining sense of political
comment beneath the mild smut.
Robin Nedwell turns in a classic
performance, desperately putting on
the pompous, smart-suited, on-the-

ball attitude to get his position of
power, faking right-wing belief and
approval of research cuts in a Trojan's
horse attempt to finally back up the
lone voice of sanity from Clark's
Professor Loftus and resurrect some
medical values. The heartfelt balling
out in the bar when Loftus gets the
wrong end of the stick is a very
powerful moment, joyfully
counterbalanced by the final scene of
comrades-in-arms friendliness.
However, the comic gem is Geoffrey
Davies's stunning drag sequence,
lapsing into his manly tones, slipping
tiaras out of his bag and whooping
with glee at victory. Importantly,
thanks to Chapman's fondness for
just nudging the stereotypical
goalposts in the *Doctor* series, this
sequence of drag goes one step
beyond pantoland toward the more
realistic topic of medical sex changes.
Although the whole rouse is send up
by Layton's tongue-in-cheek idea to
take Davies out and Clark's stunned
double-take reaction, the comedy is
typically multi-faceted.

Written by **Bernard McKenna with
Graham Chapman**
Broadcast 11 June, 1972

The Fox
A new Matron breezes through St.
Swithin's but otherwise it's business
as usual with Bingham being a bitchy
bore, the docs talking birds 'n' booze
and Loftus bellowing for Britain. A
pretty standard sort of script from
McKenna and Chapman although, as
usual with the medic Python aboard
there's realms of scientific jargon
alongside the innuendo. It's a
pleasant twist to see Clark's
tyrannical Loftus brought down a peg
or two by the new broom – his first
Matron who continually harps on
about his madcap, amorous
adventures as a young man. Nedwell
is as brash and cool as ever, groping
Winmill and plotting revenge on the
smart alec sneak of Richard
O'Sullivan, and Davies and Layton
have a grand little scene organising
and reorganising their working day
round more valued drinking time.
One gloriously *Python*esque element
comes in the shape of William

Moore's country yokel patient,
surrounded by various vegetables,
initially embracing the compost heap
trick and happily gurgling and
chuckling throughout the madness
with a carrot hanging round his neck.
However, besides that surreal bit of
business, there's a rather obvious
reference to *Dr. Who* (mid way
through Jon Pertwee's era) and a
bucketload of old smut (the
Bingham/ Bang 'em telephone banter,
Loftus crying out to Matron that she
should leave his patients' vegetables
alone and the like!). All good clean
medic fun with, once again, the plot
and counter-plot of Nedwell and the
lads resulting in smiles all round with
the beloved authority figure of Ernest
Clark.

Written by **Bernard McKenna with
Graham Chapman**
Broadcast 18 June 1972

A Night With the Dead
One of the very best *Doctor In
Charge* episodes exploring Waring's
mortal fear of the mortuary, abused
by a hard-up, betting-obsessed Stuart-
Clark and a rival in love, Bingham.
The initial sequence setting up the
fear and trepidation is brilliantly
played by Nedwell and Davies,
ushering in a typically cheerful
assistant in the morgue (why is it that
people surrounded by the dead
always rejoice in black humour and
have stomachs of cast iron??),
although he disapproves of Nedwell's
throwaway line about folk dying to
get in. A stunning rendition of *Yes,
We Have No Bananas* is a comic high
point and look out for a very subtle
inclusion of *I Ain't Got No Body*,
two years before Marty Feldman gave
the gag cinematic immortality in the
Mel Brooks film *Young Frankenstein*.
The dark humour may subside a tad
during the lustful Sullivan's longing
for Helen Fraser and his uneasy
attempts at proposing to her,
although there are plenty of surreal
giggles provoked by his engagement
ring being slipped onto a dead man's
finger, while the apt moment of
corpsing between Sullivan and
Nedwell is priceless stuff – developed
with a shared aware look between

Davies and Nedwell. However, thankfully, the spooky, nifty laughs are back on track for the overnight stay in the morgue with Davies's subtle chain rattles and window slams designed to spook Nedwell out of a bet for a fiver. O'Sullivan's overplayed ghost voice scuppers the fun but Nedwell gets his night in shiny nightie come-uppance. A well constructed, away from the norm series entry with less characterisations to clog up the fun and an excellent performance of cheerfulness covering extreme nervousness from Robin Nedwell.

Written by **Bernard McKenna with Graham Chapman**
Broadcast 25 June 1972

This Is Your Wife

The usual comic misunderstanding at the hospital, this time concerning the marriage between Richard O'Sullivan and Helen Fraser on the high-profile St. Swithin's Day, leads to manic chaos and quality low-brow comedy. For beer money, Chapman and McKenna craft a typical, untaxing arena for the usual suspects to pratfall, mince and moan about in, giving O'Sullivan some priceless moments of nervous frustration and, as always, allowing the sublime Robin Nedwell to remain the king of cool in mounting situations of confusion. A briefly seen Ernest Clark delivers some choice barking put-downs and comic observations (the nun at the orgy line could have done with an extra comeback rather than the abrupt fade but it still hits the mark), the well orchestrated attempts of Davies and Layton to save their third musketeer buddie from the supposed jaws of wedlock play with high energy and Nedwell's questioning of the sainted Saint's masculinity goes for cheap laughter and delicious confusion from the naive O'Sullivan. It's fairly average slice of *Doctor In Charge* comedy with the canteen discussions and various over-flamboyant character assassinations of Fraser. There is at least one masterpiece when Kenneth Waller's pessimistic patient goes in for operation and unwittingly faces the go slow tactics of half the doc quartet

and the record-breaking speed actions of the other two. In the end, there has to be a knuckle sandwich for the authority figure of the church, some playful find-the-ring antics in a fountain and a hilariously disgruntled, sodden marriage line-up for some title sequence snapshots. Still, the usual theme being replaced by the wedding march is the biggest surprise.

Written by **Graham Chapman & Bernard McKenna**
Broadcast 2 July, 1972

The System

Hilarious confusion is guaranteed when the hospital employs an elaborate timetable from Dr. Waring, allowing Chapman and McKenna to milk maximum, standard, knock-about fun from a simple but endearing idea. The madcap playing of Nedwell, Davies, Layton and O'Sullivan is again brought under strict control by Ernest Clark's power, and the show begins with a delicious bit of inspired bickering over which doctor is teaching which group of students. The old schoolboy humour and petty jealousies from *Doctor in the House* replace the more down to earth, pleasures of the flesh mentality of earlier shows in this series, with Nedwell's, albeit craftily pinched, idea trying to impress the boss man. Moments of inspired madness result from the unworkable rota, with O'Sullivan giving a heartfelt lecture to no students, Nedwell finding himself surrounded by bemused medics and, best of all, the delightful delivery of Layton and Davies as they deliciously buck the ludicrous system by presenting two different lectures at once just because the timetable says they should. There's a rare chance for Nedwell to wallow in hassled performance while the penultimate moment of calm kindness and understanding from tyrannical Clark is a touching injection of sentiment, gloriously ripped away by the final moment of truth.
Jam-packed with funny set pieces and, despite one camp throw-away and Layton's racist reaction, it's all a refreshing break from stereotyped bedpans and big bosomed nurses.

The laddish fun when Davies' qualified doc is stumped by Nedwell's student medical trivia teaser and the hilarious onslaught of Professor Loftus impersonations, capped by one from the man himself, are amongst the funniest scenes in the series.

Written by **Graham Chapman & Bernard McKenna**
Broadcast 23 July 1972

Amazing Grace

With the quota of regular doctor characters cut down, this memorable episode allows a great deal of prat-falling, endearing character comedy from Tony Robinson. Clumsy and inept, a full decade before his Baldrick in the *Blackadder* series, Robinson staggers round the ward in glasses, falling over apparatus, falling into people and falling out with his superior. Nedwell and Layton, more concerned with bedding Robinson's tasty nursing sister and to cover their own falsified glowing reports, set about to improve his performance in time for the distinguished inspection of Richard Hurndell's medical big wig. A sterling central support from Hurndell, this is another approachable authority figure from the Chapman and McKenna file, taking pleasure in noting medical progress and expressing concern in light of the underworked hierarchy's apparent inability to detect correct medical symptoms. Alongside the usual lengthy technical speeches (including a beauty, delivered with panache by Layton) there is a huge influx of basic innuendo comedy, delightfully chatting up the local nurse populace with mind-wondering mentions of football via balloons/breast obsessions. There's a well judged bit of working class banter with a missing 50 pence piece and a financially concerned, Diana Dors-like mother, but basically this episode is yet another case of misleading some chap in charge and generally pulling together to get away with a bit of low-level corruption. Blessed with an excellent farce performance from Robinson and the solid rock performance of Hurdnell, the regulars happily stroll through the fun with consummate ease.

Written by **Graham Chapman & Bernard McKenna**
Broadcast 6 August 1972

Yellow Fever

A case of I don't like Chinese, with Professor Loftus disturbed to learn that a group of 20 pals of Doctor Waring's local oriental restaurant owner are coming for a guided tour round the hospital. There's plenty of mileage for Ernest Clark's booming authority and the sneaky hand-rubbing of Richard O'Sullivan to shoot off about communist plots and infiltration of the alien force, while the other doctors struggle to get away with it, with Davies, Sid James-like, flogging any old medical rubbish as national treasures. The endless translations and mortal fear of red politics does tend to wear a bit thin after a while and this certainly is hardly a vintage Chapman/McKenna episode, although the cast pull through to the bitter end and Clark plays his character mood changes with real style. Still on tenterhooks about his knighthood and with a reassuringly military word from his pal the Brig, the Chinese are embraced with open arms, shown all the modern technology with a view to international sales and finally ushered in to witness a bit of Clark magic with the operating tools. Among all the political angst, backbiting and insecure expressions are one or two pleasing wacky moments, notably the incessant shouting of 'Why!' all over the place (the Brits believe it means 'Hello' after translation complications), a relaxed bit of prop manoeuvre as Nedwell whips a pinched cigar out of his pocket and a classic put-down from Clark as Nedwell's smug command of the language is proved to be incompetence.

Written by **Graham Chapman & Bernard McKenna**
Broadcast 20 August 1972

That's My Uncle!

When Loftus is away the lads can play, but their professor's replacement seems to play the sporting, skiving, drinking and womanising game with as much vigour as them. It's a clever touch to have this bogus authority figure shock the young docs with a mirror image of their own badly behaved lifestyles and William Franklyn's smooth performance is a masterstroke. He's Stuart-Clark's uncle, thus the charming cad persona obviously runs in the family, and this characterisation is so strong that the regulars just surround him with ever ready pound notes, a line of gin and tonics (presumably Schweppes) and willingness to do his work. Semi-regular Debbie Watling, having caught the eye of Nedwell in an earlier episode, gets seduced into the super cool Franklyn world while Layton is dragged round the golf course and pays his own tip. There's some cynical comment on the private medical scheme, with Franklyn's prize patient getting a blonde bimbo, television and chocolates while forking out a fortune for a made-up ailment but at the end of the day, the docs celebrate him as a loveable rogue with their admiration backfiring as they see him into a cushy job with lots of money and Nedwell's pseudo-bird. Interesting as an episode which sees the usual charmers foiled by the kingpin and blessed with a deliciously surreal touch as Davies wheels in a dead sheep.

Written by **Bernard McKenna & Graham Chapman**
Broadcast 10 September 1972

Blackmail

The knighthood for dear old Loftus is imminent but a deal with Stuart-Clark getting away with bar fund embezzlement in order to give the Professor a nod into his exclusive club gets recorded by a chief medical rival. An enjoyable episode, with Ernest Clark's petulant outbursts fondly embracing his two chief doctor disaster areas, Nedwell and Davies, who go through the mill and beyond in order to save their jobs and, on a lesser scale, save their Professor from a scandal. There's a classic operation scene with hushed Chinese whispers about Loftus and later some good banter in Davies's posh and swish club, while Nedwell goes low-brow, hilariously bumbling round the place like a four ale bar. Typically with Chapman there's plenty of medical jargon floating about and at least one touch of bizarre humour with the notion of piranha fish in the bladder revenge, but the major knockabout fun comes along with the lads' window-cleaning disguises in order to pinch the incriminating evidence. Complemented by a burst of George Formby singing *When I'm Cleaning Windows,* some longing glazes at girls in hot pants and plenty of pratfalling, the docs go through the comedy motions with skill. The knighthood has already been secured, to be awarded in the next episode, but that doesn't stop Ernest Clark's final hiccough-curing threat and some charming three-way back-patting between the St. Swithins chaps.

Written by **Bernard McKenna & Graham Chapman**
Broadcast 1 October 1972

Series Two
The Merger

The soft face of authority, Ernest Clark, battles the sneaky face of authority, Henry McGee, when the beloved St. Swithins is threatened by a takeover bid from High Cross hospital. The classic set piece here features Loftus lecturing a bunch of students on the types of jaundice as the hapless quartet of docs bumble and fumble around him. A masterpiece of timing, the sudden disappearances and reappearances of Davies et al is hilarious stuff, endorsed by Clark's never failing petulance. That apart, this is fairly standard stuff, simply allowing the doctors to run riot in order to convince McGee and Harold Bennett (on leave from *Are You Being Served?*) that the hospital is a den of corruption and free living. Naturally they have the wrong end of the stick, believing Clark is all for the merger and after a cushy job with the new firm, thus their smoking, drinking, snogging and malpractice antics in the wards are all batting for the wrong side. There's a cracking mock argument between Davies and Layton over some poor chap's leg while Nedwell breezes through the fun with hearty laughter, cigar-puffing pleasure and relaxed, anti-patient reactions. In the end, of course, everything works out fine. The disruptions certainly backfire with ill-effect but the ever chattering verger finally points out that the old place is a historical monument and thus can't simply be bulldozed and forgotten. Again there's a pleasing community feel between the three fun-loving doctors and their barking Professor, for although there antics distress the medical system while endearing them to the audience, their affections and loyalties to good old-fashioned British traditional attitudes shine through alongside the anything for a giggle behaviour. Naturally, O'Sullivan's sour-faced medic is all for the destructive changes, rewarded with a seeming eternity bound and gagged in the company of the verger's boring waffle. Oh, and by the way, look out for Geoffrey Davies's Alan Bennett-like phone conversation conning O'Sullivan; it's a real television magic moment.

Written by **Graham Chapman & David Sherlock**
Broadcast 15 September 1973

Hello Sailor!
The last *Python*-related *Doctor* show for a very long time, Chapman was by now heavily involved with *Python* television assignments and gearing up for their major cinematic break with *Holy Grail*. Interesting, this surreal little episode cross-fertilises the old-style hospital banter with an all-together more off-the-wall approach to comedy. Indeed, the first half seems almost to be a watered down attempt to embrace all the girl-chasing, money-owning, medical-incompetent jargon while establishing the ultimate authority threat in the shape of Nedwell's enlistment into the Navy. With a choice between five years of hard graft or marriage to the stunning Angharad Rees our clever hero amazingly opts for the former, although he suddenly realises his

mistake and tries to get out of the problem. Good friends to the bitter end, George Layton and Geoffrey Davies give him a hand and it's this second-half plot development of pleading insanity which really sends this show into orbit. Despite Chapman's regular involvement throughout the early 1970s, none had even been so completely strange as this programme, delighting in Nedwell's frogman gear, expressing love for the Prime Minister, letting folk know that he's related to Queen Victoria and showering affection on his beloved Uncle Bobo, a wind-up plastic frog! There's a delicious bit of comedy business with Nedwell desperately trying to break through the stern face of authority with manic hopping, a cracking 'don't be a chicken' line from Layton, Nedwell's bemused look into camera and a totally *Python*esque piece of drilling – frog hop fashion. Naturally there's a reasonable explanation, for this is not anything goes *Python* but narrative comedy *Doctor In Charge* – and thus, the resident psychiatrist himself is a bit of a nutter, wandering round the place in frogman outfit and Nedwell has been mistaken for him! Problem solved, Rees bumbles in with a compounded difficulty and has a crash course in frog insanity – her sophisticated attempt at half-hearted hopping is a masterpiece of comic unease, with Chapman brilliantly endorsing his outlandish style on a traditional format.

Written by **Graham Chapman & David Sherlock**
Broadcast 8 December 1973

DOCTOR ON THE GO

For Your Own Good
Back to the medical fold after three years and now a respected post-*Python* force, Chapman could earn a bit of spare cash by teaming with *Who*/*Hitch-Hikers* writer Adams for this standard burst of St. Swithins farce. There's nothing very taxing here, with just average comic material stemming from Gascoigne's wealthy, arrogant, adulterous, hospital-bound

father (a quite brilliant turn from Derek Francis) causing problems all over the place, bashing Nedwell's car, disowning his son, running financial rings round Davies and causing the ultimate insult to Proud Scot John Kane by addressing him as an Irish porter! The soppy one has an enjoyable groundbreaking five minutes of drunken madness and Ernest Clark changes professional attitude when he discovers his long lost girl was whisked away by this capitalist monster. The other regulars have little to do along the way. The whole scenario works like a sub-quality *Fawlty Towers*, with our familiar faces put through the hoop by a moneyed moron – read Geoffrey Davies and the quite beautifully written horse-racing scam as Fawlty on the make and the pieces slip together perfectly. There's some half-hearted, bolshy anti-bank chatter from Kane but nothing really radical happens and this fine, if uninspired episode, just about sums up this tail-ender season of *Doctor* antics. Who's round is it...

Written by **Graham Chapman & Douglas Adams**
Broadcast 20 February 1977

DOCTOR WHO

The most fun slice of science fiction in the known galaxy with the grooviest telly theme tune of all-time, this BBC milestone began life on 23 November 1963 with the irascible, white-haired, time-travelling old buffer of William Hartnell with his hand on the T.A.R.D.I.S. steering wheel. In a mixture of H.G. Wells revelation, comic asides, political comment, wonderful acting and an unrelenting sense of patriotic pride, the show became a Beeb flagship and cult icon while almost immediately triggering comic wags and parody attempts. The first was via Peter Glaze and *Crackerjack* in 1964, although the fledgling *Python* style of John Cleese was only five years behind when, during Patrick Troughton's final season as the good doc in 1969, *I'm Sorry I'll Read That*

Again dedicated their on-going serial completely to the ethos of *Who* with Professor Prune and the Electric Time Trousers. In his final memoirs, *I Am the Doctor*, Jon Pertwee drew a parallel between the opening scene of his story *Spearhead From Space* and the most celebrated Michael Palin intros for the *Monty Python* It's Man. Who said tenuous! Years later, when Sylvester McCoy's seventh telly doctor had been pulled from the air and amidst weekly media hype concerning the return of *Doctor Who*, John Cleese himself was continually cited as one of the key names up for the part in the proposed Spielberg resurrection of the show. Finally, when the news was really hot about another American production company having a bash at *Who*, Eric Idle was definitively, certainly and without question going to play the role, remaining faithful to the British attitude of *Who* while having perfect familiarity value for Stateside audiences. The role went to Paul McGann and both Cleese and Idle denied even being contacted for the much rumoured filmic returns! In the end, the only tangible link with *Monty Python* and *Doctor Who* cropped up during the coolest doc's penultimate series in the 1979 Tom Baker classic *City of Death*. Basically, Tom the man is caught up in another one of those life and death struggles against a mini alien despot who plans to revert the creation of planet Earth, but the real beauty of this fondly remembered serial came with the lush Parisian locations (so chuffed with the first foreign shot that the doc and Romana are seen doing the tourist essentials during the first five minutes) and a delightfully witty screenplay from Mr. David Agnew (in reality the pseudonym for Graham Williams and Douglas Adams from an idea by David Fisher – the earlier Agnew credited story, The Invasion of Time was penned by Williams and Anthony Read). The richness of dialogue, connoisseur tenancies and blissful intoxication of the French atmosphere is brilliantly captured via Adams and his genius for sophisticated, funny science fiction. His childhood ambition to write for

Doctor Who came to fruition with this show, the Key to Time story *The Pirate Planet* and the later Tom Baker story *Shada*, which failed to materialise due to BBC strikes (although the remnants would later resurface on BBC video in 1991, complete with Baker links). At around the time of the second series of *Fawlty Towers*, following a suggestion from Adams John Cleese was invited to make a very brief guest appearance in the concluding episode of *City of Death* – with an hour and half filming time. As his abode was a mere six minutes from the BBC and he relished the work of Adams, the actor agreed. Thus, while Baker struggles to ascertain the Big Bang, the eruption of life on earth and the steady equilibrium of the universe, John Cleese and Eleanor Bron alleviate the tension with a stunning comic vignette. The thematic heart of the story concerns France's most celebrated painting, *The Mona Lisa*, and a load of copies drifting through various time-loops. Thus, the T.A.R.D.I.S. is safely deposited in the Louvre and it is during this climatic scenario that Cleese appears. Turning on his pompous, authoritarian act of intellect intensity, he earnestly examines the beauty of Tom's time machine, celebrating the blue box as high art. Cleese, fingers pinched and his very soul moved by this artistic ecstasy, is unfazed by the sudden appearance of Tom and co, the gradual disappearance of the box and the fact that this art which is art simply because it exists no longer exists. He merely nods with genuine passion as Bron mutters 'Exquisite! Absolutely exquisite.' The scene lasts 40 seconds! It's a masterly comic moment, played with total conviction by the satire boomers.

Did You Know? There are outstanding BBC out-takes of Baker and Cleese in the T.A.R.D.I.S. interior set happily slagging off their pal, Douglas Adams: priceless. Not only did John Cleese not see his contribution to *Doctor Who*, he never watched any episodes of the fab TimeLord.
Doctor Who: City of Death, episode 4.

Doctor Who **TOM BAKER**
Romana **LALLA WARD**
Count **JULIAN GLOVER**
Countess **CATHERINE SCHELL**
Duggan **TOM CHADBON**
Kerensky **DAVID GRAHAM**
Herman **KEVIN FLOOD**
Art Gallery Visitors **ELEANOR BRON & JOHN CLEESE**
Screenplay by **David Agnew**
Theme by **Ron Grainer**
Incidental music **Dudley Simpson**
Special sounds **Dick Mills**
Production assistant **Rosemary Crowson**
Production unit manager **John Nathan-Turner**
Director's assistant **Jane Wellesley**
Assistant floor manager **Carol Scott**
Film cameraman **John Walker**
Film recordist **Graham Bedwell**
Film editor **John Gregory**
Studio lighting **Mike Jefferies**
Studio sound **Anthony Philpott**
Technical manager **John Dean**
Senior cameraman **Alec Wheal**
Visual effects designer **Ian Scoones**
Electronic effects **Dave Jervis**
Vision mixer **Nigel Finnis**
Videotape editor **Rod Waldron**
Costume designer **Doreen James**
Make-up artist **Jean Steward**
Script editor **Douglas Adams**
Designer **Richard McManan-Smith**
Producer **Graham Williams**
Director **Michael Hayes**
Broadcast BBC1 – 20 October 1979

THE DRESS

This delightful short film was directed by Eva Sereny, stills photographer for Steven Spielberg, on a meagre budget. It's a contemporary morale fairy tale concerning an unfaithful husband who, having bought a posh dress for his mistress, finds renewed love for his wife. Michael Palin took on the leading role to help out Sereny and to tune up his acting skills. A quick two-week shoot, just after one of the many rewrites of American Friends, this is a charming piece of work and a very disconcerting chance to see Palin in adulterous mood. The film won a BAFTA for Best Short.
Forever Films/National Film Finance

Corp – Paramount British Pictures.
MICHAEL PALIN
PHYLLIS LOGAN
DERRICK BRANCHE
DAVE HILL
RACHEL PALIN
Screenplay by **Robert Smith**
Story/ Director **Eva Sereny**
Photography **Robin Vidgeon**
Editor **Mike Birdsell**
1984, 25 mins

EAST OF IPSWICH

An award-winning play from Michael Palin detailing teenage sexual awakenings in a boring British coastal resort and capturing the fictionalised essence of his first meeting with wife Helen in 1959 at the same place. Rawle-Hicks is superb as the young Palin figure, struggling with kindly, repressive parental influences, yearning for female company and making his bumbling transition into manhood during a few days in Suffolk. Originally developed as one of David Putnam's *Real Love* series of dramas (initially planned to hit television and then transfer to cinemas – an idea abandoned before Palin's project came to fruition), Palin's attention to period detail and gentle satirising of certain British types makes for an enchanting piece of work. Rock 'n' Roll and James Dean had created this thing called a 'teenager', but in 1959 British youth culture was still the quiet rebellion of a coffee bar and the skiffle sound of Lonnie Donegan, where dangerous highlights constituted staying out until ten at night and grabbing cordial snogs up a darkened alley. The stark contrast between religious-organised party games on the beach and the pseudo-American pleasures of smoky jazz clubs and sex on the common is cleverly intertwined in the closing section of the play, illustrating the lustful longings of teenage British chaps with their restrained desire for the English rose and, in Richard Burrill's case, a blast of uncontrolled Dutch passion. You can almost smell the two-day-old bed linen and undercooked meals, complementing the endless church-based outings, cricket on the beach, sizzling sausage evenings and middle-class sexual tension.

This stuffy, angst-ridden, gently nervous middle-classness is personified in the great performances from John Nettleton and Pat Heywood as the overly concerned parents, instilling a desire for unspoilt countryside, British heritage and nice romantic couplings with daughters of distinguished businessmen. Palin creates an unforgettable vignette of boredom and restraint in the Scrabble sequence, with his youngster's total disinterest contrasted with amazement at his father's shameless getting away with outlandish words. Heywood's knowing silence is perfection. The supporting cast is awash with distinguished acting talent, adopting many faces from the collective pool of past *Python* projects, notably the ever reliable Charles McKeown as the illness-obsessed, over-energetic, over-enthused and over-familiar troublemaker Mr. Hargreaves. Sheila Fearn is his wife, epitomising the slightly conceited figure she played in *Time Bandits*; *Faulty Towers* guest-stars Allan Cuthbertson and the priceless Joan Sanderson respectively capture the spirit of overbearing, humourless fathers and dictatorial guest house owners with a dash of friendly regard mixed with the overbearing, bullying attitude. Players from *The Missionary* add to the fun – Janine Duvitski's bemused, warmly knowing maid, Roger Brierley's cheerful, fun-organising vicar and, best of all, Graham Crowden, as the uncomfortable headmaster desperately trying to impart sexual knowledge to the young Burrill. Eagerly latching onto the conversation geared towards dog behaviour and away from the more forthright lust of the male animal, Crowden perfectly sums up the uneasy, embarrassed face of authority leading the supposed innocence of youth through the maze of life via the least awkward route. A classic tale of post-war British attitudes from the charming viewpoint of one boy's experience.

Mr. Burrill **JOHN NETTLETON**
Mrs. Burrill **PAT HEYWOOD**
Richard Burrill **EDWARD RAWLE-HICKS**
Mr. Horrobin **ALLAN CUTHBERTSON**
Mrs. Horrobin **ROSEMARY MACVIE**
Julia **OONA KIRSCH**
Anna **PIPPA HINCHLEY**
Miss Wilbraham **JOAN SANDERSON**
Headmaster **GRAHAM CROWDEN**
Dancing Teacher **JUNE ELLIS**
Betty **JANINE DUVITSKI**
Mr. Macklin **TIMOTHY BATESON**
Edwin Macklin **JOHN WAGLAND**
Keith Macklin **STUART MANSFIELD**
Mr. Hargreaves **CHARLES McKEOWN**
Mrs. Hargreaves **SHEILA FEARN**
Mrs. Argonaut **PHYLLIDA HEWAT**
Reverend Phelps **ROGER BRIERLEY**
Rebecca Phelps **MICHELLE JORDAN**
Rachel Phelps **JAYNEE JORDAN**
Ice Cream Assistant **WARREN SAIRE**
Motorbikers **TIP TIPPING & WAYNE MICHAELS**
Jazz Band **THE SOLE BAY JAZZ BAND**
With thanks to **The Southwold & Reydon Corps of Drums**
Screenplay by **Michael Palin**
Music **George Fenton**
Production managers **Elinor Carruthers & Ian Hopkins**
Production assistant **Thelma Helsby**
Costume designer **Charlotte Holdich**
Make-up **Jan Nethercot**
Editor **Ken Pearce**
Designer **Sally Hulke**
Photography **Nat Crosby**
Stunt arranger **Nick Gillard**
Producer **Innes Lloyd**
Director **Tristram Powell**
73 mins, Broadcast BBC2, 1 February 1987

ELEMENTARY, MY DEAR WATSON

This Comedy Playhouse special, although not written by John Cleese, was the star's first attempt to break into his own series in the wake of *Monty Python*. Officially still part of the squad, this pilot aired on the exact same day as the last episode of *Python* series three. Sadly, the purposed series was not forthcoming, for Cleese made a perfect, sardonic, superior Sherlock Holmes and his Watson, Willy Rushton, kept in place the style of sixties satire boomers as sophisticated comic actors. Cleese would later have another crack at playing the great detective in *The Strange Case Of The End Of Civilisation As We Know It* – itself an interesting failure.

Sherlock Holmes **JOHN CLEESE**
Dr. Watson **WILLIE RUSHTON**
Screenplay by **N.F. Simpson**
Producer **Barry Took**
Director **Harold Snoad**
BBC1 18 January 1973, 30 mins

ERIK THE VIKING

Based on the concept of Terry Jones's children's book *The Saga of Erik the Viking*, although bearing little resemblance to any of the actual stories, this is a much under-valued, good fun romp through the myths and legends of Norse folklore. Having thought of grabbing Jim Henson's Creature Workshoppers to bring the fantastical characters to life (in the end Jones was roped in as scriptwriter for Henson's *Labyrinth* instead) the writer/director decided the book was the book and the film should be, to use a phrase, something completely different. Thus while retaining the central character and including wonderfully cinematic ideas from the book such as the Dragon of the North Sea attack (King Kong-like figures and life-size head model for Tim Robbins close-up shots) and the Edge of the World, Jones resurrected an old abandoned scene he had written with Michael Palin during one of the aborted *Python* film writing sessions. The idea of a nervous Viking feeling guilty at killing a peasant girl formed the start of the adventure and gave Jones a free hand to tackle the essence of Norse mythology along the way. Although it was probably a fair bet to steer clear of anything remotely

involving high sea-geared adventure following Chapman's *Yellowbeard*, this film, boasting major input from Jones and a stunning supporting performance from Cleese, could have suffered from an audience expecting great chunks of *Python*esque comedy. As it happens, although the humour is off-the-wall, most of the film delights in flights of magical adventure. Like a reworked *Thief of Baghdad*, its humour complements the sheer fun of the adventure rather than driving it along and, indeed, if you tackle this film with an open mind, ready for some blistering fantasy, a sprinkling of madcap comedy and a mouth-watering cast, you are in for a good time. Naturally, it doesn't all come off, but things are a lot better than the reviews from critics of the day would suggest. The basic idea of a nice Viking becoming sick of the continual killing, pillaging and raping, is an effective one and the wide-eyed innocent, thigh-slapping performance from Tim Robbins (after *Howard the Duck* but before mega stardom with *The Player* and *Bob Roberts*) is an energetic, optimistic and likeable one. The historical detail (notably in the pre-title sequence of fire, Viking screams and primitive dwellings) is up to the expected excellence of Terry Jones' other directorial works, although some of the ranting, raving antics of Erik's fellow Viking pals may be a bit laboured at times. But Erik has seen the light, haunted by the intelligent comments from the ill-fated, unraped Samantha Bond at the film's close, effortlessly debunking the Vikings' circular argument of voyage for rape, while revealing the humanity and spark of imagination deep within Erik's bombastic culture.
This opening scene is the perfect example of what the film is all about, combining typical sitcom dialogue from married couples with a historical base, driven home by the poignant death and farewell speech from Samantha Bond. This film is not going for low comedy on the high seas but a humorous twist of old legends made into fun for a modern audience. The early star cameos from a dodgy-eyed, hellfire, ageing Viking,

Mickey Rooney, and a still seductively voiced prophet (Eartha Kitt) are brief but memorable. Notable is Kitt's glorious intonation of the mystic 'great winter', filling Robbins with the desire for a voyage of discovery and to free the gods of the old world. Like John Goldstone's later ocean romp, *Carry On Columbus*, Robbins has a crew of social misfits and his plans are heading for disaster thanks to the blacksmith philosophy that war means good sword business. Thus, a fast mind-changing, much missed sex beast travels with Tim while a wonderfully sneaky, under-played, almost whispered turn from Anthony Sher does the old Uriah Heep act and slimes about. It's the old battle between good and evil, with Robbins and his men facing Gilliam-like adventures with sea dragons (a very impressive bit of film-making à la *Night of the Demon*, which is slightly marred by a pretty ropy creature) and bickering among themselves. Robbins's farewell speech, revealing the pessimistic horrors that await them, is delivered in a gloriously flamboyant, energetic, upbeat style, as Rooney looks on with amazement, while his motley band of brothers includes McInnery, (fresh from the last series of *Blackadder*) over-acting with perfect grace all over the place, McKeown as his father, turning on the Feldman/*Yellowbeard* whining, Freddie Jones as the bluff and bumbling religious nut who desperately tries to convert his heathen pals to Christianity, and John Gordon Sinclair, the everyman of the group, embracing fear like a friend, with a line fine in seasickness and self-pity. The hilarious arrangement and rearrangement of ship seating plans is exquisitely played by the star ensemble, with Robbins getting the final laugh with an amazed 'That doesn't matter!' when it's suggested that all the beard-wearers are on the opposite side to all the moustache wearers. It's the only copper-bottom *Python* moment in the script but fits in exactly with the lavish fantasy feel of the project and if the Viking ramble scenes get a wee bit noisy, well, hey... that's war for you. The stark, Shakespearean might of the storm at sea is beautifully contrasted with the lush environment in which the lads find themselves, instantly improved even further by the encha-nting appearance of Imogen Stubbs. Projecting friendship, lust and hilarity into the proceedings with her bare legs condemned as disgusting by this unmerry band of seafaring folk. Stubbs, in her seduction of Robbins and warm affection for his innocence, casts a spell of charm over the film and unlike many of these comic adventures, creates an endearing and emotive romantic lead opposite the star. Naturally, for *Python* followers, this sequence is also important for Terry Jones' appearance as the King of Hy-Brasil, the Celtic version of Atlantis. Totally overplayed and foppish beyond the call of duty, Jones grabs the magical quality of his script and blossoms with unashamed love, unashamed pleasure and a very ashamed lack of musical ability. Giving a hangdog expression and begging for honesty in their critical approach to the claptrap the music-makers produce (not enjoying the truth when it hits and nervously watching the suppressed laughter of the Viking brigade) this is Jones in up-front mood, on top of the world and over-playing for Britain. It's grand stuff. His Neroesque emperor of excess is a huge slice of fun and, if rather taxing after a while, there's mileage in his invisible search for the scantily clad lover figure of Robbins in his daughter's room and, his last scene defending the premise of survival and refusing to believe that his world is crumbling about him, mock the eternally optimistic, petulant belief in the stability of reality. This is a wondrous world of Norse myths, of magical horns for calling the gods, of mystic places where the dead of battle find a home and of the eternal struggle against evil oppression. The final onslaught into the land of ice is probably the most visually outstanding element of the film, with the boat and crew frozen, the very stars dropping all around them and a faint hint of *I Saw Three Ships* on the Innes score giving this overall display of snow

and lights a Christmas tree appearance. The ultimate entrance into the world of the dead is a haunting experience, with friends, foes and relations staggering round the cold, cheerless room in a state of bloody decomposition. Freddie Jones who, like Terry Jones, was affected by the magic cloak, is the only one not affected by the vision of death and destruction, and it's this ultimate disassociation from the folklore of his people that saves our hapless group of wanderers. However, despite a sterling cast, no-one comes close to the brief but telling performance from John Cleese as the evil Halfdan the Black, historically a rather decent Norwegian chap but here given the teeth-bearing nastiness of Cleese in full outrage mode. Constructed as a Fawlty-like, bloodthirsty madman, his initial, endearingly dark scene is reminiscent of his friendly Robin Hood in Gilliam's *Time Bandits*. Polite, dignified and quietly spoken, Cleese dishes out various horrific punishments to those who have offended him, and is complemented by a stunning symbol of evil, the vulture at his shoulder. Delivered with calm delight, Cleese mildly hushes anxious cries of terror and casually condemns men to stomach-churning deaths with a meek look of apology. His interest is caught by Sher's sneaky crawl into his favours and then it's no more sort-of Mr. Nice Guy. Instead he crops up on the ocean waves with a crew of skull-attired henchmen and a custom-made chomping battleship (Cleese chuckles, 'Open wide!' as the stern cranks apart). Faced with attack by Robbins and the chaps, Cleese sits with bemusement as this apparently invisible nutter bombards his ship and mockingly whips the cloak off and on for shock effect. Still unaffected by all this, he simply looks around and mutters, 'What'. Hilarious stuff. However, his comeuppance comes via a clever cinematic tie-in with the Wicked Witch of the West's demise in *The Wizard of Oz* (just replace house with ship) and it's goody cheers of triumph all round.

This film may have its flaws, but

there's no doubting that it's great to look at, good fun to experience and made with a genius eye for imaginative expression. Don't pass this one by.

Erik the Viking
Prominent Pictures in association with AB Svensk Filmindustri – Orion/UIP
Erik **TIM ROBBINS**
Erik's Grandfather **MICKEY ROONEY**
Freya **EARTHA KITT**
King Arnulf **TERRY JONES**
Aud **IMOGEN STUBBS**
Halfdan the Black **JOHN CLEESE**
Slavemaster **TSUTOMU SEKINE**
Loki **ANTONY SHER**
Keitel Blacksmith **GARY CADY**
Sven's Dad **CHARLES McKEOWN**
Sven the Berserk **TIM McINNERNY**
Ivar the Boneless **JOHN GORDON SINCLAIR**
Thorfinn Skullsplitter **RICHARD RIDINGS**
Helga **SAMANTHA BOND**
Harald the Missionary **FREDDIE JONES**
Snorri the Miserable **DANNY SCHILLER**
Ernest the Viking **JIM BROADBENT**
Jennifer the Viking **JIM CARTER**
Erik's Mum **MATYELOK GIBBS**
Unn-the-Thrown-at **TILLY VOSBURGH**
Leif the Lucky **JAY SIMPSON**
Ingemund the Old **JOHN SCOTT MARTIN**
Thorhild the Sarcastic **SIAN THOMAS**
Grimhild Housewife **SARAH CROWDEN**
Mordfiddle the Cook **BERNARD PADDEN**
Ulf the Unmemorable **BERNARD LATHAM**
Thorfinn's Parents **JULIA McCARTHY & ALLAN SURTEES**
Ivar's Mum **SANDRA VOE**
Thorkatla the Indiscreet **AELA CONNOLLY**
Leif's Pregnant Girlfriend **SALLY JONES**
Ornulf/Chamberlain/Dog Soldier **ANDREW MacLACHLAN**
Bjarni/Halfdan's Guard/Musician **TIM KILLICK**
Thangbrand/Citizen/Dog Soldier **GRAHAM McTAVISH**
Gisli the Chiseller **CYRIL SHAPS**
Eilif the Mongol Horde/Musician **PETER GEEVES**
Prisoners **PADDY JOYCE, COLIN HARPER, HARRY JONES, BARRY McCARTHY & GARY ROOST**
Hy-Brasilian **NEIL INNES**

Odin **SIMON EVANS**
Thor **MATTHEW BAKER**
Horribly Slain Warrior **DAVE DUFFY**
Even More Horribly Slain Warrior
FRANK BEDNASH
Music **Neil Innes**
Editor **George Akers**
Producer **John Goldstone**
Written & directed by **Terry Jones**
Filmed Malta, Norway and England
12 Cert. 107 mins, 1989

AN EVENING WITHOUT SIR BERNARD MILES

The second Amnesty concert included just the two Pythons, John Cleese and Terry Jones, although comic and music contributions also came from Pete Atkin, The Bowles Brothers Band, Connie Booth, Julie Covington, Jonathan Miller, Peter Ustinov, John Williams and the totally fab Peter Cook. Performed on 8 May 1977, the show, *An Evening Without Sir Bernard Miles* (in homage to the founder of The Mermaid who, would you believe it, wasn't in the production), was directed by Terry Jones and formed a hour-long ITV special on 10 September 1977. The best-selling record, *The Mermaid Frolics*, featured Cleese and Connie Booth performing a legendary version of *At Last the 1948 Show*'s Book Shop sketch, Cleese and Jonathan Miller performing Words... And Things and Terry Jones resurrecting memories of his Oxford Mafia days, with the definitive record of Forgive Me from *The Oxford Revue*. Peter Cook's new monologue, *E.L.* Wisty From Beyond the Veil, is a masterclass in comedy and makes this bit of vinyl invaluable.

FAERIE TALE THEATRE

This series of classic fairytales for

contemporary audiences was the brainchild of actress Shelley Duvall who decided to round up the cream of film talent for this much celebrated series. For the very first show, *The Tale of the Frog Prince*, she contacted her friend Eric Idle to write and direct. This decision made the series an instant award winner, gaining Idle an Ace Award for this pilot classic.

A Platypus Production with Mercury Pictures in association with Lion's Gate Films
The Frog/Prince Robin **ROBIN WILLIAMS**
Princess **TERI GARR**
RENE AUBERJONOIS
CANDY CLARK
ROBERTA MAXWELL
MICHAEL RICHARDS
DONOVAN SCOTT
Written, directed & narrated by **Eric Idle**
Executive Producer **Shelley Duvall**
Producer **Jonathan Taplin**
Showtime, 53 mins, 1982

The Pied Piper of Hamelin
Despite the success of the first show, it would be another three years before Idle would actually appear on screen in one of Duvall's *Faerie Tales: The Pied Piper of Hamelin*. Robert Browning explains the phrase 'pay the piper' by relating the tale of the Pied Piper in verse – David Bowie was due to play the part but over an informal dinner Idle's comments resulted in Bowie saying he wasn't doing the acting but simply writing the songs. On his return, Idle's answerphone was buzzing with messages from Shelley Duvall pleading with him to take over and he considered it his Richard the Third, injecting serious, full-bloodied, codpiece-wearing dramatics into the realms of children's fantasy.

Did You Know? This show was filmed in Toronto for original star David Bowie's tax purposes.

A Platypus Production with Glord Television Entertainment in association with Lion's Gate Films
The Pied Piper/Robert Browning **ERIC**

IDLE
TONY VAN BRIDGE, KERAM MALICKI-SANCHEZ, PETER BLAIS, PETER BORETSKI, JAMES EDMOND TOM HARVEY, KENNETH WICKES CHRIS WIGGINS
Written & directed by **Nicholas Meyer**
Producers **Bridget Terry & Frederic S. Fuchs**
Showtime 47 mins, 1985

FAIRY TALES

Written by Terry Jones during the summer of 1978 for his daughter, Sally, the book's 30 short stories included The Corn Dolly, The Silly King, The Wonderful Cake-Horse, The Fly-By-Night, Three Raindrops, The Butterfly Who Sang, Jack One-Step, The Glass Cupboard, The Wooden City, Simple Peter's Mirror, The Sea Tiger, The Witch and the Rainbow Cat, The Snuff Box, The Man Who Owned the Earth, The Wine of Li-Po, The Beast with a Thousand Teeth, Dr. Bonocolus's Devil and The Boat That Went Nowhere. The stories were adapted for radio, television – East of the Moon, adapted by Neil Innes and including his songs was later released on video – and record – a 1982 disc featured the stories read by the likes of Bob Hoskins and Helen Mirren.

By **Terry Jones**
Published by Pavilion Books – hardback 1981 Reprinted by Penguin Books – paperback
Illustrated by **Michael Foreman**

FAMILIES AND HOW TO SURVIVE THEM

Following the break-up of his marriage to Connie Booth, suffering the insecurities of all men of true genius and nursing suspected psychosomatic illness, John Cleese found help from his therapist, Robin Skynner, over three and a half years between 1974 and 1977, and this book is a lighthearted, accessible but incisive look at human problems through a conversational format between the man of science and the comic client. Taped, informal and jargon-free discussion the working title was *Kitchen Shrink*. Chapters include Why Did I Have to Marry You? – love and relationships, I'm God, and Let's Leave It Like That – the arrival of a new baby, The Astonishing Stuffed Rabbit – baby's self-identity, Who's in Charge Here? – a child's development in sexual understanding and guilt and What Are You Two Doing In There? – concerning continued sexual relationship after birth of baby. Written by Robin Skynner & John Cleese, published by Methuen, 1983. A follow-up Methuen publication in 1989, *Life and How To Survive It* by Robin Skynner & John Cleese tackled the differences in family life in terms of dysfunctional behaviour and in wider terms within business, politics and religion.

FANTASTIC STORIES

A companion piece to *Fairy Tales*, this is a collection of longer children stories by Terry Jones.

Written by **Terry Jones**
Published by Pavilion Books, 1992
Illustrated by **Michael Foreman**

FAWLTY TOWERS

The classic beyond-words misadventures at 16 Elwood Avenue, Torquay, became the major post-*Python* achievement of John Cleese and, indeed, the inspiration came on Tuesday, 12 May 1971 when the *Monty* crew stayed in a Torquay hotel (Gleneagles) during a BBC shot. Hotelier Donald Sinclair subjected the team to shoddy treatment, dismissive contempt, refused Graham Chapman a brandy and threw major insults directed at Gilliam's American-style eating habits (cutting all the food up and spearing the desired pieces). All the Pythons left the following day – except Cleese. When the Pythons became five in 1974, the BBC were very keen to give Cleese his own follow-up series and together with his wife, Connie Booth,

he began plotting.
Originally, they toyed with the idea of comedy developing from the differences between male and female attitudes (although Bird and Bron had successfully covered that), but then an old favourite cropped up. In 1973 Cleese had used the Fawlty-like figure in a *Doctor At Large* (No Ill Feeling) with Timothy Bateson spreading guest house doom and gloom. Producer Humphrey Barclay suggested at the time that the idea had series potential and, although at first dismissing such an idea, Cleese quickly resurrected it for his BBC series. The situation is simplicity itself; the regulars can encounter any amount of new characters within the framework with no major explanation and the no-fuss narrative allows more time for wall-to-wall jokes and comic possibilities.
The all-important figure of Basil Fawlty grew from the suppressed anger of the writers, Cleese and Booth, as well as that of Cleese's father, with the character becoming, arguably, the best loved member of British humour's roster of likeable failures – Steptoe, Hancock, Rigsby, Trotter, Meldrew. *Fawlty Towers* saw Cleese and Booth spend six weeks on each intricate script, tuning it to perfection, scoring a rare feat in situation comedy tradition by hitting the floor running, selecting for a limited number of episodes and leaving each one a real classic. By the time series two was screened in 1979 Cleese and Booth were divorced, but the acidic touch of sparring genius was still in evidence and these are some of the crispest, funniest and body-convulsing pieces of comedy you could ever wish to see. As a small but beautifully marked collection, the 12 priceless half hours rank alongside the funniest shows of all time – NO exaggeration!

Series 1
A TOUCH OF CLASS
The one where Basil's upper class pretensions are used against him by a con man. This first episode of *Fawlty Towers* sets up the characterisations for the entire run. Cleese, first seen struggling with a typewritten menu,

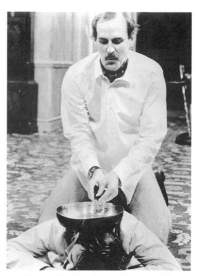

Classic Basil – *Fawlty Towers* with Cleese and much put-upon Sachs

is petulant and aggressive, Scales is in full nagging mode (ordering the picture hanging and directing Cleese, seen shutting his eyes out of blind obedient frustration). Booth is cool, calm and collected in the face of a crisis. Sachs mugs around the place with Barcelonian elegance and Ballard Berkeley, obsessed with strikes and the latest cricket score, bumbles with style. Oh, and look out for an uncredited appearance from the Miss Tibbs and Gatsby, clearly not played by the familiar faces of Flower and Roberts. Similar in style to the second series' Psychiatrist episode, this show features Robin Ellis as a leather-jacketed, smooth-talking, relaxed type of guy whom Cleese hates out of jealousy. His easy, skilled manner in the Spanish language when talking to Sachs and his ultimate, undercover, tough guy role in the proceedings perfectly offsets Cleese's retentive, patriotic Britishness. Fawlty's scream of 'Right!' as the late-rising couple timidly seek his attention is definitive, and the running theme throughout the series – Cleese and his obsession with hobnobbing with the rich and powerful – immediately comes into play here causing the confrontation with Michael Gywnn's shady, bogus Lord. In one of the most celebrated Fawlty scenes, the Lord struggles to fill out the registration card while Cleese (on line to Mr. O'Reilly and skilfully establishing the story-line for the second episode) breaks into his confusion with aggressive and abrasive observations. In a moment of pure comic richness, Cleese finally twigs his noble guest's high standing, pauses and mutters 'Go away!' as he replaces the phone receiver. It is the ultimate example of Cleese's character putting the landed gentry before anybody else and his unflagging dedication to ingratiation. The farcical attempts at impressing the Lord, moving guests from the window table and scraping around for pleasant words with offers of free tit-bits, leads the cunning Gwynn into his plan to relieve Cleese of his priceless coin collection and a couple of hundred quid. The amazed reaction when Gwynn requires a cheque to be cashed is a classic mixture of stunned nervousness and uncontrollable joy, with meek mumblings of 'I'm so happy!' His manic grin and pompous 'El Naturalmente!' has come to be a powerful punch of British comedy excellence. From the first, Cleese is denied the finer things in life to which he is partial – his snatch of Brahms is hardly out of the player before Scales vigorously switches it off; con-

versations are rudely interrupted by pressing aspects of his job and once scorned the venomous bite of retribution is delivered with wide-eyed angst.

Although it is easy simply to see this opening episode as a vehicle for developing characterisation and introducing the setting, it is far more than that. Within this first half hour the character of Basil Fawlty is delivered lock, stock and barrel into the audience's imagination. Perfect from the start, Cleese's performance is a masterpiece of childish emotion, outburst and disgust. The unforgettable scene when Gwynn's supposed valuables are shown to be two common house bricks is a milestone, highlighting Cleese's total disbelief, desperately clinging onto the hope that if he bangs them together, shakes them and takes a good sniff they may be revealed as precious objects. The final realisation of defeat results in muffled moans and introspective collapse. A flawless performance. At the close, his pride may be damaged but the unity of Fawlty Towers employees have pulled together to save the day. With screams of 'Bastard!' and held-back attempts at a good thrashing for the dodgy Lord, his anxiety is released but his desire for upper class clientele is

thwarted. In one of my all-time favourite Fawlty moments he literally attacks a plotted plant that lurks behind him. The man is on a knife edge, constantly in the running for success but always falling foul of outside influence, his wife's mentality or, more often than not, his own misunderstandings.

Did You Know? When this first episode aired, those considered in the know began rumours that the hard-done-by, much put-upon Manuel was based on Terry Jones – a comic interpretation of the Cleese/Jones loggerhead situation during heated *Monty Python* discussions. Cleese totally denies any such idea with bemused and amused disbelief. It is widely believed that the Major is a warm, rose-tinted version of Cleese's dreaded Latin teacher at St. Peter's, Captain Lancaster, whose earnest reading of *Three Men in a Boat* had the young pupil in hysterics. The actual location for the exterior of Fawlty Towers is not in Torquay but Woburn Grange in Buckinghamshire. Cleese accepted his *Fawlty* BAFTA from Eric Morecambe, Ernie Wise and Princess Anne. The immortal names Basil and Sybil actually came from a couple of members of The Communist Party that *Python* film editor Julian Doyle mentioned to Cleese.

Let's all stick together. The *Fawlty Towers* staff in more relaxed pose

A Touch of Class (sign gag: Fawlty Towers with a slightly dislodged 'S')
Basil Fawlty **JOHN CLEESE**
Sybil Fawlty **PRUNELLA SCALES**
Manuel **ANDREW SACHS**
Polly **CONNIE BOOTH**
Lord Melbury **MICHAEL GWYNN**
Danny Brown **ROBIN ELLIS**
Major Gowen **BALLARD BERKELEY**
Sir Richard Morris **MARTIN WYLDECK**
Mr. Mackenzie **DAVID SIMEON**
Mr. Waring **TERENCE CONOLEY**
Mr. Watson **LIONEL WHEELER**
Written by **John Cleese & Connie Booth**
Film cameraman **Len Newsob**
Film editor **Bill Harris**
Costumes **Mary Woods**
Make-up **Cheryl Wright & Jean McMillan**
Production assistant **Mike Crisp**

Lighting **Clive Thomas**
Sound **Mike Jones**
Music **Dennis Wilson**
Designer **Peter Kindred**
Produced & directed by **John Howard Davies**
19 September 1975

THE BUILDERS

The one where cheap hotel alterations embrace the glorious anti-talent of Mr. O'Reilly, a prominent garden gnome and an unforgettable umbrella attack. Although it's an almost impossible choice and, even as I write, *The Anniversary Party* and *Basil the Rat* tap me on the shoulder, this episode has to be the finest of all time. Absolutely flawless in construction with not one second of screen time wasted, the leads are at their most powerful and the supporting cast is sheer perfection – none more so than David Kelly's sublime Mr. O'Reilly with a carefree 'lick a' paint!'/tea and biscuit philosophy. In one of the greatest scenes of Prunella Scales' career, she spits out insult after insult coupled with physical abuse, as the smiling Irish construction worker desperately tries to protect himself. Beloved as the one-armed dishwasher in *Robin's Nest* and, later, resurrecting poor building memories with the Roy Kinnear comedy *Cowboys*, this is David Kelly's finest half hour. The inter-play between defeatist pessimism from Cleese and Kelly's upbeat attitude is outstanding, with perhaps the ultimate example of the three-tier joke coming with Kelly's 'If the good Lord...' comments. Priceless.

With the Fawltys out of the way for five minutes of screen time – the building error is made in their absence – Andrew Sachs is given full rein as the hopeless but keen head of the organisation. Brilliantly latching onto Cleesian mannerisms while answering the phone ('Yes, yes, yes!' in frustration), embracing surrealism (the phone receiver panned across the empty foyer) and pathos (a shell-shocked realisation that it is the dreaded Fawlty talking) all combine for perhaps his greatest series moment. Sachs has a classic sequence

with the garden gnome, spots Fawlty within Booth's sketch and generally has a grand time prat-falling for Spain during his five minutes of despotic power. Booth, napping and out of the way, sets up the Irish trio's misreading of the plans, a superb whack by proxy via Cleese's telephone instructions and the majestic jumping back in amazement from the man himself as he sees his hotel in a state of rearrangement. It's a show packed with the best things in Cleese's comedy bag of tricks, notably his condescending childlike delivery to the two old dears (as well as giving a nod to the original source of material for the show – the hotel Gleneagles pays host to Miss Tibbs and Gatsby during the construction work); a flamboyant defence of his dress sense; patriotic juices flowing throughout; hard-done-by doldrums at every turn (his reaction to Booth's 'What's the point of being alive!' a class example); absentminded surrealism (the plonking of a second cap on top of the one he's already wearing, feeble excuses made up as he goes along (the virus ploy concerning builder Stubbs and the no-go contract); tongue-in-cheek self-abuse (when he maniacally blames himself for the building mistakes); irrelevant, *Python*esque incorporations of unconnected famous outsiders (Denis Compton and not Kissinger in this episode!); biting comments (the masterpiece – 'Don't drive over any mines or anything!'); self-satisfaction (the Sugar Plum Fairy tune setting up the fantasy land of completed building work behind the back of his wife); frustration with inanimate objects (the stranglehold on the garden gnome); outrageous plays for sympathy (the quickly activated leg wound) and toe-curling attempts to avoid conflict (as his wife lets rip into O'Reilly). Ironically – and here's the major joke of the series – when there's cause for complaint, as in this case, Cleese backs away from confrontation with embarrassment and a sheepish attitude. Desperately he tries to make up for his wife's understandable anger with feeble excuses and whispered apologies

contrasted with natural, everyday little problems which bring out the ranting monster in him. This show sees Cleese in totally definitive style – a landmark in television comedy and, yes, I'm off the fence, the best ever *Fawlty Towers*.

Did You Know? Cleese considers his performance a poor one since the audience's reaction was very muted – he later found out a great chunk of them were tourists from Iceland! In fact, when first screened, *Fawlty Towers* wasn't a major hit – the first series was repeated in January 1976 and the cult began. By the November 1985 repeat this first series received audience figures of 12.5 million, the record for BBC2. Famous fans include ex-president George Bush and distinguished film directors Martin Scorsese and Bernard Tavernier.

The Builders (Fawlty Tower)
Basil Fawlty **JOHN CLEESE**
Sybil Fawlty **PRUNELLA SCALES**
Manuel **ANDREW SACHS**
Polly **CONNIE BOOTH**
Major Gowen **BALLARD BERKELEY**
O'Reilly **DAVID KELLY**
Miss Tibbs **GILLY FLOWER**
Miss Gatsby **RENEE ROBERTS**
Stubbs **JAMES APPLEBY**
Delivery man **GEORGE LEE**
Lurphy **MICHAEL CRONIN**
Jones **MICHAEL HALSEY**
Kerr **BARNEY DORMAN**
Written by **John Cleese & Connie Booth**
Music **Dennis Wilson**
Film cameraman **Stanley Speel**
Film editor **Bob Rymer**
Costumes **Mary Woods**
Make-up **Jean Speak**
Production assistant **Tony Guyan**
Lighting **Geoff Shaw**
Sound **John Howell**
Designer **Peter Kindred**
Produced & directed by **John Howard Davies**
26 September 1975

THE WEDDING PARTY

The one where Basil's moral fabric is stretched to breaking point with frantic coupling all over the place and a flirty French piece is after his body. It's very apt that this wonderfully written but under-rated episode has a seductive continental figure caught up in the middle of the British anal-retention comedy, for in style and structure this is *Fawlty Towers* in French farce mode. The heat of the English Riviera obviously breaks down Connie Booth's barriers, as she wanders round the place in skimpy gear and snogs her fella while setting up an attack on Cleese with a full-bodied rant, misquoting her guy's name as Turnip, dispelling the rumour about topless afternoon teas while, much to Fawlty's annoyance and voiced through his torrent of condemnation, he has his sexual interest raised at the same time as he is condemning her attitude. Immediately after balling out about Booth's appearance Cleese answers the ringing phone with 'Fawlty Titties'. It seems everybody in the hotel is at it. Or at least, in the ultra-sensitive, morality-obsessed eyes of Cleese they are. From his wife's opening chatter with a male guest, blessed with Scales' piercing laughter (the most amusing grotesque expression of fun since Betty Marsden in *Carry On Camping* and leading to some delicious Cleese put-downs including his *How To Murder Your Wife* cinematic reference), love is clearly in the air. Cleese, grinning, trying to impress (*formidable!*) and bowing to his French admirer's every whim, sets up a misunderstanding of hidden passions with the sex-hungry young couple. As with the characters of Robin Ellis and Nicky Henson, this life-loving, passionate pair are the nemesis of Cleese's patriotic stiffness. Fawlty is disgruntled by April Walker's suppressed laughter during 'Yes thank you!', angered by whispered comments about his suit and totally outraged when it transpires the couple are not married. Barking on about the 'law of England', happily allocating two single rooms miles apart and desperately trying to keep his wife's easy-going acceptance of the situation out of it, this is Cleese in full chest-puffing action, striding through the mire of the human condition and morally correcting everything around him.

Very much a forerunner to the series two episode, *The Psychiatrist*, his outmoded and obsessive self-righteous attitude is highlighted as misinformed and unreasonable but, through Cleese's powerful comic performance, the audience can still laugh at his misfortune and celebrate the man as a likeable character of dissent. Once that seed of corruption is planted nothing will shift it and even the most innocent of actions fuels his disgust. The best example here is the chemist discussion. The audience are informed via a brief scene with the couple and Booth that a chemist is required for batteries to operate an electric razor. Cleese, obviously with the sex obsession still in his mind, infers the chemist request relates to condoms, shoots his mouth off about disgusting behaviour, shockingly reacts to the half-asked enquiry about borrowing a couple and, ultimately, realising his mistake, continues with his disgusting rant, ducks out of eye-shot and buries his head in his hands. A prime moment of Cleese building the comedy up to fever pitch. The general fruity behaviour of stepdaughter hugging stepfather, Booth hugging friend's stepfather, rushing out of hotel room doing up her uniform and satisfied male groans, all embrace the same comic trick of leaving Cleese in the dark and the audience all-knowing, while this manic farce is counterbalanced by pathos via Sachs's birthday speech (cruelly destroyed by Cleese), his pleasure at the umbrella gift and drunken love towards his employer. Again with the audience/character knowledge working two ways, the angst-ridden battle between Cleese and Sachs takes on homosexual overtones and the continual flirting of the French temptress takes Cleese's moral fibre to breaking point. She has a shared passion for classical music (she recognised Chopin and doesn't repeat Scales' trick of moaning about his playing of it), flattery (making Lord Byron look like a tobacconist indeed!), understanding speeches (hoping that Mrs. Fawlty is appreciative) and sly, knowing ways of seduction (she begs for her

window to be fixed – forgotten from earlier in the episode – believes Cleese leaves his tape player in her room on purpose – and is not averse to discussing her naked sleeping rituals with the grinning Cleese). She is the ultimate test of Basil's character, who comes through with flying colours with tall stories about his wife's return and manic, unnecessary play-acting. There's even a rare bedroom vignette of the marital hell he is fighting to preserve – Cleese reading *Jaws,* Scales smoking, stuffing in chocs and periodically laughing at her periodical. For all this, the pay-off to the scenario is the show's greatest moment, with the reality of relationships sinking in, a massive pause, one final concern about Booth's involvement and an earth-shattering, play the game, did that make Britain great, flamboyantly caricatured delivery of his wife's solution – 'I'm so sorry I made a mistake!' It's a masterpiece, folks!

Did You Know? When Prunella Scales got married in real life, to that grand actor Timothy West, at Chelsea Register Office in 1963, the hat she wore was borrowed from the wife of Andrew Sachs. Small world.

The Wedding Party (Fawty Tower)
Basil Fawlty **JOHN CLEESE**
Sybil Fawlty **PRUNELLA SCALES**
Manuel **ANDREW SACHS**
Polly **CONNIE BOOTH**
Major Gowen **BALLARD BERKELEY**
Mrs. Peignoir **YVONNE GILAN**
Mr. Lloyd **CONRAD PHILLIPS**
Mrs. Lloyd **DIANA KING**
Alan **TREVOR ADAMS**
Jean **APRIL WALKER**
Miss Tibbs **GILLY FLOWER**
Miss Gatsby **RENEE ROBERTS**
Bar guest **JAY NEILL**
Written by **John Cleese & Connie Booth**
Music **Dennis Wilson**
Costumes **Mary Woods**
Make-up **Jean Speak**
Production assistant **Tony Guyan**
Lighting **Geoff Shaw**
Sound **John Howell**
Designer **Peter Kindred**
Produced & directed by **John Howard Davies**
3 October 1975

THE HOTEL INSPECTOR

The one where an irritating spoon salesman is mistaken for a high profile hotel guide writer. There are certainly less complicated threads to this half hour, although that doesn't stop it being one of the funniest of all *Fawlty Towers* episodes. Latching onto the simple comic notion of mistaken identity and boasting a sublime performance from Bernard Cribbins, Cleese can take his alter ego through the gamut of emotions from disgruntled condescension to flagrant boot-licking. Straight from the outset Cribbins is the bane of Cleese's life, interrupting his unsuccessful attempts to light a cigarette à la Maigret and storming in with mesmerising speeches of flowery language. Far from impressing the snobbish Cleese, who would himself, happily use elaborate language to impress, a taste of the same medicine merely frustrates him, questioning his sanity, moaning with contempt and viciously sending him up with over-played mirroring of his delivery. Cribbins, giving a peerless performance, is, in the eyes of Cleese, the real guest from hell, for although his requests are reasonable, however much Cleese tries to avoid doing his hotelier duties Cribbins keeps on demanding them. Thus, when the typical Brit in the place finds his request for a diagram of the location or a taxi cab number denied, that would be it. Cribbins' Northern edge and happy determination soon allows gritty anger to break through for major action. The all-time classic scene in this episode has to be the pens/Ben's box misunderstanding, Cleese and his abbreviated Post Office, the wonderful confusion of Cribbins and the final wham bam gag as bemused James Cossins is asked his opinion about the map and Cleese blurts 'P off!' The reaction is priceless. Cleese's spellbound amazement at the fact that someone might want to contact the annoying Mr. Hutchinson, a quick resurrection of the *Python*esque Henry Kissinger mention and the truly immortal Scales put-down concerning the perming of her ears all add to the Fawlty bombastic myth. However, not

long after Cribbins whizzes through his elongated request for a certain Red Indian television documentary does Cleese click that this nutter could be a certain hotel inspector. Immediately the emphasis changes from total disregard to total dedication, laughing off his every whim for ice buckets and fresh vegetables. It's just that everybody else suffers instead. The unforgettable corked wine routine with Cossins is a masterpiece, enhanced by Sachs at his most nervous, Cleese at his most pompously incorrect (his superior wine knowledge is sadly lacking) and some magical interruptions from a very dissatisfied Cribbins. Confusion concerning the table and a re-ordered meal leads to massive loads of the wrong food being served to this supposed V.I.P. as Cribbins gets more and more frustrated, culminating with his elephant's ear on a bun outburst, some straight talking and straight fighting. The revelation of Cribbins and his profession, initially morally shocked that his wife listened to a guest's phone call, causes Cleese the warrior to explode. Now convinced that Cossins is his main man, it's all-out attack from Cribbins, bowing and scraping to Cossins, and quick, custard pie-styled revenge from Cleese and Sachs. But let's not forget the classic Cleese begging to Cossins at the close, Cleese's raspberry fuelled 'Spoons', the torn-up, never to be seen again omelette which the Major happily begins to eat, and the final, angst-ridden scream that signifiers Cleese and his major attempt to get a good hotel write-up could be in serious jeopardy. A classic.

The Hotel Inspectors (Fawty Toers)
Basil Fawlty **JOHN CLEESE**
Sybil Fawlty **PRUNELLA SCALES**
Manuel **ANDREW SACHS**
Polly **CONNIE BOOTH**
Mr. Hutchinson **BERNARD CRIBBINS**
Mr. Walt **JAMES COSSINS**
Major Gowen **BALLARD BERKELEY**
Miss Tibbs **GILLY FLOWER**
Miss Gatsby **RENEE ROBERTS**
John **GEOFFREY MORRIS**
Brian **PETER BRETT**
Written by **John Cleese & Connie**

Booth
Music **Dennis Wilson**
Costumes **Mary Woods**
Make-up **Jean Speak**
Production assistant **Tony Guyan**
Lighting **Geoff Shaw**
Sound **John Howell**
Designer **Peter Kindred**
Produced & directed by **John Howard Davies**
10 October 1975

THE GOURMET NIGHT

The one where Basil bans riffraff, gets saddled with a drunken chef and dishes out some serious grievous bodily harm to his clapped-out car. The ultimate display of Cleese in prime pretension mode, desperately trying to move away from the standard Brit git clientele and embrace the cream of polite Torquay society. Naturally, these upper class types are highlighted as condescending and inconsiderate towards Fawlty's type, but that doesn't stop the irritating compliments and embarrassed attempts at avoiding conflict from the wild, hair akimbo hotelier. The hilarious comic strands are introduced gradually and allowed to simmer in the imagination before being used for their major impact. Notably, the episode begins with the car problems, with Fawlty desperately going for the easy-fix solution while Scales nags away about garbage treatment. The idea of the unreliable vehicle is set up, alongside the chef besotted with Manuel, buying a Booth sketch, showering continental love all over the place and giving his old employee the off-the-wagon look of professionalism. In a typical *Fawlty Towers* development, the best laid plans of class and culture begin to go horribly wrong – seen in the classic spoilt child scenario, who moans about the high quality grub and pines for convenience out of a bottle. Fawlty beautifully controls his temper regarding these 'proles', this outspoken child, the loving mother and henpecked husband (barked at by his wife in strict contrast to the nurturing treatment she gives her son) which immediately vindicates him and his dream of self-improvement.

However, when the news filters through concerning the cancellation of four of his gourmet guests the old venom squirts out. His bombastic treatment of his beloved permanent elderly duo is contrasted with a self-congratulatory grin and silky introduction to the Colonel – a sublime performance from Allan Cuthbertson – and his diminutive wife. The resulting misunderstanding and Cleese's awkward attempts to avoid mentioning 'smallness' cause a vignette of priceless material, increased with Cleese's faux pas about the dead daughter. With the arrival of the Twitchens Cleese almost gets things back together again with calm, normal small talk, warm thanks for supporting the gourmet venture and effortless charm.

However, problems are on the way with Booth's gloriously farcical drunken chef explanation full of cooking terminology, Cleese goes into wild duck impersonations, a couple of *Python*esque rants about Henry Kissinger and a hilariously muffed intro between his guests, with Cuthbertson's nervous head twitches proving too much for Fawlty. The four guests are united in a common opinion of their host's weirdness and, basically, the game is lost from that point on. Kurt, out for the count, hardly helps matters with the uncooked mullet scenario; a manic tussle with the chef results in Cleese sticking his head into the mousse, establishing the 'hair in my mousse' juxtaposition (with Cuthbertson's wonderful bellowed reaction) and the final solution boils down to their old pal André and his high street restaurant. A change in menu dictates that if you don't like duck 'you're rather stuck!' and a lightning dash to the eatery produces a rather small though succulent duck dish plus sauces. The car problem gag is skilfully avoided here in favour of its inclusion during the second mad dash (the first duck having been trodden on), thus building up the laughter potential to maximum overdrive as Cleese tears into his vehicle with thrashing twig and thrashing tongue. Meanwhile, trying to hold the fort, Booth struggles through *I'm Just A*

Girl Who Can't Say No, Sachs plays Spanish guitar and Scales regales the bored guests with risqué tales of Uncle Ted, as Cleese, one abandoned car and a bit of speedy footwork later, finally presents a dessert dish to the outraged gathering.

With an explorative dive into the trifle Cleese utters the immortal final words, 'Duck's off. Sorry!' A classic of British comedy.

Did You Know? Cleese considers the finale of *The Gourmet Night* the single best scene he has ever written. Video Arts subsequently hired out this episode to the London Hilton and British Holiday Inns.

The Gourmet Night (Warty Towels)
Basil Fawlty **JOHN CLEESE**
Sybil Fawlty **PRUNELLA SCALES**
Manuel **ANDREW SACHS**
Polly **CONNIE BOOTH**
Andre **ANDRE MARANNE**
Kurt **STEVE PLYTAS**
Colonel Hall **ALLAN CUTHBERTSON**
Mrs. Hall **ANN WAY**
Mr. Twitchen **RICHARD CALDICOT**
Mrs. Twitchen **BETTY HUNTLEY-WRIGHT**
Major Gowen **BALLARD BERKELEY**
Miss Tibbs **GILLY FLOWER**
Miss Gatsby **RENEE ROBERTS**
Mr. Heath **JEFFREY SEGAL**
Mrs. Heath **ELIZABETH BENSON**
Master Benson **TONY PAGE**
Written by **John Cleese & Connie Booth**
Music **Dennis Wilson**
Film cameraman **Stanley Speel**
Film editor **Bob Rymer**
Costumes **Mary Woods**
Make-up **Jean Speak**
Production assistant **Tony Guyan**
Lighting **Ron Koplick**
Sound **John Howell**
Designer **Peter Kindred**
Produced & directed by **John Howard Davies**
17 October 1975

THE GERMANS

The one where Sybil is in hospital with an ingrowing toenail; Basil desperately tries to hang up his moose's head; the fire drill back at the hotel goes a bit wrong; and, oh, there are some Germans staying... Universally accepted as the crowning

glory of *Fawlty Towers* (although in my opinion several other shows are far funnier), this, as with the best football matches, is a definite show of two halves. In fact, the immortal clash with the German guests is a very minor element to the fun, although it's stored up for the comic showdown and the threat of their appearance is foreseen from the start. Berkeley's old military warhorse is hardly keen on the idea, with deliciously surreal tangents concerning women, India, Germans and, as Connie Booth wonders, German women. Berkeley's restrained 'Bad eggs!' has the polite distaste of an old soldier, whereas Cleese, with his vicious 'Bastards!' is the ridiculed, furiously patriotic, post-war face of xenophobic bigotry believing that if Germans are unable to speak English it's their own fault.

In terms of character development this pride in his country is perfectly in keeping with the Fawlty we know and love; however, although his uneasiness about the prospect of German visitors is keen, in an attempt to slightly lessen the 'not mentioning the war' gags and unsubtle references to Nazi big wigs, the sub-plot includes a bash on the Cleese bonce and mild concussion. Thus, with bandaged head, mistaken identification of Booth and off-kilter antics, Cleese can exorcise the demons of prejudice under the cover of a temporary loss of moral code. Besides all that, the basic sight of Cleese resurrecting *Python*esque silly walks, doing the Hitler impression after his bemused 'I can't do Jimmy Cagney' and replacing menu jargon with wartime symbols is very funny. Despite allowing the Germans to be quite normal characters, hurt by memories of the war and allowing them the final tongue-in-cheek dig at the close, the sheer energetic delivery of Cleese firing on all cylinders blows away any competition. Indeed, the invasion of Poland observation remains not only the most quoted line from *Fawlty Towers*, but one of the great moments in the history of British television. No mean feat. However, as I've said, there is far more to this show than the classic

Germanic rant. Cleese delights in the painful prospects for his wife's post-op recuperation (following a manic jump back in surprise at the doctor) and skilfully contrasts the medical situation with his less restricted home truths following his own admittance – the quiet dog put-down to Brenda Cowling becomes the more overtly personal observation about her ugliness. The Moose antics are excellent, embracing Sachs and his English learnt from a book (listen out for a throwaway reference to his hamster, later resurrected for the last show). See Berkeley's amazed reaction to this alleged wonder of modern technology and Cleese, at his petulant best, as Scales' phone call stops him doing the precise thing which she has phoned to remind him to do. The final collapse of this beauteous beast is the last straw and brilliantly leads into the many disasters of the fire drill. Pompous, supercilious and outraged, Cleese unwittingly activates the burglar alarm and sets his guests into fire drill mode. The ensuing 'more than his job's worth' detailed explanation and spoilt drill is wonderfully detailed comedy – Cleese's whimpered, stuttered cries of 'Fire!' are powerful indeed, while the anger forced towards the Lord above and the skilful prop by-play, with the typewriter and telephone employed as helpful glass breakers, is perfectly timed. In truth, the final, most celebrated section becomes a bit obvious and ranting at times, although as a piece of break-neck farce it's probably Cleese at his best. Somehow, the quick gear change is rather too quick, although one can forgive anything which shows Cleese maniacally opening one bleary eye to see if the coast is clear. The continual slips into talk about piano wire and consideration that his German speaking guests are a wee bit odd all add fuel to the Fawlty fire, although even in this manic state the old attempts to cover his opinions are in play – after one too many mentions of the war he blurts out, 'Korean!' in a feeble cover-up effort. Thus, Fawlty the out-patient and Fawlty the man aren't that much different, while his

cry of 'Who won the bloody war anyway!' certainly rallies British audiences together, in a two-edged celebration of victory and warm mocking of the British mentality to remember victories for years. To top it all, Cleese sends out a shockwave of final abuse that the Germans have no sense of humour and, after only 30 years since the close of World War II, Cleese's understanding and inspired treatment of a tricky subject should be celebrated as a career milestone. As with 1918, 1945 and 1966, the Brits come out on top again!

Did You Know? Cleese hates this episode because of its flaws such as the anticipated moose falling and Sachs aiming his head for the smashing tray, convinced that fans are being kind when they praise this classic! During the long gap between series one in 1975 and series two in 1979, there were suggestions for *Fawlty Towers* Christmas specials and even a movie version. The latter was very seriously considered, based on a Spanish holiday which would include Cleese and Scales encountering a hotel manager even ruder than Cleese. Ultimately John Cleese preferred a more close-knit, one-set, burst of catastrophic comedy with the Fawltys captured on a hijacked plane, delayed at Heathrow, recaptured by the all-conquering Cleese through sheer frustration who twists heroics by hijacking the plane himself when the pilot cancels the flight. A sort of *Clockwise* with laughs! In the end Cleese and Booth decided against the idea, feeling it would take the situation of *Fawlty Towers* beyond recognition and, above all, beyond its breaking point. The outcome was six belated new television episodes and a huge, permanent full stop to the series. Years later in an interview Cleese was happily philosophical about the decision – 'We'd got six hours of Basil which was not bad. Shakespeare only got three and a half from Hamlet, and look how he's lasted.' Others were desperate to recapture the old Fawlty magic – when Cleese was approached for a part in Tony Palmer's *Wagner* with Richard

Burton he was distressed at the cameo role, to all intents and purposes nothing more than a quick Basil-like rant. When the producers promised Prunella Scales would play his wife Cleese turned the part down flat. In 1976 Cleese seriously considered opening a restaurant called Basil's in partnership with Andrew Leeman. Although a Knightsbridge location was found, the idea was abandoned.

The Germans
Basil Fawlty **JOHN CLEESE**
Sybil Fawlty **PRUNELLA SCALES**
Manuel **ANDREW SACHS**
Polly **CONNIE BOOTH**
Major Gowen **BALLARD BERKELEY**
Mrs. Wilson **CLAIRE DAVENPORT**
Miss Tibbs **GILLY FLOWER**
Miss Gatsby **RENEE ROBERTS**
Sister **BRENDA COWLING**
Doctor **LOUIS MAHONEY**
Mr. Sharp **JOHN LAWRENCE**
Mrs. Sharp **IRIS FRY**
German guests **WILLY BOWMAN, NICK KANE, LISA BERGMAYR & DAN GILLAN**
Written by **John Cleese & Connie Booth**
Music **Dennis Wilson**
Film cameraman **Stanley Speel**
Film editor **Bob Rymer**
Costumes **Mary Woods**
Make-up **Jean Speak**
Production assistant **Tony Guyan**
Visual effects **Peter Pegrum & Ken Bomphray**
Lighting **Ron Koplick**
Sound **John Howell**
Designer **Peter Kindred**
Produced & directed by **John Howard Davies**
24 October 1975

SERIES 2
COMMUNICATION PROBLEMS
The one with the deaf old fusspot and Basil's Hanging Gardens of Babylon outburst. The most obvious of comic devices, the irritating guest with hearing problems, is taken to heights of comic genius with this milestone *Fawlty Towers* episode. Although the four principals are on their usual excellent form, it is the new angst force of Joan Sanderson's peerlessly played Mrs. Richards, that

makes this show such a classic. Typically smug, frumpy, awkward and hearing things only to her advantage, she rips through the hotel like a demented stray cat, complaining about everything, misunderstanding situations and aggressively blaming it all on someone else. The stunned confusion over lavatory paper and writing paper is brilliantly played, with Connie Booth's wide-eyed, eager-to-please delivery contrasting with the self-righteous outrage of the old lady. However, naturally, it's opposite the towering figure of angst himself, Cleese's Fawlty, that the comic gems really fly. I would wager that a poll determining the favourite Fawlty moment would be a toss-up between the German dining party and the stunned reaction to Sanderson's steely-eyed dismissal of her bedroom window view. Her petulant comment about Torquay not being good enough is all that Cleese needs for an unforgettable, spiralling assault of absurdity, frustratingly trying to prove his point and hearing nothing but complaint upon complaint. The surreal, totally British notion of her having a hearing aid, switched off to save the battery, almost goes by uncommented on by Fawlty, merely used as a vehicle for biting mime-play and the source of an unusually cutting, remark from Booth. Clearly, even Cleese's manic creation can't be blamed for reacting against this one. The sub-text involves Cleese gambling on horses, which results in wads of unaccounted-for money floating around the hotel – Cleese's winners, Sanderson's alleged stolen cash, the money recovered from the antique shop and the money in the form of an antique vase. Confusion upon confusion, counterbalanced by madcap subterfuge and Ballard Berkeley's pricelessly forgetful Major, add up to major quality comedy. In a move away from just total irritation with everybody, Cleese shows a less anally-retentive side to the character, being civil to a departing, satisfied guest (it is he who suggests the winning horse), doing a brilliantly impromptu rendition of *Camptown Races* on hearing of his lucky win,

skilful bouncing of ice into his drink, a *Python*esque delight in his idea of sticking a bat up Sanderson's nightdress and even scrubbing 32 pence off a mildly uncertain guest queuing for his bill. The show also contains two outstanding set pieces, with the definitive battle between Fawlty and Manuel concerning the confused horse names (Dragon-Fly/Nit-Wit) and the necessity to keep the news of the winning streak away from Sybil. Cleese, in quiet, petulant mood, mutters the immortal line – 'I could spend the rest of my life having this conversation!', while the sublime manic miming of the horse's name is hilarious beyond the call of duty. Booth's suggestion of small size, as Cleese fumbles around his trouser fly area is a masterpiece while the breathing dragon motif (resurrected from an earlier action dedicated to his wife) allows Booth a moment of realisation, composure and remembrance. Class stuff. When his financial gain crumbles around him, Cleese's character crumbles too, into a pathetic, childish babble, effortlessly snapped into mock outrage as Sanderson complains of a missing tenner. But alone and with a kiss to God, his problems are vanquished and Cleese has a final moment of delight when his triumph has come and he's in profit at last. Sadly his joy is very short-lived, but Cleese is a wonderful picture of total ecstasy as he laughs with glee and greedily cuddles his new-found wealth. The shocked silence between the four when the awful horse-backing truth emerges and life gets as low as it possibly can, is a high point in television farce.

Communication Problems (Fawlty Tower)
Basil Fawlty **JOHN CLEESE**
Sybil Fawlty **PRUNELLA SCALES**
Manuel **ANDREW SACHS**
Polly **CONNIE BOOTH**
Mrs. Richards **JOAN SANDERSON**
Major Gowen **BALLARD BERKELEY**
Terry **BRIAN HALL**
Miss Tibbs **GILLY FLOWER**
Miss Gatsby **RENEE ROBERTS**
Mr. Thurston **ROBERT LANKESHEER**
Mr. Firkins **JOHNNY SHANNON**
Mr. Mackintosh **BILL BRADLEY**

Mr. Kerr **GEORGE LEE**
Mr. Yardley **MERVYN PASCOE**
Written by **John Cleese & Connie Booth**
Music **Dennis Wilson**
Costume **Caroline Maxwell**
Make-up **Suzan Broad**
Lighting **Ron Bristow**
Sound **Mike Jones**
Videotape editor **Howard Dell**
Production assistant **John Kilby**
Design **Nigel Curzon**
Producer **Douglas Argent**
Director **Bob Spiers**
19 February 1979

THE PSYCHIATRIST
The one where a couple of 'three doctors' and a bronzed love god represent both ends of the human evolutionary scale, while a blonde Australian and some mental confusion cause Basil a problem or two. One of the most interesting episodes exploring Basil's suppressed attitude to sex (note his clipped, whispered pronunciation of the word), manic outrage at the thought of happy couples enjoying some happy coupling in his hotel and the struggle between pretence/terror when faced with a professional opinion that may delve too deeply into his inner turmoil. And apart from all that, it's pretty damn funny too! Nicky Henson is a joy as the supercool, open-neck shirted dude covered in gold medallions and cruising round the place radiating confident sexuality.

Cleese, stilted, stifled and respectful, finds everything he hates embodied in the character, although his shallow considerations of his gold trinkets is vindicated by Henson's couldn't care less, unromantic comment that one of them comes from 'Colchester, I think'. The mental battle between repressed feelings and outer cool creates moments of high tension comedy, although Cleese can only enjoy them privately, allowing himself a little giggle when he has put the vocal boot in particularly well. This expression of inner feelings in private is later developed in the marital farce of sex obsessions and hidden fantasies, triggered by the arrival of Luan Peters' well-endowed Aussie and some hilarious groping misunderstandings. Nicky Henson is the ultimate enemy: lucky in love, lucky in deception and projecting a likeable, 'one of the lads' attitude to everyone. His throwaway gag about the Torquay guide and other short books disturbs Cleese's Thatcherite beliefs and patriotic pride; his dismissal of the hotel food provokes more unsubtle references to apes and a glorious French restaurant put-down (note the extreme detail in the script when the French translation for the home of fine cuisine, restaurant The Apple of Love, is situated in Orchard Street). On the other side of the coin is Cleese's embarrassment at Scales' feeble sap joke and a chest-puffing speech expressing his medical leanings – wonderfully debunked and devalued by Scales' perfect delivery of... 'run a hotel!' Even before the Abbotts arrive, Scales latches onto the undercurrent of enjoyment, equating fun with sexiness, while enjoying perhaps her finest *Fawlty* moment with the immortal listing of her mother's manifold mortal fears, much to the chagrin of Henson. Naturally, once the medical slant becomes apparent, Cleese is a bundle of pent-up emotion, sexual nervousness and wide-eyed fear, hilariously misreading the idle, small talk on holiday plans as being about sex and generally behaving even more oddly than usual out of sheer panic. It's a sterling farce performance, complemented by Nicky Henson's casual order of champagne, wall-tapping cover-ups, some antics on a ladder, pathos-sprinkled marital home truths from a gobsmacked Scales and a crowning moment of visual comedy with Cleese casually leaning on the door and falling into Henson's room. However much Fawlty tries to be relaxed and self-controlled, he will never emulate the easy manner of Nicky Henson. Always remaining uncool – the basic essence of why Basil Fawlty remains a powerful comic creation. Even his outstanding gear change from sarcastic cockiness to warm charm when he welcomes Henson's white-haired old mother doesn't fool any of the assembled mass. His puritanical

attitude and multi-faceted insecurities are always bubbling beneath the surface or rampantly illustrated, notably at the close of this episode as he hops around the landing with his head buried deep in his arms. It's these weaknesses that make the audience love him.

The Psychiatrist (Watery Fowls)
Basil Fawlty **JOHN CLEESE**
Sybil Fawlty **PRUNELLA SCALES**
Manuel **ANDREW SACHS**
Polly **CONNIE BOOTH**
Mr. Johnson **NICKY HENSON**
Dr. Abbott **BASIL HENSON**
Mrs. Abbott **ELSPETH GRAY**
Major Gowen **BALLARD BERKELEY**
Terry **BRIAN HALL**
Raylene Miles **LUAN PETERS**
Mrs. Johnson **AIMEE DELAMAIN**
Miss Tibbs **GILLY FLOWER**
Miss Gatsby **RENEE ROBERTS**
Henson's girlfriend **IMOGEN BICKFORD-SMITH**
Written by **John Cleese & Connie Booth**
Music **Dennis Wilson**
Costume **Caroline Maxwell**
Make-up **Suzan Broad**
Film cameraman **Alec Curtis**
Film sound **Bill Chesneau**
Film editor **Susan Imrie**
Studio lighting **Ron Bristow**
Studio sound **Mike Jones**
Videotape editor **Neil Pittaway**
Production assistant **John Kilby**
Design **Nigel Curzon**
Producer **Douglas Argent**
Director **Bob Spiers**
36 minutes...
26 February 1979.

THE KIPPER AND THE CORPSE
The one where Basil deals with an untalkative, rather dead chap in the hotel. A classic scenario which sees Cleese at his most elegantly manic, brilliantly keeping the audience's sympathies while lugging a dead guest around and desperately trying to fool his unsuspecting colleagues. Other sideline entertainment includes Geoffrey Palmer's doctor who yearns for sausage and Richard Davies (for years that Welsh bloke in *Please Sir!*) giving an excellent supporting performance of disbelief, desperately trying to get into his locked hotel

room, unaware that Cleese, Sachs, a dead body and a deadbeat body are already in occupation. Davies's emotions move from reasonably willing to pass the day with Booth to barely suppressed anger.
However, the most important supporting turn, be it dead or alive, is from Derek Royle, years before over-acting himself to death in *'Allo, 'Allo*. The basic strands of confusion are established before the pale Royle's arrival (some themes like the little man with the new, red-haired bimbo are not developed), but Cleese, in notable angst-ridden mood, makes sure he goes to bed fully mocked, rocked and unsettled. The ignored 'Goodnight' unleashes an inspired rant about hardly being the Gettysburg Address while the sickly guest really tries his luck with a request for breakfast in bed, being brought down to size by both Cleese's glorious rudeness and Scales with a torrent of kindness. Naturally, the comic height comes with the following morning's discovery of the guest's demise. Cleese, as petulant, inattentive and self-opinionated as ever, wanders into the room, plonks down the breakfast tray and mouths off about socialism, strikes, concerts and cathedrals, disgusted at not 'getting a bloody word' out of the man. It's Booth's late milk delivery that reveals the facts, with Cleese in overload mania mode, desperately trying to get rid of the (supposedly) incriminating kippers. There's a glorious scene of battling mentalities as Palmer's doctor is stunned at Cleese's misreading of the guest's silence, setting up a legendary Cleese onslaught about Burma railways and suggesting prior warning from guests not likely to make it through the night. The relationship between the doctor and the hotelier is a telling one, beginning with ingratiating kindness (prepared to get the man some ham sandwiches because of Cleese's social standing pretentions), desperately shared humour (Cleese tackles television terminology for the ill-fated sausages saying normal service will be resumed) and pompous outrage (amazement at Cleese keeping the body in the

kitchen and apparent total stupidity in clocking dead humans). The resulting farce embraces attempts to hide the truth from his other residents (Cleese brilliantly tells the truth to Miss Gatsby, thus making the whole idea of a death in the hotel ridiculous and tapping into the shared notion that sudden fatalities among his clientele would, indeed, make Cleese happy), antics in a cupboard and mistaken identity between Leeman's friends and the undertakers. Cleese's stunned reaction on seeing their work pal in the basket is a masterpiece of expressive comedy – 'Not much!' – while the various threads of disaster, including a brief disturbed interlude with a new chap and his blow-up doll, come to a head. Sachs and Booth turn in excellent work (both are attacked by the little dog and both throw themselves into farcical manoeuverings of the dead body round the hotel), although Sachs has a classic moment of snarling reaction to the pampered pet, while Booth – desperately trying to save the face of her mad employer – suggests that the basket contains linen rather than Mr. Leeman, to which Cleese energetically shouts 'Brilliant!' before recovering his posture. The attempts to hide, move and store the unfortunate dead guest embrace everybody else in the building, with the macabre sense of comedy developing into a manic crescendo of complaints, shock and anger, rounded off by Berkeley's surreal address of the dead body and the blessed relief in the security of the basket for poor old Cleese.

Did You Know? This classic episode was selected by the BBC as their entry for the 1979 Montreux Festival (following the originally chosen dismissal of the *Goodies* show). However, the judges were dismayed at the stock funny foreigner characterisation of Manuel and the episode came nowhere. Nevertheless, Cleese had two last laughs – his narration on *To Norway, Home of Giants* won for Norway! Meanwhile, he could count his money and blessings from the 1977/1978 overseas sales of *Fawlty Towers* series one –

bought by 45 television stations in 17 countries none of whom seemed to take offence at Manuel's characterisation.

The Kipper and the Corpse (Fatty Owls)
Basil Fawlty **JOHN CLEESE**
Sybil Fawlty **PRUNELLA SCALES**
Manuel **ANDREW SACHS**
Polly **CONNIE BOOTH**
Dr. Price **GEOFFREY PALMER**
Mrs. Chase **MAVIS PUGH**
Mr. White **RICHARD DAVIES**
Mrs. White **ELIZABETH BENSON**
Major Gowen **BALLARD BERKELEY**
Miss Tibbs **GILLY FLOWER**
Miss Gatsby **RENEE ROBERTS**
Terry **BRIAN HALL**
Mr. Leeman **DEREK ROYLE**
Mr. Xerxes **ROBERT McBAIN**
Miss Young **PAMELA BUCHNER**
Mr. Zebedee **RAYMOND MASON**
Mr. Ingrams **CHARLES McKEOWN**
Guest **LEN MARTEN**
Written by **John Cleese & Connie Booth**
Music **Dennis Wilson**
Costume **Caroline Maxwell**
Make-up **Suzan Broad**
Film cameraman **Alec Curtis**
Film sound **Bill Chesneau**
Film editor **Susan Imrie**
Studio lighting **Ron Bristow**
Studio sound **Mike Jones**
Videotape editor **Howard Dell**
Production assistant **John Kilby**
Design **Nigel Curzon**
Producer **Douglas Argent**
Director **Bob Spiers**
5 March 1979

WALDORF SALAD

The one where a transatlantic guest proves more than a match for Basil. Although not a vintage episode, this show examines Fawlty's proud, flawed patriotism and finds his rude willpower unable to contain the explosive rants of his bombastic American visitor satisfactorily. In half an hour Cleese and Booth hold the fundamental difference between the two cultures up to a magnifying glass and make more in-depth and penetrating observations than the whole of Cleese's *A Fish Called Wanda*. In many ways the film develops the retentive attitude of the British against a more fun-loving

American freedom, although in this *Fawlty Towers* episode it is more evenly balanced and tongue-curlingly effective. The scene is set with a dining room of quietly complaining guests, mumbling about the quality of meat and slowness of service, brilliantly brought into cold reality by Cleese's explosive enquiries as to whether everything is all right – quickly confirmed with meek grins and whispered thank yous. It is the British aversion to confrontation shown in definitive terms. While the evening meal causes flurries of activity and hopeless incompetence, Scales, as the gossiping lady of luxury, passes an awkward while talking about the pricelessness of solitude with a guest who quite clearly wants some solitude himself. Cleese, in the meantime treating his paying guests like the customary dirt under his feet, wanders around with lamb dishes, wishes a bon appetit with a coda raspberry and ingratiates himself to the stunning English lady. Just about to remonstrate, pompously shooting his mouth off about the uncouth rubbish he has in the hotel, and to one guest none too subtly mocking the outrageously loud American complaining about the bad weather and the driving on the wrong side of the road. We the audience are, of course, privy to the gag that this chap is, in fact, her husband, and, as it happens, the last person about to stand for sloppy hotel accommodation. Bemusement over the cultural differences in food and drink follows (Fawlty is stumped with the Screwdriver as a drink and the components of a Waldorf salad); Scales effortlessly engages the partner in charming small talk, counterbalancing Cleese's unmovable devotion to the rain and fog of Blighty in light of the sun and fun of California. But basically, our hero has taken on far more than he can chew, whipping 20 quid off his guests to keep the kitchen open past nine o'clock, falling for Brian Hall's karate chat and then booting him out for his Fin fun in preparation to tackle the meal himself. The basic stupidity and Englishness of Cleese, mocked but never to the limit, may string out this episode a bit too much, but one of the greatest literal critiques of all time appears in his unfavoured description of Harold Robbins as 'pornographic muzak!' – pure genius – while he desperately tries to fob of the streetwise backchat of his American guest with alternative hotel-based food like the Ritz salad, complemented with various, long-winded tales of undelivered food and physical injuries. The Americans' obsession with kicking arse and with financial gain are condemned in disgruntled manner by Cleese's spirit of British strength, while his initially supportive Brit guests prompt a proud, chest-puffing speech of national unity. The glory moment, as usual, is short-lived and Cleese rants about Nazi mentalities, ushers his guests away like Jews to the gas chamber, briskly walks out of his hotel and, noting the heavy downpour, registers into his own hotel with a delicious array of problematic American food desires – in bed. Touché Sybil.

Waldorf Salad (Flay Otters)
Basil Fawlty **JOHN CLEESE**
Sybil Fawlty **PRUNELLA SCALES**
Manuel **ANDREW SACHS**
Polly **CONNIE BOOTH**
Mr. Hamilton **BRUCE BOA**
Mrs. Hamilton **CLAIRE NIELSON**
Mr. Arrad **NORMAN BIRD**
Mrs. Arrad **STELLA TANNER**
Mr. Johnston **TERENCE CONOLEY**
Mrs. Johnston **JUNE ELLIS**
Terry **BRIAN HALL**
Mr. Libson **ANTHONY DAWES**
Major Gowen **BALLARD BERKELEY**
Miss Tibbs **GILLY FLOWER**
Miss Gatsby **RENEE ROBERTS**
Miss Gurke **BEATRICE SHAW**
Miss Hare **DOROTHY FRERE**
Written by **John Cleese & Connie Booth**
Music **Dennis Wilson**
Costume **Valerie Spooner**
Make-up **Suzan Broad**
Lighting **Ron Bristow**
Sound **Mike Jones**
Videotape editor **Neil Pittaway**
Production assistant **John Kilby**
Design **Nigel Curzon**
Producer **Douglas Argent**
Director **Bob Spiers**
12 March 1979

THE ANNIVERSARY PARTY

The one where Basil's surprise backfires, Sybil storms off and Polly does a bit of impromptu playacting for the benefit of a gaggle of Fawlty's friends. The sword of Damocles and a bit of militant back-chat between Booth and Hall sets up the impending doom of bluff and counter-bluff in this masterly half hour, whose delicious black humour, twists and characterisations out-Ayckbourn Alan Ayckbourn to rank as one of the most powerful ensemble pieces you are likely to come across. Cleese, wallowing in self-satisfaction at the hurt and pained reaction of Scales as she broods about the supposed forgotten 15th wedding anniversary, delights in over-played absent-mindedness, gives the obvious reaction take to Scales' amazed 'Say that again!' and adds insult to injury with a dry historical rummage through the dates of great battles. However, this perverse bit of fun is quickly contrasted by the sudden departure of the missus and a torrent of expectant guests and awkward questions. With a concurrent slapstick battle roaring between Andrew Sachs and Brian Hall over the glories of Spanish cooking, the three couples celebrating Fawlty's big day are fobbed off, beaten and basically lead down, round and beyond the garden path.
Ken Campbell's cynical Roger, almost immediately clocking the reality of the situation and deliciously pinpointing every contradiction in Cleese's fund of tall stories, runs riot through the hotel, commenting on the shabbiness of the place, supping gin all over the shop and tossing in the corniest of gags at the drop of a hat. His reaction to Cleese's grandiose plans to turn the bar into a sort of captain's cabin affair gets a splendid look of quiet disgust from the main man, while the dentist/doctor discussion has some great sarcastic mileage in it. The conspiracy between Cleese and Booth even surpasses the horse betting charade, with eyes mistaken for thighs (Polly says her legs are swollen, bringing on Cleese's concerned inspection), a half baked story about

Scales and her Northern double driving round the town, and Cleese's outraged outburst regarding refunding the petrol money of his inquisitive guests. The comic genius reaches fever pitch with Cleese lugging Booth upstairs, a long overdue rant from the much used and abused maid ('You want to be in a Marx Brothers film that's your problem') and the final employment of bribery to go through the Sybil-routine. Campbell's eternal wet blanket delights in every false start, awkward pause and surreally mind-numbing throwaway gag (Basil Brush et al), as Booth desperately transforms herself into a be-wigged, Brandoesque version of the absent wife, while Una Stubbs, desperately trying to preserve sanity, accepts crisps as she struggles to retrieve lost nuts. Following a priceless comeback from Cleese with his petulant enquiry as to whether Campbell reads a lot of Oscar Wilde, the ultimate pitch-black showdown with friends and the phony Sybil ends up as a hilarious waving fest of mumbled words and feeble comforting. There's a bizarre quality to the vicious attack on Pat Keen's nurse, followed by the arrival of the real Sybil, creating total amazement among the gathered throng, a quick move from Cleese, chucking her into a cupboard past the floor-reeling kitchen battlers and the shocked departure of the gaggle of pals. Delighting in an off-the-wall treatment of a fairly standard farce situation, this can be cited as Cleese's all-time masterpiece if the choice weren't so difficult. In any event, with chest puffed and one hurdle out of the way, Cleese's final line 'Piece of cake. Now comes the tricky bit' can send a shiver up the back of any Brit comedy connoisseur.

The Anniversary Party (Flowery Twats)
Basil Fawlty **JOHN CLEESE**
Sybil Fawlty **PRUNELLA SCALES**
Manuel **ANDREW SACHS**
Polly **CONNIE BOOTH**
Roger **KEN CAMPBELL**
Alice **UNA STUBBS**
Arthur **ROBERT ARNOLD**
Virginia **PAT KEEN**
Reg **ROGER HUME**

Kitty **DENYSE ALEXANDER**
Audrey **CHRISTINE SHAW**
Major Gowen **BALLARD BERKELEY**
Miss Tibbs **GILLY FLOWER**
Miss Gatsby **RENEE ROBERTS**
Terry **BRIAN HALL**
Written by **John Cleese & Connie Booth**
Music **Dennis Wilson**
Costume **Caroline Maxwell**
Make-up **Suzan Broad**
Film cameraman **Paul Wheeler**
Film sound **Bill Chesneau**
Film editor **Susan Imrie**
Studio lighting **Ron Bristow**
Studio sound **Mike Jones**
Videotape editor **Howard Dell**
Vision mixer **Bill Morton**
Production team **John Kilby, Penny Thompson & Iain McLean**
Design **Nigel Curzon**
Producer **Douglas Argent**
Director **Bob Spiers**
19 March 1979

BASIL THE RAT

The one where a combination of Government Health Inspector, two dead pigeons in the water-tank and Manuel's rather dubious pet hamster could add up to closure of the hotel. The last hurrah for *Fawlty Towers* ranks as arguably the most polished and sustained of the entire 12-show run. This is the ultimate battle between Cleese and the figures of authority that hound his life – here a wonderfully dry performance from John Quarmby as the health inspector. He first appears studying a plate of meat in the hotel kitchen and unleashing an inspired diatribe of self-service abuse and amazed reaction from a petulant, full-steam-ahead Cleese. His brilliant but unsuccessful attempt at trying to get away with his aural attack, chuckling about the glories of being British and having the style to laugh at each other, falls on infertile ground as the catalogue of health and safety requirements is reeled off with monotonous energy by Quarmby and leading to the obvious but inspirationally played mutter, 'Is that all?' Brian Hall, giving stunning support here, lobs in George Orwell's social observations, while the nub of the comedy comes from Sachs and his

beloved pet rat. The difference between Scales and her soft, understanding approach to the problem and Cleese's sledgehammer domination is a perfect blend, scuppered by Booth's humane and deceitful plan to hide the rat away with the approval of Sachs and Hall. But the major battle, as always, is between the towering Cleese and Scales, storming through a double-quick sticker and paste job to rectify the hotel's shortcomings and setting up one of my all-time favourite Fawlty moments as Scales relentlessly checks and double checks every point. Cleese and his Mastermind/stating the bleeding obvious comment, is a high point of British comedy. Building up to the discussion about letting the rat fend for itself, shocked amazement at his wife's fears and culminating with the classic gang of mugger field mice scenario. This is pure class in a glass stuff. Cleese, in a desperate attempt to cheer up the overly depressed employee, employs the definitive use of the three-tier joke situation, making two reasonable 'why don't you' suggestions for a fun night out but finally losing the patient he has found and stuttering to a climactic, 'Why don't you cheer up, for Christ sake!' Absolute textbook material. Meanwhile, Booth is seen getting an attack of Fawlty mannerisms snubbing a departing client; a classic episode from the first series is referred to with the vermin/German misunderstanding between Cleese and Berkeley; and the Anglo/American divide is viciously lambasted with Cleese's sneaky Mickey Mouse delivery of Booth's sugary lie. The ratatouille confusion is one of the canon's most celebrated threads with Sachs careering round the place like a distressed turkey, Cleese embracing television iconology with his George Burns farewell 'say goodnight to the folks, Gracie!' and causing farcical nightmares with the poison-impregnated bit of veal, reunited with the clean bits of meat and popping up on various plates in the dining area until the very end. The Holmesian deduction to determine

the poisoned portion, complete with Cleese's bemusement at the major concern for the cat, allayed fears upset by the moggie choking on a fur ball and the hilarious, wrenching impersonation from the man himself all adds up to stomach-aching hilarity. The high pitch of laughter is slightly lowered with the Franklyn/Neville dining room element, but there's no denying that the final burst of explosive, rat action (however, unconvincing the furry rodent may look in that biscuit tin) is a major peak in the series. With stunned reaction from the inspector, small talk on the weather from Scales and the flaked-out body of Cleese quietly dragged away, an end to a comedy milestone is marked. They certainly don't come much better that this.

Did You Know? Ever keen to pinch a golden idea, American television tried a couple of versions – *Snavely* with Harvey Korman in the Fawlty role got to the stage of filming a pilot in 1978 but died a death, while a six-part series appeared on NBC in 1983 under the title of *Amanda's By the Sea* with Bea Arthur. Cleese enquired how the rewriting was going only to be informed that they had made only one minor cut – Basil Fawlty had been written out – sort of like *Hamlet* without all that deadwood concerning the Danish Prince. Cleese demanded his name be removed from the programme. In the late 1980s rumours were even flying that Joanna Lumley was going to tackle the Fawlty role – but forget the rest; enjoy the best.
In the wake of the show real Fawlty Towers hotels have sprung up from Torquay to Tenerife. In Sidmouth, Devon a hotelier changed his hotel name and his own from Stuart Hughes to Basil Fawlty by deed poll. In 1991 he was voted onto the East Devon District Council as a member of The Raving Looney Green Giant People's Party. Miami held a Basil Fawlty Festival with a host of lookalikes, while Marvin Kitman of New York's *Newsday* started the Basil Fawlty for Prime Minister campaign. In a mock election he won

63 percent of the vote. Finally, at the birthplace of *Fawlty Towers*, Gleneagles in Torquay, the late Donald Sinclair reputedly haunts the guest rooms, still causing problems!

Basil the Rat (Farty Towels)
Basil Fawlty **JOHN CLEESE**
Sybil Fawlty **PRUNELLA SCALES**
Manuel **ANDREW SACHS**
Polly **CONNIE BOOTH**
Mr. Carnegie **JOHN QUARMBY**
Major Gowen **BALLARD BERKELEY**
Terry **BRIAN HALL**
Miss Tibbs **GILLY FLOWER**
Miss Gatsby **RENEE ROBERTS**
Ronald **DAVID NEVILLE**
Quentina **SABINA FRANKLYN**
Mr. Taylor **JAMES TAYLOR**
Mrs. Taylor **MELODY LANG**
Guest **STUART SHERWIN**
Written by **John Cleese & Connie Booth**
Music **Dennis Wilson**
Costume **Caroline Maxwell**
Make-up **Pam Meager**
Film cameraman **Paul Wheeler**
Film sound **Bill Chesneau**
Film editor **Susan Imrie**
Studio lighting **Ron Bristow**
Studio sound **Mike Jones**
Videotape editor **Howard Dell**
Vision mixer **Bill Morton**
Production team **John Kilby, Penny Thompson & Iain McLean**
Design **Nigel Curzon**
Producer **Douglas Argent**
Director **Bob Spiers**
26 March 1979

• MARTY FELDMAN

Unsung comic genius, born 1932, who first got involved with the *Python* players when in 1966 he was made chief writer for *The Frost Report*, overseeing the work of Chapman, Cleese, Idle, Jones and Palin. Feldman became part of the *At Last the 1948 Show* team with Cleese, Chapman and Tim Brooke-Taylor, performing comedy for the first time thanks to Cleese's recommendation. Feldman's success led to his own BBC2 show *Marty*, which features sketches by Cleese, Chapman, Jones and Palin, with the road to mega-stardom taking in work on *The Dean Martin Show*, film assignments: *The Bed Sitting Room*, *Every Home Should Have One* (the last reunion with Took) and ATV's headlining *Marty Feldman's Comedy Machine* (with Orson Welles, Spike Milligan, Bob Todd, Hugh Paddick and Terry Gilliam on title credits). However, this show embraced the American market, knocked his surreal genius and changed the format by using experienced US comedy writers like Rudy DeLuca, Pat McCormick and Barry Levinson. In 1972 Australian live shows resurrected old material and *Marty Back Together Again* was a sadly apt title after Hollywood excess. Post-Mel Brooks and his finest film contribution in *Young Frankenstein*, Feldman's attempts to write, direct and star in his own comedy movies led to huge failure and bouts of self-destruction. His brief salvation came in the unlikely shape of Graham Chapman's woeful pirate romp *Yellowbeard*. Although frail, Feldman was having the time of his life filming in Morocco with old chums, Chapman, Peter Cook and Eric Idle around him. However, a heavy work load, ambitious stunts and his usual love of cigarettes – he was smoking some 80 a day – combined with the fierce heat and lack of oxygen in the highly elevated Mexico City. On the last day of filming Chapman heard Feldman had been taken to hospital. Apparently, following his shoot on the film, he had enjoyed a bit of tourist shopping and even done a piece of spontaneous comic business in his hotel lobby. But just an hour later he suffered severe chest pains and died of a massive heart attack. *Yellowbeard* is dedicated to his memory.

FIERCE CREATURES

Much rebuffed and rearranged movie whose pre-release history is one of trial audience reaction, expensive re-shots and long periods of re-thinking. Okay, so it didn't make much money in America and the critics only presented praise with the coda that *A Fish Called Wanda* it ain't, but for me this is one of John Cleese's most powerful, and more importantly, hilarious movies. The ten-year production history and time/pound-consuming alterations are totally and utterly justified. It certainly knocks spots off *Wanda*, simply by skilfully returning to what Cleese does best – British respectability battling against embarrassment and redundancy, fighting for his corner, fighting corruption and being very, very funny while he does it. It's an old-fashioned, outmoded England, dependent on innuendo and slapstick for much of its comedy and even recruiting old Frost faces like Ronnie Corbett into the action. A real return to Ealing comedy values here, with the British tight-knit group battling for their individuality and freedom of speech, winning over the initially ogre-like Cleese and taking on the almighty power of the dollar with bumbling and endearing Britishness. Moreover, with two Pythons in the zoo, they are not kept apart for most of the movie à la *Wanda* but happily thrown together for continual comic banter, over-zealous flamboyance and, most warming of all, unashamed embracing of their previous incarnations – during the seductive seal-lion show one spectator is heard to say 'Wonderful plumage!', Cleese sardonically suggests using a sharp stick to calm an escaped ant-eater and there's an intangible magic when Cleese/Palin clash. The lads are back with a vengeance and even the corniest of tit gags can't hold them back. Indeed, every critic worth his salt and a few who aren't, latched onto the notion that this was more like a *Carry On* movie. Well, if that means, British, funny and good natured then I'm all for it. In Cleese's eyes this was far from a sequel to his 1988 blockbuster and more like an equal, like the *Carry On*s, simply capitalising on an established and successful team and moving location. It's quiet disquieting to see our King of cool comedy embracing the most base of double meaning humour, but that doesn't stop it being funny. The quartet are all in brilliant form, even though poor Jamie Lee Curtis is called on for nothing more than a string of ever more revealing dresses – no complaints from this side.

Once again, everybody's thunder is effortlessly stolen by Michael Palin, of the four leads moving completely away from his *Wanda* characterisation and eagerly injecting great swathes of Peter Cook's *Interesting Facts* persona into his part. Rambling on about his beloved insects, ever ready with an opinion on almost everything and hilariously wandering away from every scene still rabbiting on about something or other, this is a classic supporting turn who creeps throughout the action with little actual importance to the plot but enlivening every scene with a bizarre, rollercoaster bit of business. His manic antics dressed as a bee are sheer class in anybody's book. Kevin Kline as well, scores heavily as the anxious, sex-mad, power-mad son of the Aussie big wig (a rather more coarse character study from Kline). It's *Wanda* all over again, but here his muscle-bound pretensions and corruption don't succeed in bedding Jamie Lee, his anti-British ideals are going no where (not even Curtis, never mind Cleese, gives the notion the time of day) and his childish banter simply seems to play like endearing madness. Thus it is that his averted death (test audience reaction decreed that his departure via a killer rhino wasn't funny) is understandable. The ending in the final print is a feel-good, just finale to the old fashioned farce and knockabout humour. Kline plays a complete idiot again but there's an added edge of endearing stupidity about him that lets us forgive all his half-hearted vices – the languid tortoise (shades of *Sid's Mystery Tour*) allegedly sponsored by Bruce Springsteen – 'you were born to run with this', labelled tiger and hilarious clockwork panda are deliciously manic schemes. Besides, anybody that goes for big money to save an anger-fuelled final showdown has got to be congratulated. The film isn't a masterpiece by any means, it takes a while to warm up and there are sags of misdirection along the way, but once Palin starts asking awkward questions to a pompous, self-assured

Cleese there's film magic on offer. This is a *Wanda* reunion (the likes of Aiken and Georgeson crop up in minor roles as well) with the embittered angst happily removed. It may not be a biting satirical attack but *Fierce Creatures* quietly and effectively highlights the absurdity of advertising and multi-million dollar control of the global village via innuendo, smut and class performances. Cleese, with a heart from the start, although eager to instil the fear of God into his new minions, plays his role with the befuddled panic of Fawlty on overdrive and, despite the characteristics having already passed way into our collective consciousness, there's nothing quite as rewarding or hilarious as enjoying Cleese in full-on rant mode. The supporting cast are all spot-on, whether it's the emotional bumbling of Ronnie Corbett, spending most of the last half hour waddling around in a seal suit, the laconic and militant ease of Robert Lindsay (his reaction to the five gun shots is acting class all the way), Derek Griffiths, embracing the warm love between man and animal, and Corey Lowell, oozing American sexuality while throwing herself fully into the all-out British farce of the situation. The sexual understanding of Cleese, endorsing his appeal to Curtis, and creating reams of farcical situation, are class stuff, and besides

any plot device that can get Lowell down to her undies has got to be good (in my book).

The main difference is that this film has a heart, geared towards good fun throughout, adding to this feel-good quality a cross-national understanding, teaming up to fight the heartless money makers and protect the interests of animals (while, from a clever movie-marketing point of view, still gaining support from the comically-mentioned companies with a long, closing credits roll-call). Cleese has tongue-in-cheek sexual pride with Curtis coyly endorsing his pseudo-animal sexual instincts. The final cherished embrace is what good old-fashioned comedy is all about. The character name slip at the very close is a delightful resurrection of the earlier movie, working so beautifully it almost makes me want to dig out *Wanda* for yet another reappraisal. Almost. *Fierce Creatures* is by far the funnier movie, given a further injection of touching warmth by the dedication to Gerald Durrell, founder of Jersey Zoo, and, of course, dear old Peter Cook (both of whom died in January 1995). Just another reason to stick around until the close of the final credits.

Did You Know? This is the first reunion of *G.B.H.* stars Michael Palin and Robert Lindsay, with director Robert Young. The Kline death

Something's not quite right in zooland... *Fierce Creatures*

ending grated with Cleese in a
November 1995 screening and the
producer's girlfriend, Clara,
suggested the son play-act as the dead
father. Cleese latched onto this
notion as a definitive farce idea, with
the convention of the same actor
playing both parts twisted by the
actual acting within the narrative
being less convincing than the work
of Kline the paid movie actor,
although that pay was nowhere near
Kline's usual asking fee. As with *A
Fish Called Wanda* the high-earning
lead players took a very small initial
fee in favour of a percentage of the
takings, thus the budget (including
two Hollywood attractions) was fixed
at $15 million. Unfortunately, when
the test audience results hit the fan
(firstly from Los Angeles, then New
York and Chicago) Cleese rewrote the
ending, struggled to reunite his far
flung cast (Palin, for one, was
somewhere in Borneo filming his
third travelogue) and headed back to
Pinewood. It was estimated that the
additional 15 minutes of required
footage would pile on £500,000 per
minute to the budget. The planned
spring 1996 release date was delayed
until early 1997. Lisa Hogan, who
plays the small but glam part of the
sealion keeper, started as a researcher
for Cleese's Fish Productions before
graduating to production assistant on
Fierce Creatures and ultimately
landing a role. Mad press speculation
about an affair sprang up, with the
main piece of evidence remaining
that Hogan's only other acting work
had been one-line in an Aussie soap
opera. But Hogan gives an excellent
performance in the movie and this
merely highlights Cleese's great
talent-spotting ability. The killer
rhino that dispatched Kline in the
original ending was worked by a head
and shoulders model moulded
around a Land Rover and sharp eyes
watching the film's trailer will spot
this edited sequence. The trailer was
a masterpiece of comedy as well,
with the four stars addressed in Oscar
terms, notably the punchlining,
Michael 'I knew a man called Oscar'
Palin. Class.
Cleese was fascinated with zoos as a
child when he used to skip school to

visit Bristol Zoo and watch the ring-
tailed lemurs. The films Marwood
Zoo is based on Gerald Durrell's
ideal of zoological research projects,
and although filmed at the
naturalist's location and dedicated to
his memory gets its name from
Cleese's middle name – Marwood. At
work on the script Cleese contacted
Britain's top animal consultant Rona
Brown for a list of the five cuddliest,
cutest creatures known to man – she
provided the fab five in the movie,
wallabies, lemurs, meercats,
Uruguayan coatimundies and
Patagonian maras. The final cast of
animal performers was 115 creatures
from 35 different species, 3,000 ants,
a load of uninvited 'incarnations of
former Nazi officer' wasps and a cute
rabbit left over from *The Secret
Garden*. Mocked within the film, the
producers did receive sponsorship
from the stars (Steve Martin –
wallabies/Springsteen – tortoise/Kevin
Costner – gorilla) to help finance the
film – clever stuff. Cleese approached
Margaret Thatcher for a Vulture
sponsorship deal but she declined!
The oft quoted comment that the
film was 'an equal not a sequel' to
Wanda was originally coined for
Richard O'Brien's unsuccessful
retrack of *The Rocky Horror Picture
Show*, *Shock Treatment*.

Fierce Creatures
Universal Pictures presents A Fish
Productions/Jersey Films Production
Rollo Lee **JOHN CLEESE**
Willa Weston **JAMIE LEE CURTIS**
Vince McCain/Rod McCain **KEVIN
KLINE**
Adrian 'Bugsy' Malone **MICHAEL PALIN**
Sydney Small Mammals **ROBERT
LINDSAY**
Reggie Sealions **RONNIE CORBETT**
Cub Felines **CAREY LOWELL**
Gerry Ungulates **DEREK GRIFFITHS**
Neville Coltrane **BILLE BROWN**
Pip Small Mammals **CYNTHIA CLEESE**
Hugh Primates **RICHARD RIDINGS**
Di Admin **MARIA AITKEN**
Ant Keeper **MICHAEL PERCIVAL**
Flamingo Keeper **FRED EVANS**
Sealion Keeper **LISA HOGAN**
Parrot Keeper **CHOY-LING MAN**
Vulture Keeper **TIM POTTER**
Aquarium Keeper **JENNY GALLOWAY**

Tiger Keeper **KIM VITHANA**
Buffalo Keeper **SEAN FRANCIS**
Rodent Keeper **JULIE SAUNDERS**
Woman in Red Dress **SUSIE BLAKE**
Her Mother **PAT KEEN**
Her Husband **DENIS LILL**
Inspector Masefield **GARETH HUNT**
Sergeant Scott **RON DONACHIE**
Sergeant Irving **PAUL HAIGH**
Octopus Security Guards **LEON
HERBERT & STEWART WRIGHT**
Frightened Executive **KERRY SHALE**
TV Producer **MAC McDONALD**
Zoo Secretary **AMANDA WALKER**
Man in Straw Hat **TERENCE CONOLEY**
Sealion Spectators **TOM GEORGESON,
JOHN BARDON & ANTHONY PEDLEY**
Sponsors **JENNIE GOOSSENS,
GEORGIA REECE, HILARY GISH,
KENNETH PRICE, BRIAN KING &
PETER SILVERLEAF**
Hotel Manager **KEVIN MOORE**
Assistant Hotel Managers **LESLIE
LOWE & IAIN MITCHELL**
Hotel Maid **VALERIE EDMOND**
Policeman **NICK BARTLETT**
TV Journalists **RICCO ROSS & KATE
HARPER**
TV Reporter **NICHOLAS HUTCHISON**
Student Zoo Keepers **KATE
ALDERTON, JACK DAVENPORT, JO
ANN GEARY, WILLIAM GROVE,
FRANCIS POPE, JAQUI THOMAS &
DAVID WOOD**
'Jambo' the Gorilla **JOHN ALEXANDER**
Background Gorillas **TESSA CROCKETT,
PHILLIP HILL, HOLLY HOFFMAN,
MARIO KALLI, TINA MASKELL &
ELIZABETH O'BRIEN**
Panda Performer **ALISA BERK**
Puppeteers **TIM ROSE, DARRYL
WORBEY, WILLIAM TODD JONES &
STEVE A. CLARKE**
Screenplay by **John Cleese & Iain
Johnstone**
Based on *The Fierce Creature Policy* by
Terry Jones & Michael Palin
Music **Jerry Goldsmith**
Kevin Kline Acting Double **Kenneth
Price**
Gorilla choreographer **Peter Elliott**
Stunts **Riky Ash, Jamie Edgell, Sean
McCabe, Mark Southworth, Gary
Powell, Abbi Collins, Paul Jennings,
Andreas Petrides, Lee Sheward &
Anna Stacey**
Production designer **Roger Murray-
Leach**
Photography **Adrian Biddle & Ian**

Baker
Editor **Robert Gibson**
Assistant directors **Jonathan Benson &
Roy Stevens**
Art directors **David Allday & Kevin
Phipps**
Assistant to John Cleese **Amanda
Montgomerie**
Co-producer **Patricia Carr**
Executive producer **Steve Abbott**
Producers **Michael Shamberg & John
Cleese**
Directors **Robert Young & Fred
Schepisi**
Filmed in May 1995/Summer 1996,
Pinewood Studios, Bucks & Jersey Zoo
93 mins. 1997

THE FINAL RIP OFF

An absolutely invaluable double
compilation *Monty Python* release
from Virgin who wisely repackaged a
bundle of old *Python* material once it
took over the Charisma back
catalogue. The only totally new piece
is Michael Palin's introduction,
although several of his brief links are
new (Marilyn Monroe) and the Henry
Kissinger song is a longer version
than that originally featured on the
Contractual Obligation album.
The Final Rip Off – *Side 1*
Introduction, Constitutional Peasant,
Fish Licence, Eric the Half-a-Bee
Song, Finland Song, Travel Agent,
Are You Embarrassed Easily?,
Australian Table Wines, Argument,
Henry Kissinger Song, Parrot (Oh,
Not Again!)
Side 2 Sit On My Face, Undertaker,
Novel Writing (Live From Wessex),
String, Bells, Traffic Lights, Cocktail
Bar, Four Yorkshiremen, Election
Special, Lumberjack Song
Side 3 I Like Chinese, Spanish
Inquisition Part 1, Cheese Shop,
Cherry Orchard, Architects Sketch,
Spanish Inquisition Part 2, Spam,
Spanish Inquisition Part 3, Comfy
Chair, Famous Person Quiz, You Be
the Actor, Nudge Nudge,
Cannibalism, Spanish Inquisition
Revisited.
Side 4 I Bet You They Won't Play
This Song On the Radio, Bruces,
Bookshop, Do Wot John, Rock
Notes, I'm So Worried, Crocodile,

French Taunter Part 1, Marilyn
Monroe, Swamp Castle, French
Taunter Part 2, Last Word.
Virgin MPD 1 1988
Written and performed by **GRAHAM
CHAPMAN, JOHN CLEESE, TERRY
GILLIAM, ERIC IDLE, TERRY JONES
& MICHAEL PALIN**

A FISH CALLED WANDA

Without question the most successful
feature film to emerge from the
splintered *Python* group, this is really
a pretty standard heist comedy with a
blown-up reputation. Hyped to high
heaven, a film like *Nuns On the Run*
is far superior. But in terms of box
office receipts (£127 million), *A Fish
Called Wanda* was a true British film
blockbuster, feted as the greatest
comedy film to emerge from these
shores since *The Lavender Hill Mob*.
There's no denying that the film
contains some classic sequences and
the Anglo/American quartet at its
heart does some fine work, but
there's something faintly niggly and
unlikable about the whole project.
The ultimate fusion between
*Python*esque grotesque and American
hip, *A Fish Called Wanda* proves the
perfect vehicle for John Cleese's in-
depth deconstruction of the anal
retentive attitude of some British. A
fair target for laughs via *The Frost
Report*, *Python* and *Fawlty*, this film
is a backhanded celebration of the
inferior yet pompous quality of the
Brits. True, the chief protagonist in
this line of argument, Kevin Kline's
manic Otto, is highlighted as a
complete nut, but the power of
repetition is so strong that the
adoption of crusty British accents,
digs at narrow-minded beliefs and,
worst of all, outbursts about winning
World War II are relentless
throughout the movie. Okay, it's
funny if there's a point of contrast
along the way, and in classic Cleese
examples like *Fawlty*'s *Waldorf Salad*
it was the delightfully pompous but
loveable Cleese himself. Here, under
the allure of the delicious Jamie Lee
Curtis, Cleese turns to
understandable jelly and flows along
with this surge of anti-Brit debate.

It's almost farcical in the hands of
Kline's wonderfully over-the-top
performance, but when Cleese's level-
headed barrister pontificates about
the British being dead and stuffy,
hoping to escape from this anglicised
hell via a quick one with Curtis and,
amazingly, losing out to Kline's
deranged pleas for an apology, it
batters a sensitive nerve. Fine, the
guy's got a gun or he's hanging Cleese
out of the window, but whatever
natural advantages the script
provides, it's Cleese's Englishness that
is being pricked and mocked here.
When Kline, convinced of Cleese's
importance in the crime, tries to
make it up to him (with quite funny
results), cowardly Cleese runs round
his green and pleasant land like a
frightened child, pleading for mercy
and tossing away every ounce of
dignity his character may have had.
The rather obvious contrast between
seductive American strip for passion
and tired, sex-bored British strip for
bed merely reinforces the cultural
divide between the supposed super
dude Americans and the restricted
British. Stifled by his overbearing wife
(actually a stunningly attractive and
powerful turn from Maria Aitken),
saddled with a whining, spoilt
daughter and wandering through his
highly paid, under-appreciated work
with a sigh, Cleese is the epitome of
Brit-lagged male. It's the American
influence that affects him (he goes
round saying 'Hi', gets aroused by
Jamie Lee and impressed by her
interest in his work), risks everything
to see her and finally grabs a
gangster's moll, turns his back on
home, authority and the spirit of
Britishness.
Here, the Hollywood sell out has
gone too far. The film grossed big
time in the States but is there any
wonder: Kline's torrent of none too
subtle Brit abuse even earned him an
Oscar for best supporting actor.
Gentle satire at the Brits' expense will
get the Brits laughing along and
loudest, but this sort of blanket
attack is neither funny nor clever.
Only once does Cleese bark away
about America's failure in Vietnam,
but this is at a time when he is
standing up to his midriff in waste oil

The Anglo-American cast posing for the big hit *A Fish called Wanda*

the rhythmic banter of his low-life creations, but in a British comedy film which claims to resurrect the spirit of Ealing for a modern generation it is hardly needed. Even in *Monty Python's Life of Brian* and *Nuns On the Run* swearing is used as a limited, powerful shock exclamation and is not only acceptable but funny. In *Wanda* it's common currency, losing its cinematic clout, and becoming just a device to remove this film from family-oriented comedy audiences. Now, you have just read a lot of anti-copy about *A Fish Called Wanda* which, I believe it deserves. However, it also deserves high praise. Any movie that can drag Charles Crichton out of retirement for one last bash should be celebrated, even though the homage to his own *The Lavender Hill Mob* and the Ealing ethos is negligible. Thirty years later the crooks can get away with it, but none of the four are anywhere as likeable as Alec Guinness, Stanley Holloway, Alfie Bass or Sid James. However, to take the film on its own terms, the four central performances are uniformly excellent. Jamie Lee Curtis oozes sex appeal through out and Cleese does his usual pompous act to perfection although he's hardly Cary Grant, as his character name would suggest. Mind you, *A Fish Called Wanda* is hardly *His Girl Friday* either! But it's Kline and Palin that really steal the honours. Kevin Kline's knuckle-headed, Ramboesque hit man crusades through the mess with determination and flamboyance. Despite the fact that most of the film's worse ideology is delivered via his character, there's something fascinating in his knife-edge anger. Played in Steve Martin fashion, Kline forsakes subtle acting for all-out bedlam, latching onto Sellers-like insanity (fish/terrapins in *Never Let Go*) and spouting his *Python*esque obsession with Nietsche all over the place. Two moments stand out from the rest. One is his pent-up anger being expressed in a fairly quiet fashion, storming out past Palin and hastily smashing Jamie Lee's framed photograph, which is surpassed by Kline's hilarious attempts to cover up

and the line of argument is constructed to buy him some time, stalling Kline's gun attack and allowing Palin's steam-roller revenge to make its slow progress forward. Even this final death of the American loser was changed due to test audience reaction and Kline lives to see the movie out – it's a very effective gag reappearance as well. However, this final adjustment from Cleese was one of many, many rewrites from the conceptual stage in 1984 to the finished print and indeed, that final sequence does need the laugh of Kline's survival, while Cleese also took the opportunity to give Jamie Lee a warmer personality and a clear affection for Cleese. He cleverly worked everything out, cutting out

Palin and Wendy's father in the classic Kline, Curtis, Cleese scene in Archie's house, considering for weeks the notion of Palin's dog-killing and rearranging his momentous court room scene to allow Curtis to frame her lover rather than Cleese take the bull by the horns. However, the British characters are still either pompous with an anti-Brit attitude (Cleese), bumbling idiots (Palin) or foul-mouthed criminals (Georgeson), while the script is peppered with bad language aimed against the British character, authority and way of life. Worse, it's simply tossed into Jamie Lee and Kline's dialogue just to spice up the action. Now I'm the last one to condemn a film for its use of bad language. In Tarantino's world it fits

Jamie Lee's seduction of Cleese when his wife turns up unexpected. With strained tales about the American intelligence operations and a quickly and desperately made-up name, this is Kline's high point. His character has the power to seriously irritate but there's no denying that the guy is still the coolest thing in the film. But for me, it's Michael Palin who saves the film totally. With less to do than the other three, Palin can craft his stuttering character, mixing comic pratfalling with real pathos as he destroys Patricia Hayes' pet dogs in *Tom and Jerry* cartoon fashion. Originally Cleese wanted the blood and guts of real *Python* comic violence, but Crichton wisely toned it down for a more acceptable and funny level. Palin's nervousness at Kline's mock homosexuality, his unstuttered 'good!' as he hears of childhood abuse for the black-clad madman and his sudden cure of stuttering as Kline finally meets his pseudo-end are all film high points. However, naturally, the best moment comes when Cleese and Palin meet. It's for only one scene and quite near the end (smacking of wasted opportunity akin to the Marx Brothers never meeting in *The Story of Mankind*) but when it happens it's classic stuff. Cleese is at his best waiting for Palin's stutter as to the whereabouts of the diamonds and one can't help wishing that the two old colleagues were together more. With showered praise no movie could possibly live up to, *A Fish Called Wanda* is an enjoyable crime caper and that's all, but even the legendary set pieces (Cleese stripping to Russian spouting/Palin with the chips up his nose) are hardly that inspiring. For me, only some choice moments from the cast redeem a film that's almost irredeemable, but then 50 million Elvis fans can't be wrong so I'm waiting for a Defence Council with the powers of Cleese himself to convince me of the film's overflowing merits.

Did You Know? Apart from *The Last Pawn* and *Corruption*, other considered names for the film included *Wanda*, *A Goldfish Called Wanda*, *Wanda the Parrot*, *Wanda the Policeman* and *A Guppie Called Jack*. In Japan it was released as *Wanda, the Diamond and the Good Guys*. The title star is a rare Black Lace Angel Fish and *Wanda*'s box office popularity saw a major jump in sales of the pet.

A Fish Called Wanda
MGM/Prominent Features Production
Archie Leach **JOHN CLEESE**
Wanda **JAMIE LEE CURTIS**
Otto **KEVIN KLINE**
Ken **MICHAEL PALIN**
Wendy Leach **MARIA AITKEN**
George **TOM GEORGESON**
Mrs. Coady **PATRICIA HAYES**
Judge **GEOFFREY PALMER**
Portia Leach **CYNTHIA CAYLOR**
Customer in Jeweller's Shop **MARK ELWES**
Manager of Jeweller's **Shop NEVILLE PHILLIPS**
Inspector Marvia **PETER JONFIELD**
Bartlett **KEN CAMPBELL**
Warder **AL ASHTON**
Locksmith **ROGER HUME**
Davidson **ROGER BRIERLEY**
Sir John **LLEWELLYN REES**
Percival **MICHAEL PERCIVAL**
Magistrate **KATE LANSBURY**
Copper **ROBERT CAVENDISH**
Zebedee **ANDREW MacLACHLAN**
Vicar **ROLAND MacLEOD**
Mr. Johnson **JEREMY CHILD**
Mrs. Johnson **PAMELA MILES**
Children **TOM PIGGOT SMITH KATHERINE JOHN SOPHIE JOHNSTONE**
Nanny **KIM BARCLAY**
Junior Barristers **SHARON TWOMEY & PATRICK NEWMAN**
Clerk of Court **DAVID SIMEON**
Stenographer **IMOGEN BICKFORD-SMITH**
Junior Barrister **TIA LEE**
Police Officer at Old Bailey **ROBERT PUTT**
Prison Officers **WAYDON CROFT & ANTHONY PEDLEY**
Hotel Clerk **ROBERT McBAIN**
Airline Employee **CLARE McINTYRE**
Indian Cleaner **CHARU BALA CHOKSHI**
Hutchison **STEPHEN FRY**
Screenplay by **John Cleese**
Story by **John Cleese & Charles Crichton**
Music **John Du Prez**

Production designer **Roger Murray-Leach**
Casting director **Priscilla John**
Camera operator **Neil Binney**
Sound recordist **Chris Munro**
Sound editor **Jonathan Bates**
Art director **John Wood**
Set decorator **Stephanie McMillan**
Costume designer **Hazel Pethig**
Assistant to Mr. Cleese **Sophie Clarke-Jervoise**
Location manager **William Lang**
Photography **Alan Hume**
Editor **John Jympson**
Assistant director **Jonathan Benson**
Associate producer **John Comfort**
Executive producers **Steve Abbott & John Cleese**
Producer **Michael Shamberg**
Director **Charles Crichton**
Filmed at Twickenham Film Studios and on location in London & in the interior of Oxford town hall
106 mins 1988

THE FISHER KING

With his reputation tarnished by the *Baron*, Terry Gilliam instantly redeemed himself by toeing the Hollywood line with this rich, modern fairy tale. Abandoning his desire to construct a project from scratch, Gilliam tackled someone else's screenplay, overseen by the studio bosses and marketed as a big budget production while still, uniquely, retaining the elements of fantasy and magic that were his hallmark. The subject matter – the corrupt American dream being cleansed by human emotion through the mystery of Arthurian legend – could almost have been a Gilliam concept, and his understanding of the spiritualism of character creates a believable, touching and, even, exciting film. The guardian figure of Robin Williams (as the down 'n' out Parry, fallen from educated status via tragedy) is the catalyst for redemption and the performance is in turn hilarious and tear-jerkingly painful. At the outset this seemingly insane figure lapses into disturbed renditions of *I Like New York*, baffled diatribes of fantasy in the city, religious ideology and the expected dive into crazy comic voices – the flamboyant camp delivery to confuse the white trash figures/rapid character changes from quiet introspection to blasted instructions/frantically executed performance of mystic bowel movement. However, this is gradually toned down to symbolic injections of subdued and paraphrased Groucho Marx (the perfect performance of *Lydia the Tattooed Lady* in the restaurant), caring understatement (as his singalong audience of mental patients reluctantly go with the flow he merrily shouts 'Don't Hold Back!') and underplayed comic interludes (as a coin is dropped into his drinking cup and he sheepishly gives thanks) while beneath the distasteful exterior Williams the actor reveals the soul of the misunderstood clown. As he literally strips naked in Central Park, the trappings of pain are removed to present the pure, clear but magically touched truth of the man.

The stem of the Fisher King legend, delivered while staring up at the sky, is arguably Williams' most potent acting performance, uncluttered by superfluous exaggeration. A watershed moment in the eyes of the film's chief protagonist Jack Lucas (as played by Jeff Bridges) and the audience itself. Williams makes us believe. For all that, Bridges' performance remains the most astounding, ripping through his boy wonder persona, gleefully castigating the horrors of modern American life and even slumping through the depths of human endurance only to almost get sucked back into the commercial world of angst-ridden attack from a safe, wealthy position. In a performance that sweeps into callousness, love, adventure and raw pain, Bridges translates the confused, nightmarish hurt of Williams into currency tangible to the man in the street. The supporting performances, particularly the Oscar-winning turn from a raunchy, warm Mercedes Ruehl, dutifully bow to the power of this central male bonding relationship and the film, blessed with a thoughtful screenplay by Richard LaGravenese, dispels the belief that films that say something can't also

fulfil the need for populous appreciation. Gilliam's obsession with cinema is less employed than in, say, *Brazil*, but the 1930s ideal of glamour and romance shines through in a subtle fashion – indeed, the delightful Fred Astaire-like musical convention of suspended reality when the business population of New York waltz around the train terminal was an amendment to the script from Gilliam himself. Not only that, but the very hive of this human drama is a video rental outlet (crammed with the lower treasures of the market, swamped with pornography parodies of the classics – *Ordinary Peep-Holes!* – in a world which craves Katherine Hepburn and Cary Grant), featuring even more personal references to his own belittled masterpiece when Bridges, at his lowest ebb, drinks Jack Daniels in front of a poster for *Brazil*. The use of the Pinocchio doll is a continual motif throughout the film, enforced by the tolerance and unsullied belief of childhood (the privileged boy who presents Bridges with the toy calls him 'Mr. Bum!' There's a call from Bridges himself for Jimminy Cricket as if expecting the romance of the moment to comfort him, and indeed, Williams, in an uncomfortable, damaged fashion, is the Jimminy figure the disgraced disc jockey needs – note Williams indicating the nose growing when Bridges lies about love). Walt Disney himself is name-checked, ironically interlaced with the 20th century's personification of evil, Adolph Hitler, in a powerful, heartfelt, dispensable masses discussion between broken man and pristine plaything.

All these themes of childhood innocence, corrupted, self-opinionated adulthood and belief are typical Gilliam touches, compounded by the definitive search for Arthur's Holy Grail through a labyrinth of mediaeval towers, murderous red knights and bands of travellers finding strength in unity. As with Jonathan Pryce in *Brazil,* Williams is haunted by images of faceless destruction and Gilliam's most powerful montage sequence has to be the minutes of bewildered pain

following his returned faith in human nature after a touching first kiss from Amanda Plummer's Lydia. Seen through the eyes of a close observer, Williams' accepted world of position and marriage is destroyed through the gunman's madness, graphically ripping away the ordinariness of the situation in a few seconds of violence. The powerful link between the two characters, Bridges' flippant comment causing this mild-mannered psychopath to kill, is much more than a narrative connection but illustrates the frailty of life and the importance of shared experience.

In a perfectly mapped-out fashion, Gilliam links the two lives together, changing his directorial style from the initial stunning use of extreme close-up and shadow for Bridges' conceited radio broadcast to the humbled, head-to-head understanding of later sequences. Fantasy appears through 'Dutch' angles or Errol Flynn-like sweeps, adding a sense of Camelot to Bridges' attempt to purloin the Holy Grail for his friend's sanity. The ivory tower isolation of wealth is immediately suggested in aerial shots illustrating Bridges' stretch limousine in a sea of yellow cabs and the basic, fundamental thread of respect for all fellow humans comes through in close-up shots of eyes. As with *Twelve Monkeys*, Gilliam makes use of the symbolism of eyes, notably here through Bridges, radically changing from spoilt figure relaxing with his script (looking almost Gilliamesque and later addressing an entire post-*Python* concept by ranting 'America doesn't know the first thing about funny!') to totally shocked figure when the news of the massacre breaks through, solely through the pain in the eyes – with the perfected television tagline 'Forgive Me!' ringing hollow in the wake of tragedy. The realisation of why his radio broadcast is featured on television is transmitted via a second of smug pride to disbelief. From the initial, self-referential (the use of *Hit the Road Jack*), blistering anarchy (a crunching burst of Spike Jones) and dark velvet, twilight world of unconsidered comment to the fade into unrestrained, emotive simplicity of the closing, neon-light enhanced swell of *I Like New York*, a journey of humanity is presented, embracing understanding, pride and love. For Gilliam's first assignment as 'hired director' the message of fantasy business as usual was clear.

Did You Know? The original studio package came with a teaming of Robin Williams and Billy Crystal with, importantly, a planned capitalisation of Williams from *Good Morning, Vietnam* having him as disc jockey Jack Lucas. Gilliam felt the subtlety of the piece would not support two comic performers and cast Bridges to breathe life into the flip side of his American destiny.

The Fisher King
A Hill/Obst Production
Jack Lucas **JEFF BRIDGES**
Parry **ROBIN WILLIAMS**
Anne Napolitano **MERCEDES RUEHL**
Lydia **AMANDA PLUMMER**
Sondra **LARA HARRIS**
Ben Starr, Sitcom Actor **HARRY SHEARER**
Aging Chorus Boy **MICHAEL JETER**
Radio Engineers **ADAM BRYANT & PAUL LOMBARDI**
Lou Rosen **DAVID PIERCE**
Limo Bum **TED ROSS**
TV Anchorman **WARREN OLNEY**
News Reporter **FRAZER SMITH**
Crazed Video Customer **KATHY NAJIMY**
Sitcom Wife **MELINDA CULEA**
Bum at Hotel **JAMES REMINI**
Doorman **MARK BOWDEN**
Father at Hotel **JOHN OTTAVINO**
Little Boy **BRIAN MICHAELS**
Hippy Bum **BRADLEY GREGG**
Jamaican Bum **WILLIAM JAY MARSHALL**
John the Bum **WILLIAM PRESTON**
Superintendent **AL FANN**
Porno Customer **STEPHEN BRIDGEWATER**
Stockbroker Bum **JOHN HEFFERNAN**
Red Knight **CHRIS HOWELL**
Straitjacket Yuppie **RICHARD LaGRAVENESE**
Bag Lady **ANITA DANGLER**
Drooler **MARK BRINGELSON**
Pizza Boy **JOHNNY PAGANELLI**
Receptionist **DIANE ROBIN**
Motorcyclist **JOHN BENJAMIN RED**

Parry's Wife **LISA BLADES**
Edwin **CHRISTIAN CLEMENSON**
Doctor **CARLOS CARRASCO**
Guard **JOE JAMROG**
TV Executive **JOHN de LANCIE**
Nurse **LOU HANCOCK**
Radio Show Call-ins **CAROLINE CROMELIN**
KATHLEEN BRIDGET KELLY & PATRICK FRALEY
Young Punks **JAYCE BARTOK & DAN FUTTERMAN**
Wheelchair Bum **TOM WAITS**
Screenplay by **Richard LaGravenese**
Associate producers **Stacey Sher & Anthony Mark**
Production co-ordinator **Pam Cornfield**
Photography **Roger Pratt**
Camera operator **Craig Haagensen**
Editor **Lesley Walker**
Casting **Howard Feuer**
Production designer **Mel Bourne**
Art director **P. Michael Johnston**
Music **George Fenton**
Producers **Debra Hill & Lynda Obst**
Director **Terry Gilliam**
Tri-Star Pictures cert 15,
137 mins, 1991

DAVID FROST

Mr. TV for the sixties, David Frost was born in 1940 and, following a healthy obsession with Peter Cook's genius, became the leading light of the Cambridge Footlighters and performed Cleese/Chapman material in revue. Powerful and astute, Frost signed up mountains of old Cambridge talent for his shows, notably latching onto Cleese as early as 1963's *TW3* before giving him performance television exposure on *The Frost Report*. Besides Cleese, the shows incorporated written contributions from Chapman, Idle, Jones and Palin and led to the major Cleese/Chapman classic *At Last the 1948 Show*. Other *Python*/Frostian spin-offs included *How to Irritate People*, *The Two Ronnies* and *The Rise and Rise of Michael Rimmer*, the latter the first half-hidden assault on the Frost character itself. With the freedom of *Python*, the lads could happily abuse the overshadowing, self-promoting figure of Frost, notably Eric Idle's Timmy Williams

boasting an ingratiating personality starring in his own life-based sketch written by himself in big letters followed by additional credits whizzing by in an ironical nod to *The Frost Report* and grabbing anybody that comes along to further his own talent. Other *Frost*-based *Python* japes included It's A Tree with 'super, super' mutterings and The Mouse Problem including Frost's home telephone number, while Idle later parodied the Frost/Nixon interview on *Saturday Night Live*. Indeed, at one stage, Frost telephoned Idle and suggested he could become the seventh member of the just forming Python team, linking the sketches with jokes and observations. Idle told him to 'Piss off'.

However, whatever the secret feelings and public banter, it remains a fact that without David Frost giving up his contract with John Cleese and enabling him to work with five other writer-performers for the BBC in 1969, we may never have seen *Monty Python's Flying Circus*.

THE FROST REPORT

David Frost, *the* kingpin of television with a huge wealth of talent, rounded up comedy pros from the Oxbridge pool for a new, hip live sketch series (almost the final live comedy show), with the usual suspects from his Cambridge experience joined by Jones and Palin whom Frost had seen performing at the Rehearsal Room, atop The Royal Court. Frost put the major burden on John Cleese – having contracted him in America as major on-screen and writing contributor – and, naturally, Cleese, in turn, roped in his old writing partner Graham Chapman. Crucially important in the development of *Monty Python*, the regular weekly script conferences recruited Cleese, Chapman, Idle, Palin and Jones in the same room at the same time for the first time. Each had bumped into the other over the years and knew of their work via college revues, but by now Cleese was a major comedy star and Palin, meeting him for the first time, was in great awe of this legendary Cambridge figure who had written great material about a chap watching stones, worked on Broadway and done a load of other impressive stuff.

Cleese as performer worked brilliantly with Ronnie Barker and Ronnie Corbett, with the three of them personifying Britain's different classes in the most celebrated satirical sketches included in the shows – written by Marty Feldman and John Law. Cleese, pompous, upper-class and poverty-stricken, Barker, avuncular, middle-class, wealthy but vulgar, and Corbett, timid, lower-class and knowing his place, were visually perfect for the comic ideas. Indeed, the three proved so popular that when the sketches were resurrected for *The Two Ronnies* several years later Cleese happily agreed to repeat his role. Cleese was, of course, the oldest of the *Python* group, indeed, a good four years older than the youngest member, Michael Palin, thus he would lead the meetings and, as a result, became the head of the *Python* family. The productions were organised by the Scot, Jimmy Gilbert, who approached Terry Jones and Michael Palin in 1966, having been impressed by their earlier BBC material. Initially they were restricted to very minor bits and pieces such as Frost's witty ad-libs, although such gems as the karate champion cutting a cake were clear signs of Jones & Palin firing on all cylinders – Barker's chop causing a nearby house to collapse.

By the second series, Jones and Palin were writing *Python*esque party discussions between Cleese and Corbett concerning the rigorous fun of Hendon's exciting lifestyle compared to Cleese's adventurous antics (very Two Rons) while Eric Idle, used to writing on his own, came through his Cambridge experience with acidic genius intact, often collaborating with Tim Brooke-Taylor and even0 Graham Chapman, when Cleese was more preoccupied with performance. Idle's forte was in linear comic discussion, brilliantly crafting Frost's CDMs (Continuous Developing Monologues) and leaving a mark with a Ronnie Barker item

concerning the notion of staggering Christmas to avoid major hassles. With a Peter Cookian obsession with words for words' sake, Idle's comic style was clearly on the way up. The sheer volume of material generated by this army of writers resulted in continually good quality television, with Cleese often pushing for his sub-standard sketches to be vetoed in favour of better stuff from the other writers. Cleese, of all the Pythons, was at the forefront, for his performance work was on live television, often in front of 14 million viewers.

Classic sketches clearly suggest the wonder of *Python* to come: like Matter of Taste, featuring the petulant Cleese as a wine connoisseur opposite Frost's hopelessly inept palette; the grammar-school quiz parody *Top of the Form* borrowed from Cambridge and featuring both authority-edged Cleese and gibbering student Cleese (the wombat/playing wom material); Adventure, with Cleese's intrepid interviewer talking with Frost's insurance salesman (having been led into thinking he would be a deep sea diver – sort of Peter Cook meets John Cleese 1971 vintage) and the over-protective mother smothering her undergraduate son (Cleese) on his return from university.

Frost himself would deliver the links, sounding amazingly like Eric Idle's *Python* persona, feeding the angst-ridden, confident figures of Cleese with nervy characteristics (his 'I once trod on an orange!' during the Adventure interview is pure *Python* nowhere man stuff), a healthy Cook admiration (clearly highlighted in the spiralling Hilton monologue), the Argument sketch influencing Age of Contradiction news report (complete with *Python*esque sex change eye-witness) and the typically Idle moment as a newsreader gets engrossed in a sexual scandal story he's broadcasting, prove that Frost was excellent as both comic sounding board and comic talent scout. The pressures and fund of talent paid off when the show won the Golden Rose of Montreux in 1967 (with *Python*-geared items including the Jones/Palin karate sketch, very Gilliamesque

closing credits and Cleese in authority, church/law, mood) and a second series was commissioned. Frost and Gilbert, aware that the writers were on minuscule salaries, allowed the likes of Palin and Jones (on a mere £14 a week between the two of them) to play minor supporting roles to supplement their earnings, while their writing duties were also enlarged with whole sketches like Judges in a Playground illustrating legal dignitaries letting off steam on the swings and roundabout. At least one classic Cleese/Chapman sketch would crop up each week – notably Goat Skit, String and the legendary Courier Skit, while Idle merrily rolled off Frost's comic monologues by the yard. Cleese fully established his upper-class authoritarian persona with deliciously straight-faced condemnation of dreadful zookeeping on Frost's part (shades of *Fierce Creatures* some 30 years later), a glorious, corrupted, snobbish, grammar school mocking, character assassinating, double-standard schoolmaster embracing a gym constructed by students, ethnic minority baiting and home-made burials, the groanworthy, university-pedigreed, camp copper quickie ('Morning Super/Hello Wonderful!'), *Richard III*-like legal figures and earnest bulletin newsreader with plenty of question-driven shock headlines but no substantial news. It was quickly made clear that Cleese was less imposing in the roles of ineffective, timid police victims and patriotic-questioning anonymous German heroes.

Although the spectre of satire was still in evidence, Frost was quick to realise that the boom had blown over and, thus *The Frost Report* was more about hilarious sketches than putting the world to rights via humour. As an extra cabaret bonus each show would feature a song from Julie Felix. Be honest! The show proved a superb training ground for *Python* and while the *Do Not Adjust Your Set* lads found useful places for earlier rejected sketches, Cleese and Chapman happily incorporated unused Frost material for their first few *Python* contributions.

Did You Know? Unshown in the West Country's TWW Region, Cleese's major involvement in *The Frost Report* went unnoticed by his father who send him a letter saying that Marks & Spencers were looking for a personnel director if the money was getting tight and the career going nowhere. Mind you, by the close of the second series, Cleese, as was his wont, was bored with *The Frost Report*.

The Frost Report 1st series – BBC1 10 March – 9 June 1966 (13 x 30 mins) Authority, Holidays, Sin, Elections, Class, The News, Education, Love, The Law, Leisure, Medicine, Food and Drink, Trends. 2nd series – BBC1 6 April – 29 June 1967 (13 x 30 mins) Money, Women, The Forces, Advertising, Parliament, The Countryside, Industry, Culture, Transport, Crime, Europe, Youth, Show Biz.
Performed by **David Frost, Ronnie Barker, John Cleese, Ronnie Corbett, Sheila Steafel & Julie Felix**. Marty Feldman made chief writer and programme associate by Frostie, overseeing the likes of Barry Cryer, Dick Vosburgh, Neil Shand, Peter Vincent, David McKellar, Tim Brooke-Taylor, Bill Oddie, Tony Hendra, Herbert Kretzner, Keith Waterhouse, John Law, Bob Block, Willis Hall, Peter Tinniswood, Frank Muir, Denis Nodern, Barry Took, Dick Vosburgh, Peter Lewis, Peter Dobereiner, David Nobbs and David Frost himself as well as John Cleese, Graham Chapman, Eric Idle, Michael Palin and Terry Jones.
Music **Dennis Wilson**
Musical director **Harry Babinowitz**
Film editor **Ray Millichope**
Film associate **Jim Franklin**
Graphics **Roy Laughton**
Producer **James Gilbert**

Two record releases gathered the pick of the shows, *The Frost Report On Britain* and *The Frost Report On Everything,* while *Frost Over England,* a special 30-minute television compilation, was broadcast on BBC1, 26 March 1967. Linked by new Frost/Anthony Jay material and featuring Cleese/Corbett/Barker

performing the class sketch, this won the Montreux Gold Rose in 1967. The final flurry of *Frost Report* action was a 40-minute festive edition, *Frost Over Christmas* which appeared on 26 December 1967, although the format was happily reworked for the ITV company Rediffusion as *The Frost Programme.* Actually on-air smack between the two seasons of *The Frost Report* this ran from 19 October 1966 until 4 January 1967 and also featured Corbett, Barker and John Cleese. Regular *Frost Report* writer Michael Palin replaced Cleese as on-screen comic support for *Frost On Sunday,* making its debut on the first Sunday of broadcasting under the new LWT banner. Despite suffering from the strike that affected *We Have Ways of Making You Laugh* (with Idle/Gilliam), Head of Light Entertainment Frank Muir acted as floor manager to drag the project through. Again Ronnies Corbett and Barker were in the cast, along with Josephine Tewson, with the first series, broadcast 4 August 1968 to 5 January 1969. 23 episodes of 50 minutes, lead to series 2 from 4 January to 29 March 1970 (not 8 March), with 12 episodes of 50 mins.

FULL CIRCLE

The third and biggest Palin travelogue encompassed ten episodes and a journey through Alaska, Siberia, Japan, Korea, Vietnam, Philippines, Malaysia, Java, Australia and New Zealand. The show's working title was *Palin's Pacific,* while old cohort Eric Idle suggested the programme should be broadcast as *Palin's Rim.* The opening episode, bumbling through Alaska and into Russia, encompasses all sorts of treasures, whether it be the sight of territorial bears, a vain search for reindeers or a healthy meal of fish soup with vodka, but the indelible highlight was Palin's passion rendition of a Russian marching song, comically continuing after his helpful chorus stop with booming delivery and made-up features. Delights in the oriental include hilariously split drink coupled

with typical British niceties, a long over-due meeting with Japan's biggest *Python* fan (sporting an I Love Michael Palin T-Shirt), some thought-provoking comment on man's inhumanity to man (the 1945 bomb/Korean war), Zen meditation questioning and some pretty Zen-like antics in a mock Holland. The poignant memories and modern cruelty of Vietnam were set in stark contrast with Palin's Beauty contest judging and *Wind in the Willows* references. Palin effortlessly continued to demystify remote foreign travel via bumbling Britishness. Another major BBC worldwide smash with video and book sales soaring into the charts but by the end Palin's sight seeing ventures seemed to have allowed the profitable horse to be flogged to death.

Did You Know?
There were plans to feature John Cleese in a gag spot, quietly reading a newspaper in the middle of nowhere and exchanging a brief greeting with his fellow Python.
Episode one was planned for 31 August 1997 on BBC1 but the tragic death of Diana, Princess of Wales touched the nation and dominated the communication airwaves. Palin's show was screened on BBC2, repeated again on BBC1 the following Sunday and re-run on 7 September. After all that travelling Palin still maintains his favourite places are the west coasts of Ireland and Scotland.

Full Circle written and presented by **Michael Palin**
Photography **Nigel Meakin**
Sound **Fraser Howell**
Production Assistant **Jane Sayers**
Post-production **Vincent Narduzzo & Marc Eskenazi**
Editor **David Thomas**
Series producer **Clem Vallance**
Director **Roger Mills**
A Prominent Television Production for the BBC
7 September–9 November 1997, 10x50 mins

FUNNY GAME, FOOTBALL

A rare comedy football album preceding Frank Skinner and David Baddiel by 20 years and performed by a mystic collection of talents billed as The Group. Among their number were character actors Arthur Mullard and Bryan Pringle, cartoonist Bill Tidy and a couple of Pythons – Michael Palin and Terry Jones. Highlights include Terry Jones as the whining woman facing the football converting skills of *The Missionary*, a very *Python*esque quiz show with Palin asking Jones' nervy contestant barrel-loads of football trivia and I Remember It Well, a wistful discussion about football glories past between Palin and Jones. Funny Game, Football – Piraeus Football Club, Crunch!, Rangers Abroad, An Open Letter to George Best, The Missionary, Sir Alf Speaks, World War III, Newsnight with Coleman, Soccer Laureate, Bower Boys, Scilly Season, Government Policies, I Remember It Well, Floor's the Limit, Director's Song, Blackbury Town, A Joke

Starring **TERRY JONES, MICHAEL PALIN, ARTHUR MULLARD, BRYAN PRINGLE, BILL TIDY, JOE STEEPLES** and **MICHAEL WALE** as The Group
Written by **Joe Steeples, Bill Tidy & Michael Wale**
Music by **Neil Innes**
Charisma Perspective CS4/EP
Charisma CB 197 – 1972

G.B.H.

Along with Dennis Potter's *The Singing Detective*, G.B.H. can rightly claim to be the most powerful piece of television drama of the last 25 years. Any review could never do full justice to such a towering, thought-provoking programme – it's simply one of those things you must watch. Basically tackling the corrupted, champagne socialist ideal of Liverpool, the 11-hour marathon of emotion boils down to the fundamental battle between two people – the embodiment of super cool, well off 'new labour' in Robert Lindsay and the working class, determined face of the people in Michael Palin. There are many fascinating elements along the way but the tension, dramatic power, nerve-wracking assault and twisting mind games that build up between the two are electric.

Wallowing in Potteresque obsession with childhood memories and misunderstood guilty secrets, Lindsay's controlled face covers a haunted imagination, put-upon past and disturbed spectre of supposed insanity. Palin, dealing with a mental problem during this jobless, partyless mid-life crisis, consulting Jean Anderson and disturbing his doctor with a massive list of imaginary aliments, calming himself down with hand grips and wandering round the place in a naked daze, highlights the embarrassing reality of insanity. Clearly, these two opposing elements of working-class/moneyed socialist ideals are very close. Again, as in Potter, the power of the thought is important, with Lindsay's honest, cloth-capped, true labour figure continually reflecting himself onto the stylised and stylish world of 1990s politics where memories of Harold Wilson are mocked and cold power is hurled into the realm of mob rule. The question of class is mocked and revealed as cancerous; more lightweight examinations of better low position are embraced (note the cheeky reference to Willy Russell's *Educating Rita* and the casting of Julie Walters as Lindsay's dysfunctional mother) and the supporting cast is universally exemplary. Of special note is Jimmy Mulville's nervy, spineless researcher, William Gaunt's brilliantly controlled episode one cameo dismissing the ludicracy of the new system (his petulant line concerning the four Ns in his name is a masterpiece). David Ross who shines as the poetry spouting, tortured, worn figure of old-fashioned education. Michael Angelis turns in a typical but vibrant performance as the adulterous bohemian and John Sharpnel goes out in a burst of misunderstood fury. The starry guest spots include mysterious girl from the past, Lindsay Duncan and bombastic, military-geared and wonderfully eccentric Daniel Massey who enliven the proceedings, but it's Palin and Lindsay that carry this milestone series. Lindsay's is the more showy of the two roles, falling from status of media darling to babbling embarrassment, with unforgettable nervous arm jerks getting ever more pronounced and wallowing deep in Daleks, Tom Bakers and sea devils at the infamous hotel *Dr. Who* convention.

But Palin, the lone voice against blanket strike madness, battling to protect his special needs children, delivers a subtle, slowly building characterisation of purity. He lapses into Milliganesque to entertain his Henley Street pupils with lashings of funny voices, putting on his Peter Falk private eye act, masking his feelings in front of the kids with manic, back to front jacketed foreigner science explanation and defusing the tense basketball based meeting with Lindsay with music trivia (*16 Tons* – Tennessee Ernie Ford). Comedy is used to sharpen the brutality of this story. The children love him (poignantly giving him an Ella Fitzgerald album which later comes in very handy), his emotion at the loss of a pupil and his gradual wearing down of Lindsay highlights strong character and determination – where Palin's interest is the community Lindsay frets about his hair loss. Palin is little England, taking on the tide of capitalism, where he denies tension with a cup of tea. His calm put-downs to gutter journalists and his steely gaze as the approaching might of Lindsay's avenging angel parts the picket line like the Red sea marks this out as Palin's most valuable acting performance. He captures the paradox of Jim Nelson perfectly, strong in public – weak in private, with his continual feet washing, cupboard antics (the silent realisation that he is not alone is almost *Python*esque before the angst-ridden outburst) and fear of crossing bridges shows the man of courage crumbling from within. The holiday interlude, with kindred spirit Daniel Massey, embraces pure drama and hilarity – with nightmarish fire imagery, panicked hiding of photographic evidence and a Dick Barton-styled car chase ending in religious misunderstanding, but the programme's most powerful moment is the final confrontation between Palin and Lindsay.

The entire plot has been building up to this moment, back in the traditional labour club where Palin can shine and Lindsay collapse. Palin's impassioned speech, condemning the crowd for reading just one book and following the Mob instinct, is peerlessly performed – almost doing for Britain what Kevin Costner did for America in *JFK* – and earning himself the powerful last image, a triumph of jazz music, lighting and self-confident performance. The heart of the script is in Palin's performance, but the dramatic height has to be the subdued two-hander between the protagonists in the club toilet just before the showdown. Lindsay and Palin are both victims, both anger and embittered. Compassion is displayed and the whole concept of the drama is captured with quiet restraint. For me, it's the greatest moment in the programme and one of the most compelling pieces of television acting you could wish to see. This is a masterpiece.

G.B.H. – 1. It Couldn't Happen Here
2. Only Here On A Message
3. Send A Message To Michael
4. Message Sent
5. Message Received
6. Message Understood
7. Over and Out

Did You Know? Despite the violence involved the title *G.B.H.* actually stands for Great British Holiday – there are two, Palin's family chalet and Julia Walters' at the seaside. Alan

Bleasdale originally wanted Michael Palin to play the part of Michael Murray. Ultimately the powerhouse role went to Lindsay with Palin happily tackling the complex emotions of Jim Nelson. Considered a very brave and commendable piece of casting at the time – this was Palin's first dramatic role – Bleasdale explained that ever since he had seen the Dead Parrot sketch he saw the serious acting potential in Palin's eyes.

G.B.H. (Films) Ltd for Channel Four
Michael Murray **ROBERT LINDSAY**
Jim Nelson **MICHAEL PALIN**
Mrs. Murray **JULIA WALTERS**
Barbara Douglas **LINDSAY DUNCAN**
Grosvenor **DANIEL MASSEY**
Mr. Weller **DAVID ROSS**
Minders **JOHN HENSHAW, AL BRIERLEY & SEAN NAUGHTON**
Teddy **ALAN IGBON**
Young Michael Murray **STEPHEN HALL**
Eileen Critchley **JANE DAWSON**
Schoolmistress **DEE ORR**
Caretakers **BERT GAUNT & DAVID SCASE**
Franky Murray **PHILIP WHITCHURCH**
Peter **ANDREW SCHOFIELD**
Monica **AYESA TOURE**
Stan **JAMES TOMLINSON**
Red Neck Councillor **NORMAN MILLS**
Joseph Cartwright **CLIFF HOWELLS**
Terry **PAUL BUTTERWORTH**
Hunningdon **WILLIAM GAUNT**
Young Barbara **MICHELLE ATKINSON**
Judge Critchley **CLIFFORD ROSE**
Miss Hutchinson **SERENA HARRAGIN**
Two-Bouncers **IAIN ORMSBY-KNOX**
Robby Burns **DANIEL STREET-BROWN**
Geoff **BILL STEWART**
Black Waiter **JAKE ABRAHAMS**
Diane Niarchos **JULIA ST. JOHN**
Laura Nelson **DEARBHLA MOLLOY**
Martin Niarchos **MICHAEL ANGELIS**
Dr. Jacobs **JOHN SHRAPNEL**
Mervyn Sloan **PAUL DANEMAN**
Lou Barnes **TOM GEORGESON**
Joey Thug **PAUL OLDHAM**
Billy Thug **GARY MAVERS**
Macker Thug **WAYNE FOSKETT**
Scrawny Thug **CHRIS HARGREAVES**
Fifth Thug **CARL BARRY**
Joel **IAN HARTLEY**
McKenzie **CHRISTOPHER HALLIDAY**
Bubbles **PETER-HUGO DALY**
Bubbles' Friend **STEVE HALLIWELL**
Philip the Researcher **JIMMY**

MULVILLE
Presenter **JIM POPE**
Conservative Speaker **TONY BROUGHTON**
Conservative Aid **JOHN CAPPS**
Radio Journalist **PETER FAULKNER**
Susan Nelson **ANNA FRIEL**
Jessica Nelson **HAYLEY FAIRCLOUGH**
Mark Nelson **EDWARD MALLON**
Frank Twist **COLIN DOUGLAS**
Michael Murray Snr **NIALL TOIBIN**
Proacher Terry **DAVID NICHOLLS**
Poacher Vic **FREDDIE FLETCHER**
Grandfather Burns **ARTHUR SPRECKLEY**
Mr. Burns **PETER ARMITAGE**
Punk **VINCENT KEANE**
Sylvia **DEBRA GILLETT**
Dr. Goldup **JEAN ANDERSON**
Distinguished Gent **WILLIAM FRANKLYN**
Teenager **SHARON MUIRCROFT**
Schoolchildren **OLDHAM THEATRE WORKSHOP**
Screenplay by **Alan Bleasdale**
Photography **Peter Jessop**
Camera operator **John Maskall**
Editors **Anthony Ham & Oral Norrie Ottey**
Assistant directors **Chris Newman, Tim Vine & Peter Deakin**
Production manager **Caroline Hewitt**
Art director **Andrew Rothschild**
Music **Richard Harvey & Elvis Costello**
'The Love Song of J Alfred Prufrock' & 'The Waste Land' by **T.S. Eliot**
Designer **Martyn Herbert**
Executive producer **Verity Lambert**
Producers **David Jones & Alan Bleasdale**
Director **Robert Young**
6 June–18 July 1991 – seven shows, Channel Four, 11 hours

GEORGE OF THE JUNGLE

The big Disney movie for Christmas 1997. John Cleese adds some comic class to this live action resurrection of the 1960s cartoon. The humour falls somewhere between Tarzan Escapes and Carry on Up the Jungle.

Walt Disney Pictures./Mandeville Films
Voice of an ape **JOHN CLEESE**
Director Sam Weisman
Cert U 93 mins

TERRY GILLIAM

Born 22 November 1940, Medicine Lake, Minneapolis, Minnesota, Terry Vance Gilliam was educated at Birmingham High School, showing skill at an early age in drawing by amusing himself and family with strange alien figures. His father was a travelling salesman for Folger's Coffee, later becoming a carpenter. Terry had one sister (born 1942) and one brother (born 1950) – now a detective with the L.A. Police Department. Gilliam entered Occidental College as a Physics Major, but after six weeks decided this was not for him and opted for a more helpful career move as an Arts Major. However, due to an instant dislike of the art history professors, Gilliam changed once more, becoming a Political Science Major and finally graduating with this degree. His career ideas were also a case of chop and change, harbouring a desire to be either a film director or an architect.

A summer job in an architect's office during his College days put paid to the latter idea, while an early interest in drawing cartoons saw his keenest interest channelled into the magazine *Fang*. Originally established as a poetry appreciation publication, Gilliam and a bunch of pals reinvented the college magazine and injected subversive comedy into the bored life of a talented student. During his senior year, Gilliam became editor of *Fang*, happily ripping off the style of Harvey Kurtzman's *Help!* magazine and eventually sending him copies of his work. While the Brit-based Pythons were worshipping *The Goon Show*, Gilliam's formative years were obsessed with Kurtzman's influential comic book *Mad* and both his writing and drawing work predominantly reflected this.

An encouraging letter from his hero persuaded Gilliam to abandon a depressing career in an advertising agency and journey to New York after his graduation. He walked straight into the job of assistant editor for *Help!* Although animation was far from his mind, the comic

A stunning Terry publicity pose – note the *Life of Brian* poster

invention displayed in his work was biting, black and, above all, very funny. Crucially, it was during work on *Help!* that Gilliam met John Cleese for the first time, but the magazine eventually folded, Gilliam toured round Europe for about six months and eventually returned to New York, broke, jobless and staying in Kurtzman's attic. Moving back to New York, Gilliam found employment as a freelance illustrator on comics like *Surftoons* and a book with Joel Siegel, *The Cocktail People*. Siegel was working at the Carson Roberts advertising agency and got Gilliam a job there too, working alongside Stan Freberg's comedy-embracing ex-writing partner. Hired as copy-writer and art director, Gilliam was given a fairly free hand, although the constraints of office life soon took their toll, and he was reduced to working on dodgy advertising promos for Universal's poverty row film output. Gilliam lasted with the firm for a matter of months before his English girlfriend and his own wanderlust dragged him to London. Arriving in 1967 Gilliam found a footing as a freelance illustrator (contributing material to the comic book *Car-Toons*) and art director on *London Life* although he was fast becoming disillusioned with the magazine rat trap and called on

his only British television contact, John Cleese, for help. Cleese introduced Gilliam to producer Humphrey Barclay (who would go on to produce *Doctor in the House*) involved in 1967 on a little programme entitled *Do Not Adjust Your Set* with Michael Palin, Terry Jones and Eric Idle. Indeed, Barclay, having initially bought two sketches off the animator, even wrote a letter keeping Gilliam out of the American Army while he worked on the show. With the landmark piece Elephants, Gilliam found his niche with cut-out animation, grabbing influence and indeed raw material from the great masters. If inspiration wasn't forthcoming Gilliam would journey to The National Gallery and plunder images from heroes like Albert Dürer, Doré and Bronzino's *Venus and Cupid* – the foot of Cupid becoming the icon for a *Python* generation. However, Gilliam's non-judgmental appreciation of artistic imagery found him equally at home rummaging through the pages of 1920s Sears and Roebuck catalogues to create the most potent 'look' of *Monty Python* comedy. He had an airbrush technique which, in combination with his deliciously warped sense of humour, created twisted versions of 'cherished images'. Gilliam was the missing link which fused *Python* as a unit and, uniquely, was given total control over his animations. The others would provide the closing idea for an often uncompleted sketch and the beginning of the next one, and, as often as not, Gilliam would turn up with a can of film, camera ready for insertion into the episode. His best and most violently funny material came from sitting at his desk, pent-up with frustration and weariness, at two or three in the morning, while the various sound effects either came from the cheesy BBC library or Gilliam himself. Indeed, the only connection his five cohorts had with the work was quickly recorded voice-overs (and sometimes script suggestions while recording them), although they never saw the rough animation work and could only judge when the reels were screened at around 3 o'clock on the day of studio recording. The most independent of the group, even his work was sometimes tampered with – notably when Gilliam and Jones had put an episode to bed and director MacNaughton shortened his beloved elongated, unstopping tree animation breaking through the skyline into space. Gilliam's animation was heavily influenced by the anarchic American television comedy of Ernie Kovacs and he found delicious potential in the twisting of cinematic convention in Buster Keaton's *Sherlock Jnr* which he first saw at a 1960s revival in New York. Gilliam's vision was the over-riding binding force which kept the British genius of *Python* together.

His *Python* exposure worked as a major springboard for other assignments, notably impressing Marty Feldman, who incorporated his work into *Marty* and subsequently retained him to create the title sequence for *The Marty Feldman Comedy Machine*. Gilliam also worked on the titles for Vincent Price's *Cry of the Banshee* and an ABC television *After-School Special* on Shakespeare entitled *William*. Eventually he resurrected his *Python* greats for a book, *Animations of Mortality*, and the film *And Now For Something Completely Different*, for

which Alexander Walker noted in his *Evening Standard* review that the animator is 'Always best when he draws blood'. *Python* made Gilliam wealthy, so he surrounded himself with priceless images by Dalí, Max Ernst and his favourite artist, Bosch, and living in a handsome Highgate Heights Victorian house with his wife, make-up expert Maggie (married in 1973), who had worked on *Python*, and daughter Amy Rainbow (born 1977). Holly Dubois (who appears in *Brazil*) was born in October 1980 and Gilliam's son, Harry Thunder, followed in May 1988.

Python also gave him an opportunity to direct films, co-working with Terry Jones on *Monty Python and the Holy Grail* and graduating to his scatological movie solo debut *Jabberwocky* for Sandy Lieberson – Gilliam had turned down his offer to direct the Beatles-cover laden documentary *All This and World War II*. Following *Jabberwocky* Gilliam pushed for his script of *The Ministry*, later to become *Brazil*, and toiled with a fantasy idea called *The Minotaur*. With no takers showing interest Gilliam tried for a commercial children's adventure film, roped in Michael Palin to add a lighter touch to his grotesque obsessions and whacko – *Time Bandits*. The fantasy trilogy, young boy – *Time Bandits*, young man – *Brazil*, old man – *The Adventures of Baron Munchausen* provided Gilliam the director/writer with major hassles with narrow-minded studio heads and astronomical budgets. He thought about roping in Michael Palin to add something to his conception about the Minotaur and began planning a film version of the DC comic *The Watchmen* for producer Joel Silver (written by Alan Moore and Sam Hamm it would tap into the dark underbelly of American comics à la Tim Burton's *Batman*, although its projected December 1990 release never came).

Eventually, he broke his golden rule of only directing his own scripts (which had seen him decline both *Enemy Mine* and *The Princess Bride* following the success of *Time Bandits*) and accepted the

comparatively easy option of simply directing a Hollywood-based movie. No writing, no Pythons, just Gilliam directing – *The Fisher King* proved enjoyable and successful. In 1992 Gilliam was planning a remake of *A Connecticut Yankee in King Arthur's Court* but this project came to naught and 1994 saw him finally signed up to direct Bruce Willis in the futuristic nightmare of *Twelve Monkeys*. A mega-success which allowed Gilliam studio money, total artistic freedom (within reason) and the muted chance to direct European arthouse style within the big budget commercial cinema world, he was suddenly hot news with aborted and toted projects including *The Defective Detective* (in the Gilliam mind since at least 1989) with Nicholas Cage, *Down and Out in Las Vegas* with Johnny Depp, *The Trial* a very promising sci-fi Western with Bruce Willis and even the long awaited *Time Bandits II*.

GOODBYE AGAIN

An ill-fated attempt by ATV to resurrect the comedy magic of Peter Cook and Dudley Moore in *Not Only... But Also*. Despite pure class from the headliners, these hour-long shows were bolstered by big name music guest stars to rocket the series into the American market. Sadly, despite guests like Donovan, Ike and Tina Turner, Anne Bancroft, Mel Torme and Warren Mitchell, the series lasted only four episodes. Show three guest starred John Cleese. 14 September 1968 – with Taffic, John Wells and Rodney Bewes. Colour

THE GOODIES

Totally brilliant BBC series of surreal comedy from Tim Brooke-Taylor, Graeme Garden and Bill Oddie which is every bit as inventive and important as a certain *Monty Python's Flying Circus*. Although hardly as universally influential as *Monty Python*, *The Goodies*, with a unique mix of outrageous visual humour, brilliant team chemistry and Oddie's fab music, created a cult favourite which lasted throughout the 1970s on BBC television. Travelling the same route to fame as Chapman and Cleese – Cambridge Footlights, *I'm Sorry I'll Read That Again*, *At Last the 1948 Show*, *Doctor in the House*, *How to Irritate People* – The *Goodies* made their last series for the Corporation in 1980, transferred to ITV for just six episodes over 1981/82 and eventually joined forces again for narration on children's favourites *Bananaman* (including subversive subtext along the way) and Billy Bunter on BBC radio. Naturally there was great rivalry between the Pythons and the Goodies (note the disgruntled reaction to five Gumby clones and the *Python* theme in the 1975 show *Scatty Safari*), although following the departure of John Cleese from the *Monty Python* television shows and a belated new series of *I'm Sorry I'll Read That Again* reuniting Cleese with Brooke-Taylor and Oddie in 1973, it was only natural that this battling banter should be incorporated into *The Goodies*. Thus, in a show that ranks alongside the all-time great *Goodies* episodes like *Kitten Kong* and *Earthanasia*, John Cleese guest-starred in the Christmas 1973 special, *The Goodies and the Beanstalk*. This 45-minute special boasts Alfie Bass as the tiny bellowing giant, the dog rendition of *Anything you can do*, the over-sized geese depositing golden eggs, the homage to Hitchcock's *The Birds*, the Goodies performing *Who Wants to be a Millionaire* while impersonating the Marx Brothers and Eddie Waring's hilarious self-parody of *It's A Knock-Out*. Just when you think it's all over, John Cleese has his moment. Down and out, Timbo desperately tries to flog his empty bean tin, embraces another load of panto conventions by giving the old object a rub and with a burst of smoke and of familiar Sousa, a turbaned Cleese, in BBC announcer gear, begins with 'And Now For Something...' just before Tim gives him a filthy look and mutters 'Push off!' With outlandish facial expression Cleese has his revenge with a forceful comment on *The Goodies* with 'Kids' programme!' before vanishing. Brooke-Taylor

clasps his hand over the freshly imprisoned Genie Cleese, much to the delight of Garden, and the final credits roll. Class stuff.

The Goodies and the Beanstalk
Starring **TIM BROOKE-TAYLOR GRAEME GARDEN**
and **BILL ODDIE, ALFIE BASS, EDDIE WARING, JOHN CLEESE, CORBETT WOODALL, ROBERT BRIDGES, MARCELLE SAMETT, TONI HARRIS, HELLI LOUISE, MARTY SWIFT, ARTHUR ELLIS**
Written by **Graeme Garden** and **Bill Oddie** with Tim Brooke-Taylor's biro
Animal trainer **Michael Culling**
Music **Bill Oddie** and **Michael Gibbs**
Costumes **Rupert Jarvis**
Make-up **Jan Harrison & Lyn De Winne**
Visual effects **John Horton**
Design **John Stout**
Sound recording **Bill Wild**
Dubbing mixer **Peter Lodge**
Lighting cameraman **Alan Featherstone**
Camera operator **Ian Pugsley**
Film editor **Ron Pope**
Producer **Jim Franklin**
Broadcast 24 December 1973

THE GRAND KNOCKOUT TOURNAMENT

...or, is this the end of the monarchy as we know it? Often blamed for starting the downfall, allowing the fun-loving youngsters a free hand to try for victory and hardly play the British game, this is a manic final celebration of *Knockout* insanity. John Cleese and Michael Palin were roped in to join in the fun and games and both were interviewed by Hal Linden for the American transmission of the programme (12 August). A Royal charity special of the beloved *It's A Knock-Out* featured Cleese throwing food at Palin as he tries to cross a slippery pole above water in The ASDA Marathon and a spot of manic jousting. Most of the other games reflected the heavy advertising sponsorship for the Save the Children Fund, with McDonalds restaurants, Canada Life Assurance Lovers, Harrods, King of the Castle, The

Britannia Building Society Cooks played along with Call Out the Guard, The Ghost of Alton Towers, Knock A Knight, King of the Castle and The Uninvited Guest. Organised by Prince Edward and held in Alton Towers the other Royals going for the common touch were Princess Anne, and the Duke and Duchess of York. Andrew's Green team included Michael Palin with John Travolta, Judy Simpson, Sharon MacPeake, Fiona Fullerton, Anneka Rice, Steve Podborski, Nigel Mansell, George Lazenby, Ian Charleston, Gary Lineker and Griff Rhys Jones, while Cleese joined Christopher Reeve, Tessa Sanderson, Sarah Hardcastle, Kiri Te Kanawa, Toyah Wilcox, Steve Cram, Barry McGuigan, Eddy Grant, Peter Blake, Nicholas Lyndhurst and Duncan Goodhew in Edward's Yellow team. Other celebs included Meat Loaf, Tom Jones, Jackie Stewart and Kevin Kline – joining the two Pythons just prior to filming *A Fish Called Wanda*. Les Dawson and Su Pollard provided some fun on the sidelines, Rowan Atkinson and Barbara Windsor oversaw the event as Lord and Lady Knock – Yes! – while Cleese's anti-British US interview explained that the nation is allowed one silly day before returning to depressed and rather disorganised lives – *Wanda* here we come!

Games designer **Stuart Furber**
Producer **Alan Walsh**
Director **Geoffrey C. D. Wilson & Martin Hughes**
BBC1 North West in association with Knockout Ltd
19 June 1987

THE GREAT MUPPET CAPER

Following John Cleese's enjoyable guest appearance on *The Muppet Show* it was only natural that he would embrace the endearing creature again for this, their second big screen outing. A good friend of co-creator Frank Oz, Cleese agreed to a typically Cleesian role as a pompous and distinguished, gloriously stereotypical upper-crust British characterisation. Completing his work in a day and a half, Basil Fawlty terminology was resurrected with the casting of *Communication Problems* actress Joan Sanderson as his wife.

Universal Pictures
Starring **THE MUPPETS**
Neville **JOHN CLEESE**
Nicky Holiday **CHARLES GRODIN**
Lady Holiday **DIANA RIGG**
Dorcas **JOAN SANDERSON**
Guest starring **ROBERT MORLEY, PETER USTINOV & JACK WARDEN**
Screenplay by **Tom Patchett, Jay Tarses, Jerry Juhl & Jack Rose**
Photography **Oswald Morris**
Music **Joe Raposo**
Production designer **Harry Lange**
Producers **David Lazer & Frank Oz**
Director **Jim Henson**
97 mins, 1981

GREAT RAILWAYS JOURNEYS OF THE WORLD

A passionate man when it comes to traditional railways, Michael Palin was the ideal guest host of this endearing BBC celebration of the age of rail class. *Confessions Of A Train-Spotter* is the fascinating journey from Euston Station to Kyle of Lochalsh, Scotland via The National Railway Museum, incorporating travel by steam locomotive, Intercity and The Flying Scotsman. For the fourth show of seven broadcast in this first series, Palin was phoned out of the blue by director Ken Stephinson following a comment on a radio interviewer explaining that the train was his favourite form of transport. Palin's was the last show to be commissioned and assigned a host – the only British-based journey in the series but the most engaging.
Written & hosted by **Michael Palin**
Series Producer **Roger Laughton**
Producer **Ken Stephinson**
BBC2, Broadcast 27 November 1980

This first railway journey was instrumental in ultimately landing Palin his massive round-the-world assignment so he was more than willing to return over 15 years later for another British-based trip from

Derry to Kerry. Though it was a mere jaunt compared to his other epic adventures, Palin managed to contrast the beauty of steam with uncompromising observations about the Irish troubles and a heartfelt search for evidence of his grandmother who fled to England to escape the potato famine. A delightful old buffer with a hilarious goat story, a dignified Lord engine driver, Harley Davidson owners (complete with a Sid Vicious bike), rock 'n' rolling vicars, impromptu limericks, a spot of road bowling and an inspired word of wisdom from authoress Molly Keene all add to a priceless steam journey across the country.

Written & presented by **Michael Palin**
Photography **Nigel Meakin**
Executive producer **David Taylor**
Produced & directed by **Ken Stephinson**
1993

THE HAMSTER FACTOR AND OTHER TALES OF TWELVE MONKEYS

Extensive and totally essential 'Making of...' documentary for Terry Gilliam's *Twelve Monkeys*. This is arguably the most complete and engrossing behind scenes production you could wish for (and, hey, I've seen a lot of 'Making of...' documentaries). From the moment when Gilliam officially signs the contract to direct the movie, to post-production, critics' reaction and the opening night, everything is included and discussed in a programme that almost rivals the running time of the film it is addressing. The major delight, of course, is the extensive interview footage with Gilliam himself, scanning the scope of total excitement (in animated, enthused discussion with Bruce Willis) to total despair (in the aftermath of a near

fatal horse-riding accident and seeing the film spiral into chaos). Like a resplendent Orson Welles figure, this artistic genius struggles to find common ground with the Hollywood villainy to create a piece of intelligent work with star name quality.
Willis works through the project with directorial ideas of his own, shocked when certain scenes he loved are supposedly questioned and ultimately bonding with the malevolent director when Gilliam calls his bluff – knowing full well that a collection of scenes were played flat and lifeless because Willis wasn't happy with their set-up. From that knowing look between them both it's clear that this is a two-way attack on both cinematic language and redefining Willis's screen persona. There's some fascinating studio material, the video ball problem being a key example, some excellent, penetrating interviews with producer Chuck Avelon, co-producer Lloyd Phillips and editor Mike Audsley, while avoiding in-depth story discussion with the stars in favour of hands-on, fly-on-wall observation of the actors at work. Willis fully moulds his character, Stowe happily goes along with Gilliam's vision and there's a powerful look at Pitt learning the madness mannerisms with hand-clapping, slapping and violent room pacing.
Where this scores over other 'making of' productions is its detailed autopsy of the film – allowing Gilliam, warts and all, to react to press reviews and look quizzically at his David Letterman introduction of 'Hollywood visionary' with a mixture of amazement and disgust. The Washington preview audience material is, perhaps, the most poignant, with reactions seemingly very good in complete contrast to the filled out reaction cards that the director, the producer, writers and editor take on board. Gilliam's heartfelt 'They hate the movie!' gets no reaction save pitiful looks of helplessness but, thank God, he sticks to his guns and releases the film with only minor cuts. The Alan Smithee signed sketch, depressed, anti-film reaction to his career and mood

swings all somehow soak into Gilliam's work and go a long way to making him the most imaginative director around. To cap all this wonderful stuff, there's even an early, *Monty Python*-inspired animation sequence detailing the Hollywood hassles involved with *Brazil* and the *Baron* which perfectly, quickly and hilariously sets up the story. A flawless examination of a great motion picture in production.

A Low Key Production
Original score **John Benskin**
Executive producer **Alan Glazer**
Associate producers **Lucy Darwin & Lisabeth Fouse**
Assistant editor **Cheryl Hess**
Narrator **Keith Fulton**
Camera & Sound, edited, produced, written & directed by **Keith Fulton & Louis Pepe**
87 mins, 1995

GEORGE HARRISON

The Harrison/*Python* link is extensive and important, spanning back a lot further than you might think. The first connection with the legendary musical force and the *Monty Python* members came in an episode of *No, that's Me Over There*, a situation comedy penned by Eric Idle starring Ronnie Barker. In one show Idle made an on-screen appearance in hippie, trippy guise and the piece of music used to illustrate his cool, right-on persona was *Baby You're A Rich Man* by The Beatles, with Harrison on harmony vocals and tambourine. Indeed, while the early work of the team members was inspirational to The Beatles in film, the format of 1965's *Help!* was certainly reflected in the later structure of *Monty Python*. Most tangible of all is the direct use of John Lennon's shovelling waiter from *Magical Mystery Tour* seen in John Cleese's shovelling waiter in *Monty Python's The Meaning of Life*. The emergence of *Monty Python* in 1969 helped get Harrison through the madness and media backbiting surrounding the Beatles split, and he was quoted as saying that 'The only thing worth getting

out of bed for is *Monty Python's Flying Circus*'. In the aftermath of the greatest group of all-time split, Harrison longed for a rest from the embittered wrangling, hoping for a breakthrough of the legal binds and a chance to unite The Beatles, The Bonzo Dog Doo Dah Band and the *Monty Python* team for rock 'n' roll comedy sessions. That pipe-dream, alas, never came together, although the basic seed saw semi-fruition with the 1975 *Rutland Christmas Special* which recruited one member from each of those groups. George Harrison, Neil Innes and Eric Idle. Harrison and Idle had met the previous year when Eric and Terry Gilliam travelled to America to promote *Monty Python and the Holy Grail* chatting with the ex-Beat backstage at the Director's Guild in Los Angeles after a screening of the film.

The result was a firm friendship between Harrison and Idle leading to a high profile guest-starring turn on *Christmas with Rutland Weekend Television*. The sessions were legendary, with Idle drunk for most of the recording and George continually wanting to perform *The Pirate Song*, in a clever reverse of the celeb's yearning for respectability on *Morecambe and Wise*. In one of Idle's favourite gags, Harrison the Rock God appears on stage in stunning white robes and cool dude style, begins the spine-tingling guitar riff intro to *My Sweet Lord* and crusades into *The Pirate Song*. It's excellent stuff and the lyrics for the pirate ditty feature in all their splendour in *The Illustrated Songs Of George Harrison* – credited as an Idle/Harrison composition. Following Harrison's problematic attempts to perform *The Pirate Song* on *RWT* it was only fitting that for Eric Idle's first appearance on *Saturday Night Live* in October 1976 his performance of Harrison's *Here Comes the Sun* was interrupted by the cast.
Also in 1976, Idle, who had practically directed the *Rutland* episodes, was invited by Harrison to direct his two promotional films for singles from the *33 1/3* album. The Beatles had started the trend of

videos as far back as 1966's *Paperback Writer/Rain* and Harrison continued the practice – Idle organised and directed the films over a three-day shoot, brought in familiar *Rutland* people for support and presented Harrison's songs *Crackerbox Palace* and *True Love*. Idle even contributed funny voices to Harrison's classic single *This Song* – dealing with the legal wrangle over the *My Sweet Lord/He's So Fine* similarities – screeching 'Could be Sugar Pie Honey Bunch' and 'No sounds like Rescue Me!' with *Python*esque delight. The following album, *Extra Texture*, also featured contributions from Idle who willingly did radio spots in England for the album promotion. Harrison returned the favour when he donned Mountie gear and appeared on stage with the *Python*s during their *Lumberjack* finale at New York's City Centre – he was hardly recognised by any of the audience. In 1973 Harrison produced the single release of Michael Palin's weather forecast version of *The Lumberjack Song*.
Eric Idle's fascination with The Beatles impact stretched back to his Lennon-McCartney styled Hallelujah chorus which was used by Cleese, Chapman and the like for the Broadway presentation of Cambridge Circus. During *Rutland Weekend Television*, Neil Innes had penned the Beatlesque song *I Must Be In Love* and inspired Idle to create The Rutles. A huge hit when screened in the Beatles-geared, Idle-hosted *Saturday Night Live*, a UK/US feature film co-production was the result in 1978. The sweetest joke of all was Harrison's willingness to make a return to his own slightly warped past with a cameo as an ageing man interviewing Michael Palin. Clearly enjoying these regular interludes from guitarist hero to comic guest star, Harrison was distressed when Idle informed him that owing to EMI's withdrawal of finance the new *Monty Python* film would not be made. Harrison loved the script, loved the Pythons and wanted to see the movie – the cliché saw Harrison buy the dearest cinema ticket in history, put up the money for production and

establish the hugely successful HandMade Films to make *Monty Python's Life of Brian*. Harrison even made an extremely brief guest appearance in the film as Mr. Papadopoulis, caught up in a manic crowd, muttering 'Hello!' in thick Liverpudlian and looking stunned by the whole thing – as Michael Palin noted some ten years later at a celebratory dinner, Harrison was obviously amazed at being trapped in a mass of people screaming for someone other than himself! Following the major *Brian* money-spinner Eric Idle met Bob Hoskins at a party. In the same no-go area with a pet project called *The Long Good Friday*, the film had been altered to a television drama which dictated great swathes of violence being edited from the final print. In order to plug HandMade as much more than a comedy outlet, Harrison bought the project from Lord Grade. The result was another winner and, although during its ten years at the top HandMade's biggest projects would be *Python* oriented, the company boosted the quality, quantity and credibility of films in this country. Meanwhile back at his day job of being a legend, Harrison teamed up with Bob Dylan, Jeff Lynne, Tom Petty and Roy Orbison for the feelgood jamboree of The Traveling Wilburys in 1988. The first album has an introduction written by Michael Palin while the second album release (Wilbury Vol. Three – 1990) has a piece penned by Eric Idle, under the name of Tiny Hampton, currently leading the search for Intelligent Life amongst Rock Journalism at the University of Please Yourself, California. Idle also cropped up as a butler alongside John Candy on the Harrison, Lynne, Dylan, Petty video for Wilbury Twist. And after all that, Harrison's son, Dhani, was the most impressed when he found out Idle had voiced a character in *The Transformers: The Movie!* Harrison remains a key figure in Pythonology, certainly the most energetic and vocal fan, even plugging The Rutles in Beatles Anthology overdrive on VH-1.

HELLO SAILOR

A wonderfully surreal first novel by a Python, this Eric Idle work takes in political corruption, royal scandal, the Vietnam war, military madness and an outlandish extension of the space race. A work of inspired lunacy, cleverly latching onto publishing conventions and altering the perspective of the novel form, Idle actually wrote this in 1970, five years before its first publication. In fact, the first line came to him during a bout of flu in the early *Python* days and immediately after recovery he sat down to finish the novel. It sold over 20,000 copies in paperback.
Hello Sailor By Eric Idle, published by Futura, 1975

HELP!

No, not the Beatles movie, but an influential magazine edited by Harvey Kurtzman. Following his major success with Cambridge Circus in the States, John Cleese was invited to star as Christopher Barrel, a man who falls in love with his daughter's Barbie doll in a fumetto (photo feature) *Christopher's Punctured Romance* for the May 1965 issue of the magazine. Written by Dave Crossley, photographed by Martin Iger and also featuring Cindy Young as John's wife, Wilma, the piece was a huge success. At just about the same time assistant editor Gloria Steinem handed the reins of control over to a certain young chap by the name of Terry Gilliam who supervised the Cleese photo shoot. Small world, isn't it?

HEMINGWAY'S CHAIR

Only the second novel written by a Python, following Eric Idle's *Hello Sailor* by one entry in this book and some twenty years, Michael Palin's work concerned the Hemingway obsessed postman Martin Sproale. A deconstruction of the small town, harmless, train-spotterish postal worker (reeling off the great man's long list of diseases and how many times he hit his head when drunk), American academia adds both interest in his life and literal substance to his hero-worship. Working like a contemporary Ealing comedy, Palin's narrative is never really 'Pythonesque' as the critical blurb would have us believe, but a richly sketched, character driven, indictment on modern efficiency gone mad. This is the endearingly, only slightly apologetic picture of a little community man fighting against the modern age of money-making, technology, mergers and smooth-talking business. The actual chair is merely a Holy Grail of Sproale's driven character surge, a wondrous remnant from Hemingway's boat which acts as both an impossible dream and inspiration for action. An excellent, balanced piece of work, Sproale's small-mindedness is questioned against a backdrop of a willingness to change to fulfil the destiny of his hero. The character is reassuringly flawed yet sympathetic.

Did You Know? As part of the book's press promotions Palin recorded a comic tape explaining that the novel is 'on sale at all good bookshops, some shoe shops and the odd butcher. VERY odd butcher...'
The novel is set on the Suffolk coast where Palin met his wife Helen and to where his parents retired – 'It has a complete lack of drama but when my mother was alive I could walk along the beach and think melancoly thoughts – knowing there was a cup of tea and a muffin at the end of it.'

By **Michael Palin**
Published by Methuen 1995/1996
Paperback edition Mandarin

HOLLYWOOD SQUARES

Following the completion of *Monty Python's Life of Brian* Graham Chapman rented a house in Hollywood for a time, appearing for a week's run on this popular game show in a promotional act for the new film. Exactly the same as the Brit version, *Celebrity Squares* with Bob Monkhouse calling the shots,

Chapman struggled to get some anarchic comedy into the format, bouncing feeble bits of banter off host Peter Marshall, endorsing 'Ni!' as the ultimate get out of awkward situations saying, desperately trying to find some off the wall, off-the-cuff laughter from Shakespeare, Cary Grant and the Queen's handbag but succeeding in nothing more than giving his best film a damn good plug. Among his fellow celebs was Vincent Price who, incidentally, was among the first group of panellists on the pilot episode of *Celebrity Squares*. Graham Chapman appeared on the shows broadcast 5, 6, 7, 8 and 9 November 1979.

HOT AIR & FANTASY – THE ADVENTURES OF TERRY GILLIAM

A documentary on the making of Terry Gilliam's ambitious 1989 project, *The Adventures of Baron Munchausen*. A tale of struggle rather than pleasure, Gilliam, with much interview material, and star *Python* icon Eric Idle, labour the point about financial problems, filming difficulties and mammoth setbacks – including trained horses denied entrance to the country/trained dogs down with liver complaints/disastrous weather conditions, you name it! This is a fascinatingly optimistic celebration of the artist fighting against a tidal wave of oppression and finally delivering the goods. The interviews are excellent and enlightening, the clips are well chosen and, best of all, there's a mesmerising insight into Gilliam the director working on set. Add to that, footage of a relaxed Gilliam letting his fantasy run free with a ride on a bathing elephant's back, some great material with the Baron's cohorts getting the aged make-up treatment, Gilliam finding empathy with the Baron, singing a snatch of the main man's theme and a priceless vignette from interviewee Oliver Reed, spurting on about the plot and deliciously imparting, 'Does that make sense – it does to me!!'

Special Treats, Interviews with **Winston Dennis, Terry Gilliam, Eric Idle, Charles McKeown, John Neville, Sarah Polley, Oliver Reed & Ray D. Tutto**
Narrator **David Castell**
Music **Michael Kamen**
Camera **Rinaldo Palmadessa, Steve Jellyman & Kevan Debonnaire**
Sound **Robert Rossi, Richard La Motte & Peter Brown**
Video editor **Damon Heath**
Thanks to **Daniela Edelburg, Prominent Features, Janet Ramsey & Eugene Rizzo**
Producers **Colin Burrows & David Castell**
28 mins, 1989

HOW TO IRRITATE PEOPLE

With numerous film and television assignments on the go, Graham Chapman and John Cleese were asked by mentor David Frost to fashion a comedy special to try and break into the American market. Frost, with contacts in Westinghouse Systems in the States, gave the two writer/performers a chance to structure some material around everyday situations that really irritate. Cleese, having married Connie Booth, was keen to involve her. Eager to work with Michael Palin, he also roped in the *Do Not Adjust Your Set-*er as actor only. Tim Brooke-Taylor, from their *Cambridge Circus/1948* days also came aboard and Frost acted as executive producer. The sketches were very much in the mould of typical Cleese/Chapman stuff of the day, self-contained, manic comments on the madness of life with a twist of convention breaking through the logical, everyday surroundings. Several were later reworked or refilmed for *Marty* and *Python* with half-baked sub-classics like the airplane cockpit and the Cleese/Booth dining scene standing alongside real ground-breakers like the car salesman sketch which later resurfaced as the parrot. Cleese, as the link man in almost 'And Now...' mode, keeps the whole thing together (although for the studio audience recording he had to do the show in

order, thus changing for his part in each sketch, donning the smart gear and then changing again) and finally realises the whole point of this exercise – that the entire concept was to irritate. Despite failing to spearhead the Frost clan into America, this is a fascinating collection of tryouts and almost-classics which would flower into *Monty Python's Flying Circus*, *Marty* and *The Goodies*.

Did You Know? David Frost presented *How To Irritate People* in America as part of a series of Sunday night comedy specials on the Westinghouse Network, alongside programmes showcasing Tommy Cooper, Ronnie Barker and Frankie Howerd.

Starring **CONNIE BOOTH, TIM BROOKE-TAYLOR, GRAHAM CHAPMAN, JOHN CLEESE, BARRY CRYER & MICHAEL PALIN**
Written by **John Cleese & Graham Chapman**, 1968

ERIC IDLE

The last Python to attend Cambridge, the inventor of Nudge, Nudge and the owner of a mind for comic language on a par with Peter Cook, Eric Idle was born 29 March 1943, at Harton Hospital, South Shields, County Durham, lived in Oldham and Wallasey as a child and attended boarding school at Royal School, Wolverhampton, from 1952. His father, who had served in the RAF during the war, died in a car crash in 1945. Idle journeyed to Cambridge in 1962 to study English at Pembroke College, having a 'very English' obsession with words and sharing Chapman's love of *The Times* crossword, although, thanks to *Beyond the Fringe*, he was hooked on the idea of the Footlights. Both Cleese

and Chapman were already heavily involved but, via his own Smokers show, Idle was invited to join the club immediately in March 1963.

By the time of *Footlights '63*, which took the Edinburgh Festival by storm at the same time as Terry Jones was batting for Oxford's comedy team, Idle was appearing alongside Richard Eyre, David Gooderson and Humphrey Barclay. Anything produced at the time was very much in the shadow of *Cambridge Circus*, but Idle wrote, directed and performed in the 1964 Edinburgh effort and met Oxford-based Michael Palin for the first time. By 1965 Idle was elected President of the Footlights club, instrumental in changing the no-woman rule for the Footlights and allowing the likes of Germaine Greer into the club. He also found time to write and star in the 1965 revue *My Girl Herbert*. Despite Idle's reservations about the project, he toured Britain with the show and played three weeks at the Lyric Hammersmith in a hugely successful close to his Cambridge experience. Idle followed this with regular cabaret work at London clubs like The Blue Angel (with John Cameron) and The Rehearsal Room before heading off to Leicester for

rep. theatre experience. Credits included *Oh! What A Lovely War* and the farce *One For the Pot* for the Christmas season, but Idle hated the restriction and spent most of his spare time (and a few occasions when he should have been on stage!) penning contributions for the John Cleese radio classic *I'm Sorry I'll Read That Again*. Idle was sharing a flat with Graeme Garden in the late 1960s and it was he who got Idle, Jones and Palin involved in his *Twice A Fortnight* venture.

It was a natural step forward in 1966, when Idle was offered the chance to join scores of Oxbridge writers on *The Frost Report*, a role which led to his scripting Ronnie Corbett's sitcom *No – That's Me Over There* and vital involvement in ATV's *Do Not Adjust Your Set*. *Monty Python's Flying Circus* in 1969 saw him become one of the country's most prolific writer/performers and it was also a year that saw his marriage to Australian actress Lyn Ashley on 7 July during the final week's filming for *Python*'s first season – the couple had one son, Carey (born 1973) – but divorced in 1975.

During *Python* he produced, wrote and starred in his own radio series *Radio Five On Radio One* – a sort of set-up for *Rutland Weekend Television* which was his major post-*Python* venture, while embracing the various team film/stage credits and importantly cracking the American market with high profile appearances on *Saturday Night Live* and *The Rutles* – during which time Idle had his appendix removed at Arab Hospital, St. John's Wood. Producer Lorne Michaels invited Idle to guest star on *Steve Martin's Best Ever Show* in 1981, but unwilling to journey to America Idle instead secured a budget, took a crew down to Stonehenge, directed and performed an academic parody *Did Dinosaurs Build Stonehenge?*, edited it on video and sent it to the US. Cachet with the old crew saw his cameo in *National Lampoon's European Vacation* with Chevy Chase, following which Idle spent some time with Chase writing a script for an unfilmed entry, *National Lampoon's Vacation Down Under*.

After *The Rutles* Idle planned a film version of Gilbert and Sullivan's *The Pirates of Penzance* with a Victorian setting. He travelled to Penzance and discovered the perfect castle location for a realist feel to the movie. Although the screenplay was ready and able it clashed with Joe Papp's Broadway production with Kevin Kline as the King, and while producer Ed Pressman bought Idle's version for filming he eventually invested in Papp's interpretation as a recorded stage show. Kline would have suited Idle if the productions had been merged, although he really wanted Albert Finney or Michael Caine, while Bette Midler was up for the Pirate Queen, but all the Gilbert & Sullivan setbacks proved perfect training for Jonathan Miller's 1986 English National Opera production of *The Mikado* which starred Idle as Ko-Ko.

The first Python to write a novel (*Hello Sailor*) and stage his own play (*Pass the Butler*), Idle's writing and performing career has embraced Hollywood cameos (*Casper*), brief US television stardom (*Nearly Departed*) and British sitcom (*One Foot in the Grave*) although this comic powerhouse still has a pile of uncompleted, unfilmed and rejected projects. *Splitting Heirs*, a long nurtured idea, was finally made in 1993, but there were rumours that a forthcoming Hollywood comedy would boast a screenplay by Idle and John Sessions, while among his favourite projects on the boil was a musical space comedy *Road to Mars* (although it was later rechristened *Outta' Space*). An updating of the Bing and Bob classics with Idle and somebody else cracking gags in a weird futuristic setting, the film would endorse the 1930s *Flash Gordon* look of the future, akin to Gilliam's nostalgia in space vision. Other screenplays yet to be filmed include a TV documentary about a fictitious Hollywood producer *The Legendary Sid Gottlieb*, a farce based round a modern re-telling of Faust, *Taxi to Hell*, and a musical concerning one of Idle's chief passions, cricket, told through royal journalist scandal, *The Back Page* – a piece later performed on BBC radio as the low-key but superb *Behind the Crease*. Idle spends a great deal of time working on film/television script ideas in his home at San Fernando Valley, California (with ex-*Playboy* model Tania Kosevich, whom he married in 1981, and their daughter Lily, born 1990), but he still has home roots with a property in St. John's Wood, North London.

I'M SORRY I'LL READ THAT AGAIN

While celebrating the free-wheeling fun of *Cambridge Circus*, George Seddon in his review for *The Observer*, noted that the show 'will start nothing'. He couldn't have been further from the truth, for from its collective cast sprang one of the longest running BBC radio comedy shows of all. With the popularity of *Cambridge Circus* on the West End stage and the BBC employment of John Cleese as writer and Humphrey Barclay as producer (although they were both officially recruited as 'writer-producer') it was only natural that the revue graduates were ripe for radio exposure.

Thus it was that the entire *Cambridge Circus* cast came together for a one-off radio version in December 1963. So successful was it that the gang came together again for a trial run of three episodes, incorporating elongated material from the original show, and utilising the first major public performances of John Cleese and Graham Chapman. Senior producer Ted Taylor steered the fledging radio clowns through the early days, overseeing the much truncated recording of Cleese's classic *Judge Not* sketch and other items from *Cambridge Circus* during sessions on 10, 17 and 24 March 1964. Initially due to go out under the title *Get Off My Foot* (an old Frank Randle catchphrase, Max Miller movie and totally irrelevant here) these shows were broadcast on 3, 10 and 17 April, latching onto the typical apology from any fluffed broadcasting line – *I'm Sorry I'll Read That Again*. As a

prelude for their New Zealand and New York performances, this radio experience was invaluable and the shows, an instant success, prompted the BBC into commissioning a full season of 13. However, by this stage, in October 1965, the cast had gone through important changes. Indeed, the second series contains no Pythons at all, for Chapman had dropped out of the enterprise to renew his medical career and Cleese had opted to stay in America after the *Cambridge Circus* shows. Filling in for the absentees was Cambridge Footlighter Doctor Graeme Garden, joining forces with his fellow Goodies-to-be for the first time and adding his own surreal sense of awful puns and cleverness. When Cleese returned to England in 1966, the show retained Garden and bunched up to slot Cleese back into place. Garden was absent from the third series, owing to a midwifery course in Plymouth, during which he nevertheless still regularly contributed scripts for the show. Despite, and indeed, because, the Oddie/Garden scripts were chock-full of obvious, childish, silly comedy, there's no doubting that this show is a vital flagship in the history of British radio, clutching to the manic format of *Round the Horne* and twisting it for a university-based audience. Indeed, all the writer-performers were heavily influenced by *The Goon Show* and yearned to create their own equivalent for the 1960s, in *I'm Sorry I'll Read That Again*, they achieved it with flying colours – combing *Python/Goodies* style with borrowed Milligan/Cook ideas and with a BBC authority figure, promoted to producer after the fourth series, the broadcasting send-ups were rife and hilarious. Throughout, bad jokes ruled although, naturally, there were surrealist riffs and *Python*-like sequences along the way, notably Beethoven's Fifth Symphony playing backwards, a pre-Terry Jones musical mice sketch with Fritz and his musical hamster and deconstructed fairy tale legends for contemporary audiences! Relying heavily on the familiarity of stock characterisations, corny one-liners and knowing comedy, the team

ploughed through a decade of cracking material, guaranteed to reward the studio and listening audience with a barrage of specially constructed dreadful jokes, which were greeted with groans of approval. As with Milligan's mile-stone, there was a loose, flexible storyline and the second half was usually given over to a long, winding sketch.

Once the lion's share of writing fell on the shoulders of Garden and Oddie, the reliance on familiar catchphrases and stock characters fully took over and by the fifth series it was less like a comedy show and more like playing in the Cup Final for the cast, slipping in their lines between hearty heckles and uncontrolled response from the audience. Cheering, groaning at the awful puns, knowing the key comic loops off by heart and saying them along with the cast, it made inspired comic expression more and more difficult and Cleese, in particular, became incensed by the reaction. His anger would lead to continual outbursts of 'Shut Up!' or sarcastic cries of 'Obvious!' when the team got a laugh through clichés and poor gags – a vintage example being the chestnut 'what do you do with a wombat' line (you play wom with it!). Naturally, of course, this delighted the audiences even more and eventually Cleese's dislike of the programme was written into the scripts akin to Kenneth Williams and his search for artistic prowess in *Round the Horne*. Nevertheless, he was still not averse to embracing tongue-in-cheek condemnation of Shakespearean comedy with a straight snippet from the Bard followed by amazement that the audience thought their comedy was a bit off! Cleese delighted in his usual collection of strict officials and bemused orators, playing earnest BBC reporters, confused cricket commentators, offensive quiz-masters, camp Nazi officers, dismissive theatre critics, straight-laced racist policemen and bombastic bank managers with consummate ease. However, despite staying with the series until the bitter end, Cleese found the relentless pun-based format rather restrictive and became increasingly disillusioned with his position. Indeed, his involvement diminished as the show when on, but through thick and thin Cleese stuck with his £32 an episode role for over 100 shows, even after walking away from his beloved *Python* in early 1973. By the end of the programme, Cleese was hardly getting any dialogue at all (more by choice than anything – notably a hilarious notion of babies thinking themselves old as toddlers gives all the gems to Brooke-Taylor's neurotic cherub while Cleese feeds laugh lines). He even had a clause written into his contract excusing him from rehearsals – and this element was skilfully included into the ethos of the show. Certainly, following the initial *Cambridge Circus*-oriented shows, Cleese as writer was hardly bothered, preferring to inject his material into *Python* and happily stroll through the *I'm Sorry I'll Read That Again* scripts, contribute the odd sketch and rewrite on the day of performance. His memorable John and Mary duologues, written with Bill Oddie, did fire his imagination and over the years these became more and more surreal.

The acting experience and ability to work an audience and time a laugh was invaluable for later *Python* stage performances and despite reservations, Cleese threw himself into a series-based love of rodents, particularly ferrets. Publicity shots of the cast featured loads of stuffed creatures and Cleese's pride and joy was his song *I've Got a Ferret Sticking Up My Nose* – to the tune of *Rose of England*. Bill Oddie composed over 140 songs for the shows (occasionally helped out by Eric Idle's lyrical contribution) and Cleese's Ferret effort was recorded for posterity with Chapman and Brooke-Taylor during their *1948 Show* days. Indeed, Cleese was always eager to include the number in the live *Python* shows but faced veto from the other members. Years later, another vintage *I'm Sorry I'll Read That Again* ditty, a refrain in honour of Oliver Cromwell to a Chopin tune, was reworked by Cleese and Idle for the

Monty Python Sings album. Series 6, showcasing the classic serial Professor Prune and the Electric Time Trousers – sort of Doctor Who meets Tommy Trinder – presented Tim Brooke-Taylor's performance as Spot the dog getting Ahhs from the audience on every Woof, much to Cleese's mock disgrace. There was an over-indulgence in bad puns but everything is done with such a good heart, the cast are brilliantly talented and there's an air of feelgood insanity running through all the programmes, reflected in the barrel-scraping but joyous Fish 'n' Quips session with every fish joke known to man included. The team, in homage to Spike Milligan's comedy teaching worked with the theory that if you repeat a word enough it will become funny – hence the obsession with Teapot (which leaked into *Goodies* and *1948 Show* language) – and, like Milligan, delighted in getting dubious character names like Martha Farquar – think about it – past the BBC censors while allowing more obvious, innocent but slightly saucy sounding words to be edited. Cleese, Hatch, Kendall, Brooke-Taylor, Garden and Oddie were all cast in the 1978 Radio 2 pantomime *Black Cinderella Two Goes East*, alongside dream guest star Peter Cook, but an official resurrection of *I'm Sorry I'll Read That Again* was a long time coming. Finally, for the glorious 25th celebrations, the BBC roped in the old team for one last show, ushering in the sound nobody wanted to hear again as the World War II siren merges into the strains of Angus Prune. An hour-long special with grand Jack the Ripper dramatics recreated from the 1973 season, Spike Jones like China Town repeats and all the old favourite characters: the first half delighted in rounding up the team. It ribbed the various sitcom ventures and birdwatching antics of its stars in the intervening years – David Hatch, now Head of BBC Radio Comedy, was ever ripe for authority-mocking. Cleese, throwing himself joyously into the renewed cornyness of it, performs the five-bar gate gag (*In Spring, Spring, Spring* – lifted by Oddie from the Goodies'

Beastly Record) with the maximum dose of brilliant disdain. Cleese, highlighted as a mega-rich, ageing crazed comic, circling the universe in his spaceship, *Ferret One*, and desperately trying to escape Basil Fawlty comments, chucks in ex-parrot references, injects a priceless Video Arts training film parody, takes over the BBC (Broadcasting By Cleese), resurrects the *Python* silly walk for radio and once more sings the glorious *Ferret Song*. Bemoaning the lack of interest shown in these two comic masterpieces during the making of *Silverado*, showing a rare touch of pitiful nervousness, condemning Kevin Kline for changing his latest film title from *A Ferret Called Wanda* and, best of all, attacking Michael Palin's travelogue – '80 days... more like 80 years' – this is Cleese in relaxed, self-parodying mood and the result is priceless. There's even time for a vicious 'Shut up!' directed at his adoring audience. It brought a radio landmark to a suitably rounded close.

Did You Know? The immortal Angus Prune, who lent his name to the show's title theme, was the embodiment of the typical viewer the cast considered was tuning in and the name was adopted for a beloved slot in the show, Prune Play of the Week, and ultimately took over the whole proceedings with series eight broadcast on 'Radio Prune'. Angus Prune was also often listed in the roll call of performers with other nutty intruders including T. Briddock and A. Gibbon OBE. Apart from their classic clash on *The Goodies*, John Cleese and Bill Oddie teamed up as part of The Superspike Squad for an International Athlete's Club fundraising single, *Superspike, Parts 1 & 2* (Bradley 7606).

Cambridge Circus starring **Humphrey Barclay, John Cleese, Graham Chapman, David Hatch, Jo Kendall, Tim Brooke-Taylor & Bill Oddie** Music by **Burt Rhodes and his Quintet** Producers **Humphrey Barclay & Edward Taylor** Broadcast 30 December 1963. *I'm Sorry I'll Read That Again* pilots

Written & performed by **Tim Brooke-Taylor, Anthony Buffery, John Cleese, David Hatch, Jo Kendall & Bill Oddie**
Music by **Burt Rhodes & His Quintet**
Producers Humphrey Barclay & Edward Taylor
Broadcast 3, 10, 17 April 1964, Friday 9.30pm on the Light Programme.
1st Series (9 shows) starring **Brooke-Taylor, Garden, Hatch, Kendall & Oddie**
Music **Bill Oddie** supported by the **Dave Lee Group** (and throughout the entire run until 1988)
Producer **Humphrey Barclay** (sole producer for series 2, 3 & 4) – 4 October to 6 December 1965, Mon 10pm.
2nd series (13 shows) starring **Brooke-Taylor, Cleese, Garden, Hatch, Kendall & Oddie** (cast now complete and remained unchanging) – 14 March to 6 June 1966, Monday 10pm (shows 6–13 repeated from Saturday 23 April, 12 noon, show 4 repeated 13 June and show 3 repeated 20 June).
3rd series (14 shows) – 3 October to 6 December 1966, Monday 10pm (repeated following Saturdays at 2pm – except show six airing at 1pm).
4th series (14 weeks) – 23 March-23 July 1967, Sunday 5pm (repeated the following Monday at 10pm).
5th series (14 weeks). Producers **Humphrey Barclay** (just off to become Head of LWT Light Entertainment) **& Peter Titheradge** – 14 April to 7 July 1968, Sunday 9.30pm Radio 2 (repeated the following Friday at 1pm). Christmas Special – 26 December 1968.
6th series (13 weeks). Producers **David Hatch & Peter Titheradge** – 12 January to 6 April 1969, Sunday 9.30pm Radio 1 & 2 (repeated following Wednesday at 7.45pm).
Special, *The I'm Sorry Christmas Show* – 25 December 1969, 8.45pm.
7th series: A New Improved Whiter-Than-Blue Radio Wash-Out (13 weeks). Producers **David Hatch & Peter Titheradge**. – 15 February to 8 May 1970, Sunday 8.45pm Radio 1 and 2 (repeated the following Wednesday at 6.15pm). Christmas Special – 31 December 1970, 10pm Radio 4.
8th series: Producers **David Hatch & Peter Titheradge** – 6 July to 28 September 1972, Thursday 12.25pm

Radio 4.
9th series: from 4 Nov 1973. 25th anniversary special. Producer **Richard Wilcox** – 25 December 1988.
Most of the *I'm Sorry I'll Read That Again* scripts were written by Bill Oddie and Graeme Garden but, notably in the early years, the other cast members John Cleese, Graham Chapman, Tim Brooke-Taylor, Jo Kendall, David Hatch, Humphrey Barclay and Antony Buffery contributed, as well as Eric Idle, John Esmonde, Bob Larby, Brian Cooke, Johnny Mortimer, Peter Vincent, Chris Miller, David McKellar, Les Lilley, Alan Hutchison, Elizabeth Lord, Chris Stuart-Clark, Chic Jacob and David Lund.

IN THE BEGINNING

No, nothing to do with that dodgy George Martin prelude to *The Beatles Anthology 3*, but a totally charming, streetwise cartoon version of God's creation of man. There's plenty of irreverent humour delivered with panache in the sombre tones of Michael Hordern, tapping into the tongue-in-cheek horrors of modern life mixed with modesty while expressing his own importance, working class ethos from Adam and Eve (with Enfield's chauvinistic kitchen sink comment) and there's even a Beatle beetle gag when a crawling creature rips into the apple and comments that he knows all about good and evil in a thick Liverpudlian accent with Lennonesque features.
But it's a classic performance from John Cleese as the tempting snake that steals the show. He enters and exits humming Rossini's *The Storm*, and it's all wise-cracking banter, as Cleese dismisses the warning not to eat the forbidden fruit, delivering his lines like a fairground con artist, highlighting the need for clothes and sporting a rather fetching top hat. He loses this along with his stick-like arms and legs when his failed attempt to defend his actions results in divine retribution and a mutually agreeable job-plan change to satanic force, working in cheerful unison with Hordern's God. Sneaking around the place with corrupting utterances and

a wonderfully cunning delivery, Cleese's snake is a great contribution with a touch of Terry-Thomas.

A Word Pictures production in association with Dd DIVERSEdesign
In The Beginning – Snake **JOHN CLEESE**
God **MICHAEL HORDERN**
Adam **HARRY ENFIELD**
Eve **JANET McTEER**
Screenplay by **Bud Handelsman**
Animation **Catti Calthrop**
Colourist **Roz Calthrop**
Backgrounds **David Chaudoir & Paul Trainor**
Associate producer **Anuradha Vittachi Armstrong**
Producer **Peter Armstrong**
Director **Steve Billinger**
MXMXCII, 12 mins

NEIL INNES

With a major connection with pre, during and post *Python* projects, Michael Palin considers Innes to be the seventh Python. Born December 1940, Innes studied art at Norwich Art School with Viv Stanshall and moved on to Goldsmith's College, London University, before forming the Bonzo Dog Dada Band in 1966. The Dada reference reflected their artistic leaning, although they later removed the intellectual handle altogether for the more obvious comic charms of Doo Dah. (Besides, the band members were fed up of explaining the Dada meaning.) Their trumpeter went off to become part of the record company's invention group, New Vaudeville Band, and he cropped up on *Top of the Pops* while the lads were still struggling. Eventually that struggle paid off when the band released their first album, *Gorilla* in 1967, worked with The Bee Gees and Cream, made two tours of America, working with The Byrds and Joe Cocker at the Fillmore West, and reaching the peak of coolness with a guest turn playing *Death Camp for Charlie* in the Beatles film *Magical Mystery Tour*. Indeed, Innes scored a personal success with the band's only number one, *I'm the Urban Spaceman*, produced by Apollo C. Vermouth, alias Paul McCartney. The band became resident guests on *Do Not Adjust Your Set* but after a brief spell of popularity broke up in January 1970. Innes joined another band, The World, immediately afterwards and got roped in with Grimms in 1971 before reuniting with the Bonzo band for one final album. By now his old *Do Not Adjust* cohorts had semi-founded *Monty Python* and Innes earned £25 for warming up the *Python* studio audience, actually getting the chance to write and perform in the Cleeseless fourth series.

Despite working with other bands, such as The Scaffolds, post-Bonzo, his real love was wacky musical comedy and the *Python* brigade were glad to have him around. He brought lyrical class to *Monty Python and the Holy Grail*, teamed up big time with Eric Idle for *Rutland Weekend Television* and took on the John Lennon role for *The Rutles*. Innes became a major part of the *Python* live shows (injecting remnants from Bonzo days, belting out the likes of *The Idiot Song* and *The Old Gay Whistle Guest* as well as performing in the sketches), featured in the filmed Hollywood Bowl concerts, cropped up in *Monty Python's Life of Brian* and acted as a talented good luck charm through various *Python*-related projects – Gilliam's *Jabberwocky*/Palin's *The Missionary*/Jones' *Erik the Viking*. Later he scripted and provided songs for the Emmy nominated series *East of the Moon*, a television series based on the book *Fairy Tales* by Terry Jones. Following the hour-long musical special *The Rutland Weekend Song Book*, producer Ian Keill suggested a 13-part series starring Innes. Although he toiled with the title *Parodies Lost,* the purposed series was eventually whittled down to six and became the belated BBC2 show *The Innes Book of Records* featuring a guest starring turn from Michael Palin in the first show, resurrecting *Python*esque memories by lying under a bridge just outside Bristol in nothing but his underpants, wanting to be prodded by the famous

BBC stick and cavorting around as a policeman. Palin also cropped up as a record producer on the Innes single, *Recycled Vinyl Blues*, utilising eight old discs being melted down to make a new one (thus featuring snatches from familiar, cleverly acknowledged, tunes) and a bit of *Python*-inspired banter at the beginning. The show warranted a record release, presented pop videos of his greatest comedy songs and even included an appearance from a certain *Urban Spaceman*. Indeed, as well as resurrecting his song *When Does a Dream Begin* from *Python*'s fourth series, the shows also saw the first airing of the 1996 Rutles comeback single *Shangri-La* with Innes in Superman garb surrounded by a chorus of holiday campers.

INTERLUDE

A sixties reworking of the classic Ingrid Bergman/Leslie Howard film *Intermezzo*, injecting this romantic drama of a love affair between a symphony conductor and a reporter with hip understanding, contemporary backdrops and, surprisingly, the marital reconciliation in the original film. Mind you, it is Virginia Maskell (the eternal cheated wife from *Only Two Can Play*) so you can't blame the old buffer. Director Kevin Billington invited John Cleese to spice up the action a bit with a glorious comic interlude in this rather sour-faced *Interlude*. Playing the memorable supporting part of a seedy, pompous television Public Relations man, Cleese turns on his usual supercilious behaviour for some brief scenes opposite Oskar Werner and Barbara Ferris. However, its attempt at old-fashioned romance in the context of swinging sixties attitude was ribbed by many critics – Wilfrid Sheed wrote 'If you laughed at *Brief Encounter* you will roar over this one.'

Columbia/Domino
Stefan Zelter **OSKAR WERNER**
Sally **BARBARA FERRIS**
Antonia Zelter **VIRGINIA MASKELL**
Lawrence **DONALD SUTHERLAND**

TV PR Man **JOHN CLEESE**
Mary **NORA SWINBURNE**
Andrew **ALAN WEBB**
Natalie **GERALDINE SHERMAN**
Humphrey Turnbull **ROBERT LANG**
George Selworth **BERNARD KAY**
TV Director **HUMPHREY BARCLAY**
Written by **Lee Langley & Hugh Leonard**
Photography **Gerry Fisher**
Music **Georges Delerue**
Production designer **Tony Woolard**
Director **Kevin Billington**
113 mins, Technicolor, cert A, 1967

ISADORA: THE BIGGEST DANCER IN THE WORLD

Tony Palmer, who later recruited Jones and Palin for *Twice a Fortnight*, was a friend of a friend of Michael Palin and invited him to jump aboard this bizarre and wonderful Ken Russell version of the life of Isadora Duncan, played here by Vivian Pickles. Although it sounds like a 1950s sci-fi film along the lines of *Attack of the 50 Foot Woman*, this is the usual mix of bizarre characters, musical themes and drama docu-mentary. Palin, desperate to get any sort of BBC television exposure after his work on *Now!* was cast as an undertaker and joined three other people playing musical instruments on top of a hearse as it passed through London. By sheer coincidence, one of his fellow morbid players was Eric Idle, whose role extended to a memorable vignette involving Isadora's children. Cast as Death's chauffeur, Idle's character parks his car, with the dancer's two children aboard, goes to hand-crank the vehicle but leaves it in reverse, so the car trundles into the Seine and kills the children. His reappearance with Palin mocking the serenity of death is a typical Russell image.

Isadora Duncan **VIVIAN PICKLES**
ERIC IDLE, MICHAEL PALIN
Assistant Producer **Tony Palmer**
Director **Ken Russell**
BBC1 22 September 1966

JABBERWOCKY

Depending on your mood, this is either a pretentious incoherent mess or a piece of art bristling with images of stark beauty. I still have major problems with this cult favourite. It's certainly a unique piece of film-making but the stifling atmosphere is relentless and, at the end of the day the constant stream of excrement, urine, arse-flashing, dirt, deformed limbs, self-mutilation and pure filth can get a bit too much. Although the immortal poem is embraced at the outset, this is more like Lewis Carroll after a very heavy night out with the lads, projecting a totally bizarre, other-worldly quality with the fresh-faced, charming innocence of Michael Palin plonked in the centre like a refugee of sanity tossed into bedlam. The humour sort of creeps up on you and there are massive swathes of material which are disturbing, hilarious and even more disturbing because you find them hilarious.

Although this was the first independent film-making venture for a Python, co-written by old *Help!* employee and American chum Charles Alverson, it was originally planned as a short BBC project. However, producer Sandy Lieberson suggested it would make a better feature film and the process began. The budget was tiny (£500,000), the writer-director was eagerly learning as he went along and the *Python* expectations were deliberately being avoided. Everybody involved was struck by the sheer professionalism of this saga of shit – indeed folk were quite looking down their noses at the amateurish manoeuvres of another fresh-faced film-maker across the crowded studio as George Lucas put together *Star Wars* (clear failure all the way!) Gilliam was more than a bit

panicked at the prospect. It's no wonder that he wanted to clutch beloved icons of *Python* to his chest – Palin's lead performance and a very brief cameo from Terry Jones in the pre-credit sequence.

This is *Monty Python and the Holy Grail* territory with Gilliam's concerted effort to lift away a lot of the obvious humour and replace it with more realistic historical details, thus he skilfully moves away from the surreal, slightly off-the-wall mugging of the team into the realms of nightmarish fantasy. The cast is rich indeed, interestingly plundering the invaluable vein of main-stream British comedy successes and twisting his actors' familiarity into haunting distortions of their popular personas. Alongside his nervy central *Python* star turn, Gilliam gathers together one of *Dad's Army*'s magnificent seven, a *Carry On* legend, Steptoe's son and a Likely lad.

There's even a stunning central turn from that survivor of the Music Hall circuit and newly discovered Brechtian master, Max Wall, staggering round his draughty old castle, suffering the elongated, mind-numbing list of names, titles and achievements on his entrances (setting up the great gag near the end with his shock when the introduction is shortened) and grouching about the place like an ancient turtle. With its bleary, flickering candlelight, dusty floors and muffled screams, Wall's castle is hardly more comfortable than the hovels of his kingdom (although the Chepstow/Pembroke castle locations have a grand quality and wealthy blokes ride on horseback through the masses and reveal the great divide between the rich and poor). The villagers of Palin's acquaintance consider travelling a distance of two miles as the ultimate adventure; filth and disorder is everywhere; meanwhile the might of military power and the threat of the supernatural battle it out.

Anyway, Gilliam's effort to move away from the *Python* label involved deliberately restructuring the first part of this film as almost totally lacking in comic content, and indeed, when revisiting *Jabberwocky* one can

see that towards the end much more comedy is included – notably as *Carry On* faces play William Wycherley comedy with Harry H. Corbett's randy old Squire, amorous fun with Alexander Dane and the bellowing bluster from Bernard Bresslaw's cuckolded husband. Corbett's Robert Newtonesque rogue is the film's high spot, embracing the ethos of the film's filth obsession with vigour and having a whale of a time over-acting, storming through the action with flashing grin and ready wit. Bearded, bleary-eyed but retaining his Steptoe laugh, Corbett triggers the film into comedy mode, with Palin's disastrous attempts to improve the efficiency of the metal works, the manic chase for his beloved turnip, employing football crowd cheers on the soundtrack as peasants boot the item away and Neil Innes with his continual drum beating as the King's roll call is delivered.

The very first sequence, featuring a heavily disguised Terry Jones as the poacher, is perhaps the most effective of the entire film. Indeed, if audiences were expecting *Python* this pre-title sequence would certainly have put them straight immediately. Beautifully directed, there is an air of sinister menace, helped by foggy location, eerie music and effective aerial shots that give us a monster's eye view. The attack, when it comes, is quick and gory. It's still seen through the monster's point of view, with Jones screaming into close-up camera, falling silently to the floor as a mass of bones and steaming fresh with the quiet atmosphere punctured by the sound of birds flying away. The title flashes across the screen in dripping red letters and we enter Gilliam's darkest world.

Palin's ever cheerful, lovestruck character is a continual joy, although his good nature is never enough to defeat the decay of the environment around him. Shunned by his dying father, rejected by his love and used by most people he meets, Palin wanders through the film like a lost soul. Abused by the Fishfinger family, even when he saves their lives, mocked by the guards, trapped into

A cast roll-call for *Jabberwocky* (Neil Innes, Deborah Fallender, Max Wall, John Le Mesurier, Warren Mitchell, Michael Palin, Annette Badland and Brenda Cowling)

the bloodthirsty, dismembering life of a Knight's squire he finally wanders past great piles of Jabber-poo and carcasses for the final show-down. With stunning use of *Night On Bare Mountain*, Gilliam sets up the monster's entrance with chilling skill and despite being set in Bosherston quarry and having that delightfully shabby quality of a Hartnell *Doctor Who* monster, the *Jabberwocky* battle is brilliant cinema. On a minute budget and working as hands-on director, Gilliam himself journeyed to a local abattoir to pick up bits of cow stomach to form the skin of the monster, placed the 'man in the rubber suit' performer in the monster costume backwards to give the walking motion a more alien quality and filmed sequences with a child in Palin armour to give his makeshift creature the illusion of height. More importantly in terms of the fledging film-maker, Gilliam cleverly conceals the Jabberwocky for as long as possible, setting up brief glimpses through Palin's helmet before the final revelation of the wobbly creature. But if you haven't suspended your disbelief this far in then there's no hope for you; if you have, this is Palin's loveable bumbler winning through and defeating the external threat. But even here, denied his true love but embracing fairy tale-convention, getting the Princess and

Royal endorsement, Palin's success is a failure to him. A film of total extremes, there is too much filth all over the shop but Gilliam's artistic style pulls it off, contrasting beautifully filmed silhouetted compositions juxtaposed with images of arse-scratching and shitting out of windows. Now that's extremes for you! Besides, Palin's eager-to-please niceness, the bickering sequences between Max Wall and John LeMesurier, the great majestic sweep of mediaeval music and Harry H. Corbett's never say die, good-time chap are more than enough to leave a more than pleasant aftertaste.

Did You Know? Despite the presence of three Pythons in the production, Gilliam was desperate to move away from the blanket of comedy that bound him. Indeed, his one instruction was that *Python* would not be used in the film's advertising – in reality, certain American releases changed the title to *Monty Python's Jabberwocky*...thanks!... although, with the quick buck to be made, a return to *Python*esque mediaeval territory and half of the *Monty Python* members involved, one can hardly blame them. Gilliam's personal favourite screening was at a low-key festival attended with Palin in Spain, where no *Python* preconceptions were in evident and

the film played without subtitles – the working-class audience loved the visual beauty of the piece. Gilliam's style was inspired by comic illustrations drawn in the margins of illuminated mediaeval Bibles, celebrating the humour and joy of bodily functions with crapping animals and cheery monks flashing their bums, with only minor elements coming from Tenniel's illustrations for *Alice Through the Looking Glass*. Gilliam made do on his limited resources by borrowing discarded bits of the *Oliver!* set at Pinewood, latching onto leftovers from *The Marriage of Figaro* and even writing a scene specially incorporating a cellar based round a lavish set being used by Blake Edwards for *The Revenge of the Pink Panther*. Sadly, annoyed at the prospect of Gilliam making use of his material, Edwards destroyed the set together with an accompanying catapult that Gilliam also wanted. Unperturbed, Gilliam rewrote the scene, changing Palin's entrance into the castle from the cellar scene to the appearance through the toilet system and linking to the urinating guard sequence. It was just the removal of one of the shit gags and the insertion of a piss visual, but Edwards was hardly playing the white man, was he? Gilliam's part as Man with Rock was originally earmarked for Dudley Moore.

Jabberwocky
Umbrella (Goldstone/Lieberson)
Dennis Cooper **MICHAEL PALIN**
The Squire **HARRY H. CORBETT**
The Chamberlain **JOHN LE MESURIER**
Mr. Fishfinger **WARREN MITCHELL**
and introducing, again, King Bruno the Questionable **MAX WALL**
The Other Squire **RODNEY BEWES**
1st Herald **JOHN BIRD**
The Landlord **BERNARD BRESSLAW**
3rd Merchant **ANTHONY CARRICK**
1st Merchant **PETER CELLIER**
The Princess **DEBORAH FALLENDER**
Bishop **DEREK FRANCIS**
Man with Rock **TERRY GILLIAM**
2nd Herald **NEIL INNES**
Poacher **TERRY JONES**
Guard at Gate **BRYAN PRINGLE**
2nd Merchant **FRANK WILLIAMS**

2nd Guard at Gate **GLENN WILLIAMS**
The Prince **SIMON WILLIAMS**
Griselda Fishfinger **ANNETTE BADLAND**
1st Fanatic **KENNETH COLLEY**
Mrs. Fishfinger **BRENDA COWLING**
Fanatic's leader **GRAHAM CROWDEN**
Mr. Cooper Senix **PAUL CURRAN**
Landlord's Wife **ALEXANDER DANE**
Armourer **BRIAN GLOVER**
Wat Dabney **JEROLD WELLS**
Flagellant **TONY AITKEN**
3rd Squire **PETER CASILLAS**
Flying Hogfish Peasant **DERRICK O'CONNOR**
Apprentice Armourer **DEREK DEADMAN**
Fanatic **JANINE DUVITSKI**
Ratman **ROY EVANS**
Old Man with Petition **BILL GAVIN**
Peasants **HAROLD GOODWIN & JOHN GORMAN**
4th Peasant & Fanatic **JULIAN HOUGH**
Door Opener **DES JONES**
Sister Jessica **GORDON KAYE**
Spaghetti-eating Fanatic **CHRISTOPHER LOGUE**
Crescent & Red Dog Knights **DAN MUIR**
MR PUGH'S PUPPET THEATRE
Red Hetting & Black Knights **DAVE PROWSE**
King's Taster **GORDON RAWLINGS**
Kevin Fishfinger **SHERIDAN EARL RUSSELL**
The Monster **PETER SALMON**
Scubber **HILARY SESTA**
Sergeant at Gate **JOHN SHARP**
Bandit Leader **GEORGE SILVER**
3rd Peasant **TONY SYMPSON**
Screenplay by **Charles Alverson & Terry Gilliam**
Music **De Wolfe**
Associate producer & additional photography **Julian Doyle**
Production manager **Bill Camp**
Production supervisor **Joyce Herlihy**
Special effects **John F. Brown & Effects Associates**
Monster creation **Valerie Charlton, Clinton Cavers & Jen Effects**
Stunt arranger **Bill Weston**
Camera operator **Simon Ransley**
Photography **Terry Bedford**
Editor **Michael Bradsell**
Production designer **Roy Smith**
Art director **Millie Burns**
Costumes **Hazel Pethig & Charles Knode**

Make-up & hairdressing **Maggie Weston, Elaine Carew & Scota Rakison**
Construction co-ordinator **Bill Harman**
Executive producer **John Goldstone**
Producer **Sandy Lieberson**
Director **Terry Gilliam**
Umbrella Entertainment Technicolor
On location in Wales and London/Shepperton Studios
We would like to thank the Rev Charles Dodgson for the use of the poem
Technicolor, 101 mins, 1977

JAKE'S JOURNEY

Wonderfully surreal children's fantasy playing like a cross between *Monty Python* and *Doctor Who,* this stimulating pilot for a CBS series was never even screened. The initial call came from Witz End Productions suggesting an American series filmed in England, based on Mark Twain's *A Connecticut Yankee in King Arthur's Court.* Chapman liked the book but wanted more flexibility and suggested the time-travelling element which seemed to hit the right buttons with the makers. The mediaeval flavour of Twain inspired Chapman to tackle elements of *The Once and Future King* (dealing with Merlin as tutor to Arthur) as well as bizarre moments reshaped from Carroll's *Alice in Wonderland.* Happy to have some sort of input in the structure of the piece, Chapman was keen to write the series (besides, the huge amounts of absurd money flying about for just over 20 minutes of screen time was too good to turn down), and by November 1987 Chapman and Sherlock had put some ideas together for the network. Still, the writers didn't have a completely free hand, with a scene set in 1939 Europe being cut (much to Chapman's chagrin, included to illustrate that Jake could travel anyway), while his love of delicious *Python*esque was provided by a giant lobster involved in a cycle race and some off-the-wall banter with a manic witch – although this hilarious scene was also edited by the makers. A $1.2 million budget was put up for the pilot, 16-year-old Chris Young addressed teenage American

youth caught up in magic and Chapman's old pal, Peter Cook was roped along as the King. Chapman, also wrote a small character role for himself as the miserable Queen who wouldn't speak because she was too mean to give away words. Working with Cook to perfection, Chapman was eager to let others do the acting while he concentrated on the show's structure. However, the casting of Sir George, the crusty old Knight who befriends Jake and appears wherever he lands in time, was a late and elongated decision. The team wanted the same actor subsequently to star in the series and, at the eleventh hour, Chapman himself landed the part – complete with heavy armour, hassled filming times and a sense of knowing exactly what the scriptwriter wanted! Although untested, NBC commissioned several episodes during the US Writers Guild strike and these scripts were mainly concerned with the mediaeval/*Connecticut Yankee* element of the series, although Chapman had enthused about ideas for later shows, including a pre-war Austria, the Elizabethan period, Ancient Rome, Greece, Egypt (which would be filmed on location in Spain) and a futuristic struggle on another planet. By late 1988 the programme was finally coming together, but despite every other executive at NBC loving the project, network president Lawrence Tisch rejected it. Following this hive of activity coming to naught, Chapman was disillusioned with the project and, becoming ill with the cancer that would kill him, his energy for re-promoting the idea was flagging. The Disney Channel took up the option in early 1989 but before anything else could be developed Chapman died. *Jake's Journey* died with him.

Starring **GRAHAM CHAPMAN** as Sir George/Queen
King **PETER COOK**
Jake **CHRIS YOUNG**
Screenplay by **Graham Chapman & David Sherlock**
Producers **Marc Merson & Allen McKeown**
Director **Hal Ashby**

JOHN CLEESE'S FIRST FAREWELL PERFORMANCE

A making of *A Fish Called Wanda* with the peerless John Cleese holding court, seen at work on the film's structure, nervously filming under-rehearsed love scenes with Jamie Lee Curtis and watching the masterly Charles Crichton at work. This is an excellent record of the making of a smash hit comedy with jolly, feelgood interviews, plenty of *Monty Python* memories and even a clip of Cleese and Palin as the Scot and the gynaecologist. Iain Johnstone's interviewing technique is incisive and effective, pushing Cleese on his two marriages and getting a brilliantly intelligent answer, pushing the question of squashed doggie censorship and getting a brilliantly intelligent answer and, justifiably, pushing on the American bias and getting a brilliantly intelligent answer. If you haven't seen the film Cleese's skill and passion would convince you of anything. There's some priceless location footage of Kevin Kline filming his 'death' sequence, a good contrast between his spell-binding performance as Donald Woods in *Cry Freedom* and his manic attack on Cleese, nerve-jangling clips of Cleese filming the fifth story hang-a-thon complete with resurrection of his 'Brian' footballer interview style from *Python*, rehearsal play with Kline's fish abuse and some grand Cambridge reminiscences on the career that might had been as Cleese goes through his courtroom motions. However, for all that, the best moments come with Palin and Cleese in conversation on the wonderful detail of Palin's descent down a luggage chute. Surreal, charming, and in homage to Pete 'n' Dud the two ex-Pythons spin a mesmerising train of thought on great acting down chutes, historical figures who had tried and succeeded and knowing banter about their own self-importance. There's nothing more delightful than two excellent comedy pros amusing each other and there's some sort of perverse and satisfying pleasure in the fact that these few minutes of spontaneous fun are far funnier than anything in the finished movie.

Interviews with **JOHN CLEESE, MICHAEL PALIN, JAMIE LEE CURTIS, KEVIN KLINE & CHARLES CRICHTON**
Film extracts by kind permission of UIP and *Python* (Monty) Pictures
Special thanks to **Anne Bennett, Rosemary Goodfriend & John Cleese**
Production manager **Pat Lett**
Post production **Crow Films**
Camera **Philip Chavannes & Peter Coppins**
Sound **Chris Moore**
Video editor **Spencer Hill**
Director **Iain Johnstone**
A Kentel Production, BBC 18 October 1988

TERRY JONES

Born in Colwyn Bay, Wales, on 1 February 1942, the son of a bank clerk, Jones grew up in Claygate, Surrey, and was educated at a Church of England primary school and Royal Grammar School, Guildford, from 1953 where he finished as head boy. He showed intense interest in modern poetry from the age of five. Until he was 15 he yearned for an academic career, ultimately seeing the light in the Bodleian library where he suddenly realised he didn't want to spend his life writing words about other people's words. Notwithstanding this, he grabbed the chance of a university education, impressively being accepted by both Oxford and Cambridge. While harbouring an interest in attending the latter due to its dramatic credentials, he had appeared in the Haymakers production of *Time Remembered*, Jones had no serious theatrical desires and a sense of loyalty for Oxford's offer coming in first saw the student continue his history studies at St. Edmund Hall College in 1961. He became involved in the college magazine, *Isis*, which was more studious than satirical, but eventually pressure from fellow students and his tutor released his renewed interest in performance and Jones joined The Experimental Theatre Company.

Performing everything from comedy to Brecht, it was during his time with the ETC that he met fellow Oxford history student Michael Palin in 1963. Jones, an upper class man, was impressed with Palin's cabaret work and the two wrote the first recognised piece of *Monty Python* material together soon after. Originally conceived for the revue Loitering Within Tent, their first collaboration was the immortal Slapstick sketch, looking at the evolution and implications of physical comedy, years later becoming a favourite element of the *Python* live performances. Based on an original idea by Bernard Braden's son, Chris, the sketch later cropped up in the Oxford Theatre Group's 1963 Edinburgh staging of ****. Although Palin wasn't involved beyond his co-writing contribution, this revue launched Jones on a career in comedy, returning for his third year at Oxford with invaluable West End experience and a high reputation. He energetically embraced the new Experimental Theatre Group production of *Hang Down Your Head and Die*, an emotive comic message piece set in a circus ring and dealing with the theme of capital punishment. Alongside Palin's cohort Robert Hewison, David Wood and Palin himself, the piece was staged at the Oxford Playhouse 11–22 February 1964 and Jones, spanning mime, song (notably *All That Gas*) and knockabout humour, was singled out for his stunning work as the white-faced victim, screaming before being dragged away to the gallows as the other cast members eagerly took the climactic applause. The show proved successful enough to warrant six weeks at the Comedy Theatre, London.

His final year at Oxford saw Jones writing and performing in *The Oxford Revue*, alongside Palin, and successfully taking the show to the 1964 Edinburgh festival. It was here that both Jones and Palin made their television debut, when a Scottish film crew did a brief feature on them, including extracts from the revue and *Hard Day's Night*-like cavorting from the lads. The brief London run of

Terry Jones in serious mood – apart from joke nose and glasses, of course!

The *Oxford Revue* led Jones to a collaboration with Noel Carter on a pantomime parody, *The Poor Millionaire*, which was penned over a weekend and with Jones now living in Lambeth, Willie Donaldson, who had been instrumental in staging *Beyond the Fringe*, gave him £50 to write a comic play called *The Love Show*. With nothing but the title, Jones began constructing a historical, off-the-wall look at sex through the ages, eventually decamping to his parents' house in Esher and getting old Oxford pal Michael Palin aboard. In the end, *The Love Show* never materialised but it did bring Jones and Palin together for the first time in 'civvy street'. While Jones was toiling away at *The Love Show* he was given a further £200 to write a TV play called *The Present*. Again this play, although completed, went unperformed, but the money was more than useful and fuelled a career-defining decision in Jones' life. With his girlfriend still at Oxford and the relationship floundering, Jones considered either returning to his old College to get some sort of work or really going for the London connection and find some television break. Strolling over Lambeth Bridge he decided to stay in the capital and finally landed a job as a copywriter

for Anglia Television. Frank Muir contacted him and gave Jones a fairly undefined office job for the BBC which involved script editing, looking at incoming comedy material and actually writing odd bits for *The Kathy Kirby Show*. It proved to be six months' invaluable experience of watching shows in production, although his position was always uncertain and a six-month director's course with director Ian Davidson was not completed by Jones due to peritonitis. Notwithstanding, at the end of the course, much to his amazement, he was made a production assistant, a job which lasted for another six months. Gradually, with Palin in tow, Jones began writing material regularly for BBC television, even performing some of their little sketches on film for Ian Davidson's *The Illustrated Weekly Hudd* in 1965.

The first joke of Jones' to appear on television was for *The Ken Dodd Show*. A visual gag, from an idea by Miles Kington, it featured a policeman's walking race. Having met the legendary comedian back stage at the London Palladium, been instructed in theatrical superstitions and jumped aboard for his television breakthrough, Jones successfully sold the idea to Dodd's production team.

Indeed, when the *Review of the Year* commented on Dodd's huge success in 1965, the clip used was Jones' policeman material! Adept at linking comic material for BBC variety shows, Jones would often get the call for humorous bits and pieces, notably for Lance Percival and *The Billy Cotton Bandshow*, which featured a five-minute sketch entitled The Body. Working like an early version of *Python*'s Reg Pither, it was the first television work Jones directed. While still recuperating from peritonitis, Jones was approached to contribute to the Beeb's serious arts programme, *Late Night Line-Up*. Screened at 11 o'clock, every night, it packed a cross section of reviewers into the tiniest studio in the TV centre to discuss the major points of interest derived from that evening's television. Jones was briefed to liven up the Friday night broadcast with a bit of comedy business, organising the *Late Night Revue* section and roping in pals, Michael Palin, Robert Hewison and Barry Cryer.

Writing and performing the material themselves, one farcical bit of business concerning Batman and Robin went beyond the serious insights that the presenter favoured, guest reviewer Dennis Potter stormed on about wasting his time with total rubbish and the fledging Pythons were shown the door. But fear not, the crazy, frightfully serious format would be later mercilessly ribbed by *Python*'s It's the Arts and the like. By now, of course, Jones had left the employ of the BBC to concentrate on pure comedy writing, notably contributing material with Palin and the other Brit Pythons to *The Frost Report*.

Another satirical comedy series from the makers of *TW3*, *The Late Show*, running for six weeks from 15 October 1966 to 1 April 1967, also called on the Jones/Palin partnership. Tuning their skills as writers and comedy performers with a Samurai spoof (*Hibachi*), filmed interludes including commuters making their way through jungles and slapstick in style of Antonioni art cinema, there were often dramatic elements to the comedy and the chance to work opposite such masters as Eleanor

Bron, Humphrey Barclay, John Bird and Barry Humphries. Indeed, the two worked closely with John Bird on the 1967 show, *A Series of Birds*, produced by radio comedy guru Dennis Main Wilson who had worked on *The Goon Show* and *Hancock's Half Hour*. It was Main Wilson who brought in Jones and Palin as additional writers who structured the narrative of the comedy in these self-contained stories. The eight-week run from 3 October 1967 proved unsuccessful; the most popular story was one which spanned two episodes, thus allowing the audience to warm to Bird's characterisation. Much to their surprise, the two found themselves credited as script editors for the programme although their contribution amounted to just a few helpful ideas to gauge audience reaction to the show's material. The script, what there was of it, didn't arrive for attention until the day of performance. The show's brief, embracing both political satire and fantasy within the half-hour stories, resulted in Jones and Palin rewriting chunks of the material.

Away from television Jones and Palin were offered the chance to write a traditional pantomime for the Watford Civic Theatre, and eagerly redefined the form with their version of *Aladdin*, presenting a basic retelling of the familiar tale with slight twists of anarchic comedy including the boring Prince Fong with his very boring song. The production was performed in 1968 and proved so popular that Jones and Palin were asked to write the 1969 show, *Beauty and the Beast*. Meanwhile, television stardom had come with *Do Not Adjust Your Set* and *The Complete and Utter History of Britain* (springing from a suggestion from Terry's older brother, Nigel, born 1940) which immediately led to *Python*. Jones the performer was sometimes under-estimated in *Python* but his work is perhaps the most fascinating, brilliantly personifying the bowler-hatted man in the street, embracing silent slapstick myth, stomach-churning grotesques, lustful heroics and, almost always, called on to play the judge in Cleese's court

room skits (complete with his difficulty with R prouncements, lapsing into nervousness and joyfully undermining his acting authority). Above all else, Jones was superb when playing the everyman surrounded by madmen, whether it was Cleese's callousness, the Bruces or the Nudge Nudge man. *Python* also resurrected an old interest in television production with Jones sitting in on editing sessions for *Monty Python,* always filming five minutes of excess material to allow judicial cutting. Initial problems of interference arose with producer Ian MacNaughton, and by the Cleese-less Series Four, the team were completely denied the luxury of these extra five minutes. Jones went on to direct the *Python* film cannon (a body of work which has grossed in excess of $100 million) as well as notable directorial ventures like *Personal Services, Erik the Viking* and *The Wind in the Willows*. In 1976 he embraced the old academic life he had rejected for comedy by publishing *Chaucer's Knight,* wrote a serious screenplay, *1381,* detailing the peasants' revolt when the people fought against repression and took over London, and has penned a series of children's book over the years. *Fairy Tales, The Saga of Erik the Viking, Nicobobinus, Curse of the Vampire Socks* and *Fantastic Stories* remain some of his proudest achievements, hugely popular, used in school assemblies and influenced by Chaucer's way of writing in common speech – easy but rewarding, affectionate, not condescending and enjoyable family fun. Between 8 April 1987 and 13 May 1988 Jones wrote scores of pieces for *The Guardian*'s input column published every Wednesday in the *Young Guardian* supplement. Initially approached for four pieces, his comments on everything from nuclear power, *The Sun* and the *Obscene Publications Bill* to Margaret Thatcher, the poll tax and the Zeebrugge disaster formed the book, *Attacks of Opinion,* published by Penguin. He still writes occasionally for the paper. His home is in Dulwich, South East London/Grover Park South of

Camberwell, shared with his wife photosynthesis biochemist Alison Telfer (they married in 1970), two children (daughter Sally, born 1974, son Bill, born 1976) and his dog Mitch (although his idyllic family life rests alongside an 'open marriage' arrangement). The house contains his beloved top study which is bowed with the weight of history books. Jones, a lover of life's finest things, financially supported *Vole*, an environmental magazine edited by Richard Boston in a Campaign For Real Life (subsequently helping the venture with The Dartlington Trust) and sponsored his own fondness of real ale by helping to reopen Penrhos brewery in Herefordshire and vocally support CAMRA. Guest starring in *The Young One*s, directing a television Indiana Jones and hosting *Paperbacks* kept Jones busy in between pet projects and his *Python* fame continued to bring offers from high profile film-makers. Jim Henson invited him to script the fantasy *Labyrinth* and shortly after, Steven Spielberg and Joe Dante consulted Jones with regard to *Gremlins II*. Jones presented an outline of possible storylines, all based round the characters from the first film, and a forgotten rule which allowed the endearingly destructive creatures to return, but none of his suggestions were taken up in the finished film which went all out for cinematic in-gags and satirical comments on American business notions.

THE KNIGHT AND THE SQUIRE

A Terry Jones penned children's book concerning the misadventures of a boy and his trickster companion in 14th-century England.

Written by **Terry Jones**
Illustrated by **Michael Foreman.**
Published by Pavilion, 1997

LABYRINTH

With a reputation for children's literature, Terry Jones was approached by Jim Henson to script this magical fantasy film which utilised Muppet-like characters and real actors, including a certain David Bowie as the Goblin King. Jones had contacted Henson's office with a view to make a film of his book *The Saga of Erik the Viking*, only to be told that Henson was trying to get in touch with him with regard writing *Labyrinth* – ironically Henson's daughter Lisa was reading the *Viking* book and suggested Jones as a suitable writer for the goblin project. In fact, Jones had briefly met Henson in 1975 during initial *Python* inroads into the US but really gained inspiration for *Labyrinth* thanks to Brian Froud's conceptual drawings for the film's puppet creations. Jones had a deep plan for the all-powerful Goblin figure to be shown as a fraud, merely using the mystery of the labyrinth to project illusions of strength and protect his fragile existence, but in the end this wasn't what Henson had in mind. Jones, injecting allegory and meaning to the fantasy was shocked at the notion of this central Goblin character being a singer (Bowie or Michael Jackson were up for the part and thus Henson wanted to exploit the musical potential and marketing angle). He also wanted the character to appear all the way through, though Jones kept the centre of the labyrinth, the King's liar, as the *Wizard of Oz*-like surprise close to the movie. Very little in *Labyrinth* is pure Terry Jones, but he was justly proud of the Pit of Hands sequence, brilliantly realised by the film-makers. Despite limited influence on the film, the association with artist Brian Froud did lead to the book, *The Goblins of the Labyrinth*, which loosely bases character descriptions and stories on the figures from the Henson project.

Labyrinth
Henson Associates/Lucasfilm Ltd.
Released by Tri-Star Pictures
Sarah **JENNIFER CONNELLY**
Jareth **DAVID BOWIE**
Screenplay by **Terry Jones**
Story by **Jim Henson & Dennis Lee**
Producer **Eric Rattray**
Director **Jim Henson**
101 mins, 1986

THE LAST MACHINE

'Right from the start, cinema dealt in illusions, dreams, miracles, spectacles of all kind... a new art of the imagination', Terry Gilliam, who hosted this five-part celebration of the moving image, summed up the work of pioneers that still influenced his own cinematic flights of fancy. In tow with The British Film Institute, this imaginative, informative and historically priceless drama-documentary series spearheaded the BBC celebration of film's centenary. Ultilising Gilliam as both film fanatic and comic performer, the series used stylised dramatics to recreate landmark events in early film history, in conjunction with actual rarely, if ever, seen archive footage.
Part 1 – The Space and Time Machine. 1895 and how cinema re-flected the Victorian obsession with travel.
Part 2 – Real Lives. Early news and documentary films, many of which were faked, the earliest use of colour film and the emergence of sound.
Part 3 – The Body Electric. First images of women, mainly erotic, pulling in the audiences with Edison's 1895 peep-show of New York dancer Annabelle Moore raising temper-atures. The rise of censorship, the multi-camera photography of Eadweard Muybridge (played by Bryan Pringle), suffragette Emily Davidson at the Derby, the artistic body images of Marcel Duchamp/
Fernand Léger and the start of comedy.
Part 4 – Tales from the City. The use of modern city environments, the first regular film shows and the onslaught of the gangster movie.
Part 5 – The Waking Dream. Exploring the earliest fantasy and horror films.

The Last Machine, presented by **Terry Gilliam**. Also featuring **Fiona Shaw, Allan Corduner, Peter Eyre, Bryan Pringle, Paul Rhys and Malcolm Sinclair**
Written by **Ian Christie**
Director **Richard Curson Smith**
7th January – 4th February 1995
8pm-8-40pm, 5 x 40 mins. BBC2

LAST OF THE SUMMER WINE: Welcome to Earth

The longest running television situation comedy of all time kicked off with Bill Owen, Peter Sallis and Michael Bates fighting hard to avoid going quietly into old age, and with Owen and Sallis joined by Brian Wilde, the late Michael Aldridge and Wilde again, the viewing figures remained healthy for 25 years. The series attained such a high profile that even John Cleese willingly made an extremely brief guest starring appearance in one episode. In a cross between *Close Encounters Of the Third Kind* and *E.T.* our three hapless heroes do the 'bicycle across the moon' scene and crash into a Northern Cleese waiting for aliens. Complete with outrageous accent and striped bobble-hat, his shocked and stunned stock character reaction to this outer world life form is worth waiting for.

Did you Know?
The pilot for *Last of the Summer Wine* was in the 1973 batch of *Comedy Playhouse* with Cleese's ill-fated *Elementary, My Dear Watson*.

Compo **BILL OWEN**
Clegg **PETER SALLIS**
Foggy **BRIAN WILDE**
Ivy **JANE FREEMAN**
Nora Batty **KATHY STAFF**
Edie **THORA HIRD**
Howard **ROBERT FYFE**
Marina **JEAN FERGUSSON**
Pearl **JULIETTE KAPLAN**
Glenda **SARAH THOMAS**

Wesley **GORDON WHARMBY**
Guest starring **JOHN CLEESE**
Written by **Roy Clarke**
Produced & directed by **Alan J. W. Bell**
BBC1 27 December 1993

LAVERNE AND SHIRLEY

Eric Idle had met Penny Marshall in 1974 when, along with Terry Gilliam, he was in America promoting *Grail*. Then married to Rob Reiner, Marshall remained friends with the *Python* and invited him onto her hit American sitcom – the first time a *Python* member had performed such an assignment. This *Laverne and Shirley* episode, the series being a successful spin-off from *Happy Days*, saw the unique teaming of two America-high profile Brits, ex-Herman's Hermits front man Peter Noone and Idle, crashing through the usual US comedy style with rock 'n' roll lifestyle, fun-loving, corrupt attitude and a love of dope. Although they don't perform their oft-mentioned popular B side *Fits Me Like A Sock*, this episode was the only show in the series initially banned from syndication broadcast because of the positive drug references – a fact Idle remains proud of to this day.

The basic plot highlights this British rocking mentality as a bit of a drag, promising to marry the girls only to escape huge tax demands, but it's a happy ending with the boys paying for their bus fare back from Las Vegas and it made further vital inroads for Idle into lucrative American circles.

Starring **PENNY MARSHAL, CINDY WILLIAMS, MICHAEL McKEAN, DAVID L. LANDER, ERIC IDLE, PETER NOONE**
Song: *Love, Love, Love* written by **Eric Idle & Stephen Bishop**
ABC-TV, Broadcast 24 February 1981

A LIAR'S AUTOBIOGRAPHY Vol. VI

Despite the obvious untruth contained in the title – this is the first and only volume of memoirs – Graham Chapman's riveting and hilarious account of his first 37 years is mainly accurate and stimulating material. Brilliantly mingling Python memories, comic fantasy and subtle deceptions, Chapman's frank discussion on his private life and mental drive that enhances all his work makes this essential for the *Python* fan and lover of grand literal skill. Despite bucking the system effortlessly – he cheekily includes a chapter nought – this is not the manic gag-inducing ramblings of a comic genius on an ego trip. The very first chapter candidly deals with his alcoholism and struggle to give up the booze. His life at Cambridge forms a major part of the book, while classic contributions in *At Last the 1948 Show* and, even, *Monty Python's Flying Circus* are covered in just over a chapter. There are priceless memories from the Python's experience in Tunisia filming *Brian*, the compromising German shows and live performances in America, real affection showered on his old pal Keith Moon, as well as more off-the-wall moments like a barrage of name dropping and extracts from the Oscar Wilde sketch. Pure brilliance. And as Michael Palin's old writing cohort Robert Hewison plucked from the text for his *Evening Standard* review, it's 'an intercoursingly good read'.

A Liar's Autobiography Vol VI by **Graham Chapman**, with **David Sherlock, Alex Martin, David Yallop & Douglas Adams**
Published by Methuen 1980
Issued as paperback by Magnum Books

THE LIMERICK BOOK

A collection of children's limericks by Michael Palin, published by Hutchinson Books, 1985

LOOK AT THE STATE WE'RE IN!

With his Video Arts head intact, John Cleese oversaw this entire series of six ten-minute films, tackling various maddening aspects of life in contemporary Britain. Planned over lunch with Roger Graef (with whom Cleese had collaborated on Policeman's Ball) the first film, *The Organisation*, looked at tax inspectors (starring Anthony Sher, Rik Mayall, Adrian Edmondson/writer – Chris Langham), followed by *Secrecy* (Harold Kingsby JOHN CLEESE, Mrs. Duvet DAWN FRENCH) broadcast Sunday 21 May. *Local Government* starred Hugh Laurie and Imelda Staunton, written by Chris Langham, Guy Jenkin's Legal System headlined Robert Hardy and the place of Royalty was questioned in *Nanny Knows Best* with Geoffrey Palmer and Prunella Scales (written and directed by Sean Hardie). However, by common consent, the series masterpiece was last to be broadcast, *The Status Quo*, written by and starring the great man himself, John Cleese, at his petulant, manic best as the Politician for Leaving BRITAIN Where It Is. Kicking off with the stirring refrains of *God save the Queen*, Cleese rips into his Party Political Broadcast, directed by Hugh Laurie (who actually directed this film as well with the clever out-of-focus, off-camera work of an operating television studio), briefly outlining that everything works fine and the public can get stuffed! A definitive inspection of the *I'm Alright Jack* ethos this is, after all, billed as A Party Political Broadcast on Behalf of a Few Dozen Men in Suits. Going ballistic at the word power (ranting on about big desk, chauffeur-driven cars and female interviewees, resorting to *Python*esque use of the word written on a cupboard and ultimately exercising his prerogatives by grabbing Sarah Stockbridge's breast), Cleese waffles on politics with a smile and insincere good cheer. Complaining about the use of *Cheek to Cheek* as not being weighty enough, droning on about British iconology like cricket and cliff walks, ultimately resurrecting Fawltyisms with his orders to writer Langham as 'waiter!', while replacing cold truth with muffled, mumbo jumbo of constitutional reform, everything (down to the pigeon outside the window) is false. The setting, the promises, the smile – everything is a lie, delivered with misunderstanding, venom and pomposity, dictating to the few, jokingly mentioning the millions who have had a hard day looking for work and, finally, becoming the straight-faced clown he is via Stockbridge's make-up job. Cleese is peerless in this stuff and with a final rant about those ungrateful buggers, a swift look at his watch and a stroll off for lunch, the message of introspective government is driven home. The final, *Python*esque scratched record correction of music to Status Quo's *Whatever You Want* rips into action, pleasing the politician in a link between high energy rock and idyllic English countryside.

A Video Arts/Sisyphus Production for BBC *Look At The State We're In!*
The Status Quo
Politician **JOHN CLEESE**
Director **HUGH LAURIE**
Writer **CHRIS LANGHAM**
Make-up Girl **SARA STOCKBRIDGE**
Written by **John Cleese**
Producers **Roger Graef & Margaret Tree**
Director **Hugh Laurie**
BBC2 4 June 1994.
Look At The State We're In! – The Debate, hosted by **Sue Cameroon**, was broadcast on 5 June 1994

THE LOVE BAN

Alternatively known as *It's a 2' 6' Above the Ground World*, this was yet another officious supporting film role for John Cleese and the last in a long line of notable comic cameos before big screen stardom began with *Monty Python and the Holy Grail*. *The Love Ban*, a would-be hilarious so-called sex comedy, tackles the touchy issue of a Roman Catholic couple (Hywel Bennett and Nanette Newman) going on the pill and the comic problems which ensue with such a laden style that most of the nudge-nudge humour and interesting controversy is lost in mugged

performances and under-written dialogue. Despite being in the hands of film pros Betty Box and Ralph Thomas, this is certainly more in the *Percy* mould rather than *Doctor in the House*, with Hywel Bennett, as usual, giving a wonderful performance, but struggling against Christmas sentiment and hipster attitude. Once again John Cleese, accepting this during a financial blackspot which also included whipping off *Doctor At Large* episodes for television, gives the most enjoyable performance as a contraceptive lecturer. Sort of *Monty Python* without the bite.

British Lion/Welbeck
Mick Goonahan **HYWEL BENNETT**
Kate Goonahan **NANETTE NEWMAN**
Jonathan Goonahan **RUSSELL LEWIS**
Sean Goonahan **SIMON HENDERSON**
Father Andrew **MILO O'SHEA**
Lecturer **JOHN CLEESE**
Susan Goonahan **SALLY-ANN FERBER**
Lucy Goonahan **CLAIRE McLELLAN**
Albert Baker **NICKY HENSON**
Jacki **ANGHARAD REES**
Joyce **GEORGINA HALE**
Miss Partridge **MADELINE SMITH**
Pregnant Girl **JACKI PIPER**
By **Kevin Laffan**, from his own play
Photography **Tony Imi**
Music **Stanley Myers**
Animation **Bob Godfrey**
Editor **Ray Watts**
Art Director **Anthony Pratt**
Producer **Betty E. Box**
Director **Ralph Thomas**
Eastmancolor, 96 mins, Cert AA, 1972

LOVE POTION

Graham Chapman served as executive producer for this comedy romance directed by *Monty Python* film editor Julian Doyle. Lending Doyle's directorial debut some classic comic clout, Chapman's role was purely supportive. Doyle followed this romantic tale by directing Rik Mayall and Richard O' Brien in *Shock Treatment*. 1987 U.S.A.

THE LUMBERJACK SONG

The most celebrated musical number from the original television series, this has become a major source of reference for an entire post-*Python* generation. First cropping up after the Palin/Jones barber diatribe in Series one, episode nine, Palin's mad chomping, Connie Booth's tearful heroine and the bemused chorus of manly Mounties (Cleese, Chapman and The Fred Tomlinson Singers) must rank as one of British comedy's most familiar, totally bizarre images. It certainly proved immediately popular enough to reappear in the 1971 film *And Now For Something Completely Different*, following on from the almighty Dead Parrot, while two years later Palin rerecorded the song as a single (Charisma CB 268 – the B-side featured a standard rendition of *Spam Song*). This new version presented Palin as a weather forecaster, lapsing into fantasies about giant trees and finally throwing aside his broadcasting duties to sing the *Lumberjack* anthem. A wonderful resurrection of an old favourite, the most interesting aspect of the disc was that its producer was none other than George Harrison. Indeed, Harrison joined the Pythons on stage to sing the *Lumberjack Song* during their New York performance and Palin or Idle joyfully donned checked shirt and woollen hat for every live *Python* show, performed by the entire cast as the finale to the first Amnesty International concert in 1976.

THE MAGIC CHRISTIAN

Infamous Peter Sellers comedy of excess which attempted to capture Southern's anti-establishment sixties essence with fresh *Python* blood injected into the screenplay. Following

13 re-writes Sellers contacted new kids on the block, John Cleese and Graham Chapman for help. With the offer of £500 a week and in an ironical incorporation of the 'money will buy anybody' theory of the movie, the writers could hardly refuse. Both believed that their endorsement of the film helped appease an uncertain Sellers and clinched the high budget to afford the appearance of Ringo Starr (having already cropped up in Southern's *Candy*), although in the end very little of what Chapman and Cleese wrote was included in the finished film. Having knocked the original screenplay into some sort of shape, the writers were understandably peeved to see the makers revert to the version which had already been rejected.

However, Chapman and Cleese did see their work bolster the movie with one of the best scenes, featuring Sellers, Ringo and Cleese in an examination of money over art - with Sellers amazing Cleese's Sotheby's chap by buying up a Rembrandt, mutilating the work by cutting out the painted nose and discarding the rest. The petulant delivery of Cleese, already in definitive *Python* put-down mode, continually turns away from Ringo and Sellers until serious money is mentioned and the frosty exterior falls away to reveal a man obsessed with huge amounts of cash.

Chapman also cropped up on screen as one of the Oxford rowing team, gallantly expressing disbelief at attempted bribes to throw the Boat Race in an uncredited but enjoyable piece of straight-faced pride. As with the pre-*Python* writers, this psychedelic sixties trip celebrated the greed of mankind via a well paid array of stunning guest stars. It was certainly a case of take the money and run which saw Christopher Lee agree to play the good Count Dracula for a quick gag appearance, Laurence Harvey solemnly deliver a striptease version of Hamlet's soliloquy (an idea pinched from a far more satisfying rendition in *The Pure Hell of St. Trinian's*) and Yul Brynner perform Noel Coward's *Mad About the Boy* in drag to an unimpressed

Roman Polanski. If cinema notables like that could swallow their pride for a few quid, what chance the rest of us! Any film which closes with bowler-hatted businessmen wading through blood, urine and manure has to put its money where its mouth is. Mind you, despite its chequered history and critical bemusement, *The Magic Christian* is a very good piece of late sixties film making. Sellers is wonderfully urbane throughout, putting on a deliciously foppish upper class accent (during hassles concerning a hot dog and a parking ticket), while Ringo (in the aftermath of Fab Four fall-out) merrily bounces the comic insanity off his surrogate father figure and injects the perfect essence of with-it, working class man of the time. A Lennon-a-like is briefly spotted boarding the exclusive cruise ship of the title, McCartney penned the classic Badfinger sing-a-long and repeat-a-thon *Come and Get It* while eccentric British treasures (Hattie Jacques, Dennis Price, John LeMesurier) effortlessly hold their heads above the tidal wave of flashing lights, quick cut-away images and drug culture coolness. By far the funniest, and warmest, moment comes with Spike Milligan's bumbling traffic warden, affectionately having his arm interlocked with Sellers as his thirst for money is tested. It's a brilliant, reassuringly straight-forward, comic sequence which amazingly rests wonderfully well amid a film of unforgettable, potent, but undeniably bizarre images. A scantily clad Raquel Welch whipping half-naked female rowers is one that will stay with you – first class travel will never be the same again – and, reflective of its time, the film addresses violence, racial issues and the class system. A fascinating film and one which bears repeated analysis if you can get your head round the first few minutes and just go with the flow. Despite the limited involvement of Chapman and Cleese, this was both a valued learning process and the ideal environment for those immediate pre-*Python* months.

Did You Know?
The most famous Chapman/Cleese contribution, The Mouse Problem, was edited from the shooting script. Later rejected again by Marty Feldman, it eventually appeared in *Monty Python* and became heralded as a classic. Sellers was initially thrilled with the sketch before returning the following day rather disgruntled, removing it because his milkman didn't think it was funny! Much of Ringo Starr's scene-stealing comedy business also fell foul of the whims and fears of Sellers.

Commonwealth United/Grand Films
The Magic Christian
Sir Guy Grand **PETER SELLERS**
Youngman Grand **RINGO STARR**
Dame Agnes Grand **ISABEL JEANS**
Hon. Esther Grand **CAROLINE BLAKISTON**
Captain Reginald K. Klaus **WILFRID HYDE-WHITE**
Oxford coach **RICHARD ATTENBOROUGH**
Laurence Faggot **LEONARD FREY**
Hamlet **LAURENCE HARVEY**
Ship's Vampire **CHRISTOPHER LEE**
Traffic Warden 27 **SPIKE MILLIGAN**
Solitary Drinker **ROMAN POLANSKI**
Priestess of the Whip **RAQUEL WELCH**
Nightclub Singer **YUL BRYNNER**
Pompouff **PETER BAYLISS**
Sotherby's Director **JOHN CLEESE**
Oxford Stroke **GRAHAM CHAPMAN**
Ginger Horton **HATTIE JACQUES**
Winthrop **DENNIS PRICE**
Sir Lionel **MICHAEL TRUBSHAWE**
Lord Barry **DAVID HUTCHESON**
Sommelier **CLIVE DUNN**
Fitzgibbon **FRED EMNEY**
Auctioneer **PATRICK CARGILL**
Duke of Mantisbriar **GUY MIDDLETON**
Waiter **GRAHAM STARK**
Sir John **JOHN LE MESURIER**
Lord Hampton **JEREMY LLOYD**
Ship's Guide **DAVID LODGE**
Hot Dog Vendor **VICTOR MADDERN**
Edouard **FERDY MAYNE**
Police Inspector **FRANK THORNTON**
with **MICHAEL ASPEL, ALAN WHICKER & MIKE BARRETT**
Screenplay by **Terry Southern, Joseph McGrath & Peter Sellers**, based on Southern's novelAdditional material by **Graham Chapman & John Cleese**
Photography **Geoffrey Unsworth**

Editor **Kevin Connor**
Production designer **Assheton Gorton**
Art director **George Djurkovic**
Sound **Brian Holland**
Executive Producers **Henry T. Weinstein
& Anthony B. Unger**
Producer **Denis O'Dell**
Director **Joseph McGrath**
1969, 95 mins

THE MAGNIFICENT SEVEN DEADLY SINS

Despite a writing and/or performance roll-call featuring such major comic talents as Spike Milligan, Harry H. Corbett, Marty Feldman, Joan Sims, Ray Galton, Alan Simpson, Peter Butterworth, Leslie Phillips, Bernard Bresslaw and Harry Secombe, this compendium of sketches put together by director Graham Stark continually falls flat. However, one of the better episodes is 'Wrath', written by Barry Cryer and Graham Chapman. Basically the authority-baiting struggle of two veteran military types against a trumped-up, power-mad Park Keeper. With stunning, playful, petulant performances from loveable pranksters Ronald Fraser and Arthur Howard, the object of their murderous plans is a typically 'jobsworth' turn from Stephen Lewis – an 'I 'ate you Butler!' seems to be continually playing on his lips, as he denounces Fraser's distinguished, proud chap as 'too old', faces wanton destruction of park property (park bench/bin) and childish, lavatorial antics with laxative powers. Complete with seventies glam girl, groovy mood music, stylised comic slapstick and laboured sight gags, this successfully mixes anarchy death wish with cultured manners (all friendly sharing of sandwiches, *ITMA*-like Cecil/Claude niceties and matter of fact killing plans). There are a couple of priceless movie references, with the *Pyscho* theme accompanying Fraser's ill-fated, dampened knife attack and a manic Lewis bike display embracing *Butch Cassidy and the Sundance Kid* memories via the tune *Raindrops Keep Falling On My Head*. The subject matter is perfect for Chapman but it is not until the final twist in the

fork-tail, after life ending that his delicious sense of paradoxical comic values shines through.

Tigon: *The Magnificent Seven Deadly Seven Sins*
Starring **LESLIE PHILLIPS, JULIE EGE, HARRY H. CORBETT, JOAN SIMS, PETER BUTTERWORTH, BERNARD BRESSLAW, SPIKE MILLIGAN, HARRY SECOMBE, BRUCE FORSYTH, DAVID LODGE, IAN CARMICHAEL & ALFIE BASS**
'Wrath' section written by **Barry Cryer & Graham Chapman**
George **RONALD FRASER**
Kenneth **ARTHUR HOWARD**
Jarvis **STEPHEN LEWIS**
Photography **Harvey Harrison Jnr**
Music **Roy Budd**
Produced & directed by **Graham Stark**
107 minutes, 1971

MARY SHELLEY'S FRANKENSTEIN

In the wake of *Bram Stoker's Dracula* in 1992, its chief rival in the greatest horror story of all-time stakes was redone and dusted in a faithful and affectionate nod to the original book. Latching onto the literal tradition of the piece from the start, with the chilling reading from Mary Shelley's diary and the shocking appearance of the title from a mire of darkness, this is a lavish production which skilfully blurs the edges between text and the creative, drug-induced poet's fest of the Byron/Shelley excesses in Switzerland that formed the background for the story's conception. Robert De Niro's horrific, unremorseful creature showed yet again that Hollywood's big guns were happy to embrace this new obsession with horror cinema (Gary Oldman's blood-sucking for Coppola/Jack Nicholson adding to the werewolf myth with *Wolf*). But it's a stunning piece of work from Kenneth Branagh, both as director and on-screen monster maker, that makes this film such an impressive and breathtaking work. The creation sequence is arguably one of the most powerful moments in the entire genre.
As per usual, Branagh surrounded

himself with the cream of British and American acting talent, notably his almost ever present talisman, Richard Briers, Helena Bonham Carter, Tom Hulce, Ian Holm and John Cleese as the quietly obsessive Professor Waldman. Cleese's brief but totally mesmerising contribution comes during the plague-ridden, medically challenged, filth-encrusted sequences set in Ingolstadt, 1793, where experimental ideas are considered occult and the driven energy of the young Frankenstein shines like a beacon of exploration. Cleese plays his part like an aged, failed and world-weary version of Frankenstein (indeed, the part could have been perfect for Peter Cushing) as it happens Branagh bravely and typically ignored the fact that Cleese was pigeonholed as comedian and cast him in perhaps the most effective film role of his career. His time on screen is a bare ten minutes but, like Orson Welles in *The Third Man*, Cleese is at the very core of the story, giving an eye-catching and unforgettable performance as well as reinforcing the obsession within Frankenstein to preserve and recreate life within the narrative structure. The classic three-way ape arm sequence with Cleese, Branagh and Hulce is a masterpiece, with comedy (Hulce's amazed reaction) and scientific passion as the two like-minded men of genius connect. Cleese is a man who has seen the horror and felt the angst of Branagh's idealistic dreams but the presence of a man who shares his ambitions rekindles a long lost sense of discovery. Branagh's direction sets up Cleese perfectly, with his reputation for bizarre experiments surrounding him in mystery before his first speech. He is a quickly vanishing figure in a flowing black cloak and a sinister knowing face from within a carriage, but his finest moment comes with his very first appearance. With Branagh's eager student in the gods of the lecture hall, point of view camera angles and Robert Hardy's condescending gaze when condemning original thought, Cleese is glimpsed in half light. Upon hearing Branagh's enthusiastic pleas for the knowledge of forbidden sciences Cleese, interested by what he hears, shifts position out of the shadows and looks upwards. It is a spell-binding moment. While poor old Hardy flamboyantly rants and raves, Cleese effortlessly steals the scene with no dialogue whatsoever. This is the work of a fine actor.

Mary Shelley's Frankenstein
Tri-star Pictures in association with Japan Satellite Broadcasting Inc. and The IndieProd Company An American Zoetrope Production
Creature/Sharp-featured man **ROBERT DE NIRO**
Victor Frankenstein **KENNETH BRANAGH**
Henry Clerval **TOM HULCE**
Elizabeth **HELENA BONHAM CARTER**
Walton **AIDAN QUINN**
Victor's Father **IAN HOLM**
Grandfather **RICHARD BRIERS**
Professor Waldman **JOHN CLEESE**
Professor Krempe **ROBERT HARDY**
Victor's Mother **CHERIE LUNGHI**
Mrs. Moritz **CELIA IMRIE**
Justine **TREVYN McDOWELL**
Claude **GERALD HORAN**
Felix **MARK HADFIELD**
Marie **JOANNA ROTH**
Maggie **SASHA HANAU**
Thomas **JOSEPH ENGLUND**
Landlord **ALFRED BELL**
Screenplay **Steph Lady & Frank Darabont**
Script supervisor **Annie Wotton**
Music **Patrick Doyle**
Costume designer **James Acheson**
Editor **Andrew Marcus**
Production designer **Tim Harvey**
Photography **Roger Pratt**
Casting **Priscilla John**
Creature make-up & effects **Daniel Parker**
Camera operator **Trevor Coop**
Art directors **John Fenner & Desmond Crowe**
Associate producers **Robert De Niro & Jeff Kleeman**
Co-producers **Kenneth Branagh & David Parfitt**
Executive producer **Fred Fuchs**
Producers **Francis Ford Coppola, James V. Hart & John Veitch**
Director **Kenneth Branagh**
Filmed at Shepperton Studios & on location in the Swiss Alps, Technicolour 120 mins, 1994

SPIKE MILLIGAN

The grand old master of British comedy, Spike Milligan is arguably the key figure in the development of 20th century humour. It is unlikely that without him, there would have ever been any such thing as *Monty Python's Flying Circus*. Worshipped by Graham Chapman, John Cleese, Terry Jones, Eric Idle, Michael Palin, Terry Gilliam, Peter Cook, Marty Feldman, Kenny Everett and every other player worth his salt in the anarchic comedy invasion, Milligan's mix of surrealism, innuendo, silly voices, sound pictures and anti-establishment comment in *The Goon Show* cut a swathe through post-war entertainment and changed the face of comedy beyond recognition. Celebrated by the new generation of television comedians, Milligan's own small screen work in *A Show Called Fred*, *The TeleGoons* and *Q* set the trend for *Python* to follow. Although often perturbed at his ideas being incorporated in the work of others (*Monty Python*/Richard Lester) without getting full credit, Spike could never really complain about Cleese and the gang. At every avenue the team would fete their comic guru, using his classic Goonish short *The Case of the Mukkinese Battlehorn* to support *Monty Python and the Holy Grail* and eventually the forces merged on screen for *Monty Python's Life of Brian*. Spike, blissfully unaware of the filming, just happened to be in Tunisia on holiday when the Pythons gave him the call. Tossed into robes and open-toed sandals, Milligan's bearded cameo has a few words of mumbled dialogue, no narrative importance and ends up alone in the dust with a look of bemusement – but in that look, my friends, shines 30 years of inspired lunacy. Milligan clearly enjoyed the experience, for some four years later he cropped up again for another madcap support opposite Eric Idle in the Graham Chapman comedy *Yellowbeard*.

THE MIKADO

Classic Gilbert & Sullivan Japanese-based operetta reinterpreted by Jonathan Miller, relocated in the Grand Hotel on the English coast in the 1920s and revitalised by Eric Idle's energetic performance. With a sterling cast, including the young and ever glamorous Lesley Garrett, Idle's comic persona was perfect for the Executioner, Ko-Ko, continuing the usual practise of updating the list within *I've Got A Little List* to feature mentions of Ronald Reagan as part of his punishment agenda. Luckily, television and album versions were made for posterity.

Did You Know?
Idle had worked with Jonathan Miller on the BBC production of *Alice in Wonderland* and being a huge fan of *Beyond the Fringe* was happy to tackle the project – indeed Dudley Moore played Ko-Ko in Los Angeles with Idle resuming the part in Houston.

The Mikado **RICHARD ANGAS**
Nanki-Poo **BONAVENTURA BOTTONE**
Ko-Ko, Lord High Executioner **ERIC IDLE**
Pooh-Bah **RICHARD VAN ALLAN**
Pish-Tush **MARK RICHARDSON**
Yum-Yum **LESLEY GARRETT**
Pitti-Sing **JEAN RIGBY**
Peep-Bo **SUSAN BULLOCK**
Katishka **FELICITY PALMER**
Written by **Gilbert & Sullivan**
Additional lyrics for *I've Got A Little List* by **Eric Idle**
Produced & directed by **Jonathan Miller**
The English National Opera production first performed at the London Coliseum 18 September 1986

THE MIRRORSTONE

With shades of Wilkie Collins's *The Moonstone* in the title and a children's mind for magic, this was another successful storybook from Michael Palin. It tells the tale of a young boy, good at swimming, who sees strange reflections, is mystically brought to another world by Wizard Salaman, inventor of the Mirrorstone, and involved in his eager needs to retrieve the object. Palin, Seymour and Lee share writing credit on the cover as the book boasts some wonderfully detailed hologramatic features.

Written by **Michael Palin**
Conceived & designed by **Richard Seymour**
Illustrations by **Alan Lee**
Published by Jonathan Cape Books, 1986

MISLEADING CASES

Gentle court room mockery which allowed a beloved, aged eccentric to raise an eyebrow, cheerfully parody the system and react with amazed disbelief at all around him. In full *Python* stardom, Cleese was invited to inject a typically pompous attitude.

Mr Justice Swallow **ALASTAIR SIM**
Sir Joshua Hoot **QC THORLEY WALTERS**
Guest starring **JOHN CLEESE**
Producer **John Howard Davies**
BBC2, 1970

MISSING PIECES

A fairly standard comedy suspense script is given a golden touch by Eric Idle's leading performance packed with a barrow-load of rare physical comedy and his usual sardonic, off-kilter observations. The basis plot thread, concerning two bumbling pals who are chased by various interested parties on the trail of a valuable knife, provides a suitably Hitchcockian (sort of *North by NorthWest* meets 1954's *The Man Who Knew Too Much* via *Notorious*), winding road, knockabout thriller with some feel-good buddy moments, a slice of romance, some stunt-heavy action, a dash of John Huston's *The Maltese Falcon* (valuable artefact/Mr. Gutman) and plenty of obvious, Vaudevillian-styled jokes. The credit sequence is a very successful contemporary stab at slapstick humour, with Idle's notable sight gags including a full-on rush into a reversing lorry and a classic bit of

marathon-convention twisting with his grabbing of a beggar's cup, drinking the money within, spitting it out and eagerly handing it on to another beggar. Idle handles the irony well and it's a very effective, underplayed moment.
Robert Wuhl's performance could never be described as under-played however, and although his wild-haired, cherubic babblings tend to grate after a while, there's no denying that he has some good moments along the way, relishing some typical anti-lawyer observations, a knowing look into camera when his instrument is praised and a wry comment about the room cleaning in the aftermath of the raided apartment. His character gets under the skin, appealing enough for the audience to swell with pride and really celebrate his final success. Besides, at the end of the day, he provides the perfect sounding board for Eric Idle's work. What more can you ask? Idle certainly wouldn't have dreamt of writing some of his sequences, but he plays the corny old gags and sight humour with great conviction, tackling remnants and in-jokes to grand old timers of film comedy. There's the obvious Abbott and Costello nod with the 'Who died?'/'Ya!' banter, the knock-about, do anything for a laugh style of The Three Stooges runs throughout the film, the cowardly incompetent caught up in dangerous situations recalls vintage Bob Hope ('Oh, that Mr. Gabor' when the gun appears), the memorable interlude song *High Energy*, pitched centre of Sinatra's *High Hopes* and the Road movie's *Put it There Pal* brilliantly captures traditional buddy love, Idle's desperate attempt to hide from the Chinese madman not only echoes his own *Nuns on the Run*, but more importantly, his hiding place is pure Marx Brothers class from *Monkey Business*, he embraces Stan Laurel-like drunk antics from *The Bohemian Girl* and finally, the skyscraper climax comes somewhere between *Quatermass and the Pit* and low-grade Harold Lloyd. But whatever he's doing, Idle makes it worthwhile. He has a hilarious early sequence in the bathroom, singing *Today, I'm*

Going To Love Everybody into his mouthwash, getting confused with the telephone and generally doing some pretty nifty prop juggling in a sort of less cool variation on Woody Allan's masterpiece bathroom scene in *Play It Again Sam*, with just a dash of Peter Sellers in *The Party* for good measure. This link is extended with the petulant doctor's reaction to the multitude of paper towels, while enjoying some subtle play with the skeleton. Later he has a classic exchange with James Hong's fortune cookie guy, flamboyantly and obviously trying to draw Idle's stupid attention to the concealed note. It's a classic moment.
There's brain cells somewhere along the way, for Idle tackles Holmesian detective work with ease, counterbalancing bizarre renditions of Beethoven in the car, escaped lunatics and a one-armed hoodlum from Bob Gunton in the grand tradition of *The Fugitive* with painfully corny but funny wine-related gags, unsuccessful multi-faceted, over-security for his pad and a priceless *Python*esque notion of humorous sympathy cards. The pseudo-American accent is betrayed by the typically British 'Sorry!' as he defeats the bad guy and even the rather crummy foster parents discussion with the lawyer is well played. If you can imagine a sort of *Dumb and Dumber* with a higher intellectual level crossed with *North by NorthWest* you just about have *Missing Pieces*. It's almost a classic and I doubt if there's an original gag cracked in the entire film but that doesn't matter, there's a real sense of a good time being had by all - ideal for some 'turn your brain off' entertainment.

The Rank Organization & Aaron Russo Entertainment/Orion Pictures release
Missing Pieces
Wendel Dickens **ERIC IDLE**
Lou Wimpole **ROBERT WUHL**
Jennifer **LAUREN HUTTON**
Mr. Gabor **BOB GUNTON**
Baldesari **RICHARD BELZER**
Dr. Gutman **BERNIE KOPELL**
Sally **KIM LANKFORD**
Hurrudnik **DON GIBB**

Krauso **LESLIE JORDAN**
Ochonko **LOUIS ZORICH**
Scarface **DON HEWITT**
Paul/Walter Thackery **JOHN DE LANCIE**
Chang **JAMES HONG**
Marlon **JANICE LYNDE**
Mrs. Callahan **MARY FORGARTY**
Chauffeur **BRUCE KRONENBERG**
Elissa **STACEY ANN LOGAN**
Joseph **DEREK MEADER**
Myra Gluckman **KATE STERN**
Father of the Bride **PAUL KEITH**
Bernice **SHARON BROWN**
Nurse **ANDREA GARFIELD**
Young Chinese man **DARRYL CHAN**
Mrs. Waldham **LOUISE TROY**
Woman at Concert **GLORIA STROOCK**
Man at Concert **LEONARD STERN**
Chinese Man **RICHARD KWONG**
Receptionist **KELLIE JO TACKETT**
Attendant **LOU MYERS**
Mountain Man **RICK ZUMWALT**
Dog Walker **ALISA McCULLOUGH**
Production designer **Michael Z. Hanan**
Music **Marvin Hamlisch**
Song: *High Energy* music by **Marvin Hamlisch**, lyrics by **David Zippel**
Performed by **Eric Idle & Robert Wuhl**
Light Cavalry Overture by **Franz von Suppa**
Serenade, Opus 8 by Ludvig Von Beethoven, arranged by **Natham Birnbaum**
Editor **Evan Lottman**
Photography **Peter Stein**
Casting **Julie Hughes & Barry Moss**
Costume designer **Bobbie Read**
Eric Idle's tailored wardrobe by **Hart, Schaffner & Marx**
Production designer **Michael Z. Hanan**
Stunt co-ordinator **Joe Dunne**
Unit production managers **Lou Fusaro & Bill Carraro**
1st assistant director **Alex Hapsas**
Script supervisor **Martha Mitchell**
Camera operator **Tony Cutrono**
Art director **Mark Zuelske**
Set decorator **Doug Mowat**
Executive producer **William C. Carraro**
Producer **Aaron Russo**
Written & directed by **Leonard Stern**
1991 89 mins

THE MISSIONARY

Michael Palin's first solo film venture and one of the many backed by the

What's a nice girl like you... Michael Palin tries to show Tricia George the errors of her ways – *The Missionary*

new HandMade label, this is really a polished *Ripping Yarn* and brilliantly done (indeed, Palin once expressed interest in re-editing the *Yarns* for a cinema release). During work on *Time Bandits*, Denis O'Brien and George Harrison asked Palin to come up with a script idea of his own; the result was this stifling return to exploring emotion-concealing pride of British history with a more understanding, balanced style of writing. Gentle and understated, Palin's solo writing credit retains brilliantly written parodies of the British upper classes, highlighting the sickening, money-loving, bloodthirsty, champers guzzling, xenophobic attitude of the rich, while celebrating the eccentricity of organised religion and superior attempts to smooth the pleasures of the underprivileged. Palin's performance, typical of *Ripping Yarns,* is meek and mild, incorporating just a dash of adventure and sexual interest into his collected, God-fearing British characterisation and, as with his BBC shows, he wisely surrounds himself with a distinguished collection of seasoned thespians. The ever-wonderful Maggie Smith, who would later work with Palin in *A Private Function*, contributes a quite stunning mixture of landed gentry wealth and free-spirited sexual energy. Denholm Elliott, who had guest-starred in *Across the Andes By*

Frog, gives a peerless performance as the Bishop of London, nervously explaining the job Palin is required for and peppering his speech with sporting terminology, while fellow British film icon, Trevor Howard, personifies the stuffy, over-privileged, self-opinionated, *Times* letter writer, pontificating against everything and anything that may affect his position as uncontrolled, wealthy bore. David Suchet has an unforgettable Scottish monologue pledging his healthy body to the worship of Smith, a doddery old Roland Culver plays doddery and old with skill, Graham Crowden does a good job of his under-used country vicar and Timothy Spall's bumbling manservant - with some hilarious fertility symbol dropping business - all give the project class.
But it's the stately Michael Hordern, both providing off-screen narration and on-screen delight as the absent-minded butler, that effortlessly steals the film. Staggering round the enormous Ames estate, his hound-dog expression, misunderstandings and petulant behaviour creates some glorious material, particularly opposite the sheepish Palin and the *Python*esque madness of countless misdirections. Palin, both as writer and actor, brilliantly addresses the attitude of the time, tasting the freedom of Africa while finding his girlish fiancée and her filing system of letters a massive contrast to the good

time had by all on the streets of London. Palin's mixture of sexual willingness (all for God's message, of course) and schoolboy personality makes an appealing central figure but despite a fairly short running time there are occasions when the film runs out of steam and stretches the situation to breaking point. But the audience are made to care for the characters and the final falling from grace with dignity is a warm and affecting experience. Besides, the closing credits with Neil Innes's cockney chappie reprising his Music Hall ditty is enough to please anybody. A light and easy film which skilfully puts across its moral debate with Palin's persuasive use of charm and innocence.

HandMade Film: *The Missionary*
Rev. Charles W. Fortescue **MICHAEL PALIN**
Lady Ames **MAGGIE SMITH**
Lord Ames **TREVOR HOWARD**
Bishop of London **DENHOLM ELLIOTT**
Rev. Fitzbanks **GRAHAM CROWDEN**
Corbett **DAVID SUCHET**
Slatterthwaite **MICHAEL HORDERN**
Deborah Fitzbanks **PHOEBE NICHOLLS**
Ada **TRICIA GEORGE**
Emmeline **VALERIE WHITTINGTON**
Lord Fernleigh **ROLAND CULVER**
Lady Fernleigh **ROSAMUND GREENWOOD**
Parswell **TIMOTHY SPALL**
Singer in Gin Palace **NEIL INNES**
Mission Girls **DAWN ARCHIBALD**
FRANCES BARBER
DEBBIE BISHOP
CERI JACKSON
JANINE LESLEY
SASHA MITCHELL
FRANCINE MORGAN
SOPHIE THOMPSON
SALLY WATKINS
Gym Trainer **DERRICK O'CONNOR**
Small Boys at Mudflats **TONY FAWCETT, JASON BARR & EDMUND BUMSTEAD**
Arthur Pimp, the Long haired Man in Gin Palace **DAVID LELAND**
Emily **ANNE-MARIE MARRIOTT**
Usher at Wedding **HUGH FRASER**
Best Man at Wedding **PETER BOURKE**
Millicent **JANINE DUVITSKI**
Fernleigh's Maid **TILLY VOSBURGH**
Fernleigh's Butler **ARTHUR HOWARD**

Fernleigh's Doctor **HUGH WALTERS**
Friends at Raggy Masterson **JULIAN CURRY & CHARLES McKEOWN**
Majarajah **ISHAY BEX**
Lord Quimby **TONY STEEDMAN**
Lady Quimby **DAMARIS HAYMAN**
Young men **DAVID DIXON & ANTON LESSER**
Sir Cyril Everidge **FRANK MILLS**
Majarajah Boy **YESSEL SHAH**
Schoolmaster's Voice **JOHN FORTUNE**
Screenplay by **Michael Palin**
Art director **Norman Garwood**
Costume designer **Shuna Harwood**
Editor **Paul Green**
Music **Mike Moran**
Put On Your Ta-Ta Little Girlie written by **Fred W. Leigh**
Sung by **Neil Innes**
Production manager **Graham Ford**
Assistant director **Gary White**
Camera operator **Dewi Humphreys**
Set decorator **Ian Whittaker**
Photography **Peter Hannan**
Executive producers **George Harrison & Denis O'Brien**
Producers **Neville C. Thompson & Michael Palin**
Director **Richard Loncraine**
Filmed at Lee International Studios & on location in England, Scotland and Kenya
86 mins, 1983

MOM AND DAD SAVE THE WORLD

Also known as the equally risible *Dick and Marge Save the World*, this wacky, fast-paced sci-fi comedy with America taking on a threat from an alien planet makes *Independence Day* look like... well... *Independence Day*. One of the major delights is a *Python*esque cameo from Eric Idle which crops up towards the end. Bumbling around with aged anarchy, forgetting things, trying to explain his history, delivering Pertwee-like observations ('I have reversed the polarity on the magno-beam, you are now safe to leave!') and imprisoned in a cell with nothing but the figure of Kathy Ireland clad in fur bikini (played like Racquel Welsh in space) to keep him sane. Tapping into Michael Palin's memorable prisoner from *Brian*, Eric fully embraces his old legacy - instead of Graham Chapman

saying 'What!' it's Jeffrey Jones.

Warner Brothers/Mercury
Marge Nelson **TERI GARR**
Dick Nelson **JEFFREY JONES**
Tod Spengo **JON LOVITZ**
Sirk **DWIER BROWN**
General Afir **THALMUS RASULALA**
Sibor **WALLACE SHAWN**
Semage the King Raff **ERIC IDLE**
Rebel **KATHY IRELAND**
Screenplay by **Ed Solomon & Chris Matheson**
Music **Jerry Goldsmith**
Producer **Michael S. Phillips**
Director **Greg Beeman**
1992, 87 mins

MONTY PYTHON AND THE HOLY GRAIL

The team's first feature film proper, this reunited the six members for the big screen after John Cleese had walked away from the television ventures; capitalised on the historical comic genius of the writing of Jones and Palin (relishing this major canvas for injecting contemporary types and mannerisms into a mediaeval Britain setting); highlighted Graham Chapman's superb acting skill in a stolid, sustained acting performance; allowed the sublime Eric Idle to mug away with vigour; and, vitally, saw the cinematic directorial debuts for both Terry Jones and Terry Gilliam. Apart from all that, it's also one of the five funniest films ever made in this country. It may lack the structured polish of *Life of Brian* and even sag into rather unfunny territory about two-thirds of the way through, but *Monty Python and the Holy Grail* has more class comedy in its first hour than any film deserves. Not so much a parody, more a conventional mediaeval epic with heaps of very silly things going on, there's a sense of special occasion, for although the television team had only just split up, all members are united for this major onslaught on the film market.
Basically made up of disjointed sketches, complete with class Gilliam animations, outlandish touches of absurdity and even a couple of jolly

ditties from Neil Innes, the film does play like an elongated, focused *Python* TV show, although there is chance for the intellectualising of humorous academic history to take full flight and the on-going, running gags, notably concerning the flying behaviour and coconut grasping attributes of the swallow, gradually gain momentum throughout the film. More so than their reheated compendium in *And Now For Something Completely Different*, the team work harder to treat cinematic convention with the same contempt as the television series had shown to small screen convention. Within the hilarious, anti-subtitled comments during the subdued, European cinema styled credits and the garish, Hollywood glitz, complete with *Sgt. Pepper*-like mock cinema conventions the Pythons contrast art-house with commercialism. However, rather than take cinematic form over the hot coals, *Grail* decides to simply mock historical concept via typically insane *Python* logic, inject some mild religious mockery via Gilliam's bossy God animation and revel mainly in tried and tested comic ideals. With the added bonus of superb period detail and some of the team's funniest material you can forgive everything, even the baffling and unsuccessful lapses into educational television historical presentation parody with John Young's on-screen historian, the contemporary police investigation and the final arrest of our Round Table heroes in place of a proper ending.

While Chapman's brush with alien forces in *Brian* mocks filmic excess, there's a sense that *Brian* is just the six lads play-acting in a muddy field rather than going for all-out believability. Mind you with such high class play acting, this is only a superficial complaint. From the moment we enter this murky, mist-swirling landscape, dripped in poverty-stricken contempt the Pythons can let loose with surreal, dysfunctional and totally brilliant madness with the clip-clop of coconuts ushering in King Chapman and skivvy Gilliam – this is pure film magic. Instantly, we can see the team

happily embracing an affectionate and knowledgeable grasp of history while riding full-on through the pomp with manic arrows of comedy puncturing everything in sight with convincing murky backdrops.

Graham Chapman, as with his landmark Brian, is allowed to play his comedy straight surrounded by a galaxy of grotesques and here, in deep discussion about weight ratio of swallows, are Michael Palin and John Cleese undermining the absurdity of coconut travel with a typically spiralling conversation.

Idle's biting characterisation wastes no time in digging in with class deconstruction with his identification of Chapman as a King because he isn't covered in excrement while sugar-coating the pill with the painfully hilarious 'bring out your dead' sequence, bending the red-tape, committing murder and commenting on the class divide all in the name of being a good neighbour.

For many the film's ultimate highlight is Palin's bolshy Dennis condemning Chapman's bemused King with a string of communist complaints and structured pointers for a more acceptable social doctrine. With his filth collecting mother (Terry Jones – 'Well, I didn't vote for you!') in tow, his working class fury (embracing the classic challenge on the Lady of the Lake legend), mapped out plans for a communal system and outraged reaction to being addressed as just one of the masses – despite Chapman's limited knowledge – this is a classic of repressed British comedy observation.

Next up in the laughter stakes is Cleese's glorious Black Knight, battling on against Chapman's super cool figure with dismembered limbs, gushing blood ('just a flesh wound') and determined sarcastic taunts. The head-bashing, monotonous chanting monks, although a real downer for *Carry On Columbus*, successfully link this highlight with the legendary witch ducking sequence. The absurdity of judicial punishment, later further explored with *Brian*'s Stoning scene, allows Connie Booth's witch to both latch onto modernity with 'It's a fair cop' and address the

viewing audience, while Terry Jones, pseudo-intellectual, throws in a mention of bird and coconut experiments with John Cleese gloriously over-acting with an impassioned 'Burn her!' Jones is superb, conducting the whole thing like a schoolroom lesson with Idle and Palin struggling to impress and Cleese, sheepishly nervous, holding back with his correctly perceived suggestion.

In the end, beyond the hilarious contrasts between burning a woman when proven a witch and dunking an innocent one, Chapman's celebrated interjection and Jones, impressed beyond measure, proves that absurdity works all the time. The storybook feel of the adventure is heightened by Gilliam's luscious illustrations and Palin's narration, with the film twisting the essence of telling tall tales with the monstrous hand defeating the human. The notion that this is just a play and its characters merely players is further incorporated via the wonderment of the Pythons at Camelot with Gilliam pricking the bubble via his unimpressed throw-away comment – 'It's only a model!' Cinematic tradition within this historical believability is again injected via Neil Innes's impromptu singing of the *Knights of Camelot* song, complete with lyrics referring to Clark Gable, a *Python*esque favourite Spam and the ultimate of desperate rhyme, push the pram a lot. Even here, the team can comment on the cruelty of the period while remaining funny, with the jovial strapped up prisoner happily clapping along to the tune deep within the dungeon and the helmet banging antics overflowing to the helmetless surf who is, naturally enough, knocked cold. As with Jones's earliest treat, Slapstick, pain directed at other people is still disturbingly hilarious. Retaining the Gilliam animation as sketch links, his regal-looking God with booming Chapman voice effortlessly merges with the real-life sky footage and sets the seal on the holy quest for the grail.

But in *Python* it's the irrelevant details which make the whole so satisfying with the principal example having to be the peasant slapping the river with a fish. It's just a quick visual laugh, slotted in as the lads ride past and no comment is directed at the scene – this is the essence of *Monty Python* at its purest. Later a carpet is beaten with a cat as Idle's handy shrubbery salesman bumps into Chapman's Ni-cursed Monarch, ultimately reeling with the prospect of chopping down a tree with a herring – this is the stuff to confuse and amuse. The initial sarcastic encounter with John Cleese and his outrageous French accent (again pinpointed by the script as playing within a film) throws up the most oft quoted parts of the film with elderberries and hamsters imprinted on the mind for all time highlighting these Frenchie types as perfectly rude swines, effortlessly winding up Chapman and bringing on some put out, Brit-manners upheld reaction. The British insulted are the British defeated here, with the typical cry of 'Run away!' as the surreal landslide of stuffed farm animals results in the half-baked and over-played Trojan rabbit scene. At least Innes wasn't squashed by a 16-ton weight! The Pythons still weren't averse to having a go at television culture as children's history programming is feebly mocked with the waffling and condescending figure of authoritative knowledge brutally cut down by the Knights. From here on it's every man for himself as each of Arthur's God-fearing Knights make their own bumbling way to the glories of success. Eric Idle's cowardly Sir Robin, complete with pessimistic madrigal singing from Innes and a bickering reappearance from Palin's militant Dennis, creeps through the forest trying to avoid any sign of danger before bumping into the camp, self-condemning Three-headed Knight (courtesy of stunning squeaking from Terry Jones, Graham Chapman and Michael Palin). Gilliam makes pre-*Jabberwocky* use of grotesque comic figures from Mediaeval bibles with a swimming hole montage of bum-flashing monks before Michael Palin's ultra-innocent Sir Galahad discovers a rain-sodden

castle entrance and finds himself in a Carol Cleveland led sex haven. With a gorgeous collection of fresh nymphets on display, Palin's Jim Dalesque British nervousness is taken to extremes with a delicious *Carry On* wallowing in base innuendo and surfeit of *Are You Being Served?* Pussy gags, justified in *Python* terms with Cleveland's pleas that she thought this material was going to be cut, but the boys wrote it and decided to keep it in. More fundamental tongue-in-cheek script questions concerning Cleese's sexuality battles against the non-stop, barrel-scraping farce, brilliantly topped off with a *Carry On* celebration of pals rescuing sex hungry Brit from free-wheeling sex fest – one almost expects some downtrodden Sid James moaning and Terry Scott to swing into view! With Palin's narrator independently resurrecting the swallow theory and embracing the art of performance with an enthused celebration of 'smashing acting', Chapman's stunned scene with Gilliam's manic, hairy nutter latches onto the idea of filmic sequence while setting the scene for Rowan Atkinson's wise woman chat in the Ben Elton/Richard Curtis classic *Blackadder II*. Then it's the Palin/Jones landmark – the Knights who say 'Ni!', which the other Pythons weren't too sure about but has now passed into our collective comic consciousness. Desperate for a shrubbery and setting Chapman and his lads the task to end all tasks, this manic screaming Viking-like forest dweller takes the film to the heights of surreal nonsense. Even the burst of contemporary police activity pales besides the wild-eyed muttering of Michael Palin. Gilliam enjoys a totally unconnected bit of jumping weather fun before Cleese's Sir Lancelot has his moment of glory, trying to out-hero his trusty steed Concorde (a brilliantly self-deprecating cameo from stiff upper-lipped and 'proud to be British' Idle). Longing for some terrified damsel in distress to aid, the situation Cleese stumbles upon is the classic Jones/Palin Northern brass kingdom scenario, with Palin's mouthy swamp

magnet keeping his wimpish son, Jones, behind locked doors, effortlessly stopping anti-realism bursts of song and injecting a sense of outraged frustration with the misunderstanding guards of vacant Chapman/Formbyesque Idle. Jones, displaying his genius for mime, secretively scribbles his plea for help and gingerly fires it out on an arrow while his guardians look on happily. Cleese's cliché-ridden, Errol Flynn-like Knight jumps into action, gallops into view like Omar Shariff in David Lean's *Lawrence of Arabia*, tries to kill everybody in sight and leaves the place looking like an exaggerated *Hamlet* climax. The period detail of making merry wedding festivities is breathtaking, while the shocked reappearance of Jones (believed dead) and Cleese's nervous, spluttered 'Sorry!' give this realistic image of historical carnage a maniacally comic twist.

The message, of course, lies in Palin's money-mad, social-ladder climbing businessman hailing the murderous Cleese as his guest of honour and allowing Jones a weedy final stab at his song. With each Knight a relative failure, the lads reunite for a progress report following Gilliam's multi-eyed monster. The almighty Cleese gives one of his most compelling performances, as the horned enchanter Tim, rolling his Rs, muttering 'Quite!' with perfection and quietly spinning his fateful warning concerning the killer, small, white rabbit. With a smattering of skulls and Chapman's critical amazement at his co-writer's acting ('What an eccentric performance!') the foolhardy Gilliam tries his luck with the squawking glove puppet before Idle's Derek Nimmo-inspired religious reading of instructions for the holy hand grenade goes round in ever madding circles. The genius discussion concerning Castle Argghh... (a location which crops up later, complete with Cleese French insults) and Gilliam's Black Beast (which is clearly green) vanishing, thus saving the film's cast thanks to the animator's fatal heart attack, fade to the climatic Bridge of Death sequence, resurrecting Gilliam's masterly hairy old nutter from his scene 24 chat with Chapman. Easy questions, with a few tricky ones tossed in, see great swathes of Chapman's men meet their end in the Gorge of Eternal Peril before the inquisitor is fooled by his own question concerning those damned different species of swallow. A very belated intermission, the arrest of Cleese's Lancelot by interlopers from 1974 law-enforcing and a return from the French taunters, using insults as the ultimate weapon, more or less rounds things off, with the final battle quickly curtailed by the arrival of modern policemen, stopping the historical goings-on, arresting our hapless heroes, Roger Cook-like, blocking the film cameras to avoid the public gaze and thus finishing the film with no fanfare. At the cinema screening there was brief mediaeval play-out music but what ever way you cut it this is an easy and slightly unsatisfactory closure. Seemingly with no way to finish the movie and lacking an everlasting supply of Gilliam animations to cross-fade and merge into, the only way out was a sudden cut to black. Jones decided that with nothing else to say he would simply run out of film and stop the story, hoping for 30 seconds of total darkness, some dreadful muzak and some sort of closing moment – cinemas across the country were not willing to play ball so the audience are left in the air but, so what; the previous 90 minutes includes some of the most cherished comedy moments ever committed to film.

Did You Know?
Typically, Terry Jones was very keen to do a *Python* film, while John Cleese was very much against the idea. Having been swept along with Victor Lownes and his promises of huge wealth from *And Now For Something Completely Different*, Cleese was rather disinterested in *Python* altogether – be it television or film. The others had discussed the possibility of their own, totally original film since the beginning of *Python* series three with Jones/Palin writing reams of historical pieces and

contemporary material (later reworked for series four). The unconvincing remnants of this crossing-the-ages style is the dysfunctional historian/policeman thread in *Grail*. Michael White, the producing brain behind the film who had had a finger in the *Cambridge Circus* pie, produced *The Rocky Horror Show* and eventually headed *Comic Strip*, found backing money from Led Zeppelin, Pink Floyd (before their pre-*Wall* financial mire) and three record companies. The budget was so tight (£229,000) and the costs so high that although Neil Innes wrote great swathes of score, orchestra time was out of the question – in the end vast chunks were lifted from commercial mood records.
Despite the high quality of the film, the Pythons knew major splits were taking hold, notably here with the two directors on one side and the actors on the other. Whereas on television MacNaughton got the attacks and Jones could fight for the *Python* voice in the editing suite, here the group was controlling performance, writing and direction, with no-one to blame but the members of the group itself. Tension was also stretched thanks to the fledgling directing skills of Jones and Gilliam and the fact that all the team were working for virtually nothing in order to get the film made with the limited budget and wallow in the hoped for profits – thankfully those profits are still pouring in today. Although battling with alcoholism, Graham Chapman rallied the disgruntled crew together for a drink-fuelled, sing-a-long party on the eve of rumbling threats of decamping from the two weeks of suffering in a rain-sodden Scottish location. The following day, Jones and Gilliam presented the first ever rushes of *Grail* and highlighted what a cracker they had on their hands – from that day on it was all hands to the pumps. Although not credited on the film, the photo of Sir Not-Appearing-In-This-Film is Michael Palin's son Thomas. The *Monty Python* team selected the classic 1956 short film *The Case of the Mukkinesse*

Battlehorn starring Peter Sellers, Spike Milligan and Dick Emery as the support film for *Holy Grail* – perfect homage to comic leaders and a very funny beginning to anyone's cinema trip. *Grail* did great business in Russia (with audiences enjoying the anti-religious material and encouraging unfulfilled plans to perform the live *Python* show in Moscow) but its most important feat was to break into America. Appearing just as the old television back catalogue was gaining air time, *Grail* saw major publicity and high profile interview sessions. All the Pythons travelled to the States and attended the American premiere in New York (*Variety* later published a photograph of fans lining up for the screening at 5.30am while many cities saw armour-clad folk handing out flyers and waving gigantic *Grail* banners), following which Gilliam and Idle concentrated on the West Coast publicity and Chapman and Jones targeted Chicago – answering questions at the MidWest opening and handing out coconuts to the first 500 customers. The team, like The Beatles a decade earlier, came with vast qualities of material which immediately washed over the States in a tidal wave of appreciation. Not only that but Mr. Hip himself, Elvis Presley, loved the film, owned a private copy at Gracelands and watched it five times.

Python (Monty) Pictures Ltd in association with Michael White
Monty Python and the Holy Grail
Starring **GRAHAM CHAPMAN** as King Arthur, Hiccoughing Guard & Three-Headed Knight
JOHN CLEESE as Second Soldier with a Keen Interest in birds, Large Man with Dead Body, Black Knight, Mr. Na (village blacksmith interested in burning witches), A quite extraordinarily rude Frenchman, Tim the Wizard & Sir Lancelot
TERRY GILLIAM as Patsy (Arthur's trusty steed), the Green Knight, Soothsayer, Bridge-Keeper & Sir Gawain (the first to be killed by the rabbit)
ERIC IDLE as The Dead Collector, Mr Blint (a village ne'er-do-well very keen on burning witches), Sir Robin, the guard

who doesn't hiccough but tries to get things straight, Concorde (Sir Launcelot's trusty steed), Roger the Shrubber (a shrubber) & Brother Maynard

TERRY JONES as Dennis's Mother, Sir Bedevere, Three-Headed Knight & Prince Herbert

& MICHAEL PALIN as 1st soldier with a Keen Interest in Birds, Dennis, Mr Duck (a village carpenter who is almost keener than anyone else to burn witches), Three-headed Knight, Sir Galahad, King of Swamp Castle & Brother Maynard's Keeper

With

The Witch **CONNIE BOOTH**

Zoot & Dingo **CAROL CLEVELAND**

The First Self Destructive monk, Robin's Least Favourite Minstrel, The Page crushed by a rabbit & The Owner of a Duck **NEIL INNES**

Old Crone to whom King Arthur said 'Ni!' **BEE DUFFELL**

The Dead Body that claims it isn't & the Historian who isn't A.J.P. Taylor at all **JOHN YOUNG**

The Historian who isn't A.J.P. Taylor (honestly)'s Wife **RITA DAVIES**

Also appearing Either Piglet or Winston **AVRIL STEWART**

Either Winston or Piglet **SALLY KINGHORN**

Also also appearing **MARK ZYCON, MITSUKO FORSTATER, SANDY ROSE, JONI FLYNN, LORAINE WARD, SALLY COOMBE, YVONNE DICK, FIONA GORDON, JUDY LAMS, SYLVIA TAYLOR, ELSPETH CAMERON, SANDY JOHNSON, ROMILLY SQUIRE, ALISON WALKER, ANNA LANSKI, VIVIENNE MacDONALD, DAPHNE DARLING, GLORIA GRAHAM, TRACY SNEDDON, JOYCE POLLNER & MARY ALLEN**

Camera operator **Howard Atherton**
Camera focus **John Wellard**
Camera assistant **Roger Pratt**
Camera grip **Ray Hall**
Chargehand electrician **Terry Hunt**
Lighting **Telefilm Lighting Service Ltd** and **Andrew Ritchie & Son Ltd**
Rostrum cameraman **Kent Houston**
Sound recordist **Garth Marshall**
Sound mixer **Hugh Strain**
Boom swinger **Godfrey Kirby**
Sound maintenance **Philip Chubb**
Sound assistant **Robert Doyle**
Dubbing editor **John Foster**
Assistant editors **John Mister, Nick**

Gaster, Alexander Campbell Askew, Brian Peachey & Danielle Kochavi
Sound effects **Ian Crafford**
Continuity **Penny Eyles**
Accountant **Brian Brockwell**
Production secretary **Christine Watt**
Property buyer **Brian Winterborn**
Property master **Tom Raeburn**
Property men **Roy Cannon, Charlie Torbett & Mike Kennedy**
Catering **Ron Hellard Ltd**
Vehicles **Budget Rent-A-Car Ltd**
Construction manager **Bill Harman**
Carpenters **Nobby Clark & Bob Devine**
Painter **Graham Bullock**
Stagehand **Jim N. Savery**
Rigger **Ed Sullivan**
With special thanks to **Charlie Knode, Brian McNulty, John Gledhill, Peter Thomson, Sue Cable, Valerie Charlton, Drew Mara, Sue Smith, Charlie Coulter, Iain Monaghan, Steve Bennell, Bernard Belenger, Alpini McAlpine, Hugh Boyle, Dave Taylor, Gary Cooper, Peter Saunders, Les Shepherd, Vaughn Millard, Hamish MacInnes, Terry Mosaic & Bawn O'Beirne Ranelagh**
Songs **Neil Innes**
Additional music **DeWolfe**
Costume designer **Hazel Pethig**
Production manager **Julian Doyle**
Assistant director **Gerry Harrison**
Special effects **John Horton**
Choreography **Leo Kharibian**
Fight director & period consultant **John Waller**
Make-up artists **Pearl Rashbass & Pam Luke**
Special effects photography **Julian Doyle**
Animation assistance **Lucinda Cowell & Kate Hepburn**
Lighting cameraman **Terry Bedford**
Special effects **Olaf Prot**
Costumes **Siggi Churchill**
Designer **Roy Smith**
Editor **John Hackney**
Executive producer **John Goldstone**
Producer **Mark Forstater**
Directed by **Terry Gilliam & Terry Jones**
Made on location in Scotland at the 14th-century Doune Castle, Castle Stalker, Killin, Glen Coe, Arnhall Castle, Bracklinn Falls, Sherriffmuir, in a forest just outside London (for The Black Knight sequence) and completed at Twickenham Film Studios
Technicolor
Premiered March, 1975, Los Angeles,

opening in London 3 April 1975

THE MONTY PYTHON INSTANT RECORD COLLECTION

A compilation collection of classic tracks from the first five Charisma *Python* discs featuring heavy editing, rearranged links and one brand new recording of Summarised Proust Competition. The original album packaging, designed by Terry Gilliam, folded out into a box boasting the spines of some outlandish record titles but later pressings made do with just a single sleeve or gatefold cover with a picture of the stacked record collection inside – thus ruining the joke, although store managers reputedly insisted that the originals kept breaking open and unfolding in the shop.

The Monty Python Instant Record Collection – Side 1: Introductions, Alastair Cook, Nudge Nudge, Mrs. Nigger-Baiter, Constitutional Peasants, Fish Licence, Eric the Half-A-Bee, Australian Table Wines, Silly Noises, Novel Writing, Elephantoplasty, How To Do It, Gumby Cherry Orchard, Oscar Wilde Side 2: Introduction, Argument, French Taunter, Summarised Proust Competition, Cheese Emporium, Funerals at Prestatyn, Camelot, Word Association, Bruces, Parrot, Monty Python Theme
Charisma (CAS 1134), 1977

MONTY PYTHON LIVE AT CITY CENTER

Record of the *Python*'s hugely successful New York stage show from 14 April 1976 features selections from the Drury Lane material as well as a couple of Neil Innes rarities (*Short Blues* & *Protest Song*), freshly resurrected *Python* favourites (World Forum) and some newly written American-geared links. The actual shows were the first major breakthrough for *Python* in America and notably included guest spot, unheralded Mountie appearances from, on separate occasions, Harry

Nilsson and George Harrison for the *Lumberjack Song*, while Leonard Bernstein attended. Plagues with sound problems via dodgy mikes, the record company recorded the first few (worst) performances because they wanted the record out while the three-week run was going on. It was only released in the US.

Monty Python Live at City Center – Side 1 Introduction, Llama, Gumby Flower Arranging, Short Blues, Wrestling, World Forum, Albatross, Colonel Stopping It, Nudge Nudge, Crunchy Frog, Bruce's Song, Travel Agent.
Side 2 – Camp Judges, Blackmail, Protest Song, Pet Shop, Four Yorkshiremen, Argument Clinic, Death of Mary Queen of Scots, Salvation Fuzz, Church Police, Lumberjack Song
Arista (AL 4073).
Performed Wednesday 14 April–Sunday 2 May 1976

MONTY PYTHON LIVE AT DRURY LANE

A record of the classic Theatre Royal stage show which began in February 1974 and boasted the team's greatest hits, a bit of Neil Innes and Cleese/Chapman reclaiming several classic sketches from *Cambridge Circus*/*At Last the 1948 Show* for *Python* immortality. Eric Idle's whispered, unbriefed presenter, desperately trying to identify celebrity audience members, translates the manic shrieks of chanting, covers the visual Chapman wrestling with a history of the Drury Lane Theatre and reacts against Cleese's cricket-obsessed secret service chappie. The familiar old Python favourites like *Nudge* and *Argument* are greeted like old friends while the belated appearance of the parrot almost rips the roof off – boy, is it worth waiting for, with Cleese elongating his rant into infinity with 'he's f***ing snuffed it!', Palin taking over Idle's narration with a plug for the old sketch expedition and the audience hand-clapping along to the *Liberty Bell* reprise. Vintage classics

like *Four Yorkshiremen* are embraced to the *Python* bosom, the mock racist, animal-abusing, vomiting bad taste of *Cocktails* was new for the show, while oldies, *Slapstick*, and newies, Terry Gilliam's *History of Flight*, were added for this classic record exclusively released to the British market.
Innes does a bit of pre-Rutles Beatling with *The Idiot Song*, Carol Cleveland appears and the team effortlessly keep the *Python*-loving audience in the palm of their hands. Idle's 'couple of digger deviants' during the anti-poofie Aussie audience participation is pure class (clearly appreciated by Cleese), Chapman throws himself gloriously into the fantasy spinning of Yorkshiremen and Gilliam gets in on the act with his brief leg ditty. Terry Jones' Karl Marx is as hilarious as ever, Idle scores with his dubious 'Thank you Karl', comedy thy name is Cleese, with an impassioned cry of 'Albatross for Christ's sake!', Chapman's Colonel keeps comic conventions ticking along merrily, but the priceless highlight must be Michael Palin's scratchy rendition of Sir Henry Irving performing a vintage *Dead Parrot* sketch. Totally essential record of live *Python* and a 'little bit cheeky!'

Monty Python Live at Drury Lane
Side 1 – Introduction, Llamas, Gumby Flower Flowering, Secret Service, Wrestling, Communist Quiz, Idiot Song, Albatross, Colonel, Nudge Nudge, Cocktail Bar, Travel Agent
Side 2 – Spot the Brian Cell, Bruces, Argument, I've Got Two Legs, Four Yorkshiremen, Election Special, Lumberjack Song, Parrot Sketch Charisma CLASS 4.
1974

MONTY PYTHON LIVE AT THE HOLLYWOOD BOWL

With the King it's the 1968 comeback telly gig, with Queen it was Live Aid and for the Pythons, it's this cracking concert film. An invaluable record of their greatest ever live performance.

Filling the void for superb surreal comedy between Spike Jones and *The Simpsons*, *Monty Python's Flying Circus* had become a huge cult favourite in America. Post-*Brian*, interest was at fever pitch and the Pythons took on super-stardom at the Bowl. A brilliant mix of old, old telly favourites, obscure sketches from earlier incarnations, vinyl class from *Contractual Obligation* (Jones's *Never Be Rude to an Arab*/*Sit on my Face*) and some grand newies, this is a collection of the most important and hilarious sketches of the post war years. The old classics like *The Ministry of Silly Walks*, *Crunchy Frog* and *Nudge, Nudge* are greeted with tidal waves of applause, notably once Idle wanders on stage with just a pint of beer and cheesy grin, not a sausage is uttered before the crowd go berserk. The sketches are pretty much left untouched, with Jones retaining his businessman symbol of the bowler hat and Carol Cleveland's spiced-up ('blow-job!'/Palin pushing her breast for buzzer) receptionist for the argument sketch talking about services in pounds.
Even when amendments are made they are very slight and tongue-in-cheekily pinpointed – the World Forum is still choked with football trivia, Coventry et al, although the phrase is changed from F.A. Cup to English football cup, while Pearl Carr and Teddy Johnson are elbowed in favour of Jerry Lee Lewis. Eric Idle talks in terms of dollars, while discussing jello rather than jelly, it's garbage and trash cans, and Palin, looking for some money to improve his silly walk, requires a Federal grant. But in basic terms, *Python* came and conquered with very little alteration, the team having built up a major cult following in the 1970s via regular television exposure and finally making their stage debut in the States in 1976. This really was British comedy in rock stadium terms, packing in huge audiences to chant along to the tag-lines.
Interlaced within the stage antics here are filmed interludes and vintage Terry Gilliam animation, all projected onto a large screen and incorporated into the live

performance. The team adapt their twisting of conventions to suit the media, with Palin's fairground barker delivery of the Chapman wrestling match, the definitive rendition of the *Albatross* sketch with unprompted members of the audience shouting out 'What flavour is it!' before Terry Jones takes up the line and Chapman castigating Jones for talking to the audience at the close of the *Crunchy Frog* sequence. Chapman questions Cleese in usherette mode, noting he's not a real woman and Cleese hilariously injects a bit of *Brian* terminology with 'Don't oppress me!' This is a polished, fun performance of eight great entertainers, featuring the momentous battle of wits between Cleese as the pope and Idle as Michelangelo discussing *The Last Supper's* 'mother of a blow-out!' (originally written and performed by Cleese and Jonathan Lynn for *A Poke in the Eye (With A Sharp Stick)*, the immortal *Philosopher's Song* with three Gilliam created stand-up Aussies with fully movable lips to join in with the communal singing and the legendary Graham Chapman school of jape, putting straight-faced and boiler-suited Palin, Jones and Gilliam through their slapstick comedy paces. The 'Hey Vance!' from Chapman, causing the built-up, double whammy sight gag is a masterpiece while the lecture concerning the 'dispatch of an eatable missile' sees Chapman's authority of the absurd reach new heights.

Gilliam enjoys a brief, ill-fated resurrection of his 'Legs' song, Jones suffers a similar fate with his radical, pseudo-xenophobic *Arab* and Neil Innes, fully embraced as part of the clan, performs his classic Bonzo Dog Doo-Dah number *I'm the Urban Spaceman*, complete with mistimed and energetic Vaudevillian hoofing from Carol Cleveland. Innes, featured on guitar for the Bruce sing-along and cropping up in several Gilliamesque minor parts, also resurrects the spirit of The Rutles with the greatest track the band never recorded. With audience members clearly celebrating the Liverpudlian boy's legacy, with a banner reading ' I think it was the trousers', Innes gives

the ultimate performance of *Idiot Song*, grinning warmly to the crowd and creating comic magic. Alongside this injection of post-Rutles mania, there is an inclusion of a sketch from outside of the Stateside-familiar canon, Palin, Jones, Chapman and Idle performing, in definitive *Monty Python* terms, the *Four Yorkshiremen* sketch from *At Last the 1948 Show* (thanking Feldman and Brooke-Taylor during the closing credits). If a greatest moment had to be chosen it would have to be Idle's Smoketoomuch rant. Boring Palin's Mr. Nice Guy to distraction, Idle's performance is a towering masterpiece, going on for ever. Extended even beyond the record version, this is Idle's inspired madness of monologue at it's absolute peak. Chased by Cleese and wandering round the audience droning on about the perils of foreign travel, Idle's delivery is perfectly moronic and monosyllabic even invading into Chapman's opening material for the next sketch. Idle performs a breathtaking piece of work – flawlessly. Clearly the Pythons relish the experience of audience involvement, with Palin enjoying a sniggering ad-lib alongside Eric Idle's ultra-camp Q.C. and the final sketch collapsing into corpsed mayhem with Jones cracking up, Idle fighting back the laughter as he rambles on about jug-fish and rat-based puds, Chapman's schoolboy stumbling in with talk of a dead bishop and the Church police over-acting with pride. It's a glorious encapsulation of good fun *Python* with the lads breaking up at the shaky props, corpsing moments and uncomfortable strap-on mikes, finally breaking down into Idle's audience confiding speech about not wishing to be involved in such a shambolic sketch and ripping into a rare performance of the *Lumberjack Song* with Palin stuck in the Mountie chorus. It's a cracking close to a cracking show with the closing credit sequence reflecting warm back-stage laughter between the team and a final command to Piss Off! (later picked up and developed by Rik Mayall and Ade Edmonson for the *Bottom* stage shows) directed

at the chuffed audience. Although in the same snip and paste filmic category as *And Now For Something Completely Different*, this is a precious record of the lads, live and in your face. Priceless.

Did You Know?
The Pythons performed four shows at the Hollywood Bowl in 1980 (26-29 September – plus an open dress rehearsal on 25 September) and although a major concert return to American fans, a chance for some quick dosh and some invaluable tuning of comic performance, this was really a fill-in between film projects. Stuck after a stolid 13-week writing session with no thematic centre the team had good, albeit unrelated, sequences set in 1880 and 1980, filmic parody, historical moments but no firm plot. Cleese was happy to use all the material and construct a sketch film but the others felt this would be backtracking after the narrative style of *Brian*. In the end, of course, they did return to sketch format, albeit with a much stronger linking thread, creating *Monty Python's The Meaning of Life* from their disjointed writing sessions. But before taking the plunge on that decision they took the relatively easy way out and filmed their greatest hits in front of an adoring audience. Destined for either HBO or Showtime, this edited highlights package rearranged the running order of the show for cinematic pace and received only limited big screen exposure, cropping up on video and television almost immediately, but it stands as the only valued visual record of *Python's* unique six-pack, live and proud.

Monty Python Live at the Hollywood Bowl
Thorn EMI
The *Monty Python* Begging Bowl Partnership
Written & performed by **GRAHAM CHAPMAN, JOHN CLEESE, TERRY GILLIAM, ERIC IDLE, TERRY JONES, MICHAEL PALIN & NEIL INNES**
With **CAROL CLEVELAND**
Production co-ordinator **Anne Henshaw**
Stage manager **Mollie Kirkland**

Production design **John McGraw & John Miles**
Sound **Stan Miller**
Wardrobe **Day Murch & Hazel Pethig**
Props **Charles Knode & Bill Peirce**
Makeup **Ve Neill & Maggie Weston**
Promotion **Clog Holdings & Larry Vallon**
Press **Patti Wright**
Python's U.S. co-ordinator **Nancy Lewis**
Music production **Andre Jacquemin**
Title music **John Duprez & Ray Cooper**
Editor **Jimmy B. Frazier**
Lighting design by **William Klages**
Video control **John B. Field & John Palacio**
Audio recordist **Ed Green**
Script supervisor **Sandra Pearson**
Unit manager **David R. Horne**
Production manager **Steve Terry**
Technical directors **John B. Field, Jimmy B. Frazier, Ken Holland & Gary Matz**
Camera operators **Dave Hilmer, Mike Keeler, John Lee, Dave Levisohn & Wayne Orr**
Technical operations supervisor **Steve Deaver**
Videotape operator **Bill Conroy**
Maintenance **Bill Feightner & Bert Weyl**
Assistant audio **Jeff Fecteau, Chris Seidenglanz & Larry Stephens**
RTS phonelines **Kenneth Nunn**
Camera assistants **Dan Andresen & John Mayon**
Audio utility **Rich Brown & Mike Wilson**
Audio re-recording **Jerry Clemans**
Opticals designed by **C.D. Taylor**
Rear projection **Background Engineers**
Assistant videotape editors **Mark Bernay & Ken Laski**
Production associate **Joanne Fish**
Recorded in Imagevision by **Compact Video Service, Inc.**
Concert film assembly **Arden Rynew**
Post production supervisor **Sandra Pearson**
Post production director & editor **Julian Doyle**
Concert film co-producer **James Rich, Jr.**
Filmed sequences directed by **Ian MacNaughton**
With thanks to **Marty Feldman, Angus James, David Lipscom, Tim Brooke-Taylor, Arista Records, Inc. & Charisma Records Ltd**
Executive producer **Denis O'Brien**
Concert film produced & directed by

Terry Hughes
premiered, New York, 25 June 1982
78 mins.
Showtime – 8.30pm (except Sunday, 28th September 8pm) Tickets from $10 – $16

THE MONTY PYTHON MATCHING TIE AND HANDKERCHIEF

The original pressing for this milestone album featured a pull-out inner sleeve with notes and a gloriously colourful illustration of the cover's tie and hanky, partially visible through a hole in the cover, which pulls out to reveal some poor chap being garrotted on the gallows (while wearing the aforementioned tie and handkerchief). A further Gilliam masterpiece (with the dead chap having his tie and hanky inspected by an onlooker), printed on green paper details the record credits and comic business concerning the background to this landmark series on Mediaeval Farming. More importantly, the B side twisted convention as only *Python* could with two separate grooves of totally different material. Each consisted of about 20 minutes of *Python* and the selection played was determined by which groove your needle found first. Fans sometimes waited years to hear the other stuff! The recording technique had been employed for 78s as early as 1911, but the *Python* team not only resurrected the idea after many years but marked its first use on a long playing record. Although a later American release resurrected these Python extras (Arista AL 4039) other reissues opted for a normal cover design and consecutive B-side. Boring! When the album was released in the States in 1975 Arista released a single (AS 0130) featuring edited versions of Who Cares, the Elephant, Infant Minister for Overseas Development and Pet Shop Conversations but nothing can compare to this, the original and best, Charisma release. The sides are not itemised or differentiated (both are marked side 2), while the double play side adds further to the confusion (in fact, the

record is merely given away as a free gift with the tie/hanky set!), but the accepted running order is as follows: Side 1 begins with a political debate with pepperpot Chapman, militant Palin, gleeful host Idle and Hitler-based question from 'the fiercely erotic' Carol Cleveland leading to absolutely nothing before the radio broadcast is quickly turned off to make way for a resurrection of one of the team's joint television favourites, the Dead Bishop on the Landing/The Church Police, with Idle turning his nose up at Jones and the jug fish. Cleese interviews Chapman's surgeon for Who Cares? in a sketch variously known as Mr. Humphries the Elephant or, definitively, Elephantasoty, a surreal, typically Chapmanesque take on medical matters with his transplant obsessed doctor waiting for accidents to happen, gleefully bounding off at the sound of car crashes and eagerly detailing the quality of life one human now enjoys as a useful piece of furniture. Even more typical *Python* fare is presented in the Thomas Hardy Novel Writing piece, with Palin's enthused sports host building up the crowd, awaiting Hardy's first words for *The Return of the Native* and tossing out of words as mental defeats – a total delight. Cleese's Word Association on Tonight's the Night, brilliantly played at a rate of knots with football obsession, use of well-known phrases and peerlessly surreal connections superbly works like Ronnie Barker with a degree while a classic exchange between Chapman & Idle ('hot enough to boil a monkey's bum!') establishes the Bruces and, for the first time, the much celebrated elongation of the Aussie fest with the *Philosopher's Song*. Meanwhile it's 4 June 1973 and Palin's earnest voice-over tells the tale of a file clerk's day where nothing happened. Aided by menacing music and Palin's hushed delivery, this non-evident murder mysterious taps into Hitchcockian dismembered limbs that aren't there and even the not-to-be appearance at the Old Bailey (complete with gavel knocking) before we enjoy a brief vignette of the clerk (Jones) with

Carol Cleveland as bored Brummie assistant. A perfect deconstruction of *Scotland Yard* conventions. Doctor Chapman explains the human brain, whooping cough and looks on as Jones's pepperpot tucks into some tasty dog before Palin's anxious narrator returns to introduce the celebrated Cheese Shop (the 'I don't care how f***ing runny it is' mix). Idle whisks us back to Hardy's novel writing, in between the defunct Wasp Club of Jones and Cleese's Tiger Club before John's Great Actor can really dig into the dreaded Shakespearean performance with a self-gratifying, number of words per character obsessed, limited expressions, 'happy prancing!' chat with Idle.

Side 2a: So, if your needle hits a Background to History then you're in for, as far as I'm concerned, the purest, funniest and cleverest piece of recorded material in the entire *Python* repertoire with Chapman's introduction of a Mediaeval Open Field Farming discussion encompassing a ploughing reggae, Oxon theory from Manchester University retold in Ronettes style, Professor Moorehead going all Gary Glitter with his impassioned 'There's evidence' and Palin (in a cross between Peter Sellers and Nigel Planer) bursting into heavy Beatles style. Cut the scene to Chapman searching his local record shop for First World War Noises and a booth extract of Palin/Jones in trench discussion before a stuck record gets our hapless customer complaining. Idle's no help, for the young lady is 'off dead'; there's a gloriously Milliganesque sound picture conjured up with Gilliam's torture chamber grotesque and a Hancockian silence before our WW1 Johnnies are back in action with mouth organ atmosphere and Palin's tense officer with the sexual interest in dogs. But before things gets too graphic and normal, the record sticks again and Chapman's complaint that his record has stuck also sticks – ahh! CDs, you can't fool the public like this! Meanwhile, Palin introduces Boxing Tonight with Kenneth Clark and this slice of *Python* class comes to an end

with the post of Oxford Professor of Fine Art well and truly decided. Side 2b: Now, just put your needle back to the start and if you haven't already heard this, settle down for some fresh *Python*ing about with Cleese's Infant Minister for Overseas Development, Jones whining on and Palin's exploding Mrs. Nigger-Baiter, before it's fast rewind back to London 1892 for Oscar Wilde's Party. Pet Shop Conversations takes the parrot to sick extremes with the familiar Palin/Cleese clash haggling over buying a cat/terrier before settling on major re-shaping of limited livestock into desired creatures. The restructuring compromise is made perfectly dangerous as Cleese only agrees if he can watch – sublime. Idle's Farming phone-in never really gets going, with the pyschiatrist guests doing their best, a confusing party line and finally Jones' Goonish caller who was left a question for the show in a will. With some class no-nonsense nonsense to finish on, there's nothing else for it but Idle to sigh 'That's all we've got time for.' Indeed, it is, but this is arguably *Python*'s finest, most ambitious and complex use of the recorded medium.

The Monty Python Matching Tie And Handkerchief Charisma CAS 1080
Recorded 'on quite a nice day in late September 1973'
Producers **Andre Jacquemin, Dave Howman & Terry Gilliam**
Music **Neil Innes**

MONTY PYTHON ON SONG

A double single release featuring the George Harrison *Lumberjack Song*, *Spam Song*, *Bruce's Song* from the Drury Lane tapes and, finally, Eric the Half-A-Bee (MP 001).

MONTY PYTHON SINGS

One final compilation album just to disprove that 1987's *The Final Rip Off* wasn't the final rip off, this priceless collection of *Python*'s greatest hits formed part of the 20th

anniversary celebrations and is dedicated to Graham with love from John, Terry G, Eric, Terry J and Michael. Besides the usual suspects from *Grail*, *Brian* and *Life*, there is the classic *Money Song* which started the musical tradition way back during the original BBC shows, the George Harrison-produced *Lumberjack Song* making its album debut, a longer version of Chapman's *Medical Love Song* featuring a new verse and chorus in addition to the familiar *Contractual Obligation* version and, perhaps best of all, a magical studio take of Terry Gilliam's short but sweet ditty *I've Got Two Legs*. The only totally new *Python* track is *Oliver Cromwell*, utilizing a Chopin melody (resurrected from *I'm Sorry I'll Read That Again*) and featuring lead vocals from John Cleese and backing choruses by Eric Idle. The collection also included the printed lyrics and so, for the first time, fans could sing along to *I Like Chinese* with confidence, while Gilliam's new gaping mouth illustration was worth the asking price alone.

Monty Python Sings – *Always Look On the Bright Side of Life* (words & music – Eric Idle), *Sit On My Face* (words – Eric Idle, music – Harry Parr Davies, arranger – John Du Prez), *Lumberjack Song* (words – Terry Jones & Michael Palin, music – Terry Jones, Michael Palin & Fred Tomlinson, arranger – Fred Tomlinson), *Not the Noel Coward Song* (words & music – Eric Idle), *Oliver Cromwell* (words – John Cleese, music – *Polonaise No. 6 Op. S3 in Ab* by Frederic Chopin), *Money Song* (words – Eric Idle & John Gould, music – John Gould, arranger – Fred Tomlinson), *Accountancy Shanty* (words & music – Eric Idle & John Du Prez), *Finland* (words & music – Michael Palin, arranger – John Du Prez), *Medical Love Song* (words – Graham Chapman & Eric Idle, music – Eric Idle & John Du Prez, arranger – John Du Prez), *I'm So Worried* (words & music – Terry Jones, arranger – John Du Prez), *Every Sperm Is Sacred* (words – Michael Palin & Terry Jones, music – David Howman & Andre Jacquemin), *Never Be Rude to an Arab* (words & music – Terry Jones, arranger – John Du Prez), *I Like*

Chinese (words & music – Eric Idle, arranger – John Du Prez), *Eric the Half-A-Bee* (words – Eric Idle & John Cleese, music – Eric Idle), *Brian Song* (words – Michael Palin, music – Andre Jacquemin & Dave Howman), *Bruce's Philosophers Song* (words & music – Eric Idle), *Meaning of Life* ((words – Eric Idle, music – Eric Idle & John Du Prez), *Knights of the Round Table* (words – Graham Chapman & John Cleese, music – Neil Innes), *All Things Dull and Ugly* (words – Terry Jones, music – *All Things Bright & Beautiful*), *Decomposing Composers* (words & music – Michael Palin, arranger – John Du Prez), Henry Kissinger (words & music – Eric Idle, arranger – John Du Prez), *I've Got Two Legs* (words & music – Terry Gilliam), *Christmas In Heaven* (words – Terry Jones, music – Eric Idle), *Galaxy Song* (words – Eric Idle, music – Eric Idle & John Du Prez), *Spam Song* (words – Terry Jones & Michael Palin, music – Michael Palin, Terry Jones & Fred Tomlinson, arranger – Fred Tomlinson)
Producers **Eric Idle** & **Andre Jacquemin**
Enginnered & mixed by **Andre Jacquemin**
assisted by **James Saunders** at Redwood Recording Studios
Co-ordinated by **Kath James**
Virgin MONT 1
1989

MONTY PYTHON'S BIG RED BOOK

Methuen looking for comedy writers from outside the publishing medium as with *Punch* authors A.P. Herbert, Sellar & Yeatman, approached the Python team in March 1971. Influenced by children's colour illustrated books the Pythons happily threw themselves into the project – the book title was inspired by Chairman Mao's doctrine and the recently published controversial *Little Red School Book* – to add to the standard Python silliness, the cover was blue to heighten confusion. Gilliam's cartoons rescued from oblivion by Eric Idle, presented the publishers with 70 pages of camera-ready artwork in dribs and drabs. Idle took television material as a starting point but added new pieces to bolster

the original *Python* humour with loads of original photos, new artwork, script extracts and the like! In *The Bookseller* – 10 July 1971 – 'The Ford Motor Company recommends *The Monty Python's Big Red Book*' ad – was exposed as a lie in a footnote. Cleese sent a memo to Methuen's general sales rep, as alias Colonel Muriel Volestrangler, condemning the publication – 450,000 copies formed the initial sales with the popular paperback reissue emblazoned with the legend 'New hard-back edition' and *Python*'s literary Guild's introductory offer of one free tub of dung (plus, a dead Indian monthly – tick if required!). The launch party was a Newsreader Ball due to the team's obsession with the ethos of television news – reflected in their use of Bosanquet and Richard Baker in the shows. A letter of endorsement from Television Newscasters was included. Contents: 'Romeo and Juliette' featuring Ken Shabby & Rosemary, Why Accountancy is Not Boring by A. Putey, Campaign Literature for the Silly Party, Batley Ladies' Townswomen's Guild, Sports Page with Jimmy Buzzard & Ken Clean-Air System, The Importance of Being Earnest – A new version by Billy Bremner, Sir Kenneth Clarke – Are You Civilized?, The Greatest Upper Class (Twit) Race in the World, Goat's Page, Johnson's Novelties ('Guaranteed to break the ice at parties'), Letter Retracting the Endorsement of the book, Lumberjack Song, Whizzo Chocolate Assortment, How to Walk Silly, Poems of Ewan McTeagle, Piranha Brothers.

Written by **Graham Chapman, John Cleese, Terry Gilliam, Eric Idle, Terry Jones & Michael Palin**
Edited by **Eric Idle**, designed by **Derek Birdsall**
Published by Eyre Methuen
1971

MONTY PYTHON'S CONTRACTUAL OBLIGATION ALBUM

As the title suggests, this was *Python* fulfilling a strict contract and contains all new *Python* material with a healthy roster of classic songs (over half the album is musical) – plundered several times since for various compilation projects. Short but sweet, the musical bad taste note is struck with a rousing chorus of *Sit On My Face*, threatened with legal action as the delights of oral sex are set to the tune of the old Gracie Fields song *Sing As We Go* and nobody at *Python* had bothered to clear copyright. From the outset, this was a hastily cobbled-together project and with typical irreverence Gilliam constructed a makeshift sleeve with blurred Charisma track listings/spine details and simulated ripped information on the record itself. The hand-written footnote – 'Can T.G. do a nice eye-catching cover to help it sell? E.I. Not really worth it. T.J.' captured the mood perfectly and Idle's initial announcement, plugging this as skilfully crafted by British comedians, ends with a suggestion that it be filed away at the back of your record collection.
Although many prime bits of *Python* are premiered here, notably the peerless Henry Kissinger, the team are still not averse to re-evaluating old material and String from *The Frost Report* gets the full Cleese rant and Idle's bemused treatment, with John's keen as mustard salesman desperately trying to flog 122,000 miles of the stuff. He shrinks into oblivion as the refrains of Never Be Rude To An Arab from Terry Jones embraces anti-xenophobic attitude via a xenophobic attitude in a reverse of Noel Coward's *Don't Let's Be Beastly To the Germans*. An explosion ends Jones in his prime before Idle resurrects *Python*'s address of all nations with *I Like Chinese*, a cracking piece of song-writing with Speedy Gonzales-like Chinese accompaniment, a latching onto deep, meaningful philosophy and culminating with the ultimate devotion to Chinese food.

Michael Palin's brilliant Bishop monologue, intoning the creation of earth with *War of the Worlds*-like solemnity, sci-fi menace and power clangs, breaks down into fumbling advertising with his continual fish obsession. Chapman and Idle bitch in the studio and Palin's delightful 'Oh damn!' links into some babbled talk of doctors arriving and Graham's masterly *Medical Love Song* unashamedly telling disease as is it. The following item, *Farewell to John Denver*, was subsequently replaced after legal action from the singer. In the original, a thinly veiled parody of *Annie's Song* culminated with the strangling of Denver. In the more widely known version, Jones breaks into the brief silence with a humble apology, explaining this brief lull is due to legal restrictions. The item is so short that nobody would really have noticed if the piece had been totally removed, but that was not the *Python* way and, now, the Denver truth is more celebrated than ever before. As it happens, Jones introduces Palin's *Finland* song, allowing a Peter Cook-like burst of nonsense about Mr. Griffiths of Hemel Hempsted and his collection of credit cards. Side one concludes with *I'm So Worried* by Terry Jones, an unforgettably morose, rambling contribution with more false endings than *Sh-Boom!*
Idle kick-starts the flip side with *I Bet You They Won't Play This Song On the Radio*, a cheerful ditty with almost every other word bleeped out of existence, while Palin's erudite preacher goes into nubile girl rubbing territory and the killjoy actions of the Lord. Jones, with pinched nose and elongated phrases, plods through the unique strains of *Here Comes Another One* before Chapman breaks in with 'That's it, is it?' and the listening audience is treated to a full orchestra, funky *Starsky and Hutch* arrangement and a lilting Western version. A plundered sketch from *At Last the 1948 Show*, Bookshop, is given its definitive rendition with Cleese going into full rantathon mode and Chapman doing an excellent Marty Feldman with a lust for Edmund Wells' reworked Dickens, the

expurgated version of *Olsen's Standard Book of British Birds* and *Biggles Combs His Hair*. 'Funny!' Idle's lumbering song, *Do Wot John* acts as a bridge to a hilarious comment on the modern music scene, *Rock Notes*, with more fish obsession in the *Dead Monkeys* earlier incarnations and Terry Jones, in Paul Robeson tribute mood, strolls through the equally lumbering *Muddy Knees*. Jones, Palin and Idle join forces for a new sketch, Crocodile, tackling commentary on the British team for the sport Being Eaten By A Crocodile. Jones as Sergeant Major and Palin as Cookian contestant cannot impress Idle who cuts through the *Python* logic twisting to challenge the concept of being chomped by a 'bloody great crocodile'. Handing back to the studio, Palin goes into the delicious *Decomposing Composers*, utilising bits of Mozart and Beethoven to stunning comic effect in an affectionate tribute. Chapman turns in a virtuoso performance, bickering with himself over Bells and attacking an impending church of England invasion which would have given Gilliam plenty of food for thought in visual expression. Terry Jones is allowed to see the album out with the truly earth-shatteringly boring *Traffic Lights*, crawling along in hilarious fashion until the final promised rhyme of Bamber with Amber breaks down to an exhausted 'Oh God!', angelic choir boys reinvent environmental praise in *All Things Dull & Horrible* and things come to an end with A Scottish Farewell, none other than the beloved *Here Come's Another One* done to bagpipes. For the second time, Jones is blown to bits. Hardly the most emotive *Python* album, with no clever use of the recorded medium, this does, nevertheless, contain a bumper feast of memorable *Python* items and saw their last original gathering on vinyl. Charisma released *I Like Chinese*, *I Bet You They Won't Play This Song On the Radio* and *Finland* as a single (CB 374), while Arista produced a 12 inch promotional sampler for American radio broadcasts (SP 101) and released a single version of *I Bet*

You They Won't Play This Song On the Radio (AS 0578) including a mono version on side A and a stereo version on the B side.
Monty Python's Contractual Obligation Album Charisma CAS 1152. 1980

MONTY PYTHON'S FIRST FAREWELL TOUR

A three-week run of live one night performances across Britain beginning in Southampton and coming to a close on 24 May, 1973. During the run, Palin's birthday (5 May) fell on the night of the Birmingham show and Eric Idle got his mother, a dead ringer for Mary Whitehouse, to present the birthday boy with a cake. Cleese, ad-libbed 'No!' and grabbed Palin, instead of the usual Dead Parrot sketch get-out of the 'Do you want to come back to my place?/Yeah, all right' gag and Idle, in gold MC jacket, introduced his mum as Whitehouse. Palin clocked, ran with the gag and fooled the audience into thinking Whitehouse had played ball.

MONTY PYTHON'S FLIEGENDER ZIRKUS

The Pythons first became involved in German television when an enthused Bavarian TV producer approached the BBC with a view for a special version broadcast in 1972. Although there were some new items on the agenda, familiar classics like *The Lumberjack Song* and Graham Chapman's Bomber-Harris self-wrestling were remade and performed in German. The script was translated, the Pythons struggled through and the audience did convulse. In 50 minutes, totally made on film, the show kicks off with a female announcer (who tops and tails the show) being dragged into a lake by a frogman and things get more and more manic from there on in, with a sketch Live from Athens (featuring the death of a torch burner), an aborted documentary on Albrecht Dürer, Michael Palin's Bruce talks about kangaroos/Dürer/Fosters/life and everything (remember this is a Brit doing an Australian accent performed in German!) and a cut-out Anita Ekberg singing in praise of Dürer to the tune of Robin Hood/Dennis Moore. The restrictions obviously push the Pythons over the edge at times but this is never anything less than totally fascinating with Part 4 of *The Merchant of Venice* from the Bad Toltz Dairy Herd momentarily breaking into the Dürer obsession; our torch-bearing chap plugging cigarettes; a Frenchman who's only been to the bathroom once in five years (immediately confirmed by such distinguished associates as Nixon and the Pope); the charming rendition of *Little Red Riding Hood* with Cleese ultimately becoming manageress of a Holiday Inn in the United Arab Republic; a *Python* convention filled with applauding Women's Institute members and those priceless Pepperpots in Munich to promote shopping as an Olympic sport. There's an interesting, if half-hearted comic attempt to address the analysis of comedy with the tracing of the joke through historical footage featuring cavemen, Columbus, the Greeks, Mediaevals and Egyptians. It's certainly patchy stuff but the running gags, introspective references and surprisingly effective performances make this a vital part of *Python*'s legacy. Besides, there's one true classic in the television debate show parody *Stake Your Claim*, with Norman Vowles of Gravesend claiming he wrote all Shakespeare's work. Despite the show being screened opposite an England/Germany football match the audience was healthy, the critics liked it and the Pythons were invited back for a second show in October 1973. This was a much more ambitious, audience-friendly piece of *Python*, aimed at the German market but filmed in English (much to the cast's relief). Subsequently dubbed the 'lost' show – although it isn't – this second German venture was labelled Schnapps With Everything and boasted 40 minutes of totally new *Python* material, injecting German

elements only in the top and tail fairy tale sequences, the odd Gilliam German newspaper and a caption or two. The majority of sketches are pretty dodgy to be honest, although Cleese, in British stiff-upper lipped announcer mode, strolls the streets of Germany detailing the alarming habit of businessmen and their craving for a bit on the side explained away as the result of tax concessions or even too much citrus fruit in the diet. Idle and Palin punch off unsuspecting dolly birds, and this line of thought extends throughout the whole show. Indeed, in typical *Python* style, sketches weave and divide into each other and back again, with the Idle hosted television show about sycophancy between Chapman and Palin playing like a half-baked, rejected BBC skit. Indeed, it's quickly broken into by Cleese, whose sex obsession pulls the ideal opportunity to channel anger, backtrack, get him dragged away and halt the interview sketch completely. The pre-title bit of Eastern European business with Chapman's William Tell is like a warm up for *Grail*-like realism without being terribly funny but there's an instant saving grace in Gilliam's reworked opening credit sequence, featuring among other things, a Lon Chaney Snr tree – what more does the world need? There's some good *Ripping Yarns*-like stuff (continual references to heroes not seeing their aunties for long periods of time!!) with Terry Jones and his mouse reserve taking one step further down the absurdist path with a fish park and a clever embrace of Western film convention including Gilliam's mice stampede. However, the Western malarkey goes on a bit, despite Gilliam hamming it up as Gabby (in homage to Western icon George 'Gabby' Hayes), lapsing into Benny Hill's *Yakkety Axe* theme, some manic chicken-panning and the sudden shock of discovering his find is nothing more than fool's chicken! A bit of Cleese Hitleresque ranting and Palin's straight-laced fellow leads into the classic moment of the show – the Philosophers' International football match with the Greeks and Germans wandering round the pitch simply

considering the ball and its place in the order of things. Punctured by Cleese and his announcing of Chapman's Colin Bomber-Harris wrestling match, the football warms up with Terry Jones resurrecting his World Forum performance as Karl Marx, jogging onto the pitch for a bit of controlled thinking. The Greeks finally get the idea and, via Palin's commentary, the Germans' reasoning for disallowing the goal brilliantly careers through philosophical thought before latching onto football terminology with Karl's belief that it was off-side.

It's gloriously daft in the best Python tradition and mesmerisingly contrasted with some harrowing shock imagery from Gilliam, presenting arguably his most powerful set of animations. Then it's back to Idle's non-starter television skit with a black screen allowing ten seconds of sex, a reappearance from a vindicated Cleese and head-on into the jaw-achingly elongated contact lenses/hearing aid shop. It's a perfect *Python* environment but the endless train of ideas with Cleese, hard of hearing, selling hearing aids and Palin (as Dr. Waring in a nod to the old *Doctor In The House* shows) struggling through as the contact lenses guy who can't see, quickly gets painful. Apart from the clever incorporation of the items on sale being employed by the doctors to absolutely no avail, Eric Idle's petulant customer gets some good lines in among the prat-falling. Jones, as a disgruntled madman, storms in with a knife for a suitably manic ending, while Idle steals the limelight with a Groucho Marxian one-liner direct to camera. Imagine the dirty fork sketch without the comic chemistry and you're nearly there! The final section, written by John Cleese and Connie Booth and variously known as Happy Valley or The Princess with Wooden Teeth, is an interesting departure into the realms of European fairy tales. Again this is stretched to breaking point but Booth's wooden-toothed Princess is a classic creation and Terry Jones, spending most of his time being grumpy and bashing out *Goon Show* meets Yoko Ono compositions on his organ, gives a towering comic contribution as King Otto. Indeed, Jones so relished his part that he tentatively suggested taking up the reins for a feature-length version of this sketch and its long *Python* life saw an abridged version performed on *Monty Python's Previous Album* and a live rendition crop up in the Drury Lane shows. Dismissing would-be suitors like Cleese with impossible, death-dealing tasks and moaned at by his adulterous wife (Chapman), Jones makes things easy for Palin's pimple-nosed, pretentious, scumbag sort of a bloke. His buck-toothed, cockney Prince Walter, struggling with his task of buying 20 Bensons from the shop, is the major saving grace here, although Chapman has a whale of a time as the red-nosed Judge and there's some mind-blowing dragon fighting from Eric Idle. Gilliam's manic Witch is a masterstroke, getting the curse a little too complete, injecting the reference to aunties for the last time and causing a mad chicken rush from the Western sketch. Patchy to say the least, but important as the last television *Python* venture to feature John Cleese and containing enough complete madness to satisfy anybody.

Did You Know?

When EMI pulled the plug on *Life of Brian*, the team's first thought was to go back to these German shows of 1972 and 1973, edit them down to an hour of the best material, write another half hour of sketches during September/October 1978, stick them all together and have a cheap, effective little *Python* movie. Thankfully, *Brian* was saved and these Germany rarities remained unseen until resurrected for a major *Python* retrospective at New York's Museum of Broadcasting on 17 and 24 February 1989. When filming the first German show, the Pythons were taken to a historical concentration camp site. Arriving too late to enter, an argument erupted and Graham Chapman made his infamous, inspired cry of 'Tell them we're Jews!'

Von und mit **Graham Chapman, John**

Cleese, Terry Gilliam, Eric Idle, Terry Jones & Michael Palin
und als gast **Conny Booth**
Animation **Terry Gilliam**
Szenenbild **Michael Girschek**
Kostume **Monika Altmann-Kriger**
Schnitt **Hilwa Von Boro**
Ton **Heinz Terworth**
Maske **Georg Jauss & Josef Coesfeld**
Kamra **Justus Pankau & Ernst Schmid**
Produktionsleitung **Peter Sterr**
Produzent **Thomas Woitkewitsch**
Regie **Ian MacNaughton**

MONTY PYTHON'S FLYING CIRCUS

Hugely influential television comedy series – witness the rest of this book! The Alternative Titles suggested included – *The Aming Flying Circus. Arthur Buzzard's Flying Circus. Arthur Megapode's Cheap Show. Arthur Megapode's Flying Circus. Arthur Megapode's Zoo. B.B. Circus. Baron Von Took's Flying Circus. Bob Python's Flying Circus. Brian Stalin's Flying Circus. Brian's Flying Circus. Bunn, Wackett, Buzzard, Stubble and Boot. Charles Ind's Flying Circus. The Comedy Zoo. Cynthia Fellatio's Flying Circus. The Down Show. E.L. Megapode's Flying Circus. E.L. Moist's Flying Circus. E.L. Thompson's Flying Circus. E.L. Trotsky's Flying Circus. E.L. Turbot's Flying Circus. The Fly Circus. The Flying Circus. The Full Moon Show. Gwen Dibley's Flying Circus. A Horse, A Spoon and A Basin. The Horrible Earnest Megapode. Human Circus. It's Them! It's T.H.E.M. The Joke Zoo. The Keen Show. Ken. The Laughing Zoo. Limb's Flying Circus. Man's Crisis of Identity in the Latter Half of the Twentieth Century. Megapode's Cheap Show. Megapode's Panic Show. Megapode's Atomic Circus. Megapode's Flying Circus. Myrtle Buzzard's Flying Circus. Nigel's Flying Circus. Noris Heaven's Flying Circus. Norman Python's Flying Circus. The Nose Show. O. 1 2 3. Ow! It's Colin Plint! Ow! It's Megapode's Flying Circus. Owl Stretching Time. The Panic Show. The People Zoo. The Plastic Mac Show. The Political Satire Show.*

The Royal Philharmonic Orchestra Goes to the Bathroom. Sex and Violence. The Sparkling Music and Stars Interview. Stephen Furry's Flying Circus. Sydney Moist's Flying Circus. Them. The 37 Foot Flying Circus. Vaseline Parade. Vaseline Review. The Venus De Milo Panic Show. Whither Canada? The Whizzo Easishow! (Guaranteed to last half an hour! Money back if not!). Will Strangler's Flying Circus. The Year of the Stoat. The Zoo Show.

Series One – Recorded from August 1969 and broadcast on BBC1 around 11pm from 5 October, several of the shows latched on to some of those discounted titles for sub-headings. Conscious that *Python* was following Spike Milligan's *Q* shows and a great admirer of the man's work, the team were keen to recruit Spike's Ian MacNaughton. Unavailable at the beginning, John Howard Davies produced the first five shows. MacNaughton eventually fully came on board and apart from being helped by Jones, Palin or Gilliam on location scouting trips he worked closely with Jones on the final edits of the show. The healthy competition and rivalry between the team always seemed to break down to an Oxford versus Cambridge situation with the visually oriented Palin, Jones and 'honorary Oxford guy' Gilliam, on one hand, and the vocal prowess of Chapman, Cleese and Idle on the other. Indeed, Michael Palin maintains that all six writer/performers were very much individual forces from the outset, almost beginning to break up as a unit from the first meeting on 13 May 1969. Cleese, the recognised star force as far as the BBC were concerned, was the rebel of the gang, defying his straight authority image with delicious irony. Palin and Jones just had a ball like the old student pals their were continually going off in surreal wordplay tangents that only their understood and their found amusing. Gilliam was the most isolated of the group, working on his creative flights of fancy away from the rest, Chapman spend most of his time injecting wonderfully manic suggestions into the show while projecting an affable, charming personality to each and every crew and cast member, while Idle usually sat around with his head stuck in a book. The written material would be voted into the show which always meant Idle (usually writing on his own) had to sell his ideas twice as powerfully to get any headway at all. The acting assignments were far less complex – usually, if a person had written a piece their would play it. Cleese was always chosen as the official figure or straight-faced lawyer; Chapman usually grabbed the medical characters; Jones the working class nutters or judges and Palin and Idle seemed to interchange between the other character parts. Gilliam cropped up occasionally, always as some mindless and often wordless grotesque. At heart, Python was a writing team and if one thought another could convey his words better then their were no qualms about letting them have the screen time. The distinctive theme tune of Sousa's *The Liberty Bell* was quickly selected from a standard BBC album of marches which both Palin and, particularly, Gilliam wanted. The American warmed to his countryman's sound, immediately hooked by the bong! that starts the whole thing off. He made that bell much louder, rearranged and edited the piece to a 30-second extract and, bingo, the unforgettable refrain of *Monty Python's Flying Circus*. With the scripts in place, the unique *Python* look and sound together and a freshness of approach about to revolutionise television, *Python* humour was untested, unconventional and disliked by many senior people at the Corporation. But the team had been given a 13-week, no questions asked assignment and what they got was this...

EPISODE 1

A momentous chapter in the history of British television; one can only hazard a guess at the BBC1's audience reaction to this first broadcast attack of pure *Python*. Suffice to say that Palin's It's Man, Ursula Andress/*Dr. No*-like

appearance from the ocean choking and desperately chasing after the camera followed by the subdued tones of Cleese and the sound of Sousa is simply television magic. By no means one of the best episodes of series one, this does, nevertheless, establish *Python*'s style and, more importantly, fearlessness of stepping into bad taste, clearly highlighted with the variety show parody 'It's Wolfgang Amadeus Mozart' played by Cleese à la Liberace. Shifting between show biz and sports, the composer presents Famous Deaths in an *Opportunity Knocks/It's A Knock-Out* style with Idle's Eddie Waring-a-like on scores and Ghengis Khan's demise fighting for pole position. The request death, poor old Graham Chapman as Bruce Foster relaxing at home before unexpectedly pegging out, leads to Nelson's contemporary departure (from a high-storey building), and the running motif of squashed pigs, squealing throughout this opening show. In its primitive fashion, this also establishes the stream of consciousness style of *Python* with Jones the teacher crossing out pigs on his blackboard before lumbering into the rather laboured teaching Italian to Italians sketch, with the pupils confounding the master with their skill and the one benefiting student, Chapman's German stereotype, re-directed to the German class.

The team are very much finding their feet here, but Gilliam's animation hits the floor running with a surreal montage of pigs, head removals cracked like eggs and advertising glories for Whizzo butter. Perfectly intercut into a pepperpot 'spot the different taste' compared with a dead crab, the characters' inability to realise they are involved in the very sort of consumer test they're condemning begins to turn the television psyche in on itself and this is heightened with Palin's nervy presentation of 'It's the Arts'(having difficulty with delivery and seeing his Arthur Jackson summing up finished off by Cleese's naked Viking). The Cleese/Chapman Sir Edward Ross interview is the first recognised classic to make an appearance,

stripping away the pretensions of modern cinema to wallow in personality/voice of the people familiarity via 'pussy cat' and 'Eddie baby' comments. This priceless dialogue continues with the less celebrated 'It's the Arts' look at Picasso's attempt to paint while riding a bike. The absurdity of the notion is counterbalanced by natural sporting appendages, such as a detailed look at the route, Chapman's mournful biking champ and Cleese's excitable commentator on location, fuelling the bizarre quality of the piece with frantic observation of a mass of artists cycling by, extending the visual humour with Toulouse Lautrec while continuing the pig references. In between all this artistic pedalling is a landmark interview with Arthur 'Two Sheds' Jackson, the misunderstood composer brilliantly brought to angst-ridden life by Jones, desperate to get away from his nickname, while Idle continually drives the irrelevant but obsessive point home.

With back projection of the garden shed in question and half-hearted attempts to get things back on the classical music trail, this is a *Python* classic. A mock newsreel fires Gilliam's imagination with a rampage through a Victorian photo album; a trapped figure (voiced by Jones) struggles to attract attention from someone; nastiness embraced with broken fingers; rebellion of the age with naked images hidden from the law; bizarre dancing soldiers and a final, long anticipated pig attack. It's all a fascinating prelude to a *Python* masterpiece, The Funniest Joke in the World, which runs to the end of this episode. In mock, old campaigner style, linked by Chapman's military presence, the team expertly deconstruct the art of warfare in terms of the art of comedy. From Palin's opening hysterics as Arthur Scribber the performance and visual impact is uniformly perfect. Jones, as the sincerely shocked reporter talking about sudden, violent comedy, Idle as the joke writer's ill-fated mother, Chapman's bumbling, fearless policeman and Cleese, evil personified as the heartless Nazi officer, create a surreal world of death by sense of humour, deploying uniformed singing of laments from the police (Cleese/Palin/Idle) and ultimately translating this one-liner into a weapon. Prancing through coloured smoke like *Dad's Army*, incorporating archive footage of Neville Chamberlain's pre-war 'joke', illustrating bravery through Palin's brilliantly stiff upper-lipped prisoner of war rejecting Chapman threats, allowing a briefly spotted bit of dying laughter from Gilliam and Idle's German joke (tuned into by the bemused Jones/Palin on the home front), this mini history of World War II concludes with Idle's lament for the unknown joke and the finality of battle signified by a football referee's whistle. *Python* was here to stay.

Did You Know?

While giving no more than 90 minutes studio time and an extra half hour maximum was nothing new from the BBC, even for projects they weren't sure about, the initial audiences were another thing – often very much like the host of wildly applauding ladies from archive Women's Institute footage that graced the early shows. Most expected a standard comedy variety show and tended to treat the traditional stand-up, warm-up comic with more respect than the show they had come to see, although friends and relations including Connie Booth and Ernest Jones were vocal in the laughter department while the rest of the audience sat uncertain. Eventually, with the cult audiences on the same wavelength attending the crowded recording sessions, reaction was more vocally appreciative and the Pythons themselves began making brief pre-show appearances until they practically ran the warm-up sessions using various musicians they had discovered on holiday or like-minded people like Neil Innes.
Naturally, the location budget wasn't that much for this first series, with the team enjoying just two weeks outside filming. But as time went on, more and more was filmed away from the studio (four weeks for the second series, five for the third) and, thus,

allowing, the Pythons more time and more control over the final presentation. Filmed on location, the first ever, classic It's Man spot was set in Bournemouth. The immortal Sousa march theme has now became part of *Python* world culture. Following years of dormant disuse, it crops up at *The International Horse Show*, rehearsing brass bands overheard during a Charles and Di interview at Horse Garden Parade, Chinese players on the eve of the British handover, various football matches, many other sporting events and even in orbit, when a tape of *Python*'s opening riff featured among the possessions of a British astronaut. Sketches like the Lingerie Shop Robbery, Johann Gambolputty's It's the Arts doco and The Dirty Fork were all wanted in this first episode by various team members but only cropped up later. The Italian Lessons sketch was also intended to be longer with a nationalist fight while the war jokery featured a Churchillian speech and contemporary studio debate. Show 1, as broadcast, also features Michael Palin's pet *Python* name Gwen Dibley – his writer of the world's funniest joke lives on Dibley Road, Dibley. Other mentions throughout the *Python* TV years are: The Dibley Boy's school hosting *Seven Brides for Seven Brothers* (series 2, episode 5) and the failed film director L.F. Dibley.

Series 1 Episode I 'Wither Canada?' was conceived, written and performed by **John Cleese, Michael Palin, Graham Chapman, Terry Jones, Eric Idle**
Also appearing were **Carol Cleveland & Terry Gilliam**
Makeup supervisor **Joan Barrett**
Costume supervisor **Hazel Pethig**
Animations by **Terry Gilliam**
Film cameraman **James Balfour**
Film editor **Ray Millichope**
Sound **John Delany**
Lighting **Otis Eddy**
Designer **Roger Liminton**
Film direction **Ian MacNaughton**
Producer **John Howard Davies**
5 October 1969

EPISODE 2
This is the one. Despite being number

two in broadcast order, this classic episode was the very first half hour of distilled *Monty Python* presented to a bemused and totally gobsmacked BBC studio audience. A television landmark indeed, and it's good to see that the show includes a handful of vintage *Python* pieces heralded by a glorious It's Man moment and Cleese in pompous over-drive announcement mood. The very first sketch proper, one of my all-time favourites with Graham Chapman's pondersome farmer and Terry Jones superb as the city businessman, is the perfect meeting of *At Last the 1948 Show* and *Do Not Adjust Your Set*, beautifully written and structured to allow insanity to seep into a normal situation. Chapman's laid-back delivery ranks with the best acting of his career, capping the laugh brought on by the manic, off-screen (and thus cheap to film) behaviour of his flock by discussing 'A clever sheep!' by the name of Harold. Rounded off, this is a prime sketch but the beauty of this fledging Python group is found in the radical development of the idea.
For an *At Last* episode, Chapman's comic resolve would cut to another sketch. Here Cleese and Palin baffle the nation as two wind-up French experts, breaking down the stereotypes (berets/striped shirts) for their own comic invention (handing over fake moustache for kick-starting mannerisms/Cleese's silly prancing), revealing the deluxe inside of a flying sheep and coming down to earth for the obvious laugh by slipping in the word 'poof' in their outrageous French diatribe. A group of Cleese, Chapman, Jones and Palin pepperpots (the grotesque house-wives were labelled 'pepperpots' in the original scripts although never referred to as such within the shows) link into a definitive television situation parody with Cleese's supercilious, meticulous and self-conscious BBC interviewer discussing the multi-buttock assets of commoner Terry Jones, cleverly skipping round the subject with layers of careful phrases for the Jones seat before his restraint is replaced with angst-ridden attempts to see the evidence and stand tall for the

viewer's rights. Idle, in 'And Now For Something Completely Different' mood, wastes some time by starting the sketch again before Cleese realises what's going on and Jones explains that he thought this was the continental version. Again the team take this multi-body parts idea one step beyond with Graham Chapman's two-noses skit before Michael Palin's smooth host introduces the infamous Terry Jones creation, Arthur Ewing and his Musical Mice.

All this violent madness is dismissed by Carol Cleveland, looking as saucy as ever, wandering into the classic Marriage Guidance sketch with Michael Palin's wonderfully ineffectual Arthur Purty. Basically, the sketch just highlights the total lack of spine in Palin's accountant character, with even Idle inadvertently obscuring Palin's camera line and Palin himself injecting the clever touch of nervously pulling his socks up as Idle lusciously glazes at Cleveland's legs. It is laying the groundwork for *Python*'s total disregard for the accepted norms of comedy – with Cleese's Clint-like philosopher instilling some spirit into Palin only to fall at the first hurdle, get slapped by a rubber chicken-wielding knight and prompting the team's response to this sort of stuff – 'So much for Pathos!' In time, even that familiar Knight figure would bite the dust – coming too close to comedy cliché and visual catchphrase for the team, akin to the hated reliance on easy gags in *I'm Sorry I'll Read That Again*.

A complete change of pace comes with the refined, historical footage of Terry Jones as Queen Victoria joined by Chapman's Gladstone, breaking from sedate filmed archive material into a brilliant parody of Robert Youngson's 60s silent comedy compilations with over-enthused commentary, wacky antics, jaunty theme music and manic sound effects. This is a prime example of the seamless force of *Python* comedy, even without Gilliam's animation, for the still image of Jones as the Queen becomes a photo on the mantelpiece of Jones the housewife in the fondly remembered reverse kitchen sink

sketch. The idea is simple enough – Chapman's working class chap is a high-profile playwright expressing the struggles of the common man while living in Hampstead and globe-trotting. Idle is the refined public school figure who waxes lyrical on the value of working down the mine. Jones is the mother and wife defending both points of view of her loved ones, taking in her hard done-by stride the nightmarish hell of gala lunches and her hubby's writer's cramp. It's sixties iconology twisted, played to perfection and giving more than a knowing reaction to the champagne lifestyle of the John Osborne set. As if to bring folk back to their bewildered state, it's almost a return to the bloke with three buttocks before it is hastily realised that the idea's been done to death. Then comes the chap with nine legs who has run away ('Bloody hell!') and thus, in desperation, it's Cleese as a Scotsman on a horse – like the Colonel, the Knight and the Its Man, he's a regular cameo character in series one. A recurring image of Chapman's nose act and Harold, the successfully flying sheep, links to John Cleese hosting the religious debate show *The Epilogue* with almost Crazy Gang references (Monsieur Edward Gay) hints of the Idle novel to come (Dr. Tom Jack – author of *Hello Sailor*) and a physical fight for the existence or non-existence of God. Once the idea is set up (pure violence in place of thought process) the joke is finished so no time is wasted before Gilliam's Western cowboy rides into the scene and dies. The grave is watered and grows hands which are cropped and collected; the legendary flute statue kisses to play a tune; the granny-eating pram eats some grannies before turning on its master and fades to the classic Cleese/Chapman sketch, The Mouse Problem. Along the way this had been rejected by both Peter Sellers and Marty Feldman but here the lads really go for it with Palin presenting this serious television examination of the situation, Cleese reliving his experiences as Mr. A (although in a knowing comment on television convention his real identity

is given), while Jones is spot on as the understanding, quietly spoken interviewer nodding in sympathy as Cleese remembers the cheese being handed around.

But the high point comes with Graham Chapman's pseudo-psychiatrist, lapsing into his magician's act with lovely Carol Cleveland in assistance and expressing his sexual attraction to mice, much to the unease of Palin. The continual use of 'I know I have!' builds to a frenzy with his cheery, innuendo-fuelled phrase about getting it out in the open. This is Chapman highlighting that with the right script and a little less of the bottle he was arguably the most penetratingly hilarious Python of them all. The famous men extension of the mouse idea, with Jones as Napoleon keeping a firm hold on his cheese under his coat and Idle's rough and tough Viking, perhaps take the idea beyond its limitations although the man on the street survey, with Cleese extremes and Chapman, again stealing the moment with his understanding regular Joe summing up with 'I'd kill 'em!' is excellent. The mouse party footage is spell-binding, done in perfect fly on the wall documentary style as the threads of the episode are wound up with Palin shooting Harold as he flies overhead and the pro-religious result of the epilogue coming in during the final credits. This is a prime *Python* show.

Did You Know?

This monumental piece of television history enjoyed Barry Took as warm-up man and went before the cameras at 8.10pm in Studio 6, BBC Television Centre. An unedited playback of this show on 1 September proved the Pythons had succeeded. Material cut from this show included Pepperpot discussion on the pros and cons of French philosophers as opposed to German ones and a brief Palin interview with The Amazing Kargol and Janet. That definitive man of insignificance, Arthur Putey, is referred to as both A. Posture and A. Pewtie in the original script. Arthur was a favourite *Python* name

The first official publicity shot – comedy revolution 1969 style

particularly with Chapman, who used it in homage to one of his favourite actors, Arthur Lowe.

Series 1 Episode II 'Sex and Violence' was conceived, written and performed by **John Cleese, Michael Palin, Graham Chapman, Terry Jones, Eric Idle & Terry Gilliam**
Also appearing was **Carol Cleveland**
Makeup supervisor **Joan Barrett**
Costume supervisor **Hazel Pethig**
Animations by **Terry Gilliam**
Film cameraman **Jimmy Balfour**
Film editor **Ray Millichope**
Sound **John Delany**
Lighting **Otis Eddy**
Designer **Christopher Thompson**
Film direction **Ian MacNaughton**
Producer **John Howard Davies**
12 October 1969

EPISODE 3

Palin's It's Man was by now a signifier for warm affectionate laughter and his intro here, chased by an off-screen big cat, is a classic. Already *Python* was playing havoc with television announcements, erroneously explaining that this episode is 12B before lurching into the obsession for recognising different types of trees: a line of enquiry which will crop up throughout the episode – right up to the final credits. Initially the Larch idea invades Eric Idle's court case, with our cheerful, crafty

cockney delivery of parking offender, Mr. Larch, metamorphosing into an articulate intonation complete with Olivier-style *Richard III* vocals. A return to the Judge Not days of *Cambridge Circus*, Chapman's witness – a whining, nattering, gossiping old bore by the name of Fiona Lewis – rips into a legendary, ever-mounting diatribe, much to the petulant dismay of Judge Terry Jones and cynical defence counsel Cleese, embracing the medium with knowing looks into camera and warning raised finger on words like 'womb', 'KGB' and 'Wooden leg'. The typically Cleesian dead witness in a coffin takes the court joke to macabre heights, while Palin's Cardinal Richelieu figure embraces history in a totally surreal context, unfrocked by Chapman's flat-footed, bumbling Inspector who unashamedly begins his window-cleaner song, latterly accompanied by a prancing Cleese and a judicial chorus. The rubber chicken-carrying knight and a bit more Larch sets the scene for one of *Python*'s most celebrated inventions – the legendary Bicycle Repair Man, instilled with bucketloads of Palin's quiet confidence. Again this defies the expected, with Cleese and Chapman in Superhero gear exclaiming 'But how!' as Palin's busy, well-controlled maintenance chap goes about his business. It's

gloriously silly and hilarious – the hallmark of *Python*. The spirit of the American dream philosopher is embodied in Cleese's commie-hating BBC announcer who quickly lapses back into his gent persona before Eric Idle's warm-hearted children's story-teller comes on the scene. One of those more adult-geared sketches which couldn't quite get into *Do Not Adjust Your Set*, Idle's enthused reading of Ricky the Magic Pixie, totally engrossed with the untypical sexual goings on is quickly usurped by another story smothered with lost innocence, each new tale moving up dubious avenues with Idle's shocked reaction to transvestites, contraceptives and melons! The sense of corrupted childhood is continued with Gilliam's masterly animation of joyful playing rabbits squashed by a hippo before a seaside competition is established with a contribution from two of the boys – a little sketch set in a restaurant. Taking the notion of 'the customer is always right' to the limit, Chapman's easy reaction to his dirty fork leads to a chain reaction involving Idle's humble manager, Cleese's manic, brain-damaged chef and the other *Python*s all queuing up with exclamations and apologies. Chapman scores heavily with his shocked 'It wasn't smelly!' before consciously setting up the required punchline about the knife and delivering the line with knowing, comedy convention-twisting amazement. The message is that the preceding material is no funnier with a close and soon even this tongue-in-cheek acknowledgement of the norm would be abandoned. Here, following the seaside setting, the sketch is treated like a bathing beauty contestant with Palin's cheerful 'bit vicious in parts but a lot of fun'. Gilliam's Purchase a Past cartoon, with cut-out photographs and other people's memories making up for their boring lives – at a cost – is among his most potent work, with police dressed in pig-gear and the nightmarish spectre of vintage, sepia-coloured strangers invading your home. The milkman trap is an enjoyable throwaway skit, if only for Palin's nervous, expectant expression.

Cleese's bored newsreader, unaware of the stereotypical robbers breaking in and stealing him away lock, stock and barrel, with a further larch mention, continues unabated with his professional broadcast and, of course, chucks in a quick 'And Now For Something Completely Different'. But the episode's key moment comes with sniggering kiddies Palin, Jones and Idle, laughing at the mere mention of 'Bottom' and pushing forward a little sketch written by Eric called Nudge, Nudge. Immediately it's set up as childish, base innuendo, channelled through Idle's school-capped youngster, nervously putting sexual awakening into comedy. It may say more about my sense of humour than that of Idle's, but this has always been the high point of *Python* comedy in my opinion. Idle's Nudge, Nudge man has, since, became the ultimate King of Cool, fuelling a thousand drunken bar room laughathons with nods to blind bats, photographs and say no mores all over the place. The joke, of course, is that Idle's self-confident character is a total loser, trying to discover sexual tit-bits from the experienced but refined bowler-hatted man of Terry Jones. Time has almost removed the final revelation and Idle's nudge, nudge dialogue ranks with Shakespeare as capturing the spirit of the British. He's just so damned wicked and remains Idle's ultimate contribution to *Python* power! With no material anywhere close to Nudge, Jones blows the ref's whistle off screen, Palin's It's Man looks stunned and the credits roll. What could follow total class?

Did You Know?
Originally the Larch concept was not included and Idle's Harold Larch was dubbed Millet. Graham Chapman was due to play a fourth schoolboy in the Nudge, Nudge schoolyard interview.

Series 1 Episode III, 'How to recognise different types of trees from quite a long way away' was conceived, written and performed by **Graham Chapman, John Cleese, Terry Gilliam, Eric Idle, Terry Jones & Michael Palin**

Also appearing was **Ian Davidson**
Makeup supervisor **Joan Barrett**
Costume supervisor **Hazel Pethig**
Animations by **Terry Gilliam**
Film cameraman **James Balfour**
Film editor **Ray Millichope**
Sound **John Delany**
Lighting **Otis Eddy**
Designer **Christopher Thompson**
Film direction **Ian Macnaughton**
Producer **John Howard Davies**
19 October 1969

EPISODE 4
Introduced as episode Arthur part 7 – Teeth, this show signposts Graham Chapman's bombastic Colonel as purveyor of sanity and common sense, importantly being ridiculed by the comic form due to his obsession with protecting authority and striving for a justification of the initial introduction. It's Eric Idle's religious crooner, linking the material and enjoying some unabated snogging while rejoicing in the glories of belief, that shows the hypocritical but joyous attitude of *Python* to its fullest – merging into the art galley sketch with Cleese and Chapman slapping imaginary kiddies and eating artistic masterpieces. Projected within the sketch as the ultimate desecration of these works of art, Palin's expert clearly highlights *Python*'s reinforcing of the anarchic behaviour by consuming a small masterpiece himself before facing the camera and hiding his outrageous endorsement of destruction. Palin's seductive helper has her dreadful gag mocked and emotionally exposes the situation of her acting responsibility by moaning that it's her only line – a cry reiterated by Gilliam's Viking guy almost immediately afterwards. But that's not before Chapman can puff out his chest, defend the honour of military service and rant on about the army being a real man's life. There's a lengthy section of the show handed over to Terry Jones and a splendid Edwardian gent mime struggling to undress on the beach – some 20 years before *Mr. Bean* and illustrating the Keaton-influenced Jones as the great mime performer singled out in *Hang Down Your Head and Die*. Wrapped in a towel,

receiving bemused glances from contemporary onlookers and embracing slapstick comedy with vigour, Michael Palin's disgruntled bloke lights his fag but is mistaken for a Peeping Tom by Jones. This is a classic moment – toss in Chapman's policeman with the blown cover with the removal of deck-chairs and you're in pure Chaplin territory. Indeed, the *What the Butler Saw* segment plays like sophisticated Benny Hill but the entire interlude is merely building up to Jones, in his element, happily stripping on stage. With the music and the crowd the scene shows that when seen in a performance, not only does human frailty and embarrassment go out of the window but the whole notion of undressing in public becomes socially acceptable. Humiliating laughter becomes appreciative applause. Cue Chapman's Colonel again bumbling through his 'it's a man's/dog's/pig's life' in the modern army which naturally leads to a bit of military discipline courtesy of John Cleese and a fresh fruit obsession. One of *Python*'s seminal classics, this is the full version with Idle's priceless mania about being attacked with a pointed stick, a crash course in banana defence, Jones meekly wielding a load of raspberries, the obligatory 16-ton weight, Palin's obstacles desperately trying to curtail Cleese's absurdity and the final release of a tiger. Played with every ounce of manic grotesque energy in Cleese's body this is a masterpiece of British sketch comedy. A multitude of visuals and soundbites, with split screen, a return from a sexed-up singing Idle, a filmed insert of wind-up rickshaw and bathing toff, some more fresh fruit and Chapman complaining that the show was supposed to be about teeth, all jumbles up and comes at you for a manic prelude to the Bookshop sketch. With iconology posters plugging Desmond Morris's *The Naked Ape* and Frank Sinatra's *The Detective*, this is not the classic *At Last the 1948 Show* skit but a battle of espionage and double bluffing played out between Cleese and Idle. Finally this is all about teeth, in a very round about way, with Idle's not so innocent request for *The Illustrated History of False Teeth* kick-starting a whole mini James Bond movie with Palin bounding with heroics, Terry Jones as Brian the manic dentist injecting a theatrical dry (again this is the comedy exposed as just graduates goofing off), Carol Cleveland as every man's ideal dental nurse and Cleese cheerily explaining all the plot twists for Idle's benefit and, more obviously, for the audience. Highlight is Graham Chapman's supercilious mastermind, stroking a stuffed white rabbit in homage to Blofeld's white cat, breaking into delicious over-acting ('Dead and never called me Mother!' is peerless) before a spy lunch break is called as Idle reveals himself to the watching millions as Arthur Lemming of the British Dental Association – cue little ditty, a link to the opening credits, a further abuse of the 'man's life' motto, some totally ballistic Chapman over-reacting and a quick prod at the sleeping It's Man. Pure class.

Did You Know?
This episode was going to feature the Bed Buying sketch and the Hermits, both used in show 9. The edible picture frames were made of flour and water paste.

Series 1 Episode IV 'Owl Stretching Time' was conceived, written and performed by **Graham Chapman, John Cleese, Terry Gilliam, Eric Idle, Terry Jones & Michael Palin**
Also appearing was **Dick Vosburgh**
Carol Cleveland
& Katya Wyeth
Makeup supervisor **Joan Barrett**
Costume supervisor **Hazel Pethig**
Animations by **Terry Gilliam**
Film Cameraman **James Balfour**
Film editor **Ray Millichope**
Sound **John Delany**
Lighting **Otis Eddy**
Designer **Roger Liminton**
Film direction **Ian MacNaughton**
Producer **John Howard Davies**
26 October 1969

EPISODE 5
With the *Python* audience clearly

hooked on this radical collection of nonsense and social ribbing, the team could safely allow less than inspired half hours to escape onto the nation's screens. With some true class already in the audience's subconscious, Palin's rowing It's Man and Cleese's moronic delivery of the title could hold their heads up high with pride and usher in the dodgy comedy of Confuse-A-Cat. A large chunk of the show is given over to the heart-wrenching story of a suburban lounge near Esher with Jones as the domineering housewife, Palin as her hen-pecked hubby and a super cool Chapman doing his vet bit peering over his glasses and giving forth knowledgeable opinions on the fate of cats in a rut. It all gets a wee bit out of hand with the appearance of Cleese and his three-ring circus of ranting stage antics constructed like a military operation. After far too much Long John Silver boxing, Idle/Jones costume changes, Cleese policeman mugging and Penguin frolics it's almost a relief to welcome in Bewilderbeast and finally curtail this sketch. Gilliam's knitting moustache and granny link lead to Palin's over-worked attempted customs fraud, desperately trying to get past with his selection of goodies but continually telling the truth about his crimes and gingerly hiding his mistake.
It's all funny stuff but Idle's defrocked vicar takes the biscuit before Terry Jones hosts the ultimate anti-television sketch desperately trying to discuss the implications with a stuffed cat and a stuffed lizard. From the very start this situation, with its stripped down and raw humour, remains a classic *Python* moment of challenging comedy. The terminology of television journalism is rather more obviously dissected with the man in the street interviews including Jones up on the roof and Carol Cleveland who, in anybody's book, is quite clearly not a man. The Gumby influence is heightened, the familiar chicken-wielding knight returns and Idle's chess-playing is disturbed by the noisy entrance of copper Chapman on a drug raid. Latching onto the notorious officer

who made a Cromwellian attack on British rock stars by drug busting his way to the top via Donovan, the Rolling Stones and eventually John Lennon and George Harrison, here the suspicious substances are quite blatantly planted on the unsuspecting victim (albeit the joke is lightened and extended by the thick-eared copper mistakenly providing his brown paper bag of sandwiches). Moronic moans from Cleese's lower class characterisation and the race prejudice of Palin transposes into Idle's laid-back newsreader (stepping in and out of a picture of himself like some sort of inverted Keaton in *Sherlock Jnr.*) and latching onto almost *Carry On* territory introducing *Match of the Day* with the romantic movie. Complete with Idle interruptions, the passionate slobberings of Terry Jones and Carol Cleveland fades into acceptable cinematic sex (and a none too subtle homage to the Jon Voight/Sylvia Miles romp in John Schlesinger's *Midnight Cowboy*) with a montage of black and white footage before the subliminal use of archive material (gushing water/collapsing chimneys/Richard Nixon et al) is revealed as nothing more than Terry's sad obsession with his projector and film collection as poor old Carol patiently waits for the earth to move. That nasal, 'Just one more, dear!' says more about the British stereotypical sexual male than a library of academia. The final movie is, in fact, Gilliam's comment on the weakling, with a clichéd sand in face on the beach situation, a Jayne Mansfield-like glam girl and a pseudo-American muscle man offer. However, nothing in this show can compare to the sublime Cleese/Chapman confrontation at the manager training course with the meek and mild Graham, desperate to impress, continually falling into the malicious tricks of his inquisitor. The surreal, elongated 'Goodnight!', bell ringing and manic counting down from five finally lulls Chapman into a string of funny faces, squawks and shameless humiliation. It's an archetypal but rarely celebrated *Python* exchange. Palin's elder statesman, languishing in the position of Careers Advisory Head, laments his early ambitions for a life in medicine or art before Idle comes into his own as the comic book burglar gaining entry into Miss Cleese's abode by false pretences, explaining that he's really after her valued possessions but, in reality, living up to her worse fears by attempting to sell encyclopaedias – the only option is a Milligan/Feldman dive through an open window.

Did You Know?
Chapman's interviewee was originally named Stig rather than David Thomas and the It's segment was due to see Palin tossed over the side of a cliff. The Confuse-a-Cat sketch came about when Cleese was writing at Chapman's penthouse. They noticed a neighbour's cat which never moved from one spot whatever the weather – cue comic twisting.

Series 1 Episode V 'Man's Crisis of Identity in the Later Half of the 20th Century' was conceived, written and performed by **Graham Chapman, John Cleese, Eric Idle, Terry Jones & Michael Palin**
Also appearing was **Carol Cleveland**
Research **Sarah Hart Dyke**
Makeup supervisor **Joan Barrett**
Costume supervisor **Hazel Pethig**
Animations by **Terry Gilliam**
Film cameramen **Max Sammett & Alan Featherstone**
Film editor **Ray Millichope**
Sound **John Delany**
Lighting **Otis Eddy**
Designer **Christopher Thompson**
Film direction **Ian MacNaughton**
Producer **John Howard Davies**
23 November 1969

EPISODE 6
The It's Man is wanted on the phone and before the show even begins we are trailed for next week's Arthur Figgis episode. The BBC bemoan the cost of continual captions, a signature runs amuck across maps and a burst of classical music heralds the in-depth culture programme *It's the Arts* with Graham Chapman the earnest host. Celebrating an undervalued German composer with

a lengthy, long and winding road of a tongue-twisting name, Chapman delivers the absurdity of the situation with wonderfully straight skill. In his introductory profile, Chapman completes the name twice and begins a third time before a filmed insert welcomes Terry Jones as the great composer's only living relative. Cleese, in definitive BBC interviewer style, asks the question in complete detail, with Jones, doddering and muttering his answer in full, heightening the madness of the humour by pausing after the composer's name and then giving the composer's wife a complete name check as well. Despite Cleese's rather anxious pleads to answer things quickly, the interviewee dies before any information is imparted and the host digs the grave on the spot for his guest. Gilliam's animated montage, including a knight, an extraordinary Liverpudlian Lon Chaney Snr (in *Phantom of the Opera* mode) and the legendary statue fig-leaf picking censored moment seamlessly link into Michael Palin's mouthy gangland boss who continually avoids breaking the law and briefs his lads on how to do the ultimate job of buying his new watch – involving skilful stuff like walking into a shop and paying for one – before Terry Jones gets a bit miffed and suggests chucking in a few illegal elements like some sustained parking after the metre has run out to make the job more exciting. ('We never break the bloody law!') A typical touch of insanity from the Palin/Jones writing team, extended by Terry's money purloining vicar, Michael's Scottish interlude and the typically dumb-bell copper of Cleese recognising the different filmic qualities as he wanders out of the filmed insert and into the studio for the almighty Crunchy Frog sketch. Terry Jones, the relaxed business brain behind Whizzo Chocolate Co., astounds Cleese and his vomiting assistant Chapman by admitting that the material included in his delicious sweet meats are raw, rather unpleasant items! It's a miniature version of the themes Jones and Palin would develop for their 1973 television play *Secrets*, but here the

writing is rich, concentrated and peerlessly performed by Jones on a wild, flamboyant tangent of enthusiasm about his product. ('Our sales would plummet'.) The disastrous effect of listing ingredients in detail in comparison to the succulent, pleasant honesty of the chocolate is a masterpiece, enforced by Cleese's nonplussed commands to Jones as he addresses the viewers at home.
Palin's obsession with the narrow-minded, little man lost persona of the officious businessman is seen in his much-copied city stockbroker wandering past exciting and outlandish events (Mel Smith and Griff Rhys Jones did a very effective take on the idea for *Alas Smith and Jones*). The basic gag is that this non-entity is so wrapped up in facts and figures that he strolls past naked shop assistants, monstrous figures attacking bus queues, soldiers on manoeuvres, invisible cab drivers, dead people and rampant snogging, only to fulfil his fantasies via the pages of *Thrills and Adventure* magazine.
Idle's Red Indian theatre-goer sketch is an almost forgotten gem, with Chapman's petulant Brit stunned by his Leatherhead rep experiences (with a name check for Idle's Sandy Camp from the drug planting sketch in episode 5) and the ancient teaching of happiness through acting, the genius of Cicely Courtneidge and the sheer majesty of the Dorking Civic Hall. There's even a chance for some self-referential comment on Terry Jones and his choc attack with Idle's brave-face enjoying a crunchy frog.
Cleese's friendless policeman, a Scotsman on a horse yet again and a filmed insert of a Highland wedding are all blown away by Gilliam's brilliant granny-eating pram animation, complete with surreal black humour and the obligatory 16-ton weight. Hardly a taxing reference to Fox, 20th Century Vole allows Chapman to eat the scenery with a deliciously over-played movie mogul, terrorising his gang of six nervous writers with pathetic storylines and snap judgements. A comedy concerning a dog piddling on a tree

with star headliners Rock Hudson and Doris Day gets the yes men yessing for all their worth, with concerns of pinko subversion corrupting the meeting. Palin hilariously puts on a mock faint rather than giving any comment at all, while the madness of the Hollywood machine plays the swinging sixties game of movie-making by putting up David Hemmings as the weirdo hippy. What else? With nowhere else to go the sketch and show finishes with the gag seamlessly leaking into the closing credits for the first time.

Did You Know?
This episode was originally due to begin with Palin, Cleese and Idle desperately trying to remember the name of Jones in a pub, mistaking him for everyone from James Stewart to Anthony Newley via David Frost – he turns out to be Arthur Figgis, a rather boring accountant. Cleese's Scotsman on a horse was actually performed by stuntmen – the close-up of the Python was actually filmed with him sitting on a bicycle! The City Stockbroker boring day sketch by the rare combination of Graham Chapman and Eric Idle, brilliantly sends up the Day in the Life sketches Jones and Palin had written for Marty Feldman. The Saltzberg film parody was also a left-over from Feldman, written by Cleese and Chapman for *At Last the 1948 Show* when Marty was due to play the producer. At rehearsal, Feldman dropped out of the sketch and it remained unused until Chapman gave it his all for *Python* – with added vitriol following their movie madness experience with *The Magic Christian*.

Series 1 Episode VI Produced by **Irving C. Saltzberg Jnr.**
An Irving C. Saltzberg Productions Ltd. and Saltzberg Arts Films, Oil, Real Estate, Banking and Prostitution Inc, Co-production.
From an original idea by **Irving C. Saltzberg Jnr.**
Written by **Irving C. Saltzberg & Irving C. Saltzberg**
Additional material by **Irving C. Saltzberg** and **Graham C.**

Chapmanberg, John C. **Cleeseberg**, Terry C. **Jonesberg**, Michael C. **Palinberg**, Terry C. **Gilliamberg**, Eric C. **Idleberg**
Also appearing was **Ian C. Davidsonberg**
Credits by **Irving C. Saltzberg**
Research by **Sarah C. Hart Dykeberg**
Makeup by **Joan C. Barrettberg** based on an idea by Irving C. Saltzberg
Costumes by **Hazel C. Pethigberg Jnr.**
Animations by **Terry C. Gilliamberg**
Film Cameraman **James C. Balfourberg**
Film editor **Ray C. Millichopeberg**
Sound **John C. Delanyberg**
Lighting **Otis C. Eddyberg**
Designer **Jeremy C. Daviesberg**
By permission of **Irving C. Saltzberg** Tax Loss Motion Picture Inc.
BBC Producerberg **Ian C. MacNaughtonberg** (Mafia Films) Inc. **Jnr.**
The Endberg
BBC C. TVBerg Jnr.
30 November 1969

EPISODE 7

A very important episode if in retrospect one of the most unfunny *Python* exercises of all time. After a collection of brief, linked sketches, the entire programme is handed over to one, extended playlet as the cringes and non-start laughs become rife. It starts off brilliantly with a prompted It's Man (note the obvious filmic cut-away) and a fun Eric Idle sketch which covers up cultural embarrassment over train-spotting by explaining that his obsession is camel-spotting. Apart from the sheer madness of the piece, the cleverest element is the character name of Mr. Sopwith as in the Sopwith Camel. Gilliam begins the 'You're no fun anymore' ball rolling with continuations from Dracula, Captain Bligh and the chicken knight. A high-powered financial meeting fingers Palin's minute business discrepancies and Jones reiterates the no fun anymore by-line. Idle reappears tied to a railway-line, a fitting fate after his camel subterfuges, Palin has a few Jewishisms about his licence fee and in his other persona introduces the major bulk of this episode – A science fiction spectacular that all the lads have contributed to. It opens

with the loving couple of Chapman and Idle (looking like something out of *The Meaning of Life* 15 years early) wandering along the railway station of New Pudsey. Their fate, despite a nearly lost to the wind hat, is put on the back burner in favour of Michael Palin's boring city gent, tax official and gardener (still strolling through life's adventure from episode 6 and suddenly turning into a Scotsman). With suitably sinister *Night of the Demon*-like sound effects, the mysterious deed is done and Graham Chapman's laid-back, pipe-smoking, old school tie scientific boffin (the major redeeming feature of this X-farce X-file) pontificates for England, deducing that Scotland is a non-tennis playing country and the alien invasion of Blancmange-like Wimbledon wannabes are obviously bettering their chances as the first intergalactic winners. Chapman's wondrous train of thought and Cowardesque observations are perfectly contrasted by the rather saucy bimboisms of Donna Reading excelling in a one-off *Python* venture in the absence of Carol Cleveland – flashing her legs with pride, walking into misunderstandings of Chapman's rhetorical mutterings, pouting and licking her lips seductively into camera for further big screen offers.
As a high-powered satire on the B movie science fiction genre this is all good fun (Reading's exclamation of 'Them!' brings on shocked incidental music which is hilariously familiar from a thousand fifties chillers), but the *Python* team more than lose their way when Chapman and Reading are not on screen. The entire Scottish obsession thing doesn't really come off, with Jones and Palin mugging desperately to impart the storyline with massive orders of kilt-making contracts (although Palin's masterly confusion about his client being 'Not really a man!' is certainly worth the wait). The over-crowding of Scotland, heightened by the English decamping leaving just one footballer, the ref and Idle's solitary fan at the match, links to the tennis spot with Idle's doubles player trying to justify his team structural habits to Cleese's

policeman (more interested in the way five can play doubles than any strange sightings of alien attackers). With discussion name checks for *The Rise and Fall of the Roman Empire* and Googie Withers, Idle's detective inspector finds everything hilarious before correcting himself to be a tragic, slapping disrespectful impersonator and wading into cannibalistic terrain. The final pseudo-BBC report from the Wimbledon finals, with Palin's Scotsman batting the monstrous blob, the returning couple of Idle and Chapman ('just panned off us!') eating the offending substance and Palin playing all the points against himself to win the match rather than sailing through by default, takes the sci-fi story and this *Python* to its close. It's a blessed relief when the credits come and the Pythons were very sharp to stick this one away in the middle of the run. It drags beyond belief but Chapman and Reading brilliantly save the day as well as the episode.

Did You Know?
That huge invasion of Scotsmen included most of the crew dressed in kilts – totally against union rules but helping out the Pythons.

Series 1 Episode VII You're No Fun Any More was conceived, written and performed by **Graham Chapman, John Cleese, Eric Idle, Terry Jones, Michael Palin & Terry Gilliam**
Also appearing was **Donna Reading**
Research **Sarah Hart Dyke**
Makeup supervisor **Joan Barrett**
Costume supervisor **Hazel Pethig**
Animations by **Terry Gilliam**
Film cameramen **Max Sammett & Alan Featherstone**
Film editor **Ray Millichope**
Sound **John Delany**
Lighting **Otis Eddy**
Designer **Roger Liminton**
Produced & directed by **Ian MacNaughton**
7 December 1969

EPISODE 8
Episode 12B, praising the delights of Full Frontal Nudity which never really comes despite the It's Man's

improved position of glam girl adoration and flowing champers, quickly destroyed by an exploding bomb. A war newsreel proclaims the setting as Unoccupied 1970 with Chapman's definitive Army Colonel confronting a cheery Eric Idle who reasons why he wishes to leave the army, distressed at the working with dangerous real guns – having expected toy ones. However, Idle soon finds his very silly argument usurped by the appearance of Jones and Palin as sarcastic, sadistic Mafia chappies, accidentally breaking things on purpose, promoting their protection racket and grinning with malicious intent, much to the unimpressed attitude of Chapman. A rare writing collaboration between John Cleese and Michael Palin, here for the first time, Chapman emerges from within the sketch format and actually challenges the quality of the piece in which he is appearing. Stopping the show for being very badly written and not giving him a funny line yet, Chapman halts Idle's attempted reappraisal of his concerns about guns, rebuffs the entire *Python* philosophy with an attitude of not being able to think of a good punchline, and prompting the Mafia men of Jones and Palin to question whether the British public would understand this television terminology before queuing up a Gilliam cartoon. The overall title is embraced with an old man and nudity before Palin's respected art critic fumbles through a comment about the nude in his bed and Miss Wyeth can bawl about her only line being debunked as groan-worthy humour. The manic bed buying sketch with Terry Jones and Carol Cleveland confronting the eccentric sales techniques of Chapman and Idle runs round and round after its own tail for too long but still hits the comic button with surreal multiplying of measurements, bag-over-the-head antics when ever the word mattress is mentioned, T.V. in-jokes (Mr Verity and Mr Lambert) and mutual standing in a tea chest to calm everybody down. Once Cleese wanders on and joins in with a hearty rendition of *Green and Pleasant Land*

you may as well give up hope and join in as well.
The typical *Python*esque trick of allowing archive crowd footage to also sing along, Carol's reiteration of the 'it's my only line' complaint (more than fair comment on the underwritten female parts in the show as well as simultaneously poking fun at the bimbo glam girl parts the lads *had* written) and the obligatory man in the street section sees the thing invert into itself, the previous sketches condemned as silly, the bed farce condemned as even more silly and the silly stakes raised even higher with a filmed interlude concerning the contradictory situation of a hermit commune. Palin and Idle enjoy a brilliantly irreverent, slightly camp take on the isolated lifestyle (sort of *Hancock's Half Hour*: The Wild Man of the Woods fun with Tony and Kenneth Williams for a post-*Round the Horne* generation). Again the *Python* viewer is included within the comedy discussion, with an exclamation that filmed material makes no real difference to the punter at home, although Chapman clearly doesn't think so as he attacks the in-shot film crew on the mountain side as Gilliam's insanity tidies things up. The classic legs akimbo dancing mermaid signals the ultimate comic moment for any self-respecting *Python* fan as bated breath across the nation awaits John Cleese, hair slicked back, sinister raincoat buttoned tightly, rattled cage in hand and the immortal words, 'Hello Miss!' I'm sure the majority of readers could quite happily recite the rest for themselves. The Dead Parrot sketch has become far more than simply the most celebrated and repeated piece of *Python* comedy. This Chapman/Cleese masterpiece has become the benchmark for any other piece of comedy sketch material before or since. With a total life of its own, the joyous performance of Cleese and Palin ranks with the best comedy of this or any other century. Amazingly, judging by the audience reaction, it was treated with enthusiastic, if hardly uncontrollable, titters on its first

performance. No matter, the Norwegian Blue and this debate on the British way of getting one's money's worth not only runs the gamut of synonyms for 'death' but sees the team submit their most impressive and recognised contribution to world culture. Of course, in this original television version, the fun goes on even longer with the pet shop man's brother being a wag, Terry Jones assuring the irritated ex-parrot owner that he is right, Cleese looking directly into camera for support, Jones embracing yet again the feel of performers performing – explaining that it's hard to pad these things out to 30 minutes – and Palin's shifty, so nice you could forgive him anything, guy desperately trying to cover over his ploy with the immortal 'It was a pun'. Chapman, crusader for non-silly comedy, stops the parrot pleasures from going too far out and finally justifies the title with some full frontal material – which turns out to be Terry Jones flashing Boo! at unsuspecting passers-by. Such a classic episode has to end on a high and it does – the landmark Hell's Grannies, with Idle's television psychologist explaining the fate of Bolton – a frightened city – under attack from these layabouts in lace with their swinging sixties attitude of making tea not love. Chapman's bemused policeman steals the scene with his stunned comments about the grannies blowing their pensions on such luxury items as a tin of meat for the cat. As with earlier *Python* skits, the team take the idea beyond its natural closure, incorporating bully boy babies and lethal Keep Left Signs. However, with the Pythons challenging even their own conventions with this show, Chapman's Colonel can stumble into shot and dismiss the entire thing as far too silly while highlighting Idle's unconvincing long-haired vicar. With their own anarchic style now pinpointed as anarchic from within the comic structure, anything could happen.

Did You Know?
At the start, the long-winded buying a bed sketch was even longer,

embracing other silly words like 'pesos' for 'lettuce'.

Series 1 Episode VIII Full Frontal Nudity was conceived, written and performed by **Graham Chapman, John Cleese, Eric Idle, Terry Jones, Michael Palin & Terry Gilliam**
Also appearing was **Carol Cleveland, Katya Wyeth & Rita Davies**
Research **Sarah Hart Dyke**
Makeup supervisor **Joan Barrett**
Costume supervisor **Hazel Pethig**
Animations by **Terry Gilliam**
Film Cameramen **Max Sammett & Alan Featherstone**
Film editor **Ray Millichope**
Sound **John Delany**
Lighting **Otis Eddy**
Designer **Geoffrey Patterson**
Produced and directed by **Ian MacNaughton**
14 December 1969

EPISODE 9
A mine-infested field greets Palin's It's Man and the lads dive straight into surrealism with the feted *Llama* song live from Golders Green featuring Idle and Jones screaming their way through, Cleese enthused and grinning, giving translations (look out, there are llamas!) and Chapman, looking divine in evening dress and astride a motorbike, crusading into the action. Although a popular *Python* stage addition, this rag-bag of shrieks quickly fades in comparison with the rest of the show. For a start, it features Cleese uttering those immortal and forever over-used words And Now For Something Completely Different for the first time, while Palin displays the impressive attribute of a tape recorder up his nose. John Cleese is at his eccentric peak as the befuddled, double vision adventurer Sir George Head OBE. The delicious self-belief in what he sees is taken to ultimate extremes as he mulls over the fact that last year's expedition was building a bridge between the two peaks – Idle's embarrassed and rather uneasy reaction to the dawning knowledge is pure comic genius. Idle's relief at finding an ally in Chapman's flamboyant mountaineer is very short lived as he begins to run amuck across the office. His final

outburst against the absurdity of Cleese creates the pregnant pause, heightened by the final realisation that Cleese is vindicated in his double vision belief. This is *Python* in definitive terms and a very rare sketch from the Cleese/Idle writing partnership. But, as Al Jolson might say, you ain't seen nothing yet, for after Gilliam's encyclopaedia salesman it's all systems go for The Lumberjack. Michael Palin, enjoying one of his finest moments, has his lumberjack shirt showing under his bloodied barbershop overalls as he nervously scrubs his hands. Wallowing in cinematic iconology from *Psycho*, Palin ferociously tries to control his murderous tendencies with customer Terry Jones. It's all a masterpiece of macabre comic power as the hair-fearing barber mock-cuts the businessman's locks, uses tape recorded, Geoff Hurst-fuelled footballing chit chat (turned off while the tape is still audible) and nearly gets away with it before he breaks down, explains his (again *Psycho*-like) mother's 'face your fears' attitude and ultimately lapses into his fantasy occupation of a... what else?... lumberjack. Palin, outlandish chewing action and beloved Connie Booth in place, goes into genius overdrive with flamboyant leg slapping and transvestite under-tones as Cleese, Chapman and The Fred Tomlinson Singers cover uneasy reaction with hearty singing on the chorus. Peerless stuff.
Rubber Man of Zurich Awards and sex on television gives Chapman a stunning bit of Professor Gumby sycophantic nutter fun with *Only Make Believe* and Palin turns on his smooth presenting skills for Ken Budda and his inflatable knees as Jones continues to listen to his barber's tale of hair, depression and missed opportunity. The Upper Class Twit of the Year prototype, with a rabble of hunting, fishing and shooting brain-deads highlighting old fashioned, outmoded and peerlessly debunked attitudes is juxtaposed with a more down-to-earth, obvious bit of humour via a quick Benny Hillesque visual gag by flushing out a courting couple who turn out to be two men.

However, the old familiar easy jokes are slowly being stripped away by this stage and the chicken knight is saddened when informed he isn't needed this week – although, of course, in *Python* logic he is needed albeit just to be told he isn't needed. Cleese's And Now link man is happily nestled in a hen house and ushers in the loving couple of Carol Cleveland and Graham Chapman, soft toy department romantics whose night of passion is disrupted by the reappearance of Idle's Nudge, Nudge man, with Milligan-pinched gags (Dung!) and a load of manic friends – Cleese and Jones as the touchy, feely couple from hell, Palin's wonderfully repulsive Ken Shabby (alongside incognito goat) and even a scantily-clad, over-sparkling Terry Gilliam camping around the place and chatting up the gang. It's six Pythons and the ultimate glam girl all together now in one bizarre, sing-song orgy, roller-coaster of a sketch – indeed, Chapman plays it dead straight, acting like Kenneth Horne surrounded by a galaxy of Williams, Paddick and Pertwee grotesques. But here, Cleese shoots Chapman and that never happened in *Round the Horne*, despite what our Ken thought about the scripts.

Did You Know?
Palin's barber tape ran for much longer in the original script while the grotesque Chapman house party was totally different, with people arriving for dinner seven hours late and the host politely entertaining in his pyjamas.

Series 1 Episode VIIII The Ant, An Introduction was conceived, written and performed by **Graham Chapman, John Cleese, Eric Idle, Terry Jones, Michael Palin & Terry Gilliam**
Also appearing was **Carol Cleveland, Connie Booth & The Fred Tomlinson Singers**
Research **Sarah Hart Dyke**
Makeup supervisor **Joan Barrett**
Costume supervisor **Hazel Pethig**
Animations by **Terry Gilliam**
Lighting **Otis Eddy**
Film Cameraman **Alan Featherstone**
Film editor **Ray Millichope**

Sound **John Delany**
Lighting **Otis Eddy**
Designer **Jeremy Davies**
Produced & directed by **Ian MacNaughton**
21 December 1969

EPISODE 10

One of the most potent It's Man appearances has the camera pan across a row of pig carcasses hanging on hooks joined by Palin's ragged fellow who looks more terrified than normal. He utters the immortal word and kick-starts this fine episode. By now, all was signposted play with Cleese and Idle waiting to take part in the robbery sketch. The BBC summons, recruiting Mr. Average 'I can't act!' Palin grudgingly accepting the nagging comments concerning Mrs. Brando's son and that nice Mr. Redford. The notion of instant television and the cross between reality and the home audience view of small screen entertainment is embraced with Palin's walk-on (off!) part, irrelevant to the comic item and quickly dismissed for the bumbling, sophisticated, cliché-ridden (tiny black mask/striped shirt), controlled Milliganesque (full of fine, fine rambling) Cleese, literally pointing his handgun right onto Idle's calm and cool shopkeeper's nose. Graham Chapman's ingratiating television link man laughs hilariously at the item, points out the homosexual references (his camp lapses and interest in muscle magazines), tugging at the sacred cow of established sitcom and stabbing that other television icon, David Frost, with the wooden chat show It's A Tree with Idle's Frostian Arthur Tree. Typically manic in *Python* terms, with an audience made of a forest landscape, Cleese's multi-talented block of wood (writing the history of the world, film work and plenty of charity) and Idle's 'super, super' host whines on and on into some wood-related Gilliam animation, embracing tired music hall tunes with furniture impressions of Long John Silver and Edward Heath. A celestial choir heralds the vocational guidance counsellor. Only in *Python* does the central character, here, Cleese's authority figure, join in

with the tail-end of the singing before Palin's intensely dull interviewee wanders in.

The team relished pinpointing the boredom of Chartered Accountancy, mainly because there had thankfully escaped such intense jobs themselves. Here they find the definitive image in Palin's rambling, smiling, eager but disconnected fellow who is unaware of the sketch tradition – unlike Cleese, who painfully dismisses the gay banter to get on with the comedy, reacting brilliantly to Palin's boyish desire to be a lion-tamer, gently explaining that the last essential skill required is to have your own hat and setting up the *Fierce Creatures* philosophy of tame/vicious animal after Palin's misunderstanding over the ant-eater. The newly filmed version for *And Now For Something Completely Different* enjoyed the luxury of roaring lion footage, rather than a small photograph and Cleese's impersonation, but Palin's reaction here is perfectly timed, leading into the charity appeal for this boring collection of financial experts. A familiar favourite, the larch, the return of Chapman's ever more effeminate presenter and Terry Jones, complete in homo-baiting Viking attire, makes a perfectly disconnected build-up to a stunning sea-scape shot, a potted history of British heroics and the newest name on our roll-call of greats, Ron Obvious.

Having enjoyed Palin's definitive Nowhere Man, we are now treated to Terry Jones, bobbing up and down, jogging on the spot, gullibly believing in himself and cheerfully explaining his aim to jump across the English Channel. Cleese, in BBC interviewer mode, listens with amazement before cornering the devious brains behind the scheme, Palin's sharp-suited, fag-smoking Italian wideboy. As always, the characterisation owes much to vintage Peter Sellers and it is very much down to Palin's joyous playing that keeps this departed nag flogging sketch fresh, flashing past pitiful failure at the jump, an ambitious, quickly curtailed attempt at eating Chichester cathedral, a tunnelling journey from Godalming to Java and various other no-hoper attempts. It ends with the death of Jones, Palin's merciless continuation of the twisted management, audience muttering (reflecting the quickly constructed robbery sketch) and comment on sad endings. A quick resurrection of the glories of dead parrot, with Cleese/Palin in Pet Shop Mark II would later be re-recorded for vinyl but never burrowed into the nation's consciousness to the extent of 'Bereft of Life'. However, the animal abusing and promised mutilation of Palin's cocky, cockney assistant (happy to restructure an unwanted terrier into cat/fish/parrot format) plays well with the sickness fully being heightened by Cleese's initially shocked reaction warming to perverted eagerness to watch the operation. It's really *Python* trying to shock for shock's sake but the Palin/Cleese acting tension is as potent as ever and Chapman's off-stage interactions provide a perfect balance.

However, as the team push the boundaries further back they both distil repulsion and pre-empt critical boredom with the disconcerting structure of the show by suggesting that this sketch is predictable, making the item even more unpredictable. Cleese addresses the audience, stepping out of character and out of television constraint, stepping into the shoes of Joe Businessman and discussing the programme within its own convention. Both Chapman's Julius Caesar and correction of the Christmas Show presentation work as fleeting soundbites for the next sketch, with Idle's Gorilla-suited wannabe librarian, spanning the audience hilarity of a wild animal trying for such a job, passing through the slowly dawning expectations of perverted vicar (Jones) and penetrating chairman (Chapman), instilling a desire for wild creatures in authority and finally reverting to performance tradition by being revealed as a man in a skin. The seed for Rowan Atkinson's Gorilla sketch in *Not the Nine O'Clock News* is here, embracing memories of Peter Cook's *One Leg Too Few* from *Not Only... But Also* and taking the

notion into the realms of surreal logic with the appearance of a real white dog for the job. *Python*'s Points of View interlude follows with Idle's money for silly observations, Cleese's dignified captain and the 3,000-year-old ramblings of Terry Jones, in homage to the legendary Mel Brooks/Carl Reiner recordings. The ancient one's request for two people in bed is answered with Jones/Palin as yet another married couple, with the continual interruptions from various lovers (Idle's Frenchman, Cleese's Brit, Chapman – in an early celebration of Biggles – and Ian Davidson's Mexican rhythm combo). Palin's easily appeased queries keep going until the comic ideal is broken; Palin's figure is himself enjoying extra-martial activity and this further breaking with tradition ends with Gilliam's (predictable!) finish with the Liverpudlian Sperm Whale and various animal consumers.

Series 1 Episode X was conceived, written and performed by **Graham Chapman, John Cleese, Eric Idle, Terry Jones, Michael Palin & Terry Gilliam**
Also appearing were **Barry Cryer, Carolae Donoghue & Ian Davidson**
Research **Sarah Hart Dyke**
Makeup supervisor **Joan Barrett**
Costume supervisor **Hazel Pethig**
Animations by **Terry Gilliam**
Film Cameramen James Balfour**& Alan Featherstone**
Film editor **Ray Millichope**
Lighting **Otis Eddy**
Sound **Jack Sudic**
Designer **Martin Collins**
Produced & directed by **Ian MacNaughton**
28 December 1969

EPISODE 11

By this stage, the Pythons were definitely in full flow, allowing their dysfunctional sense of television structure to go completely overboard. The episode begins with a typical *Python* favourite, a look at a boring BBC2 education programme with retentive presenter and dragging dialogue. Here it's Chapman's Professor R.J. Canning, desperately trying to get *World of History* off the ground but immediately suffering and

condemning an onslaught of interruptions. Death plays a vital part in this show, with the immortal undertakers film running throughout and an ashen-faced Terry Jones brilliantly wandering onto the *History* set to address the audience. Codes and conventions of television are broken; outside broadcasting situations invade the studio with surreal use of comic device and personality, but by now nobody was going to be surprised or shocked by the abnormal. If anything, the public would have been more surprised if the Chapman show had got past two minutes. As it is, the undertaker film breaks in with some outlandish bad taste, cross-fading into the murder mystery sketch with Chapman's familiar pompous middle-aged father figure and Carol Cleveland revealing as much of her legs as the shortest of short skirts could manage. This is a typical example of the *Python* sketch that is really going nowhere, included because of the absurdity of the situation and to offer Cleese the opportunity of some valued mental attack. The structure of clichéd, Christie-like police inspector dialogue is broken up and delivered in various combinations and the assembled masses' shocked repeating of Cleese's name, Tiger, leads to the distress and panic of Cleese himself. Basically, the sketch consists of Cleese fancying Cleveland (after all, he's only human), desperately trying to discover the murder that isn't there and finally being done to death himself. Note the cartoon-like use of obvious murderous motives with the arrow through the neck and, most telling of all, the big bottle simply marked 'poison'. It's Wile E. Coyote slapstick in human form. After this, all the Pythons tend to stagger in dressed as various police personnel with Idle's Fire and Jones as the more restrained and less gullible There's a Man Behind You.

Even so, the team labour the same gag over and over again unrelentingly and even embracing the sheer absurdity that the viewer can only wonder at what outrageous name the next law-enforcer will have. In the same way, the team incorporate the obvious lavatorial humour at the beginning of the episode, condemning its infantile properties via letters and shocked audience reaction but still reinforcing it as obviously funny material through the use of names like Knickers and Bottom for the easy laugh. The team cleverly highlight these comic ploys simply to get an easy laugh, thus allowing them to get the humour from the low-brow dialogue and, most tellingly, a higher appreciation of humour from their forced questioning of it.

But above all this, there's the Eric Idle intellectual football interviewer to savour, cascading through flowery questioning for Cleese's brain-dead striker, Jimmy Buzzard. Taking his lead from *So Little Time* with Peter Sellers and his fund of stock answers for idiotic teen pop stars, Cleese is a visual bag of confused reaction, struggling to find any meaning in Idle's flights of fancy and delightfully looking around when he drags out a totally inept but bog standard interview response from the bowels of his brain. So thrilled is he, that he eagerly repeats the response. This surprisingly brief interlude remains a key *Python* favourite but it does, in fact, quickly pale when the almighty Interesting People slot storms into view.

Michael Palin is at his silky smooth best, with ever ready grin and enforced button-pushing for instant applause. The shameless face of quick editing, shock tactic television with an over bearing host and conveyor belt system of star guests this is the chat show as freak show, with everybody from the wee voiced Jones in a matchbox as the half inch Howard Stools (bowel humour meets surrealism) to Jones again, resplendent in flowing robes as A. Bayan, stark raving mad and damn proud of it. This is viewing for curiosity's sake only – the nutters of the world paraded in front of a gaping audience all out for a cheap thrill and a giggle. Palin plays up to the bemused and amused studio audience with brilliant timing, pausing and giving encouraging, in-character reaction, while repeating

'Yes a fraud' when some *Python* audience folk are happily taken along with the feel of Interesting People and react accordingly. Eric Idle's pseudo-invisible Mr. T. Walters, the most boring man in the universe, brilliantly elongates certain words like past, glance and walk in a monotone, sing-song manner which is inspired, while Cleese happily hams and barks as the shouting man, distressed at the apparent death of his half-inch chum.

However, as throughout this episode, it's Terry Jones that really shines brightest, presenting one of his greatest vignettes as Mr. Maniac, a cross between Robert Louis Stevenson's Edward Hyde and Alice Cooper, complete with startling manic hair and staring eyes, he rejoices in a Peter Cook-like bit of banter with hypnotised bricks. The show takes a downward slide with a continued sporty feel (the cricket bashing in the boxing ring) and the return once more to the undertaker film with grave-diggers staggering out of the hole (several times in a sort of Mack Sennett silent comedy homage), eventually followed by escaping convicts, police, tracker dogs and finally Palin's inanely grinning beach lad. A quick link from Jones as an angelic manager chappie effortlessly brings us to the classic *World of History* reprise, with Chapman's Professor Channing quickly usurped by a certain A.J.P. Taylor, voiced by John Cleese twittering on about legalisation history or something, though few could care as the stuff is mouthed by a delectable Carol Cleveland, in undies, cavorting about on her bed. What more could the great British public want? History is suddenly fascinating, with injections of bits of fun (strip-tease/Palin's European windbag professor snogging the scantily clad bimbo squirming beside him) before Cleveland returns once more with some suggestive fondling of an egg whisk.

Steady lads! That's almost too much for one classic episode but wait, there's the Gumby view of history (don't hold your breath) and Eric Idle's mad interpretation of Pearl Harbour

courtesy of The Batley Town Women's Guild – the six lads bashing each other in the mud. This final piece of uncontrolled nonsense is anchored to serious historical comment with a throw away mention of Nazi war atrocities before even the ever patience BBC can't hold back the closing credits any longer. Without containing one true all-time, copper-bottom *Python* milestone, this show easily stands as one of the most consistently hilarious first series efforts.

Did You Know?
Material cut from this episode and never used was the tale of Herbert Arkwright who eats buffalo and a punch-drunk interviewer talking to the incompetent and nervous prospective boxing champion Henry Pratt.

Series 1 episode XI – Conceived, written & performed by **Graham Chapman, John Cleese, Terry Gilliam, Eric Idle, Terry Jones & Michael Palin**
Also appearing were **Carol Cleveland, Ian Davidson & Flanagan**
Animations by **Terry Gilliam**
Research **Sarah Hart Dyke**
Make up supervisor **Joan Barrett**
Costume supervisor **Hazel Pethig**
Film cameramen **James Balfour & Alan Featherstone**
Editor **Ray Millichope**
Sound **Jack Sudic**
Lighting **Otis Eddy**
Designer **Geoffrey Patterson**
Produced & directed by **Ian MacNaughton**
4 January 1970

EPISODE 12

Although erroneously billed as episodes 17 to 26, this is the penultimate entry for this ground-breaking first series, kicking off with Terry Jones, a vicious grizzly bear and a signal box outside Hove setting for the quickly defunct The Naked Ant, sliding almost immediately into the Goswell Road falling from a high building sketch. One of the most celebrated *Python* vignettes, its basic message of human life being over quick, gambled monetary gain is happily distinguished by the sheer brilliance of the writing and the straight-faced, eager playing of Idle and Cleese. It's a typical example of *Python* humour, with the outlandish behaviour outside of the team members being at first disbelieved, then accepted as the norm and finally fully embraced as a simple part of life's playtime (the dead mother eating sketch works in the same way). Sustained for just a few minutes, the falling idea is one of the most inspired in the *Python* range, blessed with a hasty letter of complaint (incorporated into the overall narrative of the sketch) and rounded off with a priceless bit of work from Gilliam, with a shapely 1920s bathing belle effortlessly breaking the fall of a blockful of businessmen.

Like the 1953 Daffy Duck short *Duck Amuck* (yes, Warners were pretty radical and ground-breaking too), Gilliam's hands appear within the frame as the illusion of cartoon life is created and a swinging, tripping sixties experience burst of coloured flowers covers up the switch to Palin's earnest introduction of yet another dodgy television show, *Spectrum*. Taking the pompous, overbearing host figure usually reserved for Chapman, Palin goes for it, with quick, short delivery, completely nonsensical obsession with the meaning of everything (questioning what he means by words, what he means by mean etc, etc) and a rattling, rhythmic style of speech (cleverly linked with the click/clack rhythm of a train on the track via the archive footage). Indeed, Palin's over-anxious presenter could have come from the world of Ronnie Barker's official loonies on *The Two Ronnies* (a show that Palin contributed to in the early seventies) and it remains one of my favourite and least heralded bits of *Python* comedy. Give that man a round of applause for comic genius beyond the call of duty. Next up, Idle's Nazi comment at the close of episode eleven is opened up to include three Germans hiding away in a respectable British guest house. Terry Jones, in definitive middle-aged dreary drag mode, wanders through her humble little slice of Britain, bemused by the bombastic and suspicious behaviour of her guests.

Idle is in his element with a typically rambling monologue concerning his arduous journey to the area (turning the uncomplex convention of small chat, good journey and that kind of thing, into a nightmarish analysis of the trials of modern motoring). His teeth-achingly hilarious use of common speech and stupid, would-be humorous defusers of situations (the priceless 'warm and wet' cliché when offered tea) sets this man out as one of Idle's most ambitious and hilarious small, dull folk of provincial England. His nonplussed attitude to the presence of John Cleese's outlandish Milliganesque Adolf Hitler (sorry, Mr. Hilter) allows the simpleton to ignore outraged Germanic outbursts and ill-informed Britishisms and only worry about the road situations and the dubious quality of the map. It also taps into Peter Cook's obvious use of a Mr. Hitler in his E.L. Wisty monologues, while Adrian Edmondson continues the tradition with his Eddie Hitler in *Bottom*. Palin, shaven-headed, grinning with pure Nazi evil and smoking his fag à la cockney wideboy, embraces British cricket terminology and World Cup 66 memories of good old Bobby Charlton in an attempt to disguise his nationality (using the obvious but still effective comic ploy of transposing words to get the affect just slightly wrong, i.e. chips and fish, and the like).

The manic satire is full of subtle moments (notably Minehead spelt Meinhead on Hilter's political campaign paraphernalia) while the Brit in the street is highlighted as every bit as corrupt and dangerous as the Nazi mentality via typical *Python* interview soundbites. The first, Idle's mother who explains her pre-offered baby was bitten rather than kissed, gets the audience cracking up and the team eagerly take the opportunity of slipping in blatant social comment under the sweetened attitude – the classic example being Jones as the squawking woman agreeing with their Coon attitude but admitting she is mental (sort of Alf Garnett without the padding), alongside Chapman's immortal Tory politician

droning on and on about nothing in particular (foaming at the mouth like a screen-tested *Godfather* Brando and pratfalling with dignity and genius). In the light of such powerful and hilarious material the only way forward was complete and utter insanity with the silly-voiced policeman sketch, featuring Terry Jones desperately trying to report a burglary only to find that his cop shop is packed with mad law-enforcers who can only register different stupid intonations. The magic really hits home with Eric Idle's appearance, talking normally to Jones, shrieking at Cleese and rumbling at Chapman, who merrily sings instructions to the squad car lads, leads into a miaowing pig and a quick snapshot of Richard Nixon for a bit of politics there! The universally acclaimed 127th Upper Class Twit of the Year packs a real punch towards the close of this episode, with the five key performing Pythons going through their pronounced teeth, landed gentry paces with staggering step and bemused expressions. The complete and unabridged version (rearranged and shortened for the movie *And Now For Something Completely Different*) this is a masterpiece of *Python*, taking elements from Milligan and Feldman television with the unique blend of Cleese and the lads at full power. Cleese and his Fawlty-like commentary gives the entire thing a sort of BBC sports coverage authority while class moments like the kicking of the beggar and insulting of the waiter are hilarious comments on the pompous authority of moneyed idiots with no respect. Spoilt, brattish, girl-shy, completely incompetent and totally without tolerance, these five raving madmen are definitive *Python* grotesques, none more so than Graham Chapman, acting like a nutter in a peerless comic contribution of insane babbling as the seven equally dodgy spectators watch aghast. Death (a motif continued with Terry Jones's deceased letter writer that follows) is again instrumental in the situation, the only kind way out for these social dissenters and the only way to win in this ultimate race to be the world's first class lunatic. The perverse attitude of the wealthy reflects badly on the working classes inability to destroy themselves in such a sporting fashion, complemented by Gilliam's honest British Tommy, who, via a Kenneth Williams-like intellectual is insulted, mocked, condemned and finally screwed up for Terry Jones's pipe fodder, surging into Chapman, Connie Booth and Michael Palin's unkempt Ken Shabby on the courting question. The symbols for a respectable upper-class marriage are in place, the Archbishop and Abbey are considered for the service, money is no object and even this filthy lower-class toilet cleaner follows the expected conventions of seeking the father's approval. The niceties and motions are painfully gone through as Chapman's father figure expresses homosexual interest in Palin. He shamelessly coughs his guts up for the world and its mother, as the entire concept is filtered through like a television soap opera, complete with photo caption 'story so far' round-up (incorporating Lon Chaney's *Phantom of the Opera*).

There's just time for a bit of inspired political silliness from that inspired political silliness maestro Graham Chapman as Lambert Warbeck of The Wood Party lecturing the nation, falling through the earth's crust and desperately carrying on with the help of TV johnnies Idle, Gilliam and the longest piece of BBC rope. Idle's apologetic looks into camera are superb while Chapman, summoning up all the British determination in his control doggedly continues with gulps, emms and pregnant pauses (later semi-adopted for Rowan Atkinson in the best man section of his Wedding routine) while desperately flinging himself about the cheaply decorated BBC impression of the centre of the earth – sort of mid-Jon Pertwee *Doctor Who* without the budget. Outstanding.

The entire episode is rounded off with various incarnations from the just savoured half-hour barking No!, including Terry Jones and his signal hut besieged by mad bear from the very opening, Palin's earnest

television chappie and the man's fine Nazi characterisation, getting a quick nudge from Cleese as he corrects Nein! to the English! As the It's Man continues on his pinball mission from the opening credits the viewer can at last sit back and relax following 30 minutes of non-stop *Python* class.

Did You Know?
The legendary Upper Class Twit sketch was a late, handwritten addition to the script.

Series 1 episode XII – Conceived, written & performed by **Graham Chapman, John Cleese, Terry Gilliam, Eric Idle, Terry Jones & Michael Palin**
Also appearing were **Connie Booth, Ian Davidson & Flanagan**
Animations by **Terry Gilliam**
Research **Sarah Hart Dyke**
Make up supervisor **Joan Barrett**
Costume supervisor **Hazel Pethig**
Film cameraman **James Balfour**
Editor **Ray Millichope**
Sound **John Delaney**
Lighting **Otis Eddy**
Designer **Geoffrey Patterson**
Produced & directed by **Ian MacNaughton**
11 January 1970

EPISODE 13
From the moment everyone's favourite It's Man crops up from inside a coffin (in a throwback to the undertakers running gag from show 11) you know your are in for a grand time, with a petulant John Cleese and whining, dragged-up Eric Idle staggering into the abusive restaurant sketch. Idle delights in his finest moments of comic expression with a dismissive, continual complaint on his lips, droning on and on as good old Cleese tells it as it is to anybody who cares to listen. After years of suffering the vitriolic outpourings, no amount of heart-wrenching, soul-searching pauses can bring a good word for the old bat. After Terry Jones makes a pleasant welcome and the sickly smug Michael Palin dishes out the place's strict veggie rule, the comedy begins to ebb away and, by now past master at the quick get-out, Idle is allowed to step out of reality (if indeed the character ever existed

in reality) and embrace comedy terminology like punch-lines and canned applause, desperately looking around to pinpoint the source of this erroneous outbreak of the studio audience's presence. Before long it's *Terry and June* time, with obvious, self-mocking cornball jokes, brief, easy to please one-liners and Chapman's standard old buffer, cross-balanced with a mountain of surreal *Python* bad taste with cannibalism overtones (of the highest order), Idle's untouched bit of tasty vicar and Jones, happily joking with the prospective consumers of his flesh – was Douglas Adams watching a few light-years before Peter Davison cropped up in A *Hitch-Hiker's Guide to the Galaxy*? By now the very fact that the cast question the validity of a comic idea without an ending was accepted by each and everyone tuning in although the rare example of cinematic parody with the Pearl and Swine (as in Pearl and Dean) adverts highlighting sex sells anything, is a rather uncomfortable prologue for the extremely short but unforgettable Albatross sketch. Cleese, in glorious bombastic mood, literally bellows meek Terry Jones into the ground with obvious insults and dumbfounded reaction to his normality-geared questions relating to the bird's flavour. Although this classic scene lasts hardly a minute, subsequent sketches would enforce the power of the vignette with continual shouts of 'Albatross'. Lest we forget!

Meanwhile, a Rottingdean policeman in the shape of John Cleese is propositioned by the breathless Palin and homosexuality in the force is highlighted, authority is mocked and questioned but above all, officialdom baiting is shown to be simply hilarious fun. And a quick edit of old footage even has the grannie brigade applauding the freedom of sexual choice. The next up, Idle's manic hospital sketch, is more about grammar than surgical life, with Idle's doctor going through the old elongated 'Me Tarzan' variation with initially inspired and ultimately quickly dwindling results, so much so that the sketch dies, Idle thinks better of it and grudgingly shouts out 'Albatross' to put everyone out of their misery. *Python* makes the effortless get-out both charming and totally functional, allowing these scraps of comic ideas to work themselves into the show's framework and quite blatantly see themselves mocked and tossed out again – all in front of the viewer's gaze. Priceless. Historical Impressions is much more like vintage *Python*, with Palin's silky host Wally Wiggins and a stunning array of famous dead people hamming up some contemporary personalities – notably the unforgettable Julius Caesar version of Eddie Waring custody of a wonderfully over-acting Eric Idle. Succinct, the sketch is pure gold dust, lurching on into Cleese patronising a couple of school kids (Palin and Idle) and mirroring this typically condescending treatment of the young with a similar playing interview with 42-year-old Chapman and his insurance chum Palin – note the dream fairy from Idle who had a quick chance to mutter No along with the rest of the world at the close of show twelve. There's no real joke here, except the clear exposure of adults' failure to address children with common sense and respect. As a vehicle for this, nothing could be better than Cleese's sugary looks into camera, hiding complete contempt and disinterest with over-played warmth. The resulting police adventure (thanks to the bowler hatted lads request) sees the first appearance of a certain Harry 'Snapper' Organs, later to be immortalised by Terry Jones in series two but played with quiet reserve here by Palin, repeating his Good Evening greeting in full Peter Cook mode and delighting in the use of occult, magic and mysterious doings to combat crime – an incredibly silly and hilarious expose of dubious, Masonic elements from within the force. The crime theme continues with Palin's Mr. A.T. Hun yearning to be arrested by Terry Jones, skilfully balancing his false moustache until the man can handle the pressure no more and simply rips it off and chucks it into his hat – much to

Palin's delight. It's yet another clodhopping look at coppers with Chapman relishing the chance to don a dashing blue frock, Palin's real historical identity being traced by machinery and a class Cleese cartoon to link into the psychiatrist sketch. Although shamelessly undervalued, this major piece of *Python* is typical of their turning the conventions of television comedy on its head. The delectable Carol Cleveland can question the power of the dialogue, dispute Cleese and his forlorn attempt to highlight his position as psychiatrist rather than just doctor and see the identity problem solved by the knowingly enforced ploy of a telephone conversation. Terry Jones skilfully undermines the originality of the situation and basically the sketch is simply one of false starts, absurdity and deconstruction of the comedy format. Palin throws in a comment about the insanity of mind doctors, the Albatross is hastily resurrected and the scene swiftly moves to Chapman's office, introduced with young Graham drawing glasses and 'tache on Cleese's portrait to make it resemble himself. The one-set television show is mirrored and mocked, Cleese's telephone ploy is laboured and strengthened and the team parody the cheapness of BBC production with affection, hindsight and authority, even before they themselves can open mouths to do it. As the sixties came to its natural close, on a high of freshly laid out *Python*, Eric Idle's withering, clichéridden hippie figure full of squatters rights, 'Hey man's and free love, captures the inapt attitudes of a generation as he downs the authority of the police, dismisses money as unreal (bringing on an inspired throwaway line from Chapman) and swinging with a naked journalist babe, who looks amazingly like Carol Cleveland scantily clad once more... Gilliam cries that the series can't end on this note and before the It's Man is chased off by undertakers and Cleese intones a tongue-in-cheek reference to the prospects of another series, the team say farewell with the mutilation of a tinted baby which sounds like Donald Duck on acid.

How else could the last gasp of a passionately flawed but unsurpassed decade of opportunity, youth culture and British cool come to an end?

Did You Know?
An additional part of the A. T. Hun sketch, featuring the police solving crimes sent in by viewers, was cut from the final script.

Series 1 episode XIII
Conceived, written & performed by **Graham Chapman, John Cleese, Terry Gilliam, Eric Idle, Terry Jones & Michael Palin**
Also appearing were **Carol Cleveland, David Ballantyne**
Animations by **Terry Gilliam**
Research **Sarah Hart Dyke**
Make up supervisor **Joan Barrett**
Costume supervisor **Hazel Pethig**
Film cameraman **James Balfour**
Editor **Ray Millichope**
Sound **John Delaney**
Lighting **Otis Eddy**
Designer **Geoffrey Patterson**
Produced & directed by **Ian MacNaughton**
18 January 1970

Series 2
Even during the first series the BBC were more than a tad unhappy about both *Python* mercilessly ribbing the corporations programmes and also the team's fearless baiting of authority. However, the press reaction was enormously encouraging, while a select but vocal young cult following had erupted and thus, somewhat reluctantly, the BBC commissioned this landmark second series recorded from June to October 1970. Of course, it cannot be over-stressed that the top dogs of the BBC were very pleased with *Python*, naturally, because – let's make no bones about this – even if a show was successful but the Beeb hated it that show would disappear (witness *Dr. Who* in 1985 and 1989). Thus, many considered *Python* exactly the sort of youth-geared, challenging, societyquestioning sort of comedy the BBC should be making. Even so, despite the comedy being at a peak of excellence many at the BBC were continually mopping their brows and

tutting – as Graham Chapman later observed the gang were forever restricted to 'a shed near the front gate'.

Of course, some ten years later when Michael Palin's It's Man adorned the front cover of the *Radio Times* and the team's biting genius was celebrated with the 1979 tribute show *The Pythons*, the BBC smiled all the way to the bank. However, by that stage, the six were well past the front gate, far away from the television studios and safely in the classic archive. But in 1970, the Pythons faced further hassle from the schedules, with Scotland running the show on different nights and several regions obtaining an opt-out cause which meant that some weeks *Python* was screened, while other weeks the team were replaced by the region's own programming.

EPISODE 1

The team kick-start their second series with one of the greatest half-hours of comedy ever created. Jam-packed with class moments it is interestingly less spasmodic than the first series, dropping in copious amounts of material although handing over almost the whole of the closing half to one thematic masterpiece – Ethel the Frog. However, before Snapper Organ gets going there's Cleese's BBC announcer chappie behind bars uttering the immortal words 'And Now For Something Completely Different' and leading into the nemesis of polished continuity, Palin's earth-shatteringly brilliant It's. I don't think any one word can send a more powerful comic shiver down the spine than 'It's', simply because the soul knows that *that* music is on the way... Pure unfathomable magic.

Just to further reassure the viewing public that the boys were back in town with a vengeance, the first full item is a television parody, *Face the Press*, with Chapman's gloriously gowned politician locked in mortal verbal debate with a patch of brown liquid. The initial joke, Chapman's twofold answer, climaxing with a high-pitched whine, is hilarious on the low-brow level and intellectually

serves to pinpoint the irrelevance and lack of interest in political opinion as Idle's grinning host rambles about fashion and trivia over the top of the answer and reintroduces the viewer just as Chapman is coming to a close. Cleese, in drag, taps into *Round the Horne* Omipaloni speech, before Jones in middle-aged old pepperpot mode (straight out of the glorious traditional of panto and *Carry On*) is shocked into action by Gilliam's strangely unnerving clown, knowingly wandering into The New Cooker Sketch, emblazoned across the screen with the subtlety of a Cecil B. DeMille epic. The definitive incorporation of the 'more than my job's worth' British workman, Palin and Chapman tut, shake their head and do they best to help in their own retentive, constrained fashion, dictated to by detailed rules and regulations from a mysterious head office. Palin particularly grabs this little pompous figure of semi-authority, laughing at the pure absurdity of the rules but upholding them strictly with pride and determination. The crowd of brown-jacketed, bespectacled workers gradually increases until, before long, the entire world seems to be teeming with the faceless image of conformist bureaucracy.

Gilliam's dreaded, all-over shaving cartoon smooths the link between the cooker and the Idle pervert, slobbering and wheezing into a corner shop and desperately trying to uncover the sex ad amongst Terry Jones's collection of pure and innocent items. In many ways this is Idle's nemesis of innuendo humour, discovering sex in absolutely everything but when finally confronted with the blatant plug for a blonde prostitute this dirty-minded shuffler is at a total loss. After so many years of imaging the pleasures of the flesh in every situation, Idle's eye twitching pseudo-flasher, like the Upper class twit of old, can't come to terms with the reality of sex; he can't recognise its existence outside of 'nudge, nudge say no more' terminology. Above all this, anything with Idle getting over-heated is a joy for comedy lovers with a

connoisseur's palette.

Thankfully, before the sketch is allowed to drift away into nothingness, Idle's dysfunctional shop customer is usurped by John Cleese, with a silly walk and a respectable request for *The Times*. The Ministry of Silly Walks is one of those *Python* mega-bites that has grown and developed out of all proportion from its original incarnation. The bane of Cleese's life and perhaps, second only to the parrot, in the hearts and minds of *Python* followers, the Silly Walks routine is a masterpiece of sustained surrealism in a situation of normality. Written by Jones and Palin from an idea by Cleese and Chapman (the Cambridge lads thought of a Ministry of Anger crossed with the notion of silly walking – thanks to some poor chap desperately climbing uphill past Graham's house – and handed it to the Oxford guys) it is played with straight-faced seriousness and intent; one can almost imagine the government funding scores of slightly unusual walkers across the country. And if only for Terry Jones's sliding, almost kneeling jaunt past Cleese and several amazed passers-by, this is worth a fortune in blues-defusing material. Palin's weedy, chartered accountant sort of guy, embarrassingly inept in the art of silly walking, struggles to impress the master, who idly strolls round the room, legs akimbo and a vocal delivery resonant with authority. Again, when the material comes to an abrupt close it is merged into vintage *Python*ified footage of silly walks through the ages (complete with Palin's grinning, camera-aware, Little Titch styled effort – rumoured to have originally been part of Jones' wacky Queen sketch – and the outstanding Chapman finale, hopping off into oblivion). The mock French routine, with half Brit bowler and half onion seller doesn't come together fully, despite the glorious over-acting of Cleese and Palin which is worth a look. The convention baiting system of passing over the moustache for motivation (a throwback to show one) still has some comic mileage.

However, Idle's BBC globe

announcement brings on the ultimate pièce de résistance in *Python* folklore, the major examination of the notorious Piranha Brothers on the exposé show Ethel the Frog. Undoubtedly one of the all-time masterpieces of *Monty Python's Flying Circus*, the legend of Doug and Dinsdale is played out via archive photos and film, interviews with surviving and even departed witnesses with the standard mocking of the police via Terry Jones as the definitive Snapper Organs. This obvious Kray parody was both timely and daring at the time, knocking the cockney working class slump situation, lightening the school day angst by the cheap laugh (the Chapman and Jones silent interview) and allowing Cleese, the world's perfect anchor man for this sort of comedy genius, to playfully pinpoint the cutting edge of satire. Palin as interviewee steals the scene, whether it be his fearful, chain-smoking, cheek-scarred nervous wreck or, best of all, his dark shaded, wideboy hustling, escort agency bloke. Crafted from years of listening to Peter Sellers and notably latching onto his cocky vocals from *The Trumpet Volunteer*, this is one of the great *Python* characterisations. His seedy attitude and painfully unconvincing attempts at covering up his sex business culminates with a dubious phone call from a client being attributed to his mother. The timing of the closing phrase makes a comedy devotee weep with joy! Pure class.

Chapman's lazy-eyed drawling witness is great value and Idle is a delight as the over-enthusiastic, forgiving type, whilst Cleese, revealing the hidden fear of Spiney Norman the Hedgehog stops the flow brilliantly in its tracks by exposing and addressing a bit of *Python* iconology via his female impersonator line. The finale is handed over to Jones, running through his bewildering array of inept theatrical disguises, tapping into the notion of the uniformed face of policing as mere play acting (complete with Chapman's camp co-star) and some priceless snap shots of Jones in costume, including Ratty

from *Toad of Toad Hall* (some 25 years before Jones would play the scaly lead on film). The transformation between bitchy backstage banter and the dignified uniformed policing is a powerful undermining of macho authority. The less than rave reviews for his performing prowess are a scream, particularly Cleese's wonderfully delivered put-down. Even Chapman's glorious double fluff on his manic television pundit doesn't stop it being one of the coolest moments in the show but sadly, no sooner does Gilliam's rather light and almost transparent giant hedgehog pop his head round the houses than the credits roll and one of the most precious *Python* shows is no more. Rewind the tape and start again is my advice!!

Did You Know?
Eric Idle had promised to get the entire Chelsea football team to liven up John Cleese's initial announcement but clearly he couldn't because they don't appear. The script is unofficially dubbed 'Give Us Money, Not Awards!'

Series 2 episode I – Conceived, written & performed by **Graham Chapman, John Cleese, Eric Idle, Terry Jones, Michael Palin & Terry Gilliam.**
Also appearing were **David Ballantyne John Hughman Stanley Mason**
Animations by **Terry Gilliam**
Research **Patricia Houlihan**
Make up **Penny Norton**
Costumes **Hazel Pethig**
Visual effects designer **John Horton**
Film cameraman **James Balfour**
Editor **Ray Millichope**
Sound **Peter Rose**
Lighting **Otis Eddy**
Designer **Robert Berk**
Produced & directed by **Ian MacNaughton**
15 September 1970

EPISODE 2
One of the greatest of all *Python* starts (Terry Jones as a far from magnificent man in his flying machine) leads into one of the most celebrated chunks of *Python* ever, the Palin/Jones masterpiece concerning

the rather unexpected appearance of the Spanish Inquisition. The trio in red are instrumental throughout the entire show right from the first sketch as Graham Chapman's impenetrable Northern worker jabbers on to Cleveland about the trouble at mill in 1912 Jarrow. Bemused and embittered about his accent proving difficult, Chapman utters those immortal words ushers in the signifier for screen terror (a shock musical explosion on the score) and a wildly flung open door revealing Palin, Jones as Biggles the insecure member of the clan and Gilliam (actually getting some fairly important dialogue to deliver) as Cardinal Fang, the maniacally grinning crackpot. Palin's act of terror and deadly power is just that, an act, desperately trying to get his chin-tingling monologue right and struggling through misunderstandings, incorrect instruments of torture and dismissive attitude from his would-be captives. Chapman's disgruntled and disinterested repeated delivery of his initial shock reaction is perfection, while the diabolical laughter/acting captions tap into the 1965 Beatles movie *Help!* (with John Lennon deliberately over-playing bits of straight-faced guffawing). Chapman's Northern chappie is hastily whipped away by Cleese, complete with goatee beard and BBC manner (whose line 'I'd like to be in programme planning but unfortunately I've got a degree!' is arguably the most introspectively telling piece of *Python* ever, detailing the power in the hands of the ignorant and that the considered nonsensical, throwaway, kid-worshipped culture of comedy houses the real genius), shipped into contemporary space and plonked into a raring-to-go sketch with Eric Idle's copious amounts of hilarious, novelty items guaranteed to break the ice at parties. This is an archetypal bit of Idle insanity, going round and round in more and more hilarious circles until the moment of comic climax comes with no punchline from Chapman's stooge character. The sketch is defunct as Cleese titters at the gag himself (predicting an entire series from the unused tag while pinpointing, even now, that while it was not required, there was a tagline in existence somewhere). A classic piece of Idle is simply allowed to come to the abrupt halt the way the writer clearly did.

A bit of bizarre Chapman head cartooning develops into a toilet obsession, with a nudie book of plumbing glimpsed in the hands of Idle's character for the outlandish political abbreviations sketch. This is a perfect example of *Python*'s skill in turning half-completed jokes into a total show of dysfunctional but praised material.

Sex is again highlighted as taboo, tentatively suggested as a possible new tax increment (just as Talbot Rothwell was working a similar notion into his *Carry On Henry* script) but the Terry Jones figure of retentive authority has to resort to calling sex 'thingy', unable to speak directly within this intellectual gathering of officials. It's all part of this mad, contrasting vision of Britain, populated by Colonel Blimps ranting on about taxing all foreigners living abroad and bringing back hanging, while the shabby nutters like Palin's It's Man (actually getting a bit of a line here) ramble on about Raquel Welch and the unattainable and, perhaps, unmanageable dream of Hollywood fantasy. All this sheltered talk of sex naturally sets the scene for Carol Cleveland's customary and expected flash of shapely leg, deliciously ripping up a clutch of old Uncle Ted snap shots before expressing natural surprise and heralding the major bulk of Spanish Inquisition activity.

Unlike other comedians outside of the university sphere whose historical parodies were basically gleaned from movies or television, the *Python* team wallowed in knowledgeable pretension with lengthy round-ups of historical facts before tackling the humour, seen in definitive terms in this Jones and Palin masterpiece. It doesn't matter that these 16th-century henchmen are transported to 1970 with dodgy comfy chairs and cups of coffee, the team still lay factual ground rules for their comic deconstruction of the system.

Gilliam's Confessional artwork may seem to go on forever, but the medical element is good fun and besides, it acts as a fine preparation for the seminal Semaphore Version of *Wuthering Heights* – so damn cool. Cleveland is stunning as Katy, Jones is wonderfully poised as Heathcliffe, the location filming adds the perfect mood to the insanity of the situation and the aged guy sleeping with signals is beyond criticism. Okay, the team tend to labour the point home with three other classic movies told in various mad fashions (although the clippette of Caesar on an Aldis Lamp is not to be missed!) but so what! There's a complete change of scene (as this gag is pretty much self-contained) allowing Chapman to relish the chance to play older than his years again as a distinguished judge presiding over a parlour game influenced court. ('How can you find someone not Esther Williams!') With the serious undertones covered by charades this is a load of kids ignoring court dignity and having a damned good time. Importantly, the seriousness is always just under the surface with a particularly inspired bit of acting from Idle hilariously repeating the discovered phrase, 'Call the next defendant', before immediately changing his posture and repeating the words in stern court fashion. Terry Jones as a defrocked judge still clinging onto power, faces the temptation of the flesh that lead to him being in the dock and brings on a demented onslaught from a Chapman bound for South Africa having a final British court fling with a totally outlandish sentence. Jones' reaction is a masterpiece and the final *Python* twist on the Inquisition plot occurs just when everybody is expecting the guys in red to appear (audience and narrative players alike) and they don't turn up. Stepping out of the context of performance and addressing the others in relation to the credits rolling over the image, Palin's final outburst is priceless stuff. The key to *Python*'s laboured gag is that when familiarity seems to be getting totally ridiculous, the rules are quickly changed.

Series 2 episode II
Conceived, written & performed by **Graham Chapman, John Cleese, Eric Idle, Terry Jones, Michael Palin & Terry Gilliam**. Also appearing were **Carol Cleveland & Marjorie Wilde**
Animations by **Terry Gilliam**
Research **Patricia Houlihan**
Make up **Penny Norton**
Costumes **Hazel Pethig**
Film cameraman **James Balfour**
Editor **Ray Millichope**
Sound **Peter Rose**
Lighting **Otis Eddy**
Visual effects designer **John Horton**
Designer **Ken Sharp**
Produced & directed by **Ian MacNaughton**
22 September 1970

EPISODE 3

In between exploding stuffed animals and Cleese in full BBC flow, this one kicks off with Carol Cleveland's kit off again (no complaints from this reviewer), happily stripping down to her black undies and beyond (off camera I hasten to add) much to the bemused interest of the straight-laced face of broadcasting authority. Michael Palin's well mannered but slightly petulant archbishop figure, repeating his lines for a later show (which never came) in various fashions (including a telling Milliganesque/Eccles version), gets collared by Jones in the middle of nowhere and inadvertently sucked into the Flying Lesson sketch, a bizarre track across countryside wilderness with Cleveland's rotary action secretary and elements of normality (the tea lady, hallway conferences, forced Good Mornings) within the surreal situation of the great outdoors. Caves and manholes alike, Cleveland wanders through them all without a care, handing over to an identically dressed clone secretary (like the New Cooker sketch, the work force are highlighted as a faceless conveyer belt of cheap labour).

The actual sketch (when at last it arrives) is pretty dodgy, although Chapman's barking mad flying instructor (hanging from the room) goes gloriously overboard with embittered comments about Jones and his pompous attitude, while Jones himself bites back with put-downs, pointless bickering about hanging from a piece of bloody wire and a storming out. Perhaps the best moment comes with Chapman's finished phone call, as he drops the receiver on the phone and mutters 'missed!' when the instrument fails to hit its target. It was a long shot at the best of times! The plane theme is continued with Jones (two years later) carrying a different Chapman incarnation (full of Woosterisms like 'Bally piece of luck' and the like) before an onslaught of continuity corrections almost take over the show. Idle's airman is himself later corrected by all and sundry as the fabric of television history is ripped apart by a trainspotter attitude. Michael Palin's plane-bound bounder, inapt (even in this age of Michael Caine cool, glasses are a sign of weakness), apologetic high-jacker staggers into the cockpit waving a gun and demands (in the nicest possible way) to be taken to Luton. The niceties and good-natured banter between Palin, Jones, Cleese and Cleveland defuse the situation, lessening Palin's wavering power even more so (look out for the classic moment as Palin gingerly moves his gun swiftly away from Cleese as the pilot makes an innocent but sudden move) and finally ending in a compromising solution involving a haystack near Basingstoke. The gag is that Cleese, in sinister shades, turns on his Roger Moore manners and orders Palin's bus to go to Cuba. It's always the way!

One of Terry Jones's *Python* masterpieces, Ewan MacTeagle, takes the writing of begging letters to a new art form, showered with intellectual praise and discussion, searching for a hidden meaning in his mundane words, in a surreal, spiralling *South Bank Show*-styled examination from world leaders in literally expression. Basically it highlights the bogus quality of intellectualising poetry, debunking the flowery elevation of drivel to a pedestal of artistic genius. Besides, it sets up the immortal Palin gynaecologist comment from beneath

Cleese's pedantic Scot and allows Jones to bumble, ham and fume with grand style. And thus to the final part of the show, ushered in with Idle's fluffed milkman psychiatrist entrance, deliciously tapping into the conventions of diary delivery with the added *Python* twist of case histories, money-obsessed society and the break-up of mental stability. Palin repeats his Scots medic gag, the notion of a Jersey Cream Psychiatrist's outfit is wonderfully idiotic and Idle embraces the running continuity gag through the show by quickly rectifying a misleading comment from within the narrative of the sketch.

This is self-contained comic madness with no peer, chucking in everything from the familiar cartoon violence signifier of the 16-ton weight and character name changes midway to the hastily halted 'if I could walk that way' chestnut from Chapman's potty old dear. Onwards and upwards to Michael Palin's hosting of It's the Mind and the final five minutes of repeated, repeated and repeated material as déjà-vu invades the senses. The mysterious, black and white montage of opening credit shots (complete with the bizarre Jones and the egg pic!), phone class, television links, unexpected glasses of water and, finally, the milk float arrival, is shown again and again. Clearly the Pythons get away with just over 20 minutes of material within a half-hour plot, but who cares – the repeats are ever more hilarious, the Palin reaction is a masterclass in suppressed nervous confusion and the whole thing takes ingenious ridicule to new heights. As the credits roll the repeated action could happily go on and on into comedy eternity and it saved film as well!

Did You Know?
Election Night Special was due for inclusion here but the déjà vu stuff got so out of hand it was shifted to episode 6.

Series 2 episode III
Conceived, written & performed by
Graham Chapman, John Cleese, Eric

Idle, Terry Jones, Michael Palin & Terry Gilliam.
Also appearing were Carol Cleveland, Jeanette Wild
Animations by Terry Gilliam
Research Patricia Houlihan
Make up Penny Norton
Costumes Hazel Pethig
Film cameraman James Balfour
Editor Ray Millichope
Sound Peter Rose
Lighting Otis Eddy
Visual effects designer John Horton
Designer Ken Sharp
Produced & directed by Ian MacNaughton
29 September 1970

EPISODE 4
One of Terry Gilliam's most florid and enjoyable cartoons – the sluggish caterpillar into the gloriously technicolour moth – begins this episode just before the other lads line up in full Gumby mode to painfully introduce the Architects sketch. It takes a damn long time for the BBC cameraman to get the idea of what these five moronic nutters are groaning on about, but before long Chapman's official figure of respectability is shooing the white-hankied ones away in preparation for, you've guessed it, the architect sketch. This is a sketch of two halves, Brian. Firstly John Cleese, appears as confidence personified before his elongated and full-bloodied explanation of his slaughter house design raises concern from Palin and Jones – on the look out for a block of flats. Overtaken by the embryonic spirit of Basil Fawlty, Cleese explodes with pent-up anger, frustration at being overlooked as a mason and biting condemnation of the puerile minds of officialdom denying the flamboyant rights of the struggling artist. By contrast, Idle's candidate, smooth, charming and erudite, suffers from a painfully faulty model of his proposed building, collapsing, igniting and crumbling with blatant signposted graphics highlighting that this is *Python* satire, folks. In the end, Cleese and his masonic obsession is vindicated, Idle's cost cutting plan (satire but all the more powerful after the very notion of satire has been

mocked and pacified) is accepted and a long winded, on-film humiliation of obsessive masonic activity follows. A BBC apology for any offence the masonic item may have caused is quickly slotted in, covering the BBC's backs via a blanket of extended comic expression. There's some more over-played Gumby activity before Chapman's on-screen pinpointed straight man embraces comedy convention as Michael Palin's devious insurance lad goes into overdrive. A shabby, shady geezer in the tradition of Palin's Ethel the Frog persona, Devious is a glorious *Python* grotesque, eagerly offering nude ladies with policies, avoiding dodgy questions and quoting any old price to secure Chapman's Aston Martin contract. By now common practice, the narrative is interrupted by Idle's appearance as a worried vicar; Chapman expresses concern over whether he has any more lines and Palin's helpful consultation of the script – 'Are you man?' – tap into performance exposure. The gag is going nowhere but who cares; this is class in a glass stuff from the trio, conflicting religious nervousness and hard-nosed business via unrehearsed play-acting with hilarious results. Besides, it's just a sideline sketch for the ATV crime-busting parody *The Bishop*. A C. of E. Films production. The opening credits from Gilliam are a mini masterpiece, done in glorious black and white, stop motion caption cards, silhouettes, rotating camera angles and fading negative images perfectly in keeping with the wonderfully sixties kitsch flavour of *Man in a Suitcase*, *The Saint* and *Department S*. Terry Jones has a field day as the American gangster-battling hero; that pesky 16-ton weight prop pops up once more for some more harmless cartoon-like violence and the several failures of this less than impressive crime-fighter play in flashback as the scene comes back on itself into Palin's insurance office. And yep, you've guessed, Palin's shocked reaction starts up the same title sequence once again (which is, believe it or not, repeated for a third time a wee bit later on). The gang get away with it, of course, but cleverly

inject an official BBC apology for the alarming amount of repeats in this show.
Taking the laboured gag one step further than the previous episode's *It's the Mind* routine, here are the Pythons freely admitting that they are taking this joke a bit too far for its own good but, hard luck, they had gone and been and done it anyway. By the by, along the way in this ecclesiastical confusion, look out for the kind plug for the latest Peter Sellers movie, *Hoffman*. Eric Idle's youthful documentary film-maker is quickly chased off by Chapman's drag creation, going into Benny Hill fast speed action with his crew at the very mention of a possible drug story round the corner, while the normality of British life is wonderfully turned on its side again with the literal notion of an installed poet. Palin's 'play it by the book' poetry reader (a relation to that new cooker bloke) has a quick butchers at Idle's reciting Wordsworth in the home of voluptuous sex beast, Terry Jones, and almost wanders into *Terry and June* land with coy innuendo, domestic sitcom conventions and shifty, sexual unease. The barrier of small talk is stripped away (although *Python* being *Python*, Palin must do a spot of real forecasting, stepping out of character, adopting a BBC culture and whipping down his chart!) before Eric Idle's television announcement sets up the discussion programme (turned off by Jones) which we later rejoin only to discover that the show within the show is, in fact, discussing the sketch in which it has just been turned off in! Getting all this...? Complete glorious bad taste is embraced for Cleese's chemist shop sketch, sternly shouting out embarrassing ailments and opting for a bit of Frankie Howerd with the chest rash customer, although again, the BBC, bless 'em, quickly stagger in, highlighting the clean up TV campaign by insisting on the removal of certain words which the team happily repeat over and over again in case anybody is unsure of what those dreadful words are. In a satirical attack on the madness of petty censorship, police arrest various

naughty word offenders and Terry Jones opens up the less naughty chemist shop sketch. However, after a repeated halt on this line of enquiry, this too is stopped in its vulgar tracks, only to be replaced by Palin's not at all naughty chemist sketch. Palin, grasping his over-flamboyant assistant with glee, tosses in reiterated T sounds in his delivery (taking Jon Pertwee's *Navy Lark* mannerisms to breaking point), joyfully inspects his fragrances for essence of various fish, gives a brief mention to an unsuitable parrot version (tapping into collective knowledge of series 1, episode 8) and finally allows Eric Idle's customer to address the audience to explain the conventions of television acting. Longer and longer periods of time away infringe on Idle's search for TV reality (correcting the clock and playing for time), while there's a classic shot of Palin waiting in the studio for his entrance. Breaking the conventions of TV, *Python* cleverly reverse this trend by actually showing Palin breathlessly running through the streets and ignoring intrusive interviewers, surrounded by more willing soundbite contributions from everyone from Palin's Spanish inquisitor to Palin's Ken Shabby. Chapman's bombastic copper rounds off the proceedings with mouthy officialdom, while the Beeb apologise for the last time and go out with an over-indulgent mire of American homage which invades the entire concept of *Python*ology during the closing credits.

Series 2 episode IV – The Buzz Aldrin Show
Starring **Buzz Aldrin**
with **Graham Chapman, John Cleese, Eric Idle, Terry Jones, Michael Palin & Terry Gilliam**. Also appearing **Sandra Richards & Stanley Mason**
Script by Buzz Aldrin and Neil 'One Giant Step for Mankind' Armstrong
Animations by **Terry Gilliam**
Research **Patricia Houlihan**
Make up **Madeleine Gaffney and Buzz Aldrin**
Costumes **Hazel Pethig**
Film cameraman **James Balfour**
Editor **Ray Millichope**

Sound **Peter Rose**
Lighting **James Purdie**
Visual effects designer **John Horton**
Designer **Robert Berk**
Produced & directed by **Ian MacNaughton**
20 October 1970

EPISODE 5

Following Palin's BBC globe announcements and the titles, we are introduced to Cleese's And Now... link man in a greasy spoon cafe somewhere in England (the Grillomat Snack Bar, Paignton, actually), allowing him a whole string of self-aware and singly uninventive menu and food-related speeches to bring some sort of enforced coherence to the sketches. Clearly amused by his own ingenuity, Cleese giggles and guffaws with the excitement of a school boy as this episode's only copper-bottom *Python* classic rumbles into view. Blackmail, hosted by Palin's ever-smiling, glittering bow-tied and ocelot-jacketed cool guy, is the ultimate introspective investigation into tacky television, complete with Terry Gilliam's naked organist, homosexual references and the humiliation of wealthy landed gentry nobs. The black and white footage of Terry Jones and the seductive Carol Cleveland taps into the conventions of seaside naughty humour, perfectly playing like a flickering, black and white 'What the Butler Saw' while the Jones telephone call effortlessly leads into a monumental bit of extreme silliness from Graham Chapman. His droning on about putting things on top of other things is quickly defused by Cleese's timid debunking of the art and the entire thing collapses into knowing references to outside broadcast film quality from within the surreal, semi-normal universe of studio audience recording.

Having enough of this concept, the team simply chuck in some Nazi soldiers and a hasty attempt at Prisoner of War drama, complete with Gilliam's concern at the unashamed presence of every cliché save the cheerful cockney sergeant, only to be cheered by the sudden influx of cockney sparrowisms from

Terry Jones. The episode limps onto a discussion programme from a couple of normal working class nutters – the wannabe talker but put-down Eric Idle and the post-dead parrot *Python* figure of John Cleese, who dominates with outraged utterances and off-kilter Cookian observations. Although further unconnected ramblings about phone services were edited, this sketch is clearly going nowhere; the scene cuts to the things on other things committee going through the human drainage system, while Cleese is brilliantly brought into parallel with Gilliam's work via a split screen, a marvellous and clever image which even Idle, tongue in cheekily in character, praises. Idle's house guest in a self-destroying room goes on far too long, despite the seductive appearance of Carol Cleveland's short lived maid and the wonderfully petulant delivery of Chapman's family retainer. Clearly clutching at anything, Palin's 'swollen leg' rehearsing archbishop is happily resurrected while the committee find solace in a school hall and settle down to a painfully stilted interpretation of *Seven Brides for Seven Brothers*, with Chapman's demented Head, Palin's timid man of God and a few absentees in the cast, resulting in just four brothers with two brides. Gilliam's Twiddle Dum and Twiddle Dee of ghoulish animation, Teddy and Neddy enjoy a brief piggy bank hunt which links into this episode's finest moment with Eric Idle's alternatively charming and abusive butcher. Palin's shocked reactions are a total joy and although the joke is repeated it never loses the mood, with Idle's insults piled on, and the niceties and considerate boy insinuations forming some much needed comic genius. The John Cleese boxing scenario doesn't really go anywhere, tapping into the all sportsmen are thick and/or boring theory of his footballer Jimmy Buzzard, while trying to emulate the documentary style of Ethel the Frog. Cleese's brain-dead moron fails to notice Palin's trainer dallying with his missus, needs his head sawn off to wake up fully and wins his matches

by fighting Connie Booth's *Alice in Wonderland* schoolgirl complete with blonde ringlets and Cliff Richard obsession. Cleveland's shapely sparring partner gives the actress some decent lines without simply relying on her figure to get the message across, while Graham Chapman's manager, complete with dark glasses and shameless abuse of trust, is certainly worth waiting for. Hardly a classic piece of *Python*, episode 5 is a standard romp past the by now, fairly familiar actions and reactions against convention, but even Cleese's anchor man seems off form, despite a notable closing sequence on board a bus with intertextuality back to the silly walk scenario from episode one. Average fare but who can handle big stuff all of the time!

Did You Know?
The original script credits the writers as Terry Palin, Eric Jones, Michael Cleese, Graham Gilliam, Terry Chapman and John Idle.

Series 2 episode V
Conceived, written & performed by **Graham Chapman, John Cleese, Eric Idle, Terry Jones, Michael Palin & Terry Gilliam**.
Also appearing **Carol Cleveland, Ian Davidson, Connie Booth, Mrs. Idle**
Animations by **Terry Gilliam**
Research **Patricia Houlihan**
Make up **Madelaine Gaffney**
Costumes **Hazel Pethig**
Film cameraman **James Balfour**
Editor **Ray Millichope**
Sound **Peter Rose**
Lighting **James Purdie**
Visual effects designer **John Horton**
Designer **Richard Hunt**
Produced & directed by **Ian MacNaughton**
27 November 1970

EPISODE 6
Television deconstruction forms the start of this episode, with Eric Idle's enthusiastic host of *It's A Living* pontificating on the fee system of the BBC, before Palin's globe announcer gets himself worked up into a manic state over time-checking details. However, it's an inspired Enoch Powell animation and a different slant

on the opening credits that really gets the show on the road, with Gilliam's clever image of blackness remaining while the familiar refrains of *The Liberty Bell* play as normal. Only when the light switch is found and activated does the original Gilliam credits spring into life, from the middle portion featuring the chicken man on the conveyor belt machinery. It's inspired stuff and even Cleese refrains from his usual And Now For Something Completely Different to fully readjust the opening proceedings. The public school prize giving sketch is basically various criminals and no-goods masquerading as distinguished people from the church in order to grab the goods themselves (sort of Sid James with a degree), although Palin cleverly avoids injecting the obvious innuendo reaction to his introduction, finding the laugh via the stately ladies smile of sexual remembrance. Idle's bogus archbishop is a masterpiece of timing, Chapman seems a bit less at ease as the outlandish oriental figure and Jones, struggling on for the death knolls of the joke, steals some laughs as the inspector before all hell breaks out with Cleese and military protection in the finale *If* homage atmosphere.

Indeed, this similarity is pinpointed by Chapman's film review show (screening the clip we have just witnessed) which draws parallels with the classic 1969 anti-educational authority angle of Lindsay Anderson's *If*. Seedy, crazy director Terry Jones, hilariously bemoans his fate at making these mini piles of guff just as the likes of Hitchcock and Kubrick are beating him to it. A well sustained piece of work, Chapman, all official charm and sharp suits, and Jones the embodiment of the hard done by, hopeless artist, make this the highlight of the show. Certainly the various VIPs in wicker baskets don't even try to give it a run for its money, with outside broadcasting embracing pleasant locations and dodgy poetry from Palin's dragged up old dear – the appearance of Terry Jones's completely barking Samuri warrior is

a Godsend.

The following sketch, dealing with hopeless inept or unappetising free gifts with various offers, does hit home, notably thanks to Chapman's dizzy Indian (rather than the promised dead one because it was probably a faulty cooker), infiltrating into the domestic bliss and sophistication of Palin's dinner party with a deconstruction of the prized incentive to order luxury items. The team come out and expose the ploy as infuriating and pointless, reversing the outlandish garishness of advertising by hiding these disgusting freebies in the small print. Incentive as embarrassment. The similarly geared police link, with Jones proudly boasting about 'What's all this then' T-shirts, Gilliam's motorised pig and his own intertextual reference back to the silly walk classic, act as memorable titbits before Eric Idle's ingratiating and irritating media guy, Timmy Williams, oozes into view. Clearly based on the worst possible elements of David Frost, full of Kenneth Williams camp, false love for all and continuous performance for the press, Idle is a towering picture of affection – creaming himself with desires to please everybody and make his life as easily, media-friendly as possible. Terry Jones and his heart-wrenching plight are nothing in the light of German television deals, Cleese's biography and Chapman's eagerly scribbled newspaper piece. Idle's moment of true greatness comes with his disinterested and totally expressionless pause as the camera recording his entire life is momentarily switched off. Chapman's huge-hooted Raymond Luxury Yacht cod interview tackles television embarrassment with Palin and even a half-hearted racist insinuation about anti-Semitism – hastily denied and thus suggesting cultural hatred comes from within the culture rather than out of it – however, the two aren't around long enough for people to decide before seductive giggles accompany Gilliam's sexual athletics and a topless Mona Lisa.

The Marry Me language

misunderstanding in the marriage bureau provides a classic example of Eric Idle's definitive, long winded, sexually ambiguous tomfoolery, brilliantly reversing the supposed nervousness on Terry Jones's part over Idle's comments about his actually marrying him rather than marrying him to somebody else, by finally revealing that Jones's actual choice for partner was another man rather than embracing convention. Gilliam's cancer-ridden fairy tale prince (with the deliberately obvious over-dubbed voice of Palin changing the illness to gangrene to protect the sensibilities of the audience on repeat screenings and video releases), still manages to include the racist observations from the busy body neighbours before the final hurdle arrives with the *Election Night Special*. The team fall over themselves trying to outdo each other's Peter Snowisms and Ian Davidson is restricted to knowing, camera loving observations of how many times he has appeared on television. The studio material is an easy parody of the hectic BBC attempts to clutch straws, counterbalance and counter-guess the election results, throwing themselves into mental states of excitement via swingometers, importantly sending thank-yous to Spike, getting simple innuendo-drenched giggles from the Arthur Negus/Bristol observations and insipid, half-baked expert opinions. However, the real joy comes with the outside links with the candidate results, delighting in various mad representatives of the incredibly popular Silly Party. Cleese's straight-laced reading of bizarre names is a masterpiece but he outdoes himself with the final Silly Party chap. The name seems to go on forever, getting more bizarre and uncontrolled as they go along, in a mix of respectability and John Lennon's *Revolution 9*. Remaining perhaps the absolute pinnacle of clutching your guts absurdity from the team, the madness is almost unrelenting for what seems like hours. Totally class stuff.

Did You Know?

The Pythons incorporate the name of series film editor, Ray Millichope, in this episode – one of the human pyramid of politicians, he is the leader of the Allied Technicians' Union.

Series 2 Episode VI Conceived, written & performed by **Graham Chapman, John Cleese, Eric Idle, Terry Jones, Michael Palin & Terry Gilliam**. Also appearing **Rita Davies, Ian Davidson**
Animations by **Terry Gilliam**
Research **Patricia Houlihan**
Make up **Madelaine Gaffney**
Costumes **Hazel Pethig**
Film cameraman **James Balfour**
Editor **Ray Millichope**
Sound **Peter Rose**
Lighting **James Purdie**
Visual effects designer **John Horton**
Designer **Richard Hunt**
Produced & directed by **Ian MacNaughton**
3 November 1970

EPISODE 7

This starts a trend of beginning the show with a completely different show, well before the *Python* credits confirm the channel surfer has found the anarchic group in action. Although to be fair, this episode's Attila the Hun Show soon tires of convincing historical narration and blood-stained footage and goes straight into John Cleese and the deconstruction of American television situation comedies. Contrasting the frivolous, wise-cracking, good-looking family with the brutal figure of Attila, the team brilliantly inject throwaway slaughter gags and bad taste, family fun entertainment with knowing winks to the home audience. All the conventions are mercilessly debunked, with Carol Cleveland's dizzy blonde bimbo of a wife, the black manservant Uncle Tom (Eric Idle going perfectly over the top in a direct incorporation of the racist treatment of Rochester in *The Jack Benny Show*) and the sickeningly enthusiastic audience reaction to the entrance of familiar series characters. A few minutes of sustained satire really hit home before Cleese's straight-laced Beeb announcer is super-imposed over some stock, shock footage and *Python* officially begins.

Graham Chapman's medical vignette – with Cleveland's stripper routine while being examined and scrutinised by some shady, rain-coated pervs – could have come directly from his *Doctor* scripts (and indeed, a similar misunderstanding with medical students and decorators occurs in Bernard McKenna's *In Place of Strife*, an episode of *Doctor In Charge* broadcast on 3 November 1973). The stripping logo is retained for Terry Jones, as he disrobes in order to liven up his boring political policy, complete with Eric Idle's wide-eyed dribbling host, while the entire ministry system is viewed via pop star terminology with hippie groupies and free love.

Jones, now in the role of a disgruntled father, taps into television documentary mode when he admits to his wife (Idle) that he's been talking to the television people again, a continual process for airing burning issues, and Chapman's jocular, semi-serious incognito rat-chaser, ferrets out their sheep invasion people, delivers a class visual gag with mice on a string and introduces the Third test rouge which backfires and becomes reality (several times) with Cleese and his team. Idle's excitement at getting the Dorset village Wains Cottage mentioned on telly exposes the Chapman rat-catcher sketch as a sketch, and is itself repeated a second time. In the surreal, time-loop *Python* logic of Gilliam's animation, the eventual outcome of this build-up of material is the immortal Killer Sheep, allowing the American genius to go completely wild with a Jimmy Durante sound-alike, black eye-patched sheep leader. The Carol Cleveland/Eric Idle scientific horseplay with the breaded boffin having no clue, repeat no clue, repeat no clue about anything, quickly sinks into confusion with even the writer questioning the quality of his lines, before help is at hand with Michael Palin's News For Parrots. Seven and a half hours of minority television (the nub of the satire) is condensed into the *Python* chief creature obsession (the parrot) and that of The Goodies (the gibbon), political scandal from Idle (complete with innuendo-fuelled references to no portfolios), a repeat of the parrot material with Wombats in replacement and a snatch of the parrot's version of *A Tale of Two Cities* (embracing the cockney rhyming innuendo via Cleveland's resurrection of Jane Russell's blouse-stretching bed bending from *The Outlaw*, and playing the game for parrots with self-mocking pretty boyisms all the way).

If this all gets a bit too much then take solace in the glorious village idiot life of Cleese's Arthur Figgis, coherently and articulately discussing his important cultural purpose for the BBC cameras before turning on the insane gibberish for the local population. It is a John Cleese classic, full of silly walks, falling over, stark raving mad behaviour and brief interludes of sane observation – notably on the arrival of Palin's fellow idiot. Other delights along the way include Chapman's business-minded banker, M. Brando (complete with Palin's Hollywood call gag), the concept of getting a university degree in village idiocy and Idle's traditionalist, self-taught pontificator, before the real idiots are highlighted in the Upper Class Twit brigade of the city (sub-titled to pinpoint their plummy observations and, in-fact, repeating most of the jokes from the Upper Class Twit of the Year sketch). All this pretentious behaviour leaps into the next sketch, deconstructing cricket commentary with Chapman's Goonish behaviour, Idle's drunken old bore with a string of ancient statistics and a state of play which praises every thrilling non-move. Eventually the manpower is seen as obsolete and a far more active load of home furniture has a bash with leather and willow – even resulting in a table being out (leg before wicket) – quite bizarre.

Naturally, in terms of the team's comic extension, other sports get the furniture treatment in a quick burst of *Python* insanity but this is soon forgotten in favour of John Cleese's patronising game show host and Terry Jones, irritating for England, as the thick old bat who has successful wild stabs in the dark, sets up some racist bickering and even manages to mention Spam before its major *Python* appearance in episode 12. The 'open the box' terminology is taken directly from telly quiz shows and the enthusiastic roll-call of would-be penguin sweet meats is hilarious, even more so in light of the prize on offer. Tim Brooke-Taylor had, in fact, given us the definitive rendition of this sketch opposite Cleese for *How to Irritate People*, it had cropped up with Marty Feldman in *At Last the 1948 Show* and would be reshaped for Amnesty International, but this *Python* resurrection is more than sufficient for world immortality.

Series 2 episode VII conceived, written & performed by **Graham Chapman, John Cleese, Eric Idle, Terry Jones, Michael Palin & Terry Gilliam**. Also appearing **Carol Cleveland, Ian Davidson**
Animations by **Terry Gilliam**
Research **Patricia Houlihan**
Make up **Madelaine Gaffney**
Costumes **Hazel Pethig**
Film cameraman **James Balfour**
Editor **Ray Millichope**
Sound **Peter Rose**
Lighting **James Purdie**
Visual effects designer **John Horton**
Designer **Robert Berk**
Produced & directed by **Ian MacNaughton**
10 November 1970

EPISODE 8

Television's obsession with sport begins episode 8, with the BBC's proud roll-call of variety ending up with cricket as almost the entire programme schedule and other sport in between. This tongue-in-cheek, hackneyed complaint to the Beeb's hotline is continued right up until the familiar *Python* tune when the first two notes of *Sports Report* are edited into a bit of Sousa. Gilliam makes a subtle adjustment to the expected animation when the immortal foot crashes down, shatters and is replaced by an urban jungle which quickly decays. A comment on the brief span of modern society which, via the historical discovery of the toe

and some hasty prehistoric hysterics, links to the television formatted *Archaeology Today*. A one-gag exercise with Palin's public schoolboy closet pervert obsessed with height, almost licking his lips at Cleese's 6 foot 5 inch frame and hammering into poor old Jones with minute comments and withering looks. The outside broadcast is weird to say the least but Cleese is so goddamn cool, notably when mouthing his part of a duet (vocalised by Terry Jones) on *Today* with Carol Cleveland, that the whole works really well – playing like a study of academia via Western movie values. The emphasis of height equals pride is taken to logical *Python* conclusions and the brave rants act like a semi-dry run for the immortal Black Knight sequence in *Monty Python and the Holy Grail*. Chapman's plea for insanity is definitive stuff with his dignified and sincere delivery contrasted with the outlandish appearance of a hatchet buried in his head, allowing his calm Voice of God manner to suddenly descend into glorious madness with uncontrolled squawking and roving eyes. The inane meets the insane. Anything goes with direct delivery to the camera and Eric Idle's delightful vignette basically centres around the fact that his drag persona doesn't know her name and assumes the identity of anything that comes into her head. At one stage setting up a priceless bit of Leapy Lee's *Little Arrows* and a mention for the Middlesex/Arsenal legend Denis Compton. Cleverly Gilliam's manic punch-drunk boxer knocks Idle out before the joke can go on too long and collapse.

The next sketch, the infamous 'change my wife' banter, has been condemned as *Python* sexism, but surely Idle is simply highlighting that this is the sort of narrow-minded, bigoted and self-righteous attitude that his streetwise nutter would have. Besides, it's far too funny to be condemned for anything and sensitive audience members should either wallow in the sheer bemusement of Terry Jones or simply keep out of my way. The notion of changing a wife which doesn't quite measure up is just

an extension of the idea of changing any other goods on the market. This is *Monty Python* after all; it's a comedy observation of the way we live our lives and a magnification of the absurdities around us. And classic stuff it is too. There's just no point in complaining about a beloved and vital British institution, it's not a way to make friends and influence people! Anyway, just to counter balance any problems, Cleese blows his whistle, takes Idle's number and books him for attempting the idea – akin to the arresting of people who used forbidden words on the BBC in episode 4. It's a satirical dig at those people who may take it seriously and be offended, but importantly highlights that the Pythons were aware of what they were doing and conscious of enforcing sexist attitudes by mocking their own comedy. Clever, eh!

The sketch is abandoned, fading into an obvious bit of name misunderstanding between Palin and Chapman, seized by the throat by Gilliam's animation and transmogrified with some delicious gangster mockery with the dreaded chicken heavy Eggs Diamond. Keep your eyes peeled for a special guest appearance from Spiney Norman. The Cocktail Party sketch is very much in *The Two Ronnies* mould, with Palin struggling to hide his embarrassment at Terry Jones and John Cleese as the Gits – the idea would later be toned down and elongated for Cleese's *Fawlty Towers* episode The Gourmet Night. Basically these repugnant figures are happy to live with ridicule as Palin nervously announces them to his wife, Carol Cleveland. It's glorious obvious humour and Cleese's spitting in the handbag has to be seen to be believed! It's so nightmarish that the lads seem to want to address any adverse comments again by a tongue-in-cheek presentation of a nice version of the sketch. But enough of that when there's Graham Chapman's great white Aussie hunter on the look-out for insects to kill.

With one of the all time great opening lines, Chapman's manic, fearless slayer of defenceless creatures ranks as one of *Python*'s top characterisations. Behind the laughs it's a serious indictment on the cruelty and absurdity of blood sports with the human race abusing the natural world, on the surface it's just hilarious comedy performed with relish. The judicial authority figure was always a favourite *Python* target and the camp Palin and Idle figures are probably the finest examples of madness behind the power. Palin's creation of his booming Northern, on-stage voice is a classic. An interlude from gossiping pepperpots Idle and Chapman (dropping female clichés about shopping and buying nothing, finding the job of making a cup of tea a taxing day's work etc) sweeps into John Cleese's completely barmy Ludvig Von Beethoven, desperately trying to work the old keyboard magic with his continuously jabbering old woman chatting in his earhole. Chapman makes the perfect irritant and the usual *Python* practice of carrying the gag through other similar sketches presents Eric Idle's unforgettable Jewish William Shakespeare washing up, Terry Jones as a hen-pecked Michelangelo, swapping names for their various works of art and finally coming full circle with Cleese, his Mynah bird and a nice touch of Jimmy Durante's record of *The Lost Chord* playing in the background. Class stuff. Thankfully to round up an excellent bit of *Python* it's back to the gloriously irreverent Idle and Palin in legal mode, with Eric's relaxed smile at the close of the sketch expressing a good time had by all. Unmissable.

Series 2 episode VIII conceived, written & performed by **Graham Chapman, John Cleese, Eric Idle, Terry Jones, Michael Palin & Terry Gilliam**. Also appearing **Carol Cleveland**
Animations by **Terry Gilliam**
Research **Patricia Houlihan**
Make up **Madelaine Gaffney**
Costumes **Hazel Pethig**
Film cameraman **James Balfour**
Editor **Ray Millichope**
Sound **Peter Rose**
Lighting **James Purdie**
Visual effects designer **John Horton**

Designer **Richard Hunt**
Produced & directed by **Ian MacNaughton**
17 November 1970

EPISODE 9

One of the all-time classic opening scenes with an array of bikini-clad glam girls posing to the refrains of *A Pretty Girl is Like A Melody* only for the whole atmosphere to be debunked by the presence of John Cleese, similarly clad, for the And Now announcement. The 'how to recognise various parts of the body' material which runs throughout this episode and is skilfully used to link the sketches, naturally starts with the *Python* foot, embraces various, discreetly covered naughty bits, and the huge false hooter of Chapman's Throat-Wobbler character, cropping up again a bit later in this very episode. The identification of the kneecap links into the much celebrated and imitated Australian philosophy sketch, full of Bruces, beer drinking, sheep dipping and anti-poofery. Although perhaps mocking the very notion of stereotyping, the sketch is hilarious throughout, notably Cleese's straight-faced and straight-laced enforcement of the vital rules of Aussie happiness and acceptability. The contradictory interview between Palin and Jones doesn't really get started before there's an almighty piece of brilliance between Messrs Chapman and Cleese, performing a prime slice of *Python* japery via a discussion on plastic surgery. It gets a bit silly but, after all, that's the whole name of the game and the two are clearly having a great time just being wonderfully, deliciously and uncomplicatedly stupid together. The entire point of *Python*.

The two contrasting military moods between the anger drilling and, the more familiar, camped up approach step aside for some inspired 1950s B-movie take-off Gilliam madness with the Killer Cars (if sheep then why not anything else!), the 'out of the frying pan into the fire' appearance of a giant cat and, ditto, the giant, dismembered hand. Idle's gangster airport sketch with Palin going into

devious overdrive and the opportunity to suspiciously pick your time of flight and price of ticket is a half-hearted reheating of several earlier ideas and the following re-enactment of the first heart transplant takes off from where Idle's Pearl Harbour extravaganza left off (indeed, it's the exact same footage!). Okay, it's more intertextuality because the gang are up front about the repeat, with mentions of the previous Batley Woman's Guild effort, but the fact remains that by this stage the Pythons were reworking vast quantities of old material. The underwater version of *Measure For Measure* is good fun but even this is laboured into the ground with other like-minded productions. When, a bit later, John Cleese links some sketches with a dry, 'They must be running out of ideas!' he's exactly right, although they can still claim to be the first group to crack a Mrs. Thatch gag here and the pepperpots discussion between Cleese and Chapman with regard the television-based penguin is a masterclass in comic acting. Chapman's exasperated 'Intercourse the penguin' clearly hits home with Cleese. Now the team are really going for it, almost mentioning the unmentionable and loving the sense of dangerously knocking back the boundaries of television respectability. There's some typical derision at the expense of British provincial towns before the lads fully pull out the stops for the detective finale. Palin's mildly challenged inspector turns the tables on Chapman's posh delivery (look out for Cleese's delighted reaction to Chapman's work) by some familiar refrained mockery (dished out by Chapman to Terry Jones in the Flying lessons sketch) and Jones rips into an Elvis-like jiving blues singing copper, promoting a Katie Boyle-like appearance from Eric Idle and a celebration of the *Eurovision Song Contest* style via the boys in blue. Chapman's manic foreign jabberings incorporating bizarre lyrics about bang bangs and tiddlers could be a genuine winner if you use your imagination, and not too much of it either!

Did You Know?

Gilliam was going to make an addition to the opening credits – the chicken chappie was to be carrying a banter proclaiming 'How to Recognise Different Parts of the Body'. Barry Humphries claimed *Python* stole Bruce off him, having enjoyed success with a comic hero called Bruce earlier, but the sketch writers John Cleese and Eric Idle both denied this – simply addressing the fact that every Australian they met, including Idle's director friend, was called Bruce.

Series 2 episode IX conceived, written & performed by **Graham Chapman, John Cleese, Eric Idle, Terry Jones, Michael Palin & Terry Gilliam**.
Also appearing **Carol Cleveland, The Fred Tomlinson Singers, Vincent Wong, Roy Gunson, Alexander Curry, Ralph Wood, John Clement**
Animations by **Terry Gilliam**
Research **Patricia Houlihan**
Make up **Madelaine Gaffney**
Costumes **Hazel Pethig**
Photography **Joan Williams**
Film cameramen **James Balfour & Terry Hunt**
Editor **Ray Millichope**
Sound **Peter Rose**
Lighting **James Purdie**
Visual effects designer **John Horton**
Designer **Richard Hunt**
Produced & directed by **Ian MacNaughton**
24 November 1970

EPISODE 10

Probably the weakest entry in series two, the first 15 minutes are an elongated comic inspection of art cinema and the bending of historical facts in Hollywood myth making. The show starts with Carol Cleveland's forlorn bride, sat in a rubbish dump holding a cabbage – hardly the most inspiring beginning for comedy. It's all done in neo-realism style, sending up the Brigitte Bardot persona via Vittorio de Sica European art movies with Terry Jones as the babbling, dark shaded, dapper, fag smoking guy, improvising sub-titled dialogue and making one of the most boring motion pictures in history. The Bardot link is reinforced

with the films characters being cited as Brian and Brianette but that's not the end of the sequence, instead we are subjected to more dodgy cabbage humour, pretentious black and white montage footage (notably featuring Chapman and the piano plus the other team members in various guises) inter-cut very badly with Jones and Cleveland in full Euro flick mode, repeating the pained, non-happening of the previous stuff with the added humiliation, in terms of the foreign film being parodied, of the microphone being all too obviously in shot.

Clearly having more than enough of that, the scene shifts to a location report on the film *Scott of the Antarctic*, sending up the *Carry On Camping*esque fact that snow is faked on the beach and allowing Cleese's manic, incompetent and furiously babbling Scottish director to gabble on about drink, garbage and avoiding film small talk. With filming in process, Palin's Hollywood hunk is highlighted in Alan Ladd terms with heights strapped to his feet, while Cleveland does the perfect blonde bimbo starlet, Miss Whore, playing her scenes from within a trench and getting rather tetchy when asked to get out! Palin's muscle-bound, muscle-brained cinematic icon is memorably bumbling and conceited and his distress at the lion fight being cut, due to the Antarctic setting, creates the only really successful joke in this scenario. Idle's flamboyant American producer suggests a fight with a penguin as an alternative. Maybe it's the over-enthusiastic audience laugh track or maybe it's just desperation after ten minutes of sub-standard material, but that line cracks me up every-time. Basically all this stuff is one long elaborate build-up for the change of title to Scott of the Sahara, with Palin finally getting to grapple with the wonderfully unconvincing lion (the fight, complete with Sam Peckinpah slow motion and blood squirting with the lion skilfully brandishing a chair, is worth the dross, believe me!). The gag is stretched with the Mr. Tickle-like killer penguin battling Terry Jones and no-one can lose their

clothes more elegantly while being chased by a toothsome chest of drawers than Carol Cleveland. After 15 minutes of this filmic nonsense the *Python* credits finally arrive, heralding Terry Gilliam's animation, continuing the teeth theme with one of his greatest piece of work, Conrad Pooh's Dancing Teeth. The delayed start to the dance is spot-on. And finally, there is a glimmer of real class *Python* with Cleese, post-parrot trauma, struggling into a post office only to face another Palin job's worth, bemused at his request for a fish licence for his pet fish Eric – despite his collection of Eric tagged creatures, the immortal Eric the half a bee would come later on vinyl in *Monty Python's Previous Record*. The cat/dog licence banter is pure Python genius but it's a very long time coming and pretty lonely. For no sooner has the Lord Mayor decreed his decree much to the amazement of Mr. Cleese Esq, than the Mayor's rugger match kicks off, followed by the footie between the Long John Silver impersonators and a load of medics – showcasing more goals than an Ian Wright convention. Palin's sycophantic laughter results in a swift disappearance under the beloved 16-ton weight and, with a sigh of relief, the team can put this one down to experience.

Did You Know?

Mercifully, much of the Scott of Antarctic material was cut, including a further interview with Idle's producer character, a dreaded attacking tarantula that rings like a telephone and Jones discussing the fundamental depth of his characterisation. His character was also originally due to be chased by a roll-top desk rather than the set of teeth in the final print. The manic, long-armed penguin was, in fact, a one-foot model orchestrated by Gilliam.

Sereis 2 episode X conceived, written & performed by **Graham Chapman, John Cleese, Eric Idle, Terry Jones, Michael Palin & Terry Gilliam**. Also appearing **Carol Cleveland, Mrs. Idle**
Animations by **Terry Gilliam**

Research **Patricia Houlihan**
Make up **Penny Norton**
Costumes **Hazel Pethig**
Film cameraman **James Balfour**
Editor **Ray Millichope**
Sound **Peter Rose**
Lighting **Otis Eddy**
Visual effects designer **John Horton**
Designers **Robert Berk & Ken Sharp**
Produced & directed by **Ian MacNaughton**
1 December 1970

EPISODE 11

Reeling from the previous episode, the lads signpost the initial sketch with Idle's entrance through the window, knowing looks to Cleese and on-screen itemisation of jokes. It's a mild satire of nepotism in business where anything can be forgiven if you're related to the boss and Idle's disastrous attempts to promote coffee (including a free dog gift – an echo from the Indian offer in episode six) perfectly bring out Cleese's petulant, calm condescension. The sketch, sagging, links to Idle's prize winning film and the obligatory introduction. However, again the conventions of *Python* style are altered with the stuck record during the idyllic scenery, repeated with Cleese's BBC announcer and, even more potently, used once more when the familiar theme and credits stick momentarily. Palin's stripping Ramsey MacDonald (originally scripted as Stanley Baldwin) continues the authority baiting thematics with a rather lacklustre air and even John Cleese's manic *Exchange and Mart* editor, desperately trying to sell everything and anything to prospective employee Terry Jones doesn't even seem to be firing on any cylinders. Gilliam's Chinese invasion is a class bit of animation though, followed up by his satirical attack on American advertising in terms of world peace, latching onto conventions (the 'not white car') and impressive looking graphs to impart absolute rubbish. The other team members redeem themselves with a glorious, strangely uncelebrated look at the Agatha Christie range again, pinpointing the minute clue of train timetables and elongating it into the entire form,

structure, narrative power and character obsession for all the suspects. Death, destruction and family values count for nothing when a seat reservation is in the offing. Palin's foppish rotter, Tony, is a brilliant stereotype of the over-ambitious rep. actor, even incorporating the vocal impediment of Ws for Rs from Michael Medwin's tongue in cheek dramatics in *Curtain Up!* As with Ewan's Scottish poems, the playwright, one sad rail nut by the name of Neville Shunt (Jones), is heralded as a genius by Cleese's fast talking, pretentious television critic, denying the claims that Shunt's work is just a load of rubbish about railway timetables and, via quotes from every highbrow source available, rambles on about the mystic beauty of his work. Of course, it is all just a load of rubbish about railway timetables, but who cares! Fellow television boffins Palin and Jones, struggle to avoid dental/teeth references as they introduce Chapman's distinguished, well-endowed in the mouth region, big-toothed film director. A brief snippet from his historical masterpiece quickly outstays its welcome but that old stand-by, interviews with the general public, produces a hasty reiteration of the title sticking from Eric Idle's businessman and a rare chance for Carol Cleveland to don character make-up and play an old dear instead of one of the Pythons themselves. And fear not, class *Python* lovers: there's a chance to wallow in the team's attack on organised religion via Idle's crackpot beliefs told in game show style (with Gilliam's nude organist from Blackmail), ideals of wealth and sexy glam girls, Cleese as Bruce the Archbishop complete with Aussie symbolic can of beer, the Gumby slant on faith, Palin as both Ken Shabby and a devious-styled wideboy for naughty fun, Jones as the lunatic angle and, finally, the embodiment of respectability in Chapman's Most Popular Religion Ltd. The theme is completely worked into everyone's subconscious via Gilliam's sickly smiling preacher continually revealing the dark devil of corruption from

within. It's a track taken to unsurpassable heights in *Life of Brian* but here, as there, this is the team skilfully exposing the hypocrisy of organised religion rather than religion itself. As such it speaks volumes. Although a fondly remembered *Python* element the Spike Milligan-inspired 'How not to be seen' spot goes on for an age, with sporting interviews and guest turn singing padding out the basic *Q*-like idea of blowing up members of the general public (the basic concept was featured in lighter terms with Milligan's Nation Anthem scenario where members of the public were tested to see who would stand for her Majesty). However, even though the Pythons flog the idea to death don't turn off before the very end (the very idea anyway!) because the team finish with a concerned BBC announcement explaining that you have just missed *Monty Python's Flying Circus* and a very quick montage of images from all the proceedings sketches are flashed before your eyes. Priceless.

Did You Know?
The Arthur Crackpot Handbook, plugging the glories of greed is good, was cut from this show.

Series 2 episode XI conceived, written & performed by **Graham Chapman, John Cleese, Eric Idle, Terry Jones, Michael Palin & Terry Gilliam**.
Also appearing **Carol Cleveland**
Animations by **Terry Gilliam**
Research **Patricia Houlihan**
Make up **Penny Norton**
Costumes **Hazel Pethig**
Film cameraman **James Balfour**
Editor **Ray Millichope**
Sound **Peter Rose**
Lighting **Otis Eddy**
Visual effects designer **John Horton**
Designers **Robert Berk**
Produced & directed by **Ian MacNaughton**
8 December 1970

EPISODE 12
By now it was fairly common practice for the shows to begin with misleading opening credits for other shows. However, this episode's *The Black Eagle*, a dramatic tale of

smugglers and the like, remains the best and most sustained example of this. Unlike material such as *The Attila the Hun Show*, this slice of BBC historical drama contains no *Python* team members as trigger points for the *Python* explosion, nor any funny lines. Even the credits, unlike the parodies of *Morecambe and Wise*, contain no obvious comic content and many viewers furiously swapped channels believing they were missing *Python* somewhere else. It is only as the camera pans across the forbidding coast line that the camera catches sight of John Cleese's And Now For Something Completely Different announcer and the *Python* madness begins.

Mind you, when it finally does get under way, how better than with the immortal Hungarian phrase-book sketch, continuing the historical grandeur of the opening item with on-screen, explanatory legend of 1970s Britain, before the masterly Cleese staggers in with book in hand. The exaggerated and over-played word, Want, can cause grown men to collapse with hilarity and has effortlessly passed into our collective culture heritage, with the format giving the perfect opportunity for the Pythons to include abuse, sexual comments and innuendo-drenched Bellamy Brothers hit within a frame-work of misunderstood foreigner and corrupted Brit publishing house (opening the court scene with Palin's flamboyant Derek Nimmo impersonation – quickly capsized by Idle's prosecuting counsellor). Back on the bench is Terry Jones, far from the stigma of Chapman's outlandish sentencing, with an enjoyable reappraisal of the parlour game slant in that sketch via Idle's gleeful yes/no cross examination. Cleese is clearly enjoying the comedy as much as anyone when Chapman blasts out with 'I didn't know an acceptable legal phrase' and the entire thing rushes headlong into *Sun*-styled captions (Cutie Q.C. and the like). Gilliam's memorable American cop cum Kubrick's *2001: A Space Odyssey* brilliantly resolves itself in football significance just in time for Eric Idle's cheesy introduction of World Forum.

A *Python* masterpiece, this legendary gathering of major historical figures (notably Jones as Karl Marx and Gilliam's passionate Che Guevara) turns the intellectual debate into a joyful football and pop trivia game. The bemused reaction of Jones is comedy, pure and simple! Idle's brilliance lies in the perfect incorporation of game host mannerisms (all 'bad luck there Karl', three-piece suites, enquiries about nervousness, zooming camera on answering panellist and clever manoeuvring of his contestant onto the right studio floor spot). It's that perfectly detailed even though the Coventry City trick question lost its contemporary power in 1987 when the team actually did win the FA Cup). Michael Palin's public-schoolboy based, patriotic narration for the First War World drama is quickly curtailed by Cleese; the flamboyantly effeminate director of Terry Jones hastily removes a bizarre array of unrequired extras and the caption writers have a bit of short-lived fun, before it's back to Ypres, Idle's girl-troubled Tommy and the strong, right arm of Palin. Before things really get going there's a classic revolutionary art gallery scene with characters from the great works of art walking out of their frames and striking for better conditions. The chat between Jones and Chapman is superb and remains one of the best, unheralded moments in the *Python* canon. Linking in with all the strike talk, the scene quickly cuts back to a BBC comment concerning the abandoned Ypres sketch and the reappearance of the lads, complete with brave, armless and quietly embittered John Cleese desperately trying to carry on with British pluck. In contrast, Chapman is the definitive cowardly officer, side-stepping every fair or foul way of ascertaining the chosen man to lay down his life, forever moving the goal-posts, pontificating about muddles and insisting that rank doesn't enter into the equation when clearly it does! Note the delight on Cleese's face as he realises the audience have got the joke.

The Royal Hospital For Over-Acting,

full of dubious King Rats and Richard IIIs (initiating a generation of *Python* fans who delighted in shrieking 'A horse, a horse, my kingdom for a horse' in an outrageously loud and uncontrolled way through playgrounds nationwide and continue to cheer up boring social functions with lapses into *Python*ology) effortlessly remains as the greatest twist on the NHS in *Python* history. Idle's reformed Shakespearean thesp is a masterpiece and Gilliam does a great double whammy with his ghoulish *Hamlet* performances. Palin's outrageous Gumby flower arranging is short-lived but memorable (later a favourite of the live shows) before the almighty Chapman and Idle cross words with Jones in the Spam routine. Taking its inspiration from the classic Peter Sellers record *Balham – Gateway to the South* ('Honey's off, dear!'), the Pythons pinpoint one moment of that landmark George Martin recording and run with it. The chant of the devoted *Python* scholar, Spam is a masterpiece of sustained absurdity which happily invades the Viking chorus within the cafe and is woven into the closing credits of the show.

Did You Know?
One of the most celebrated Jones/Palin pieces for *Python*, Spam was disliked by both Cleese and Chapman because its madness had no root in believability, but it made both Gilliam and Idle laugh so, thankfully, it got in.

Series 2, episode XII – Conceived, written & performed by **Spam Terry Jones, Michael Spam Palin, John Spam John Spam John Spam Cleese, Graham Spam Spam Spam Chapman, Eric Spam Egg and Chips Idle, Terry Spam Sausage Spam Egg Spam Gilliam**
Also appearing on toast **The Fred Tomlinson Spam Egg Chips and Singers**
Animations by **Terry (Egg on Face) Gilliam**
Research **Patricia Houlihan and Sausage**
Make up **Penny Penny Penny and Spam Norton**
Costumes **Egg Baked Beans Sausage**

and Tomato Oh and Hazel Pethig Too
Film cameraman **James (Spam Sausage Egg and Tomato) Balfour (Not Sundays)**
Editor **Ray (Fried Slice and Golden Three Delicious) Millichope (Spam extra)**
Sound **Chips Sausage Liverwurst, Pheasant, Spam, Newsagents, Chips and Peter Rose**
Lighting **Otis (Spam's off dear) Eddy**
Designers **Robert Robert Robert Robert Berk and tomato**
Produced & directed by **Ian (Mixed Grill) MacNaughton 7/6d**
BBC Spam TV Service not included
15 December 1970

EPISODE 13

To finish off this second series of inspired genius, the Pythons present the Royal edition with no And Now For Something Completely Different. Instead it had flustered comments from Cleese explaining that Her Majesty, although at present watching *The Virginian*, is expected to tune into the show and that all audience members should stand. The artists, of course, will continue as normal – like sure they will. The titles, not as normal, are a brilliantly lavish, regal affair from Gilliam and the impending moment of royal patronage is forever evident, notably in the first sketch via Cleese's upper class twit official.

The sketch is a classic, with a load of Welsh miners debating about historical inaccuracies and legalisation, full of bloody this and bloody that as Eric Idle's bombastic leader counter-acts and corrects reams of highbrow information. The working man as thinking man. After a no go with the Toad elevating sketch, Chapman's nutty television interviewee, apparently famed for saying things in a very roundabout sort of way, contradicts himself with straight to the point answers before that little twist has outstayed its welcome and he throws himself into outrageously long bits of dialogue. The following slice of telly absurdity, with various guests who only say either the end, the start or the middle of words, elongates the Chapman piece to breaking point and approaches a sort of *Two Ron*s

sketch on LSD. Gilliam's bad taste, bad breath ad with dragons and nubile young tit-bits was, in fact, taken up by Listerine for a series of ads featuring the voice of Willy Rushton – talk about low-art imitating parody – and Gilliam's next animation interlude embraces the nice side of cartoons with an innocent Bambi-lookalike and Palin's happy frolicking through a painted backdrop à la *Song of the South*. Palin, years before the fish-obsessed Pythons gave us *The Meaning of Life* and *A Fish Called Wanda*, takes his audience through the sex life of the pike, before there is a slightly jokey and amended apology for giving out incorrect information regarding the fish's staple diet. Just to bring this madness to a surreal conclusion there's a superficially smiling Chapman tapping into waiter terminology with his enquiry about whether 'We are enjoying the show!' before Jones contributes the ultimate train-spotter, interviewing himself about stealing bird-watchers' eggs before the comic idea is expanded with various human abusers and users of defenseless creatures being used and abused in the same way. However, this slight idea is replaced by impressive regal music, a quick gag appearance from Spiney Norman and the extravagantly fan-fared insurance sketch, watched for all of two seconds by Her Majesty. The comedy within the insurance sketch is unimportant and fairly non-existent; it is merely an excuse for Cleese and Idle to play to the royal watcher, a joke sportingly continued when we switch to Reginald Bosanquet's respectful standing during the News. A grand, unique and ground-breaking bit of hands across the channels there.

The intensive medical care unit run like a military operation is pretty funny for a while, with various patients running themselves into the ground for health, fitness, Queen and country, but Cleese and Chapman's love for hospital madness results in the sketch going on a tad too long (sorry lads!), although there's some good, obvious innuendo (enjoy the runs) mixed in with the insanity and

television doctor convention via a quick burst of the *Dr. Kildare* theme. Chapman includes another dig at the landed gentry docs who are purely in it for the loot and Cleese's familiar announcer is seen promoting the importance of the Hospital for Link men, desperately searching for an example of a link and turning the *Python* convention on its head by cutting to the mountaineering sketch only to find that the team haven't written one. An obvious link denied and thus, in a round about way, Cleese is cured, momentarily, of his link obsession!

Documentary footage of allied troops reworked as schoolgirls on a trip leads into the manic pepperpots of Chapman and Palin running a torpedo submarine, before Cleese resurrects the old stand-by of angry letters and the gang are tossed into Noel Coward like dramatics adrift in an open boat. Chapman's highlighting of the innuendo-fuelled question from Palin 'How long is it?' destroys the tense atmosphere of the scene and all are in turmoil before the drama is resurrected and the all-important cannibalistic text is revealed. With hurt feelings when Cleese's leg is condemned as gammy, bickering as to whom is going to eat whom and a final delicious menu of human bits organised, Carol Cleveland's waitress wanders in front of the marine backdrop and takes the order to the tune of outraged mock reaction from the studio audience. There's only one way to go from there and that's ever onward, into the infamous and outrageous eating dead mother scenario from Cleese and Chapman. It's a sick but perfectly *Python*esque concept and although cold feet prompted the team and the BBC to include cries of amazement and disgust from off camera, almost blotting out some of the dialogue, this is a major step beyond the realms of accepted BBC decency... wonderful. What a way to end a series!

Series 2, episode XIII conceived, written & performed by **Graham Chapman, John Cleese, Eric Idle, Terry Jones, Michael Palin & Terry Gilliam.**
Also appearing **Carol Cleveland, Ian**

Davidson
Animations by **Terry Gilliam**
Research **Patricia Houlihan**
Makeup **Madelaine Gaffney**
Costumes **Hazel Pethig**
Cameramen **James Balfour & Terry Hunt**
Editor **Ray Millichope**
Sound **Peter Rose**
Lighting **James Purdie**
Visual effects designer **John Horton**
Graphics **Bob Blagden**
Stills photography **Joan Williams**
Videotape editor **Howard Dell**
Designer **Robert Berk**
Produced & directed by **Ian
MacNaughton**
22 December 1970

'Is this a dead parrot I see before me?'...

Series 3

Cleese was restless towards the end of
series 2, but wisely kept going
through the 13-strong third series
recorded from December 1971 to
May 1972 to contribute some of his
finest work. Cleese, rather bored with
the whole thing, was becoming
involved less and less, while his
shared ideal with Graham Chapman
in writing sketches with inbred logic
was at loggerheads with the bizarre
excess of Jones/Palin pieces. Indeed,
Cleese maintains that he only created
two totally new items for series three
– Dennis Moore and The Cheese
Shop. Great chunks do stretch the
Python ethos to breaking point, but,
on the other hand, when it's good
(Flag-seller/Oscar Wilde/The Money
Programme) series three boasts some
of the best material in the entire
canon – like The Beatles White
Album, there's a totally sublime six-
parter here, but why fudge the issue,:
here's the six lads, all systems go. Hit
and miss it may be, but who cares?
Terry Gilliam created a new set of
title credits – complex industrial pipes,
the irreplaceable squashing foot
(twice), pregnant medical extraction,
hopping bloke in car, exploding teeth,
palm tree sunset – and Terry Jones's
nude organist (taking over from
Gilliam in series one's Blackmail)
became a regular opening sequence
image alongside Cleese's announcer
and Palin's It's Man.

EPISODE 1

This starts with a typical Jones/ Palin
sweeping shot of Icelandic mountains
in 1126 for the much heralded Njorl's
Saga before latching onto the nude
Jones, Cleese, It's, the credits and, the
first sketch proper: Idle's Michael
Norman Randall in the dock charged
with mass murder (20 dead all on or
around 19 December 1971). Jones, as
the judge, delivers his string of
victims with perfect timing; Cleese is
a woolly self-effacing prosecuting
counsel, Palin makes a cheery jury
foreman and a battled Chapman as
humbling policeman, but it's Idle's
peerless praise for all concerned,
sincerely apologising for all the
trouble his bloodthirsty rampage has
caused, that really makes this scene.
A warm character against a faceless
list of dead bodies, Idle's heartfelt
tributes, pleading for a life sentence
and his dishing out of so much
affectionate thanks makes this lesser
known *Python* courtroom scene one
of the best and most powerful (a
good-natured manner can wipe away
any crime) – ending with Jones
momentarily wavering on his verdict
and the collection of law-abiders
giving Idle's likeable killer a rousing
chorus of *For He's A Jolly Good
Fellow*! Gilliam's cracking prisoner

forms the perfect contrast to this
leniency, finishing off the last line of
the song à la Sher Khan in *The Jungle
Book* and escaping through his own
broken body, hotly pursued by the
Palin-voiced detective. Through a
stunning maze of Gothic staircases,
The Third Man-like sewers (the
crook's veins and, thus, having our
hero wade through the blood of the
escapee) and an *Indiana Jones*-like
rolling onion/apple down to the pit of
the stomach, this stands as one of
Gilliam's finest pieces.
However, it's quickly back to Njorl
(part II) with Cleese's detached
narrator breaking into the screen to
explain his use of the word 'terrible'
to a questioning Norse Palin. Idle's
elongated introduction delays Jones
mounting his horse, Jones begins to
explain the problem before himself
getting into elongated narrative,
while Cleese breaks the diatribe with
an appeal for help in starting this
BBC costume classic from the
viewing public. Introducing himself
as the third voice we heard, fobbing
off another Palin interjection and
happily oblivious to his secretary's
cleavage spraying, Cleese unveils
plans for backing from The New

Malden Icelandic Society.
In the best part of this rather lumbering, over-used Saga, our hapless hero journeys to New Malden, a chance in music indicates business opportunity travelogue, Palin's Mayor welcomes a bemused, fur-clad Jones before everything falls apart, the Malden team are reprimanded, permitted to have another go and cut the action back to Iceland's Land of Dark Forces. However, just as convention is recaptured, the battling warriors display MALDEN on their chests, advertising banners are held aloft and amidst fighting action, subliminal messages of 'Invest in Malden' are projected, desperately explained by Palin's wideboy Malden chap in a complaint phone-call from BBC Cleese.
The result, Njorl's Saga, part III, which limps onto Chapman's programme planner explaining his reliance on sport 'it's not your highbrow bleeding plays which bring in the viewers, you know' with his massive five-year sentence reflecting on Jones the Judge and Idle's cheerfulness. Gabbled introductions, taken to the limit of audience tolerance, breaks down for the mummified defendant (note Idle's embrace of low-brow humour and the biggest laugh coming with 'Can you raise any part of your body!') while the team run the gamut of taboos with blasphemy (screw the bible), homosexuality in high places (Jones is off to a gay lib meeting and refers to Dad's Army's Frank Williams as 'Maurice'), police corruption (Chapman believes he doesn't need a reason to charge the convict and Jones quickly hushes him up as the cameras are on him) and police brutality (with Palin's manic PC PanAm bashing people about the head, playing with his truncheon, 'Oh, Yes!', and cracking up as Chapman momentarily reacts to the audience).
Everything is performed like a show, with the real seriousness of the issue as nothing to the public persona of those involved – even Palin's lowly, numb-skulled copper embraces the ideal with his thank yous and magician's twist – 'for my next piece

of evidence'. It's guest player Frank Williams who breaks off this sketch, looking deep into Gilliam's impression of inside the bandaged bloke (with Palin's detective still crawling around inside) and forging into Idle's sex obsessed Stock Market reporter, a fore-runner to show 3's Money Programme, and seeing his burst of inspired gibberish curtailed by a bucket of water from Gilliam's pepperpot creation. This old shopping lady, whisked away in a Doctor Who-like time scoop and booted out into the town centre, leads into the classic Cleese/Chapman peppers exchange with sadistic treatment of a newly dead cat and Graham's wonderfully sick treatment of a disliked budgie, breaking into a squawking rant about mutation birds terrorising the sewers and linking back to Gilliam's link with greeting for a full sized Mrs. Cut-Out who shuffles by. A typically high octane discussion on Sartre and the question of freedom breaks out in the laundrette with Cleese, having met the French couple on holiday, deciding to phone them up. Python's insane logic is shown in definitive terms when the hunt for a Paris phone directory initially comes up with one for Budapest – as though this is perfectly normal in a British laundrette. There's another name check for North Malden with Idle's Whicker-like host, another drag through the Njorl's Saga credits for a brief pepperpot invasion of Iceland (the show was due to end with Jones' horse receiving a custard pie in the face) before Parisian clichés, organ music, tarts and striped shirts, identity the correct destination. Palin, the usual fag-out-of-the-mouth British pepperpot, introduces the family goat who keeps the excess pamphlets in order by eating them and a well gone, unseen philosopher's agreement with Cleese puts another Python show to bed, quickly rounded off with the masterpiece, Whicker's Island. The impressionist's dream, Alan Whicker's intonations, glasses and ever ready microphone is mocked by Idle, Cleese, Chapman, Jones and Palin in a never ending, crossing-over of earnest interviewers, hanging

round the pool, sipping drinks and chatting to the only person left to chat too, Chapman's very Whickeresque Vicar. Sheer madness in the best Python tradition this very short, very funny moment ranks with the best of series three material.

Series 3 episode I *Whicker's World* was conceived, written and performed by **Alan Whicker John Cleese, Whicker Graham Whicker Chapman, Alan Michael Palin Whicker, Eric Whicker Whicker Idle, Terry Whicker Jones, Terry Alan Gilliam**
Also appearing **Alan Whicker, Mrs. Idle, Connie Whicker Booth, Rita Whicker Davies, Nigel Whicker Jones, Frank Williams** as the Boy Whicker
Make up **Alan Whicker & Madelaine Gaffney**
Alan Whicker costumes **Hazel Pethig**
Animations by **Terry Whicker Gilliam**
Mr. Whicker kindly photographed on film by **Alan Featherstone**
Edited on film by **Ray Millichope**
Mr. Whicker's sound by **Alan Whicker, Alan Whicker & Richard Chubb**
Mr. Whicker was entirely lit by **Jimmy Purdie** (assisted by Alan Whicker)
Mr. Whicker was designed by **Robert Berk**
Produced and directed by **Alan Whicker Oh, & Ian MacNaughton**
A BBC Whicker Colour Production
19 October 1972

EPISODE 2

Hard on the heels of The Kon-Tiki Ra 1 & Ra 2 is the long awaited tale of Mr. and Mrs. Brian Norris's Ford Popular, with the suburban pair of Palin and Chapman grinning with inane glee as the theory of ancient Hounslow to Surbiton emigration is discussed! Python took the idea to glorious extremes again with Idle's narration pinpointing the final clinching piece of evidence with the compatible betta-cutta lawn mowers, leading to a major expedition seen off by one small boy with a Union Jack and recorded with surreal Palin banality in diary form. Chapman's photographic record and sandwich making keeps up morale until the discovery of the Kingston By-Pass, journeying along that 'silvery turd' the Thames and magically hitting on the notion of taking the 3.47 train via Clapham. He plants his flag and reverses his notion to become immortalised as Wrong-way Norris. The usual beginning combination of Jones, Cleese, Palin and titles ushers in ultra-talented school-boys Idle, Jones and Gilliam, desperately trying to keep their high flying skills from the notice of dogged headmaster Palin, frowning on this amazing extra curriculum activity resulting in feats of medical genius, obviously picked up from that hugely popular children's television show *How To Do It?* (and nothing to do with *Blue Peter* at all).

For me, this is one of the most effective and enjoyable *Python* television parodies ever, done with total affection with the perfect 'Hello Alan, Hello Jackie!' exchanges capturing the Peter Purves/Valerie Singleton era for an entire generation. Chapman, holding on to the obligatory *BP* pet, Cleese and Idle (in drag again) promise major advances in world peace and musical prowess, taken to heights of sheer comic bliss with John's sincere cheesy grin and 'Thanks Jackie – Great idea!' It's spot-on stuff and done totally without malice while, followed with Cleese's baby treatment as Minister for Overseas Development, these few minutes of pure *Python* are priceless. The ultimate comment on all the team's middle-class mothers, Cleese clearly exorcises a few demons here, aided and abetted by Jones as his mum and a sublime piece of racist coyness in Palin's Mrs. Nigger-Baiter, a name summing up the repressed angst behind the friendly irritation. Human life is considered worthless, friendship counts for nothing – this is the mother as seen through *Python* eyes. Therapeutic or what!

Idle's new vicar, trying to flog brushes and encyclopaedias with a continual 'I'm not religious', proves a useful diversion before Chapman (with medical hat on once more) rips into the disastrous healing properties of dynamite with Idle's man of God. Unable to break the doc's concentration as he details the failure of his work (84 dead), and a quick jibe at traditionalist, family-geared humour

('people laughed at Bob Hope') it's saved from wringing out the gag into nothing by Gilliam's inspired animation of a human body chart, fed up of being prodded and walking off the edge of the filmic image. By this stage, even the link was becoming conventional, shown to be exactly that and proved to be ineffective. Gilliam grabs a rare chance of on-screen stardom (albeit short-lived) as the classical musical expert almost interviewed by Eric Idle for Farming Club, quickly booted out only to see the programme utilise his knowledge with The Life of Peter Ilytch Tschaikovsky and a debate whether he was a genius or 'just an old poof who wrote tunes' – ideas covered in the BBC publication *Hello Pianist*. Cleese runs through homosexual terminology, embraces knowledge with the idea that the great composer was born in a Ken Russell movie and hands over to Palin's overtly camp speaker (Maurice, music critic and hairdresser) for some effeminate ideals. Chapman's earnest expert, obsessed with size in relation to other things, points out the composer was much smaller than Nelson's Column while Terry Jones, as Robin the frantic guest, details the great man through his scale model complete with naughty bits via intertextuality to series one. It's back to Palin camp before a Harry Houdiniesque attempt to play Tschaikovsky while escaping from a sack, with Carol Cleveland's ever reliable Rita in attendance. Onwards and upwards to Trim-Jeans Theatre, a rather laboured idea, trying to recapture the magic of Bruce with Palin, Idle and dragged-up Chapman putting on the Oz for their terrific product, weight-reducing via amateur dramatics. A typically *Python* idea but the playing lacks conviction and the writing quickly runs out of steam as Jones, before and after, highlights the results, Chekhov's work is employed, Gielgud and Richardson 'thespian off' the pounds and The Great Escape, utilizing an effective genuine musical bridge, illustrates major weight lost of the cast. Gilliam's smooth host, fighting a battle between his hippie,

thought-provoking mouth and lavish, shallow, showbiz brain, finally nails his disobedient lips to his face in order to introduce the Fish Slapping. It's a bare 20 seconds, with Palin's small attack countered with Cleese's huge clout into the water, but not only has this priceless visual remained one of *Python*'s most cherished moments it also summed up almost entirely what the US consider Britcom to be! Gilliam's animation quickly ties up the loose ends with an extension of World War II played out beneath the sea, with a Nazi fish swallowed by a bigger British ship (all walrus moustache and 'Fritz!' chat) before an even larger Japanese fish finishes the thing and leads to stock sinking ship footage and Terry Jones, as the Captain, orchestrating the rescue of his staff by continually amending his 'women and children first' to include any costumes his lads find (Red Indians/Spacemen and Idle's confused mix of 15th-century merchant and Renaissance man). Another unjustly ignored *Python* gem, the aftermath of rescue, with Cleese's swarthy South American mercenary, hardly gets going before the BBC financial plight is mentioned, extras talking up the cost of programme making, the stunt rings up another twenty guineas and Idle's continuity announcer, naked from the waist up and reading by candle light, hastily denies the rumours of BBC budget collapse. The Cleese interrogation begins again but the Republic atmosphere is distilled by *Puss in Boots* thigh-slapping, audience participation, trouser-vanishing and irrelevant flashback visual wobbles with no money for the sequence (quickly filled in by an energetic Jones with tales of weird creatures and bravery). But it's no good, the set removers break into his desperation, Palin's Irish pepperpot and her husband (Chapman) find The Horse of the Year Show taking place in their kitchen and Idle closes the whole show down with a simple 'That's all!' Discarded scraps of paper herald the credits. But it's not quite all over, someone's turned over to ITV and yes, my word, that's a fab, cool, bearded Ringo

Starr, alongside a flirting, eyelash fluttering Lulu, all for the It's Man interview show. Palin's half-forgotten BBC employee, in usual tatted suit, sheepishly wanders out, greets his audience with a hello, good evening and welcome, finally back in the television limelight before, shock horror, he says the dreaded word It's, signalling the pale *Python* titles to run over the image as Lulu wanders off and Ringo goes for it with a peeved look, quick exit, dragged back recovery and fisticuffs with the ragged host. That's *Python* clout for you...

Did You Know?
For the final anti-chat show, hosted by Palin's It's Man, the original script called for 'four extraordinarily famous guests' and the Pythons were desperate to get the first television reunion of The Beatles. Realistically, the team tried to secure John Lennon and Yoko Ono as the surprise guests but ultimately Graham Chapman, who had become friendly with Ringo Starr during *The Magic Christian* days, managed to tempt the fab's drummer into *Python* legend. Priceless stuff.

Series 3 episode II conceived, written & performed by **Graham Chapman, John Cleese, Eric Idle, Terry Jones, Michael Palin & Terry Gilliam**. Also appearing **Julia Brecks**
Animations by **Terry Gilliam**
Research **Suzan Davies**
Make up **Madelaine Gaffney**
Costumes **Hazel Pethig**
Visual effects designer **Bernard Wilkie**
Film cameraman **Alan Featherstone**
Editor **Ray Millichope**
Sound **Richard Chubb**
Lighting **Jimmy Purdie**
Designer **Robert Berk**
Produced & directed by **Ian MacNaughton**
25 October 1972

EPISODE 3
With credits for *The Money Show* and Eric Idle's straight-laced introduction, this quickly soars into classic *Python* mode with obsessions based round cash and the peerless *Money Song*, celebrating Idle's insane love with an order to forget your

Marxist ways. It's one of the classic opening moments and with a quick flash of Terry Jones's nude organist, Cleese's announcer and Palin's It's Man it's headlong into the official *Python* credits. The Elizabeth I drama with speech impediments and scooters is totally mad, but Chapman is spell-binding as the Queen and Terry Jones, staggering onto the set, is unforgettably bizarre as the oriental Visconte impostor. Cue Cleese, in definitive thick-skulled detective mode, establishing the running link for the show of the Special Forged Film Directors Squad. With Gilliam in assistance, Cleese rattles off a potted history of the film-maker's great works, giving special mention to the impeccable Dirk Bogarde and celebrating the efficiency of good old Nazi Germany. The scene, momentarily curtailed for a bit of Gilliam cops and robbers animation, phases into the classic Cleese/Chapman Church Police sketch with Idle's jug-fish menu, rat-oriented deserts and a deceased Bishop on the landing. Chapman's schoolboy is perfectly breathless and eager to inform but it's Palin's Hitleresque copper with a croak that steals the scene. Gilliam's hand of divinity breaks into the real sketch world and links to some stunning Edwardian space-hopper material before Idle, Cleese, Chapman and Cleveland machete their way through some Edgar Rice Burroughs jungle vines into a little bit of British sophistication in the middle of the dark continent. Sort of like *Carry On Up the Jungle* with A levels, Palin's blacked-up restaurant owner battles the elements and his plucky British clientele is dragged off by a bloke in a gorilla suit. His shocked close-up is too much for the Beeb's sensibilities and our gaze is cut to scenes of orgy and blokes in animal costumes in Ken Russell's *Garden Party* before the lesser of two evils takes us back to Cleese in the jungle.
Terry Jones has a classic moment as a native chappie who struggles to find his line in the script and this obviously promising idea is extended with Jones (now proudly donning a 'Our Hero' badge) desperately trying

to get the lines from a brain-addled Palin. The emphasis is all wrong, he reads stage directions, and, in the masterstroke, he gives a brilliant performance just a bit too early and finally loses the dramatic edge for a bland reading of the line. A case of Python labouring a point to perfection. But back in the jungle, Cleese tosses in a misunderstood great expedition reference (complete with photo snapshot of the Great Exhibition!), the very nature of filmed stuff is questioned to reveal a camera crew and Cleese's gobsmacked reaction to the camera crew being filmed reveals yet another camera crew. Ending in glorious disarray, Idle wanders through a handy door in the middle of nowhere to arrest the supposed director Michelangelo Antonioni, lapsing into a potted cinematic history of the great man's works over the closing credits.
But wait, your watch isn't wrong, there's another six minutes of *Python* to come and what a six minutes... One of the all-time great comedy moments, the legendary Argument sketch. It's passed into our nation's collective consciousness but however many times you see Chapman's vicious torrent of abuse, Cleese at his most petulantly determined and Palin gradually getting more and more frustrated it just cannot possibly fail to make you laugh. You eat, you sleep you convulse at the argument sketch. That's it. The concept is pure *Python*, brilliantly twisting the everyday conventions of office terminology and surreally shifting them upside-down and round about. Resurrected many times since, this is the definitive rendition with Idle's complaints bloke, Jones banging people on the head and Idle's light entertainment squad chap bursting in to arrest the team for doing exactly what he's just done. As Palin moans at one time, 'What a stupid concept', but it works every time and sadly the extra minute of *Python* promised never comes.

Series 3 episode III conceived, written & performed by **Graham Chapman, John Cleese, Eric Idle, Terry Jones, Michael Palin & Terry Gilliam**. Also appearing

Rita Davies
Carol Cleveland
The Fred Tomlinson Singers
Animations by **Terry Gilliam**
Research **Suzan Davies**
Make up **Madelaine Gaffney**
Costumes **Hazel Pethig**
Silly extra music by **John Gould**
Film cameraman **Alan Featherstone**
Editor **Ray Millichope**
Sound **Richard Chubb**
Lighting **Jimmy Purdie**
Designer **Robert Berk**
Produced & directed by **Ian MacNaughton**
31 October 1972

EPISODE 4

Vintage footage heralding blood, death, devastion, war and horror like a trailer for the next coming attraction does, indeed, lead into such a titled programme with affable Michael Palin as host and a *Call My Bluff*-like jingle setting the scene for Eric Idle's earnest Shakespeare anagramist. A typical Idle sketch, using words to weave nonsensical pictures which Palin easily makes sense of, this is a sort of *Python* meets Ronnie Barker piece with *Hamlet* and *Richard III* retold in anagram form before, Palin the pedant highlights that really Idle's last utterance was a spoonerism. With a disgruntled response, the elongated introduction of Jones the organist, Cleese the announcer and Palin the It's links to the opening credits.

The anagram gag runs throughout the programme, with Terry Jones's pepperpot in a 'beat the clock' spot rearranging the jumble of words to form the intro to the Merchant Banker sketch (an idea which invades the sketch itself with Cleese's profession name block appearing as an anagram). A slimy, money-obsessed Cleese authority figure, with a chart depicting How Rich I Am on the wall, this is one of those unsung *Python* masterpieces, with the definitive Sellers-like little man characterisation of Terry Jones desperately trying to get some money for the orphans and explaining the foreign concept of charity. Forgetting his name for the moment, injecting

Nazi-references into his babble and struggling with the notion of happiness, Cleese's reaction to Jones' sheepish comment 'You're a rich man!' brings on a priceless torrent of agreement and the ever widening gap between kindness and meanness is peerlessly brought to life by the two – with Jones pleading for the pound and Cleese believing the offered flag a bit small for a share's certificate. The penny dropping, but with Cleese only grasping the financial gain wheeze of charity, lends the comedy a gloriously cynical, dark edge. With the trap door replacing the usual 16-ton weight (which turns up later), a quick word from Viking Palin and Cleese embracing *I'm Sorry I'll Read That Again* mannerisms with 'Shut up!', the repeated musical fanfare for a couple of pantomime horses allows the sketch to step beyond madness, with panto convention of foot banging for horse language to be juxtaposed with carnage as the two beasts wage a life and death struggle merely to claim the one job position for bank pantomime horse.

The life and death motif goes into over-drive with Cleese's mock documentary narration of tinted sea lion footage, uninteresting limpet attacks (complete with inappropriate sinister music), a still shot of an ant attack on a wolf, with misleading action-packed voice-over/white arrow pinpointing the non-event, a clever piece of bawling between various television naturalists and finally, full circle to panto land with a goose killing Terence Rattigan. The theme is taken to extreme with the manic, top-heavy Panto Princess Margaret, hilariously tracking down a silver tray of breakfast before Gilliam puts the comedy out of its misery by animating the shooting of the narrator.

The killer house concept (familiar from series two's killer cars) tackles similar grand with B-movie sci-fi nervousness as these inanimate objects devour mankind – the grizzled American House-Hunters, track down, label them for destruction and allow NCP car parks to claim one parking spot, used for a score of vehicles, one on top of the

other. The toilet visit behind a clump of trees is a clever touch but the team are clearly repeating themselves by now, merging into another Chapman attack on the military with Mary (Army) recruitment Officer continuing the anagram theme (as well as allowing a nice nun sight gag) as Idle applies for the position in a comedy sketch and enjoys an effeminate diatribe with the main force's man. After initial disbelief, Chapman throws himself into this line of enquiry, plugging the various units before enthusing wildly about the colour continuity of the Durham Light Infinity – his impassioned 'This is Good. This is Real!' steals the show. But the real treat within the sketch is that, just as you forget Idle was an actor after a job, the actor reminds you, complaining about the size of his part and detailing his wealth of dialogue as 'Really, really, I see and really!' Ever happy to oblige, Chapman changes the scene to a bus, again hogging the limelight and getting laughs with a glorious string of bottom of the barrel, music hall one-liners – the potty gag, leaks, singing *It's Not Unusual* and embracing Max Miller-like patter with a joyous 'all in here tonight!' Wonderfully over-the-top, it's a real treat to see Chapman step out of uniform and really go for the consciously manic attitude with relish. On film, Jones the standard boring accountant repeats a failed bus fare purchasing gag-line to comic effect, utters 'good morning!' and simply walks past people much to everyone's uncontrolled hilarity. Idle is still complaining as Chapman's slapstick clown antics bring on huge laughs as the red-nosed figure assures his stooge that it's his white-washed jacket, custard-pie-smeared face and fish-adorned trousers that is the real funny thing. Chapman addresses the entire concept of knockabout comedy before we enter The Bols Family and Palin's pontificator (backed with the question – Is the Queen sane?) going well over the top with flamboyant hand movements to indicate a pause between spoken words, castigating The End credit coming up, desperately trying to stop his tv viewer from nipping into the kitchen and basically playing the comedy like a Ronnie Barker monologue. Idle's swift globe interruption keeps the laughs coming as Cleese's manic depression voice-over guy staggers back into the limelight (with help from supportive wife, Cleveland and good pal, Palin) explaining the hard times and confidence-sapping tough breaks he's suffered. Finally getting through the announcement, Richard Baker's reading of the news is masked by off-camera celebrations of Cleese's feat with the respected BBC frontman latching onto Palin's earlier arm movements for pauses, injecting even more outrageous actions and ultimately, enjoying the tail end of his broadcast with sound. Baker tosses in another obscure reference to Mauldlin and continues the running anagram obsession of the show with his introduction to the late night film. Cue James Bond-like credits from Gilliam, brilliant use of the red and black design, and Terry Jones, in shocked still photography ready to fully embrace Bondian convention to usher in the rather tedious action adventures of a pantomime horse – although it's interesting to see *Carry On* master Talbot Rothwell tongue-in-cheekily listed as writer (alongside Mireille Mathieu). Incorporating the Dick Barton theme and throwing in all the panto figures from the earlier sketch (including the Princess Margaret) it all gets a bit manic but there's some grand touches – with the panto Russian/British horses riding real horses (quite bizarre) the appearance of Idle's Upper class twit and, best of all, Carol Cleveland's seductive Bond girl crying with joy 'I'm so bleeding happy!' Priceless stuff. Cleese adds extra Upper Class weight to the fun with his mock Sports commentary and finally lapses into doco tones for a beautifully self-deprecating moment condemning the madness as English comic actors in a life and death struggle against a rather weak ending. Peerless get-out ploy!

Series 3 episode IV Tony M. Nyphot's Flying Risccu saw codvenice, twitner dna fordeperm yb **Hamrag Rachman John Ecles Rice Lied**

Torn Jersey (5.5) Michael Lapin
Marty Rigelli
Sola gearappin **Carol Cleveland**
Atchseer yb **Suzan Davies**
Kame pu **Madelaine Gaffney**
Mutesocs **Hazel Pethig**
Mainations yb **Terry Gilliam**
Cuffs Laviseet **Bernard Wilkie**
Pishcarg **Bob Blagden**
Male Fancimarm **Alan Featherstone**
Mole Trifid **Ray Millichope**
Dosun **Richard Chubb**
Lightgin **Jimmy Purdie**
Redensig **Ian Watson**
Decodurp yb **Ian MacNaughton**
BCB LURCOO ETH NED
6 November 1972

EPISODE 5

One of the best series three efforts, this gem of a show kicks off with the immortal Proust sketch from Jones/Palin. Heralded by Fringe heroes Alan Bennett and Jonathan Miller as highlighting the intellectualism of *Python*, it's really just taking university pretensions and relating them via Miss World beauty contest conventions – we are promised contestants in both swimsuit and evening wear mood. In fact, the entire concept is anti-highbrow with the girl with the biggest tits winning and ushering in the *Python* closing credits five minutes into the show! The actual task at hand is impossible (that's the joke) although Chapman does cover most of the main points of *A La Recherche du Temps Perdu* in the allotted 15 seconds, earnestly giving an overall appraisal of the book before lurching into chapter detail as the buzzer goes. Palin's wonderfully inapt contestant desperately trying to get started but failing miserably ('Big bloke...'), The Fred's choral effort going all round the houses in perfect harmony but with no time to get started ('Proust, in his first book wrote about, wrote about...!' etc), a cricket top-heavy line-up of judges and Terry Jones, given a rare chance to put on the glitzy host persona instead of Palin or Idle, all enhance this deliciously manic piece of comedy but it's Chapman's nervous, stooping chap who walks away with the honours.

Indeed, at the time, this section was the source of BBC outrage with his listed hobbies as golf, strangling animals and masturbation. The BBC blanked out the offending word so the gag was only apparent to studio audience members and lip-reading television viewers, thus the huge laugh reaction the word received lost its meaning to most – and worst still, Idle's petulant golf observation completely floundered without Chapman's outrageous comment. Thankfully, the uncensored version was screened during 1979's tenth anniversary celebration season and in subsequent repeats. Palin's breast-fixated announcer goes on about Mount Everest, gets ticked off, starts again and gets the wave of madness from the slightly eerie clown figure. The international hairdressing expedition goes on a bit, incorporating fairly obvious camp moments from Idle and Chapman, a splendid Gilliam advert for Ricky Pule's Saloon (interestingly tackling cinematic marketing targets and allowing Jones/Cleveland to provide words for Anton Walbrook and Diana Wynyard cut-outs from *Gaslight* to trial the up-coming, same-sounding, Oh James/Oh Beatrice, Fool over you movie à la *Brief Encounter*), a silent Cleese under the dryer and a priceless reaction to his cup of tea served by Palin.

It's back to class stuff with Jones in definitive mother mode, telephoning Palin's disgruntled fireman who insists it's a wrong number. Jones and her son, a wonderfully numbskull Cleese, desperately try to keep their pet hamster alive to no avail (its little eyes just close and a copy of *The Charlie George Football Book* is its only funeral shroud). If all this wasn't enough, Chapman's hilarious Zulu brother turns up in full tribal gear rabbiting on about his exploits in Dublin ('Tings are pretty bad!') and getting embroiled in the insistent telephone enquiries about shoe sizes. Cleese's bellowed 'Right out!' is worth its volume in gold alongside Palin's smartly turned out announcer (note the bizarre hand in the flower arrangement) before it's back to

Cleese, Jones, Chapman and the socialising fire brigade, talking in unison, indulging in some sherry, getting Graham's Dublin diatribe and continuing the shoe size running gag. Jones, stepping out of the context of the spiralling comedy, addresses the television audience to introduce Eric Idle's Veronica Small and super Party Hints concerning dealing with communist up-rising and the like. A bit of door-to-door, Gilliam's reds under the beds business, clockwork statesmen and puking guts up, leads to the almighty telephone exchange sketch with Chapman leading insignificant Cleese around his team of vocal stereotypes, be it Jones as the waffling, contradictory, cover your back politician, Idle's controversial South African ('Kill the blacks!'), Palin's glorious Northern chap ('Can you smell gas or is it me') and Gilliam camping it up like a good 'un, brilliantly lapsing into colourless mode while accepting thanks for his work.

But it's Chapman's joyous run through various vocal characterisations, notably the whining Clive Jenkins and the Miller/Idle-like wise-cracker, all gags and cheeky smiles, that dominates here. The priceless Sandy Wilson version of *The Devils*, with the telephone boys going into Busby Berkeley country, is a flawless surge of ideas, while the lapse into Proust singing and a call to start again effortlessly flips back to the Mount Everest focal point, linking into the classic Bounder of Adventure (Palin) confrontation with Idle's unaware Mr. Smoke Toomuch. Carol's saucy offer of a trip upstairs has Idle shocked, Palin's old joke about his name gets the same reaction and the difficulty with letter c/ease with letter k problem highlights Idle is more than a tad odd. A masterpiece of train-of-thought insanity (actually written by Chapman/Cleese but performed by Idle because he was the only one who didn't mind learning it!) the travel customer from hell goes on and on about clichéd problematic situations on package tours (badly made tea, dodgy Manuel waiters, postcard with our room marked with

an X, greasy food, bleedin' Whatney's Red Barrel, singing Torremalinos et al) with Idle getting the laughs as Palin, brilliantly supporting the performance with just a few interjected phrases, adds to the magnitude of the piece with quiet, inane smiling breaking into manic outrage with a screamed 'Shut your bloody gob!' and a phone call to the police. Just when you thought there couldn't do another self-referential U-turn, Palin's phone conversation leads to his shoe size being asked for and Carol steps out of the sketch to lead us away from the still rabbiting Idle and onto the waiting set of *Thrust* – a television discussion programme hosted by bemused Chapman and welcoming guest talker Cleese as coughing, mumbling, Nina Mouscuri-lookalike Anne Elk. The world-shattering Brontosaurus theory, finally blurted out by Cleese, after some glorious round-the-houses chat with a suitably worried looking host, results in Chapman's gobsmacked 'That's it, is it!' and the simple insanity of the situation (a delightful uncluttered, nonsensical completely irrelevant slice of *Python*) embraces all the recurring themes of the show (both Chapman and Cleveland's receptionist grabbed into the shoe size phone quest, Cleese throat-clearing, an order to start again, the waving clown, a Proust singalong) and culminates in anarchic team action. Arguably the pick of series three and you'll get no argument from me!

Series 3 episode V– The All England Summarised Proust Competition
A BBC co-production with Mr. LT. Briddock 2379, The Terrace, Hoddesdon
Conceived, written and performed by **Graham Chapman, John Cleese, Eric Idle, Terry Jones, Michael Palin and Terry Gilliam.**
Also appearing **Carol Cleveland & The Fred Tomlinson Singers**
Research **Patricia Houlihan**
Make up **Madelaine Gaffney**
Costumes **Hazel Pethig**
Animations **Terry Gilliam**
Graphics **Bob Blagden**
Film cameraman **Alan Featherstone**

Film editor **Ray Millichope**
Sound **Richard Chubb**
Lighting **Bill Bailey**
Designer **Robert Berk**
Produced & directed by **Ian MacNaughton**
13 November 1972

EPISODE 6

With vintage Edward Heath footage and black and white material of the lads in pepperpot mode, tackling wartime unity, beating the put-upon men at their own game, looking down on those nasty foreigners and waging war on the pornographic grip on art – cleaning up *Othello* and clothing naked sculptures – this is filmed in delicious mock 1940s newsreel style with a glorious sense of xenophobic narration juxtaposed with 1973 clear-up anarchy with Mary Whitehouse iconology. It's headlong into the trio of familiar intros from Jones, Cleese and Palin before Gilliam's animation merges into the Gumby decampment at Harley Street. Both patient (Palin) and doctor (Cleese) complain of hurting brains and Palin's initial attack on the office, screaming for medical authority and bashing his way through Cleese's desk like an uncontrolled child, is unsung *Python* genius at full volume.

One of Palin's most cherished series moments he is clearly breaking up as Cleese looks for his brain problem down his trousers and Palin splutters 'in my head!' as if there's more than one in your average Gumby. A specialist is clearly needed and with reassuring burst of the *Dr. Kildare* theme who else is called on but Graham Chapman, looking every inch the sophisticated surgeon before he asks for moustache and the like from his nurse and slowly builds up his costume to transmogrify into another Gumby. A masterly feat of performance, not originally in the script, which eventually leads to Palin on the operating table surrounded by all the Pythons and others, mugging on with Gumby mannerisms. Palin provides the vocals for Gilliam's pompous, authority chappie trying to waffle on about the meaning of life but finding the television image upside down, only covering half the scene, becoming a tiny space in the middle of the set or vanishing completely as unhelpful adjustments are made – it's a stunning running commentary on the construction of image but before long it's into the joys of the Essex Badminton Championships, watched by Chapman in drag and leading to the smashing of the set by her ballroom dance partner, Jones, allowing Cleese, jobless television announcer and travelling wildlife documentary host, to perform in the comfort of the couple's home. Consciously groaning at the old man with a moustache gag, Jones and Chapman are equally dissatisfied with this unrivetting monologue, complaining about the nerve to put it on, struggling to turn this rubbish off, facing the invasion of television convention into the home and, like the entire population, settling down to interested, albeit rather disgusted, viewing once the subject of sex is approached. Its initial interaction with his audience, pleas for a second chance as it's not much of a subject and gloriously full-bodied energy as he describes this randy seafood as whores, homosexuals and making Fanny Hill look like a dead pope. Highlighting the rampant homophobia of Mr. and Mrs. Average Britain with their outraged stamping, breaking down the boundaries of television's power to address its audience (the polite handshake between host and viewer is masterly) and, above all, damn funny stuff from the team, this is a real series three gem, highlighting that when the right material was at hand, even the ever increasingly disgruntled Cleese could still spin the old magic. There's Terry Jones as link man, Chapman's briefly seen man in the street and some choice Gilliam baby animation, as a removed dummy results in the goo-goo waffling family unit sucked into oblivion, while more nonsensical waffling is promised by Michael Palin's host outlining the latest, newsworthy happenings of various manic parliamentarians, including the kick-starting Minister for Not Listening to People.

Not happy with having ripped apart television convention for all time, now the Pythons cross-fade and merge typical clichés to form a train of comic consciousness with Palin fading into the classical serial, lapsing in the Tuesday documentary in a hand-over to Idle's Whicker-like presenter with financial figures to embrace children's storytime and Gilliam's adventures of Porky the Pig. The style seemingly reverts to the Tuesday documentary although the change is only fleeting and the ever-faithful BBC caption proclaims that 'No it hasn't' before Terry Jones, in a sublime piece of performance, runs through a party political broadcast in religious thought mode and then into *Python* footballing footage for a cross between *Match of the Day* and the romantic movie – all slow motion and snogathons. The typical Jones/Palin plan across beautiful landscape moment is enhanced by Idle's polite apology to politicians with nicely put sorrys merging into acid-dripping condemnations all in the name of making amends for any offence the earlier, much more innocent insanity-drenched, stuff may have caused.

The pretext for all this scrolling monologue is the naval expedition discussed for television by Cleese's roving reporter and involving a load of slightly effeminate chaps all bearing names of 1940s Hollywood glam stars, witness Palin's wonderful Player's cigarette-clichéd sailor, Sir Jane Russell and Idle, going for the full with-it, swinging sixties, 'hey man' attitude as Dorothy Lamour. Cleese himself, affected by this *Python* madness, slowly changes into Long John Silver with each cut-away resulting in another familiar Newtonesque element (be it parrot, patch, 'Jim Lads' or peg leg – the whole transformation is brilliantly started with a seemingly impromptu cry of pain as the leg begins to turn!). Jones, the BBC replacement for the obviously crackers Cleese, takes over, leads into serious praise for the Royal Navy (incorporating a priceless psychedelic Gilliam advert) and chats with Graham Chapman's personification of upright authority.

It's hardly fresh by series three, but there still wasn't anybody quite so cool at debunking military pretensions as Chapman and his promise that 'there is no cannibalism in the Navy and when I say that there is some' is simply perfection. As if proof were needed, various minions are seen chomping on dismembered legs, much to Graham's annoyance and leading to a classic camera blocking moment.

Although the wackiness is removed from the naval figures, the mission is hardly devoid of wackiness itself, with Chapman searching out a lake in the middle of 22 Runcorn Avenue much to the shock of Palin and diverted by his wife – Idle – to the basement apartment. There we see Jones and Palin (equipped with aqua lungs) sitting quietly in their living room, under water, complaining about the bleeding damp and the bloody sharks, communicating by signs and leading to Jones giving the naval officials a disconcerting two-finger salute.

That's the end of all that madness as Cleese introduces Eric Idle's Mr. Badger to discuss the *Magna Carta*. This boring Scot gives his answer in mime and a shell-shocked Cleese speaks for a nation when he condemns him as the silliest man he has ever met but doesn't hide his strange fascination as he invites him to dinner. Complete with finger-up-nose grossness and obsession with whiskey, Palin's waiter reacts to his wasted part and the banality of the material through pinpointed clenched teeth. Cleese suggests this is the silliest sketch he's ever been in, the other two seem in total agreement and thus they decide to stop it. This is, after all, *Monty Python* and they can do that sort of thing – see you next week suckers...

Series 3 episode VI – conceived, written and performed by **Graham Chapman, John Cleese, Eric Idle, Terry Jones, Michael Palin & Terry Gilliam**
Also appearing **Mrs. Idle**
Make up **Madelaine Gaffney**
Costumes **Hazel Pethig**
Animation **Terry Gilliam**
Visual effects designer **Bernard Wilkie**

Film cameraman **Alan Featherstone**
Film editor **Ray Millichope**
Sound **John Delany**
Lighting **Jimmy Purdie**
Designer **Ian Watson**
Produced & directed by **Ian MacNaughton**
20 November 1972

EPISODE 7

Audience expectations are quashed with the unique appearance of Terry Jones the organist fully clothed, quietly creeping onto stage, sitting down to play and immediately having his clothes whipped off on the first note, only to be joined by naked quartet members Chapman, Idle and Cleese before the usual credits roll. The Adventures of Biggles, a favourite of Chapman's, sees him adopt a leather flying helmet and healthy anti-homosexual attitude as he tries to dictate a letter to his seductive secretary. Everything gets a bit out of hand with misunderstandings, brutal killing of Palin's effeminate Algy, uneasy acceptance of Gilliam's even more effeminate, homo-denying Ginger, totally irrelevant diatribes about Chapman's Spanish connections and a belated appearance of Cleese's pantomime Princess Margaret. Allowing this 'demented fictional character' to run amuck, Chapman addresses the hidden sexuality behind the celebrated adventure stories while perversely questioning his own sexuality via the homophobic figure of English heroics. However, following Chapman's Lemon Curry interlude, Cleese setting up the forthcoming attraction, Biggles Flies Undone, and Gilliam's aerobatic animation including the collapse of the city of London and a throwback to series 1, episode 1's flying sheep, it's onto the totally illogical and strained mountaineering venture up the North face of the Uxbridge Road, with Idle's earnest climber and Chapman (quite splendid as the matter-of-fact headmaster and mother of three, Bert). The idea is a quickly realised, quickly defunct one (indeed, Cleese's interviewer encapsulates *Python* in an instant with his observation that all this is

crazy) and with speeded-up camera work the expedition tumbles out of sight as Palin's Viking latches onto the lemon curry question. The typical Jones/Palin juxtaposition of normalities has Terry in drag stuffing his chicken while Mike staggers in from a hard day's work on his lifeboat. The meeting of suburban niceties and heroic dangers disperses to allow yellow-coated Palin/Chapman machos a discussion on business and sip tea as Terry's housewife of 24 Parker Street braves the open sea to pick up a batch of cakes from Chapman's floating tea shop. There is an interaction with Cleese/Idle playing pepperpots on ocean-bound surveillance and an embracing of visual madness as Palin's seadog takes off his tray and jumps into the sea. Stirring television design and the music heralds Eric Idle's stony-faced presentation of Storage Jars which basically belittles historical importance in favour of glass containers, heightened by Terry Jones's haggard report from war-torn Bolivia. Gilliam's celebrated television viewer, Henry, the mechanical destruction of his eyes and Palin's nagging wife tag-line is elongated to include the animated chap's setting up of the next segment, The Show So Far.... which culminates with a slightly suspect programme controller fairy, the sudden transformation of Henry into frog and a nervy Terry Jones recapping on the totally disconnected, totally manic *Python* experience so far. Delivered with no comic emotion, self-aware nervousness and a sense of laying bare the bones of *Python* to discover nothing funny merely completely stupid. Going beyond what's been before him to herald what is yet to come, Jones sets up his own hammer head-banging exit, Palin's It's gets in on the lemon curry act and a quick succession of investigative reporter snapshots of Cleese leads into one of series three's greatest moments, the immortal Cheese Shop.
Stripped of its genius this is very much *Python* by numbers, with Cleese, in definitive mode, putting on the flamboyant superlatives and

running through a connected list of diary pleasures. Lacking this magical spiralling of the themes of death from the parrot, which this reunion between customer Cleese and shop assistant Palin clearly tries to emulate, the Cheese Shop remains the perfect example of Cleese's logical train of manic consciousness, getting more and more frustrated with the lack of named cheeses as the bazooka playing/dancing of businessmen Chapman and Idle go on relentlessly. Basically the point of the sketch is a total waste of time, ending in the clichéd *Python* result of a gun shot and Cleese's sardonic comment into camera. All this cheese madness with its throwaway Clint Eastwood closure is made relevant by a sweeping Western landscape, Idle's over-enthused cinema critic, backed by silent icons The Keystone Kops while waffling on about the sainted Cheese Western moment and further twisting the convention with the infamous Sam Peckinpah version of *Salad Days*.
It is rare, so late in *Python* history, to get a concentrated ten minutes of recognised classic material and this brilliantly realised cinematic parody works so well thanks to Palin's typically jolly persona, the darling young things iconology of tennis, striped jackets, pianos, summer picnics and goshes all round. The use of slow motion violence is perfectly blended with Julian Slade ideals, notably Chapman's dashing chap staggering around with a keyboard through his stomach while a handless Cleese spurts all over the shop and a pained Palin, with a tennis ball in the eye, kick-starts the transition between cheerful musical and bloodbath. As Idle explains, it's all 'pretty strong meat' before his own Peckinpah homage death provokes an official BBC apology from Cleese.
Again the team were pre-empting any comeback their audience may have made by making a joke about the whole thing (sorry to everyone in the world), pinpointing exactly what some people would do (don't phone) and finally going for the tongue-in-cheek sympathy vote (all the team come from broken homes),

personalised for full effect (especially Eric). In the clear, Idle can apologise for his colleagues' overdone apology. *Python* can twist television convention just a bit further, with Richard Baker's mock news flash reiterating elements from the show (storage jars and lemon curry) before a Jones/Palin conceived interlude, with crashing waves on a beach, wastes a bit more time, ushers in Cleese's historical figure to explain the time padding and finally reappear once more to inform the still tittering audience that there's no more jokes. But nobody would turn off, just in case...

Series 3 episode VII – conceived, written and performed by **Graham Chapman, John Cleese, Eric Idle, Terry Jones, Michael Palin & Terry Gilliam**
Also appearing **Nicki Howorth**
Research **Suzan Davies**
Make up **Madelaine Gaffney**
Costumes **Hazel Pethig**
Animations **Terry Gilliam**
Visual effects designer **Bernard Wilkie**
Graphics **Bob Blagden**
Film cameraman **Alan Featherstone**
Film editor **Ray Millichope**
Sound **Richard Chubb**
Lighting **Jimmy Purdie**
Designer **Ian Watson**
Produced & directed by **Ian MacNaughton**
27 November 1972

EPISODE 8

As Eric Idle says, 'If it's long, it's by Michael and Terry' and they don't come much longer than this episode dedicated to Mr. Reg Pither's Cycling Tour. A self-contained half-hour script, mainly culled from a rejected Palin/Jones BBC effort, this is what *Ripping Yarns* would have been like if the other Pythons would have been in on the act. A much longer script, heavily edited by Jones and MacNaughton, the entire concept comes from the Oxford camp although the ending was disliked by the other team members and several sequences enjoyed rewriting sessions by all the Pythons. However, this is the nearest *Monty Python* ever got to straight narrative comedy in the television series and breaks so far away from traditional *Python* that the familiar

Liberty Bell title sequence is completely abandoned. Suitably, Palin and Jones take the central characters, with the other players popping in and out in various cameo disguises. It's Palin's joyfully unaware, bobble-hatted, bespectacled nice guy that creates the warm, almost Ealing comedy gone insane atmosphere, helped with catchy, flowing, pastoral music, breezy North Cornwall countryside location and a blissful look of contentment as he takes a ride on his bicycle. The audience expects an accident almost at once but the direction keeps the idyllic scene going for some time; the crash comes from behind foliage and the blissful riding sequence is resurrected several times before the end. With his huge pump getting caught in his long trousers, Palin's mind-numbing bore discusses his plight with a peerlessly petulant roadside cafe worker – Idle – thinking about going to the bank for his customer's meagre change, disgruntledly accepting much praise for his banana and cheese sandwich before Palin's off again, records another crash in his diary and pours out his hard-boiled eggs plight to Cleese's disinterested garden-attending housewife. Gilliam's briefly spotted creature looks over the hedge as Palin's bike goes for another burton with Mike's archetypal simple-natured chappie, unaware of his trivial waffling but consciousness of not wasting people's time by reversing the pressure onto himself – 'I can't stand around here chatting all day!' – has crash after crash, slowly realising that both short trousers and a smaller pump could be the solution. A female Idle directs him to the perfectly signposted place, a misunderstood consultation with Doctor Idle results in Palin's need for professional advice being appeased (and an excuse to show Carol Cleveland in nurse's uniform again), our hapless heroes fruit cake seems to be slightly damaged on one side, directions are finally delivered thanks to a chemist filling out his prescription and the all-too familiar happy biking music and footage sees Palin on his way. The pause in the music, awaiting the crash which

doesn't come, is noted in Palin's diary as a short-lived escape from his usual plight, before unself-consciously breaking into a tense pub scene between adulterous husband Cleese and flirty mistress, Cleveland, with Palin's helpful offering of Tizer and naive pinpointing of the age difference causing the final breakdown of the relationship and providing the sexually interested Palin a golden moment of rear-guard action which he totally ignores. Instead, he accepts a lift from equally dull and obsessive Mr. Gulliver who drones on and on about corn beef rolls and his revolutionary new theory about creating crash-proof grub, with an energised tomato chucking itself out of harm's way until the car actually crashes and Jones, in a concussed state, ends up thinking he's Clodagh Rogers! Palin, returning the favour, hoists the bandaged Jones onto his bike, lugs him round to a very unhelpful Nurse Chapman (bring back Carol) and lapses into half-hearted physical comedy with Cleese's clumsy Dr. Woo and a manic attack on the out-patients. Meanwhile, Palin and Jones, having escaped from the white ward madness, sit round a camp fire as Palin ponders on Jones's new found ambition to get to Moscow. For you see, despite French fans (Cleese and Idle) singing a snatch from *Jack in the Box*, Jones has changed identity again. He now believes himself to be Trotsky, signs his musical fan's autographs accordingly, becomes obsessive with Stalin and ushers in a brief bit of archive footage of Lenin singing *If I Ruled the World* (originally to develop into Gilliam's ad for *Lenin's Chartbusters Volume III*, sadly cut from the show). A snogging couple, still under the misapprehension that this is Clodagh Rogers, stop their kissing and start singing – *Jack in the Box*, of course – as Idle's military type illustrates the journey of Palin and Jones via his French map.

Palin taps into television convention, breaking into narration mode but quickly stopping to allow his own voice-over recording to continue the job, as the bike pulls up at a handy

Y.M.C.A. – Young Men's Anti-Christian Association – fronted by a less than cheerful Gilliam. A rousing rendition of *God Save the Queen* heralds Palin's consultation with the British Consulate, a rather suspiciously Oriental man played with gloriously flamboyant style by Chapman, injecting his coy Mr. Robinson with all the comic mastery of Kenneth Williams' mad dictator from *Round the Horne*, desperately trying to justify his Englishness with rants about bakewell tarts, mistiming his colloquialisms with 'Buttocks Up!' and finally submerging this classic vignette into total madness with the appearance of Cleese's wild Mr. Robinson and a load of Communist types all screaming Bingo! Jones, meanwhile, has found his goal, as obvious under-cover secret police (Cleese, Chapman and Idle – complete with dark glasses and sharp suits) drag Palin off to Moscow for a hastily conjured up clambake. Employing the 1930s musical trend of roll-over town names against a backdrop of train travel, Carol's cabbie whisks our biking chum in to see Cleese's Russian general rant and roar, decide to continue without the sub-titles and proudly present the long lost power of Trotsky. Jones, having once more altered his mind, breaks into Eartha Kitt cabaret mood with a seductive rendition of *Old Fashioned Girl*, with the removal of a fur boa arousing the Russian hierarchy, another mental change to Edward Heath displeasing his audience and Idle's Nudge, nudge comedian milking the laughs, while Palin, thrown into a cell and damaging his Mars bar, faces death by firing squad. Wonderfully naive, refusing a cigarette, twisting the last-minute telegram convention with the message re-enforcing the death penalty, further twisting convention by making Idle's mother figure a dream rather than the awakening moment from a firing squad dream and helpfully showing the incompetent Russian marksmen how to fire their rifles, Jones and Palin escape from this mounting picture of angst-ridden espionage adventure with a quick and easy 'scene missing'

caption.
Everything's back to normal, Palin's pleasant biking theme ushers in the parting of the ways and contination of a North Cornwall tour while Gilliam claims the last, classic moment with the full emergence of dodging monsters Maurice and Kevin for a cracking resurrection of *Jack in the Box*. This is a very strange *Python* episode and the single story, group treatment of Jones/Palin ideals would never be attempted again. Disliked by the studio audience and critically ignored on first broadcast, The Cycling Tour stands out today as a very brave experiment which, although undeniably patchy, does endear Palin's central eccentric to the audience who are willing to restructure their *Python* expectations.

Series 3 episode VI – conceived, written and performed by **Graham Chapman, John Cleese, Eric Idle, Terry Jones, Michael Palin & Terry Gilliam**
Also appearing **Carol Cleveland**
Make up **Madelaine Gaffney**
Costumes **Hazel Pethig**
Animations **Terry Gilliam**
Film cameraman **Alan Featherstone**
Film editor **Ray Millichope**
Sound **Richard Chubb**
Lighting **E.C. Bailey**
Designer **Chris Thompson**
Produced & directed by **Ian MacNaughton**
3 December 1972

EPISODE 9

A routine flight of East Scottish Airways with Cleveland caressing Captain Palin and Cleese looking in control, is rudely interrupted by Idle's stock Scottish characterisation threatening the plane with a bomb unless he's paid £1,000. Reworking vintage Marty Feldman material, Idle's wonderfully uncertain hi-jacker forgets the whereabouts of his prime weapon, lets the information slip and endearingly tries to cut his losses for the sum of £1. Chapman's clip-board wielding director stumbles into the cockpit action, exposes the scene as performance and highlights this Scottish interloper as completely ruining the sketch which he has orchestrated – that's deep for you.

Continuing this inspection of fundamental television motivation, Jones the nude organist is surrounded by hangers-on; and desperately taking an interest in his flamboyant attempts to analyse his position, Cleese's 'And Now...' announcer discusses the intrinsic meaning of laughter, while Palin's It's Man simply does his job without any debate – it's *Monty Python*'s answer to *Glass Onion* and absolutely brilliant stuff. The title sequence and obvious ten seconds of sex seems rather lame in comparison while Chapman's elongated introduction of a revolutionary new housing project using characters from 19th-century English literary goes into *Python* insane obit with Little Nell leading the Bristol experiment, while Terry Jones, disgruntled with his battling factions from Milton's *Paradise Lost*, works the good and evil characters on different shifts to get the motorway interchange going. Jones again takes this notion even further with his mad, staring hypnotist inducing blocks of flats, with Palin's Ken 'very Big Liar' explaining the usefulness of the scheme and Chapman's architect, Clement Onan denying the fact that tenants must believe in the work. Idle, whose concentration begins to crack, finally dismisses problems with living in another man's imagination, turns his back on a nice villa and accepts his lot, while Jones's sexy, ever faithful assistance, Janet, in an array of alluring black and white snaps, deals out outrageous criminal punishment on almost everyone she comes into contact with and forces Jones, as typical *Python* policeman, to explain away the issue is mocked and trivialised with raucous singing hopelessly muffled by our shifty law-enforcer. Gilliam and Jones, mortuary workers with a healthy lot of work thanks to the police policy, tune into 'talk, tunes and damn right tomfoolery' with Shirley Bassey's Mortuary Hour, quickly covering up the groan-worthy Radio 4 gag (with three miniature radios within their set) and Cleese's totally bizarre black clad, blonde-wigged boss figure. Chapman's Mayor is a standard authority eccentric while Palin's tiny-brained V.I.P. (with skilful head-banging from assistant Cleveland) holds up the show with massive, Pintersque pauses, manic misunderstandings, lapses into 'I'm a good little doggie' insanity and, finally, with his brain back in place, a myriad of aged Hugh Grantisms with a stream of excellent, well played and jolly good exclamations as he's wheeled away. A quite unsettling piece of disconnected, disconcerting acting. The quiz answers, interrupted by Idle's recurring Scottish irritant promising not to disrupt the show for money and thus, forfeiting the payment straight away, receive little interest from the reactivated inhabitants of the slabs and hastily the scene cuts to Gilliam, off duty and relaxed, showing how his cut-out figures operate. An on-screen apology from the animator leads into the actual animation link he was discussing (a rather weak affair with a huge policeman causing panic among the houses of the neighbourhood and mass scarpering followed by the totally inspired flying saucers metamorphosing into First World War soldiers).

A 55-year jump presents the second leg of the Men's Hide 'n' Seek – all very Marty Feldman and Python by numbers but by no means less funny for that, with Jones on the look out for British favourite Chapman. With plane, bike and castle corridors forming his plan, Chapman allows the laughs to go to Jones, earnestly looking around within a few feet of the start of play, skipping through London streets and ultimately handing over to a Palin link some five years into the contest for an update and then six years further on with just twelve hours to beat Chapman's time. Across the globe, the seeking goes on, mounting into a frantic, logical madness which is the hallmark of Python. The final outcome is fairly obvious, although, again, no less funny for that and Palin's smoothie seaside host, a favourite from series one, taps into the youth market for this sort of comedy, reference points Montreux success and introduces another little winner the lads have

put together – as if to finally, literally, knock the old Python clichés on the head, Cleese wanders across the beach and wallops Palin over the head with old favourite the rubber chicken. Handing the item back to series one's redundant Knight in Armour, there's a hint of silly walking (greeted with enthusiasm by the studio audience) as Cleese violently kills something and strolls into semi-wedded bliss with Carol Cleveland for the Cheap Laughs sketch. Jones and Chapman are priceless as the whoopee cushion loving, red-wigged, pratfalling couple, bursting into the refined life of Cleese with custard pies and bodily functions. However, the trouser-dropping agony of the evening is left to the imagination as the camera pans across the madcap devastation, Idle's Scots man tries not to interrupt (with another old stand-up, the 16-ton weight making itself known), the beach iconology is once again embraced with a passer-by giving a donkey a ride, later twisted for the Cheap Laughs ideals with a pantomime goose and finally Cleese's dignity gets sucked into base hilarity with the low-brow humour of a Tupperware party having secured a feast of laughter from his neighbouring clown obsessive. Effortlessly fazing into the next item the marriage bed of Cleese/Cleveland shoots up to reveal the backdrop title of Idle's television investigation programme Probe, discussing the dangers of bull-fighting from the human point of view. Here Cleese, in definitive Blimp mood as Chairman of the British Well-Basically Club, with effeminate lapses into Lionel Blair territory among the military persona before the lights go out; the idea is quickly curtailed and Idle's Scots bloke promises to put them back on for a pound. Gilliam makes a wonderfully complex cartoon out of the simple action of turning on a switch, with Palin's nervy voice-over leading into the long abandoned trees growing into infinity before hitting the roof of the universe, a Hitler historical by-line and on into space exploration with the discovery of Algon One. A cracking piece from

Jones/Palin, the wonders of the planet are totally ignored by British broadcasters in favour of how much everything costs in comparison with home, whether the shopping facilities are adequate and what the female aliens are like (As Jones said, 'It's like going to the sun and asking Where do we sit?') Palin's Peter Snow-like observer panics at the thought of a lack of sexy lingerie, with Idle's bearded expert making reassuring noises as the scantily-clad space bimbo is spotted running across the quarry. Replacing the sheer wonderment of discovery with sheer wonder at breast proportions, this Jones/Palin notion brilliantly sums up the misplaced emphasis television gives to moments of amazing importance and, far more interesting than that, makes a hilarious close to this very fine Python episode. It only remains for Idle's Scottish gent to read the credits of the show for the princely BBC salary of 40p, sitting in a Ronnie Corbettesque leather chair, dismissing the gang as 'the usual lot' and saying goodnight to the folks before retiring, care of the Python 16-ton weight.

Series 3 episode IX Conceived, written and performed by the usual lot (**Graham Chapman, John Cleese, Eric Idle, Terry Jones, Michael Palin & Terry Gilliam**)
Also appearing **Carol Cleveland, Marie Anderson, Mrs. Idle**
Make up **Madelaine Gaffney**
Costumes **Hazel Pethig**
Animations **Terry Gilliam**
Visual effects designer **Bernard Wilkie**
Graphics **Bob Blagden**
Film Cameraman **Alan Featherstone**
Film Editor **Ray Millichope**
Sound **Richard Chubb**
Lighting **Bill Bailey**
Designer **Bob Berk**
Produced & directed by **Ian MacNaughton** for 92p and a bottle of Bell's whiskey
10 December 1972

EPISODE 10

The very absurdity of Python is deconstructed in the opening section of this series three classic, with Jones in Tudor attire, attending to Chapman's ordinary 20th-century bloke after some part-time work. The viewer familiar with *Python* comedy is hardly troubled by this moving of historical time-zones with Chapman's disgruntled requirements of normal jobs on the buses or with the underground as Jones merrily flogs his merrie England ideal. However, Jones is quickly revealed as a sham, whining about the poor job satisfaction rate, boasting about notable ex-clients (Shakespeare was a temp) while finally admitting his last job secured was in 1625, until finally dismissing this historical nonsense completely and dishing out the porn magazines. The very nature of comic performance is mocked with the Jones monologue merely breaking off for Chapman's 'I see!' and Terry's sheepish clarification that all his dialogue is completed. The dirty books business is uncovered in full with hidden stock rooms, flashy Idle plugging Teresa the Nun and Bum Biters to Cleese's Cornwall Church architecture lover and Gilliam's ancient old pervert staggering to the counter with a lifetime's worth of debauchery.

However, all this illicit madness is curtailed by Palin's sudden arrival, finding his undercover policeman sucked into the Tudor world of Sir Philip Sydney, fighting against the tidal wave of 'hey, nonny no'isms as his suspects file away before reversing this anti-cross-century sketch of misunderstanding by wandering through the door into genuine Tudor England (à la *Mr Benn*). Returning to the ideals of the programme's start, Palin's 20th-century misfit embraces the codes of olde England, jigging, merry-making and diner regaling with vice squad tales, continuing his battle against filth with a porn raid of sheepishly landing Spaniards (with Jones eagerly injecting a Goonish 'No!' into the confrontation) only to return home a hero to find his depraved wife (Cleveland) getting stuck in to the latest hot stuff, Gays Boys In Bondage. Attributed to Shakespeare and brilliantly timed as Palin's good lady wife reads from the work ('mounted police with a difference!'), all hell breaks loose as contemporary law-enforcer (in the authority-mad, sex obsessed shape of

Chapman) breaks into this historical setting, Palin's confused copper is hoist by his own petard, shipped back to modern times and unwarily staggers pass historical, linking evidence with a poster advertising Shakespeare's Bondage masterpiece – perfectly encapsulated by Gilliam's vignette with animated campness, Palin's Olivier-voiced grandeur and blacked out naughty bits for the artists. A nude Jones at his organ appears in cartoon form ushering in the personification of a normal happy couple, Cleese and Cleveland, becoming very disturbed by Palin's red-haired Rev. Arthur Belling, labouring the rather obvious point that he doesn't want to disturb anybody and thus making his disturbing presence even more pronounced. Pure *Python* insanity ensues with a very disturbing display of plate smashing, crab batting, doll fondling, foam spraying and violently loud noise-making. Naturally the *Python* will is too strong, the normals get embroiled in the white foam madness and visit the vicar's haunt of 'Loonie-up-the-cream-bun'.

The clever use of an exterior shot, delayed comic techniques and the obvious punchline of the whole congregation vocalising insanely, is perfectly achieved, before the real-life Jones, Cleese, It's and the credits start the show officially – by now, the *Liberty Bell* was appearing more and more belatedly, if, indeed, at all – with Gilliam's animal firing range (incorporating a sheep, horse, cat, Mickey Mouse, a piggy bank, a Disneyland Bear Country inhabitant and, even a nude Shakespearean performer) shaking the audience back into the groove for a quick Safari Snowball and the painfully (albeit deliberately so) played dubious words sketch. Idle and Jones inject mammoth pauses and arch raised eyebrows as the awkward quest for a clear telegraph message tackles the never very promising misunderstanding between pat and bat, surrounds the rubbish in Victorian card floral design and happily acknowledges the dreadfulness of the piece via Cleese's bemused voice-over. Even if it was

awful, *Python* could use it safe in the knowledge that, as long as they played it by numbers and highlighted how bad everything was supposed to be, nobody would question the real quality. Gilliam returns to his old sketch linking position with the Idle nonsense folded up, transported by horse and unfolded again to reveal an old stand by, the television format parody, this time *Is There?* with Cleese discussing the life after death subject with, suitably enough, three dead people. It makes fascinating television... and even the re-heated *Two Ronnies* idea of a medical condition causing words to come out in the wrong order, wrong words cropping up and mentions of Esher orgies is a relief, particularly when the doctor/patient relationship is brought to life by Cleese and Palin. It's Cleese's moment of glory though, with his Dr. E Henry Thripshaw fighting for recognition, plugging his T-shirts and finally orchestrating the film version of his disease. Historical stuff set in Syria, the title Gilliamized into Cecil B DeMille type and seemingly endless footage of battling is brought to a jolting halt by Chapman's slow-talking film critic, wasting film like a good 'un, chatting to the dissatisfied writer (Cleese finds the point of his disease has been missed) and proudly unveiling the doctor's cut of the movie with screaming battle culminating with an orderly visit to the G.P. It's still funny, but the Pythons are clearly padding and this show limps to a close with Palin's barrel-encased introduction of Silly Noises and his sherry-loving vicar guzzling bottles of the stuff as an uneasy, politely refusing and gradually dumb-struck Chapman sits back and thinks of *Brian*! The idea goes nowhere (although beyond the dialogue, the subtle set detail of a bust with elongated nose and glasses is effectively bizarre); the fact that this mild-mannered man of God has the universe's biggest supply of sherry is hardly earth-shatteringly hilarious and even a delayed cameo from Idle's British Sherry Corporation chap doesn't ignite the sketch. As usual, if all else fails, *Python* tips the thing over the edge, with Spanish gaiety, Carol's Carmen Miranda homage, Jones bellowing out gibberish and general anarchy making up for comic ideas. A quick after-credits reappraisal of dirty books/Dr. Thripshaw merchandise doesn't save this second half.

Did You Know?

Great realms of the script were never used, including a long version of Eric the Half a Bee (edited for *Monty Python's Previous Record*), Cocktails (which cropped up in the Drury Lane stage shows), a skit about a big-nosed sculptor and, most famously of all, the filmed but never screened 'wee-wee wine-tasting' sketch – a Jones/Palin sketch that the BBC and, surprisingly, even John Cleese rallied against.

Series 3 episode X conceived, written and censored by **Michael 'Bulky' Palin Terry Jones 'King of the Lash' John Cleese 'A Smile, A Song and a Refill' Terry Gilliam 'An American in Plaster' Graham 'A Dozen Wholesale' Chapman Eric Idle (Actual Size. Batteries Extra)** Also appearing **Carol Cleveland** ('Four revealing poses' Hard publications, Price 40p) and, in a variety of interesting positions, **The Fred Tomlinson Singers** under their leader 'Butch' Tomlinson **Rosalind** ('Afore ye go') **Bailey** now available from BBC Enterprises price 30p and a bottle of Bell's Body Make up **Madelaine Gaffney** & The BBC Naughty Ladies Club Unusual Costumes & Leatherwear **Hazel Pethig** & The Naughty Lads of 'Q' Division Rostrum Camera Mounted by **Peter Willis** (Massage in your own home or hotel room) Animations and Erotic Cartoons **Terry Gilliam** & Miss Hebbern 043-7962 Graphic Details **Bob Blagden** 'Denmark has never laughed so much' Red Lighting **Bill Bailey** Heavy Breathing & Sound **Richard Chubb** Film Cameraman & 'Rik' **Alan Featherstone** 'Men, it can be done' Blue Film Editor **Ray Millichope** 'What Your Right Arm's For' Designed by **Bob** 'Big, Black, Butch and Beautiful' **Berk** Produced & directed by **Ian**

MacNaughton who is assisting police with their enquiries Une Emission Nocturnale Par Television Française et BBC TV Copyright BBC TV: £5 in a plain wrapper 21 December 1972

EPISODE 11

Sport on television was a frequent *Python* target and Boxing Tonight is a classic example, with Nosher Powell's muscle-bound lug easily defeating Chapman's ponderous, historical diatribe delivering Sir Kenneth Clark, to take over his Oxford University post. But it's quickly and seamlessly merged with Cleese taking over from Idle's ref, addressing the ringside audience with the immortal words 'And now...', ushering Jones the organ into shot and allowing an exhausted It's Man to do his opening credits stuff.

But it's the classic Dennis Moore saga, a running theme throughout, that makes this such a priceless episode. One of Cleese's few major contributions to this third season, it's a shameless rip-off of the Richard Greene song of the 1950s ITV hit *The Adventures of Robin Hood*, with an obsessive thirst to relieve wealthy folk of their lupins and a deliciously cultured performance from Cleese, creating a *Python* masterpiece. With lyrical music and BBC drama-geared filming through trees as a prelude, the initial 'stand and deliver' by-play and shocked Cleveland/Jones coach-riders reaction merely heightens the potent effect of Cleese's bumbling, apologetic explanations about gun firing practice, via staggering tree identification discussions with Vicar Idle and razor-sharp interactions from Chapman. The beauty of the piece lies in it's sheer, other-worldly madness, with Cleese's unhinged persona pleading for lupins, being treated like the nutter he seems to be, only to be vindicated and rewarded when the 'normal' characters relent and give up the lupins. While Cleese doth protest too much, his line of thought is ultimately proved as justified – the landed gentry do value and horde their lupins – it's the contrast with the poor couple (Palin and Jones) that later takes the

comedy to its pinnacle, with a heartfelt outcry at more 'bloody lupins' and the slow realisation that these underprivileged really want a huge swag bag of jewels and clothes. The characters surrounding Cleese the do-gooder (mainly both Palin and Jones in poor – pre-*Holy Grail* rebels – and wealthy – concealed history lesson interludes – positions) seem to have emerged from a contemporary time-zone, reflecting both modern knowledge and television historical drama terminology. Cleese himself bravely skates round the edges of society, nervously trying to overcome his desire for flowers, do good by everybody (his pause to consult the list of requirements is both hilarious and surreally apt) and finally face both the lyric forgetting, voice-over singers and the very nature of his impossible job of redistribution of wealth. The show ends with the credits playing over a confused three-way split of money, with Cleese trying to be fair to all.

In between this prime slice of *Python*, the team serve up other gems, notably the total self-parody of the Idle/Chapman pepperpot astrological sketch. In terms of Python as a team, this is Jones and Palin deliberately constructing a parody of the word-obsessed sketches of Chapman and Cleese. Simply twisting television formats no longer seemed enough; the group needed to twist television as seen through the eyes of *Monty Python*. Admittedly this piece was written as a joke, with Jones and Palin fully expecting it to get the boot at the first read-through – instead Cleese and Chapman loved it, seemingly unaware that their style was being remorselessly sent up. Indeed, Chapman seems happy to go with the flow in performance, even pulling down the chant-along sheet of alternative words for audience interplay. However, Idle, in a deliciously self-aware performance, fully grasping hold of the over-the-top, introspective style of comedy, rants about what the stars say (the rather obvious Petula Clark misunderstanding merely setting up the cascade of words) and speeding through the piece with wide-eyed energy. The Roger Moore/Tony Curtis interlude and promise of Duane Eddy's school friend paying a call ushers in the, literal, fly by night, doctor of Terry Jones, cursing his little black bag and robbing his client. The resulting 'medics for money' sequence tends to go over old ground with less passion than before (despite the highlight of a white-coated Chapman reacting violently to a passing stethoscope). We see the Palin/Cleveland hospital with Gilliam losing some funds, medical charts highlighting the financial situation, Jones displaying his flashing reflex test and the laden, unsurprising animation continuing the 'cash over health' ideal as a bowler-hatted businessman is mowed down by a getaway ambulance.

However, Gilliam scores with a brilliantly disturbing exploding man-frog image, encompassing cooker/cuckoo clock mannerisms in a drama through the looking glass for the glam age. The Great Debate: TV4 or Not TV4, chaired by Idle with a politically geared Cleese, Palin's laid-back television critic, a gloriously stereotyped Jewish executive from Chapman and a mild-mannered Jones very briefly addressing the notion of a fourth major channel, is again, an obvious comic interlude but no less funny for that, while the Crofting Queen Victoria, Palin's BBC announcement and the sudden enforced silence when he begins to plug ITV keeps the TV-aimed barbs sharp. Fresh bursts of Dennis Moore keep things ticking along nicely, but the Ideal Loon Exhibition is a real mismatch of half-baked craziness for craziness' sake – a reheated remnant of the Upper Class Twits. The nation stream in to pay for silliness – in a way this is a comment on the viewing population tuning into *Python*'s brand of comedy – while memorable images (Chapman suspended through two tyres/Italian priests in custard) are some what diluted by repeated elements from *Python*s past (the gynaecologist lunch break gag/manic cliché-ridden Frenchmen going berserk/Idle's camp judge mincing about – reflected in the comforted losers at the very end of the show

alongside a final health/finance visual). Gilliam contributes a rather excellent bit of work with the newspaper lovelies thief (cleverly linking in with Idle's beauty contest winning judge), incorporating a typically thick-eared copper from Jones and the old portable hole gag, while Idle's poetic utterances to a less than impressed off-licence assistance (Cleese) allows the performers to recapture class *Python* shop sketches of old. Cleese's gradually warming admittance of once suffering from stories effortlessly fades into a final burst of the formerly lupine-crazy Mr. Moore. After the credits there's further mention of the black masked bandit during Michael Palin's gloriously xenophobic game show *Prejudice*, allowing the Blimpish British spirit of superiority to run amuck, challenge a few tried old notions and gleefully wallow in anti-foreigner diatribes, safe in the knowledge that they have a get-out clause of satirising those who believe this philosophy rather than mock the misguided condemnation of other nations. The notion that Brits need something to hate in the countries they visit is priceless; Palin's silky charms were never silkier; Carol Cleveland gives a stunning run-down of biting derogatory terms for the Belgians and the whole thing goes into bad taste overdrive with the culling of homosexuals (heightened with the camp interjection from within the Dennis Moore storyline).

Series 3 episode XI
Conceived, written and performed by
Graham Chapman, John Cleese, Eric Idle, Terry Jones, Michael Palin & Terry Gilliam
Also appearing **Carol Cleveland & Nosher Powell**
Make up **Madelaine Gaffney**
Costumes **Hazel Pethig**
Animations by **Terry Gilliam**
Visual effects designer **Bernard Wilkie**
Film cameraman **Alan Featherstone**
Film editor **Ray Millichope**
Sound **Richard Chubb**
Lighting **Bill Bailey**
Designer **Chris Thompson**
Producer **Ian MacNaughton**
4 January 1973

EPISODE 12

A grand episode, kicking off with Michael Palin's *A Book at Bedtime*. With a cheery smile and confident hello he begins to read Walter Scott's *Red Gauntlet* but immediately struggles with the words, tripping up at every turn and nervously looking into camera like a sheepish schoolboy reading out in front of class. It's a brilliant twisting of the polished broadcaster, enforced with the petulant arrival of Cleese, brashly reading through the start of the book before himself stumbling over the very next piece of text. It's funny once, so why not do it again: Idle turns up and finds Scott's prose a bit tricky as well. Chapman's bemused technician wanders in and the four masterly Pythons cross fade to a filmed insert of the lone Scots Piper and Terry Jones training his sharp kamikaze regiment (complete with Palin's soundbite about good money and further recommendation from Idle). The authoritative Cleese, already with a special assignment for these fine kilted lads, highlights the waste of manpower in all this training as the regiment is whittled down gradually to just a crazed Graham Chapman – who still comes out of manic killer mode to acknowledge his officer ('Thank you sir'). Palin's business man, visiting a kamikaze advice centre, juxtaposes the convention of bowler hat and pomp. As he does so, the Feldman/Milligan leap out of a door leading to death – which then returns the scene to Jones/Cleese and the regiment – sets up the recurring funny phrase for the evening: No time to lose. Getting over the failed dry run, Palin's businessman visits a No Time advice centre to chat with eye-rolling Idle about this wonderfully helpful observation. It's everywhere – on a board, a pull-down blind, an obviously pointing hand, whiskey bottle, upturned coat-tails – as Idle is dumbfounded at his client not getting the hang of the thing. It works like a drug-induced Peter Cook piece and the Palin/Idle playing is flawless, contrasting flashy self-confidence with tear-drenched, mistimed insignificance.

As a suitable bridge between ideas, Gilliam enlarges on the Toulouse/To Lose word play with post-Impressionist painters depicted via Western imagery. The regiment/advice centre treads merge completely with Jones using the phrase and receiving intercut praise from Idle, while Chapman embarks on his mission and immediately tries to kill himself by jumping out of the moving army van. Like a suicidal Dopey, he continues running round to the front of the vehicle to get mowed down while Cleese's military buffer lectures his wife, and Gilliam, Jones and other wandering folk (including some bloke with a stuffed flamingo) stop off to join the ever increasing crowd of stumbling readers trying to help out Palin's bedtime book host. A map detailing the regiment's path becomes a religious shaft of light and merges with Gilliam's stunning Neanderthal man animation, brilliantly ripping off Kubrick's opening scene from *2001: A Space Odyssey*, with skeleton smashing bone, slow motion technique and cross-fade from stone man implement to space-bound ship complete with classical music burst – the fall from the sky is pure Gilliam maliciousness.

Next up it's a familiar *Python* obsession, with penguins, allowing Cleese's medical television host to link new research with these clever 'little bastards' based in Australia. Now, despite Chapman's wonderfully over-the-top Aussie doctor, demonstrating useless experiments in penguin brain size in contrast with human brain sizes ('waste of time theory'), this line of enquiry goes on a bit, with various extensions of the tennis-loving Aussie situation, with Idle's changing room lecture and Chapman confusing the ball game with scientific game. There's a spirited dig at BBC planners which redeems things and Terry Jones, as the aged Einstein-like buffer, has a good time struggling with a hopeless experiment with non-speaking humans. Ultimately the penguin population take over the BBC and everywhere else, filling in for Prince Philip, Richard Nixon et al in world

power terms in a Gilliam montage sequence culminating with red banner bird power. The Russo-Polish border stuff (including a delightful continuation of Palin's reading problem with 'bolder' crossed out) limps on through Idle's mock foreign rambling (complete with subtitles) and Cleese's gibberish with sub-titles from around the world – it's all to set up more kamikaze material with Chapman crashing through the window and the disposal squad being called in. Again the previous sketch comic line is embraced (the whiskey bucket bears the legend Vooka); this includes a masterly piece of acting from Palin and Jones, sweating as they perform their task, enjoying extreme close-ups for maximum impact and incorporating the stirring *Mastermind* theme into the soundtrack.

Going nowhere, the human bomb idea is taken to the limit, but those nerve-drenched expressions are worth any amount of suffering. The Spot the Loony section is much more up to scratch, with Idle sporting a cheesy, showbiz grin, presenting the panel of complete loonies and running the mountain-backed scenic film footage for a chance to loony spot. The photograph section (undermining Katie Boyle's celebrity status and making life a lot easier by crediting the loony as A Loony during the historical sequence – a clip from *Ivanhoe, 1953*) runs through some literary genius with Chapman's Walter Scott (alive, contemporary but still, in true Jones/Palin form, kept to historical detail with correct birth and death dates) puts the blame on Terry Jones as Charles Dickens – with a priceless Jewish 'You bastard!' The Walter Scott theme is continued with Cleese's outside broadcast, his diatribe brought to a halt by Palin's Alan Whicker-like forestry documentary maker, borrowing his microphone and wandering off with it. A beautiful comic idea, the two battling broadcasters with, aptly enough, their respective writing partners, Chapman and Jones, are ready to fight together for the programmes. A rugby tackle, use of the *Dick Barton* theme, speeding cars,

continual Cleese waffle about gothic novels and Palin's energised action all vanishes as our hapless book at bedtime reader reappears, Idle's loony buzzer sounds over footage of Edward Heath and the closing credits are seen out with continual loony spotting as Idle's announcer can't read the title for next week's show. *Python* comedy could now happily judge the more mainstream situation comedies of the BBC, tongue in cheekily and affectionately sending up the establishment with trailers for classics like Dad's Doctor (note the exact use of *Dad's Army* typeface) with Terry Jones, kilted and white-coated, grinning merrily and looking forward to titty gags galore and naked nubile glam girls; Dad's Prooves, detailing the unnatural sexual acts between Jones as a judge and Gilliam once more the glitzy old queen; The Ratings Game (incorporating Palin's still from the loony antics and another dig at the planners, On the Dad's Liver Bachelors At Large (using a *Python* team pic, mickey taking Chapman and Cleese's involvement in *Doctor At Large*); Limestone dear Limestone (sort of Patrick Cargill meets rock obsession) and Up the Palace, wacky adventures of the royal family. It all makes up Idle's promised fest of Comedy Ahoy! and the end of *Python* signals the end of BBC transmission as the set is switched off and the image fades to that familiar wee spot of telly transmission. Wonderful self-deprecating deconstruction of the industry in which the team worked.

Did You Know?
The show was due to begin with Cleese and Idle as members of the Conservative and Unionist Party putting across their messages through the art of dance.

Series 3 episode XII
Conceived, written and performed by **Graham Chapman, John Cleese, Eric Idle, Terry Jones, Michael Palin and Terry Gilliam**
Research **Suzan Davies**
Make up **Madelaine Gaffney**
Costumes **Hazel Pethig**

Animations **Terry Gilliam**
Graphics **Bob Blagden**
Film cameraman **Alan Featherstone**
Film editor **Ray Millichope**
Sound **Richard Chubb**
Lighting **Jimmy Purdie**
Designer **Robert Berk**
Produced & directed by **Ian MacNaughton**
11 January 1973

EPISODE 13

It hardly ranks with the heady, classic days of series one, but this final burst of full, six-packed television *Python* is a brilliant example of the form, completely challenging the way viewers react to the conventions of the small screen and actually beginning with the genuine Thames St. Paul's reflected image and familiar jingle. Even the most astute armchair audience would momentarily think they had the wrong side on, particularly as the chirpy David Hamilton promises us a great night with Thames television before slipping into smooth mode with a knowing introduction for a 'rotten old BBC programme' and the *Python* titles. There's a sense that this is definitely the end of an era, with BBC familiarity corrupted as never before and the entertainment establishment mocked to breaking point – Eric Idle's balding, crying, ingratiating luvvie host for *The British Show Biz Awards* (an amalgam of David Frost/Richard Attenborough) – whose overblown affection for dead theatrical legends (Sir Alan Waddle brought on in an urn by Gilliam, complete with bow tie) and thankful celebration of the appearance of David Niven's fridge (also donning a black bow tie) make for hilarious, heavily barbed interludes throughout the show. However, even more importantly, the Pythons inject intertextuality at every corner, reappraising old situations not by repeating or altering previously told gags but by including brief homages to past glories (the Dummy Princess Margaret as guest of honour/Chapman's pepperpot talking on the phone and checking her shoe size – note the huge recognition reaction from the

audience – the pepperpot stroll down the road passing a stuffed penguin and a couple of unexploded Scotsmen/the award nominees including Richard Baker repeating his 'Lemon curry' exclamation). Sketches are heralded as part of the British entertainment scene with Idle's initial presentation of the Oscar Wilde piece leading into this fondly remembered bit of *Python* excess. Merely questioning the over-celebrated witticisms of the King's favourites, Chapman's Wilde is wonderfully foppish and biting, scoring points off Cleese and, latterly, the Irish gall of Palin's George Bernard Shaw. The notion of the Emperor's clothes, with everybody laughing uproariously simply because the Monarch finds it amusing, is counterbalanced by childish one-upmanship with the literal genius figures fighting to soar the reputation of the others. Palin's ice-melting raspberry, celebrated as the height of wit, pinpoints the facility of satire and Gilliam's party cut-out merely takes the idea of social niceties via crudity one step further. The gate-crashing, Tarzan-swinging, male chauvinist bursting animation of Charwoman simply works as a good, quick, get-out sequence, allowing Idle to waffle on about the glories of foreign film-making and a typically British-geared *The Hard Test Match* with neon-realism scenes of slow-motion cricket, heavy with death over-tones, religious symbolism and all-out sex. The resulting debate between Cleese's dark director and the Yorkshire cricket team (with Chapman's hilarious complaint about no Geoff Boycott) again taps into the notion of the television audience with Jones/Chapman pepperpots turning over, only to get back to Idle's show biz pontificating. The peppers, lurching into the new brain sketch (with new money translation for the old money references) limps along with familiar, nonsensical outbursts from Jones, Palin's business as usual salesman and Chapman's self important female. Cleese, with a running character of Peter Cook-like strangeness (with a false leg for signing and apologises from

Chapman as he drops the pen!), helps things along to the blood donor sequence, established via Jones and the bat flapping misunderstanding at the start, and given the grotesque *Python* twist as Idle yearns to give urine instead of corpuscles.

But by now, the *Python*'s bad taste had become predictable and Cleese's outrage at Idle's presentation of urine stolen from his own body smacks of insincerity, while the elongated wife-swapping from Redcar fails to gel, despite Idle's Eddie Waring-like commentary and a fine bit of David Coleman presenting from Palin, with a *Saturday Swap Shop* attitude quickly superseded by sexual politics in horse-racing terms. Indeed, the most effective element crops up during the wife-swapping closing credits with the team linked with each other's wives while Chapman is linked with Mr. Sherlock, his partner David Sherlock. Naturally, in this self-reflective episode, the closing credits are dragged into the award ceremony with the team chasing the tail of comedy by presenting the entire cast of The Dirty Vicar sketch before performing the item and concluding with Idle breaking into the madness to call the whole thing a day. Television created purely for the award system. As it happens, the sketch is hardly that impressive, purposely constructed as glorified smut with Jones going sex mad, molesting the girls and momentarily calming down to dignified, controlled tones. It simply stands as *Python*'s ultimate comment on the self-gratifying, congratulatory ethos of television.

Did You Know?

The original script is credited to Thomas and William Palin with additional material by Cynthia Cleese – the Python children at the time.

Series 3 Episode XIII, Grandstand
A BBC Inside Broadcast was conceived, written and performed by **Michael Palin and Mrs. Cleese, Eric Idle and Mrs. Palin, John Cleese and Mrs. Jones, Terry Gilliam and Terry Jones and Mrs. Idle, Graham Chapman and Mr. Sherlock**

Also appearing **Carol Cleveland and Mr. and Mrs. and Mrs. Zambezi, Caron Gardner and Mr. A**
Make up **Miss Gaffney and Mr. Last**
Costumes **Hazel Pethig and Mr. Clarke**
Graphics by **Bob Blagden and 'Naughty' Rosy**
Animations by **Terry Gilliam Rabbi Colquhoun**
Film Cameraman **Alan Featherstone and Miss Weston**
Film Editor **Mr. Ray Millichope and His Orchestra**
Sound **Richard Chubb and Mrs. Lighting**
Lighting **Bill Bailey and Mr. Sound**
Choreography by **Jean Clarke** and an unnamed man in Esher
Designer **Chris Thompson and Mrs. Armstrong-Jones**
Producer **Ian MacNaughton and 'Dickie'**
A BBC TV and Mrs. Thames Production
18 January 1973

SERIES 4 – Monty Python

The time had finally come for John Cleese to have the courage of his convictions and leave *Monty Python*, finally totally fed up with 'being told to turn up at 8am on Monday morning at Wakefield railway station, dressed as a penguin'. He had been very unhappy doing series three, got bored with the format during series two and even as early as midway through series one experimented with breaking up the writing formats (penning sketches with Palin and Idle) to dispel the familiarity of comedy. So, it was a long time coming, but eventually with the proposed series four Cleese opted out of any more television *Monty Python*. The BBC were almost on the verge of cancelling the fourth series; Eric Idle wasn't happy about continuing with a depleted team and although he performed extensively did little writing for the show. Terry Gilliam's appearances increased but his disillusionment with the series saw him contribute only a fraction of his usual animation work. Graham Chapman, bereft of his usual writing partner, drifted in and out of scripts with other members of the team as well as Douglas Adams. Thus, this fourth series really saw the solid and firing on all cylinders domination of

Michael Palin and Terry Jones, which without the powerful battling sounding board of Cleese, became dominant over the entire project. All the other Pythons, including Jones, felt the happy balance of *Python* was dishevelled by Cleese's absence. Material edited out of the screenplay for *Monty Python and the Holy Grail* and written by John Cleese found its way into series four, so by the slenderest of means the complete team did come together for the programmes.

EPISODE 1

Arguably the worst episode of *Python* ever put out and hardly the best starting point for such a crucial change-over series. In many ways this show is trying to bridge the gap between *Flying Circus* and the five-strong team with various intercut sketches and a myriad of television clichés (Chapman's contradictory announcer is one of the best and most sustained elements) while moving towards the more connected, narrative format pioneered by the Jones/Palin series three effort The Cycling Tour.
The overall theme here, The Golden Age of Ballooning, is powerfully brought to life by Gilliam's multi-image title sequence and burst of classical music but the comic inspiration is simply not there. There's the effective touch of Palin's fag-sucking, disgruntled plumber spouting historical facts as a sort of lavatorial prologue but the bulk of the show is handed over to the cod French utterances of Idle and Jones as the Montgolfier Brothers veering from excited plans about balloon construction to nervous admission of washing difficulties. It's as funny as it sounds (!), with Jones getting more and more paranoid, Chapman's stately butler figure introducing erroneous guests and unhistorical scene shifters cleaning the way for Gilliam's film show of brotherly cleanliness. The animator's usual genius is lacking in this bath-as-boxing-match sequence and it's a blessed relief when this ballooning celebration part comes to an end. Unfortunately, Chapman's earnest

BBC chap, brilliantly having a dig at the usual book of the film (taking the idea to extremes with toilet seat cover and the like) immediately presents part two, featuring the brothers in love although hastily avoiding any homosexuality/incest confusion, with Cleveland's bodice squeezed figure hanging around the place as Jones falls from his balloon obsession. It's a shame that the extended on-screen time Carol enjoyed in this fourth series didn't offer more fruitful material but she happily holds her own, nags and embraces low-brow sexual misunderstanding from Idle. It's interesting to note that *Python* was increasingly going for the common dominator and really playing typical *Python* madness strictly on auto pilot. The extended confusion about Palin's French King, quickly trying to work out which one is still alive to lend credence to his subterfuge is effective, while the usually hilarious historical awareness (spouting dates, enjoying shared knowledge) is over-worked and under-written. Chapman's King George is never fully developed, Jones (still in bath robe) just becomes irritating and only Palin's gloriously broad Scottish intruder, eagerly pinching plans and bumbling through his mission, makes anything of the script. The embarrassed pauses, small talk and Benny Hillesque chase sequence simply look like padding, but by now *Python* was beyond popularity and into cult.
The uncontrolled studio audience, who just five years earlier had hardly tittered at the dead parrot sketch, now laughed uproariously at everything. *Python* had become the Emperor's Suit of Clothes. Unconnected amendments to the ballooning structure (Idle/Chapman political discussion interrupted by Palin's balloon commentary, The Three Degrees-like invasion of George's court, Idle's huge false ears) all seem silliness for its own sake, Cleveland as sex object is yearned for by Idle, Chapman's minor butler figure milks the audience applause, eagerly takes his fellow artists' appreciation while the would-be snoggers look on during the opening

credits which are so far into the show that they hardly seem needed. As it happens the titles for series four are one of Gilliam's great pieces, embracing the old with the rolling coin dropping into a slot and starting a grainy black and white film of *Flying Circus* imagery (complete with descending foot) while crashing out of its muffled version of the theme into full colour, full blast heralding of Gothic, gory, glorious *Monty Python*. A constant delight during this series, the titles do nothing to change the quality of the script with more from Chapman's continuity announcer, Idle's sex obsessed Norwegian Party spokesman (Chapman's panel of experts is cleverly delivered and goes on for an age) and ballooning's part six with Chapman's Zeppelin pushing out various dignities who call his airship a balloon. The vintage archive mime of Jones, the failed inventor, works well, while the Germanic Jones/Palin couple discussing Yorkshire puds and sorting out the dead government in their house is almost Goonish in its excellence, but this is too little too late.

Did You Know?
Material cut from this show included Gilliam's animation illustrating his home country becoming the New Scotland, complete with a bagpipe version of *Stars and Stripes*, and a sequence taken from the life of Benny Zeppelin.

Monty Python was performed by **Graham Chapman, Eric Idle, Terry Jones, Michael Palin & Terry Gilliam** Conceived & written by **Graham Chapman, John Cleese, Eric Idle, Terry Jones, Michael Palin & Terry Gilliam** Also appearing **Carol Cleveland, Peter Brett, Frank Lester, Bob E. Raymond & Stenson Falke** *George III* song composed/arranged by **Neil Innes** Make-up **Maggie Weston** Costume **Andrew Rose** Film cameraman **Stan Speel** Sound recordist **Ron Blight** Film editor **Bob Dearberg** Sound **Mike Jones** Lighting **Jimmy Purdie** Visual effects **John Horton**

Production assistant **Brian Jones** Designers **Robert Berk & Valerie Warrender** Produced & directed by **Ian MacNaughton** 31 October 1974

EPISODE 2

The fondly remembered Michael Ellis episode features the major contribution from John Cleese and a very strong performance from Eric Idle as the misunderstood ant purchaser (sort of Cary Grant's *North By Northwest* trapped in Lewis Carroll land) with the old Carol Cleveland secretary music enhancing the vicious string of visual opening gags (Palin's store doorman kneed in the groin/Idle's misparked bike/Carol's clumsy flame-thrower customer). The seed of the episode and its highlight is the laboured discussion on ants with Chapman's bizarrely masked assistant channelling surreal services to the supposed Michael Ellis. Idle's shocked amazement and desperate impersonation of this manic behaviour is a real laugh-out-loud moment, compounded by Jones as the smooth, almost Cleesian manager with slicked-back hair and thin moustache. Palin's disconcertingly sinister delivery adds to the wonderful weirdness of the scene but it's his energetic sales pitch for ant accessories which not only builds the comedy to its full potential but reveals the clear interaction of Cleese. The ant obsession may be laboured (the handy television course on ant language with Chapman's waiter gesticulating madly compounded by the tagline anteater attack/the ever drunker Chapman in drag with a Victorian poetry reading on ants full of delightfully obvious, albeit hardly in the *Python* tradition, Shelley/Sherry misunderstanding/Palin's hasty removal of book squashed remains) but the team inject a real charm to the material whether it's Jones as the eternal mother figure nagging on about the drug-addicted tiger, Palin's Edith Evans-like attendant or the ingratiating toupee salesmen all obviously wearing their product and convinced Idle is an

ashamed wearer as well.
The use of running characters has shifted to narrative convention (Cleveland's customer is playing within the confines of the complaints department sequence as is Chapman's military buffer obsessed with his work in Norway), off-the-wall surrealism takes on a more conventional look simply because it seems mild in the wake of *Python*'s first flurry of invention and Palin's blood-stained television doctor directly interacting with his viewer, pausing, then continuing, is clichéd. In many ways the funniest episode of the series it nevertheless highlights the cracks forming in the *Python* armour. However, the ending (the store's Michael Ellis week comes to a close), deceptively dismissed as weak by Idle, forms the springboard for a multitude of alternative endings presented by store assistant Jones. Whether it be the slow pull-out, sunset, chase, happy or cliché-ridden football summing up is illustrated until finally Jones suggests the sudden end and the screen cuts to black. It's a brilliant effect.

Did You Know?
The ant-buying scene in a modern day Harrods-like department store was the first submission from Cleese and Chapman for the *Holy Grail* film. It was cut from the script and utilised here when Jones/Palin penned the coconut material and made the film theme clear. Re-worked for television a scene between Chris Quinn and the Icelandic Honey Salesman was edited from the show – it later appeared in episode six!

Monty Python was performed by **Graham Chapman, Eric Idle, Terry Jones, Michael Palin & Terry Gilliam** Conceived & written by **Graham Chapman, John Cleese, Eric Idle, Terry Jones, Michael Palin & Terry Gilliam** Also appearing **Carol Cleveland & John Hughman** Make-up **Maggie Weston** Costume **Andrew Rose** Film cameraman **Stan Speel** Sound recordist **Ron Blight** Film editor **Bob Dearberg** Sound **Mike Jones**

Lighting **Jimmy Purdie**
Visual effects **John Horton**
Production assistant **Brian Jones**
Designer **Valerie Warrender**
Produced & directed by **Ian MacNaughton**
7 November 1974

EPISODE 3

Within a very disjointed final burst of television activity this third show can happily stand tall alongside the finest examples from the full team efforts. With a comic unity, brilliantly constructed, post-*Beyond the Fringe* Second World War comic comment and a real sense of performance (particularly from Palin and Jones) this was a really worthwhile joint effort. Neil Innes plays a major part via his linking musical theme and right from the *Steptoe & Son* parody opening – with cheerful cockney down 'n' outs Jones and Palin swaggering down the street for BBC's comic caper *Up Your Pavement* this is rich *Python* material indeed. Contrasting sharply the working class ideal with the cross-cultural acceptance of the Galton & Simpson masterpiece, the tramps rummage through litter bins to discover half-guzzled bottles of champagne and find their chummy, crafty wheeler dealer image enhanced by Palin's happy-go-lucky, chuckly commentary. Clearly on a roll with the knives out for contemporary television, Chapman speeds into view in typical ATV action hero style contrasting Jason King gay abandon with *Dr. Kildare* dramatics before Idle's Naval hero documentary skit breaks for stirring patriotic music, black and white imagery and an embrace of 1944's jolly, gung-ho and Jimmy Edwards-like RAF chappies. Cue the legendary banter sketch with elongated, ambitious and unpenetrable flights of fancy which confuse like-minded airforce guys who fall into their own stream of excessive conversational description. In the, by far, best episode of the series, this is, arguably, the only copper-bottom, classic *Python* moment found in this final batch of six. Idle, in particular, delivers the gibberish perfectly, slowly getting

quieter and more introspective as he himself desperately tries to work out what he's talking about.
The comic knife is twisted and extended with Palin's new banter spouting gleefully about monkeys on the ceiling with energetic relish. Not only that, but Chapman's back as the typically disgruntled Captain, suspiciously dealing with Idle's confused chatter about spiders in matchboxes. It's all total nonsense but played with such gusto that it's a breath of fresh air and strangely different to the *Python*'s initial attack on the public's preconceptions of convention. Now Chapman can turn on his Blimpish outrage of the enemy not playing the game of war fairly (using cabbages instead of bombs), Gilliam (finally getting some pretty decent acting assignments) screaming 'Bastards!' in effective aged campaigner mode and the spirit of British military superior being ironically presented as damn fine with flag-waving, crescendo-reaching passion.
But the best is yet to come. Jones and Palin, the strongest surviving unit from the six pack of Pythons, really came into their own both in performance and writing, but nowhere more so than in the celebrated Court Martial sketch. The fine comic embrace (Basingstoke, is only part of it) for Palin's angst-ridden prosecuting officer desperately tries to get on with his business while addressing the continual interruptions and clarifying questions from the Jones judge figure. Continually explaining that the Basingstoke, Cole Porter et al in his speech is different from the judge's and our common belief ('Different one, Sir!'), the final anguish leads to Palin's new version of the other Porter's *Anything Goes* – the old pyjamas mix – and its brilliance is certainly reflected in that it was often resurrected for subsequent live performance by the team.
Throughout, Idle's dutiful, charged squaddie is meek, pleading to go home before his one chance of simple comment transforms into an accurate, erudite and impassioned speech on the futility of modern

warfare. By now, of course, social comment has filtered through and the military bigwigs can simply go all out for classic *Python* mania with a singsong reprise, colourful pixie hats and a skating vicar.
In the wake of such unique comedy the vintage war film trailer (complete with dubious love and a snatch of George Formby) seems rather old fashioned, but a subtle back step to series one delights (parrots/organ player/it's man on the ropes) is brief and potent enough to bridge the lull into a longed revaluation of past masters – the pepperpot telly watcher of Chapman (in the absence of Cleese joined by Jones) and abusing racial figures (Gilliam's punka-walla is attached to live wires in order to alert him to channel changing), groan on in typically monotonous fashion and, most interestingly, tap into the actual reality of television performance by tuning into the opening *Steptoe* pastiche of the very episode in which they are appearing. Gilliam, in another guise, can rant about the bloody repeats when the pepperpots reappear. A satirically absurd BBC programmer sketch allows Chapman to ape his own involvement in the *Doctor* television shows ('Doctor At Cake'), the general public be suggested as, and proved to be idiots (cheerfully settling down to hours of motorway coverage) and powerful, albeit hardly original, attacks on the mentality of the men on the top floor (Idle's ever growing comments misconceived as title suggestions works brilliantly).
However, no sooner does Gilliam's ever banging security guard with a sword through his head stagger in but the television screen is tuned back to those pixie-hatted military court singers.
The show continually looks back on itself and, thanks to the running theme, both musically and comically, it rarely worked better in *Python* than here. A heaving BBC centre; complaints about war drama on the box and a rather dud Gilliam cartoon (with someone resembling the teacher from Bash Street greeting a constructed beautiful day) wheezes onto Agatha Christie land with staff,

croquet, morning tea; Chapman's puffing family head; Idle sweetly smiling and Cleveland reacting violently to any words sounding remotely 'tinny'. This ongoing discussion of the awful 'tinny' words and comfortable 'woody' words takes *Python* logic beyond most people's understanding and, at the end of the day, the sketch is just nonsensical rubbish for its own sake. But if only for Chapman's progress to naughty words and his enthused delivery of 'tit' this is well worth struggling through, notably as Palin bounds in with continuous banter, murderous activity is dismissed as crap by Chapman's viewer, and the motorway, bloody repeats text of the earlier material is woven into the show. The musical variation on the *Horse of the Year Show* is standard *Python* insanity, memorably highlighted by Chapman as television trickery when the horses aren't shown to be jumping and thus suggesting that when the camera recording the viewers' reaction moves away from the horse racing so do the cameras recording the horse racing. In a further attempt to get realism BBC anchorman Peter Woods makes a round-up of WW2 appearances before Neil Innes himself ends with a grainy rendition of *When Does A Dream Begin*. A classic episode.

Monty Python (Social Class 9) was performed by **Graham Chapman, Eric Idle, Terry Jones, Michael Palin & Terry Gilliam** (Social Class 2 Arsenal 0) Conceived & written by **Graham Chapman, John Cleese, Terry Gilliam, Eric Idle, Neil Innes, Terry Jones & Michael Palin** (Social Class Derry & Toms)
Also appearing **Carol Cleveland, Bob E. Raymond & Marion Mould** (Social Class 47 Actors)
When Does a Dream Begin by **Neil Innes** (Social Class 137 Musicians) Variations on the theme by **Bill McGuffie** (Social Class 137a Other Musicians)
Make-up **Maggie Weston** (Social Class 5 till midnight)
Costume **Andrew Rose** (Social Class 35-28-34)
Film Cameraman **Stan Speel** (Social Class F8 at 25th sec)

Sound recordist **Ron Blight** (Social Class Unrecorded)
Film editor **Bob Dearberg** (Social Class Lower VIth) (Mr. Potters)
Sound **Mike Jones** (Social Class) (Slightly above the Queen)
Lighting **Jimmy Purdie** (Social Class A bottle of bells)
Visual effects **John Horton** (Social Class Ant)
Production assistant **Brian Jones** (Social but no Class)
Designer **Robert Berk** (No Social Class at all)
Produced & directed by **Ian MacNaughton** (Social Class 238-470 Scotsman) – by kind permission of Sir K. Joseph
14 November 1974

EPISODE 4

In what was a regular target for *Python*, this episode kicks off with an ATV-style car chase with groovy music contrasting the usually stuffy tradition of *Hamlet*, as played by a deliciously confused Terry Jones. Although including an excellent performance from Jones as the ambitious, restricted, innocent abroad, it is clear that the team's ideas are running out. The psychiatrist's obsession with sexual matters is repeated through various bogus medics (notably fine work from Idle and Palin, protesting too much with a string of testimonies), while Chapman's initial burst into To Be Or Not To Be recital is an effective swapping of performance symbols – highlighted when Chapman whips out a skull and casually tosses it away. In the same way Chapman wants to be Hamlet, Jones wants to be in, in a way, Chapman – a modern television figure, a private dick. Indeed, Chapman had played such a role at the start of the previous episode. But the mixed-up mind matters goes on far too long and even Gilliam has a very brief rant about the sexual problem facing Jones. The Prince of Denmark is momentarily reassured by the disorientation theory but before long Carol's nurse figure is phased out for the *Nationwide* graphics and Idle's uncannily accurate impersonation of Michael Barrett's breathless earnestness for

trivia stories. It's an easy but effective bridge to Chapman's roving reporter, John Dull, and his quest to find the truth behind comfy chairs actually resting your legs. On location at Tower Bridge, the investigation seems conclusive, but the real masterstroke comes with Palin's corrupted policeman replacing suspicion with chatty interest, joining the disgruntled television journalist, abusing privileges by lifting lunch time food for evidence, stealing beers and embarking on a detailed monologue about helmets, a reflection of the show's ongoing theme of people in uniform frantically trying to prove their authority status.
Across the bridge and unconnected to this line of enquiry is Jones in a passionate embrace with Cleveland, resisting suggestions that his young bride-to-be will allow her father to share the marital bed, quickly cutting to the uncomfortable reality with Chapman's pipe-smoking, pitch blackness boat model making authority dead loss and the sound of a coin rolling which belatedly bursts into the credit sequence.
By now it's back to *Hamlet* with Booth's Ophelia tapping into the psychiatrist sex obsession before Gilliam's Gothic slumbering skeleton animation blends into the headless boxer sketch with Palin turning on the over-optimistic, heartless promoter attitude and Idle doing well with a thick-eared yes man. There's a name check for Frank Sinatra, bloodthirsty medics revelling in the boxing action on radio and the notion that *The Robinsons* (an everyday story of people like the Archers) can be received by all radios and, thus, if one person turns off they are all turned off. The very nature of realism in soap is mocked (with overly unrealistic discussions) and reflected within society when Idle considers the programme rubbish while wallowing in a word-for-word repeat performance in her real life. *Python*'s delight in bad taste is reinforced with gleeful slaughter of pigeons (by throwing tinned food) made even more powerful via the fact it's a misconceived version of

kindness, while the Hamlet continuity gets caught up in a sporting discussion resulting in Act 2 merging with *European Cup Night*, Epsom dentists and diminutive jockey interviews.

The pick of the Epsom section comes with Palin's cigar-chomping developer but the notion is going nowhere until the Queen Victoria Handicap race. A surreal image in the style of Feldman and Milligan, this has become one of the most potent *Python* images and Idle's awe-inspiring Brian Clough reaction rounds the skit off perfectly. A performance given further weight by the now common trend of employing BBC presenters: here Jimmy Hill in Victoria garb. A disturbing Gilliam work on balloon as grapes and an all-devouring aged baby coupled with the final juxtaposition of the Hamlet and Victoria trends in the show may be a weak sort of ending but it's an ending that's good enough for me, almost restarting with Palin's man in the action whose earnest 'And then...' comes to no conclusion.

Monty Python by William Shakespeare
Dramatis Personae
Hamlet **TERRY JONES**
A bachelor friend of Hamlet's **Graham Chapman**
Quite a butch friend of Hamlet's, but still a bachelor **Terry Gilliam**
A friend of Hamlet's who, though married, still sees Hamlet occasionally **Michael Palin**
A very close bachelor friend of Hamlet's, who though above suspicion, does wear rather loud shirts **Eric Idle**
Another Part of the *Dramatis Personae*: A friend of Hamlet's who loves bachelors **Carol Cleveland**
A Jimmy Hill near London **Jimmy Hill**
A Bachelor Gentleman **Bob E. Raymond**
An Ophelia **Constance Booth**
A loonie, but not a Bachelor **Sir K. Joseph**
Additional blank verse **J. Cleese** (no relation) (of Hamlet's, that is)
Personae non Dramatis but Technicalis (some bachelors, some not) A Maker-upper **Maggie Weston**
A Costume Designer and Bachelor **Andrew Rose**
A Cameraman of London **Stan Speel**

A Sound recordist of ill-repute **Ron Blight**
An Editor of Film who is partly bachelor, and partly vegetable with mineral connections **Bob Dearberg**
A Studio Soundman **Mike Jones**
A Lighting Scotsman **Jimmy Purdie**
A Visual Effecter keen on bachelors **John Horton**
An Assistant Producer friend of Hamlet's **Brian Jones**
A Designer who prefers married men, but knows quite a few bachelors **Valerie Warrender**
A professional Producer and amateur Bachelor **Ian MacNaughton**
A Bachelor Broadcasting Corporation 21 November 1974

EPISODE 5

Python never really succeeded at science-fiction, with the series one alien invasion of Wimbledon pretty much equalling this series four effort, Mr. Neutron, in blandness. For one thing the title sequence crops up right at the start which was probably more of a shock than the usual 20 minutes in appearance, although the Housewives' Choice theme and Jones's jolly rag 'n' bones brings the crowds out and ushers in a really rather endearing bit of stupidity from Palin's boring public servant announcing the opening of a new post box. The vocal inflection of the all-important word 'box' is over-worked to breaking point, particularly as he starts the speech again... in French!... but there's no doubting that it still gets under the skin of your sense of humour. But this is merely a time filling prelude to the main business in Mr. Neutron – the most dangerous, least convincing anti-hero in the Universe. Chapman, with stark highlights, bulky yellow track suit and monotone delivery does his best with some pretty feeble material while the continual image of villain as handy home help does tend to wear very thin – although Jones as a miserable old moaner and Palin, overweight and worried, add some much needed *Python* bite to the proceedings. Still Chapman's work with Jones, as the grotty lady that does (Mrs. Scum), is a redeeming factor, with the nation's

threat waxing lyrical about love and emotion in an unemotional style, finally inviting her to join in his plans for devastation, proving his other worldliness with the banter on the ice cream competition and brilliantly stepping out of character for the Jewish questioning. The destruction of the world rubbish that results in American powers trying to bomb the guy to bits makes *Mars Attacks!* look like...well... *Mars Attacks!*, with Palin's crusty President, seen in ever increasing states of undress, more concerned about body odour than concentrated, sensible military action. By the end, thanks to a Gilliam animation, the world is left as a collapsed shell. Earlier Eric Idle's intrepid hero tries to track down top agent Teddy Salad in the Yukon, droning on uneasily about ballet with yokel Chapman and his collection of camp seventies drop-outs (the Margot Fontayne line is one of the few classic moments), while there's a laboured but enjoyable vignette in Palin's Italian restaurant with fish-obsessed Eskimo figures and Chapman's frightfully refined under-cover chap. Continual translated interjection from Idle concerned with hen-teasers adds nothing, while the chance meeting with Jones and the feted agent Salad disguised as a dog drags the show to new lows. With tempting treats including bones and meatballs Idle's continual walkies and begging finally sees the dog transform into a more manageable puppet, chatting away cagily round the camp fire. This is so ludicrous that you have to laugh, although I've never worked out just why! In Downing Street, Idle's Prime Minister slaves away at his paperwork in a restaurant with Jones's wailing violin disrupting his every thought. The obvious 'take a seat' gag with Palin's arrival sets things up nicely for Jones's romantic misunderstanding and a truly mind-blowing, repeated rendition of a tireless little ditty, *My Mistake*. This is completely mad but that's what great *Python* is all about. However, there's a real sense of low ebbs about this show, with these, hardly classic, but enjoyable moments never making up for the painful military blundering, airforce archive footage and cliff-hanging ending that's left hanging. The final saving grace is Idle's *Radio Times* representative, reading from the sainted journal (note the Circus's Flying cover), detailing the hugely expensive BBC budget and commenting on the credits as their roll by on a television set on his desk. The pleading for more time from Mr. Cotton, Palin's Conjuring Today police escape and the giant hammer attack form the most effective part of the show but it's got nothing really to do with Neutron's non-event and far too much of this episode has.

Did You Know?
Neil Innes's classic *Protest Song* was due to be performed at the end of this show but was dropped – pity!

Series 4 episode 4 Conceived & written by **Graham Chapman, John Cleese, Eric Idle, Terry Jones, Michael Palin & Terry Gilliam**
Also appearing **Carol Cleveland, Bob E. Raymond & Bloopy**
Dogs trained by **John & Mary Holmes**
Make-up **Maggie Weston**
Costume **Andrew Rose**
Film cameraman **Stan Speel**
Sound recordist **Ron Blight**
Film editor **Bob Dearberg**
Sound **Mike Jones**
Lighting **Jimmy Purdie**
Visual effects **John Horton**
Production assistant **Brian Jones**
Designer **Robert Berk**
Produced & directed by **Ian MacNaughton**
28 November 1974

EPISODE 6
The final television episode of *Python* has a political flavour with a threatened broadcast on behalf of the Liberal party, but although there is a certain amount of election fever, a masked candidate pops up at regular intervals and the final closing credits take on by-election terminology, the ground-breaking element of this show is the unforgettable Awful Family Competition, penned by Neil Innes and vividly brought to life by all five Pythons in varying elements of repulsion. Looking like perverse ghosts of Queen videos yet to come,

the team revel in a feast of unpleasantness, with Idle's nagging, worrisome mother ironing the radio and hanging the cat out to dry, Jones, by now adept at the grouchy father figure, guzzling mouthfuls of Ano-Weet cereal (note the offer of a free Pope with every packet), Palin hamming it up as the dreadfully accident-prone, pimple-adorned schoolboy continually answering irrelevant questions, Chapman, face smeared with make-up, 'bleedin' this, 'bleedin' that and slutting about the place in teenage sexual revolution and, most powerful of all, a barely comprehensible babble from Gilliam stretched out on a sofa surrounded with a fast diminishing supply of baked beans screaming for more with great passion. The Pratt heavy football team, a Tarzan-like swinging postman and the fading out of soundtrack music when Idle irons the radio are the most subtle touches in a glorious feast of the grotesque – an entirely fitting part of this climactic bit of small screen *Python*. The whole competition aspect, hosted by a glitzy-suited Palin and judged by distant members of the landed gentry, wheezes on through other more profound examples watching the show on television, an Upper Class Twit of the Year based entry and low-key comment on the nation's eating habits with mention of the heart-attacko margarine sponsorship. Chapman's door-to-door Icelandic honey week man (a throwback to the Michael Ellis episode) chatters on about the celebrations to the viewing family of awfulness (Gilliam's schoolboy eating corn plasters/a cat screaming through a hole in the wall) before the titles and further investigation reveal the entire honey promotion as a sham – Chapman's hard-done-by defence of the working man is prime *Python*, while the vintage embrace of historical documentary (in this case, the 1863 tale of Comanche Indians) acts as an unconnected introduction to the stunning Chapman/Douglas Adams penned medical sketch with doctor Graham practising his golf swings and snooker cueing action as a stabbed Terry Jones fills out trivial

questionnaires. A joyfully damning dig at the insensitivity of the profession, Chapman's headmaster-like barking (his reaction to *The Merchant of Venice* answer is priceless), Carol Cleveland's murderous Angel of Mercy and the frantic, 'do as you're told' British patient combine to make a memorably disturbing sequence. Gilliam, by now a very regular on-screen face, adds some potent clout to this line of comic expression with his humiliated patient forced to wear a paper bag over his head, mournfully ringing a bell and signalling himself out as unclean. Reflecting Chapman's medical training yet again but with an even more cheerfully cutting style than his work with Cleese, the team fail to build on the comic force with the bizarre Idle/Palin military letter dictation with Idle's superior wearing a pink ballet tutu, Palin adorned in archbishop's robes (spouting the Good Book and Raymond Chandler) and a dubious flash of mutual admiration fading almost immediately because of television restrictions. Apart from this knowing reflection of the only very slightly permissive society, this sketch falls flat and is, quite unsurprisingly, tossed aside in favour of something new. As was often the case, a stop-gap was provided by Gilliam but even his genius was failing, injecting an elongated and unfocused opera singer sequence, facing a painfully slowed-down canon shell entering his body and exploding.

It is down to Chapman again to point things in the right direction, going through his Ronnie Barker on speed routine with a direct address to the people on behalf of rich people, illustrating the plight of dating glam girls and spending lots of money with straight-faced solemnity. In a continuing spiral of television interaction, this appeal is watched by Jones' housewife, going to answer the door while cheerfully singing the old pyjamas version of *Anything Goes* from episode three. The gag itself, Idle's training the good lady in finishing other people's sentences instead of having them finished for her gets a bit too clever and involved for its own good but the two old pros tackle the role reversal insanity with gusto. Jones, marching with Wagnerian vigour to Stonehenge, acts as a mere link for Palin's African adventure but here the team is working together as in the old days, linking sketches with interesting ideas and, above all, producing top notch performances which often outweigh the scripted material. In an ironic foreshadowing of his celebrated travels, Palin's David Attenborough explorer breathlessly enthuses about the incorrect walking tree, momentarily goes into schoolboy smut overdrive with the Turkish Little Rude Tree and embodies white man naiveté with gallons of squirting sweat coupled with the shocked amazement at discovering warrior-styled cricket games in the heart of jungle. A Gilliam quickie (the old guy knitting with his feet) intercuts into this bizarre re-telling of cricket via native destruction of the British, with spears ripping off heads, piercing legs and generally causing the team of Pratts to contribute a string of ducks (apart from the really rather impressive score of Y.E.T.A.N.O.T.H.E.R. Pratt) with Chapman's dry commentary adding a touch of refined class. However, it lacks the unexpected violence of Salad Days and lapses into gore for gore's sake along the way, before handing over to the typical *Python* target, television news delivered by Idle and backed by remnants of political pleasures with Cleveland's frantic table dancing. In a burst of location reporter hangovers between Chapman, Palin and Idle, the political party announcement is concluded through unsuppressed hilarity and on that note the programme, and the series, comes to a close. It's hardly the most emotive of closes but the guitar-picked rendition of the familiar theme breaking into the Sousa march does hit the perfect note of poignancy and besides, if only for the awful family, this episode reaches the levels of previous *Python* classics.

Did You Know?
Direct reference to Michael Ellis in

the Icelandic honey week sketch was removed while Idle's briefly mentioned item on Ursula Hitler, a Surrey housewife of the 1930s who specialised in bee-keeping but kept being mistaken for her famous namesake by Chamberlain, was planned for a sizeable chuck of material which ended up in the *Python* office litter bin. The BBC, eager to carry on with a success even though the quality was clearly falling, wanted a further six *Monty Python* episodes with the five team members. Michael Palin was very keen and tried to encourage a reluctant Eric Idle to agree during a reflective walk together – Eric said No...

A Party Political Broadcast On Behalf Of the Liberal Party was conceived, written and performed by **J. Thorpe** (AGE 2), **C. Smith** (AGE 1½), **L. Byers** (AGE 0) Unsuccessful candidates **Graham Chapman** Leicester North (Lost deposit), **Terry Gilliam** Minneapolis North (Lost deposit twice), **Eric Idle** South Shields North (Lost deposit but found an old one which he could use), **Terry Jones** Colwyn Bay North (small deposit on his trousers), **Michael Palin** Sheffield North (Lost his trousers) Most unsuccessful candidates **Carol Cleveland** (Liberal), **Bob E. Raymond** (Very Liberal) & **Peter Brett** (Extremely Liberal & rather rude) Even more unsuccessful candidates **Douglas Adams** Silly Words (North) **Neil Innes** Silly Words & Music (North) (copyright 1984 Thorpe-O-Hits Ltd) Make-up & hairdressing **Jo Grimond** More make-up **Maggie Weston** Even more make-up **Andrew Rose** (Costumes North) Much more make-up **Stan Speel** (Film Cameraman) Make-up & sound recording **Ron** (North) **Blight** Rostrum camera with make-up **Peter Willis** Film editor & not Make-up **Bob Dearberg** Not Film Editor Not Make-up But Dubbing Mixer **Rod Guest** Lighting, make-up & Prices & Incomes Policy **Jimmy Purdie** Visual effects & Mr. Thorpe's wigs **John Horton** Production assistant **Brian Jones**

(Make-up North) Designer (North) **Valerie Warrender** (Far too Liberal) Producer Mr. Lloyd-George (who knew **Ian MacNaughton**'s father) A BBC-Liberal-TV-Party Production (North) 5 December 1974

MONTY PYTHON'S FLYING CIRCUS

The first vinyl spin-off from the shows came from BBC records and is basically a round-up of vintage sketches, despite being re-released as *The Worst of Monty Python*! Recorded in mono in front of a live audience, this is not just recorded highlights from the television masters but completely new versions of old favourites. A valuable audio record of the team's early successes, the Pythons themselves were led to believe that the BBC would control their recording career with more care and immediately set the precedent of studio work fashioned particularly for the audio medium. It was this that led the team to sign for Charisma records the following year. The team felt BBC Records weren't allowing them to develop, but this first vinyl release does reshape Series One sketches for the recorded medium, with more obvious sound additions of Jones padding out the record to 30 minutes, Cleese's 'Hello puss!', more elaborate Goonish coughing, Jones sign-posting the Barber Shop sketch and Cleese's running commentary of Palin's blood-removal. There's a slight alteration, with the pepperpot going mad during the Mouse problem, a Simon Dee name-check during Minehead and Palin playing the three-buttocked chap, but more importantly, the Pythons address record convention. The end of side one is announced, Idle's interviewer greets Cleese's interviewer as the bloke from the 'other side' and Graham Chapman's military figure begins Side Two with a sound check, instructs the listening masses not to mess about with the speeds and directs Cleese's disgruntled dead parrot owner to the next track. This is far more than just a collection of *Python*'s greatest hits. It's a record

quite able to hold its own alongside
the later, more celebrated, releases. A
proposed single release of Flying
Sheep/Man With Two Buttocks was
originally planned by the BBC but
abandoned.

Monty Python's Flying Circus – Side 1:
Flying Sheep, Television Interviews/
Arthur Frampton, Trade Description
Act/Whizzo Chocolates, Nudge Nudge,
The Mouse Problem, Buying A Bed,
Interesting People, The Barber/
Lumberjack Song, Interviews/Sir
Edward Ross.
Side 2: More Television
Interviews/Arthur 'Two Sheds' Jackson,
Children's Stories, The Visitors, The
Cinema/Albatross, The North Minehead
By-Election, Me Doctor, Pet Shop, Self
Defence.
Written & performed by **Graham
Chapman, John Cleese, Terry Gilliam,
Eric Idle, Terry Jones & Michael Palin,
with Carol Cleveland**
Record produced by **Ian MacNaughton**
Incidental music **Anthony Foster**
Chorus **The Fred Tomlinson Singers**
Extra sound effects **Harry Morris**
Sleeve design **Terry Gilliam**
BBC REB 73M – 1970

MONTY PYTHON'S LIFE OF BRIAN

This is the *Python* masterpiece.
Probably easily getting into people's
lists of top five comedy films of all
time, and you certainly wouldn't get
a letter of complaint from me if you
feel inclined to give it pole position. A
glorious cascade of *Python* moments,
linked by the common theme of
lampooning organised religion, this is
the most sustained and film-like film
the team ever made. A strong
narrative, a fine starring turn from
Graham Chapman, galaxies of nutty
cameos and an almost complete
refusal to mock the medium of film
which they are working in – only at
the start, the end and once in the
middle do they pinpoint filmic
techniques. Although it's hardly your
average biblical movie, the characters
within the framework of the story
don't cross the line between reality
and fiction, allowing the whole

irreverent attitude of the comedy full
scope to develop. Besides all that, this
film stands as the most polished and
cleverly crafted script the Pythons
ever put together, benefiting from five
years doing their own thing and
recapturing that unique spark which
fused the team so closely together a
decade earlier.
Terry Jones, showing a glorious sense
of historical detail in his solo
directorial debut, sets up the standard
religious film conventions (holy
chanting, the three wise men
chillingly silhouetted in front of a
wondrous sunset, nativity animals all
over the barn) ripped apart by lunatic
utterances and a mighty slap to her
baby son ushering in Gilliam's
stunning title sequence, complete
with Bond-like Shirley Bassey belting
from Sonia Jones, a majestic,
archaeological sweep to the
crumbling grandeur of ancient
buildings, a Jagger-like lolling tongue
appearing from a stone lion, flimsy
set details revealed behind convincing
stone façade and the perfect contrast
within the title structure itself – the
Monty Python section is in bright
neon lights and the *Life of Brian* à la
Cecil B. DeMille. During this
hilarious pre-title sequence of
mistaken identity, Jones as Brian's
mum, burbles and mumbles about
biting bombs and the like, while the
laughter that masks the fact that
Jesus Christ is installed in the stable
across the way and that Brian's
mirrored life is used as the source of
comedy geared together the absurdity
of total, unquestioning faith. Right
from the first sequence with Jesus
declaring his thoughts on the mount,
the concept of religion is mis-
represented and misinformed.
Humour comes from the classic big
nose (obvious ultimate insult of the
time for Palin's leper and Cleese in
Centurion mode both later adopt it)
battle between Idle and Palin, while
Jones stands as one of the most
embarrassing mother figures in the
Python cannon. However, beneath the
comic banter, the Greek/meek
mishearing and blessed cheese-
maker's mistake sets up the system of
followers rearranging and
misinterpreting the Gospel, with

Terence Baylor's pompous
observation that it obviously means
any manufacturer of dairy goods.
This thematic stance of minority
obsessives crafting the religious beliefs
to suit their own lives, runs throughout the film, notably with the anti-
woman stoning sessions ('It's just
written!'), the manic following of
Chapman's one-shoed, unambitious
prophet and the stunned silence as his
impassioned expletive doesn't get
through to them – Cleese memorably
mutters 'How shall we f*** off, oh
Lord?'
Python's stance examines the abuse of
faith for Man's personal gain,
brilliantly channelled through the
endearing performance of poor old
Graham Chapman, bemused by his
contrasting Roman/Jewish birth ties,
confused in love with his lustful
longings for Sue Jones-Davis and
foiled by the very spirit of
individuality he advocates. The
barbaric attitude of the time is
hilariously addressed via the stoning
milestone, with the 'rebel on the
football terraces' mentality from the
Jesus speech contrasted with good,
honest family fun entertainment style
of Idle's gravel salesman, with his
glib 'Local boy!' comments latching
onto boxing terminology and the
whole ethos of spectator sport giving
the act of brutal death a lighter
quality. Obviously, the entire idea of
blaspheming is mocked via John
Cleese, at his school headmaster best,
sending Idle's early stone thrower to
the back, suspiciously wondering if
there are any women present (in
reality, the entire crowd, bar Brian,
are female and thus breaking the law
as much as the poor condemned
wretch, while, a first for *Python* and,
indeed, comedy in general, the lads
are male actors playing woman
pretending to be men – the first
double bluff cross-dressers), while
injecting Basil Fawlty bite to his bitter
comments – 'Right, who threw that!'
Reinforcing the stupidity of
nonsensical punishment illustrated in
the witch dunking scene from *Monty
Python and the Holy Grail*, this
unforgettable stoning sequence revels
in the no win situation ('making it
worse!') of the innocent under-dog.

Not looking on the bright side much in *Brian* – Idle, Cleese and Palin

The double standards of a religious survival are mirrored in the double standards of Terry Jones, condemning Chapman's youth for continually talking about sex (when he isn't – merely allowing his mother's sexual obsession to reflect from his misunderstanding) and living a life as a Roman-serving prostitute as Brian spirals further into introspective confusion. In-between these heartfelt mother/son revelations one of the greatest of all *Python* interludes presents a gleefully, hoping, full of beans ex-leper characterisation from Michael Palin. Cheerfully badgering Brian for a few coins, he gladly relates the miraculous curing of his ailments by the powerful healing hands of Jesus and thus, denying him his begging trade. The line of comedy is inspired, Palin is at his most endearingly funny and Chapman's petulant denials are sheer class. When he finally relents, Palin is disgusted by the lack of financial help offered and the kicking punchline regarding the comment from Jesus really hits home as Palin hops off, skilfully avoiding a pile of horse manure with swift leg action. A vignette of pure *Python* genius. Chapman's delicious run-through every alternative phrase for his proud Jewishness remains arguably his most passionate film sequence, gloriously contrasted with his humble day job of selling such imperialistic Roman tit-bits as larks' tongues and ocelots' noses in direct homage to the

landmark Albatross selling of vintage television *Python*. The children's matinee gore fest of the lion's den balances Gilliam guts with Palin's innocence, allowing a choice bit of gleeful hamming from Neil Innes and introducing the complex, political hierarchy of the anti-Roman dissenters, led by the definitive militant, cowardice and words before the action persona of Cleese's Reg, gloriously questioning the mental failings of Idle's sex-change obsessed, baby desirer ('Don't you oppress me!'). The medical impossibility and high faluting jargon is typical Cleese/Chapman writing, while Palin's niceties shine through with hastily corrected brother/sister addressing. Meanwhile, the cardiac arrest situation on the 'pitch' and Innes victory brings a wonderful, 'up yours' to authority reaction from Cleese, swallowing his prejudices and unwillingly giving into his desire for ocelot noses and condemning the splinter groups in the movement – splitter! – the hatred of the Romans being as nothing compared to the unionist hatred of fellow supporters who don't quite see eye to eye on every single issue. Chapman's committed dispersing of the Romans leads to a wonderful Cleese attack on the physical abuse and mental humiliation of public school. Chapman's anti-Roman slogan branded on the wall of the palace is tantamount to war, but Cleese is less impressed with his Latin skills than

his revolutionary behaviour. Turning on the overbearing school punishment motif, Cleese clearly has a ball making the brilliantly nervy Chapman squirm with total fear, breathlessly trying to correct his mistake with every knowing hint from the master, energetically tugging at his ear for major effect – it's a flapper for me! A hero of the movement for doing the fullest bit of graffiti work in the history of mankind, Chapman is embraced by the brother/sisterhood of the movement, just in time for the daring kidnap plan talked to death by the cowardly Cleese and started by the almighty, unsurpassable What Have the Romans Ever Done For Us? discussion with the Jewish followers listing the important innovations from their enemy. Idle's expressions, Palin's cheerful agreement and Cleese, in ultimate bombastic mood, make this one of the funniest pieces of film you are ever likely to come across. A masterpiece of timing and spiralling comedy writing, it is arguably, *Python*'s glory moment.
Perhaps as a counter-balance to the huge laughter that sequence was guaranteed, the actual kidnap attempt itself is the film's only drop in pace. Not even the Pythons firing on all cylinders could keep the hectic pleasures going for a full ninety minutes and besides, it is only a very, very minor dip in excellence, encompassing Palin's military-minded commentary, an impressive emergence from beneath a gigantic mosaic and the final dive into Three Stooges-like eye-poking. However, just to really sandwich it between two masterpieces, Chapman's unceremonious boot into prison presents Palin's It's Man in extreme old age, Ben, the Python's answer to Treasure Island's Ben Gunn, crying 'You lucky bastard!' all over the place, jealous of Gilliam's spitting in Chapman's face, embracing inverted bigotry in the belief that this treatment is the best thing for his criminal kind and showering sycophantic devotion to the Roman oppressors. Delighting in the system, this old revolutionary now stands as the ultimate realisation of Roman

torture, offering meek devotion to the lowest of the low, laughing at Cleese's off-kilter joke ('Nice one Centurion, like it, like it!!') and smiling with affection at all but Chapman's jailer's pet! It is a classic sequence, delightfully resurrected when the old man is spied, upside down, as the crucifixion party head off for their faith at the end. At this stage it's just an audience with Palin's speech-impaired Governor – *Python*'s ultimate illustration that innuendo silliness is just as funny as satirical cleverness, with Palin stumbling over mispronounced Rs in words like 'spirit', Cleese only getting through (sorry, thwough) to him by mimicking his phrasing of throw him to the floor, and, finally, the onslaught of joke names which aren't that funny to Palin. As the guards around him suppress smiles from Palin's slow, methodical pronunciations of Biggus Dickus (how the actor himself kept a straight face, I'll never know), they gradually fail the test and explode into bursts of laughter. And if you can keep a straight face then you are seriously dead my friend. It's the film's most obvious use of stupid, naughty-sounding names, but, hey, when it's comedy anything goes, and Palin clearly has the time of his film life with the material.

Chapman's scarper through the streets, chased by Roman soldiers, breaks into the only anti-continuity, narrative upheaval in the main body of the film, when the breathless Brian is whipped away into a two-seater alien spaceship. A major *Python* flight of science-fiction fancy suggested by Graham Chapman, but very much the creation of Terry Gilliam and tapping into the popular *Star Wars* culture of the late 1970s (the aliens look like refugees from the bar, there's a suggestion of the haunting theme music and the opening sermon/wise men scenes were filmed at Matmata – the location for the *Stars Wars* desert scenes – although this bit was filmed in London!) this is a manic, off-the-wall moment unquestioned and quickly bypassed in favour of a renewal of historical pursuits.

Chapman's escape route includes perhaps my all-time favourite *Brian* segment with Idle's crafty cockney beard haggling (going through the same old routine, grabbing the *Barnum* philosophy and rhythmically shaking his head to the old 'ten for that; you must be mad!' routine), a Cleese invasion of the movement's hide-out with John Young almost going into *The Quartermaster's Store*, the Roman centurion nervously calling him a loony and, finally (à la Robert Donat in *The 39 Steps*) an impromptu address of the assembled masses, joining the likes of Gilliam's mud-clad, dismembered hands flaunting chap and Palin's bearded idiot as the new prophet on the block. Although at first his words of wisdom concerning the flowers and birds get club comedian-styled heckles from his unimpressed audience ('He's making it up as he goes along!') once the coast is clear and Chapman's unconsidered utterances cease his problems really begin. A following through the desert, including Carol Cleveland's Americanised glam girl, Cleese as a follower of bombastic authority and an uncertain Spike Milligan (who happened to be holidaying in Tunisia and dropped in for the shot) simply looks on as the mystic, uncontrollable rock star-like status of their hero dictates copying his actions (ie. the wearing of one shoe) gets out of hand. With a muttered 'Let us pray!' Spike clenches his fists, wanders out of the frame and lets the religious followers do their stuff. In the hands of a lesser man this would be nothing, but this is Spike for heaven's sake, endorsing his own followers' masterpiece with a willing, typically manic bearded cameo.

The immortal Terry Jones sequence as his holy man breaks his silence vows, protects his juniper bushes and meets the unwanted wrath of Chapman's bloodthirsty, devout horde of believers stands at the very hub of the comedy, finding miracles in the most obvious things and effortlessly highlighting their own misplaced beliefs with Charles McKeown's truly outstanding blind man contribution, celebrating his

newly found sight as he tumbles into the hole. This is the anti-obsession of religious belief in definitive terms. A night of passion with Judith may calm Brian, as he discontentedly realises that what his followers *want* to think he said is far more important than what he *really* says, although the braying crowd that meets his satisfied full-frontal figure at the window, outrages his mother, prompts Idle's impersonal question about her virginity (silence is assumed as admittance) and cracks the most telling gag about individuality as the crowd agree with one voice except Baylor, who waits for quiet and contradictory cries 'I'm not!' Anyway, it's too late, Reg and the lads pontificate about helping Brian out but the crucifixion order has already come through. Palin's thoughtful understanding counsellor chappie whispers his instructions but is happily stopped in his tracks by Eric Idle's Max Miller-like banter about freedom and islands. It is a sense of cheerful humour which will later see his release as the infamous 'Bwian' and Chapman's martyrdom for the cause. However, that's not until Idle and Gilliam have jabbered away for minutes before, ultimately, resuming their civilised, coherent chat, the military-styled crucifixion party has left and Terry Jones as the white figure of mercy has got trapped by his own kindness, ending up with Langham's cross and enriching the ever cheerful Idle with a bit of a giggle. The final crucifixion scene continues the underlining theme of human intolerance (Baylor is shocked that this Jewish sector has a Samaritan element), while Chapman's heartfelt beliefs count for nothing as his nutty colleagues sing 'For he's a jolly good fellow', his love celebrates his brave death for his uncommitted beliefs and even his own mother rejects him. For a few seconds as Chapman movingly shouts 'Mum! Mum!' and the camera remains on his beaten expression, this is as emotive as *Python* gets. It shows Chapman as a powerful film actor and brilliantly sets the scene for Idle's comic performance of *Always Look On the Bright Side Of Life*. As those who are about to die sing along with the up-tempo ditty, suicide squad's feet begin to tap and, finally, even Chapman joins in, the camera pans away to show the skyline littered with merrymaking crucifixion victims. Bad taste in the eyes of those who aren't on the wavelength, this has to be one of the greatest endings to any comedy movie anywhere. As Idle's commercially minded speech complements the continued song, the image fades to black closing a masterpiece of British humour.

Did You Know?
'I said to them, I said, Bernie – they'll never make their money back!' – the ultimate tongue-in-cheek two-finger salute to the money man who pulled the plug on *Brian*. By now, cool *Python* force John Cleese was a huge star in his own right with *Fawlty Towers* and following his powerful experiences with Video Arts, and particularly *Meetings Bloody Meetings*, he was also a kingpin round the negotiation table. However, even he couldn't stop Bernard Delfont's EMI pulling out of the film two days before filming was due to begin. Cue Eric Idle's mate George Harrison who put up £4 million, backed the movie, popped in for a cameo, established HandMade films and created the classic filmic cliché that his love for *Python* and a desire to see *Brian* resulted in 'The most expensive cinema ticket ever issued!' The filming date was put back a mere six months, the script was tightened and improved upon while the Pythons were even more committed to make *Brian* a classic. The team were already muting the possibility of another movie during the last week of filming *Grail* and, indeed, the original idea for *Brian* came from Eric Idle who toiled with a project called *Jesus Christ – Lust For Glory* which was discussed within the team while awaiting flights and publicity appearances during 1975's plugging for *Monty Python and the Holy Grail*. Although a rough draft was ready as early as Christmas 1976 and the team had been brought together for the City Center live shows the concept remained pretty much dead in the water because they

couldn't think of anything that funny about Jesus – and thus counteracting the whole misconceived controversy with the character of Jesus appearing as a straight performance role with only his words misinterpreted by the film's grotesques.
The writers were keen to highlight the torture and hardship of the time, injecting humour into the final scene while embracing warm humanity – the basis point is that crucifixion is nasty and the film is not just blindly laughing at their fate. For the actors it was a gruelling three-day filming schedule on crosses made even more chilling because each performer had his own personal cross, complete with his name on it. Early drafted ideas for this organised religion comedy eventually landed on a certain St. Brian, the forgotten 13th disciple with a demanding wife, who couldn't make the last supper because she had dinner guests and went to a club called the Garden of Juran by mistake. Titles considered were *The Gospel According to St. Brian* and *Brian of Nazareth* but the title hit another snag with the character of Jesus – they couldn't, and indeed, didn't want to, make him funny but every appearance killed the comedy stone dead. Finally all six Pythons took a two-week working holiday in Barbados, during January 1978, and came up with the idea of Brian being just some bloke mistaken for a prophet, thus allowing Jesus to remain a straight, sideline figure while Brian faced the onslaught of divine admiration. In fact, it was during this Barbados brainstorm that an EMI rep met the Pythons and promised them the £2 million budget. Only when preliminary location work, costumes and crew were already getting together a month later did the company back out.
EMI were recovering from the financial embarrassment of hastily hiring and firing the Sex Pistols when the Python film bit the dust. HandMade Films was coined as a joke name, following a recent visit by George Harrison to the Handmade Paper Mill at Wookey Hole, Somerset. Shamelessly creating media fever-pitch by uncharacteristically

basking in post-Beatles celebration, Harrison told *Evening News* (11 March, 1978) that 'three old friends might act in *Life of Brian*'.
Once George Harrison had appeared on the scene, construction crews under the guidance of Terry Gilliam started work on the sets, the team enjoyed a week of rehearsals and filming began at Monastir, Tunisia, from 16 September to 12 November 1978. Much of the work was based around the Ribat, Franco Zeffirelli's *Jesus of Nazareth* building (Brian's stoning scene, the first footage filmed, was located in the exact same place as the one in Robert Powell's epic) was next door and the team enjoyed four day's filming in Sousse (during which time Spike did his bit). A Tunisian comedian was hired to amuse the extras in readiness for Palin's speech impediment farce, Harrison popped in for his scene while taking a short break from mixing his album. In January 1979, *Life of Brian* was screened in London for an invited audience only. The finished film weighed in at two hours, 15 minutes and great chunks of class material were edited – although much of this was later reinstated. There was talk within the group to release it as it was, with an interval break, or even put it out as a two-part film, but in the end, the group decided to cut it down. Missing pieces included the shepherd in the next field, the kidnap of Pilate's wife (played by massive John Case), and, most penetrating of all, Idle's Nazi Jew Otto and his suicide army's main scene – their only appearance in the final cut is at the very end and leaves most of their comedy unexplained. After all the editing and fiddling Terry Gilliam was disillusioned, considering the end result an 'ordinary comedy'. It was hardly that – with modern stereotypes humanising/demystifying historical settings (like *Grail*) in definitive terms, by far the best film acting from all six Pythons and a script crackling with class, this is the essence of comic genius.
In 1989, following Graham Chapman's memorial service, several people urged Julian Doyle to release the full, uncut, two and a quarter

hour version of the film – *Life After Brian* – for a limited, special tribute presentation. Cleese, wary of facing a new backlash of controversy, exercised his *Python* veto to stop the idea.

HandMade Films/Python (Monty) Pictures Ltd
For Orion Pictures/Warner Brothers
Monty Python's Life of Brian
Starring **GRAHAM CHAPMAN** as Brian (Called Brian), 1st Wise Man & Biggus Dickus
JOHN CLEESE as 3rd Wise Man, Reg (Leader of Judaean People's Front), Jewish Official at Stoning, Centurion of the Yard, Deadly Dirk & Arthur
TERRY GILLIAM as Another Person Further Forward, Revolutionary, Masked Commando, A Blood and Thunder Prophet, Geoffrey & Jailer
ERIC IDLE as Mr. Cheeky, Stan (Called Loretta, a confused revolutionary), Harry the Hagler (Beard and stone salesman), Culprit Woman (Who casts the 1st stone), Intensely dull youth, Otto (Leader of the Judaean People's Front), Jailer's assistant & Mr. Frisbee the Third
TERRY JONES as Mandy (The mother of Brian), Colin, Simon the Holy Man, Bob Hoskins & Saintly passer-by
MICHAEL PALIN as 2nd Wise Man, Mr. Big Nose, Francis (A Revolutionary), Mrs. A (Who casts the 2nd stone), Ex-Leper, Ben (An ancient prisoner), Pontius Pilate (Roman Governor), A boring prophet, Eddie & Nisus Wettus
With Mrs. Gregory & Elsie **CAROL CLEVELAND**
Jesus **KEN COLLEY**
Mrs. Big Nose, Woman with sick donkey & Young girl **GWEN TAYLOR**
Gregory, Revolutionary, Masked Commando & Dennis **TERENCE BAYLOR**
Man Further Forward, Roman soldier Stig, Revolutionary, Masked Commando, Giggling Guard, A False Prophet & Blind Man **CHARLES McKEOWAN**
Judith (A beautiful revolutionary) **SUE JONES-DAVIS**
Matthias (A Stonee) & Passer-by **JOHN YOUNG**
Official stoner's helper, Revolutionary, Masked Commando, Giggling Guard & Parvus (A Centurion) **BERNARD McKENNA**
Another Official stoner's helper,

Revolutionary, Masked Commando, Giggling Guard & Passer-by **ANDREW MacLACHLAN**
A Weedy Samaritan at the Amphitheatre **NEIL INNES**
A Gladiator **JOHN CASE**
Passer-by **CHARLES KNODE**
Alfonso, Revolutionary, Masked Commando & Giggling Guard **CHRIS LANGHAM**
and
Spike **SPIKE MILLIGAN**
Mr. Papadopoulis **GEORGE HARRISON**
Written by **Graham Chapman, John Cleese, Terry Gilliam, Eric Idle, Terry Jones & Michael Palin**
Design & Animation **Terry Gilliam**
Music **Geoffrey Burgon**
Conductor **Marcus Dods**
Songs: *Brian* by **Andre Jacquemin & David Howman**, arranged by **Trevor Jones**, sung by **Sonia Jones**
Bright Side of Life by **Eric Idle**, arranged by **John Altman**
Photography **Peter Biziou**
1st Assistant director **Jonathan Benson**
2nd assistant director **Melvin Lind**
3rd assistant director **Matthew Binns**
Tunisian assistant directors **Hmida Ben Ammar, Lotfi Thabet & Slim Mzali**
Production assistants **Jennie Raglan & Nicole Souchal**
Camera grips **Frank Batt & Sadok Ben Amor**
Focus **Michael Brewster**
Loaders **Alan Annand & Hechim Cherif**
Tunisian production department **Ali Cherif, Ahmed Attia, Tarak Harbi, Habib Chaari, Claude Guillene, Jazzi Abderrazak & Mouldi Kriden**
Stills photography **David Appleby**
Chief electrician **Roy Rodhouse**
Assistant sound engineers **Dushko Indjic & Phil Chubb**
1st assistant editor **Rodney Glenn**
2nd assistant **John Mister**
Effects editor **Tony Orton**
Assistant dubbing editors **Chris Welch & Simon Bailey**
Music mixers **Keith Grant, Andre Jacquemin & Steve James**
Production accountant **Ron Swinburne**
Accounts secretary **Hafida Quertani**
Assistant accountant **Hazel Crombie**
Tunisian accountant **Ridha Turki**
Scenic artist **John Spotswood**
Modeller **Keith Short**
Construction crew **Richard Jones, Craig Hillier, Peter Verard, Robert Mason,**

Graham Bullock, Alan Seabrook, Eric Nash, Gordon Izod, Michael Melia, Roy Clarke, David Wiggins, Dennis Harrison & Bunny Southall
Electrical department **Reg Parsons, Brian Smith, Les Rodhouse, Don Matton, Chuck Finch, Kamel Kardous & Mohamed Sahli**
Animation & model department **Tim Olive, Dennis Degroot, Kate Hepburn, Val Charlton, Rupert Ashmore, Roger Pratt, Tony Andrews & Michael Beard**
Matte paintings **Abacus**
Optical effects **Kent Houston & Paul Whitbread – Peerless Camera Co. Ltd, London**
Business manager **Anne Henshaw**
Executive producer for Tunisia **Tarek Ben Ammar**
Public relations **Peter Thompson**
HandMade representative **Patricia Burgess**
Location assistants **Sallie Hampton & Christina Biziou**
Producer's assistant **Hilary Sandison**
Art dept. secretary **Patricia Christian**
Bibliography assistant **Christine Miller**
London contacts **Sally Ball, Betty Swinburne & Carey Fitzgerald**
Processed at Rank Film Laboratories Ltd. Denham, Bucks
Sound rerecorded at Trevor Pyke Sound Ltd, London W1
Dolby sound consultant **David Watts**
Music recorded at **Olympic Sound Studios, Chappell Recording Studios & Redwood Recording Studios**
Camera equipment from **Joe Dunton Cameras**
Lighting by **Lee Electrics (Lightings) Ltd**
Wigs, beards etc. made by **Wig Specialities**, London Kenneth Lintott
Costumes from **Bermans et Nathans**, London Gpil Rome, **Perruzzi**, Rome
Military uniforms from **Rancatl**, Rome
Shoes from **Pompeii**, Rome
Location catering by **Memmo** of Rome
Additional location facilities from **Trasporti Cinematografici**, Rome
Camera operator **John Stanier**
Continuity **Enda Loader**
Dubbing mixer **Hugh Strain**
Dubbing editor **John Foster**
Editor **Julian Doyle**
Sound recordist **Garth Marshall**
Make-up & hairdressing **Maggie Weston & Elaine**
Costume department **Nick Ede, Bill Pierce, Sue Cable, Zouleikha Ktari &**

He's got a very good friend in Rome... John Cleese, Michael Palin and Graham Chapman in *Brian*

Leila Turki
Props department **Peter Grant, Arthur Wicks, John Margetts, Gordon Phillips, Darryl Patterson & Geoffrey Hartman**
Make-up & hairdressing department **Susan Frear, Kenteas Irine, Diana Webber, Fatma Laziri & Famizia Choura**
Costume designer **Hazel Pethig & Charles Knode**
Art director **Roger Christian**
Associate producer **Tim Hampton**
Executive producers **George Harrison & Denis O'Brien**
Producer **John Goldstone**
Director **Terry Jones** – If you have enjoyed this film why not go and see *La Nocte*?
Filmed at Tunisia, Sousse, Carthage & Matmata
Flying saucer sequence filmed in London.
World Premiere, New York, 17 August 1979, 90 mins

MONTY PYTHON'S LIFE OF BRIAN

Unlike the *Holy Grail* soundtrack, the one for *Brian* is pretty much all the best bits from the film, an invaluable collection of *Python* soundbites, confused but made much more indispensable due to newly recorded linking commentary from Graham Chapman and Eric Idle. Both Pythons worked as producers for the album and as they were in the studio anyway they were perfect for this classic new material, with Idle as uncertain record official and Chapman distinguished voice-over artist without a clue. The album begins with a blast of Scottish mood music before Idle presents this latest stuff from 'those wacky *Monty Python* boys'. Chapman, who can't even decipher link from leek, bumbles on, Idle explains that nothing makes much sense but the kids seem to like it as Chapman struggles with quickly penned (in the pub) linking dialogue. The chemistry between the two, rarely used in the shows, is brilliant, with *Python* twisting this linking convention with precision. Whether it be talking over dramatic music, vanishing from the studio or mentioning lobster with alarming regularity, Chapman's misunderstanding narrator is a masterpiece, concerned about bad English ('During the meanwhile!') but trying everything for his long awaited £30. Idle is the voice of reason, convinced this is good enough, laid back in the knowledge that none of the Warner Brothers will care, asking for a hilariously delivered lighter performance, doing the narration himself at times of trouble and blue-pencilling Chapman's heartfelt sex link (full of 'darting tongues'). Classic stuff.

Warners released a single of the two songs from the film, *Always Look On the Bright Side Of Life* & *Brian's Song* (K 17495/W 7653) and in America a promotional album, *The Warner Brothers Music Show: Monty Python examines The Life of Brian* featured an hour-long interview with the team by Dave Herman interwoven with extracts from the soundtrack (WBMS 110).

Monty Python's Life of Brian – Side 1: Introduction, Brian Song, The Wise Men at the Manger, Brian Song continued, Sermon on the Mount (Big Nose), Stone salesman, Stoning, Ex-Leper, You Mean You Were Raped (Nortius Maximus), Link, People's Front of Judea, Short link, Romans Go Home, Missing link, What Have the Romans Ever Done For Us?, Very Good link, Ben, Brian before Pilate (Thwow Him to the Floor), Meanwhile.
Side 2: Prophets, Haggling, Brian's Prophecy, Lobster link, Simon the Holy Man, Sex link, He's Not the Messiah, He's a Very Naughty Boy, Lighter link, Pilate and Biggus, Welease Bwian, Nisus Wettus with the Gaolers, Cheeky is Released, Mandy to her Son, *Always Look on the Bright Side of Life*, Close.
Warner Brothers (K 56751), distributed by WEA Records Ltd. Producers **Eric Idle & Graham Chapman** Engineered, mixed & edited by **Anfre Jacquemin** at Redwood Recording Studios 1979

MONTY PYTHON'S LIFE OF BRIAN/ MONTYPYTHONSCRAPBOOK

Edited by Eric Idle, designed by Basil Pao and published by Eyre Methuen, this double whammy of a book features the screenplay, edited highlights (notably Idle's Otto sequence), photographs from the film, Terry Gilliam's stunning cover, with himself in biblical tableau style and a wealth of other bits of interest. Packaged as a large format, flip-over book, the scrapbook material boasts The Bruce's Philosophers Song, How it All Began: a comic strip with the Three Kings, Terry Jones and Michael Palin location filming diary extracts, A guide to what to take on filming, A Python Cinema Quiz, Brian Feeds the Multitude, 'Sharing' magazine with 'Sharing a Caravan with John Cleese', The Gilliam collection of Famous Film Titles, Cleese vs. The *Evening Standard*, Doc. Chapman's Medical Page and a bemused naked shot of the lads.

Monty Python's Life of Brian/MONTYPYTHONSCRAPBOOK written by **Graham Chapman, John Cleese, Terry Gilliam, Eric Idle, Terry Jones & Michael Palin** 1979. Methuen

MONTY PYTHON'S THE MEANING OF LIFE

Following the universal success of the hotly condemned but cinema-packing *Monty Python's Life of Brian*, Universal relieved financial security duties from George Harrison and threw heaps of money at the Pythons for a new, block-busting movie. The result, rather easily dismissible as a comedy film guaranteed to offend almost everyone, wasn't the great smash hit Universal banked on. It couldn't possible rank above the *Python* masterpiece of *Brian* and, in the eyes of non-fans today, it is a symbol of *Python* excess going too far. But this is much, much more than just the shock value of Terry Jones eating to bursting point. *Monty Python's The Meaning of Life* is a major comic expression from a seasoned team of great performers, allowed the money and freedom to do exactly what they wanted. Indeed, it was just like the old BBC days, with the added bonus of the Hollywood machine behind them and the lapsed attitude to swearing and violence

letting the team go fully for it. Moving totally away from the narrative structure of *Brian* this is polished sketch format *Python* linked by the all-covering, grand concept of the meaning of life. Taking this film as a final celebration of the glorious days of BBC *Python*, it remains a towering achievement and a more than fitting epitaph for a hugely influential group.

With the *Python*'s obsession with fish taken to new heights within the group, the six lads first appear in scaly form exchanging bits of idle small talk before the cold reality of mortality hits them and it's a real ponder on what life's really all about. Cue a stunning cut to black, the landmark Eric Idle title ditty and the most awe-inspiring set of opening credits ever to emerge from the fertile imagination of Terry Gilliam. Presenting a break-neck journey through the boredom of life and death, there's *Fantasia*-like ghouls of evil atop houses of business, passenger-gobbling trains, the old eye-ball removed telly viewer from the original shows and God's bemused weighting up between a square and round world, topped off with an injection of American iconology with millions of churned out functional families, naked save for some fetching Mickey Mouse ears. The wonders of nature as commercial efficiency, brilliantly brightened by Idle's classic song.

The film is split into seven chapters documenting the meaning of life and begins, naturally enough, with Part 1 – The Miracle of Birth – an unforgettable return to medical matters for Cleese and Chapman, highlighting the absurd waste of NHS funds and dedicated obsession with expensive equipment above human values. There's a priceless piece of timing as tons of lights and beep machines crowd the surgery, Chapman notices something missing and in perfect unison the two *Python* professionals look at each other and exclaim 'Patient!' – this is *Monty Python* firing on all cylinders. A fine use of blasting horns gives the whole musical score a sense of cod telly hospital drama, Eric Idle's working

class, cloth-capped loving hubby is quickly whisked away from the valuable machinery and the real vital thread of modern medicine is illustrated via Palin's bewildered, grey man in a suit whose total lack of knowledge of hospital matters pales when he reels off profit margins and cost-effective attitude. The actual birth is cold and brutal, hammered home by Chapman's severing of the cord with a meat cleaver and a delicious black glee in rubbing the baby with rough towels and chucking the newly born babe away from the mother. Orchestrated like a piece of drama (the cry of 'Show's over!' and the opportunity to buy a copy of the birth on both VHS and, unwisely, Betamax), Chapman has the most treasurable moment as he warns off quite naturally impending depression and violently reprimands the mother for imposing roles on her child when she enquires whether it's a boy or a girl.

The theme of birth is extended with the look at the Third World... Yorkshire – one of the most celebrated sequences in the film. Palin's downtrodden, working class lad, stumbles back to his child-ridden home with news of the closure of the factory and poverty staring him in the face. The sketch is hugely important for introducing the *Python* song into the main narrative. In the light of *Always Look On the Bright Side Of Life*'s success in *Brian* and the classic array of musical items on the Python records, *The Meaning of Life* has several classic musical interludes, with the little Roman Catholic gem *Every Sperm is Sacred*, setting the benchmark for taboo breaking, brilliantly performed material in the film. With Terry Jones's marvellous old dear taking a chorus and the Pythons getting maximum shock value via fresh-faced kids on solo moments, the entire thing bursts into a tongue-in-cheek resurrection of *Oliver!* with heel-clicking street urchins, rough-voiced babes, nannies, nuns, Brummie religious icons and even dead bodies getting in on the act. In a superbly realised jaunty musical interlude, Jones, as director, fully captures the feel-good, poor and we can handle it, working-class spirit of the Dickens musical, before the bubble of optimism is burst and the kids, destined for medical experiments, sing the song in sombre mood. However, dry those tears away, for Chapman's furiously proud Protestant, full of bloody this and bloody that, converses with his good lady wife (a fetching Eric Idle) and delights in a lengthy monologue on his sexual freedom and religion-backed ability to purchase condoms free of shame. It's an excellent performance, light years away from his, and the other members', often fluffed and muddled delivery in the classic shows. With time, money and reputation behind them, the Pythons can present their most polished and uncensored array of sketches ever. Even the weak link, the initial part of episode 2 – Growth and learning – can be forgiven as just an injection of typically *Python*esque attacking the rigours and horror of religious-based public schooling. Palin's outlandish and awe-inspired leading of the congregation is a bit too outlandish and awe-inspired, although he's fully forgiven for the spot-on delivery of the familiar phrase, 'Let us praise God!' This is a man who's been there, done that and ripped up the T-shirt. Cleese, akin to Alan Bennett's flights of religious fancy, goes all round the houses to stunning effect, memorably defending the school cormorant from vicious attack, vowing to keep China British and effortlessly illustrating the underlying insensitivity of these so-called Christian values by casually broadcasting that one of his pupils' mother has died.

Things pick up immediately with Cleese's sex education class, complete with juvenile Palin, Jones, Chapman and Idle in attendance, initially sitting quietly reading and reacting to Palin's look-out with a burst of paper-throwing and riotous action upon their master's appearance. A very forthright sexual lecture continues with these unkeen pupils looking around, tittering with nervous energy and a classic response from Idle, with 'Can we have a window open, please Sir!' The rituals of scripture practice and clothes hung on lower pegs is mocked and cleverly brought into the foreplay discussion by Chapman, Cleese threatens the unmentionable – an end-of-term exam – and the sight of Patricia Quinn stripping off for some full-on sex education demonstration still doesn't distract certain boys from staring absent-mindedly out of the window. Punishment comes with a vicious game of rugger opposite the masters, with foul play from a sidelined Cleese, forbidding *Phantom of the Opera*-styled organ music (*Toccata and Fugue in D Minor* by JS Bach) to set the atmosphere of doom and an impressive directorial cross-fade into the more tangible horrors of war with part 3 – Fighting each other. It's the old, old story of cool, dedicated officer class (Jones) protecting his squad of British Tommies (the other five Pythons), with the cold reality of war being nothing compared to his men's devotion to the strong leadership and camaraderie in evidence. Presentation clocks, Swiss watches, blood-splattered cards, cheques and even a cake, tip Jones over the polite acceptance level and into the seriousness of warfare. The sharp word more hurtful than a German bullet, Idle's bolshy, working class ethos pours out with his dying breath ('Toffs is all the same!') as the other squaddies tell it how it is. Gutted as his men fall around him like the proverbial flies, Jones bites his stiff-upper lip, ignores impending doom and sets up table, doilies and the whole works in a besieged trench in the middle of no-man's land. This is the ultimate social nicety of the true Brit carrying on with his social duties regardless and although enforcing the penetrating poetry of the next war's Keith Douglas, there is still a sense of twisted pride in the Python's delivery. Anyway, this little sequence is revealed to be a film show hosted by a contemporary kited Chapman, resurrecting his old hard-done-by, silly attitudes from 1969 with gusto. Palin's following masterpiece – with his hard-boiled, roaring and ranting sergeant allowing his timid squaddies to scarper off to spend time with kids, book reading and picture going

Where's the cheeseboard? Terry Jones in gross overdrive for *Monty Python's The Meaning of Life*

rather than enjoying his 'little scheme' of marching up and down the square – is a priceless *Python* vignette, mocking the blustering bluster of army authority but providing it with a rare face of subtle kindness.

The second leg (if you will excuse the pun – obvious later!) of the war section, tackles the African bloodbath of the first Zulu war, celebrating British pluck and officer's straight-faced continuation of clean habits and good old fashioned British decency, reaching a peak with Idle's casual bed-ridden chappie with the rather inconvenient problem of having his leg whipped off in the middle of the night. Cleese is in complete earnest, doctor Chapman tries hard to disguise the problem as a virus before, rather quickly, giving up and suggesting the nasty work of a tiger may be the cause. Palin's stunned line 'in Africa!', repeated when Cleese questions his point (desperately trying to cover up with some feeble notion of escaping from a zoo), taps into the old terminology of the letter of continuity complaint, done with the masterly under-playing of a true comic pro. Terry Jones (Celtic symbol for the working class face of *Python*) is the definitive blood-soaked minion, repeating the tiger in Africa reference before Cleese turns the screw on the social pecking order and insists that an officer's leg is far more important than total slaughter of his men – and is that the original *Zulu* rising star Michael Caine, flat on his back, mortally wounded as Cleese wanders past? It would be so right if it is! Eric Idle, excelling again at working men's rights, rambles on about the madness of getting a medal for killing in Africa but the death sentence if you kill at home, before the intrepid hunt for the upper-class Idle's leg is on. And now comes the greatest scene in the entire film, in my opinion, with those giants of comedy Eric Idle and Michael Palin trying to explain why they are in a tiger suit by weaving a totally insane, bizarre and winding load of tall tales and swinging tails, clutching at any dodgy straw from complete madness to divine instruction. There are just bucketloads of classic, absolutely mind-blowing feeble excuses and half-baked suggestions, brilliantly complemented by Idle's hilarious visual gag of looking down, allowing the tiger head to be totally visible, nervously fondling his whiskers and looking at Palin for inspiration. Without doubt, it's one of the greatest moments of *Monty Python* ever filmed. A fitting time then for a middle of the film break, ushered in by an unzipped Terry Gilliam, a refined lady host of breeding from Michael Palin and a gloriously surreal Find the Fish interlude with a swaying armed Terry Jones, a suspender-belted Graham Chapman and manic poetic pseudo-Edward Lear/Lewis Carroll utterances. Mad but it works! And it certainly gets a favourable reaction from our fishy friends with cries of best bit so far and the like before the lads start wondering about the meaning of life again and suggest that the film is building up to it. What we get is Idle's suggested blow-job on hubby Palin (it's really a case of breathing on his camera lenses, but the wipe of the mouth certainly suggests it all!) as we enter part four of our journey, into middle age.

The concept of a restaurant actually promoting the conversation of your choice is in the same league as the argument sketch, with this manic Mediaeval-style Hawaiian eating place perfectly suited to some ill-informed and uninterested small talk on philosophers and the meaning of life (cue interest from the fish tank!). It's all New England Americanisms, blessed with Palin's overly jolly tourist, Idle's soft vocals inspired by Dustin Hoffman's female alter-ego in *Tootsie* and John Cleese's waiter coming straight from George C. Scott's ranting in *Dr. Strangelove*. After a long and winding road through handy listed key names in philosophy Idle staggers onto popular music and Palin, suddenly a wee bit assertive, asks for another conversation. Cue the live organ transplant sketch, revisiting the ethos of the new cooker sketch from the old days with, again, dear old Terry Jones playing the normal, working class woman at home, with the smooth-talking anti-charm of John Cleese, stubbly efficiency of Chapman and pebble-glassed Gilliam giving up his bodily organs 'a bit premature like'. Cleese, making a super cool pass, only to get his hands on Jones's liver, sighs and, by trying to highlight the total insignificance of one human life, opens the fridge, releases Eric Idle's white-haired, pink-suited glitz kid and heralds the almighty *Galaxy Song*. A stunning gallop through the enormity of the universe, Idle's performance is breath-taking, notably his flamboyantly exaggerated rendition of the phrase, 'amazing and expanding universe!' Gilliam's graphic look at the female form in space bridges the instrumental section before Idle the man leads Jones back down to earth and mystic acceptance of the futility of her existence. A priceless slice of pure *Python* magic.

There follows a brief reprise of the Crimson Permanent Assurance pirates, attacking the deluxe board room (with Pythons, Chapman, Idle and Jones now in attendance) but it's only for a cinematic in-gag about the shameless, unprompted attack from the supporting feature, before Eric Idle's totally outrageous, smut-ridden *Not Noel Coward Song* gets into full swing. Basically running through almost every vernacular name for the penis in a few minutes, the clipped tones and jaunty tune contradict the title, with this shameless parade of naughty words tongue-in-cheekily considered 'a frightfully witty song' by some stuffed shirt. However, that moment of greatness is as nothing compared with the earth-shattering, stomach-churning, flesh-creeping appearance in the restaurant of a certain Mr. Creosote. Throwing up all over the place, stuffing himself with the entire menu – twice – abusing a silky John Cleese waiter (taking off from John Lennon's surreal spaghetti shovelling sequence in *Magical Mystery Tour*) and finally, being tempted by the dreaded wafer thin mint, exploding into a mass of half-digested muck, rancid vomit and burst rib cage. Charming. Unfairly, it's the best remembered moment in the film, even though there's an extra bonus of welcoming back *Python*'s favourite glam girl Carol Cleveland. Following some poetic, intellectual waffling from Terry Jones's anti-Semitic cleaner and a nonsensical but totally endearing wild goose chase with Eric Idle's softly spoken garlic waiter, it's headfirst into part seven and the end of the line with the big Death scene. But first, Chapman's nutter Arthur Jarrot, sentenced to death for telling sexist jokes on television, chooses his own unique method of destruction, being chased over a familiar looking cliff by topless beauties in garishly coloured crash helmets and matching undies. Sort of *Monty Python* meets Benny Hill. With some inspired kamikaze autumn leaves and a brilliantly eerie, Dickensian animation from Gilliam cross-fading into a sinister, bleak Terry Jones image of Cleese as the Grim Reaper, the spirit of impending doom enters the manic world of a quiet country dinner party. Hosted by pompous Brit chappie, Chapman, who condescendingly believes the man in black has come about the hedge, before his wife (Idle) invites Cleese in and introduces the other dinner guests including the other three Pythons – Jones and Palin in drag and Gilliam brilliantly shouting his mouth off as the flamboyant American. There's a sense of disbelief and incomprehension of Death's stately power, fingering the sinister mound of Salmon mousse as the cause for his arrival, slagging of British and Yankee traits, growling with real menace as these post-modern yuppies come to terms with their fate and finally ignoring Palin's semi-distressed cry of 'I didn't even eat the mousse!' – a joyous and unique *Python* ad-lib tossed in during the final take.

Arriving through an impressively grand gateway black hole to heaven, the commercialism delights of Mother Earth are clearly celebrated and reinforced in the after life with the place looking like an airport arrival lounge complete with grinding musique, young ladies grinning inanely and sad-looking potted plants. With the over-bearing notion that every day is Christmas in heaven, friendly waves from Terry Jones in post-liver extraction state and extras from all the film's segments, our mousse poisoned friends settle down for some glitzy, toothy entertainment from Chapman's Johnny Mathis-like man of song. The sequence is an absolute masterpiece of kitsch, ranking alongside Mel Brooks's *Springtime for Hitler* number from *The Producers* as the epitome of feel-good, bad taste. A tribute to the spirit of greed at Christmas, Chapman wanders through the realms of commercialisation with computer games, big-breasted choir girls, big breasted Santa's helpers, Calypso-styld interludes, Yo! man three kings with shopping trolleys and my favourite moment, Chapman's delicious mocking of the glories of television movies for Yuletide – 'The *Sound of Music* twice an hour and *Jaws* 1, 2 and 3'. Hastily interrupted in mid-chorus, this back to basics cinematic milestone for *Python* embraces the old media of television as Palin's refined host switches off the Christmas scene, announces the meaning of life's major points à la Oscar night and enjoys a total rant about the filth and violence in modern cinema. A hilarious venomous assault on the delightful bad taste *Python* have just dished up,

his mutant goats, chain-saw, penis-ridden notion of film entertainment ends with a deflated 'Bollocks!' and the film's masterpiece of intertextuality, as Palin sighs 'Oh well, here's the theme tune!' On a small TV set in grainy old BBC colour, the original title sequence plays for the last time as it, quite literally, floats off into the ether and is gradually faded into Idle's *Galaxy Song*. It's the most glorious of glorious closures to a collective body of great comedy work and I deny any person with at least an ounce of humility and comic affection in his body not to happily shed a tear of joy during this final moment. It's powerful stuff folks. So forget the anti-hype and celebrate *Monty Python's The Meaning of Life* as a vitally important part of *Python* culture. British comedy movies don't come a lot better than this...

Did You Know?
The writing for *Life* was the most painful of all *Python* projects, with the Hollywood Bowl shows filling in time and disagreements within the group concerning the return to sketch format following *Brian*'s flowing narrative. With scores of material and no direction, the team were considering calling the new film *Monty Python's World War III*, while a working holiday in Jamaica (à la *Brian*'s Barbados excursion) proved less than helpful. With 60 percent of the material and no clue what to do with it, several team members expressed a desire to abandon the film and the group for good. As was often the case, the project's saviour was Terry Jones, convinced that the material just needed an extra 20 minutes to became some sort of film. Palin suggested they return to England and make it into one last, farewell television series, but Cleese was less impressed with that notion. It hit Jones that it was a life story but he couldn't decide whose; Cleese suggested it could be anybody's life story and Idle blurted out – 'It's the meaning of life!'. This sparked everybody off and Cleese/Chapman immediately came up with the

opening hospital scene.

It may be made up of sketches but the film had unity, style and, above all, some of the best laughs in *Python* history. Secrets about the model work, filming and the nine-hour make-up ordeal of Terry Jones's immortal Mr. Creosote were revealed in Star Tracks: Fat City, *People Weekly*. The sequence also saw a major, relaxed session with Cleese and Jones, over a decade since 1969's creative disagreements, and now friendly, affluent and less tormented about breaking through with *Python* ideals intact. Writing the sketch together, Cleese and Jones fully went for ultimate bad taste, had a ball and got thought bucket-loads of Russian salad/Campell's Vegetable Soup. Gilliam's Crimson Assurance piece, fuelled by his fun adventure on *Time Bandits* and the pirate anticipation of Chapman's *Yellowbeard*, was originally cited to last three minutes but became so ambitious that it rivalled the main feature in filming time. With a huge budget of $80 million the team could attack public taste in luxury but even after enjoying Creosote, Cleese and Jones were as usual at opposite ends of the debate – John disliked the final cut and felt it lacked the warm, community strength of *Grail* and *Brian* (*Life* was filmed in England and thus the cast and crew came to work every day rather than lived the project through together) while Terry considered it the funniest thing *Python* had ever done. If the group couldn't decide, what chance had the great cinema-going public?

Universal/Celandine Films/The Monty Python Partnership
Monty Python's The Meaning of Life
Written by and starring
GRAHAM CHAPMAN, JOHN CLEESE, TERRY GILLIAM, ERIC IDLE, TERRY JONES & MICHAEL PALIN
With **CAROL CLEVELAND, SIMON JONES, PATRICIA QUINN, JUDY LOE, ANDREW MacLACHLAN, MARK HOLMES, VALERIE WHITTINGTON** and **JENNIFER FRANKS, IMOGEN BICKFORD-SMITH, ANGELA MANN, PETER LOVSTROM, GEORGE SILVER & CHRIS GRANT**

Dancers **LUKE BAXTER, BONNIE BRYG, CHARLOTTE CORBETT, DONNA FIELDING, ROY GAYLE, DONNETTE GODDARD, LAURA JAMES, KIM LEESON, MADDIE LOFTIN, PAUL MADDEN, KERRI MURPHY, JANE NEWMAN, GARY NOAKES, TRUDY PACK, LORRAINE MEACHER, CAROLINE MEACHER, TIMOTHY WARD, EMMA-KATE DAVIES, MICHELLE WELCH, PETER SALMON, STEVE ST. KLONIS, VOYD, GESS WHITFIELD, DOMINIQUE WOOD, WANDA ROCKIKI, SANDRA EASBY, HELEN MASON, SUE MENHENICK, LORRAINE WHITMARSH, ALISON HERLIHY, HEAVON GRANT, FLOYD PEARCE, STEPHEN BEAGLEY, LIZIE SAUNDERSON, TAMMY NEEDHAM, DAWN GERRARD, NATASHA GILBROOK, PAUL BOURKE, MICHELLE MACKIE**
Director of animation & special sequences **Terry Gilliam**
Photography **Peter Hannan**
Editor **Julian Doyle**
Production designer **Harry Lange**
Costume designer **Jim Acheson**
Choreography **Arlene Phillips**
Make-up & hair design **Maggie Weston**
Special effects supervisor **George Gibbs**
Production manager **David Wimbury**
Art director **Richard Dawking**
Sound mixer **Garth Marshall**
Camera operator **Dewi Humphreys**
1st assistant director **Ray Corbett**
Continuity **Penny Eyles**
Dubbing editor **Rodney Glenn**
Dubbing mixers **Paul Carr & Brian Paxton**
Songs by **Eric Idle, John Du Prez, John Cleese, Graham Chapman, Michael Palin, Terry Jones, Andre Jacquemin & Dave Howman**
Production assistant **Valerie Craig**
Assistant choeographer **Heather Seymour**
Location manager **Peter Kohn**
Stills photographer **David Appleby**
Set decorators **Simon Wakefield & Sharon Cartwright**
Model makers **Valerie Charlton & Carole De Young**
Gaffer **Chuck Finch**
Make-up supervisor **Mary Hillman**
Grip **Ken Atherfold**
Boom operator **Bob Doyle**
Sound maintenance **Phil Chubb**
Mr. Creosote's make-up by **Chris Tucker**

Python manager **Anne James**
Not the production accountant **Steve Abbott**
Director of Python U.S. relations **Nancy Lewis**
Assistants to producer **Tim Vaughan-Hughes & Barbara Holloway**
Opitical effects **Kent Houston, Roy Field, Paul Whitbread, Nick Dunlop & Tim Spence**
Animation **Tim Ollive, Kate Hepburn, Richard Ollie, Mike Stuart & Jill Brooks**
Art Department **Steve Cooper, Roger Cain, Andrew Ackland-Snow, Richard Hornsby, Dennis Griffin & Bob Walker**
Costume advisors **T. Stephen Miles & Gilly Hebden**
Wardrobe department **Janet Lucas, James Wakely, David Murch & Linda Eke**
Costume makers **Ray Scott, Vin Burnham, Shirley Denny, Jill Thraves, William & Lizzie Willey**
Make-up & hairdressing **Hilary Steinberg, Mike Jones & Pamela Rayson**
Wigs from Wig **Specialities**
Production department **Kieron Phipps, Callum McDougall & Paul Taylor**
Editing department **Keith Lowes, Dianne Ryder, Simon Milton, Roy Baker & Margarita Doyle**
Production accountant **Mike Smith**
Casting **Debbie McWilliams & Michelle Guish**
Special effects **Richard Conway, Bob Hollow, Dave Watson & Ray Hanson**
Properties **Brian Payne, Dave Newton, John Cole & Brian Humphrey**
Electrical department **Larry Randall, Alan McPherson, Richard Seal, Stuart Monteith & Fred Ashby**
Construction department **Mick Law, Alan Chesters, Peter Browne, John Skinner, Colin Lovering, Reg Keywood, Peter Cull, Dick Savery, Bill Sansom, Ken Powell, Melvin Coleman & Tommy Kavanagh**
Sound rerecorded at **Roger Cherrill Ltd**
Music recorded at **Britannia Row/Redwood Studios/CTS**
Lighting equipment **Lee Electric**
Producer **John Goldstone**
Director **Terry Jones**
The producers would like to thank all the fish who have taken part in this film. We hope that other fish will follow the example of those who have participated, so that, in future, fish all over the world will live together in harmony and understanding, and put aside their petty differences, cease pursuing and eating each other and live for a brighter, better future for all fish, and those who love them.
EMI Elstree Studios, Borehamwood & on location in London, North Yorkshire (Death) & Scotland (Zulu Wars)
Technicolor, released 30 March 1983

MONTY PYTHON'S THE MEANING OF LIFE

Standard soundtrack release with newly recorded linking material from Michael Palin and Terry Gilliam to smooth the transition from vision to audio. Palin, co-producing in the studio and obviously at hand, tackling the majority of newies with the top and tail fish dedications (including the hammerhead shark etc, proviso), the elongation of the First World War cake sketch with a patriotic, stirring eulogy of The Great Tea of 1914-1918 and a hilarious intro to *Every Sperm* with his babies/frying eggs equation. Chapman's peerless rant on the glories of Protestantism (preceded by a fiercely proud BBC broadcast) leads to Palin's historical glamorisation of Martin Luther's career before the Pythons use the medium perfectly and fake a record scratch to get out of it (loses something on the CD version!). During the Luther lecture one can almost imagine the Gilliam animation, and Terry himself pops up at the start of side two to explain his mainly visual contribution and discuss his 'pirate clerks' film – again the record denies him the air time and Eric Idle sails in with *The Accountancy Shanty*. The fish signal the dangers of the approaching end of side one, there's an extended version of the Grim Reaper sequence and all your film favourites are included – although the final Palin declaration of the meaning of life and the old *Python* theme is missed. The cover boasts a hilarious pontificating on the Pythons' student days, including Chapman's skill at that olde world pub game Shitties, while the album presents all the movie's songs.

For *The Meaning of Life* the songs became almost as important as the sketches, as opposed to the couple of tasty ditties from *Brian* and *Grail*. Naturally, CBS released a single (A 3495) featuring *Galaxy Song* and *Every Sperm Is Sacred* – which was extended with a longer instrumental break than that featured in the film and on the album. The single was also released in the rare picture disc format and, in keeping with the film's fish obsession, appeared in the shape of a fish bowl (WA 3495).

Monty Python's The Meaning of Life – Introduction, Fish introduction, The Meaning of Life Theme, Birth, Birth Link, Frying Eggs, Every Sperm is Sacred, Protestant Couple, Adventures of Martin Luther, Sex Education, Trench Warfare, The Great Tea of 1914-1918, Fish link, Terry Gilliam link, Accountancy Shanty, Zulu Wars, Link, The Dungeon, Restaurant, Link, Live Organ Transplants, The Galaxy Song, The Not Noel Coward Song, Mr. Creosote, The Grim Reaper, Christmas In Heaven, Dedication to Fish CBS SBP 70239 (1983)

MONTY PYTHON'S PREVIOUS RECORD

Material here is mainly studio versions of classics from series three and the German stuff but there's plenty of newies as well, kicking off with Terry Jones embracing the vinyl medium by repeatedly screaming 'Not This Record!' until the needle is ripped away and begins on some calming mood music and Idle's laid-back lecture on avoiding embarrassment. Typical *Python*, this sense of nervousness at noises and words is pin-pointed as 'part of being British' but the monotone delivery of Cleese is here to put you to the test. Disgusting noises are just too much for the public to take so Chapman is thrown in to introduce *A Book at Bedtime*. Read by Cleese, this again takes up the reins of embarrassing words with bated breath sexual references fading into classical music

and suggested costume drama with Cleese's earnest highwayman, Dennis Moore. Perhaps Cleese's proudest achievement of series three, the record keeps this campy, acceptance-seeking robber as an effective running gag throughout side one, fading out here with rambling commentary about his firearm skill before Idle's wealth obsessed *Money Programme* host bounds in with the celebrated *Money Song* and a salivating praise to finance, again continuing the use of sexual terms while almost going into *Lumberjack Song* mode at one fever-pitched moment. But then it's back to Dennis Moore successfully holding up the Lupin Express, enjoying a quick burst of his *Robin Hood*-inspired theme song and handing over to Eric Idle's brilliant Australian Table Wines monologue. Taking off from television's Bruce sketch, Idle's drunkard anecdotes, pseudo-connoisseur labelling of wines ('message is Beware') and lyrically corrupting endearing similies ('Aborigine's armpit') this ranks with the best material ever put out under the *Python* banner.

The Argument sketch is faithfully recorded with Palin's desperate client, Cleese in petulant overdrive, Chapman's wonderfully insincerely apologetic abuser, Idle quite superb as the fuming complainer and, finally Jones as the cheerful head hitter – 'what a stupid concept' – followed by the *Blue Peter* parody *How To Do It* and the pepperpot piece with Chapman and Cleese, discussing burying live cats, putting down budgies and so forth, reaching a peak with Graham's haunting picture of the mutation danger that budgie's breeding down the sewers can be. Both Palin and Idle inject innuendo-based newspaper free ads, there's more of Dennis Moore with a chorus of theme song singers who have forgotten the words and then it's onto arguably the record's masterpiece, Eric the Half-A-Bee elongated from Series 2 episode 10's Palin/Cleese fish licence sketch (famous Aqua creature owners/You must be a loony) to include the priceless song in praise of a dissected insect. Pure class. Idle's flashy celebratory introducing host of

Radio's *What Do You* quiz show fills the record with an array of outlandish sounds before the unaware Mr. Smoke-Too-Much wandering in for an adventure holiday. It's a very subdued version with Palin seeming initially distant and Idle taking a while to warm up but the rant is still hilarious. Although played with nothing like the conviction of the original television or later stage show performances, this vinyl rendition concluded with a masterpiece in Palin's frantic screams to stop Idle's droning, pleading 'for God's sake take it off!' as the needle scratches across the record in line with the Jones introduction.

Side 2 begins with Chapman's introduction of a massage from the Swedish Prime Minister which takes over from Dennis Moore as the running gag. Cleese hosts the *Silly Noises* radio quiz, unfairly giving in to Idle's wild answers, castigating his other contestants, testing the crowd with Palin's 'Ni! Ni!', *Grail* trail-blazing nob and finally highlighting game show corruption by suddenly stopping the fun. The language problems ('An expert') of Cleese's surreal Miss Anne Elk, her dino theory and Chapman's disgruntled, machine gun firing host is perfectly resurrected from the television series, while the nautical inspiring music and Terry Jones's voice-over immediately bring to mind the clichéd, camera sweep across lush scenery. In praise of the Yangste river, various cool football legends beginning with Bob Wilson, voice their appreciation of this fine natural beauty, while the lads, in football song mood, let rip with *We Love the Yangtse*. The fun continues with Idle reading the repetitive, mind-numbing A Minute Passed with Chapman getting the final laugh with his straight-laced announcement. Eclipse of the Sun, with Jones earnestly explaining that this is the first time on record for the event, is a rather laboured piece sounding like a throwback to *The Frost Report* ('Yes, you are very much mistaken!') with rain at Lord's clichés and Chapman's effortlessly underplayed confusing commentator. The Alastair Cook attacked by a duck interlude is an effective duck attack interlude. Palin's Wonderful World of Sounds, twisting nature expert conventions to perfection, magnifies animal noises all over the shop (including a few in a chemist) and goes into Peter Sellers mood as he reacts to trapped fingers. Idle takes this opportunity to plug his funeral service, with free wine glasses thrown in, Chapman, once again, introduces a massage break and this classic burst of *Python* old and new concludes with A Fairy Tale, Happy Valley – culled from the second German show and resurrecting Connie Booth's charming, wooden toothed princess. Jones has a recorded field day with his 'Ni!' styled organ songs, Palin's Prince Walter is still the funniest thing in it and Cleese, opting to avoid dramatic confusion for once, says The End and, sadly means it.

Did You Know?
Charisma released Eric the Half-A-Bee and the footballing *Yangtse Song* as a single (CB 200). The original cover art work is a brilliant Terry Gilliam creation, using the newspaper ideas from the Palin/Idle adverts (à la John Lennon's *Sometime in New York City*) only to cover up almost everything with a maniacally triple wrapped arm trying to grab a nervous, very buxom butterfly. The front cover's title is almost obscured and the only clue as to what's on the album is 'The Bee'. When the record was released in American (Buddah CAS 1063), the track listing was included, although it featured various incorrect identification of sketches – for example Silly Noises is credited as City Noises Quiz!
Monty Python's Previous Record – Charisma CB 1063 (1972)
Written & performed by **Graham Chapman, John Cleese, Terry Gilliam, Eric Idle, Terry Jones & Michael Palin.**

MONTY PYTHON'S TINY BLACK ROUND THING

A flexi-disc produced by Charisma (SO 1259) and given away free with the May 1974 issue of *New Musical Express.* Basically a promotional piece for the Live at Drury Lane album (the disc features Election Night Special and an extended version of *The Lumberjack Song*), the *Python* material was topped and tailed by new narration from Michael Palin, including a section in character as a Gumby *NME* boss. The B side consisted of *What The Press Said About Monty Python's Tiny Black Round Thing.*

THE MOVIE LIFE OF GEORGE

In celebration of the tenth anniversary of HandMade films, initially as a rescue job for *Monty Python's Life of Brian*, this Granada documentary gathered together nearly all the Pythons, other HandMade performers and George Harrison himself to tell the full story. The formation of the company is fairly well known and academically related here, but it's a joy to wallow in some class clips and enjoy the insights of the key protagonists. John Cleese, Eric Idle, Michael Palin, Terry Gilliam and, in his last television interview, Graham Chapman, all contribute soundbites about the company. Naturally, there's plenty of chat about *Brian*, with Chapman, looking ill but relaxed, happily remembering his first nude scene and the pleasures of filming. Gilliam, pontificating on his solo HandMade classic *Time Bandits*, moans about his treatment, brilliantly balanced by Idle and Cleese mock moaning about Gilliam's fiery obsessions, while other *Python*-related projects, *Live at the Hollywood Bowl*, *The Missionary* and *A Private Function*, are represented by copious clips. There's even a couple of classic out-takes with Palin from *The Missionary* and the editing is a masterpiece – cutting in with the Northern hardships from Hollywood Bowl/contrasting the light treatment of the pig in *A Private Function* with the dark realities of chicken problems in *Withnail and I/The Long Day* meat hook confrontation cutting from Bob Hoskins's explosion line to the cupboard demolition from *Time Bandits*. Although the HandMade story would shortly turn sour, there are gallons of clips from films like *Track 29*, *Checking Out*, *How To Get Ahead in Advertising*, *The Raggedy Rawney*, *The Lonely Passion of Judith Hearne* and *Pow Wow Highway*, while even here both Eric Idle and, George Harrison himself, tend to suggest that the tug of music is pulling at the hobby-styled job of film-making.
Other joys include Billy Connolly's delight at appearing in *Water* and singing his protest song, backed by 'his heroes' George Harrison, Ringo Starr and Eric Clapton, a celebrity fazed moment from Robbie Coltrane relating his suppressed, inner awe at meeting Harrison, Bob Hoskins being his usual cool self and Michael Caine relishing his chance for pure evil with his chilling cameo in *Mona Lisa*. The entire programme is inter-laced with fascinating footage from the tenth anniversary dinner at Shepperton Studios, with Michael Palin's gloriously funny speech and a mesmerising rock 'n' roll jam session with Harrison and Carl Perkins. Like the man says, 'Thank God for Rock 'n' Roll!'
But the most endearing sections are those with Harrison and Palin in quiet conversation, remembering the ornate cinemas of 1940s Liverpool, enjoying some impromptu working class humour and simply playing like a couple of old pals having an afternoon chat. I could watch tapes of those two together for hours. Magical.

Interviews with **George Harrison, Graham Chapman, John Cleese, Terry Gilliam, Eric Idle, Michael Palin, Robbie Coltrane, Bruce Robinson, Bob Hoskins, Michael Caine, Denis O'Brien & Richard Griffiths**
Special thanks to **Ray Cooper** and all at 26 Cadogan Square
Production manager **Richard Willmore**
Party production manager **Robbie Wilson**
Programme associate **Marnie Jung**
Cameras **Ric Stratton, Jeff Baynes, Chris Morphet, Simon Archer & Bob King**
Sound **Garth Marshall & Paul Corfield**
Music engineer **Richard Dodds**

VTR editors **Graham Hutchins & Bill Ogden**
Film editor **Martyn Hone**
Assistant **Salu Chowdhury**
Dubbing mixer **Aad Wirtz**
Production assistant **Sue Vertue**
Titles **Complete Video**
Executive producers **Peter Bennett-Jones & Rod Caird**
Associate producer **Michelle de Larrabeiti**
Produced & directed by **Charles Brand**
Tiger/Granada Television 1989

THE MUPPET SHOW

When I was a lad, Saturday tea-times were enlivened by ABC/CBS co-production's burst of Jim Henson television magic. The guest-star was pretty irrelevant when there were tons of corny wise-cracks from Fozzy the bear and drum-beating from that cool dude Animal. *The Muppet Show* brilliantly took the tradition of Vaudeville's song and dance, low-brow humour and glamour, cross-fertilised it with the loveable bits of cloth from *Sesame Street* and, bingo, we have a television classic. This particular episode boasts an unforgettable jug band version of *Somebody Stole My Gal*, a breathtaking cannonball catching, non-chicken involving, act from Gonzo the Great, a pleasing piano duet from Rolf and a chicken, a pseudo-pregnant Miss Piggy performing *Waiting At The Church* with Kermit and a classic bit of 'friendship till the end' material from Robin and that troll-like chap Sweetems.

However, the comic highlights come from a wonderfully petulant, Basil Fawlty-like rant from special guest star John Cleese – a friend of Frank Oz. Introduced by the green fellow as one of the 'reigning geniuses behind *Monty Python's Flying Circus*', Cleese goes through the conventions of the show with gun a-blaze, struggling with ropes to escape and complaining bitterly about working in a place infested with pigs. There's a suitably manic dressing room conversation between Cleese and Gonzo, with some painful arm-

lengthening going on, but it's the two set pieces that really steal the show. Closing with a veritable mix-up concerning his performance of *To Dream The Impossible Dream*, Cleese wanders around in dapper dress, suffers a quick change into Viking gear for some unplanned Wagner and finally reappears as a Mexican for a bit of maracas fun, proving, much to his surprise, so successful, that he plugs his new vinyl treat, *John Cleese, A Man and His Music*. However, Cleese reaches a peak with an infiltration into that timeless *Star Trek* parody *Pigs In Space* – the subtlest comment that William Shatner was a ham actor. Misunderstanding the spaceship concept and bursting onto set in pirate gear as Long John Silversteen (à la Harrison in *Rutland Weekend Television*), Cleese flamboyantly over-acts with Robert Newton-esque relish, jumping out of character and into clipped tones to address his piggy co-star and having some priceless banter with his cheeky, ever-complaining parrot. It's all Fawlty outrage and exquisite timing, incorporating some hilarious business with his detachable hook and fully reclaiming *Python*esque glories by brandishing a gun and threatening his mouthy cohort with 'Do you want to be an ex-parrot!' The stuff of legend, this outstanding guest starring turn alongside the gang lead directly to Cleese's involvement in their second big screen venture, *The Great Muppet Caper*, and stands as a glorious piece of television entertainment.

An ITC/Henson Associates, Inc Production
Written by **Jerry Juhl, Joseph A. Bailey, Jim Henson & Don Hinkley**
Muppet performers **Frank Oz, Jerry Nelson, Richard Hunt, Dave Goelz & Jim Henson**
Muppet creative consultants **Frank Oz & Michael Frith**
Music consultant **Larry Grossman**
Theme music **Sam Pottle**
Art director **Malcolm Stone**
Orchestra conducted by **Jack Parnell**
Musical associate **Derek Scott**
Lighting director **Jim Boyers**
Editor **John Hawkins**

Senior cameraman **Dennis Bartlett**
Costumes **James Dark**
Executive producer **David Lazer**
Producer **Jim Henson**
Director **Philip Casson**
21 October 1977

NATIONAL LAMPOON'S EUROPEAN VACATION

Following the success of the John Belushi cult classic *National Lampoon's Animal House*, the overall phrase was used for various slapstick, satirical looks at the American way of life. Perhaps the most popular of those branches starred Chevy Chase as the head of the accident-prone and self-righteous Griswald family, beginning with 1983's *National Lampoon's Vacation* and two years later continuing with this comic travelogue further afield. Subtle comedy is right out and much of the film is pretty corny even by the National Lampoon's standards, but there's no denying that the playing of Chase and D'Angelo is great fun throughout and any movie that can start with John Austin's sex-obsessed, suspiciously grinning quiz show host presiding over a celebration of greed and bad taste with *Pig in a Poke*, has to be worth watching. Wallowing in totally outrageous quiz categories and sending up the process viciously, the rest of the film lacks this biting edge of satire but, no matter, the British set portion of the film (their prize on the game show is, guess what, a European vacation) boasts a bundle of great comedy players and some well-judged comment on the British character. Contrasting brilliantly with the dream image of Britain (royalty/disco dancing babes, sophisticated elegance) the epitome of English hospitality is played out by Mel Smith's grumpy old scumbag, forcing his mother to carry the hotel baggage, slobbing about the place watching documentaries on cheese-making (Jason Lively's comment about only four channels and no MTV is a good one, although everyone seems to be screening that cheese doco!) and chatting away in cockney disinterest with a face full of food. It's a glorious anti-image for the Brit at home, petulantly remaining unimpressed and unbothered by his Yank guests and their television quiz catchphrases. Robbie Coltrane is pretty much wasted as a non-speaking chappie, aroused by some unsuspecting bathroom lusting from D'Angelo, although his embracing of the whistled National Anthem and nervous mop of the brow is good fun, while Maureen Lipman crops up very briefly as a saucy blonde bit mistakenly approached by Chase. British rudeness and sex obsession are counterbalanced by tourist mentions of Carnaby St, fish 'n' chips and the like, plus a couple of delightfully well-mannered and unbothered motor crash drivers. *Fawlty*'s Ballard Berkeley is great value, cheerfully shaking hands over his wrecked vehicle and injecting oodles of British eccentric charm, before a third problem on the road sees poor old Eric Idle knocked flying off his bike. A cracking cameo, this is the film's comic high spot with Idle continuing the friendly Brit attitude with cries of 'No, problems!' and 'Good heavens' as he stumbles about the place lacerated, bruised and spurting blood à la Peckinpah's *Salad Days* as he helpfully gives instructions to the family. Bridging English courage and English stupidity, Idle's 'just a leg' philosophy and plans for a brief trip to the chemist to fix major pain, is an affectionate piece of work, injecting the British spirit into the movie via a familiar face in America and via familiar *Python* spirit in the face of extreme discomfort. Once an aged Robert Dorning has witnessed the destruction of Stonehenge (after a lovely soliloquy from Chase), the tour moves on across Europe, tackling dodgy name-embossed berets and nudie shows in France, beer festivals

and frauleins in Germany and high fashion, ice-cream and robbery in Rome.
Although the movie is beginning to sag by this stage, help is at hand with the reappearance of Eric Idle, foot in a cast ('big sock really!') and projecting mad nervousness at the renewed acquaintance with the family from your worst nightmare. During a final *Italian Job* homage car chase in a mini, Idle is once again caught in the crossfire, knocked into a fountain and attacked by a disgruntled Chase. Friendly to the end, the jolly Idle suddenly remembers his dodgy leg and vanishes under the water. It is a classic, movie-saving piece of flamboyant British pride and perfectly sets up the returning home piece of Chase prat-falling and a montage of closing credit American icons including Clint Eastwood, Christopher Reeves' Superman, Bugs Bunny, MTV logo and, aptly enough, a saluting James Cagney from *Yankee Doodle Dandy* with the final image of the Warner Brothers shield.

Did You Know? Eric Idle's part took one day of filming in London and a couple of days in Italy – although this also embraced a riotous song and wine party with Keith Richards. Chevy Chase's newly scripted, fountain-based dialogue had to be cut because Idle had lost his voice due to glorious over-indulgence.
Eric Idle and Chevy Chase started work on a screenplay for *National Lampoon's Australian Vacation* soon after shooting this film, but apart from some good shark-related gags neither could come up with much and the project was shelved.

National Lampoon's European Vacation
Warner Bros. Pictures
Clark W. Griswald **CHEVY CHASE**
Ellen Griswald **BEVERLY D'ANGELO**
Audrey Griswald **DANA HILL**
Rusty Griswald **JASON LIVELY**
The thief **VICTOR LANOUX**
The Bike Rider **ERIC IDLE**
Pig in a Poke host **JOHN ASTIN**
Mr. Frogder **PAUL BARTEL**
Lady in the Bed **MAUREEN LIPMAN**
Fritz Spritz **WILLY MILLOWITSCH**
Hotel manager **MEL SMITH**

His mum **GWEN NELSON**
Rusty's German Girl **CLAUDIA NEIDIG**
Rusty's Californian Girl **MOON ZAPPA**
Taxi driver **DEREK DEADMAN**
Princess Di **JULIE WOOLDRIDGE**
Prince Charles **PETER HUGO**
Queen Elizabeth **JEANETTE CHARLES**
Announcer at Court **ANGUS MacKAY**
Man in the Bathroom **ROBBIE COLTRANE**
English Motorists **PAUL McDOWELL & BALLARD BERKELEY**
Mrs. Garland **ELIZABETH ARLEN**
Effifel Tower Girls **ISA CAROL HORIO & ISABELLE MASSARD**
Game Show Hosts **SHEILA KENNEDY & TRICIA LANGE**
Story by **John Hughes**
Screenplay by **John Hughes & Robert Klane**
Unit production manager **William Land**
First assistant director **Don French**
Casting **Marion Dougherty**
Music **Charles Fox**
Editor **Pembroke J. Herring**
Production supervisor **Dieter Meyer**
Costume designer **Graham Williams**
Production designer **Bob Cartwright**
Photography **Bob Paynter**
Co-producer **Stuart Cornfield**
Producer **Matty Simmons**
Director **Amy Heckerling**
Panavision/Technicolor
1985, 94 mins

NEARLY DEPARTED

With the impressive reaction to Eric Idle's Passpartout in *Around the World in Eighty Days*, NBC decided to try the *Python* favourite out in his own headlining situation comedy, picking up the option on the pilot and demanding a re-filmed version before going ahead. The result was *Nearly Departed*, a glorious fusion between Anglo-American cultures sprinkled with much tongue-in-cheek black humour and wackiness aplenty. The basic plot is shamelessly borrowed from the 1937 film classic *Topper*, with Idle and his wife, played by Caroline Williams, having been killed when their car meets with some falling rocks. The obvious connection is further enforced by Idle's character name Grant, carrying on from where the first film's star, Cary Grant, left off. The scenario is much the same: fun-loving, young couple refusing to lie down and die, continue to live in their old home despite new owners, getting into scrapes and finding a reluctant ally in the only person who can see them – Roland Young in the original, Henderson Forsythe here. Young, in fact, went on to star in the two sequels, *Topper Returns* and the screwball classic, *Topper Takes A Trip*. This vastly under-valued Eric Idle vehicle was an inspired, enjoyable homage to the old ethos.

One of the show's chief assets is a well constructed title song in the style of Noel Coward, briefly explaining the death experience of the two leads and sung in jolly, skippy fashion by a foppish Idle. The balance of comedy is excellent, with naturally, plenty of gags at the Brits' expense – Idle's patriotic pride in Charles Dickens is condemned as being snobbish by his wife, the neighbourhood kid condemns the disgruntled dead Idle as a dork – although reasonably because 'he was British!' But, Idle's amazed outrage is great comedy indeed; he injects surreal moments of humour throughout and one of the greatest scenes comes with a delicious attack on the aged American community, complete with vicious, tongue-in-cheek ridicule of the greed and insincerity of game shows. Both nations have their faults hilariously pointed out and the contrast between pompous swine and American slob is irresistible.

Although there are elements of toe-curling pathos, Stuart Pankin's performance (likened to Fred Flintstone by Idle and not a million miles from the truth) is a gloriously angst-ridden creation, stripping away the usual 2.4 family edge of sitcomland and embracing real, world-weary elements. Chuck in copious knowing gags about the central pair being dead, desperate attempts at continuing their life as best they can and swathes of lowbrow fun – the blonde bimbo of Wendy Schall in the shower allows Idle some shameless wide-eyed pleasures. It's a good idea (later pinched for the far inferior British comedy *So Haunt Me* with Miriam

Karlin doing the spooking) with an endearing cast of flawed characters and a quite brilliant performance from Eric Idle, effortlessly running rings round everybody else with an air of self-satisfied energy.

Sadly, however, the project was plagued with problems from the start. The pilot, *Grant Meets Grandpa*, took 18 months to get off the ground and NBC wanted the other five in the series written in three weeks. The standard obviously suffered, although distinguished director John Rich crafted some effective scenarios.

Show 2, *Adventures in Babysitting*, sees Idle and McWilliams upset because they can't visit the opening night of a symphony which their living counterparts are seeing. Grandpa is babysitting, but clears off to play poker leaving Idle in charge; he disrupts a romantic babysitting interlude; Gramp discovers family ashamed of his action and clears off, but Idle stops him. The sharp-tongued delights of the pilot are mostly replaced by mawkish sentiment but the performances are still excellent.

Show 3, *Altered States*, sees McWilliams discover an old box during renovation work on the house, containing a letter that shows Idle wasn't divorced when he married her. Show 4, *TV or Not TV*, has Lambert's television watching affecting his school grades. Idle sees *Masterpiece Theatre* in a cultural war against sport but the television is eventually banished so Idle helps out at school and deals with a bully. Sadly, despite positive reaction for the show, NBC decided not to screen the last two episodes in America and cancelled the series just when another 18 were almost on the cards. John Rich, whose credits included *The Dick Van Dyke Show* and *All in the Family*, was furious. Both shows had been allowed to develop over several series. The decision to withdraw screening of the last two programmes was a strange one and, perversely, they were probably the funniest episodes (with one, *Grant's Aunt*, allowing Idle a tour de force in comic acting as his own Aunt Millie, and

the other, *Grandpa's Date*, successfully mixing the usual pathos with British cynicism).

All six recorded shows were scheduled on BBC1 in 1990 between 8 October and 22 November, although problems even disturbed this showing, with the final episode postponed to 20 December!

Did You Know? The original title was *Ghost Story*.

Nearly Departed
Grant Pritchard **ERIC IDLE**
Claire Pritchard **CAROLINE McWILLIAMS**
Mike Dooley **STUART PANKIN**
Liz Dooley **WENDY SCHAAL**
Derek Dooley **JAY LAMBERT**
Jack Garrett **HENDERSON FORSYTHE**
Leona **JANET DUBOIS**
Perkins **HANK GARRETT**
Girl **ROBINA RITCHIE**
Josh **JASON ZAHLER**
Show 1 10 April 1989
Written by **John Baskin & Roger Shulman**
Music **Kevin Quinn, Randy Petersen & Robert Irving**
Associate producer **Kathy Landsberg**
Creative consultants **Robert Illes & James R. Stein**
Executive consultant **Eric Idle**
Consulting producer **John Rich**
Co-executive producer **Dale McRaven**
Producer **Jack Seifert**
Created & executive produced by **Roger Shulman & John Baskin**
Show 2
17 April 1989 Written by **John Baskin & Roger Shulman**
Show 3
24 April 1989 Written by **Sy Dukane & Denise Moss**
Show 4
1 May 1989 Written by **Neil Alan Levy**

NICOBOBINUS

Thirty-one chapters of wonderful adventure by Terry Jones. Nic and his mate Rosie go in search of the Land of Dragons, meeting up with the Golden Man – with a Midas touch, a ship of evil pirate monks, and a dragon that heats the palace of King Pactolus. Jones has also written an, as yet, unfilmed screenplay based on his story.

Written by **Terry Jones**. Published by Pavilion Books 1985 (hardback), Penguin books (paperback)
Illustrated by **Michael Foreman**

NO – THAT'S ME OVER THERE

A fondly remembered situation comedy for Ronnie Corbett in the immediate wake of *The Frost Report*. The first series (14 Nov-19 Dec) was written by Eric Idle, who also featured in one episode as a hippy nephew to Corbett, spouting all the usual clichéd 'Hey, man!' dialogue and really grabbing the trend of the time with the Beatles recording *Baby, You're A Rich Man* as accompanying music. Full of visual gags, Corbett's put upon, bowler-hatted office worker sparred with his wife, Rosemary Leach, neighbour Henry McGee and sexy secretary Jill Mai Meredith. Idle dropped out of the run to concentrate on developing *Do Not Adjust Your Set* but saw Graham Chapman step into his shoes as writer for the series.
The third and final series began on 17 November 1970. Chapman went on to write the semi-sequel *Look Here Now*, starring Corbett for Canadian television.

Written by **Barry Cryer, Graham Chapman & Eric Idle**
Music **Mike Vickers**
Executive Producer **David Frost**
Producers **Bill Hitchcock & Marty Feldman**

NOT THE NINE O'CLOCK NEWS

The natural successor to *Monty Python's Flying Circus* with its sketch format geared more towards political satire than television anarchism, the show made stars of Mel Smith, Griff Rhys Jones, Pamela Stephenson and Rowan Atkinson and paid tongue-in-cheek homage to its inspirational predecessor with the first episode's immortal Life of Python sketch. However, things didn't quite go as

originally planned for the series. Due for broadcast on 2 April 1979 with a cast headed by Rowan Atkinson, Chris Emmett, Christopher Godwin, John Gorman and Jonathan Hyde, at the last hurdle a General Election was called and in the usual BBC tradition which had seen *Steptoe and Son* postponed and *That Was The Week That Was* completely cancelled, this new satirical slab of comedy was put on hold. When the show finally came to fruition in October Atkinson was the only cast member retained as part of the main team, joining Smith, Stephenson, Chris Langham and, initially in second banana roles, Jones. However, the essence of *Python* was in place from the very beginning with the time slot originally following directly after the sixth episode of John Cleese's second series of *Fawlty Towers*.
Adding to the madcap flavour of this new skit show and handing over the *Python*esque baton of false television starts, Cleese agreed to film a prologue sequence as Basil Fawlty. Beginning with the familiar title sequence (with the sign reading Flowery Twats) Cleese is angrily moaning at the BBC on the phone, explaining that he won't do another show, dismissing their excuses about strikes as hardly his fault and petulantly suggesting a load of boring fill-in options. Finally, the BBC agree on a cheap tatty review, Cleese disinterestedly informs the watching viewers, he flamboyantly cues up the titles and away we go. Sadly, by the time the show went out this classic link was redundant. Retained for overseas transmissions for an added viewing hook, this classic bit of rare Cleese has subsequently been screened on *Not* repeat slots. However, back in October 1979 and in the spirit of the *Python* thing, there's another false start with Kenny Everett's short-lived relocation to the strict-minded Beeb and, after some *Python*esque caption announcements and twisted television conventions, the first sketch proper is hosted by Pamela Stephenson and pits the wits of *Python* faithful Mel Smith as film critic Alexander Walker and director

of the controversial new film *The General Sinod's Life of Christ* against Bishop Rowan Atkinson. It's full of glorious celebrations of the *Python* legend ('men, who even today, are worshipped and revered throughout the Western world'/'*Python* worshipping country!'/'I certainly didn't expect the Spanish Inquisition!') with the Christ question of Brian brilliantly challenged with the notion that Jesus Christ, in this film, is quite clearly a lampoon of the comic messiah himself, Our Lord John Cleese. Even the initials, JC are exactly the same, with references to similarities with *Fawlty Towers* within the life of 'this Jesus Christ bloke'. Python's publishing genius is incorporated by a reference to The Good Bok, their comic failings are mocked affectionately, relating the sketches that failed, paying homage to the Python clan ('these men died for us – frequently') and finally giving the dead parrot its key place as the ultimate in thought-provoking expression, explaining when two or more people are together thy shalt recite the parrot sketch – *Python* and religious terminology in perfect harmony. Over the next few years *Not* would create a string of classic sketches which can happily rest alongside the great *Python* moments, with their branching into records and books linking the two teams even more closely.
Running to four seasons, ending in 1982 and coming back with a classic 35-minute special, *Not the World Cup*, on 19 June 1982, this first priceless show clearly wipes the deck of *Python* heritage in a brilliantly forelock-touching style and closes with Andrew Sachs as Manuel twigging the contact lenses gag.

Not the Nine O'Clock News featured **Rowan Atkinson, Chris Langham, Mel Smith, Pamela Stephenson** with **Griff Rhys Jones, Jim Broadbent, Chris Emmett, Christina Gage, Olu Jacobs, Oscar James, Gerald Moon & David Rappaport**
Special thanks to **John Cleese, Andrew Sachs & Kenny Everett**
Written by **Andy Hamilton, Rowan Atkinson, Richard Curtis, Colin**

Bostock-Smith, Laurie Rowley, Peter Spence, Alastair Beaton, Barry Pilton & Chris Langham
Music **Nic Rowley, Howard Goodall & Chris Judge Smith**
Film editor **Noel Chanan**
Videotape editors **Sam Upton & Ian Prowse**
Graphics **Darrell Pockett**
Production team **Helen Murray, Patricia Rae, Marcus Mortimer, Mandie Fletcher & Rosalind Hughes**
Technical manager **Mike Chislett**
Sound **Richard Chamberlain**
Lighting **John Treays**
Make-up **Kezia de Winne**
Costume **Dorinda Rea**
Design **Paul Joel & David Hitchcock**
Production assistant **Mike Pearce**
Producers **Sean Hardie & John Lloyd**
Director **Bill Wilson**.
BBC2 17 October 1979

NOW!

Despite having to lessen the blow by consuming two pints of Guinness before recording, this was Michael Palin's first major television work, hosting a hip and happening music programme for the young generation. Cheap, cheerful and a bit ramshackle, it called upon the freshly graduated history scholar to trot around Bristol locations in outlandish Edwardian swimwear, miming to Nancy Sinatra's *These Boots Were Made For Walking* and thus, brilliantly training him in *Python* technique at an early age. Screened on Television West Wales, the musical line-up was very impressive, featuring performances from the likes of Tom Jones, The Animals, the Scaffold, the fledging Englebert Humperdinck (then singing as Gerry Dorsey) and even major comedy idols, Peter Cook and Dudley Moore appearing 20 April 1966. Palin worked on the show from October 1965 until the middle of 1966, earning enough money to moonlight on scripts with Terry Jones and push forward to the bright lights of *Python*.

NUMBER 27

An evil, flash property developer and

a 90-year-old symbol for traditional values battle it out in this Ealing-like celebration of the British character. Based on a story concerning Eton College leaving houses to students then pressurising tenants to move out, it was Michael Palin's brilliant comment on the yuppie age of greed is good. A reunion of writer-director-producer for *East of Ipswich* and a valuable meeting of Python Comic Strip generations in Palin and Planer, this is a multi-faceted, cynical, corruption of community celebration of values meeting heartless progress.

Andrew Veitch **NIGEL PLANER**
Miss Barwick **JOYCE CAREY**
Sally Veitch **HELENA MICHELL**
Clive **EDWARD LYON**
Farrant **MICHAEL PERCIVAL**
Murray Lester **ALUN ARMSTRONG**
Military man **PETER HUGHES**
Traffic monitor **JANINE DUVITSKI**
Dr. Barwick **ROBIN BAILEY**
Carpenter-Wilde **RODDY MAUDE-ROXBY**
Rennie **JOHN ROWE**
Karmel **PAUL BROOKE**
Policeman **ERIC STOVELL**
Quentin Gilbey **PHILIP McGOUGH**
Becket **PETE POSTLETHWAITE**
Maitre D' **MICHAEL GAUNT**
Louise Pratt **KATHARINE LEVY**
Hardcastle **ARTHUR WHITE**
Truck driver **DAVID LANDBERG**
Screenplay by **Michael Palin**
Music **John Du Prez**
Editor **Mark Day**
Photography **Philip Bonham-Carter**
Designer **Bruce Macadie**
Producer **Innes Lloyd**
Director **Tristram Powell**
Broadcast 23 October 1988, 75 mins

NUNS ON THE RUN

One of the best crime caper comedies you could wish to find, this late entry in the Handmade canon presented Eric Idle with by far his greatest post-*Python* big screen role, resurrecting a favourite *Python* name, Brian, (although no-one misprounounces their Rs) and standing tall, in my opinion, as the finest solo film effort from any of the team. *The Sunday Express* comments that it was

'funnier even than *A Fish Called Wanda*' and they weren't just whistling Dixie. With a feelgood, polished script and quick-fire direction from Jonathan Lynn, the laughs and action come thick and fast while the film is patriotically geared against bad guys, oriental gangland groups and the unromantic attitudes of organised crime. In an embrace of organised religion, the nuns are presented as fallible yet streetwise, understanding figures of faith. The two makeshift criminals thrown into their order finally respect and appreciate the work of the church and even the odd warm, knowing dig at the absurdity of it all is quickly humanised and counterbalanced with divine intervention.

The film works like a *Some Like It Hot* for the pop video generation and, despite wallowing in old-fashioned jokes and situations, there is an underlining hip quality to the comedy, thanks largely to the funky grooves of Yello's theme music. Some of the supporting performances are unconvincing and lightly sketched, but these pale into nothingness in comparison to the sheer chemistry at work between Eric Idle and Robbie Coltrane. Although the Laurel and Hardy link is superficial and easy, the teaming of this *Python* veteran and alternative favourite retains the endearing affection of Stan and Ollie. They bring moments of high visual comedy in the grand tradition of slapstick humour and, above all, Coltrane happily incorporates an Ollie-like wave as the two quickly dash away from Suzman's hard-bitten Sister Superior. The two are, of course, in the criminal racket, although their eagerness to repent and get out sets them aside from the murderous thugs who rule the London streets. In a powerful piece of acting from Idle, he muses sentimentally on the good old days without guns and violent mayhem. Idle is the old school villain, robbing from those who can afford it, disrespectful of the corruption of authority but, underneath it all, a damn good bloke. This caring edge is developed with his emotional scenes of devotion with the haplessly shortsighted Camille Coduri. Although played with overtones of blonde bimbo, Coduri is much more than just a British comedy glam girl; she uses classic elements of visual comedy, enjoys some brave put-downs of the criminal elite and expresses pained emotion at the thought of losing the gangster in her heart. With major help from George Harrison's *Blow Away*, the romance is a vital part of the narrative, with the final onslaught of slaps and kisses, highlighting Coduri as an independent, unstereotyped and brilliantly played character. Idle's character is very much the new man using deceit to prevent hurt, real emotional feelings and a galaxy of manic silly voices (the nun/the Irish clergyman) to create a hilariously rounded performance.

For 1990, most of the film's humour is very regressive, but regressive in the best possible way – even the dreaded 'F' word, suppressed hilariously once by both Idle and Coltrane, is held back for maximum impact at the very end of the climactic hospital chase. Lightly powered with traces of innuendo, it is Coltrane's character which seems to have stepped out of a 1970s *Carry On*, with comments about having experience of 18-year-old girls, over-flamboyant mutters of 'Cor!', various suggestive hand signals as he desperately tries to ferret out the details of the Idle/Coduri relationship and, of most note, his straight-faced painful denial in the shower sequence. Surrounded by naked nubile young ladies, the sight of Coltrane's heavily perspiring nun is one for the classic archive. Coltrane is also the lapsed Catholic element, struggling to impart titbits of information to Idle's naive queries, with the classic Trinity routine being the pick of the bunch. In a tongue-in-cheek deconstruction of the Father, Son and Holy Ghost teachings, Coltrane desperately tries to justify its complete incoherence by explaining that its very unbelievability is the root of faith. Absolutely true but cheekily punishable by the wall hanging clouting him on the head. It's a gloriously subtle moment. There are

Coltrane and Idle caught in the act – *Nuns on the Run*

plenty of obvious gags (the note almost stolen from the collection tin, Coltrane's high voice when caught during a rooftop getaway, blowing his nose on bra padding), but everything works superbly to form. It's the ideal Ealing comedy for the nineties (note the collapsing, villain-carrying drainpipe, a reference to Alec Guinness and the train-based death in that other classic crime comedy *The LadyKillers*).

Throughout the film the magical teaming of Idle and Coltrane is impeccable, whether it be in the initial, bank employee-like chat over fried grub, the knowing cell conversations or the hilarious moments in the local chemist, this is the meeting of two major comic talents in an outstanding British comedy movie. The final twist is a masterstroke, and note the cast list gag concerning this moment: while in the best *A Fish Called Wanda* tradition the good bad guys get away with it, the religious angle is well taken care of and the nasty criminals get their just desserts. A total delight from start to finish.

Did You Know? Jonathan Lynn and Eric Idle go back a long way; as Cambridge cohorts they entered the Footlights together in 1963 and when Lynn joined Cleese and co in *Cambridge Circus* on Broadway he took some Idle material with him. Later Lynn directed the first staging of Idle's *Pass the Butler*. *Nuns on the*

Run was a pet project of Lynn's and, in order to secure good business and fab performances, he approached Python's Prominent Pictures, offering the two leading roles to Eric Idle and Michael Palin. Idle was very interested but Palin, busy trying to get *American Friends* off the ground, turned it down. *Python* film savouries, HandMade, were approached, but Denis O'Brien would only take it on if Idle said Yes... He said Yes. The finished film suffered a reaction like *Wanda* to the ending and Joe Roth of Fox put up $500,000 to reshoot the close, lightening the subdued conclusion, injecting more acidic violence and funnies. In the end, *Nuns* marketing in America was muffled and the *Wanda*-style business they wanted was not forthcoming. Idle bemoans that he is still waiting for any money from this, his most important solo film venture.

Nuns on the Run
HandMade Films
Brian Hope **ERIC IDLE**
Charlie McManus **ROBBIE COLTRANE**
Faith **CAMILLE CODURI**
Sister Mary of the Annunciation **LILA KAYE**
'Case' Casey **ROBERT PATTERSON**
Sister Mary of the Sacred Heart **DORIS HARE**
Father Seamus **TOM HICKEY**
Morley **WINSTON DENNIS**
Abbott **ROBERT MORGAN**
Sister Superior **JANET SUZMAN**
Norm **COLIN CAMPBELL**

Nr. Norris **RICHARD SIMPSON**
Louis **NICHOLAS HEWETSON**
Ronnie Chang **GARY TANG**
Henry Ho **DAVID FORMAN**
Dwayne Lee **NIGEL FAN**
Ernie Wong **OZZIE YUE**
Michelle **TATIANA STRAUSS**
Julie **WABEI SIYOLWE**
Tracey **HELEN FITZGERALD**
Faith's Father **STEWART HARWOOD**
Faith's Brother **PETER GEEVES**
Hysterical Bank Manageress **IRENE MAROT**
Bank Security Guard **LOUIS MELLIS**
Policeman in Car Park **CRAIG CROSBIE**
Gatekeeper **FRED HAGGERTY**
Bewildered Policeman **MICHAEL BEINT**
Taxi Driver **TEX FULLER**
Policeman with Radio **LEE SIMPSON**
Doctor **OLIVER PARKER**
Casino Waitress **JULIE GRAHAM**
Casino Manager **DAN HILDEBRAND**
Ward Nurse **JOANNE CAMPBELL**
Chemist Shop Assistant **GEDREN HELLER**
Hospital Receptionist **BRITT MORROW**
Police sergeant **DAVID BECALICK**
Police Constable **ARAN BELL**
Tied-up Nurses **FRANCINE WALKER & SHIRLEY ANNE-SELBY**
Airport Ticket Girl **JENNIFER HALL**
Airport Policeman **JOHN PHYTHIAN**
Flight Attendants **BRIAN HOPE & CHARLIE McMANUS**
Music **Yello & Hidden Faces** (with additional tracks from **George Harrison, Steve Winwood, The Imperials & Shakespeare's Sister**)
Editor **David Martin**
Production designer **Simon Holland**
Casting **Mary Selway**
Costume designer **Susan Yelland**
Production manager **Mary Richards**
Assistant director **David Brown**
Camera operator **Neil Binney**
Art director **Clinton Cavers**
Script supervisor **Diana Dill**
Photography **Michael Garfath**
Co-producer **Simon Bosanquet**
Executive producers **George Harrison & Denis O'Brien**
Producer **Michael White**
Written & directed by **Jonathan Lynn**
Distributed by Palace Pictures
Lee International Film Studios, Shepperton & on location
92 mins, 12 Cert. 1990

THE ODD JOB

A very strange but interesting solo project from Graham Chapman slotted in between the two major *Python* films and unfairly neglected by even the most die-hard of fans. The basic storyline – a man's beloved wife leaves him; distraught, he hires an oddball guy to kill him; his wife comes back to him, but the murderer still tries to carry out his job – had originally been created by Chapman's long-standing co-writer on the *Doctor* series, Bernard McKenna. One of LWT's *Six Dates with Barker*, broadcast on 22 January 1971, it starred Ronnie Barker, Joan Sims and David Jason. Years later, Chapman saw it as the perfect film vehicle for him and reworked the original script with McKenna, adding plenty of extra padding, naturally, and small doses of additional *Python* surrealism. The result is a minor but very enjoyable comedy picture, overflowing with deliciously dark humour and some spirited work from its star. Chapman, playing a sort of cross between his old official figures from *Python* and Tim Brooke-Taylor's sitcom persona, gives a stunning central turn, playing the straight fading marriage scenes with sincerity while delighting in squawked exclamations and uncontrolled outrage. A brilliant farce performance in *Python* terms. Sadly, Chapman is slightly underpinned by sketchy supporting roles, including Simon Williams as the lascivious best friend continually trying to grope Chapman's wife, Joe Melia's rather overdone waiter, the contrasting face of the law in Edward Hardwicke's soft on the outside, hard on the inside Inspector and Bill Paterson's hard all over, aggressive, insinuating Sergeant. Diana Quick grabs her confused, bewildered and lovelorn wife role with real

conviction and Carolyn Seymour (in yet another kit-off role) does some fine, introspective work alongside her sex-obsessed elements. There's some enjoyable work from Michael Elphick and his sidekicks (including an outrageously camp Richard O'Brien), tapping into old *Python* terminology boasting about doing the catering for the Great Train Robbery and insisting that he won't protect anyone against the wrath of the American Express people.

However, it's a wonderful, manic central role for David Jason that perfectly contrasts Chapman's crumbling grip on reality. With John Lennon specs, Biggles flying helmet, casual fag puffing, black leather gear, motorbike antics and the full Jack Douglas mannerisms, Jason is a walking disaster area of mindless violence, obsession with Chapman's colour tv and dogged determination to fulfil his mission in life. The attempts on Chapman's life in the park are a joy, with flaked-out bodies all over the place, newly dug graves and inept swipes with a shovel all thrown into the mixture. It's a relatively small, anonymous part, but Jason imbues the character with an endearing edge of Norman Wisdom stupidity while still retaining the bizarre, dark quality of his cheerful dedication to murder. Obviously the overall danger and humour in the situation is stretched to breaking point here and, indeed, the basic idea of the assisted suicide isn't even mentioned until 30 minutes into the film, but still, the necessary padding isn't that dull and Chapman's comic prowess is more than enough to cover up the dodgy moments. There's a marvellous opening scene with the xenophobic doorkeeper, with Chapman's stunned, disgusted reaction as the lift door shuts being a masterclass in perfect overacting. Later his frantic attempts to try to describe Jason's appearance brings forth a rush of energetic arm flinging and face-pulling with his moment of sheer genius coming when one of his milk bottles has been laced with acid and he chases after the milkman, explaining away his sword-wielding antics to passers-by saying that the guy only left him one pint! The delivery is hilarious.

However, the film's greatest scene has to be the elongated first meeting between Chapman and Jason when the plan is hatched. Jason's cool, streetwise persona injecting major elements of train-spotter attitude, wanders about the luxury flat pontificating about the ways and means of death. It's a wonderfully played sequence between the two, perfectly capturing the film's mad core of comic ideas and dark values. Obviously, the initial idea is far funnier than the final realisation, although Jason's bumbling trail of dead bodies and Chapman's eye-popping reaction keep the laughs coming. For me, the final, dated, very kitsch seventies ending is a mistake, but this is still a very important piece of British film making. Chapman's only starring role without the involvement of any other Pythons is a masterpiece of timing, farce acting, gentle mocking of authority and sincerity in a cast of straight actors.

Did You Know? The role of the odd job man was originally intended as the major acting breakthrough for Chapman's rock mate, Keith Moon. He was also up for an appearance in *Brian* but sadly touring commitments with The Who kept him out of the fun. Besides, the production company kept on stalling over such unconventional casting, with Chapman even doing his acting work for a pittance to appease them and get the film made. Sadly, this was Moon's last chance for a new career move – he died in 1979 following the Paul McCartney party premiere of *The Buddy Holly Story*. With Moon out of the running, *The Odd Job* was eventually offered to the original and obvious choice, David Jason, who had made such an impression in the television version. Both Graham Chapman and Bernard McKenna missed the Royal Premiere of *The Odd Job* in October 1978, the two were enjoying *Python*'s finest hour filming *Life of Brian* in Tunisia.

Columbia Pictures Presents
The Odd Job

Charisma Films/Taulorda Ltd
Arthur Harris **GRAHAM CHAPMAN**
The Odd Job Man **DAVID JASON**
Tony Sloane **SIMON WILLIAMS**
Fiona Harris **DIANA QUICK**
Inspector Black **EDWARD HARDWICKE**
Sergeant Mull **BILL PATERSON**
Raymonde **MICHAEL ELPHICK**
Bernaard **STEWART HARWOOD**
Head Waiter **JOE MELIA**
Caretaker **GEORGE INNES**
Angie **CAROLYN SEYMOUR**
Mr. Kemp **JAMES BREE**
Mrs. Kemp **ZULEMA DENE**
Batch **RICHARD O'BRIEN**
Taxi Driver **CARL ANDREWS**
Milkman **DAVE ATKINS**
Police Driver **JOHN JUDD**
Police Constable **NICK EDMETT**
Barman **TOBY SALAMAN**
Boston Startler **TINY KEELING**
Old Man **DAVID HATTON**
Waiter **ANTHONY MILNER**
Ambulance Man **MARK PENFOLD**
Screenplay by **Bernard McKenna & Graham Chapman**
Based on an original play by **Bernard McKenna**
Editor **Barrie Vince**
Photography **Ken Hodges**
Art director **Tony Curtis**
Costume designer **Shuna Harwood**
Music **Howard Blake**
Production manager **John Wilcox**
Assistant director **Stephen P. Christian**
Camera operator **Neil Binney**
Executive producers **Tony Stratton Smith & Steve O'Rourke**
Producers **Mark Forstater & Graham Chapman**
Director **Peter Medak**
Filmed on location in London and at Shepperton Studios
86 mins, 1978

OMNIBUS: Life of Python

Even as early as the fifth anniversary in 1974 television was bestowing the *Python* legacy with an in-depth celebration (*In Vision*), but this 21st anniversary tribute remains by far the most absorbing and emotive. Dedicated as it is to the memory of the one and only Graham Chapman and featuring top and tail scenes from Chapman's memorial service, this really does appear as a glorious

salute to the late *Python*. Still for all that, this is naturally not a gloomy, conventional tribute and the memorial sequences are wonderfully irreverent and life-affirming. John Cleese begins the proceedings with a moving memorial to his long-standing writing partner before injecting the situation with forced but affectionate bad taste, delighting the crowd of comic masters by citing Chapman as a 'freeloading bastard' and summoning the spirit of Chapman hoping that Cleese could cause a bit of a storm by being not only the first person to have said the word 'shit' on British television but also to stand tall as the first person at a memorial gathering to utter the word f***. One can imagine Graham grinning with pleasure.

After just over 50 minutes of interviews and clips, we again join the gathering for Eric Idle's rendition of a thankfully uncensored version of *Always Look on the Bright Side of Life*, joined by a chorus from a clearly moved Cleese, Palin, Jones, Gilliam, Tim Brooke-Taylor, Douglas Adams, Barry Cryer and more. Idle completes the magic with another f*** and a touching 'God bless you Graham'. In comparison with such powerful and unforgettable footage the enjoyable ramble through *Python* treasures can be easily overshadowed, but this *Omnibus* special, brilliantly hosted by *Not the Nine O'Clock News* and *Blackadder* producer John Lloyd, celebrates the work of six fine comedy talents with affectionate understanding and respect. The Cleese/Jones tension is discussed; Gilliam joyfully crashes through several old masters and uncovers the original *Python* foot; Idle cynically predicts a lifetime of *Python* anniversaries and team member funerals while Palin wistfully remembers the past with a contented smile of satisfaction. One longs for the five to chat on camera together (à la the McCartney, Harrison, Starr material from *The Beatles Anthology*) but still, what we have here is pure undiluted gold.

Unlike the 1989 Steve Martin tribute, the much celebrated Parrot sketch is included here, alongside familiar gems like The Spanish Inquisition, The Argument Sketch and How to Defend Yourself Against Fresh Fruit. However, the real pleasure is a rare chance to savour some of the team's earliest work. Clips of Palin and Idle from *Do Not Adjust Your Set*, the totally *Python*-like clip of Jones interviewing Palin's bathing King Arthur in the manner of a post-football television spot from *Complete and Utter History*, the Speak-a English sketch with Cleese, Chapman, Feldman and Brooke-Taylor from *1948 Show* and many more, up to and including a snippet from *Not*'s Python/Christ debate with Mel Smith, Rowan Atkinson and Pamela Stephenson.

This period after the era of right-on comic expression and the emergence of political correctness dictates that the treatment of women in *Python* is addressed, but Carol Cleveland, bless her, defends the lads as being unable to pen young female roles well and is totally apologetic about this failing. Cleese, meanwhile, is wonderfully unrepentant and philosophical, while, best of all, Ben Elton – Mr. Right On himself – refuses to condemn the lads. Elton makes some fascinating observations, as does Stephen Fry, agreeing that the essence of *Python* is perhaps better in the mind rather than in reviewing old tapes, as with the best Summers, while any old excuse to wallow in almost an hour of classic clips and insightful comments from the men themselves makes this an essential introduction to the *Python* cult. An essential companion for any self-respecting *Python* fan and an essential slice of British television history in neat, easily digestible chunks. Priceless.

Omnibus – Life of Python
With thanks to **Anne James & Roger Saunders** at Python (Monty) Pictures Ltd
Camera assistants **Roger Chapman, Lawrence Gardner, Max Harrison, Phil Milliard & Carl Teitelbaum**
Production assistant **Marne Jung**
Production manager **Sue Vertue**
Electricians **Jason Hunt, Terry Hunt & Jim McBride**
Sound **Fraser Barber, Michael Lax &**

David Welch
Dubbing mixer **Colin Martin**
VT editor **Bill Ogden**
Cameramen **Mike Fox, Graham Smith & Paul Sommers**
Assistant editor **Roya Salari**
Dubbing editor **Richard Monks**
Film editor **Martyn Hone**
Associate producer **Michelle de Larrabeiti**
Executive producer **Charles Brand**
Director **Mark Redhead**
Produced & directed by **Mark Chapman**
Series editor **Andrew Snell**
A Tiger Television production for the BBC produced in association with Devillier-Donegan Enterprises

ONE FOOT IN THE GRAVE

One of the great BBC situation comedies, Richard Wilson's multi-award winning performance as Victor Meldrew ranks alongside the Fawltys, Rigsbys, Steptoes and Trotters of the world as one of television's most endearing comedy characters. From its beginnings in 1989, Renwick's scripts were spot on and the catchy signature tune, written and sung by Eric Idle, burrowed into the nation's subconscious. It was only a matter of time before Idle would himself crop up in the show and in 1991 he guest starred in *The Man in the Long Black Coat* – a 50-minute special which incorporated Victor's usual angst-ridden observations, Crosbie's under-played amazement and the ever growing feud with Cleeseian neighbour Angus Deayton. The extended air time allowed a dash of emotive pathos to creep in (as with later shows) and Wilson's powerful comic bemusement is at an all-time peak, stumbling through some delicious black humour concerning a supposed cremation urn and suffering a peerlessly produced doctor's waiting room nightmare with stony-faced outrage. Eric Idle wanders in for a couple of classic scenes, appearing initially as forbidding boots, a case-clutching hand and, finally, a sinister figure from within the fog. A Holmesian entrance, complemented by a suggestion of the Jeremy Brett/Granada theme, his

good-natured chap from the Borough Health and Public Safety goes through the motions testing Meldrew's horse manure for radioactivity. He voices a wonderful opening concern about not shaking hands and proceeds to surgically peel on his gloves for the work ahead. Overly reassuring, offering up Mars bars and even injecting a trace of the cheerful charmer as he attempts to flog some digital watches, this is a priceless minor turn from the comedy legend. Underused he may be, but there's no one on earth who could make the simple comment, 'No, no, no!' so funny and Nudge nudgian. A classic cameo.

One Foot In The Grave
Victor Meldrew **RICHARD WILSON**
Margaret Meldrew **ANNETTE CROSBIE**
Patrick **ANGUS DEAYTON**
Pippa **JANINE DUVITSKI**
Receptionist **CECILY HOBBS**
Nick Swainey **OWEN BRENMAN**
Mr. Killick **MICHAEL ROBBINS**
Special Guest Appearance **ERIC IDLE** as Mervyn Whale.
Written by **David Renwick**
Signature tune written & performed by **Eric Idle**
Arranged by **John du Prez**
Produced by **Andre Jacquemin**
Incidental music **Ed Welch**
Camera supervisor **Roger Goss**
Production assistant **Susan Silburn**
Film editor **John Dunstan**
Videotape editor **Chris Wadsworth**
Lighting director **Christopher Kempton**
Production manager **Murray Peterson**
Designer **John Bristow**
Produced & directed by **Susan Belbin**
1991

OUT OF THE TREES

Post television *Python*, Cleese ranted for England in *Fawlty Towers*, Jones and Palin tackled historical British eccentrics in *Ripping Yarns*, Gilliam moved his artistic gaze to direction of semi-*Python*esque romps and Idle trod the waters of sketch comedy. Chapman also ventured to recapture the magic of *Python* in his own series of sketches entitled *Out Of the Trees*. Only one episode was made! There were initial plans for a series, but Chapman's renewed interest in *Python* for *Brian* and the fact that hardly anybody saw or reviewed the show – it was broadcast late one Saturday night opposite *Match of the Day* – saw the BBC abandon the project. Familiar *Python*-related performer Simon Jones, *Doctor/Odd Job* co-writer Bernard McKenna and *Monty Python* collaborator Douglas Adams (along with Innes, the only non-Python to receive writing credit on the show) helped Chapman out in the venture, but the results were never more than patchily interesting with half-baked ideas concerning Genghis Khan light years from the *Python* glory days.

Starring **GRAHAM CHAPMAN** With **SIMON JONES, MARK WING-DAVEY & ROGER BRIERLEY** Written by **Graham Chapman, Bernard McKenna & Douglas Adams** Broadcast 10 January 1976, BBC2

THE OXFORD REVUE

Having written for the *Edgar Allen Magazine* (the journal of the steelmakers his father worked for) and acted (in everything from Shakespeare to *The Woodcutter* for Brightside & Carbrook Players), it was at Oxford that comedy took hold. The first major collaboration of Terry Jones and Michael Palin, this review was instrumental in a move towards anti-satire and the beginning of a fantasy attitude towards comic expression which developed into *Python*. Staged in the summer of 1964, during Jones' last year at Oxford, the cast also included Annabel Leventon, Nigel Pegram and Doug Fisher, who doubled as director. Turning their comic sights on definitive *Python* themes like British eccentricities, bumbling policemen and pompous authority types, the chemistry between Jones and Palin was electric, although much of their writing work was with John Gould, notably ranging from the gloriously surreal *I've Invented a Long-Range Telescope* to the stunning Palin and Jones effort *Song*

About a Toad. Other *Python*-geared highlights included the Goonish Last One Home's a Custard (or, *Six Characters in Search of a Song*), *Song of British Nose* and the Terry Jones classic *Forgive Me*. Storming the Edinburgh festival and playing two weeks at the Phoenix Theatre – as was now becoming the norm – The Oxford Revue was offered the opportunity to decamp to London, although the circumstances were less than inspiring. The venue suggested was The Establishment. A year before, Peter Cook and the darling young things of British comedy had reigned supreme there, ushering in everyone from Lenny Bruce to Frankie Howerd, but by 1964 the satire boom had blown over, the club was in poor repair and audience attendances were extremely low. To top it all, Palin, who was committed to university work, couldn't perform during the London run and saw his place taken by David Walsh.

MICHAEL PALIN

The youngest Python, Palin was born 5 May 1943 Sheffield, Yorkshire and grew up on a staple diet of The Goons, Tony Hancock and Peter Cook. He was improvising comic monologues about the Coronation at the age of ten and read Shakespeare plays to his mother Mary, playing all the parts. His family, headed by his father who worked for a local steel firm, discouraged him from an acting career primarily because his older sister by nine years, Angela, had tried rep and quickly became disillusioned with the lifestyle. However, Michael played minor Shakespeare parts at Birkdale Preparatory School and made his stage debut in 1948 at the age of five, playing Martha Cratchit in *A Christmas Carol* where he fell off the stage! Educated at Shrewsbury

from 1957 (in the wake of Willie Rushton and Richard Ingrams and a contemporary of John Peel), many years later (during *Full Circle* filming) Palin entertained a New Zealand Maori ceremonial gathering with his old school song, *Floreat Salopia*, instead of his usual party piece, the lumberjack. He studied history at Oxford's Brasenose College from 1962 and with only an amateur interest in acting, Palin's career ideas were aimed at advertising or the steel industry.

But once at Cambridge he began writing and performing comedy sketches with future theatre critic and fellow history student Robert Hewison, delighting in surrealist material like tape recorders in buckets, bananas – with 20 consumed in some 15 seconds, Tide soap powder ads resulting in consumption of the stuff, wacky parodies of wildlife film-makers Armand & Michaela Denis, and more familiar comic targets like RAF wartime briefings – definitively skitted by Peter Cook and Jonathan Miller in *Beyond the Fringe*. Palin performed his first material at the Oxford University Psychology Society Christmas Party while Terry Jones, in his second year, saw the freshman's work, and the celebrated Jones/Palin partnership came together to write the much used Slapstick sketch for *Loitering Within Tent*. Despite the dexterity and longevity of this material, the teaming was very much an on-off affair at this stage.

Going their separate ways, Palin continued to hone his acting skills via cabaret and plays while still writing material with Hewison. Like Jones, Palin was involved with both the Oxford University Dramatic Society and the Experimental Theatre Group, writing and performing material like *Grin* for the Summer '64 musical presentation *Keep This to Yourself* and *Etcetera, Etcetera A Weekend Revue* at the Playhouse as well as playing McCann in Pinter's *The Birthday Party*. Both Palin and Hewison would be involved in the Terry Jones revue *Hang Down Your Head and Die* at Oxford and its 44 performances in London's Comedy

Michael Palin – Mr Nice Guy

Theatre before Palin himself finally came of age with 1964's milestones, *The Oxford Revue* and *The Oxford Line* which appeared at the 1965 Edinburgh Festival. Co-writing, producing, directing and performing in *The Oxford Line*, this show opened on 23 August with a cast including Diana Quick, Mark Sadler and David Wood, with Palin material including Opener, Vicar, English, Getting To Know You, Jean-Paul Overe, Restoration Box, Battle of Wits, Brassoriania, Bananas, How Wintrop Spudes Saved the World and, in collaboration with the soon to leave Terry Jones, a sketch entitled Tinpally. The programme biography for Palin included, 'Michael aims to take up a career as a script-writer' and once he departed Oxford with his degree in Modern History in 1965 he wasted no time in joining his old friend Terry Jones in London to try and fulfil his ambition. Making a conscious break from his usual partner, Robert Hewison, Jones introduced Palin to Willie Donaldson, gaining his first ever pay packet of £50 to assist Jones on the aborted project *The Love Show* and knocking out some material at the home of Jones' parents and their cat Geronimo.

By October 1965 Palin was hosting the youth programme, *Now!* and writing comedy with Jones for BBC programmes like *The Ken Dodd Show*, *The Illustrated Weekly Hudd*, *The Late Show*, *The Billy Cotton Bandshow* and *Late Night Line-Up*. In April 1966 Palin married Helen Gibbins, the farmer's daughter he had met as a teen on holiday at Stowmarket (and later dramatised with *East of Ipswich*) and bought his first house, in Hampstead, North London, for £12,000 in 1968 (he now owns three in a row making up a palazzo on the corner of a cul-de-sac, having bought the second in 1977 for £17,500 and the third – situated in between his other two – for £180,000, the property of Downing Street caterer Clare Latimer of Clare's kitchen which now forms Palin's parlour). Palin created *The Complete and Utter History of Britain* with Terry Jones, starred in *Do Not Adjust Your Set*, contributed to Ronnie Barker's Radio 4 show *Lines From My Grandfather's Forehead*, guest starred on the first *The Innes Book of Records* in 1981, starred in Ronald Hars *The Dresser* on radio, penned a best-selling novel, *Heminway's Chair*, contributed to such publications as *The Sunday Telegraph Magazine*, *The New York Times*, *Esquire* magazine and *Punch*, became BBC's favourite travelogue host, was interviewed for Edward Whitley's book *The Graduates* (and storming out of his own house when his interviewer considered *The Missionary* unfunny), and crafted a string of personal movie successes including *American Friends* and *A Private Function*.

However, it was 1969's foundation of *Monty Python's Flying Circus* that made him one of the country's most potent comic forces. Indeed, his most celebrated performances have been in tow with his fellow Pythons, not least of which appear in *Grail*, *Life* and *Brian* (one of his favourite films, besides *This is Spinal Tap*, *Picnic at Hanging Rock* and *La Grande Bouffe*), as well as Eric Idle's *The Rutles* alongside George Harrison (aptly, Palin's favourite group is the Beatles – a man of impeccable taste), *Ripping Yarns*, *Time Bandits*, *Brazil*, *A Fish Called Wanda* and *Fierce Creatures* (his favourite people are John Cleese, and other beloved co-star, Maggie Smith). More than eager to use his public cachet for good causes, Palin fronted the BBC's *Mental Health Week* (his sister Angela committed suicide at 52; he discussed his own bouts of depression and memories of a bullying, stammering father), chaired Transport 2000 for two years and remains passionate about the nostalgia of steam railways and old cinemas – he is also on the board of Shepperton Studios. Of all the Python members, Palin was the one who looked forward most to another reunion. With the death of Graham Chapman he put these hopes behind him, but still plans to collaborate with both Terry Jones and Terry Gilliam on further projects in the future. A national institution, extraordinary writer and actor, as well as remaining the most fondly remembered pet shop assistant in history, Palin continues to spread feelgood pleasure through a myriad of projects.

PALIN'S COLUMN

Following the gruelling trips around the world and between the Poles, Palin the presenter was offered the more sedate chance to write a column for *The Isle of Wight County Press*, incorporating a homage to the lumberjack's plight by explaining that before comedy took hold he wanted to do something serious like journalism. This is his major chance. Allowing Palin to act as both host and comic charmer, each show includes copious quotes from his four printed pieces, dated 27 August, 24 September, 22 October and 12 November 1993.

A pleasing travelogue of the island's more obscure areas, each rejoices in eccentric folk and mysterious topics with show 1, *Black and Wight Magic*, taking a spine-tingling look at the hidden occult community. Briefed by the editor of the rag, Palin throws himself into the assignment, searching out the notorious Long Stone. This is the site of strange sacrifices and blood-letting, while more recently, as a local policeman explains, it has been the place where a coffin containing a doll with a nail through its head was discovered. Charming. A sea jaunt aboard the *Count Dracula* provides no leads although the Garlic festival Queen is cornily attacked by a camp, flamboyant, ashen-faced vampire, unceremoniously deposited in a wheelie bin. An ice cold swim is far more terrifying, while the delights of supernatural fun are easily bettered by Palin's early wardrobe gag, finishing his dictation and happily strolling into the piece of furniture as if it's the most natural thing in the world. However, the chief delight is Palin's wonderful old landlady Dorothy, happily making tea and totally unfazed by his black magic discoveries. She does a bit of successful predicting herself, winning some cash on the horses and whispering about not letting the neighbours know her business. So endearing is she, that although in show 2, *A Gap In The Market*, Palin is taking bed and breakfast aboard a converted torpedo boat, dear old Dorothy returns. Despite some good comic business aboard the boat with prat-falling antics and head-banging beams, Palin's rowing from Liverpool gag fails to hit home and he's soon charming his ex-landlady with a ride in a 1937 Comfy Coach and a mini-cruise on the S.S. *Waverley*, bringing on surprised 'Ooh!..'s at Palin's

reference to her regal air. Her embarrassed praise for the mention in the previous column is touching television indeed.

However, our intrepid reporter is soon on the trail of mainland folk who sold up and went out to the island – although this is a fairly non-starting project – fan mail from his black magic piece is browsed over and the pet cemetery chappie is quickly usurped by the bizarre dinosaur guy, crowding his flat out with boxes of fossils. Dubbed Dinosaur Island, this obsessive interest has clearly taken over his life and, the great thing about all of Palin's shows, his shocked amazement, is totally and shamelessly apparent throughout the piece. It comes as no surprise that the man earns the money to fund his work by desperately trying to sell dino droppings!

A bit of foolhardy solo sailing and sinking rounds off this episode, but show 3, *Old Haunts*, the pick of the series, presents the most chilling and effective moment of all. There's an emotive visit to the soon to be defunct Needles Lighthouse, a rain-sodden guest house with knitting inhibitions, an almagam of stories based round the Autumn Harvest Festival and the ghosts of the isle, but not a sign of Dorothy anywhere! The haunting aspect quickly makes far more interesting television, bumping into writer and fellow County Press journo, Gay Baldwin, and making a spooky trip to the Golden Hill Fort, originally built to withstand the French invasion that never came but now the home of half-baked tourism and a cold, ghostly presence. A British soldier allegedly hanged himself and now creeps around the Long Corridor, although an overnight vigil produces no concrete facts despite one ghost-hunter optimistically saying that 'One bang is a bonus!' – Quite! Palin, meanwhile, avoids all this stuff and plays cards with his guesthouse inmates before cycling past Bettyhaunt Lane, discovering some strange shaped, sub-*That's Life* vegetables while looking over Ventnor's Botanic Gardens with sinister whiffs of mulled wine from

ex-TB clinic days and plant-inducing classical music for the present. The callboxes continually ringing as Palin wanders past are amusing and effective, but the most interesting sequence concerns a seemingly, very good medium, by the name of Mark Brandish who gets more right than wrong and finally drags Palin into the meeting with talk of a deceased chap called Brian. The look of nervous surprise and his muttered pleas of writing a film about Brian are quite chilling – could this be Graham Chapman's last joke? Anyway, the more information that is provided the more the moment is lost, but that initial breakthrough is powerful stuff indeed. The final programme, show 4, *I Came, I Saw, I Conkered*, may be the weakest in terms of stories, but Palin is as affable as ever. Whether it's looking after his new landlady's prized best-dressed pumpkin, consoling her over judgmental rulings, tracking down a rare, wild carrot, or preventing a much needed new road, Palin injects fun and energy into every uninspiring trail. Editor Peter Hurst is back from his holiday but still playing golf, while this final column is meandering all over the place until Palin struggles to cover the Isle of Wight conker championships. Defeated, his Ealing Common, pre-prepared weapons are found to be against the rules and make their way into a Page 3 *Sun* report! – as Palin says an environment where 'something bigger than conkers' was required. However, the very real problem of a receding coastline and Palin's easy way with a bunch of schoolchildren make for great television, before he proves his theory that the world's population can be squeezed onto the Island and enjoying a brief look at Carisbrooke Castle, which housed Charles I just before the big moment.

The final section includes a current place of incarceration, Parkhurst, with life sentence prisoners putting their views across with 'dark, bleak, uncompromising humour', the controlled but fair warden and an air of the best example of an outmoded institution. There's a delightful summing up, some grand, *Please*

Release Me sound-bites, a call for the show's main man, Roger, and the endearing close of a low-key but enthralling assignment.

Palin's Column
Written & presented by **Michael Palin**
Music **Tom Palin & Sheridan Tongue**
Camera **Colin Angell**
Sound **Sam Diamond**
Dubbing mixers **Bob Jackson & Colin Martin**
Editor **Alex Richardson**
Researcher **Robyn Wallis**
Production manager **Sally French**
Meridian Executive **Mary McAnally**
Executive Producer **Anne James**
Produced & directed by **Roger Mills**
Meridian Broadcasting & Prominent Television, Channel Four, 4 June–27 June 1994, 4x 25 mins

PAPERBACKS

Literary discussion show hosted by Terry Jones who finally pushed the BBC as far as they would go when he addressed nuclear issues and the science of hypnosis alongside more conventional obsessions like Alfred Bestall's illustrations for Rupert Bear – this led to the following year's documentary on Rupert for Channel Four. Jones replaced original host Robert Kee but caused the BBC's shackles to rise after just three shows – going down too political an avenue with his interviews. The seven finished shows are riveting, fascinating insights.

Paperbacks hosted by **Terry Jones**
3 June 1981 – with **Fidelis Morgan, J.L. Carr & Paul Theroux**
10 June 1981 – with **Michael Moorcock & Joe Keeton** on hypnotics
17 June 1981 – Erotica with **Angela Carter, Reay Tannahill & Jill Tweedie**
24 June 1981 – The nuclear threat with **Charles Levinson, Robert Neild & E.P. Thompson**
1 July 1981 – Children's books with **Alfred Bestall & Jan Pienkowski**
8 July 1981 – Travel books and philosophy of life with **Iris Murdoch & Paul Theroux**
15 July 1981 – with **Robert Blythe, Peter Porter & Quentin Skinner**
Producers **Rosemary Bowen-Jones &**

Julian Jebb
Director **Nick Brenton**

PARROT SKETCH NOT INCLUDED – TWENTY YEARS OF MONTY PYTHON

The official 20th anniversary celebration from the *Monty Python* production team may lack the class of the BBC *Omnibus* tribute but this totally essential compilation of the team's best bits (minus the deceased Norwegian Blue, of course) is a glorious canter through a legacy of unforgettable comedy. Right from the opening credits this is a tongue-in-cheek ego trip for Steve Martin, embracing all the clichéd descriptive phrases (zany/wacky/anarchic/intellectual), bursting the bubble of adoration, expressing amazement that the lads could be important and British, confusing the members with the Beatles, extending the link with evidence of satanic connections (the 'Bruce' sketch played backwards and over-dubbed by Idle and Chapman), a pained reflection of the endless times these routines have been seen and an ultra-rare chance to wallow in the pretty ropey lost German show with wonderfully over-played reaction from our host. It's obviously geared for the American market (with Martin's White House reference noted for removal) with the mega-star of *Saturday Night Live* cranking up the classic *Python* memories with a joyous lack of respect and pomp. The *Python* legacy is treated with the members' usual irreverence. With that, the familiar strains of Sousa set up well over an hour of choice pickings specially chosen by the Pythons, such as World Forum, the Ministry of Silly Walks, Lumberjack Song, the Argument Sketch and Spam. Besides a clever link between the Spanish Inquisition mob boarding a bus and cutting to Gilliam's old lady at the Bus Stop animation, this is really a standard 'best of' compilation from the archives. Nothing wrong with that, but it's the big finish that really makes this collection of sweetmeats so treasurable. Steve Martin's post-credit

rounding-off muses on where the Pythons are today, revealing the fact that the team are situated in the very cupboard behind him. He opens it to reveal the team nervously looking out, closes it again and wanders off. Palin's timid cries of 'Steve, Steve, can you leave the door open please! Whole point, reunion, see us all again, Steve...' concludes with a venomous 'Bastard!' and fades to black.

Now, as a militant, naive teenage chap watching this for the first time, I was outraged that a so-called celebration could gather the team together and miss the chance of something more than this. In fact, the original plan was for Steve Martin and the Pythons to perform a totally new sketch for inclusion in the show. Each member agreed to do this, believing that one or two of the other Pythons had written the piece. In reality, none of the Pythons were involved at script level and when it came to filming Graham Chapman was so ill he was confined to a wheelchair. Although present at the recording, Chapman didn't take part and it was down to the other five and Martin to film the material, featuring the Pythons as naughty schoolchildren. Everyone involved knew it wasn't right. Having vowed never to perform other people's material, they were doing just that with an incomplete group. Hardly the best way to celebrate a 20th anniversary. In the end, the Pythons used their power of veto and opted for the brief cameo that appears in *Parrot Sketch Not Included*. Chapman is sitting with Gilliam looking dishevelled, Cleese bemused and the other three plain confused. In retrospect, this silent, simple final appearance was more than enough and perhaps, more powerful a reunion piece than even the greatest sketch of all time. Made even more touching and important with Chapman's death just a few weeks later, this is the final bit of *Monty Python* comedy and remains the perfect close. Watch, re-watch and rejoice...

Conceived, written & performed by
Graham Chapman, John Cleese, Terry

Gilliam, Eric Idle, Terry Jones &
Michael Palin
Also appearing **Carol Cleveland, Connie
Booth, Basil Tang, Marjorie Wilde &
The Fred Tomlinson Singers**
Animations by **Terry Gilliam**
Producers **Ian MacNaughton & John
Howard Davies**
Parrot Sketch Not Included
Production manager **Sue Vertue**
Producers **Charles Brand & Anne
James**
Editors **Martyn Hone & John Lloyd**
A Tiger Television Production for Python
(Monty) Pictures Ltd 1989

PASS THE BUTLER

A play by Eric Idle, its narrative
threads of transvestites, grotesque
half lives, murder, police corruption
and political intrigue make this a Joe
Orton for the eighties. Wonderfully
surreal it even has a character called
Butler the butler!

Did You Know? Idle originally
thought up the idea in France in 1979
and was in fact in the West Indies
writing *Meaning of Life* at the time
of its London run. Idle was involved
in the initial tour. He would tape the
show with audience reaction, cut and
change, as with the *Python* movies,
before honing it for the London run.
It was the longest running play in
1984 spanning Van Nuys, California
and Sweden and it's still very big in
Oslo and Scandinavia. Royalties pour
in all the time.

First performed 3 November 1981 by
The Cambridge Theatre Company,
University of Warwick, Coventry.
Director **Jonathan Lynn**.
London debut 26 January 1982
The Globe Theatre

PERSONAL SERVICES

This critically acclaimed look at the
saucy underbelly of British upper
classes and the charming Madam
who served their sexual desires was,
importantly, the first film directed by
a Python which removes any on-
screen link with a certain flying circus

– Gilliam wouldn't make the break
until 1991's *The Fisher King*. Terry
Jones here constructs an effective
filming of David Leland's hilarious,
touching and mildly shocking script,
treating the perverted lives of British
dignitaries with a gloriously
unaffected, tittering behind the hand
style. Some of the performances stray
a bit too much into overt caricature
but as a rule Jones' direction keeps a
firm grip on the subject matter,
brilliantly juxtaposing typically
British humour with the forbidden,
dark obsessions of the clientele.
Julie Walters is, obviously our main
interest, and Jones brings us into her
world with lingering looks of doubt
on various sexual adventures. We
follow her journey of discovery from
naive unmarried mother waitressing
for a living through to cool, calm,
collected acceptance of her life-
affirming position of pleasure-giver
through sex and understanding. Her
hilarious recounting of a bit of
personal service in place of rent for
her landlord is bristling with riotous
comedy and her delightfully,
unsupressed hilarity at the very
stupidity of sexual desire lightens the
entire movie – at every juncture she
giggles with amazement/
embarrassment at what she's required
to organise next and the black
leather, bound and gagged, red
flashing light sequence is pure class.
Her stunned glaze across the various
innuendo-packed prostitute ads in her
local shop – all big chests and French
polishing – almost makes the viewer
expect Eric Idle to wander pass at any
minute. Jones includes lots of florid
camera style, floating, investigative,
hand-held shots and if all the blow
outs and blow jobs get a bit too much
there's always the wonderful Walters
performance, embracing low-brow
comic commentary, romantic
ideaology, authority-baiting angst
and touching family relationships
when the tense father/daughter
situation is rectified by sex,
understanding and warm contact.
Shirley Stelfox gives a stunning
performance, over-flowing with sassy
dialogue, experienced sexual play-
acting and manipulation of her
allure. There's mind-boggling support

from Danny Schiller and dear old
Benjamin Whitrow turns in an
unforgettable picture of a restrained
Brit middle-aged nobody. Stephen
Lewis wanders in for a hilarious
underplayed cameo, Peter Cellier
embodies the cross-over between
schoolboy spanking and
respectability while Alec McCowan,
getting a bit over the top at times,
nevertheless delights us with his
adopted children's police helmet after
the raid, continual references to his
war record and cries of 'I'm a
pervert'. This element of anarchy in
old age was the major point of
fascination for Jones and is brought
out in delicious delight. Indeed, the
Christmas orgy gatecrashed by the
law forms the climactic set piece to
the film and is brilliantly
orchestrated. Beginning with an
image of perfect suburbia, Walters'
house of sex, potently backed with
Mary's Boy Child, Jones immediately
cuts from this peaceful scene of
festive cheer to the promised orgy of
pleasure within, spanning a seedy
pornography title sequence,
wheelchair-bound punters and short-
skirted girls ready for the starting
gun. If the freedom of expression and
enjoyment projected fails to convince
you, Jones vindicates the Walters
lifestyle with her caring touch of
compassion, enforcing the image of
dirty old man with cheerful put-
downs while ironically she reverts to
serving food to clients with her 'end
of bash' supply of eggs and tea. It's a
delight, again violently contrasted
with images of all-out sexual
pleasure as the police break their way
in. Despite continual and graphic
references to sex throughout, the
actual on-screen imagery is fairly
controlled, with just off-camera hand
jobs and upper slope shots standing
in for penetrative up-close sequences.
This is Jones highlighting the spoil-
sport attitude of the police rather
than all-out corruption, with their
leniency towards foreign diplomats
and important bigwigs more a
comment on the hypocritical system
than anything else. The glorious pan
out shot as Walters' clients dejectedly
wander away from the police station
is a masterly directorial image and

there's an air of good-natured, undercover rebelliousness about the film. Throughout Julie Walters gives arguably her most important and sustained film performance, while Terry Jones directs with an air for both comic and dramatic tension.

Did You Know? Despite the disclaimer at the start and end of the film, this is obviously based on the life of Cynthia Payne although the story is reshaped and re-arranged for the cinema. She even receives a credit as technical adviser and to paraphrase *Not the Nine O'Clock News*, even the initials C.P. are the same! According to a gracious Jones, the film was practically co-directed by scriptwriter David Leland who worked closely with Walters throughout the filming and presented a complete script in which huge chunks of the film's feel was already in place. Beryl Cooke designed the original poster but it was abandoned because the distributors considered it too risqué. Terry Jones discussed the issue with Jonathan Ross on *The Last Resort* and just to drive home his point, gradually stripped down to a grass skirt, aided and abetted by a very game Mr. Ross. What a pro.

Personal Services
Vestron Pictures/Zenith Productions
Christine Painter **JULIE WALTERS**
Wing Commander Morten **ALEC McCOWEN**
Shirley **SHIRLEY STELFOX**
Dolly **DANNY SCHILLER**
Rose **VICTORIA HARDCASTLE**
Timms **TIM WOODWARD**
Mr Marsden **BENJAMIN WHITRON**
Mr Marples **PETER CELLIER**
Mr Dunkley **STEPHEN LEWIS**
The Man **NIGEL LE VAILLANT**
Ron Ron **PEMBER**
Edward **EWAN HOOPER**
June **MICHELLE COLLINS**
Screenplay by **David Leland**
Photography **Roger Deakins**
Music **John Duprez**
Editor **George Akers**
Art Director **Jane Coleman**
Producer **Tim Bevan**
Director **Terry Jones**
103 mins, 1987

PETER COOK AND COMPANY

Peter Cook, quite arguably the funniest man of the century, stormed back into action with this brilliant one-off 50-minute comedy special. Showcasing Cook's genius as both performer, and above all, writer, this undervalued tour de force is semi-linked by New York cabbie, Herb Natky, lapses into Benny Hill parody with Lee Van Wrangler's cowboy song *Dying Words*, presents the deliciously eccentric ant expert Henrick Globnick and concludes with a breathtaking, variety-styled, show-stopping musical number featuring E.L. Wisty. Timed to perfection, Cook allows just the right number of false endings, embraces television convention and ends this stunning show with a delightful address to his executive producer. However, the two major comic highlights feature Beryl Reid in, quite arguably, the best written sketches in her career, with a bizarre, bee-attired plumber diatribe and the truly earth-shattering soap opera spoof *The Amnesiacs*. Importantly, Cook gives the best lines away and, indeed, two sketches are tailored for new kid on the block, Rowan Atkinson – almost running full circle from Cook's early revue skits for Kenneth Williams. The disturbing, disconcerting country shopkeeper sketch with Paula Wilcox is a masterpiece, while the babbling train weirdo plays almost like Son of Not An Asp. It also features the single contribution from Terry Jones, not actually working opposite Cook but delivering his stuffy, bowler-hatted, 'heterosexual and proud of it' thunderbolts with baggage from Nudge Nudge attacks completely intact. John Cleese resurrects memories of the Pete 'n' Dud Father and Son sketches with his earnest fatherly chat to Cook, skirting around the question of sex via fishing parables and injecting knowing looks in a vain attempt to drive the point home, although this riverside chat pales in comparison with the major Cook/Cleese partnership – out-takes of History. Recreating Neville Chamberlain's triumph return from his meeting with Adolph Hitler,

Cleese's bumbling, inanely grinning P.M. struggles to please Cook's frustrated Newsreel director, Eric Miller, desperately waves his immortal piece of paper and misunderstands the simplest stage direction. The dumbfounded expletive as the paper flies away is the biggest belly-laugh in the show and brilliantly played between these two comical giants. A work of pure genius.

Starring **Peter Cook** with **John Cleese, Terry Jones, Rowan Atkinson, Robert Longden, Beryl Reid** and **Paula Wilcox**.
Written by **Peter Cook**
Script Consultant **Bernard McKenna**
Executive producer **Humphrey Barclay**
Produced & directed by **Paul Smith**
London Weekend Television – September 14 1980

PLEASURE AT HER MAJESTY'S

A film record of the momentous Amnesty concerts of 1976, originally screened by the BBC as an *Omnibus* special on 29th December, with narrated introduction from Dudley Moore and eventually given the full big screen glory with a cinema release. With the rehearsal portions removed, a Washington impresario flogged the television show as a new *Python* movie with the rather obvious title change in America to *Monty Python Meets Beyond the Fringe*. Distinguished documentary maker Roger Graef, renowned for his *cinema verité* style, captured the powerful, pre-show effort at rehearsals and the overly enthused, 'anything for a laugh' friendliness of the performance.

A POKE IN THE EYE (WITH A SHARP STICK)

Towards the end of 1975 Amnesty International were in preparation for a charity concert to mark their 15th anniversary. Their idea was to rally a few celebrities together and present a special Sunday night show in London's West End. However, one of the first stars approached was a certain John Cleese, who not only agreed to take part but also vowed to organise the concert and invite some of his friends along. What resulted was three gala nights of the finest British live comedy imaginable, for Cleese's friends who came along included Graham Chapman, Terry Gilliam, Terry Jones, Michael Palin, Peter Cook, Tim Brooke-Taylor, Graeme Garden and Bill Oddie. Suitably opening on April Fool's Day, 1976, the show presented a wealth of classic comedy sketches and songs from *Python*, *The Goodies*, *Beyond the Fringe* and *Cambridge Circus*, while in keeping with the feel-good attitude of the project, absentee Dudley Moore saw Terry Jones step in for his *Beyond the Fringe* material while Eric Idle's place in *Python*'s Courtroom sketch saw the super-sub Peter Cook join in the fun. The Python performances included were, an introduction from John Cleese, The Last Supper with Cleese and Jonathan Lynn, Cleese, Chapman, Gilliam, Jones, Palin, Carol Cleveland and Peter Cook in The Courtroom Sketch – culled from four Python court-geared items and featuring the witness in a coffin, a debate whether Basingstoke is in Hampshire or Westphalia and a concluding rendition of *Anything Goes* by a Cole Porter rather than the real thing, *So That's the Way You Like It*, the almighty *Fringe* parody of Shakespearean performance with Alan Bennett, Peter Cook, Jonathan Miller and Terry Jones, the Argument Clinic, an upbeat version of College of Advanced Slapstick replacing the malicious pain of slapstick with cheery enjoyment from Chapman and the lads helped out by Bill Oddie, Crunchy Frog and, of course, Cleese and Palin resurrecting that dead Norwegian blue parrot, which started the show. It concluded with Palin leading the performers in a chorus of *The Lumberjack Song*, forgetting the words on one occasion and being assaulted by his cohorts. Hugely successful, both in terms of comic greatness and fund-raising for Amnesty, the three shows were boiled down to a highlights album from Transatlantic complete with Terry Gilliam cover depicting a head split

asunder emitting photos from the show and a classic 100-minute *Omnibus* special, *Pleasure At Her Majesty's*, which featured invaluable rehearsal footage and performance. A Poke In the Eye (With A Sharp Stick) Starred Alan Bennett, John Bird, Eleanor Bron, Tim Brooke-Taylor, Graham Chapman, John Cleese, Carol Cleveland, Peter Cook, John Fortune, Graeme Garden, Terry Gilliam, Barry Humphries, Neil Innes, Des Jones, Terry Jones, Jonathan Lynn, Jonathan Miller, Bill Oddie and Michael Palin. 11.30pm showtime. Prices: £150 (for not coming) £100 per box £50.07/£10/£5/£3/£2. 1–3 April 1976

POLE TO POLE

Michael Palin's second major travelthon for the BBC covers his 140-day trek between the North and South Poles, travelling through the 30 degree east longitude line covering 17 countries. Following the major success of *Around the World in 80 Days* as both a television programme and a book, the corporation quickly signed up their intrepid explorer for another bash. Although still retaining that infectious and compelling mix of dramatic tension, humanity and humour, *Pole to Pole* is far less satisfactory than the original journey. The main reason is that with the Jules Verne-based adventure there was a tangible start and end point, the thrill of the chase, nailbiting moments as Palin fights to beat the clock and duplicate a famous fictional trip. Here, time is no object and the route could be anything – as it happens the one which covers the most land and, thus, across Africa, is chosen. The programme tends to get bogged down in parts; the footage tends to sprawl uncontrolled and even the characters our man meets are less interesting than before. However, for all that, there's still no-one I would rather travel through thick and thin with, chatting with charm to all and sundry, facing hardship and injecting comic voices into every problem – indeed the first problem, where to plant your pole, is happily dismissed

with a suggestive look.
One – *Cold Start*. Looking like a refugee from *Nanook of the North*, the air transport breaks through the awful weather conditions to allow Palin to establish the journey's aim – indeed, conditions were so bad that the filming crew had to record this opening section in April 1992, after the rest of the filming had been completed! Beginning in July 1991, the early part of the massive, snowbound sea journey includes a nervous Palin getting chatted up by an over friendly Norwegian sailor (whom only a burst of Larry Funigan can appease), an outbreak of a 'happy attack', a meagre, rather sickening fish hawl and moderately successful gold planing. A meeting with a dubious Santa Claus, hilarious Palin asides, frantic vegetation whacking and the saucy Python naked again (looking nothing like Kim Basinger) are great fun but nothing comes close to Palin's bus-based, apalago rendition of Python's *Finland*. Pure class.
Two – *Russian Steps*. An arrival in Leningrad includes a Lenin look-a-like showing a rumoured Palin impersonator round, a rather moving chit chat with Lenin's bronze image, a touching music note engraved and soundtrack lavished graveyard interlude (wot no *Decomposing Composers*!) and a priceless incorporation of parrot memories with Palin's Cleeseian response 'Hello Miss!' when his liqueur coupon is in need of cashing in. A self-aware British Film Industry soon pales as Palin throws himself into the rather bland Leningrad's industry with a stimulating role as Frogman's Hand in a filmic examination of the Krayfish – as Palin notes 'a moment of film history!'. An energetic vodka drinking session results in Palin's semi-drunken desire to 'toast the fish! toast the ketchup', representing Watford, the twin town, in a mutual commemorative exchange of gifts, and a spot of mud wrestling is starkly contrasted with a poignant tour through Chernobyl.
Three – *Mediterranean Maze*. Hotel Room 411, once used by Agatha Christie while writing *Murder On the*

Orient Express, a vicious rub-down with large brillo pads, stunning news of the Russians and a cheerfully pessimistic prediction from the late Patrick Walker are as nothing for the mad Englishman antics with a blast of *Sussex By the Sea* and forces cricket on the green. A return to Egypt (the only country which overlaps with *Around the World*) sees even madder Englishmen curling the native toes with hectic renditions of *Underneath the Arches* and a very loose reading of *I'm Henry the VIII I Am*, but Palin's hilarious Shelley poetry reading while attired as a *Life of Brian*-like Roman Centurian is worth any amount of mental torture.
Four – *Shifting Sands*. Travelling through Sudan, Palin encounters unhelpful natives with misleading directions, struggles to buy anything with his unexchangable money, purchases some dodgy grub and leaves aboard a train with a much welcome gift of dates. The train's buffet car is hardly the last word in taste – Palin's tongue-in-cheek request for cucumber sandwiches speaks volumes – while there's a one-sided conversation with the freebie passers on top of the moving train. Suffering the unappetising prospect of stewed chicken and bone with day-old bread, Palin tries to pass the time with his less than chatty driver and gets seriously concerned with an old Colonial buffer's advice not to eat salads. With the threat of disease looming and the heat sweeping through, Palin survives all of two seconds on the squash court before heading into the desert, breaking down en route and finishing the episode decamped in a police compound.
Five – *Crossing the Line*. A meeting with his Livingstone, British journalist Graham Hancock, leads to a more heavily armed trip on a dirt track, with an emergency stop and being grateful for protection from youthful soldiers. Palin's obvious relief is highlighted with his nervous explosion of comic weather forecasting while everything is pretty manic in Ethiopia with a timescale still in 1984, a friendly street trouser mender and a rather charming

Manchester United fan who is mercilessly ribbed by Palin. The stunning waterfall photography is one of the most impressive moments in the show and Palin is clearly awe-struck while a torn-down Lenin statue is sat upon and Comic Relief money which provided a well for the community is justified through images of pure joy. Hilarious hat antics with uncertain exchanges and Roger Mills catching the windblown headgear at second slip tickles Palin and a touching return to the African location of *The Missionary* shows the roof that the crew put on the school is still secure. Palin, a natural with kids, addresses the pupils, says a few words about England, donates his *Around the World* blow-up globe (inflated with encouraging cries from the children) and gets the eyes shining bright with energetic football antics as the world bounces round the classroom. Fun with water to a guide who had helped Hemingway and Prince Charles add local colour and there's even time for some Johnny Morris homage hippo chatter before the final bell.
Six – *Plains And Boats And Trains*. It's a continuation of the animal theme with life on safari, glorious early morning shots of 'twin symbols of the British Empire' in the shape of lions sleepily enjoying the sun, giraffes and a crow's eye view from a hot air balloon, shades of *80 Days* again. The smartly uniformed British pilot is a whiff of home pride, images of cute lion cubs and scruff-of-the-neck tenderness boasts the 'Ahh!' factor, while the elephant family unit earnestly shifts away from the limelight. Coy age-guessing with his guides, lions chomping into a snack of wildebeest and live piano torturing all paint the African experience with good humour. The next train journey allows Palin to discuss two of his favourite subjects, football and fish, there's some wonderfully uncon-trolled giggles as his mosquito net seems to have a life of its own and the world famous non-event of the Livingstone/Stanley meet is reassuringly captured in life-size, unaffected papier maché form. It's all gloriously archaic, irrelevant but

proud.
Seven – *Evil Shadow*. A mind-bending, subdued and rather chilling consultation with a witch doctor reveals Palin's evil streak and the frantic white water rapid run would reveal the yellow streak in most of us, but the main man keeps smiling throughout, despite a cracked rib obtained by bashing a rock while swimming to the shore after the action. As with the first serial's early embrace of karaoke, here Palin comes across the relatively unknown madness of bungee-jumping, wisely tapping his head at the insanity of it all. A look round the train which carried the last remains of Cecil Rhodes and a touching moment at the grave with a simple inscription surrounded by natural beauty is contrasted with the continual threat of digging up the old boy and shipping him back home. The hectic beer garden has a glorious seventies retro feel; English conventions permeate the area; Palin receives a cow dung welcome; enjoys the enclosed luxury of the Blue Train and finally faces the fact that the *S.A. Agulhas* – the only means of transport from Africa to the Antarctic is about to sail with no room for the BBC crew.
Eight – *Bitter End*. This is the bitter end, with a hasty detour to South America, being sheepishly English as he kisses the Indian's foot on the Magela statue for luck, a packed, make-shift flight to the land of ice and some low-key Laurel & Hardy-like madness. A gloriously Pythonesque moment as Palin sits on the lavatory, looks out to white nothingness and cheerfully explains that any natural waste is shipped out to Chile leads to the funniest scene in the entire series, as our hero struggles with a totally garbled message from Helen back home. Hilariously saying anything, answering nonsensical noises with manic comments about 'clean underwear' and having fits as his detailed accounts get the same burst of radio fuzz. With a quick walk round the world, which takes all of eight seconds, Palin's second voyage of discovery comes to a close. Though nowhere near as majestic as

Dancing those pig blues away – Liz Smith, Michael Palin, Richard Griffiths and Alison Steadman in *A Private Function*

the first, these closing scenes are warm, affectionate and emotive – but only if you have sat through the entire seven hours!

Prominent Features & Passepartout Productions in association with BBC and Arts and Entertainment Network, *Pole to Pole*
Written & presented by **Michael Palin**
Camera **Nigel Meakin & Patti Musicaro**
Sound **Fraser Barber**
Dubbing editors **Jonathan Rowdon & Anne Dummett**
Dubbing mixer **Aad Wirtz**
Film editors **David Thomas & Alex Richardson**
Music **Paddy Kingsland**
Graphics **Mick Connaire & 4:2:2 Videographics Stills**
Photography **Basil Pao**
Production accountant **Una Hoban**
Location co-ordinators **The East-West Creative Association, Patricio Lanfranco Leverton, Anne Kershaw, Jake Da Motta, Film Africa, Santha Faiia, Monty Ruben, Martin Hardy, Sevim Berker, Sue Pugh Tasios, Romany Helmy, Geir Paulsen, David Rootes, Troels Muller & Kari Vaattovaara**
Production assistants **Angela Elbourne**

& Mimi O'Grady
Production manager **Mirabel Brook**
Executive producer **Anne James**
Series devised & Producer **Clem Vallance**
Director **Roger Mills & Clem Vallance**
BBC1, Autumn 1992, 8x 50 mins

A PRIVATE FUNCTION

If *The Missionary* was the Ealing side of *Ripping Yarns* than this charming period comedy was Michael Palin's complete embrace of pure character comedy without a trace of *Python*esque memories. Palin was approached for the role by writer Alan Bennett even before the first draft was completed but his endorsement and acceptance of the part resulted in HandMade backing the film. There is the canny Harrison/O'Brien policy of reuniting their star with players from *The Missionary*, Maggie Smith and Denholm Elliott. The key reason *A Private Function* is such an enjoyable film lies in its deceptively laid-back, gentle comic style. Palin's characterisation could have stepped right out the world of *Ripping Yarns*

but his nervous delivery and lack of ambition remains true to the post-war atmosphere of the piece. However, Bennett's rapid, observational humour continually breaks into this social climbing, comedy of manners. Importantly, despite being the catalyst for pig antics and social discriminations, Palin's character is very much part of an ensemble piece, nestling into the nattering, backbiting life of a Northern town, his profession (chiropodist) treated with suspicion and amazement by realms of influential men, while his home position is dictated by his domineering wife and insanely dithering mother-in-law. As with *Passport to Pimlico*, this is a comedy of rationing, self-denial and wartime unity, contrasting its obvious Ealing-like attention to character and detail with a truthful streak of bitterness. Denholm Elliott is the perfect example of this, a professional (a doctor who hates his patients), he strolls through the illegal pig rearing narrative with supercilious detachment, looking beyond the matter of life and death (in terms of both the pig and his clientele), bending the rules in order to celebrate the righteousness of royalty (the dinner is a low-key, high-octane affair to mark 1947's wedding of Elizabeth and Philip) and ringing out every laugh with the merest raised eyebrow. He never feels the need to feign interest or politeness and, as such, with nose in the air, he storms through this priceless Bennett work. The supporting cast are uniformly excellent, notably Alison Steadman as prim and proper housewife (during her initial foot treatment, a toenail clipping subtly clinks into a vase on the mantelpiece), Tony Haygate's streetwise farmer, nervously protecting his interests and boosting his law-breaking pig with scraps from all directions) and John Normington, flashing a steely gaze to all and sundry while embracing the most sarcastically biting funny line when a suggested replacement for the missing porker is a couple of turkeys ('we have 150 people coming to this function and Jesus Christ isn't one of them!'). Pete Postlethwaite (screwing with both pig detector Paterson's head and his wife) is painfully callous and there are even cameos from the likes of Eli Woods and Don Estelle but it's Richard Griffiths, his loving treatment of the pig and his eventual understanding with Palin, that gives the film heart. A failed plan to save the creature that has touched both their lives, heartbroken, thought-provoking looks at the half-digested remnants and moving, half-smiling shared eye contact highlights the power of the acting that Bennett's script developed. For all the more obvious, hilarious, filth-ridden antics of house-proud Smith and the incognito pig, rationed black marketeering ('not steak, it's status!'), one-upmanship beyond the call of duty and even the priceless, veiled *Python* in-joke with the huge, prized chiropodist foot model, the brief relationship between Palin and Griffiths lifts this charming gem of a movie from great to outstanding.

Did You Know? Betty, the 250lb Sussex Ridgeback pig who starred in the film, was more than a handful for her *Python* co-star. As he shared a car

with his overweight porcine pal, the pig tried to jump out, causing a bit of physical damage and dropping her ex-lunch on Palin's lap – he later observed that it was like trying to get a Sumo wrestler out of an igloo. *A Private Function* won three BAFTAs, Best Actress for Maggie Smith, Best Supporting Actress for Liz Smith and Best Supporting Actor for Denholm Elliot.

Island Alive/HandMade films
Gilbert Chilvers **MICHAEL PALIN**
Joyce Chilvers **MAGGIE SMITH**
Dr. Swaby **DENHOLM ELLIOTT**
Allardyce **RICHARD GRIFFITHS**
Sutcliff **TONY HAYGRATH**
Lockwood **JOHN NORMINGTON**
Maurice Wormold **BILL PATERSON**
Mother **LIZ SMITH**
Mrs. Allardyce **ALISON STEADMAN**
Inspector Noble **JIM CARTER**
Nuttal **PETE POSTLETHWAITE**
Mrs. Sutcliff **EILEEN O'BRIEN**
Mrs. Forbes **RACHEL DAVIES**
P.C. Penny **REECE DINSDALE**
Preston **PHILIP WILEMAN**
Medcalf **CHARLES McKEOWN**
Mrs. Medcalf **SUSAN PORRETT**
Father **DONALD ECCLES**
Hotel Manager **DENYS HAWTHORNE**
Barraclough **DON ESTELLE**
Ernest **ELI WOODS**
Veronica **AMANDA GREGAN**
Painter **BERNARD WRIGLEY**
Painter's Boy **LEE DALEY**
Dorothy **GILLY COMAN**
Woman **MAGGIE OLLERENSHAW**
Mrs. Beavers **JOSIE LANE**
Mervin **DAVID MORGAN**
Screenplay by **Alan Bennett**
Original story by **Alan Bennett & Malcolm Mowbray**
Photography **Tony Pierce-Roberts**
Production designer **Stuart Walker**
Editor **Barrie Vince**
Production manager **Ann Wingate**
Camera operator **Malcolm Macintosh**
Art directors **Judith Lang & Michael Porter**
Music **John Du Prez**
Executive producers **George Harrison & Denis O'Brien**
Producer **Mark Shivas**
Director **Malcolm Mowbray**
Filmed on location in London & Yorkshire
93 mins, 1984

PRIVATES ON PARADE

A sort of *Virgin Soldiers* meets *It Ain't Half Hot Mum*, this stunning filming of the Peter Nichols stage play latched onto *Python* via HandMade and a starring role for John Cleese, while remaining totally faithful to the original piece. Autobiographical (Nichols was in combined services entertainment with Kenneth Williams and Stanley Baxter), this film version is a refreshingly frank, patriotic and chest-puffing salute to the artistes caught up in the aftermath of war, where first-name terms, flamboyant mincing about and alarmingly regular chances to don women's clothing was the way of things. Topped and tailed with stiff-upper lipped movietone-style newsreel, the subject matter is reflected via comic highlights and stark contrast with British corruption, gun running and death at the hands of the oriental. The path of youth sex education, the reality of war and hardship rests painfully but effectively against the manic campness of Denis Quilley and his troupe of merry men. Quilley, resplendent in performance as a string of glam film stars like Marlene Dietrich, Carmen Miranda and even one of The Andrews Sisters, is over the top to perfection, making eyes at all the young recruits, embracing the Omipaloni talk immortalised by Williams in *Round the Horne* and dapperly skipping around the place in spotless white trousers. A poignant, touching performance, emotions masked by flagrant speech and theatricals, Quilley's stunning work, represents the spirit of artistic expression and finding an un-surpassable contrast in the stolid, official, bulldog-spirited person-ification of British duty played by John Cleese.

Playing like Basil Fawlty on a quiet day, Cleese calmly strolls through this manic camp with dignity and resolution, battling the spectres of communist corruption with a God-fearing, patriotic, royalist strength of undefeatable Britishness. Peppering his small talk to the natives with 'jolly good' hearty banter and pinpointing the cancerous, communist attack on religion with 'the gospel according to St. Marx!', he keeps the show in his control with a barked 'No smut!' remark. He highlights his blind power by simply pointing to the stage in a moment of crisis and immediately making misunderstanding Gurkhas turn away from a tense wartime situation. This is a towering screen performance. His obsessions with stamping out blasphemy, suspicious behaviour concerning his men wearing perfume (you can almost hear Williams cry 'We're boys of the service!') and rigorous, outlandish bursts of exercise create a slightly off-kilter, laughable but never completely mocked figure of brutish authority. Comedy comes from the way others perceive him and his own earnestness. Notable are the 'mind your head' chestnut, referred to again as he gingerly leaves the tour bus; a classic bit of sight humour as he boot-lickingly removes a show programme from the Colonel's comfy chair without his noticing while proceeding to sit on his own (nervously removing it from beneath him), and even breaking into oriental-bashing, cricket-laden monologue during his memorial service speech.

Like the Jim Dale film *Adolph Hitler – My Part In His Downfall,* this comic look at the British at war successfully paints multi-faceted characterisations caught up in the madness of politician's decisions, bringing home the powerful stark emotion of warfare while rejoicing in the plucky energy of the individual. Indeed, stunning supporting turns from Joe Melia (realistically towing the army line with bad language being every other word and turning in a breathtaking impersonation of Chesney Allen), Nicola Pagett (as the Welsh cum Indian glamour element of the show) and, batting for the other side, Michael Elphick (projecting a good-natured laddish attitude while happily lining his own pockets via the blood of his companions) all boost the powerful battle of art against victory played out by Cleese and Quilley. The best moment by far is a clever

incorporation of playful variety antics on stage performing the title number in contrast with hard military marching on the parade ground. The cross-fading between performance and reality is peerlessly done, employing brilliant Nichols lyrics, playful phallic banter with rifles and barrel-loads of innuendo, while during this feelgood attack, Cleese is involved in the funniest two interludes in the film. It's his rigorous desire to serve God and King that provides the source of humour, pinpointing his upper class mentality via conversations with men under his command. A thought-provoking chat with a cockney chappie, bemoaning missing out on certain battles and always arriving too late unites two elements of British pride, standing side by side and fighting for the course. The key moment comes as the lowly ranked soldier mutters 'Jesus Christ Almighty!' and receives an outraged Cleese stare in return, while the touching side of the Commanding Officer is revealed as he role-plays with Melia about counselling bereaved squaddies. The gag is a very old one but it's Cleese, picking the name Farns-Barns out of the air, and Melia's delicious subversive delivery, that makes this a comedy classic. Besides, Nicola Pagett looks stunning in her tight union jack shorts and that just about puts the cherry on top of a magic sequence. I absolutely love that bit. Conventions of Hollywood musicals are embraced, with a notable Fred Astaire and Ginger Rogers sequence filmed in black and white while breaking into colour as the dancers emerge back stage and the whistle-stop touring of travelling players running through the Burma jungle, cross-fades with applauding hands, images of the turning wheels of the van and multiple directing signposts. *Yankee Doodle Dandy* in the middle of nowhere.

This is an entertaining, moving and often hilarious film which, despite a class performance from John Cleese and emotive characterisations, failed to score a success at the box office. Interestingly the original idea of Denis O'Brien, who had bought up

the stage play rights for filming, was to exploit his companies most successful asset, the *Monty Python* team, and have each of the six members play parts in the film. The team rejected this idea, having vowed never to perform other people's written material as a group, but O'Brien kept the notion with his casting of Cleese and, following unenthusiastic test audience reaction, orchestrated the recording of some additional, more typically wacky Cleese material for inclusion. Afterward, unwisely marketed as a Python-geared film, utilising its clear pedigree to full publicity benefit, the film's trailers featured Cleese out of character and enjoying a burst of silly walking. If punters expected to see this sort of stuff in Cleese's performance they were sadly mistaken, for although this return to the Ministry's ways is included at the very end of the film it works like a relief mechanism for the chilling realities of battle. Like life itself, the film's close is tinged with sadness, half-hearted pride, forced happiness and relief, while the credits are warmed by a Dennis Potter-like farewell rendition of a show number, allowing the dead to return to the camp fun, sustained injuries forgotten and even Cleese himself to burst into song, do his comic business and happily waltz away with Quilley's epitome of dubious military behaviour. An excellent emotional escape and classic close to a much under-rated film.

HandMade Films Present
Privates on Parade
Major Giles Flack **JOHN CLEESE**
Acting Captain Terri Dennis **DENIS QUILLEY**
Sergeant Major Reg Drummond **MICHAEL ELPHICK**
Sergeant Len Bonny **JOE MELIA**
Acting Lieutenant Sylvia Morgan **NICOLA PAGETT**
Captain Sholto Savory **JOHN STANDING**
Sergeant Eric Young-Love **SIMON JONES**
Private Steven Flowers **PATRICK PEARSON**
Sergeant Charles Bishop **DAVID BEMBER**
Flight Sergeant Kevin Cartwright **BRUCE**

PAYNE
Capt Henry Cox **JOHN QUAYLE**
Pianist **NEIL PEARSON**
Infantry Officer in Jungle **DAVID GRIFFIN**
Electrician **ROBIN LANGFORD**
Drummer **STEVE DIXON**
Bass player **JASPER JACOB**
Cheng **VINCENT WONG**
Lee **PHIL TAN**
Trombonist **LEONARD PRESTON**
Trumpet player **PETER HUTCHINSON**
Woodwind **NEIL PHILLIPS**
Sikh doorman **ISHAQ BUX**
Mrs. Reg Drummond **BRIGETTE KAHN**
Climbing sailor **JULIAN SANDS**
Regimental policeman **MARK DEWRY**
Commanding Officer **TIM BARLOW**
Armed escort **MARK ELLIOT, TIM
SINCLAIR & WILLIAM PARKER**
Editor **Jim Clark**
Screenplay & lyrics by **Peter Nichols**,
based on his own play
Production designer/Costume designer
Luciana Arrighi
Photography **Ian Wilson**
Music **Dennis King**
Executive Producers **George Harrison &
Denis O'Brien**
Assistant Director **Jake Wright**
Production Manager **Remond Morris**
Producer **Simon Relph**
Director **Michael Blakemore**
1982, 93 mins. Pinewood

RENTADICK

Frightful British comedy film which, despite a script by John Cleese and Graham Chapman, stumbles from one inept set piece to another via awfully over-played star performances and an incoherent, nutty beyond belief plot. Don't be fooled by the glorious cast list, this is real rock bottom stuff, played with one eye on the fee and one on the pub. James Booth, headlining the disaster, staggers through the scenario looking like a drugged reject from a Humphrey Bogart movie (note the *Casablanca* reference near the close), while Donald Sinden, eyes aglaze and hair akimbo, over-acts for Britain as the maniacally jealous husband. The story, such as it is, chucks in everything from dubious white slavery of glam chorus girls, sinister Japanese businessmen turning into werewolf creatures, a respected detective agency corrupted by money-obsessed insiders and the McGuffin to end all McGuffins, a precious nerve gas which almost everybody involved wants a piece of. Badly acted, woefully constructed and, worst of all, just plain boring at times, the snivelling little characterisation of Richard Briers loses all endearing qualities thanks to painful overkill. Kenneth Cope, shamefully wasted, just seems to wander round the place looking for the canteen, and, perhaps worst of all, John Wells pulls faces, elongates dialogue and creeps through the film in a toe-curlingly irritating supporting turn.

But wait, it's not all doom and gloom, for with such a sterling cast of British farce talent even the most shambolic organisation can't keep Richard Beckinsale from stealing the entire film with his first big screen performance. Like Briers, Beckinsale is the typical sex-shy Brit on the loose, but the performance is blessed with subtle facial reactions, nice underplaying, nervy engrossment in a *Film Stars* magazine, effective soft focus seduction dream sequence contrasted with pratfalling elegance and a glorious bit of lusting after the ultimate glam girl, Julie Ege. Ege herself, relating the bizarre plot to journalist Penelope Keith, does exactly what she was hired to do, divert male brains away from the nonsense on screen and give the story a decorative touch. Stripping off, flirting and pouting with style, Ege does her duties to perfection. Ronald Fraser, never ashamed to overact a tad, turns on the flamboyant bluster with vigour and although hardly helped by the dialogue he's given, makes a fair stab at saving the flagging fun with moments of base innuendo ('Stick this up his rear-vent!'), reverential homage to Kenneth Williams' *Carry on Screaming!* ('Frying Tonight') and grand patriotic pride in his position of authority, pining for the Queen's speech and a bit of British discipline. At the end of the day, this is just loud rubbish, overpopulated by unimportant characters, jam-packed with *Wacky Races*-styled car chases, overdone marital farce and distilling any ounce of *Python*esque absurdity with heavy handling in performance and direction. Only once, with Kenneth Cope's manic disguise as a mouse (complete with dialogue of normality and bucket antics – and later resurrected for both *Python* and *Goodies* deconstruction) does the film fully accept its place on anarchic ground, relax and play for all-out satirical madness. It's much too little much too late, but the Goonish element to the script provides a few bright moments and, naturally, this side of the story really comes alive with the all too brief cameos from Michael Bentine and Spike Milligan. Bentine, popping up throughout, has a whale of a time as the sex-obsessed Arab, grinning and giggling with inspired lunacy, while the much welcome presence of Spike enlivens the sagging proceedings with a no-nonsense bit of nonsense as the bemused customs officer. Disrespectfully cut and pasted, interrupted by unimpressive tying up of plot threads, shamefully covered up by other bits of plot and panned away from, Spike struggles on with an ever increasing list of ridiculous items that are not allowed out of the country. It's absolutely priceless stuff, rubbish but glorious rubbish, grabbed by Spike's blacked-up chappie and completed with an incomprehensible outburst of frustration. Single-handedly Spike bucks up the last ten minutes of this mess and in terms of the script this is the film's masterpiece, if only for hearing Spike deliver some typically Goonish material penned by his natural successors. It makes *Rentadick* well worth searching out; however, you have been warned!

Did You Know? Although, the basic

idea wasn't that hot in the first place, it must be said that this finished film was a million miles away from the original intention.

With Cleese and Chapman at the helm, the film, originally called *Rentasleuth*, was planned as a vehicle for all the performers the two had been working with and writing for at the time. Thus, the likes of Ronnie Barker, Ronnie Corbett, Tim Brooke-Taylor and Marty Feldman were the planned stars of the piece, alongside supporting work from Cleese and Chapman themselves. A brainchild of David Frost, with all the talent he had amassed about him, the film was set for production in the late 1960s with Ealing legend Charles Crichton directing. Although recruiting Crichton for several training films and, of course, *A Fish Called Wanda*, Cleese was a little nervous at meeting the great man, not only out of sheer respect for his experience but also since he and Chapman had shamelessly included the ending of Crichton's *The Lavender Hill Mob* as the close of their script. However, the eventual outcome resulted in David Frost selling his rights to the piece to Ned Sherrin, a major cut in pay threatened for the writers and an adamant decision that Crichton would not be used as director. Furious, Cleese and Chapman were willing to take the cut in fee if Crichton was retained, but Sherrin refused. Out of respect for Crichton's contribution to the finished screenplay, both Cleese and Chapman withdrew their acting commitments from the film and, as a result, Feldman, Brooke-Taylor, Barker and Corbett joined them in the mass walkout.

Ultimately, on viewing the completed print, both Cleese and Chapman were horrified by the film and took their case to the Writer's Guild in order to have their names removed from the credits – thus on the final version there is only a credit for 'additional dialogue' writers and no mention of the *Python* partnership. The final film is nothing like that which was originally planned, Cleese considers his treatment the ultimate insult and has vowed never to work with Sherrin professionally again. Contrary to later claims, Terry Jones, Michael Palin, Eric Idle and Terry Gilliam were never due to be involved in this project but, certainly, the original notion sounds a vast deal more tantalising than what we have had to suffer on frequent television screenings since.

Virgin Film Productions – *Rentadick*
Hamilton **JAMES BOOTH**
Miles Gannet **RICHARD BRIERS**
Utta **JULIE EGE**
Major Upton **RONALD FRASER**
Armitage **DONALD SINDEN**
Madame Greenfly **TSAI CHIN**
West **KENNETH COPE**
Owitruss **JOHN WELLS**
Desk sergeant **DAVID BATTLEY**
Petrol pump attendant **VERONICA CLIFFORD**
Henson **DEREK GRIFFITHS**
Arab porter **ROBERT GILLESPIE**
Reporter **PENELOPE KEITH**
Japanese **DAVID TOGURI, KRISTOPHER KUM & MAX RAMAN**
Scientist **CHARLES LEWSEN**
Chauffeuse **PATRICIA QUINN**
Rivet **TREVOR RAY**
Police inspector **LEON SINDEN**
Maid **WINNIE HOLMAN**
Old lady **PATSY CROWTHER**
Removal men **MICHAEL ROTHWELL & MICHAEL SHARVELL MARTIN**
Policemen **BARRY ANDREWS, JONATHAN DENNIS & ALF JOINT**
Gatekeeper **WILL STAMPE**
Laboratory manager **ELLIS DALE**
Picnicker **MICHAEL SEGAL**
Introducing **RICHARD BECKINSALE** as Hobbs
Special appearances by **MICHAEL BENTINE** as Husein & **SPIKE MILLIGAN** as the Customs Officer
Screenplay by **John Cleese & Graham Chapman**
Additional dialogue by **John Fortune & John Wells**
Music **Carl Davis**
Title lyrics by **Caryl Brahms & Ned Sherrin**
Sung by **Dave Dee & The Kings Singers**
Production supervisor **Ron Fry**
Camera operator **Alan Boast**
Art director **Bruce Grimes**
Editor **Martin Charles**
Production designer **Seamus Flannery**
Photography **John Coquillon**

Producers **Ned Sherrin & Terry Glinwood**
Director **Jim Clark**
Eastmancolor, 90 mins, 1972

RIPPING YARNS

For me, this wonderfully detailed series of schoolboy adventures remains Michael Palin's most polished and endearing post-*Python* success. Still fuelled by totally surreal elements and intellectualism, these classic self-contained stories follow on from the more structured approach during the 1972/74 *Python* episodes (with longer and more involved pieces, notably the Jones/Palin classic Cycling Tour – a whole show without the *Python* credits anywhere), while pointing the way towards Palin's more gentle, period-based, Ealing-like comedies for an 1980s mentality in *The Missionary* and *A Private Function*. Indeed, these half-hour explorations through boyish innocence, British pride and upper class corruption could have been the way forward for the entire Python team on television. As it happened, Palin stepped effortlessly into the limelight, portraying most of the leading characters in each show, happily supported by co-writing, fellow Pythonite, Terry Jones, who injected great swathes of semi-bizarre elements into the narrative as well as one priceless manic acting turn. Interestingly, by looking at both their earlier *The Complete and Utter History of Britain* and these 1970s masterpieces, the writing contribution of Palin and Jones can be singled out from within the *Python* collective voice, historically questioning the stiff upper lipped British character and patriotic stance of the God fearing individual. While many of the military creations and figures of authority have Chapman and Cleese stamped all over them Palin, like Tony Hancock in his 1963 ITV series (recruiting Dennis Price, Kenneth Griffith, Wilfrid Lawson and the like), chooses to surround himself with seasoned stage and film actors to booster his comic characterisations. Palin's cast is enriched by the likes of Liz Smith, Harold Innocent and Roy Kinnear in character-acting overdrive. The original idea stemmed from producer Terry Hughes offering Michael Palin a chance for a solo career following the end of *Monty Python*. The suggestion was for a Michael Palin Variety Show, with introductions from the ex-Python, special guests and self-contained sketch pieces. This was not what Palin had in mind, and with Terry Jones in tow, they put together *Tomkinson's Schooldays*. Terry's brother spotted a book entitled *Ripping Tales* or something along those lines and, as with his inspiration for *Complete and Utter History*, the writers seized on the notion. The tales are populated by good chaps, heroic, slightly off-kilter, British stiff upper lipped types subtlety ribbing history. The brief was perfect for Jones and Palin. Initially, both Palin and Jones intended to perform the shows and, indeed, Jones appears in the pilot, but BBC frustrations with Jones stemming back to *Python* hassle opposite Ian MacNaughton and the feeling that this was supposed to be Palin's show caused raised shackles. The BBC hierarchy felt Jones was getting too much control on the series and it was mutually decided that he would step out of the limelight and concentrate on writing the programme. Thus Palin would play the lead and another supporting character role, originally intended for Jones, and, although this was returning to *Python*esque multi-performance he made a wonderful job of it. Despite reunions for various *Python* ventures, this is the latest project both Jones and Palin have worked on together as writers. This landmark series won the Broadcasting Press Guild award for comedy.

TOMKINSONS SCHOOLDAYS

This pilot episode is a stunning piece of work, allowing Palin to tackle a favourite target for the *Python* barbs, namely the public school system, highlighting the obvious and tangible threat of initiation ceremonies and class domination while exaggerating and mocking the situation through typically *Python*esque conventions. Most tellingly of all are those inspired by Orson Welles (he even fluffs a line and mentions sherry, a link to the famous Welles adverts), setting the scene for the yarn with elements of under-rehearsed television outside broadcasting, misquoted words of wisdom from G.K. Chesterton (helped by an initially off-camera Terry Jones) and helpless looks into camera for advice. The public school is turned into a bed of iniquity, bitterly dominated by the suave, self-confident and debonair school bully – an absolutely sublime picture of rich evil from Ian Ogilvy – and superficially run by Michael Palin's masochist, Cleese-like Headmaster (eagerly allowing the naughty boys to beat him into a state of pleasure and, in a Slade Prison governor meets Peter Vaughan's Grouty in *Porridge*, bowing and scraping in front of the school bully). In taking the idea of public school humiliation beyond breaking point, the new boys are subjected to manic sessions of being pinned to the walls, fighting the vicious stuffed grizzly bear and having escape plans thwarted by the school leopard! Palin's performance as the Head is deliciously over the top, castigating every single mutter and groan from the boys during assemblies, grinning with self-satisfied pride at his corrupt domain and delighting in outlandish acts of punishment on the weak and mild Tomkinson – Palin's other major role in the show. Tomkinson allows Palin to put on his innocent, boyish face with gusto, milking the sympathetic fate of dealing with life in the danger-soaked premises, discovering the pain and delight of alcohol, drugs and scantily clad Fillipino girls via Oligvy's bully and timidly trying to understand his parents' complex dilemmas. His father, mysteriously making numerous visits to the North Pole, allegedly to see his mistress, is greeted with Palin's inner-mind revelation that his father was supposed to be a homosexual; his mother (a stifling and sexually obsessed supporting role from Gwen Watford) is continually being discovered with lusty males cavorting about the place, while in a delicious touch of stiff-upper-lipped, no-nonsense, motherly attitude, insists on addressing her son as Tomkinson throughout (until a slip, scripted or otherwise, when she calls him Tomson only to be corrected by Palin). This initial *Ripping Yarn* is jam-packed with delights, notably Jones as the muffled and pompous lecturing explorer (greeted with a quickly condemned and then retracted heckle to speak up from one of the staff members), Palin's Head expressing the fact that some of the boys are helping the masters escape, Palin's brief Scottish abuser, eagerly bashing the boys over the head with a stick and the truly odd hopping competition, condemning several boys to death from exhaustion while allowing Palin's Tomkinson to win the day (with a little help from Ogilvy), face up to his lowly place and find himself in pole position as the new school bully. Palin's realisation that his power could change things for the good while still understanding that he must play the part results in a quite stunning change in acting style, giving Palin the opportunity to growl, beat the boys and hilariously put down his older alter ego. Depicting public school like a living hell in PoW terms, relentlessly highlighting females as either loose orientals or simple, loose country girls and fully projecting the more steady comic genius of Palin with a full quota of *Python* codes and social comments, *Tomkinson's Schooldays* was an inspired and essential bit of madness for a *Python*-starved British audience.

Did You Know? Budget busting, this pilot episode was the only show not recorded on more realistic, pristine film.

Tomkinson & Mr. Craffit the Headmaster **MICHAEL PALIN**
Mr. Ellis **TERRY JONES**
Mummy **GWEN WATFORD**
School Bully **IAN OGILVY**
With **JOHN WENTWORTH, SARAH**

CRAZEBROOK, CHAI LEE & TERENCE DENVILLE
Make up artist **Jackie Fitz-Maurice**
Costume designer **Odette Barrow**
Production assistant **John Adams**
Cameraman **Peter Hall**
Recordist **Ron Blight**
Editor **Ray Millichope**
Sound **Michael McCarthy**
Lighting **Duncan Brown**
Designer **Martin Collins**
Written by **Michael Palin & Terry Jones**
Produced & directed by **Terry Hughes**.
First broadcast BBC2 7 January 1976.
Repeated as the first episode of the first series of six *Ripping Yarns* on BBC2 – 20th September 1977

THE TESTING OF ERIC OLTHWAITE

One of the weakest in the Palin and Jones series, this one moves radically away from the bizarre and almost Goonish elements of the pilot show to a more cosy, working class, gentle form of expression. Naturally, there are still many off-the-wall elements, with Palin's Eric continually waffling on about the advantages of rainfall and the blackest kind of black puddings, but the one-joke atmosphere of the show doesn't quite hold all the elements together. Mind you, this guy is really, really boring, even driving his long suffering parents to the major act of moving home, with his father pretending to be French to avoid getting involved in conversation and his sister (Anita Carey from *Whatever Happened to the Likely Lads?* to *Coronation Street*, the perfect Northern lass) coming right out with condemnation and abuse.
Eric is basically a more simpleton variation of Arthur Purty, happily standing by as his supposed girlfriend eagerly works her sexual way through any stranger that happens to make it to her bedroom. Indeed, Eric is so, so boring that even a job in the bank is denied him, leading to a delightful cross-talking sequence between Palin's Eric and Palin's bank manager, talking in a high-pitched, monotone voice about the dangerous trials and tribulations of life in the bank. This scene is almost directly taken from a *Python* show, with comments

concerning fictitious acts of tearing men in two throughout a normal banking job only to be scuppered by the appearance of a jolly bankrobber who is mistakenly assisted by a dumbfounded Eric. The on-the-run material which takes up a good ten minutes soon outstays its welcome, but the robber's hilarious fireside chat with Eric about the smallest details of new shovels is more than enough to redeem this passage of the show. In the long run, Palin's notoriety attracts his girlfriend – who threatens her mother (a priceless Liz Smith) with running away from home and may not return until that night – the dismissive bank manager and the jovial, rotund Mayor. Despite the robber shooting the authority figure, he recovers and joyfully appoints Eric as his replacement, attracting false words of love and admiration from his parents and some eager journalistic interest, with Norman Mitchell fully throwing himself into the blackness of black puddings running gag. Complemented by a Wild West-like song and the sad Northern lad made good motif, this is a semi-*Python*esque reworking of *The Card*, with the power of simple stupidity replacing damn hard work in a lonely lad's search for position and understanding. If only for the double Palin bank discussion, this one is well worth searching out, but in light of the other rip roaring, gung-ho, action-packed, tongue-in-cheek, *Boy's Own* tales to follow, this *Ripping Yarn* unwinds a lot less ripping than most.

Did You Know? The location filming for Otterwaite was recorded in Durham because, as Palin comments, Yorkshire wasn't grotty enough! He quickly tried to hide any offence to Durham!!

Starring **MICHAEL PALIN** as Eric Olthwaite & the Bank Manager
Mrs. Olthwaite **BARBARA NEW**
Mr. Olthwaite **JOHN BARRETT**
Irene Olthwaite **ANITA CAREY**
Mr. Bag **REG LYE**
Mrs. Bag **LIZ SMITH**
Enid Bag **PETRA MARKHAM**
Arthur the Robber **KENNETH COLLEY**

Chauffeur **ROGER AVON**
Lord Mayor **CLIFFORD KERSHAW**
Reporters **NORMAN MITCHELL & ANTHONY SMEE**
Boy **PETER GRAHAM**
Boy's mother **MARCELLE SAMETT**
Written by **Michael Palin & Terry Jones**
Stunts **Marc Boyle & Jim Dowdall**
The Ballad of Eric Olthwaite by **Andre Jacquemin & Dave Howman**
Make up artist **Jean Speak**
Costumes **Linda Woodfield**
Visual effects **John Horton**
Production assistant **Eddie Stuart**
Design **John Stout**
Sound recordist **Brian Showell**
Dubbing mixer **Ron Edmonds**
Cameraman **Peter Hall**
Editor **John Jarvis**
Produced & directed by **Jim Franklin**
Broadcast BBC2–27th September 1977

ESCAPE FROM STALAG LUFT 112 B

Turning the clock back some 60 years, this show pays a tongue-in-cheek tribute to a certain Major Errol Phipps, the most dogged, determined and unsuccessful British escaping prisoner during the First World War. Palin and Jones skilfully tackle all the standard conventions of PoW movies and television plays (with the WWII classic *Colditz* particularly fresh in the minds of viewers at the time) turning all the symbols of Germanic power and British unflappability on their head. In the end the basic joke – that every other British officer is quite happy with his lot, working against Palin's escape plans but finally running off and leaving him the sole man to be guarded, only to have even the German captors leave him in the lurch – is brilliantly sustained and played. Palin's crestfallen attitude to his failed plans and decried suggestions of escape is a masterclass in under-playing comedy to perfection. The supporting cast of ever-so-sincere and proper British sorts, notably Griffin (as POW cinematic icon Attenborough), are first rate, playing the game strictly by the letter, happily serving their time and co-operating with the dreaded enemy, memorably mocking the fresh-faced, trustworthy, anti-'it's not cricket' officer. The slightly on-edge comic material works perfectly thanks to the entire British culture being played straight and with real feeling. The manic, over-indulgent escape plans of Palin are obviously hilarious and absurd, but the actor remains stern and determined. The message remains that whatever the situation, the power of being British puts one above any nationality, so much so that to be captured is an honour and to be guarding such distinguished British officers is a total, once-in-a-lifetime, unforgettable experience for the miserable Germanic worms of war. The highlight comes with Palin's unveiling of his semi-completed toilet roll glider, frowned upon by his superior officer and hastily hidden from view. The ineptitude of the idea matters not to Palin in his feverish angst to be out and bashing the Bosch once more. Palin's by now customary secondary character, the weeping, ginger-topped captive struggling to suppress his emotions over his wife's remarriage, plays to the conventions of united British military might, sharing the lows as well as the highs, as his authoritarian guide shows not the slightest bit of compassion, struggles to find the lad's prized, gift-wrapped cigarette and simply wanders off. However, despite Palin's marvellous double, the real delight in this particular episode is Roy Kinnear's frustrated performance as the vindictive German officer, desperately trying to rally his men into finding their spirit of war, cringing as he abides by the codes of captivity and, ultimately, relishing the opportunity of employing scores of men to guard the lone Palin prisoner over every waking and sleeping moment. His lapses into amazement at having to keep up the pleasantries, saying hellos, and his offering of chocolate is one for the best of British comedy compilation, with his brilliantly petulant discussion with Palin setting out this ripping yarn as one of the most consistent fun. A more restrained effort than some of the later classics, the show happily ends with madness as Palin remains alone, locks the gate and spends months

perfecting scores of escape plans (his tunnels latterly form part of the Munich underground system), before victory is ours and Palin sadly remains the only man not to escape from the camp. In a totally *Python* twist, his early death just months later at the age of 40 sees his only complete escape – later to be found a few yards from the spot he was buried. A poignant and hilarious end to a fine half hour.

Did You Know? Fittingly the distinguished narration comes from Ronald Fletcher, whose grand BBC voice flourished on the light programme from the late 1940s. After years with *Breakfast with Braden* and *Bedtime with Braden*, Fletcher became the darling of the younger set with work opposite Tim Brooke-Taylor and Bill Oddie on *Twice a Fortnight* and, eventually, being honoured with The Monty Python Award for Best Dressed Newsreader, presented by a certain John Cleese.

Major Phipps **MICHAEL PALIN**
Herr Vogel **ROY KINNEAR**
Colonel Harcourt-Badger-Owen **JOHN PHILLIPS**
Biolek **JULIAN HOUGH**
Second Guard **DAVID ENGLISH**
'Buffy' Attenborough **DAVID GRIFFIN**
Nicolson **TIMOTHY CARLTON**
Dusty **ROLAND MACLEOD**
Sergeant Major Errol **NICHOLAS DAY**
Carter **PHILIP GRAHAM**
Walcott **JAMES CHARLES**
Bo Bo **GLEN CUNNINGHAM**
Tosh **DAVID MACHIN**
Narrator **RONALD FLETCHER**
Written by **Michael Palin & Terry Jones**
Make up **Jean Speak**
Costumes **Robin Stubbs**
Production assistant **Eddie Stuart**
Design **John Stout**
Sound recordist **Ron Blight**
Dubbing mixer **Peter Claridge**
Cameraman **Peter Hall**
Editor **John Jarvis**
Produced & directed by **Jim Franklin**
Broadcast BBC2 – 4th October 1977

MURDER AT MOORSTONES MANOR
ne of the best *Ripping Yarns*, this wonderfully evocative 1920s murder

mystery parody is rich with period detail and subtle veins of bizarre surrealism. A casual attitude to death and swathes of wannabe murderers ends this choice half hour with gleeful madness, but the real pleasures are to be found in the more under-played but subversive social deconstruction. The piece begins brilliantly with Palin's young fop driving his lady love through the English countryside to visit Mumsie and Dadsie. Obsessed with cars, he happily ditches his female companion when offered the choice between flesh and machinery, cheerfully driving off and leaving the poor wreck in the middle of a rain-sodden Moor. Playing like an infantile human Mr. Toad with an unhealthy desire to discuss nothing but cars, he rabbits on at the dinner table, is dragged to bed exclaiming babblings of car noises (not quite Poop! Poop! but not far off) and is ultimately done to death with a shotgun. This early characterisation is Palin's secondary string to the Moorstones bow, quickly usurped by the silky smooth Charles, a cross between a manic Noel Coward and Peter Cook's Mr. Jolly, strolling through his elongated vowels and privileges with ever-ready shot gun and unaffected attitude to warrant murder. The underlying note of tension is naturally the feeling that even with family bodies piling up all over the place, the upper class Mother must protect her son from the outside world, chatting with only the slightest edge of concern on the telephone, carefully bringing up the old problem of Auntie's murder and showing only the merest sense of nervousness as Palin wanders off to comfort the sole benefactor of the will with a loaded gun which needs cleaning. Well, I'm reassured! The dysfunctional family, a common trend in the work of Palin and Jones, is seen in definitive terms here, with the pick of the bunch being Frank Middlemass's gloriously huffing and over-puffed figure of parental authority, continually droning on about blood, guts and swinging knee caps during his distinguished military career. This power-mad, befuddled and blustering old windbag symbolises the nemesis of warfare, boring his eldest son's fiancée into an early grave – she drowns in her own dinner (surreal or what!) – and mysteriously being brutally slain as Palin wasn't really looking. All the symbols expected of a typical murder story are employed, with Agatha Christie-like wealthy victims, mysterious country houses, a respectful, brooding butler, flighty girls with a taste for the high life (an unsubtle hint for alcohol almost ends in a round of Bovril) and idiot children abusing their money and position with a lifetime of inept dallyings. Aside from all this, Palin is supported by the choicest selection of class thespians ever assembled for a *Ripping Yarn*, tossing the outlandish dialogue and tired clichés into a cast boasting Harold Innocent, Isabel Dean, Frank Middlemass and, as the sexually eager and blood-spouting doctor, Ian Cuthbertson.

As the script cascades into bizarre mode, the acting anchors the atmosphere to the 1920s drawing room murder scene, with even the *Hamlet*esque bloodbath at the close played with frightfully good manners amidst the full-bodied hamming of Innocent. The final reaction to death, destruction and total carnage is a simply 'Oh dear!' There will always be an England.

Charles & Hugo Chiddingford **MICHAEL PALIN**
Lady Chiddingford **ISABEL DEAN**
Dora Chiddingford **CANDACE GLENDENNING**
Ruth **ANNE ZELDA**
Sir Clive Chiddingford **FRANK MIDDLEMASS**
Manners **HAROLD INNOCENT**
Dr. Farson **IAIN CUTHBERTSON**
Written by **Michael Palin & Terry Jones**
Make up **Jean Speak**
Costumes **Barbara Lane**
Production assistant **Marcus Plantin**
Designer **Martin Collins**
Sound recordist **Bryan Showell**
Dubbing mixer **Ron Edmonds**
Cameraman **Peter Hall**
Editor **Ray Millichope**
Produced & directed by **Terry Hughes**
Broadcast BBC2 – 11th October 1977

ACROSS THE ANDES BY FROG

Without doubt one of the most energetic and entertaining of all the *Ripping Yarns* with a real sparkling adventure at its heart given the natural Palin/Jones twist of insanity. The story of exploration, brilliantly set in historical context with mentions of two great early 20th-century adventurers, leads to the ill-fated and sadly neglected tale of Sneddleton's 1927 trekking experience in the Andes. Palin, wisely restricting himself to one performance, throws himself completely into this dedicated man of science, British pluck and frog obsession. Again this show tackles the familiar pig-headed and patriotically driven power of being British in a world of ill-informed natives, although Palin desperately tries to treat these not so uncomplex mountain dwellers with respect for both different culture and humanity. The highlight comes with Palin's bombastic control of a native attack on his frogs by shouting loudly and enforcing his authority on the situation, creating total silent amongst the dissenters and a hilarious babbled monologue of grievances in some foreign tongue. Palin's attitude to anything outside of his British viewpoint is perfection itself, shocked by his men's dallies with dusky maidens, even more shocked at the presentation of some well-endowed schoolgirls for a bit of exploration fun and bemused at the lack of interest from this primitive settlement whose sole obsession in life seems to be, perversely, British sports broadcasting. Listen out for Palin's radio recreation of the 1927 FA Cup final between Arsenal and Cardiff – the only time the trophy went out of England!

As with most of these shows, Palin surrounds himself with class acting from respected pros, notably here, Don Henderson's uncouth, cockney Sgt. Major, tossing in rhyming slang all over the shop and balancing Palin's upright attitude with down-to-earth observations in a sort of military-based Hancock and James double act. The mountain recce, with ancient Eileen Way (a television immortal via her shabby old

cavewoman in the first *Doctor Who* story) dragging the men through their paces at speeds unbefitting of a British officer, is real class. However, the major treasure in *Across the Andes by Frog* is the stunning supporting turn from seedy Brit bloke on the spot, Denholm Elliott, rejoicing in detailing the natives' wish that Cardiff win the FA Cup and sadly admitting that guides will be hard to find during Wimbledon fortnight. Elliot's surreal dialogue is brilliantly woven into a typically downbeat authority figure and the actor is clearly enjoying himself hugely with this awry, manic re-examination of Britain's imperial past. In a story of repression, frustration and failure, the natives finally set the frogs free to appease the God of the volcanoes while Palin's plight ends in reflective poignancy. Although naturally played for laughs and pinpointing Palin's absurdities and retentiveness, the script reflects an attitude of respect and admiration for these *Ripping Yarns* characters who set out with high hopes and find the repression of British manners and attitudes holding back their progression. A classic.

Captain Snetterton **MICHAEL PALIN**
Mr. Gregory **DENHOLM ELLIOTT**
RSM Urdoch **DON HENDERSON**
Peruvian Mountain Guide **EILEEN WAY**
Native with radio **LOUIS MANSI**
Weedy whining native **CHARLES McKEOWN**
3rd native **JOHN WHITE**
Corporal **ALAN LEITH**
Privates **KEVIN MORAN & BRIAN NOLAN**
Written by **Michael Palin & Terry Jones**
Make up **Jean Speak**
Costumes **Barbara Lane**
Production assistant **Marcus Plantin**
Designer **Martin Collins**
Sound recordist **Bryan Showell**
Dubbing mixer **Ron Edmonds**
Cameraman **Peter Hall**
Editor **Ray Millichope**
Produced & directed by **Terry Hughes**
Broadcast BBC2 – 18th October 1977

THE CURSE OF THE CLAW

Probably my all-time favourite yarn, this combines Conan Doyle adventure and Hammer horror creepiness with telling comments on the sexual repression of the Victorian era. A stunning nervous old man portrayal from Palin shuffling like Peter Cushing round his draughty, lightning-attacked house, bickering over his dead wife with sex-obsessed man servant Aubrey Morris and welcoming in a far-flung tribal expedition, off route in Maidenhead and looking for shelter. Palin's perfectly under-played performance allows the Brits in a muddle and frank sexual appetites to play off his retentive attitudes, while he relates the curse that has gripped his life through the oceans of time.

During this stunning flashback Palin is allowed to fully go over the top as the loveable, disease-ridden Uncle Jack, collecting dead rats, living in a collapsing hovel and delighting in showing off his array of pox marks. A very effective Palin-meets-Palin death scene sees Jack's wheezing utterances mix real pathos with grotesque humour, contrasting with the strained anti-fun behaviour of his parents. In Uncle Jack the spirit of adventure lives and Palin vows to return the dreaded vulture's claw to its rightful owners. Its acts of vengeance are quick and mind-bending (with Evans suffering two broken legs) while the sea voyage is plagued with sexual repression and sheltered glances. Despite finding a freedom of expression aboard, the antics on The Grimy Bastard do tend to drag on a bit, although Judy Loe is brilliantly tongue in cheek as the Blackadder's Bob-like glam girl in a pseudo-man's world. But never fear, it's back to Blighty with a vengeance. Palin junior may have failed in his task but the curse is not over by a long way.

Back in Maidenhead the threat comes full circle as the claw is revealed in Palin's hands once more, fresh from seeing off his beloved wife and a chilling act of regression fulfils our man's worst nightmare. Probably the most polished and beautifully constructed story in the series, this is real terror-based stuff lightened by Palin's shocked reaction to frank sexual matters, nervousness over

everything and swathes of slightly offbeat comedy to keep the thing in line.

Again blessed with sterling performances, notably Tenniel Evans, the piece is anchored in stolid thespian traditions with Palin bridging the gap between straight-laced dramatics and flamboyant comedy. Forget the script anomalies (Palin is born in 1881, the show's set in 1926 and it's his 60th birthday!) and enjoy a cracking bit of suspenseful fun from an invaluable series of rollicking tales.

Did You Know? No laughter track was employed on Escape & Across the Andes By Frog, while the other shows had audience reaction so badly recorded as to sound very subdued and thus were replaced. For a subsequent repeat season all six episodes were reshown to an enthusing crowd and this audience reaction remains today. The yarns were very expensive shows to put together and after the successful first season the cautious BBC commissioned just three more as the second batch. Palin considers that the nine tales took the format as far as it could go.

The Curse of the Claw: A Ripping story of fear tragedy and terror
Starring **MICHAEL PALIN** as Sir Kevin Orr & Uncle Jack
Kevin's Mother **HILARY MASON**
Kevin's Father **TENNIEL EVANS**
Captain Merson **KEITH SMITH**
Grosvenor **AUBREY MORRIS**
Young Kevin **NIGEL RHODES**
Chief Petty Officer Russell **JUDY LOE**
Lady Agatha **BRIDGET ARMSTRONG**
Young Lady Agatha **DIANA HUTCHINSON**
Ship's stoker **MICHAEL STAINTON**
Ship's engineer **VANESSA FURSE**
Written by **Michael Palin & Terry Jones**
Make-up artist **Jean Speak**
Costume designer **Robin Stubbs**
Visual effects **Ian Scoones**
Graphic designer **Ian Hewitt**
Production assistant **Eddie Stuart**
Design **John Stout**
Sound recordist **Bryan Showell**
Dubbing mixer **Brian Watkins**
Film cameraman **Peter Hall**

Film editor **John Jarvis**
Director **Jim Franklin**
Broadcast BBC2 – 25th October 1977

2nd series
WHINFREY'S LAST STAND
Arguably the pick of the Ripping Yarns certainly because it is such a damn fine, ripping yarn, starring the heroic Palin as Gerald Whinfrey, the Biggles style, (a link enforced by the dubious book references quoted in the opening book credits) all-action British gentleman cool dude who, tired of saving the known world from itself, denies a cry of help from the military and plumps for a quiet holiday instead. The problem is that the British government are faced with a devious plot from Germany to start the First World War a year early – the swines – but even Palin's single-minded plan to avoid the hassle results in his accidentally stumbling on the enemy plan.

A dignified, gentlemanly Bondian figure, Palin is clearly a man of manners, full of confidence and ability, happily reeling off his past successes and bounding around the place with Boy's Own authority. But he is no Brit dummy in a corrupt world, and the final defeat of the Germans (eagerly jumping into the arms of British troops simply to claim the distinction of a Whifrey capture) reveals the thwarted plan for a safer kind of world which can be mapped out and resolved through discussion and without bloodshed. The infiltration of British military might and a concerned aider and abetter in Palin merely allows the bloodfest of The Great War (and the promise of a rematch) to go ahead as planned. Although discussed in the narrative with the carefree attitude of a football challenge, the underlying current of the script and, importantly, Palin's pained performance, drives home the sheer awfulness of his deeds. The off-screen death at the film's close is justified and satisfying as Palin wanders off to a peaceful retirement with a glorious English sunset as backing. The main bulk of the yarn details the mysterious ghost train in which Palin finds himself, tackling the petulant station master (a recurring figure in various guises from a stately Richard Hurndell – later to take over the mantle of William Hartnell in the 20th anniversary *Who* classic *The Five Doctors*), struggling with a mini, almost unseen barmaid-cum-taxi driver, who wears his patience down with her travelogue small talk and almost drives the heroic lad over the rocky cliffs while stringing out ghoulish tales of murderous vicars and dismembered bodies. The action within Smuggler's Cottage is hilarious, with scores of suspicious home helps and perhaps the all-time masterpiece of the entire *Ripping Yarns* canon, the sealed bedroom suddenly spouting forth 28 routes of escape. With a touch of sheer genius when the race is on Palin initially chooses the broom cupboard as his exit! With only the merest element of *Python* madness (the opening scene featuring contemporary comment from the Orson Welles-like host from *Tomkinson's Schooldays*), this masterly piece of comedy embraces a more mainstream sense of the absurd, throwing in the odd moment of surrealism alongside more traditional farce, puns and sight humour. Again the acting is first rate (with Edward Hardwicke's family retainer, memorably bemused about drugging kippers, a particular delight) while the whole thing is structured as a telling comment on who should be considered the enemy and who the heartless warmongers. Major entertainment.

Gerald Whinfrey & Presenter **MICHAEL PALIN**
Mrs. Otway **MARIA AITKEN**
Admiral Jefferson **ANTHONY CARRICK**
Mr. Girlon **EDWARD HARDWICKE**
Carne **RICHARD HURDNELL**
General Chapman **JACK MAY**
Lord Raglan **GERALD SIM**
Lotte the Old Lady **ANN WAY**
Smooth German **MICHAEL SHARVELL-MARTIN**
Mr. Ferris **CHARLES McKEOWN**
Portly man **ANTHONY WOODRUFF**
Army Captain **ROY SAMPSON**
Another Eddie **PHILIP CLAPTON-GORE**
Mr. Vinney **PATRICK BAILEY**
Meat Porter **STEVE CONWAY**

Germans **Members of the Royal Marines, Exmouth**
Written by **Michael Palin & Terry Jones**
Photography **Alan Stevens & Michael Radford**
Sound **Ron Blight & Ron Pegler**
Dubbing mixer **Ron Edmonds**
Film editor **Glenn Hyde**
Designer **Gerry Scott**
Costume design **Roger Reece**
Make-up artist **Jill Hagger**
Visual effects **John Horton**
Graphic designer **Ian Hewett**
Assistant sound recordist **Morton Hardaker**
Grips **Malcolm Sheehan**
Assistant designer **Alan Spalding**
Property buyer **Enid Willey**
Lighting gaffer **Ricky Wood**
Make-up assistant **Caroline Becker**
Assistant floor manager **Julie Mann**
Assistant film editor **Brian Douglas**
Design assistant **Sarah Leigh**
Production assistants **John Adams & Sue Bennett-Urwin**
Director's assistant **Carol Abbott**
Executive producer **Sydney Lotterby**
Director **Alan J. W. Bell**
Filmed at the BBC Studios, Ealing and on location in London, Torbryan, Devon, Staverton Bridge, Devon and Cape Cornwall
Broadcast BBC2 – 10th October 1979

GOLDEN GORDON

If Whinfrey is the head of *Ripping Yarns* then this wonderfully detailed Northern period piece is the heart, awash with working class iconology, passionate and healthy obsession with football and picturesque industrial landscapes. This is Palin in definitive form, capturing the flavour of the nation's favourite game long before European star players, million-pound transfer deals and the merchandising franchise. This is 1935, when football was the working class dream, the one brief spark in a hard working, poorly paid man's struggle to survive. Palin's poignant following of his home team, having not won a game for four years, is the picture of a lowly family man who dismisses his son's enforced attempts to list the 1922 squad and his wife's (a peerless turn from Gwen Taylor) fevered declarations that another baby is on the way. The authority

figures are anti-Brit, anti-football, anti-soul sort of people; following yet another dreadful defeat, the board opts to sell the club, lock, stock and scrap metal barrel to blustering Bill Fraser – hard-nosed, brass-loving Northern business personified. However, there's a spark of working class football fan deep behind those rounded cheeks and money-oriented gaze, with Palin's impassioned, anorak-like knowledge of the football facts rekindling lost affection for the old club. Fraser's suppressed excitement, with the cold light of day desperately trying to dampen his fan persona, remains a quite stunning piece of acting. The writing is powerful, subtle and heart-warming, with the half hour starting and ending with the same scene, Palin's similar reaction to a bloody 8-1 score line. The result may be the same but the closing outburst is a united family act of delighted destruction. There's time for some glorious surrealism along the way, notably the five minutes in which the manager babbles on about the unimportance of football shorts, but all in all this is a rounded, character-driven celebration of the national game, complete with arguably Palin's most restrained and thought-provoking performance of the series. There's a real sense of feeling good and cockles being warmed as he rounds up the key legends of football's past, and I challenge any footie-geared, red-blooded, chest puffing Brit not to glow with pride when Palin trundles out his ageing team of masters. It's a sheer delight pure and simple. If you can imagine an Alan Bennett anglicised reworking of *Field of Dreams* you're halfway to the glories of this priceless *Ripping Yarn*. The smell of Yorkshire pudding and steaming half-time cup of tea is in the air, the working man is on top and all is right with the world. To cap everything off there's even a wordless walk-on part for a certain John Cleese, doing a quick double take to Taylor's baby announcement. Cancel everything to wallow in this fine piece of everyman nostalgia – class.

Gordon Ottershaw **MICHAEL PALIN**

Mrs. Ottershaw **GWEN TAYLOR**
Arthur Foggen **BILL FRASER**
Barnstoneworth Ottershaw **JOHN BERLYNE**
Cyril the Barman **KEN KITSON**
Football Manager **DAVID LELAND**
Chairman **TEDDY TURNER**
Baldy Davitt **ROGER SLOMAN**
Goalkeeper **CHARLES McKEOWN**
Footballers **DAVID ELLISON, COLIN BENNETT, MATTHEW SCURFIELD &**
Members of Saltaire Football Club
Passer-by **JOHN CLEESE**
Written by **Michael Palin & Terry Jones**
Photography **Alan Stevens**
Editor **John Jarvis**
Designer **Gerry Scott**
Sound recordist **Ron Blight**
Dubbing mixer **Ron Edmonds**
Costume designer **Roger Reece**
Make-up artist **Jill Hagger**
Visual effects **John Horton**
2nd unit cameraman **Michael Radford**
Production assistants **John Adams & Sue Bennett-Urwin**
Director's assistant **Carol Abbott**
Prop buyer **Enid Willey**
Lighting gaffer **Ricky Wood**
Grips **Malcolm Sheehan**
Assistant cameraman **Steve Albins**
Assistant costume designer **Sarah Leigh**
Assistant film editor **Christine Pancott**
Make-up assistant **Caroline Becker**
Produced & directed by **Alan J. W. Bell**
Filmed on location in Keighley, Kildwick, Saltaire, Bradley, Bingley & Guiseley, Yorkshire
Broadcast BBC2 – 17th October 1979

ROGER OF THE RAJ

Although nowhere near as emotive as the football yarn, this last ever *Ripping* adventure from Palin and Jones is an enjoyable romp through the old satirical standby of imperialism in British colonies and the 'God on our side' righteousness of the military mind. Palin's only problem is that his family are so incredibly rich that it seems impossible to achieve his dream of running a chemist shop, although 14 years of Marxist teaching during his Latin tutoring plants a seed of privileged rebellion. As always, Palin is the perfect innocent young chap naively staggering through life. Although in this show he is very

nearly upstaged by the lipsmacking cast of supporting players, notably Richard Vernon as his bewildered and really rather kindly old buffer of a father, Joan Sanderson tearing up the scenery as his bloodthirsty mother and, most treasurable of all, dear old John LeMesurier, mumbling his way through a gloriously anti-establishment speech as he joins his fellow disgraced military colleagues. It's made all the more powerful via this icon from *Dad's Army* and its feelgood embrace of Britain's finest hour. Here, with the edge of comedy mocking authority, Palin and Jones see their bravest and most forthright condemnation of the system from one of its definitive, kindly uncle figures. Despite a convincing sense of period detail and some glorious performances, *Roger of the Raj* tends to flag towards the end with insubstantial comic situations and a manic, overlong siege on the distinguished, patriotic stance of Vernon and his ilk. However, naturally there are still classic moments to enjoy, notably Palin's uneasy reaction to the copious amounts of breakfast he heavy-handedly staggers through, his memorable voice-over narration showing his fear whenever his mother addressed him and expected an answer, not to mention the final re-embracing of landed gentry luxury on Palin's own, twisted terms. This is a wry comment on the days when women had to leave the dining room to allow the men time for their talk, port and cigars, a time of strict regulations which would rather see good men kill themselves into disgrace rather than bend just a millimetre and an era of totally British supremacy against the inferior ramblings of native dissent. While Vernon's ideals of a peaceful solution and offers of tea are ridiculed, by both the narrative and the other characters, his kindly attitude is highlighted as a favourite option opposite the bombastic, spoilt, upper class fierceness of Sanderson. Although Vernon wistfully longs for the old days of slavery, it is merely to enjoy the supreme pleasure of granting

freedom to hard-done-by, hard-working folk. This plays like a subtle *Python*esque reworking of underlining *Carry On... Up the Khyber* themes, a perfect basis for a priceless *Ripping Yarn* which, nevertheless, does go to show that nine such tales were perhaps as far as the idea could have been pushed.

Roger **MICHAEL PALIN**
Lord Bartlesham **RICHARD VERNON**
Lady Bartlesham **JOAN SANDERSON**
Miranda **JAN FRANCIS**
Colonel Runciman **JOHN LE MESURIER**
Hopper **ROGER BRIERLEY**
Major Daintry **ALLAN CUBERTSON**
Captain Meredith **DAVID GRIFFIN**
Captain Morrison **CHARLES McKEOWN**
Captain Cooper **DAVID WARWICK**
The Gamekeeper **MICHAEL STAINTON**
Mutinous Officers **KEN SHORTER & DOUGLAS HINTON**
Housemaid **DOROTHY FRERE**
Stunts **Stuart Fell & Roberta Gibbs**
Written by **Michael Palin & Terry Jones**
Photography **Reg Pope**
Editor **Dan Rae**
Designer **Nigel Curzon**
Sound recordist **Bob Roberts**
Dubbing mixer **Alan Dykes**
Costume designer **Valerie Bonner**
Make-up artist **Cecile Hay-Arthur**
Production assistant **Peter R. Lovell**
Producer's assistant **Elizabeth Cranston**
Visual effects designer **John Horton**
Assistant floor manager **John Bishop**
Design assistant **Richard Brackenbury**
Costume assistant **Tessa Hayes**
Make-up assistant **Margaret Magee**
Property buyer **Eric Baker**
Assistant cameraman **Richard Gauld**
Sound assistant **John Corps**
Grips **Tex Childs**
Lighting gaffer **Ted Bird**
Assistant film editor **Arden Fisher**
Director **Alan J. W. Bell**
Filmed on location at High Halden & Godington Park, Kent
Broadcast BBC2 – 24th October 1979

THE RISE AND RISE OF MICHAEL RIMMER

This film was the original brainchild of David Frost who suggested Graham Chapman and John Cleese get together to write a film script in-between series of *The Frost Report*. Allegedly based on the fictionalised career of David Frost (in other words it is!) and causing its executive producer some paranoid moments, Peter Cook grabs the title role at the peak of his comic powers, crusading through life as an advertising guy and ultimately becoming Prime Minister. *The Card* with attitude. The location for the project was Ibiza with a three-month writing blitz, followed by a relaxing three months off, welcoming visits from Marty Feldman and Tim Brooke-Taylor just before plans for *At Last the 1948 Show* began to take shape. Huge mounds of money were floating about and their stars were in ascendancy, although the project went uncompleted and unfilmed for several years. Eventually Peter Cook was approached to take the lead and Kevin Billington assigned director, which led to one final rewrite with all four involved in the screenplay. Some good moments among the pretentious ramblings. But nothing comes close to the joyfully bizarre image of John Cleese practising balloon dancing during his tea break.

Warner Bros./Seven Arts
Michael Rimmer **PETER COOK**
VANESSA HOWARD, PATRICIA CARTWRIGHT
Peter Niss **DENHOLM ELLIOTT**
Fairburn **DENNIS PRICE**
Fromage **GRAHAM CHAPMAN**
Pumer **JOHN CLEESE**
Tom Hutchinson **RONALD FRASER**
Ferret **ARTHUR LOWE**
Blackett **GEORGE A. COOPER**
Steven Hench **HAROLD PINTER**
Sir Eric Bentley **RONALD CULVER**
Interviewer **RONNIE CORBETT**
Mr. Spimm **MICHAEL BATES**
Mrs. Spimm **DIANA COUPLAND**
Manderville **FRANK THORNTON**
Screenplay by **Kevin Billington, Graham Chapman, John Cleese & Peter Cook**
Editor **Stan Hawkes**
Music **John Cameron**
Art director **Carmen Dillon**
Executive producer **David Frost**
Producer **Harry Fine**
Director **Kevin Billington**
Cert. AA 1970, 94 mins

ROMANCE WITH A DOUBLE BASS

Following important collaborations on *How To Irritate People* and *Monty Python*, John Cleese and Connie Booth joined forces for this engaging Russian fantasy of social manners and individuality. With the lowly musician figure of Cleese and the regal Booth both caught in the same predicament (a carefree naked swim leads to their clothes being stolen), the situation results in gallant Cleese hiding the stunning Booth in his bass case and dragging her to the arranged marriage she dreads. It's a delightful story of discovery and anxiety beautifully played by the two stars and an impressive array of supporting players like Freddie Jones and Graham Crowden. Jonathan Lynn from the old *Cambridge Circus* days crops up along the way, as does Andrew Sachs, soon to be immortalised as Manuel. A low-key project which budgeted at £16,000 (a thousand of which Cleese put up himself), the original idea came from grand British character actor Bill Owen, who discussed this Chekhov adaptation with Cleese. With all the main actors on a percentage rather than a fee, the use of Henry Herbert's house for location shooting and a minuscule shooting schedule of just ten days during October 1974, this was a happy, hard-working and determined project. Released with *The Eiger Sanction*, it received warm reaction from critics although it didn't succeed in America thanks to the odd running time (the use of short subject programme fillers had been abandoned) and the nudity level of both Cleese and Booth. The Brits could take that! In March 1976 Cleese and Booth were spotted enjoying the film at a Notting Hill cinema and although the couple were separated even at this stage, the working relationship would continue to its greatest height the following year with *Fawlty Towers*, while this film saw the first professional meeting of Cleese and director Robert Young who would go on to direct numerous Cleese commercials as well as his 1997 movie, *Fierce Creatures*.

Pacific Arts Corp. Inc/Anton Films
Romance With A Double Bass
Princess Constanza **CONNIE BOOTH**
Musician Smychkov **JOHN CLEESE**
Count Alexei **GRAHAM CROWDEN**
Musician Razmakhaikin **DESMOND JONES**
Maestro Lakeyich **FREDDIE JONES**
Leader of the Orchestra **JONATHAN LYNN**
Major Domo **JOHN MOFFATT**
Musician Zhuchkov **ANDREW SACHS**
Screenplay adapted by **John Cleese, Robert Young & Connie Booth**
From an original screenplay by **Bill Owen**
Adapted from a short story by **Anton Chekhov**
Producers **Ian Gordon & David King**
Director **Robert Young**
Filmed on location at Wilton House & The Somerley Estate, Wiltshire
1974 40 minutes

RUDYARD KIPLING'S THE JUNGLE BOOK

Following the trend of classic books remade with the author's name tacked onto the front, this classic Disney adventure film was the first attempt by the studio at reworking one of Uncle Walt's old cartoon favourites into a live-action entertainment. This film works brilliantly. Lavish to look at, jam-packed with cleverly directed set pieces, some choice performances and a huge quota of laughs, *Rudyard Kipling's The Jungle Book* is a real, no-nonsense, damn fine, ripping sort of a yarn. In actual fact, the film plays more like a Tarzan movie than anything else (white man after monkey gold, baddies caught in various jungle traps), with a few subtle Holmesian references (Reichenbach Falls-like clifftop, water-plunging tussle/Baskerville's Grimpen Mire-like quicksand), while the familiar array of loveable characters from the 1967 Walt Disney masterpiece are played by real animals here – shock horror. However, although a living, breathing, growling Baloo doesn't quite have the easygoing personality of Phil Harris, there's no denying that John Phillip Scott's powerful performance as Mowgli is a massive achievement and effortlessly gives the animals around him strength, affection and endearing qualities. Somewhat overshadowed by the megabuck hype for *The Lion King*, this low-key Disney adventure doesn't shirk away from controversies, notably highlighting man's inhumanity to man and beast via Scott's jungle beast-cum-Sabuesque hero. Apart from being a very fine performance, there are several subtle traits that reinforce this intriguing mix of man and beast – notably his feline qualities both during pleasure (he purrs when Headly soothes his burnt hand with ointment) and anger (there are low growling noises when attacked by the blasted Brits). With a few notable exceptions, all the British characters are pinpointed as complete slimy swines, and those that aren't are played for laughs most of the time, but then again, in India during the 19th century we weren't the most diplomatic of races and the characterisations are never stereotypical nasties but well played bounders of the first order, notably a particularly slimy and snobbish Cary Elwes, betraying Queen, country and uniform for a chance of untold wealth. Besides, he commits the ultimate cinematic cardinal sin of longing for wealth over love – his fate is sealed almost at once, poor chap. The Brits, of course, apart from being the anti-romance and money-obsessed scumbags of the operation also are the only characters to be allowed a bit of swearing – with bloody elephant, bloody jungle, bloody this bloody the other – complemented by several boots in the same private parts (rather discreetly referred to as 'sweets' – this being a Disney movie after all!), xenophobic distrust from the natives (the well-orchestrated rope trick revenge/comments about 'Brown brother' and insincere 'No offence') and poignant longings for a return to the sanity of Sussex. Sam Neill, adopting a rather strange but never grating British accent, has his pompous moments but any officer that can show at least a bit of

affection to his daughter (ie. awkwardly holding hands) can always be redeemed, while Headly herself, looking like a young Lesley Anne-Down, turns in an excellent performance full of girlie insecurities and packed with authority, charm and level-headedness. She's pretty cool in the blood and guts trek through the jungle as well. However, despite a major level of good cinema fun contained in the movie and the fact that every British army chap looks like either Michael Palin caught up in a less funny *Ripping Yarn* or Graham Chapman on his lunch break, our chief pride in this film is a truly magical supporting performance from John Cleese, popping up all through the film and dishing out slightly pretentious, frightfully British eccentricities all over the place. He may start out like Basil Fawlty in the jungle (bemused reaction to the suggestion that a tiger is about/hilarious antics as his elephant goes out of control and he politely enquires whether someone couldn't possible lend a hand, at their own convenience and in the spirit of British decency, etc) but as soon as the hand-brake is taken off of the action and the tiger attacks for real, Cleese's doctor characterisation effortlessly bridges laughs and drama. His sombre shake of the head is all the more powerful following his initial 'Cleese as comic relief' bits, but, thankfully, the script still allows him to latch onto deliciously funny observations and knowing one-liners. Hardly ageing a day in the time between boy Mowgli going missing and man Mowgli storming through the jungle, there's a brilliant reintroduction for the good doctor with petulant monkey identification problems, a load of giggling young ladies and a wonderfully delivered tongue-in-cheek spider monkey with a moustache jape from Headly. Cleese's reaction as the penny drops is a joy. However, perhaps his best moments come with the attempt to re-establish Scott into civilisation, beginning with his inspired delight over a good old hot English bath, some behind-the-curtain splashing and his Fawltyesque emergence

dripping wet and pouring soapy water out of his shoe. His attempts at language tuition and identifying a lantern slide are classic Cleese comedy, injecting a bit of prat-falling humour with the swinging and slamming mirror, charming three-way comic banter with Scott and Headly during the 'pest' word association and a slice of boyish fun as Cleese – handing over the lantern operation to the boy –plays and mocks the notion of education with some shadow hand signals.

Two sequences stand out from the rest though, with the hilarious description of the photograph of the man with two women growing and growing until Cleese hits home with the typically British punchline and an unforgettable, throwaway line when he turns on his bemused English amazement at Scott's mistaken observation – 'That's not a boat, it's Queen Victoria!' There's a priceless comment following some charming romance between his two young co-stars: the momentous ball (full of misunderstanding, snobbishness and pathos) presents Cleese with a heart-wrenching explanation of the situation to Scott and his near death scene, with the camera giving him extreme close-up, is a touching piece of screen acting. Besides all that, there's a long-delayed but moving final, feelgood appearance, a clever inclusion of lyrics from the most popular song from the original cartoon ('The bare necessities of life...' as Cleese wanders down the stairs to the ball) and an earlier, even more subtle, mention of his 1985 movie *Clockwise* as he illustrates the art of stirring one's cup of tea. So it's tenuous... what about the very early moment as baby Mowgli is whisked away in a burning horse-drawn cart with the flames licking around the word Rose, a tiny nod to Citizen Kane's loss of youth and innocence with the burning of Rosebud – now that's tenuous! However, enough of this mild film in-joking, to conclude, this is one of John Cleese's most pleasing film performances, a majestic, well observed, multi-faceted, emotive and hilariously played piece of work which adds a major contribution to this sparkling, enjoyable, good natured Disney romp through love, terror, action, adventure and comedy.

Baloo Productions/Buena Vista
Mowgli **JASON SCOTT LEE**
Boone **CARY ELWES**
Kitty **LENA HEADLEY**
Colonel Brydon **SAM NEILL**
Dr. Plumford **JOHN CLEESE**
Screenplay by **Stephen Sommers, Mark G. Geldman & Ronald Yanover**
Editor **Robert Ducsay**
Music **Basil Poledouris**
Producers **Edward S. Feldman & Sharad Patel**
Director **Stephen Sommers**
1995, 108 mins

THE RUPERT BEAR STORY

Terry Jones celebrates the life and work of Rupert illustrator Alfred Bestall, a hero of the Python member since childhood and someone he had met while hosting the BBC literary discussion show *Paperbacks* in 1981. Taking the form of two halves, Jones explains his fascination and affection for the endearing bear of Nutley Wood and follows it with a search for Bestall, tracking him down to his cottage and interviewing the man himself. It was one of the first Channel 4 shows.

The Rupert Bear Story Written & presented by **Terry Jones**
Broadcast 9 December 1982 Channel 4

THE RUTLAND DIRTY WEEKEND BOOK

A classic publication capturing the Rutland television shows written by Eric Idle and published by Eyre Methuen in 1976. The texture of the paper reflected the subject matter, most of the material was specially written for the book, although some pieces are extended versions of television sketches and there was a wealth of photos from the series. The contents included Vatican Sex Manuel, A History of Rutland Weekend Television from 1300, RWT

Duty Log, Rutland Weekend Television TV Times, Who's Who in Rutland, Who's Had Who in Television, Accountancy and Sex by Michael Palin, Rutland Stone, Saturday RWT World of Sport Listings, Sunday Listings – Misprint Theatre presents The Wife of Christ, The Wonderful World of Sex and Rutland University Press Publications.

RUTLAND WEEKEND TELEVISION

The original concept for this classic and ground-breaking slab of genius from Eric Idle developed out of a project of Idle's during *Python*, *Radio 5*, which was a wacky sub-station of Idle comedy and music. Taking over for one hour each week on Radio One, Idle extended the notion of pirate television broadcasting for his post-*Python* bid for acceptance; John Cleese gave him the title and received a pound for his suggestion. The major historian's problem is this – if you draw a line through *Do Not Adjust Your Set*, *Monty Python* and *Rutland* it's clear that Idle continues to do the old sketch, fade-in, fade out, second sketch format. Despite *Rutland's* material being equally as good and sometimes even better than *Python*, a return to the format was never going to outshine the cult power of *Python*. While his fellow writing/performing Pythons moved onto pastures new, Idle tried to carry on as normal. Cleese, elongating his authoritative figure against the tidal wave of progress for situation comedy in *Fawlty Towers*, Palin & Jones extending their *Python* sketches examining the stiff upper-lipped attitude of Brits for *Ripping Yarns* and Gilliam finding a bigger canvas for his bizarre flights of fancy on the cinema screen. Idle happily embraced the old sketch format that *Python* had irretrievably split asunder. Having taken the sketch technique as far as it could possibly go, Idle reverted to the Spike Milligan system from which *Python* had borrowed and blown away. Like Spike, Eric Idle was at the centre of the thing, with

Neil Innes coming fully to the fore with loads of song contributions and acting pieces, alongside supporting stooges David Battley and Henry Woolf filling out the roles, à la Peter Jones and David Lodge for Spike's shows.

However, having said that, Idle's new venture was hilarious, incorporating plenty of naturally *Python*-edged satire on television programmes and certainly scoring a much bigger hit than Graham Chapman's ill-fated solo sketch venture *Out Of the Trees*. The basis concept for the *Rutland* show was a small television franchise somewhere in the middle of nowhere, whose manic shows would be shown by BBC2 once a week for at least half an hour. The claustrophobic, smallness of *Rutland Weekend Television* was enhanced by the shows coming under the wing of BBC's Presentation Department whose usual brief was for filming trailers for upcoming programmes and on which Idle had cropped up in *Up Sunday* – the only comedy series their ever did. The minuscule budget saw an entire season come in at about £30,000.

The second series was recorded in a studio in Bristol. Thus, this Eric Idle venture was recorded in a very small studio with no audience, giving it that air of small studio programming with basically no audience! This also aided the television convention bending handover between BBC2 and *Rutland Weekend Television*, extended for the second show when Idle's RWT itself hands over to the ITV station ATV, even adopting its logo to complete the gag – and bravely resurrecting *Python*'s embrace of Reggie Bosanquet. Aptly enough for Idle's off-kilter comic genius, the Rutland Weekend shows were broadcast on Mondays. The first series was linked by a continuity announcer and formed a slice of television broadcasting, with Idle's flamboyant chappie in the first show continually staggering back from an office party. As the series went on these links became ever more bizarre with Henry Woolf gradually turning into a woman delivering misleading and downright inaccurate trails for

Rutland programmes. The cosy smallness of the operation was taken to ultimate extremes when Neil Innes's complains of low budgeting materialised with his clothes being repossessed. The second series got even madder with linking material from such Music Hall-geared novelty nutters as the barbershop quartet, The Razor Blade Four and the manic Ricochet Brothers. The keys to the sketches were really elaborating on Idle's obsessive television-based material from *Python*, allowing in-depth documentary footage of the 2nd World War still being fought on The Isle of Wight, a behind the scenes look at Bathtime theatre where, in true *Python*esque fashion, great works are performed in the bath and interview deconstruction, with one memorable sequence delivered entirely in disconnected gibberish. Rich with Idle's invention, the show boasted inspired notions like the bending of spoon-bending maestro Uri Geller, angels striking outside the pearly gates, an electrical shop worker selling his soul to the devil who turns out to be an insurance agent, safari animals in the safari tour cars, the Cookian plan of saving fish from drowning and even an interview spot with Idle's mother, looking suspiciously like television clean-up campaigner Mary Whitehouse, keeping the continuity of bathtime theatre from the third show with her closing spot, chatting away in the bath. It's all television challenging, notably featuring one poor chap suffering from poor continuity who consults a doctor, on film, about his problem. Like *Python*, the sketches blended and merged throughout the episode, including characters wandering in from earlier skits and continuing their comic adventures, but it still couldn't move the format any further on.

In place of Gilliam's animations, Idle's fusing elements were the glorious songs of Neil Innes, resurrecting his old Bonzo Dog Doo Dah Band classic *I'm the Urban Song Man* and premiering numbers like *The Protest Song* which would crop up for several *Python* stage shows. There's even a ditty about wife-swapping in Stanley Holloway style, perfectly capturing the cockney cheer of the grand old man, tackling a permissive society situation with relish. By common consent, the most mesmerising musical moment wasn't an Innes song at all but cropped up at the very end of the 1975 Christmas special with guest artist George Harrison. Dressed in all the cool gear and looking every inch the Rock legend, George begins the intro to *My Sweet Lord* before breaking into the immortal *Pirate Song* – an Idle/Harrison composition which features in the illustrated songs of George Harrison. However, the major contribution from Innes was, of course, debuting his Beatlesque masterpiece *I Must Be In Love* in series 2 show 1, a sequence which developed into the priceless full-length comic gem *The Rutles* – initially billed as *The Rutland Stones*. (But that's another entry not a million miles away from this one.) While the fortunes of *The Rutles* flourished and video and record material is widespread, poor old *Rutland Weekend Television* has tended to be lost in the shuffle of television classics. Never repeated in full and never ever shown on American television because, Idle, with the full rights, was never offered enough money to let it go, RWT flounders in the mists of time, enjoying a huge cult following but rarely getting the chance to prove its excellence. Like *The Goodies*, Marty Feldman and Charlie Drake, it is an unsung, rarely repeated milestone celebrated furiously by fans but never celebrated by the BBC big wigs. Even the album, *The Rutland Weekend Songbook*, featuring studio remakes of Idle sketches and Innes songs was quickly deleted soon after its 1976 release. It's a great shame, but for those who make the effort to search out *Rutland Weekend Television*, these Eric Idle gems will never disappoint.

Rutland Weekend Television Series 1 12 May – 16 June 1975 6x30 mins
1. Gibberish, Star of the Naughty Movies – Song, Hanging, Chase Through A Priest, Sitting Under Clerics, Saving Fish From Drowning, A Miscellany of Clubs, Startime Song by Stoop Solo, World War II Still Going On the Isle of Wight, Major Who Doesn't Understand Anything, Anniversary of the Birth of Churchill's Cat, Other RWT Churchill Programmes.
2. Goodafternoon From the Goodevening – L'Amour Perdue, Cha Cha Cha, Say Sorry Again – Song, Philosophy Corner, Bodies Left to Department Stores, Intelligence Test Result, Critic Club, Talking About Great Wit, Origami, Impersonations of Medical Equipment, Communist Cooking, Kung Sooey, The Kung and I, Exposé On Normality, Blaming the Little Man at the Off-Licence, Lie Down and Be Counted – Song, Kung Dancing, Handover to ATV.
3. Warnings On Programme Content, Schizophrenia – Paranoia, Lateness, Film From Bangor, The Children of Rock 'n' Roll – Song, The Poet, Mungo Wright, Football Song, Searching for Religious Identity, God of the British Army, Thrust with Spligtherism, The Making of Bathtime Theatre, Boring – Song, The House With No Sherry, Buying People, Telegram Delivery, Television Report, Final Word with Tony Bilbow.
4. Whistle Test, Toad the Wet Sprocket in Performance, Splint with Bandwagon, Dead Singers, Rutland Weekend Theatre – Amnesia in Esher, Beauty Queen Farm, Yorkshire Showbiz Butchers, A Penny For Your Warts, Once We Had a Donkey – Song by the fabulous Bingo Brothers, The Old Gay Whistle test – Protest Song by Ray Onassis.
5. Announcers' Tryst, Solihull Wifeswapping Club, Weather-flash, Not Enough TV Shows for MPs, Urban Spaceman – Song, Your Questions Answered, Another Weather-flash, Holiday '75, Wash With Mother (Front End Loader) – Song, More Wifeswapping, Politicians on the Rain in Hendon, Selling A Soul to the Man in the Electrical Shop.
6. Announcer Complaining About the Lack of Money, Religion Today Hijacked, If You Were A Song, Rutland Weekend Cinema – Incident

at Bromsgrove, Carrot – Friend or Foe, Nelson, Execution of Charles I, Man Alive – Private Prisons Run By Suburban Housewives, Johnny Cash Live at Mrs. Fletchers, Closedown – Song O' The Continuity Announcers.
Christmas With Rutland Weekend Television – 26 December 1975, BBC2 30 mins – The Alberto Rewrite Five, George Harrison Wants to be a Pirate, Christmas Night with the Scars, Testing One Two – Song, How to Ski in Your Own Home, Giving Women As Christmas Presents, I Don't Believe in Santa Any More – Song, Overfed and Ill Vicar, Rutland Weekend Film Night – Bit of Scratchy Film, Linda Lovelace in Sore Throat, Pommy the Rock Opera, Concrete Jungle Boy – Song, Interview with Ann Melbourne, Roundup of the Year's Films, Film of HM Queen of Rutland's Year, Mr. George Harrison Sings... The Pirate Song.
Series Two 12 November – 24 December 1976 7 x 30 mins
1. Continuity Announcer Auditions, Lawyer Who Arranged His Client's Crime, Cure for Love, I Must Be In Love – Song: The Rutles in Rutles For Sales, The History of the Entire World – Episode 3 The Creation Backroom Boys, The Age of Desperation – Song, Next Week on RWT, The Effects of Inflation, Introducing Not-Necessarily-Tobacco to Civilization, That's My Mum!.
2. The Razor Blade Four, Quite Interesting People – Sheep Worrying, Madame Butterfly Collecting, Shoeshine Boy – Song, Expose on Carswapping, Godfrey Daniels – Song, Rutland Five -O, Coming Up on RWT.
3. Lance Corporal Collier Steps In, Prisoner Requests Leave, Science Lecture with a Saucer of Rancid Milk, What Makes James Burke Tick, Uri Geller Bending, Perpetual Motion Machine, Lecture, Caretaker, Recursive Documentaries, I Give Myself to You – Song, Husband and Wife, Collier Rides Again, Crystal Balls – Song, Restaurant with Strange Dress Code, Bad Habits of Killing People.
4. The Ricochett Brothers, Ill Health Food Store, The Hard to Get – Disco Song, Sprimpo (From Scunthorpe

Television), Bad Continuity, Film Doctor, Recursive Flashbacks, Classic Bad American Films – Fiddle-Dee-Dee, 24 Hours in Tunbridge Wells, Expose – The Massed Flashers of Reigate, Police Running Shops, Police Being Evicted by Squatters, Rant About Critics, Smarm to Critics, The Cast Revolts.
5. Boring Intro to Tony Bilbow Theatre, Extremely Method Actor, Flag Flog Day, Sex Problem Clinic, Song O' The Insurance Man, Accountancy Shanty – Song, I Don't Want to Fall In Love Again – Song by the Singing Gynaecologist, Escape from a Travel Agency.
6. Highwayman, Lone Accountant, Judge Jeffries, Bella the Beauty Queen – Song, Safari Park with Animals in Cars, Safari Car Park, Sexist Sketch, The Power of the Writer, Wife Swapping Poem, Coming Soon – Nixon Is Innocent.
7. Repressing Women for 2000 Years, Censorship, Showtime, The Smoke of Autumn Bonfires – Song, Playing on the Penthouse Floor – Song, An Affair in announced, Tomorrow Night on RWT – Autocue, David Frost Show Again, Return of the Pink Panther, Joining the AA, Australian Love Song, The Slaves of Freedom – Song, Angel Demonstration, William Plastic-Bidet and the Postman, Most Boring Man in the World, Competition, It's Hard to Make it When You're Straight – Song.

Written & performed by **ERIC IDLE & NEIL INNES**
Director **Andrew Gosling**
Producer **Ian Keill**

THE RUTLES

This hugely influential beat compo, bearing remarkable similarities to The Beatles, first appeared on Eric Idle's post-*Python* venture *Rutland Weekend Television*. Formulated from a favourite Idle comic moment of the earnest television outside broadcaster running after his fast disappearing camera vehicle, this basic documentary satire was linked with a Beatlesque hit that Neil Innes had written, *I Must Be In Love*. Idle put

the two of them together created *The Rutles in a Hard Day's Rut* and slipped it into the show. When the time came for Idle to host *Saturday Night Live*, he took with him two snippets of *Rutland Weekend Television* as a sort of pre-American broadcast taster. In the event, the shows were never broadcast in the States, but out of his two Rutland selections, the Neil Innes Tommy parody – Pommy, and the Rutles sequence, it was the latter that was chosen for broadcast. Throughout the *Saturday Night Live* show there was a running gag concerning the upcoming reunion of The Beatles (Indeed, Eric tries to perform Harrison's *Here Comes the Sun* while Paul McCartney, visiting John Lennon in New York, watched the show, momentarily considering an appearance together for a laugh) and Idle's clip simply fit in with the overall joke. The Rutles proved so popular that viewers began sending in Beatles albums with the Fab Four crossed out and The Rutles handwritten over the cover for signatures. With a huge interest growing in the clip, Idle was approached to make a full length version of the Rutles story in association with NBC. Thus it was that *Saturday Night Live* and *Monty Python* came together for the unforgettable story of the pre-Fab Four – *The Rutles in All You Need Is Cash*. In his book, *From Fringe to Flying Circus*, Roger Wilmut condemns The Rutles for being far too correct in historical detail and allowing a satirical study of The Beatles to escape him. However, Wilmut here misses the point. *The Rutles* is not a parody of the Beatles but rather a parody of the media reaction to the Beatles and the entire point of the joke relies on fairly detailed knowledge of the group's rise to fame and monumental career at the top. Ultimately it pokes fun at the glossy rock documentaries of Tony Palmer's ITV specials rather than the rock greats themselves. Certainly, the major quota of jokes directly concerning the group simply replaces the original with the odd Rutland-related phrase – ie. Let it

Rut, Sgt. Rutters Only Darts Club Band etc, whereas the satirical stuff comes late on with the realms of legal activity and group breakup. Above all, however, this is the ultimate comic version of the Beatles for Beatles fans due to it's very affectionate treatment of the subject. Two years later (with the assassination of John Lennon), it is doubtful whether Idle would have or could have tackled the subject with such a free, comic warmth, but in those spiralling, post-Beatles days of 1978 this major piece of work is caught in a tongue-in-cheek time bubble. Above all that, of course, is the endorsement of the product by a certain George Harrison, brilliantly hiding behind grey hair and whiskers as he interviews Michael Palin's Eric Manchester (re-Derek Taylor) as the remnants of Rutle Corp (Apple) are stripped away behind him. Although it has a running time shorter than just part one of *The Beatles Anthology*, all the major elements of Beatles folklore are tossed into the pot, brilliantly twisted by Idle's imaginative screenplay and some quite stunning reworking of old hits by Neil Innes. From the first grainy black and white appearance of the lads (jumping in unison from a truck), the detail is perfection itself, right down to the Dick Lester bald-a-like director ushering the Rutles away from the crowds à la *A Hard Day's Night*, backed by a sample from their later hit *Get Up and Go* (re-*Get Back* – you're getting the idea). Idle resurrects his bemused and confused narrator as our host taking us through those early days at the Cavern, Rutland, brilliantly addressing the speed of recording (their first album took 20 minutes, their second even longer!), Hamburg ('far from home and far from talented') and the homosexual tenancies of their manager Leggy Mountbatten (with coy interview blurb from his mother – Gwen Taylor – concerning boy's clubs and the Rutles love of tight trousers). But above all this is Innes and his Beatles-inspired songs (although it is said that he didn't listen to any Beatles material while writing the

stuff... really!) and Idle's accurate recapturing of the essence of the period. The five-piece group shot from Hamburg is uncanny; murky colour footage from the 63 Variety performance is exactly right; the quirky black and white interview footage with Lennonesque tank obsession and Ringoisms concerning desires to be two hairdressers embrace the off-the-wall wit of the group and even Mountbatten's book, *A Cellar Full of Goys*, taps into the collective memory of Epstein's *A Cellar Full of Noise*! Mick Jagger eagerly and brilliantly throws himself into the Rutles mythology, playing along with Idle's recreated history for the Beatles and memorably stringing out a tale about the lads penning a song for his group. The vintage intercut of Idle's McCartney figure gets the perfect vocal intonation on the Rolling Stones and links into Jagger's hilarious condemnation of this quickly whipped off song which was 'horrible' and unrecorded by the Stones! The American invasion is full of great moments, watching themselves on a flickering TV screen (with Idle's typical Beatles moment of feeding a sandwich to the screen), Innes, complete in Lennon leather black hat, witty, interactive press conferences, a doctored original intro from Ed Sullivan and even a wacky cameo for Bill Murray as the outlandish American DJ – but even here the humour is nothing more than direct relating of the true story. The sequence as Idle listens to this nutter on the radio is almost indistinguishable from a McCartney moment from The Beatles in Washington. Paul Simon's contribution adds name value only, while the documentary satire (Idle's wandering off to New Orleans for no apparent reason other than highlighting how expensive this kind of show can be) latches onto the old, old story of white performers stealing the blues riff from black performers, initially gleefully twisted on its head via Blind Lemon Pie's observations and finally taken to mock extremes. A resurrection of the song that started it all – *I Must Be In Love* – and some *Hard Day's* speeded-up

camera antics in a field are intercut with studio material based on the final 15-minute gig footage of the Beatles movie. But again this is an affectionate tribute, in contrast to the merchandising scam that gets past Leggy and the delicious moment when Idle's narrator speaks for the world and asks Dan Aykroyd's chain-smoking failure who turned down the Ruts, 'What's it like to be such an arsehole!' Classic moment. The Ouch! sequence, combining *Help's Ticket to Ride* skiing antics and Bahamas-based *Another Girl* footage, the Shea Stadium concert and the burning of records continue the unflawed detail, with Innes giving a brilliant, uneasy Lennonesque smile direct into camera and desperately trying to explain his reasoning behind the bigger than God/Rod outrage. There's even a chance for an inspired bit of Idle comedy detailing the fact that records were being bought just to be burnt – again, not a million miles from the truth, one supposes. The crossover point between pure rock 'n' roll and psychedelia comes with Bob Dylan's introduction not of the dreaded LSD but the even more potent tea, inspiring a cracking sequence of the lads in Pepper outfits having a quick cuppa. Sgt. Rutters who inspired a generation, is referred to as a millstone, gets the academic treatment and finally leads to Idle's uneasy admittance to being a tea user... 'and biscuits'! Coyness is replaced by coolness as the Rutles entertain the known world with *Love Life*, their class answer to *All You Need Is Love*, with garish colour, a charming opening chorus of *John Brown's Body* (as a replacement to the French National Anthem), Innes lapsing into one of the group's early hits, *Hold My Hand* (à la *She Loves You*) and even chewing gum as Lennon does on the 1967 broadcast. Now that's detail for you! The Surrey mystic and Leggy's Australian teaching job don't quite come off, although Innes in grief is a wonderful piece of acting, but the Tragical History Tour is a masterpiece of reinvented Beatles history with nuns, a camel, rabbits and the like joining the continuity-keeping policemen in a row for the pseudo-*I Am the Walrus* sequence blessed with the peerless song *Piggy In The Middle*. The tour bus costumes are amazingly accurate and the inter-cut footage of the mocked *Magical Mystery Tour*'s *Your Mother Should Know* sequence is perfection. The '68 States interview revealing Rutles Corp is an exact resurrection of the Lennon/McCartney appearance on *The Johnny Carson Show* (hosted that night by Joe Dimaggio) with Idle perched above Innes on a stool and the Lennonesque observation that the organisation will 'Help people to help themselves!' leading to Harrison's hilarious work with Michael Palin and hard man Ron Wood, highlighting the collapse and abuse of the Rutles' business empire. Perhaps the most stunning piece of the film is the extended clip from the animation classic *Yellow Submarine Sandwich*, backed by my favourite Innes song from the soundtrack, *Cheese and Onions*, and resurrecting the style of George Durning's *Yellow Submarine* perfectly, with the sequence of various opening doors, piggy banks with pig helmets, Innes sliding down a dinosaur, a brief reappearance from a Blue Meanie, clever interaction with the cartoon Rutles having a ripping time, a toothpaste mouse squeezed in a trap and a final animated note as the scene fades to white. It's a breathtaking piece of work. The final collapse is perhaps the funniest part of the show, with Idle's soppy, sloppy silly love songs, champagne antics with Bianca Jagger and dee, dee, dee lyrics contrasted with Innes hitched up with Nazi-like Yoko figure from The Pretentious Gallery exhibition, giving nutty press conferences in a shower, presenting their avant-garde flick *A Thousand Feet of Film* (backed by Bernard Bresslaw's *You Need Feet*) based on Lennon's *Self Portrait* which he explained was basically about 'my prick' and adding to the cool feel of the film with another cracking, Lennon-like song *Let's Be Natural*. Brilliantly observed comic moments are the release of *Shabby Road*, the appearance of Belushi's take on Alan

Klein, Ron Decline, in a sort of American version of Ethel the Frog (note the reprised idea that people committed suicide rather than meet him), the camera firm connection between McQuickly's in-laws (Kodak) and McCartney's (Eastman) and Idle's outrageous trudge through the dubious array of facts that lead people to believe that the quiet one, Stig, (rather than Paul) was dead. But for me, the most treasurable scenes come with Palin's petulant, laid-back explanation of the tangled legal web, Idle's caustic comment that *Let It Rot* was released as a film, an album and a law suit, and perhaps, best of all, the immortal rooftop farewell gig as Innes (in his Lennon fur coat) absentmindedly boots some poor technician chappie over the edge. It's a class moment, made all the more effective due to the absence of drawing attention to it. As a final embrace of the Anglo-American deal with the show, Idle desperately tries to coax a few words from a brilliant Gilda Radner and, suitably enough, the last words are given to Rock God Mick as he answers the question regarding the Rutles getting back together with a disgruntled, wide-eyed 'I hope not!!...' Not only an essential piece of superb Eric Idle comedy, creating a near Lennon-McCartney chemistry with Innes, but a totally essential video addition for any Beatles devotee, this is a musical, comical masterpiece of the highest order.

Did You Know? George Harrison was very hands-on with the project from the outset, screening a Neil Aspinall Beatles film for both Eric Idle and Neil Innes to help with their parody.

The Rutles in All You Need Is Cash – The Rutles:
Dirk McQuickly **ERIC IDLE**
Barry Wom **JOHN HALSEY**
Stig O'Hara **RIKKI FATAAR**
Ron Nasty **NEIL INNES**
With **ERIC IDLE** as the narrator & S.J. Krammerhead
Eric Manchester **MICHAEL PALIN**
Interviewer **GEORGE HARRISON**
Martini **BIANCA JAGGER**
Ron Decline **JOHN BELUSHI**
Brian Thigh **DAN AYKROYD**
Mrs. Emily Pules **GILDA RADNER**
Bill Murray the K. **BILL MURRAY**
Mrs. Iris Mountbatten/Chastity **GWEN TAYLOR**
Hells angel **RON WOOD**
Leggy Mountbatten **TERENCE BAYLER**
Arthur Sultan **HENRY WOOLF**
A Queen of England **JEANETTE CHARLES**
Archie Macaw **FRANK WILLIAMS**
Dick Jaws **BARRY CRYER**
With **CARINTHIA WEST, LORNE MICHAELS, ROBERT PUTT, JEROME GREEN, BOB GIBSON, PAT PERKINS, BUNNY MAY, AL FRANKEN TOM DAVIS, EUNICE, PENELOPE TREE TANIA KOSEVICH, VIVIENNE COHEN, OLLIE HALSALL, RAY TRANTER, DEBBIE WATERSON**
with **MICK JAGGER & PAUL SIMON**
Conceived & written by **Eric Idle**
Music & lyrics by **Neil Innes**
Production manager **Roger Simons**
Sound **Tony Jackson & Bruce White**
Art director **Peta Button**
Costumes **Polly Hamilton**
Make-up & hair **Elaine Smith**
Animation **Little Big Films of London**
1st Assistant director **Clive Hedges**
2nd unit cameraman **Chris Sargent**
Graphic designer **Tony Cohen**
Continuity **Pat Rambaut**
Editor **Aviva Slesin & Colin Berwick**
Location manager **Derek Parr**
Photography **Gary Weis**
Additional photography **Julian Doyle**
Producers **Gary Weis & Craig Kellem**
Executive producer **Lorne Michaels**
Directors **Gary Weis & Eric Idle**
Filmed on location in London, Liverpool, New York and New Orleans Broadcast: NBC, 22 March 1978/BBC2, 27 March 1978

Quite clearly, the song writing talents of Neil Innes were totally instrumental in creating the perfect feel of Beatles music for The Rutles and settled within the comic narrative of Eric Idle, the music proves the perfect straight(ish) backbone for the *Python*esque humour. Importantly, the songs of Innes could easily stand on their own merits and a record release of 14 songs featured in the show was put out by Warner Brother Records in 1978. Innes recruited a group of musicians who lived together in Hendon for a few weeks tuning the sound and recorded all the songs without overdubs in just two weeks. It was nominated for a Grammy for Best Comedy Recording and received a Silver disc for English sales in excess of £150,000. Complete with a stunning 20-page booklet packed with pictures from The Rutles television special, the tracks were split over the two sides with a 1962-66 and 1967-70 compilation akin to the Red and Blue best of albums of The Beatles released in 1976. Rutles fan clubs, badges, mags and even bootleg recordings of songs featured in the film but not on the disc cropped up, notably *T'anks for the Mammaries* which featured *Get Up and Go*. However, the most fascinating bootleg appearance has to be on *Indian Rope Trick*, an actual Beatles bootleg release which includes Neil Innes performing *Cheese and Onions* on *Saturday Night Live* but credited as a lost Lennon-McCartney! The record is also worth searching out for its inclusion of the Harrison/Idle classic *The Pirate Song* from *Christmas With Rutland Weekend Television*.

Rutlemania really took hold with successful launches in Austria, Belgium, Canada, Denmark, Finland, Iceland, Japan, the Netherlands, New Zealand and Norway. The album tracks selected were: The Rutles – *Hold My Hand, Number One, With A Girl Like You, I Must Be In Love, OUCH!, Living In Hope, Love Life, Nevertheless, Good Times Roll, Doubleback Alley, Cheese and Onions, Another Day, Piggy In The Middle, Let's Be Natural* – Warner Brothers (K 56459) – UK/(HS 3151) – USA. A promotional single (Warner Brothers WBS 8560) headlined *I Must Be In Love* and *Doubleback Alley*, while a promotional E.P. released on yellow vinyl (Warner Brothers Pro E723) featured *I Must Be In Love, Doubleback Alley, With A Girl Like You, Another Day* and *Let's Be Natural*. There were further plans to take the Rutles on tour or do some more albums, but these ideas were abandoned in favour of Idle's other pet projects. However, later a single release of unrelated songs to The

Rutles filmed back catalogue, *Ging Gang Goolie* and *Mr. Sheene* (EMI 2852) was credited to just 'Dirk and Stig'. Like a *Python* variation on *Photograph*, this single reunited Eric Idle and Rikki Fataar and even warranted a video directed by Eric Idle, following on from his two films for George Harrison's singles. Suitably enough the video for *Ging Gang Goolie* was filmed at the house of Ringo Starr, Tittenhurst, which had belonged to John Lennon and played host to the *Imagine* album sessions. The shot, one of the most enjoyment for all involved, included Idle, Fataar, some chaps as boy scouts and a load of scantily clad glam girls kitted out with Brownies uniforms and suspenders. Ooh er! However, apart from this brief and uncelebrated semi-reunion, The Rutles seemingly went their separate ways, but the video release of the Eric Idle comedy resulted in renewed interest in the Rutles music and, in 1990, Rhino Records reissued the original album with six bonus tracks which had featured in the programme but were dropped from the album. The classic *Get Back* parody *Get Up and Go* (dropped from the initial Warners release because it sounded too much like The Beatles classic) finally made it officially onto the record stalls, alongside new additions *Goose-Step Mama, Baby Let Me Be, Blue Suede Schubert, Between Us* and *It's Looking Good*. Sensibly these new tracks joined a rearranged repeat of the old record to form a chronological tracking of Rutles material. The Rutles – *Goose-Step Mama, Number One, Baby Let Me Be, Hold My Hand, Blue Suede Schubert, I Must Be In Love, With A Girl Like You, Between Us, Living In Hope, OUCH!, It's Looking Good, Doubleback Alley, Good Times Roll, Nevertheless, Love Life, Piggy In The Middle, Another Day, Cheese and Onions, Get Up And Go, Let's Be Natural*. Rhino Records CD (R2 75760). And it would seem that this final release of familiar but, as yet partly, unreleased Rutles sounds would be the final gasp of the pseudo-pop legends from Liverpool. However, almost 20 years after Jagger

had hoped for continued inactivity from the group, The Rutles made a high profile comeback in 1996 with a new album, new single and various television appearances, including an interview and 10 of the Best selection on the home of great music on television, VH-1. Naturally and cannily, Neil Innes latched onto the worldwide retrospective celebration of *The Beatles Anthology*, which between November 1995 and October 1996 comprised an essential haul of three double CDs and ten hours of filmed history.

The band reformed to offer the music loving world The Rutles Archaeology. An album of new songs, again wonderfully provocative but obvious tributes to classic Beatles numbers, the stunning single *Shang-lai* was issued with an accompanying video, merging vintage material of the Rutles with new studio recording sequences, à la *Real Love*. A combination of *Penny Lane* and *Hey Jude*, the tongue-in-cheek clout the band still held was illustrated with guest appearances from the likes of Peter Gabriel, Cyndi Lauder and Elizabeth Taylor for the *All you Need Is Love*-like sing-a-long sequence at the end. Although fittingly credited on the album sleeve with creating the Rutles concept, Eric Idle himself opted out of grabbing up his Rutles wig for the reunion – Innes explained that Dirk had gone into comedy! Sad but strangely apt, The Rutles, like The Beatles themselves, were down to three men for the new recordings, even though John Lennon, with a far better excuse than Idle, managed to deliver lead vocals and piano for the two new Beatles tracks... Still, there's something slightly eerie in seeing Innes, in definitive older Lennon mood, with grey hair, cool shades and haunting piano work. In terms of the album release, the first 13 tracks are supposed to be unreleased and half-forgotten tracks from The Rutles' sixties career, tucked away in a time capsule for future release. Indeed, the effective inclusion of an unpolished, laughter-ridden out-track like the official *Anthology* releases gives the new album an added affectionate quality with the track in question, *We've Arrived*, capturing the energy of Beatles music during the American invasion while latching onto White album motifs with elements from the first and penultimate album tracks (the scoring *Back in the USSR* effects and the muttered No. 2 at the close!). If anything Neil Innes does an even more impressive job of reworking the Beatles sound here, as usual finding more inspiration in the Lennon-based numbers although contributing some powerful backing vocals to *Loney-Phobia* and crafting a couple of simple but well constructed McCartney-styled love songs. Some numbers are obvious (*Major Happy* and *Rendezvous* simply recreate the first two tracks of *Sgt. Pepper's Lonely Hearts Club Band* for The Rutles) but other songs have lyrics that even Lennon and McCartney would have been chuffed to have written. There are mentions of Beatles numbers (*Norwegian Wood* on *Don't Know Why*, *Why Don't We Do It In The Road* on *Easy Listening*) and more telling, self-referential mentions of old Rutles hits (*Love Life* during the *Shang-lai* sing-a-long/*Cheese and Onions* on *Unfinished Words*), the classic *Hey Mister!* takes its lead from *Hey Bulldog*, its structure from *Yer Blues* and its basic rock 'n' roll will solve anything attitude from John Lennon's philosophy. The spirit of *Abbey Road* is perfectly captured in *The Knicker Elastic King*, complete with Ringoesque narration bridge, Lennon working class glories and even a slightly rearranged burst of the *Coronation Street* theme (McCartney included the theme to *CrossRoads* on his *Venus and Mars* album), *Joe Public* embraces the weird wonderment of *Tomorrow Never Knows* with some clever social structure lyrics, *Eine Kleine Middle Klasse Musik* (a priceless Lennon solo sound-alike hit which plays a lot better than its title parody of the Beatles German version of *She Loves You* may suggest) has Innes in fine ironic Lennon mood ('he used to travel in bath cubes'), while the deceptively simple *Easy Listening*, a coy statement of the more sedate solo

material from the post-Beatles, brilliantly contrasts old rockers slowing down with jolly harmonising counterbalancing thought-provoking, social horrors like child abuse and famine. The prize of the early selection, however, must be *Questionnaire*, a perfect blend of *Imagine* and *I Am the Walrus* elements which, hauntingly, finishes with a comment on the gun laws that killed it's inspiration. The final three selection, à la *Free As A Bird* and *Real Love*, are the Rutles today (although, of course, all the album is new material), with the legendary *Shangri-La* a mammoth single release, the jaunty, comic reworking of *When I'm 64* in relation to the year the Rutles were at their peak for *Back in '64* (with a fine *Woman's Hour* intro, some stunning lyrics about black and white images of yourself being people like you might have been, comic moments based round their famous tight trousers and the answering harmony of 'scoring porn') and, for me the best song on the album, *Don't Know Why*. A chilling performance from Neil Innes which is so close to Lennon it hurts, this song is similarly structured to *Free As A Bird* performed in Beatles style and contains some truly beautiful lyrics. If you could have the impossible and imagine The Beatles performing material like 'Looking back with 20-20 hindsight we only did the best we could, as green as any Norwegian Wood, the acid test of fame we withstood', it's poignant indeed. As with the entire Rutles history this is a glorious tribute to the Beatles, performed with understanding care and showcasing the creative genius of Neil Innes like never before. A fine comeback album which deserves more than camp, cult, comedy chart status but serious recognition as the comeback of the greatest humorous variation on the greatest of all pop combinations. The Rutles Archaeology – *Major Happy's Up And Coming Once Upon A Good Time Band, Rendezvous, Questionnaire, We've Arrived! (And To Prove It We're Here), Lonely-Phobia, Unfinished Words, Hey Mister!, Easy Listening, Now She's*

Left You, The Knicker Elastic King, I Love You, Eine Kleine Middle Klasse Musik, Joe Public, Shangri-La, Don't Know Why, Back in '64.

The Rutles:
Neil Innes vocals/guitars /keyboards
Ricky Fataar vocals/ guitars/drums
John Halsey (vocals/drums)
Ollie Halsall (1949-1992) vocals/guitar.
With **Mickey Simmonds** – keyboards, **Malcolm Foster** – bass, **Dougie Boyle** – guitar, **Bernie Holland** – guitar.
Music & lyrics by **Neil Innes**
Produced by **Neil Innes & Steve James**
Executive producer **Martin Lewis**.
This album is dedicated to **John, Paul, George & Ringo** with love from **Neil, Ricky, John & Ollie**.
Virgin Records America (VUSX 119)

THE SAGA OF ERIK THE VIKING

A story written by Terry Jones for his son, Bill and concerning the Adventures of Erik and his Viking chums through the Enchantress of the Fjord, Sea Dragon, Dogfighters, Wolf Mountain and the Spell-Hou. Comprising 27 chapters, all self-contained tales, the book forms a continual narrative of Erik's journey. Won the 1984 British Children's Book Award and inspired the 1987 Terry Jones movie *Erik the Viking*.

Written by **Terry Jones**
Illustrated by **Michael Foreman**
Published by Pavilion Books, 1983 – hardback, Penguin paperback

SATURDAY NIGHT LIVE

Broadcast from New York, the show's producer, Lorne Michaels, had, in fact, sat in on a *Python* recording session in the seventies and all his cast were *Python* fans – with *SNL* providing invaluable grounding for the likes of Chevy Chase, Bill Murray, Eddie Murphy, Dan Ackroyd, Gilda Radner and John Belushi. Eric Idle and Terry Gilliam on a visit to the States for a *Holy Grail* promotion had met Belushi who treated them like John Lennon had treated Jerry Lee Lewis. Introduced to the other members of the team by mutual friend Paul Simon, it was Idle who became the first *Python/SNL* connection when he hosted a show at the start of the second series.

2 October 1976 – hosted by Eric Idle, this features a clip of The Rutles performing *I Must Be In Love* from *Rutland Weekend Television* as well as Idle starring in sketches Killer Bees, Designer Babies and Dragnet. His attempted singing of Harrison's *Here Comes the Sun* is interrupted, while official musical guest is Joe Cocker.

20 February 1977 – Live From the Mardi Gras, *It's Saturday Night Live on Sunday*, features a guest starring turn from Eric Idle presenting an outside broadcast from an area with absolutely nothing of interest going on. An inspired idea, Idle had luckily escaped a drag presentation scene which, performed by Penny Marshall, went dreadfully wrong. Idle himself considers this bit of live television among his best written pieces.

23 April 1977 – Hosted by Eric Idle, featuring the Save England Telethon and the much celebrated David Frost/Richard Nixon interview parody with Idle as interviewer and Dan Aykroyd as the President. The show also features the Idle and Gary Weis filmed sketch Body Language (having previously concocted Drag Racing and later working on *The Rutles* movie together), as well as The World Heavy Wit Contest and Plain Talk with Idle teaming with Dan Aykroyd. Musical guest is Neil Innes, singing the pre-Rutles classic *Cheese 'n' Onions* and the subsequent comeback classic *Shangri-La*.

8 April 1978 – hosted by Michael Palin, features a clip from *Ripping Yarns* and new material of Palin performing a Sid Biggs monologue, a piece as his own manager, stuffing fish and cats down his trousers as he sings *White Cliffs of Dover*, an

escapologist version of Chekhov's *The Seagull* and a Nerds sketch playing a piano teacher. Palin also discussed at length the Pythons' problem with *Life of Brian* – with EMI having just dropped out of the picture. Indeed, he was going to wear his Pontius Pilate costume to drum up awareness of the project but decided against it.

9 December 1978 – hosted by Eric Idle, shortly after finishing filming on *Monty Python's Life of Brian* and aptly performing a travelogue on Tunisia. Idle also appears as part of a madrigal quartet, plays Prince Charles about to marry a 13-year-old girl in The Woman He Loved, a quiz host in *What Do You*, a spot in a recording studio and plays a college professor in Cochise at Oxford. Kate Bush keeps the British spirit intact as music guest.

27 January 1979 – hosted by Michael Palin who starts the ball rolling with an inspired monologue about his socks, reprises his role as Lisa's piano teacher in a second Nerds sketch and performs in the pieces, What If Superman Grew Up In Germany?, Family Classics – Chapter One of Miles Cowperthwaite and the game show *Name the Bats*.

12 May 1979 – hosted by Michael Palin who performs a Mother's Day monologue, presents the second chapter of Miles Cowperthwaite, appears as a black-market petrol salesman and even plays Margaret Thatcher on a *Weekend Update* interlude.

20 October 1979 – hosted by Eric Idle. Suffering from a heavy cold, with comic Buck Henry on the sidelines in case Idle couldn't perform, the team joke about Henry's involvement instead while Idle performs stretcher impersonations, plays a handmade store salesman, guest stars in the sketch Heavy Sarcasm and appears as the author of the book *Prince Charles Tells You How To Pick Up Girls*. Idle even crops up as a female impersonator in Hardcore II, while everything fades in comparison to Bob Dylan's magical musical contribution. Christian values rule okay and there's more hype than humour, but hey, with Idle and Dylan in one show who wants to

go anywhere else?

15 March 1980 – *Saturday Night Live* 100th Show features a pre-recorded appearance from Michael Palin in the spoof talk show *Talk or Die*.

22 May 1982 – A long drought of Python appearances on the show is broken by debutee Graham Chapman appearing briefly during the *Weekend Update* section to promote the film *The Secret Policeman's Other Ball*. Recreating his commercial, complete with half-Colonel, half-ballet dancer gear, Chapman was called in to perform the material because NBC refused to screen the original film advert.

30 October 1982 – A guest appearance from Michael Palin during promotion for *The Missionary*: He appears with host Michael Keaton and Eddie Murphy in a dressing room pre-title sequence, acts as storyteller for A Sense of Fear and features as Topol the Idiot.

21 January 1984 – hosted by Michael Palin who also brought along his 80-year-old mother as part of her birthday treat. She appears, à la Yoko, knitting on stage as Palin performs his monologue. Palin also appeared as maitre d' in the House of Mutton sketch, a restaurant which serves lamb in every dish. Musical guests were The Motels.

6 December 1986 – hosted by the stars of *Three Amigos*, Chevy Chase, Steve Martin and Martin Short, during promotion for the film. Eric Idle guest stars as a British customs officer. In 1989 Idle returned to appear in a special broadcast. It was the last Python contribution to *Saturday Night Live* before, almost a decade later, Michael Palin returned with first-timer John Cleese, to struggle through the dead parrot sketch in 1997.

Writers **Brian McConnachie, Jim Downey, Michael McCarthy Tim Kazurinski, Eric Idle, Dan Ackroyd**

THE SECRET POLICEMAN'S BALL

The third Amnesty concert established a trend and all-consuming umbrella title for the various spin-offs to come while maintaining the heavy involvement from John Cleese who both performed and directed. Fellow Pythons Terry Jones and Michael Palin pitched in alongside Peter Cook, Billy Connolly, Neil Innes, Rowan Atkinson, Chris Beetles, Eleanor Bron, Rob Buckman, The Ken Campbell Roadshow (featuring Sylvester McCoy), John Fortune, Clive James, Tom Robinson, Pete Townshend, Melvyn Bragg and John Williams. Performed at Her Majesty's Theatre on June 27, 28, 29 and 30 1979, ITV transmitted an hour-long, edited and expletive-shorn, highlights version on 22 December and the definitive record formed *The Secret Policeman's Ball* video. This featured the Python brigade resurrecting pre-*Python* sketches with Cleese and Palin performing *1948 Show*'s Cheese Shop with Chris Beetles and Rob Buckman; Cleese and Jones as Mrs. Yettie Goose-Creature performing The Name's The Game with special guest stars Anna Ford, Clive Jenkins and Mike Brearley; new boy Rowan Atkinson joining Cleese, Palin and Jones for the oft heard version of Four Yorkshiremen; the hilarious End of the World skit from Fringe with Peter Cook holding court with the entire cast of comic followers mumbling and moaning about Armageddon; and, best of all, a classic beyond the dreams of Allah version of the One Over the Eight masterpiece, Interesting Facts, performed by Kenneth Williams and John Howard in 1961 and here given the King Midas treatment by original writer Peter Cook and John Cleese. Absolutely priceless.

The video also included the extra bonus of Peter Cook, Billy Connolly and John Cleese in a merchandising advert for the concert. The obligatory record release also included Interesting Facts, The Name's The Game, Cheese Shop, Four Yorkshiremen and The End of the World, as well as Palin and Jones in How Do You Do It? and a classic meeting of *Python* and *Not* with the Palin/Atkinson sketch Stake Your Claim from *Another Monty Python Record*. Common consent, however,

gave the show's highlight over to Peter Cook's biting judicial satire Entirely A Matter For You, specially written for the occasion in a legendary 15 minutes and available on both the visual and audio versions of the show.

THE SECRET POLICEMAN'S BIGGEST BALL

Despite the name, this tenth anniversary of the first *Secret Policeman's Ball* for Amnesty was quite a low-prolif effort, marking the return to the original sketch comedians of the first shows headlining John Cleese and Michael Palin. Directed by Cleese and Jennifer Saunders, the weighty cast list included Rory Bremner, Kathy Burke, Robbie Coltrane, Ben Elton, Lenny Henry, Adrian Edmondson, Jools Holland, Steve Nallon, Roland Rivron, Willy Rushton, Dawn French, John Williams, Jimmy Mulville, John Bird, Chris Langham and the Spitting Image puppets (including one of John Cleese) all doing their bit at the Cambridge Theatre over a four-night stint. Tickets weighed in at between £9.50 and £30. However, despite *Python* treats like Cleese and Palin in the teasing Pet Shop Mark 2, Cleese and Adrian Edmondson resurrecting the classic Penultimate Supper, Palin and Cleese joining Dawn French and Chris Langham for Argument Clinic, Cleese with John Williams and Jennifer Sanders on Guitar Solo and Cleese and Palin joining forces for Biggles Goes to See Bruce Springsteen, the major coup of the show was a reunion between Peter Cook and Dudley Moore, making their first West End appearance together since *Behind the Fridge* in 1973. Performing two legendary sketches, One Leg Too Few and The Frog and Peach, Cook and Moore led the entire cast in a farewell rendition of *Goodbyee* for a classy, tear-jerking finale. Other highlights included Ben Elton's Fast Food and Drink and a reappraisal of *Python*'s Crunchy Frog performed by Robbie Coltrane, Lenny Henry, Jimmy Mulville, Dawn French and Jennifer Saunders, but the old guard once again stole the honours. Central

Television recorded the show and ITV screened a hour-long version on 28 October 1989. An extended video was released, but the usual record version was not forthcoming.

THE SECRET POLICEMAN'S OTHER BALL

This fourth Amnesty show again benefited from the talents of John Cleese, joined here by just one old Python cohort, Graham Chapman. Directed by Ronald Eyre with plenty of assistance from Cleese himself, the comedy material embraced the new *Not the Nine O'Clock News* breed with contributions from Rowan Atkinson, Pamela Stephenson, Griff Rhys Jones and Chris Langham, as well as the old guard of Alan Bennett, Tim Brooke-Taylor, Neil Innes, John Fortune and John Bird. Clive Anderson, Martin Bergman, Jasper Carrott, Jimmy Mulville, Alexei Sayle, John Wells and Victoria Wood also cropped up alongside musical contributions from Phil Collins, Jeff Beck, Eric Clapton, Bob Geldof, Sting and Donovan. Was that a show, or what! Performed at The Theatre Royal, Drury Lane on 9, 10, 11 and 12 September 1981, highlights were released on record and video, featuring A Word of Thanks from John Cleese and the gang, Beekeeping with Cleese and Rowan Atkinson, Cleese, Chapman and Pamela Stephenson in Clothes Off! and a towering rendition of *Top Of the Form* with Cleese, Chapman, Tim Brooke-Taylor, John Bird, John Fortune, Rowan Atkinson and Griff Rhys Jones. Although not appearing in the official show, the video merchandising advert was performed by Michael Palin, under the direction of film-maker Julian Temple. The American video release also included footage from the 1979 show.

THE SECRET POLICEMAN'S THIRD BALL

In terms of the talent on board, this was probably the most elaborate Amnesty concert, although the changing face of comedy is reflected in the absent of many of the original performers. From the Cambridge legends, only Bill Oddie and John Cleese were present during the run at the London Palladium from 26 to 29 March 1987. Cleese cropped up opposite Lenny Henry, Bob Geldof and Robbie Coltrane for the Ruby Wax act, while offering some hilarious assistance to the contribution from Hugh Laurie and Stephen Fry, receiving the 'Silver Dick' award which spoofs the fact that he had refused to take part in that year's show – and thus, perversely, getting him to take part. Directed by Paul Jackson with the film directed by Ken O'Neill, other performers were Joan Armatrading, Aswad, Chet Atkins, Joy Behart, Paul Brady, Richard Branson, Rory Bremner, Jackson Browne, Kate Bush, Phil Cool, Andy de la Tour, Duran Duran, Erasure, Craig Ferguson, Dawn French and Jennifer Saunders, Peter Gabriel, Paul Gambaccini, Dave Gilmour, Gareth Hale and Norman Pace, Jools Holland, Nigel Kennedy, Nik Kershaw, Mark Knopfler, Yousso N'Dour, Emo Philips, Courtney Pine, Lou Reed, Jonathan Ross, Mel Smith and Griff Rhys Jones, Loudon Wainwright III, Who Dares Wins, Working Week, World Party, Paula Yates, Spitting Image, Andrew Sachs as Manuel and Warren Mitchell injecting a bit of Alf Garnett rant. To reflect the wide range of performers, two videos were released, one for comedy and one for music.

SECRETS

At the tail end of *Monty Python's Flying Circus*, Michael Palin and Terry Jones were commissioned by producer Mark Shivas to write a one-off comedy play for a BBC2 series called *Black and Blue*. The emphasis was on satirical writing with a dark quality. The basic idea had been triggered off by a documentary on Marketing Strategy featuring a Professor from Stirling University which had interested Palin. The play involved human remains making a chocolate bar taste delicious resulting

in murderous activity in order to keep the punter happy. Fifteen years later the script would be expanded for the film *Consuming Passions*, but both Palin and Jones feel that their original television version packed more of a punch. Notably, the narrative included the element of public knowledge of human flesh in the chocolate, putting ads in newspapers for willing volunteers and attracting huge hordes of people who were happy to die for money to provide for their families. With a deliberate incorporation of the madness of modern factory methods resting alongside the black humour of the piece, it proved a successful addition to the series.

Written by **Terry Jones & Michael Palin**
Producer **Mark Shivas**
Director **James Cellan Jones**
Broadcast BBC2, 14 August 1973

SEVEN-A-SIDE

Extremely rare private recording of various greatest hits from the Oxford revues, put together by The Oxford University Experimental Theatre Club and Oxford Theatre Group themselves, preserving classic moments from *The Oxford Revue*, *Hang Down Your Head and Die*, *Keep This to Yourself* and *Etcetera, Etcetera*. Sadly, this November 1964 disc was recorded after one of Oxford's leading lights, Terry Jones, had journeyed down to London, although several of his sketches are performed, while his leading vocals from *Hang Down Your Head* (*All That Gas* and *The English Way to Die*)are contributed by Dick Durden-Smith. Michael Palin, on the other hand, was at the height of his Oxford performing career and is present on four tracks, including his self-penned and performed *Keep This to Yourself* piece Grin and invaluable material from *The Oxford Revue*. He joins David Wood and Bob Scott on the Palin/Gould number *Song of British Nosh*, has a whale of a time on *I've Invented a Long-Ranged Telescope* and finally joins the entire cast for

Last One Home's a Custard, written by Doug Fisher, John Gould, Terry Jones and Palin himself. Also featured is the Jones/Gould song *Forgive Me*, performed by Nigel Rees and *Song About a Toad*, sung by Adele Weston.

Seven-A-Side Performed by **Dick Durden-Smith, Michael Palin, Nigel Rees, Bob Scott, Susan Solomon, Jane Sommerville, Adele Weston & David Wood**
Written by **Doug Fisher, John Gould, Terry Jones, Roddy MacRae, Michael Palin & David Wood**
MJB Recording and Transcription Service, 1964

SEZ LES

The most successful format for the spiralling vocal talent and character sketches of Les Dawson was initially produced by John Duncan and ran from 1969 until 1976, chalking up 51 regular episodes, a further six special programmes and another six shows cunningly entitled *Les Sez* (which could confuse a stupid person). Anyway, a distinguished and most welcome guest player was John Cleese who, in common with his fellow Pythons, had great regard for the music hall tradition which Les brilliantly brought to the small screen. It was a real mutual appreciation society, for Les was chuffed to have such a high profile comic talent appearing on his show. The comedy contrast was lyrical – Les the working class, school of hard knocks, Northern clubs, droll, rotund, down to earth bundle of hard-done-by insecurities, John the upper class, cool, collected, superior, television generation, tall, imposing satirical force – and each joined forces to sharpen up the sketches in which they appeared together. Dawson's comedy always had a stream of surrealism running through the working class ethos observation but with the *Python*esque pomposity of Cleese this was brilliantly brought into sharp focus – notably in an intellect versus world-weariness battle in the library sketch, the Feldman-like madness of an adventure obsessed chartered accountant scaling a building and the military banter of officer/low rank counterbalanced with Roy Barraclough. The piece (concerning the destination of a train) featuring Dawson's overly Scottish Northern, complete with huge caber, arguing with officious bowler-hatted businessman Cleese is a surreal masterpiece. Both are arrogant and adamant, fighting for their respective corner of British correctness until both are proved right as the carriage splits in two. A medical sketch, dating from 1974, has Cleese in typical *Python* mood, even after leaving the official television series behind. Here his highly qualified and slightly deranged doctor goes off at completely incorrect diagnostic tangents and, after initial disbelief, Dawson goes along with it. It could have been played by Graham Chapman and Terry Jones but as it is, here we can enjoy a mesmerising clash of comedy styles fusing to perfection. Cleese and Dawson got on well together off set, with Les offering his *Python* co-star the perfect opening structure for a nerve-wracking speech – providing three totally unconnected bits of trivia, leaving a pause, explaining that this has nothing to do with his speech but reflecting how the mind wanders when one is nervous – big laugh – and into the speech proper. Their work together on *Sez Les* remains amongst Cleese's favourite and justly so.

Cleese appeared in episodes broadcast on 22 February/24 November 1974.

SILVERADO

Lawrence Kasdan, having written/directed the steamy *Body Heat*, penned *Raiders of the Lost Ark* and helped fashion the *Star Wars* trilogy with scripts for *The Empire Strikes Back* and *Return of the Jedi*, surprised fans by reverting to traditional Western conventions rather than those played out in another galaxy. Even more of a surprise was the casting of John Cleese, in a straight supporting role.

It was filmed in New Mexico with a stunning Hollywood cast and united Cleese for the first time with Kevin Kline. Although Cleese enjoys an essence of eccentric comedy, this was ostensibly a straight, all-action, rooting tooting Western movie, allowing Cleese to mould his upper-class British sheriff into a stunning support turn. The stories of learning to ride a horse, with an ever growing batch of bigger and bigger horses to stop the lofty Cleese looking silly in the saddle are legendary. Despite a wonderful atmosphere the experience enforced Cleese's Englishness, consciously giving himself a shot of the homeland by buying and reading P.G. Wodehouse and Somerset Maugham novels. In 1991 a sequel was announced but never made.

Silverado
Columbia Pictures
Paden **KEVIN KLINE**
Emmett **SCOTT GLENN**
Jake **KEVIN COSTNER**
Mal **DANNY GLOVER**
Sheriff Langston **JOHN CLEESE**
Hannah **ROSANNA ARQUETTE**
Cobb **BRIAN DONNEHY**
Stella **LINDA HUNT**
Slick **JEFF GOLDBLUM**
Screenplay by **Mark & Lawrence Kasdan**
Produced & directed by **Lawrence Kasdan**
1985, 132 mins

SIX DATES WITH BARKER

This classic LWT showcase of Ronnie Barker's multi-faceted acting skills employed some top notch writing talent. The fifth episode, *Come In and Lie Down*, was penned by John Cleese. Cleese delivered a typically *Python*esque script concerning a dissatisfied gasman who is more interested in how a psychiatrist client deals with the eccentric patients in his care. An earlier entry, Bernard McKenna's *The Odd Job*, would, of course, be extended by Graham Chapman for his 1978 feature film version and the series was obviously a power of good for the Python's ex-*Frost Report* colleague as 1971 was

the year that Ronnie Barker won his first BAFTA award for Best Light Entertainment Performer.

Come in and Lie Down by **John Cleese**
Broadcast 5th February 1971
London Weekend Television

SMALL HARRY AND THE TOOTHACHE PILLS

In this Micahel Palin story Small Harry lives with Big Alf; Alf dies; Harry is left penniless; rumours abound that Alf invented the famous Toothache pill and has left a huge house in Scotland; Harry is unconvinced but goes in search of his legacy. This is the stuff of class children's fiction.

Small Harry and the Toothache Pills by **Michael Palin**
Illustration by **Caroline Holden**
Published by Methuen, 1982

SPIES LIKE US

A hip and cool Road movie for a younger generation (even recruiting the old man himself, Bob Hope, for a *Road to Utopia*-geared, golfing gag appearance), with a hit song from Macca and Landis satisfying his obsession with movies and movie-makers via a galaxy of in-joke guest appearances. His finest example of this is the Jeff Goldblum/Michelle Pfeiffer movie *Into the Night* but here he invited director and arch Python Terry Gilliam to tackle a few days filming his cameo as a manic Germanic scientist, babbling incoherently about secret formulae. Gilliam believes that the Landis plot is to hire superior film directors and make them look like dreadful actors.

Spies Like Us
Warner Brothers
Emmett Fitz-Hume **CHEVY CHASE**
Austin Millbarge **DAN ACKROYD**
General Sline **STEVE FORREST**
Karen Boyer **DONNA DIXON**
Mr Ruby **BRUCE DAVISON**
Colonel Rhombus **ERNIE CASEY**
Test Monitor **FRANK OZ**

Jerry Hadley **CHARLES McKEOWN**
Ace Tomato Agents **BB KING, LARRY COHEN & MICHAEL APTED**
Drive-in Security **MARTIN BREST**
Dr Marston **RAY HARRYHAUSEN**
Tadzhik Highway Patrol **CONSTANTIN COSTA-GAVRAS & SEVA NOVGORODTSEV**
BOB HOPE as himself
Dr. Imhaus **TERRY GILLIAM**
Screenplay by **Dan Ackroyd, Lowell Ganz & Babaloo Mandel**
Music **Paul McCartney**
Producers **Brian Grazer & George Folsey Jr**
Director **John Landis**
1985, 109 mins

SPLITTING HEIRS

Puma problems resurrect shades of *Bringing Up Baby*, a couple of reunited Pythons, a buddy movie with comic murder tossed in and that glam sweetheart from *Darling Buds* are all tantalising prospects, but sadly this is a fairly weak effort from Eric Idle. His script fails to make British eccentricity and American over-acting gel, but Idle's frantic performance is enjoyable. Cleese, receiving a tongue-in-cheek 'introductory' credit, is brilliant as the shifty lawyer but his support is far too brief, while most laughs come from Eric Sykes as an aged buffer.

Did you know? The film's original title was another groan-worthy wordplay – *Heirs and Graces* – and Idle finished the script in 1989. It took years to finally get the go-ahead.

Splitting Heirs
Universal Pictures/Prominent Features
Tommy Patel **ERIC IDLE**
Henry, Duke of Bournemouth **RICK MORANIS**
Duchess Lucinda **BARBARA HERSHEY**
Kitty **CATHERINE ZETA JONES**
Shadgrind **JOHN CLEESE**
Angela **SADIE FROST**
Butler **STRATFORD JOHNS**
Mrs. Bullock **BRENDA BRUCE**
Andrews **WILLIAM FRANKLYN**
Mrs. Patel **CHARUBALA CHOKSHI**
14th Duke **JEREMY CLYDE**
Brittle **RICHARD HUW**

Eric Idle, Catherine Zeta Jones and Rick Moranis – *Splitting Heirs*

Jobson the doorman **ERIC SYKES**
Nanny **BRIDGET McCONNEL**
Tour Guide **PAUL BROOKE**
Sergeant Richardson **DAVID ROSS**
CID Officer **CAL MACANINCH**
Gita **ANISHA GANGOTRA**
Barmaid **AMANDA DICKINSON**
Police Constable **CHRIS JENKINSON**
Photographer **KEITH SMITH**
German Tourist **STEPHEN GROTHGAR**
Woman with dog **MADGE RYAN**
Vicar at Hunt **BILL WALLIS**
Hunt Saboteur **CAMERON BLAKELEY**
Doreen **LOUISE DOWNEY**
Old Major **LLEWELLYN REES**
French drivers **PAUL WESTON & TIM LAWRENCE**
Couple at restaurant **GARY & MICHELLE LINEKER**
Written & executive produced by **Eric Idle**
Songs: *La Mère* by **Michael Kamen & Eric Idle**/*Someone Stole My Baby*, both performed by **Eric Idle**
Production executive **Steve Abbott**
Production co-ordinator **Deborah Harding**
Photography **Tony Pierce-Roberts**
Camera operator **Philip Sindall**
Editor **John Jympson**
Production designer **Johnrd**

Art directors **Rod McLean & Lucy Richardson**
Music **Michael Kamen**
Producers **Simon Bosanquet & Redmond Morris**
Director **Robert Young**
UIP/Prominent Features 1993, 87 mins

THE STATUE

Although he wasn't originally involved in this David Niven comedy, John Cleese contributes the funniest sequences. A disconcertingly risqué load of nonsense. Niven is a respected Nobel prize winner, inventor of a new universal language, Unispeak. He wants a specially commissioned statue, sculpted by Niven's wife, to be erected opposite the American Embassy in Grosvenor Square. However, scandal erupts since the figure is nude and the male member's origin is in question! Like a Joe Orton play re-written by Christopher Wood, when the film was finished, nobody could understand what was going on so writer Denis Norden, a long standing admirer of Cleese's work (having also cast him in *The Best House in London*) penned a series of linking sequences with Niven and his psychiatrist friend, played by Cleese. In order to make some sense of the already completed footage, Cleese and Niven did an extra week's filming, including dialogue allowing Niven to explain what his life has involved and what his plans are. Cleese helpfully acts as a sounding board with interjections of 'Good idea!' and the like. It made this manic tale of a Professor's 18-foot sculpture a little more cleaner and a lot more fun.

The Statue
Professor Alex Bolt **DAVID NIVEN**
Rhonda Bolt **VIRNA LISI**
Ray Whiteley **ROBERT VAUGHN**
Pat Demarest **ANN BELL**
Harry **JOHN CLEESE**
Hillcrest **TIM BROOKE-TAYLOR**
Sir Geoffrey **HUGH BURDEN**
Mouser **ERIK CHITTY**
Sanders **DEREK FRANCIS**
Mrs. Southwick **SUSAN TRAVERS**
Mr. Southwick **DESMOND WALTER-ELLIS**
Written by **Alec Coppel & Denis Norden**, based on Copel's play *Chip, Chip, Chip*
Photography **Piero Portalupi**
Editor **Ernest Hosler**
Art director **Bruno Avesani**
Music **Riz Ortolani**
Executive producer **Josef Shaftel**
Producer **Anis Nohra**
Director **Rod Amateau**
Eastmancolor, 89 mins. 1970

STILL CRAZY LIKE A FOX

In an attempt to revitalise a flagging television series, this British-based, made-for-TV, feature-length film cast Graham Chapman in the showy supporting role of superior, upper-crust law enforcement. In one of his last assignments, Chapman effortlessly steals the clichéd plot of distinguished families and corruption in high places as the sharp witted, frightfully proper inspector with a surprise secret.

Columbia Pictures Television

Harry Fox **JACK WARDEN**
Harrison Fox **JOHN RUBINSTEIN**
Cindy Fox **PENNY PEYSER**
Josh **ROBBY KIGER**
Detective Inspector Palmer **GRAHAM CHAPMAN**
Nancy **CATHERINE OXENBERG**
Elinor Trundle **ROSEMARY LEACH**
Screenplay by **George Schenck & Frank Cardea**
Producer **William Hill**
Director **Paul Krasny**
CBS TV, 93 mins, 5 April 1987

THE STRANGE CASE OF THE END OF CIVILISATION AS WE KNOW IT

The grandsons of Sherlock and Dr John are brought in to combat Moriarty's offspring. Like the earlier Comedy Playhouse episode, *Elementary, My Dear Watson*, Cleese's attempt to play the spirit of the great detective was greeted with critical disinterest although his always slightly other-worldly performance and towering presence does the role justice.

Arthur Sherlock Holmes **JOHN CLEESE**
William Watson **ARTHUR LOWE**
Mrs. Hudson & Francine Moriarty **CONNIE BOOTH**
Dr. Gropinger **RON MOODY**
President **JOSS ACKLAND**
Klein **BILL MITCHELL**
English Delegate **DENHOLM ELLIOT**
Screenplay by **John Cleese, Jack Hobbs & Joseph McGrath**
Producer **Humphrey Barclay**
Director **Joseph McGrath**
Broadcast London Weekend Television, 18 September 1977

THE SWAN PRINCESS

In the wake of a villianous cat for Steven Speilberg (*An American Tail: Fievel Goes West*), John Cleese clearly had no qualms about endorsing this charming fairy tale from ex-Disney cartoonist Don Blueth. Playing the French frog, good Euro-friendly gags all round (!), Cleese minces and warbles his way through with effortless ease. It's hardly the most

taxing of roles but guaranteed to attract younger viewers to dig out everything else Cleesian – start with *Monty Python's Flying Circus*, series 2 episode 13!

Nest Entertainment/New Line
Rothbart **JACK PALANCE**
Prince Derek **HOWARD McGILLIN**
Princess Odette **MICHELLE NICASTRO**
Queen Uberta **SANDY DENNIS**
Jean-Bob **JOHN CLEESE**
Screenplay by **Brian Nissen**
Executive producers **Jared F. Brown & Seldon Young**
Director **Richard Rich**
1995, 90 mins

A TALE OF MEN'S SHIRTS

If classic television were classed as great works of art this would be the *Mona Lisa*, *Sunflowers* and *The Scream* rolled into one!
A special television version of an original *Goon Show* broadcast 31 December 1956, this presents Sellers, Milligan and Secombe in all their colourful, comic genius glory, suitably aided and abetted by a poe-faced announcer type chappie in the shape of John Cleese. The Goons are clearly having a whale of a time and go through the motions with joyful ease, pointing fingers, injecting all the familiar, much loved silly voices and giggled mugging. Cleese, explaining that this is the first British radio show to be transmitted on television and that the public can see words they have only heard before, introduces his comic heroes with, notably, Secombe as 'England's tallest dwarf' and the two doing the 'what, what, what personally' chestnut to perfection. The script is pretty much a repeat of the classic radio adventure, allowing Milligan to ham around the war – with Brits who will die rather than be captured (Cleese: 'Germany declared

war in all directions') and Sellers to enjoy his peerless Churchill impersonation. Spike does Eccles picking the wrong name out of a hat, Sellers does Willum Mate (the influence for Palin's God-like It's Man) explaining that 'I'm one of them, matey!' and Secombe brilliantly turning on the sophistication for the alternative ending – Sellers as the laid-back Liverpudlian lady is the show's masterpiece – while Cleese's tag-line concerning marrying the elephant can dispel with ease any uncertainties that *Python* sprang from the loins of Milligan's *Goon Show*. A magical combination of the master and the very, very promising pupil just about to graduate.

Spike Milligan, Peter Sellers, Harry Secombe & John Cleese
Thames TV August 8 1968

THE TAMING OF THE SHREW

Jonathan Miller's production formed the first programme in the third season of the BBC's exhaustive recording of the complete works of Shakespeare – 'BBC Television Shakespeare'. Miller and Robin Skynner worked on Cleese's part, transforming the essence from playful romp to thoughtful comic discourse on sexual relationships, appeasing Cleese's deep-rooted hatred of the Bard by allowing him flexibility in the role and the chance to steer Shakespeare away from the clichéd, hands on hips, bellowed style of performance which the actor's disliked.

PBS/BBC co-production.
Kate **SARAH BADEL**
Petruchio **JOHN CLEESE**
Bianca **SUSAN PENHALIGON**
Baptista **JOHN FRANKLYN-ROBBINS**
Gremio **FRANK THORNTON**
Hortensio **JONATHAN CECIL**
Lucentio **SIMON CHANDLER**
Tranio **ANTHONY PEDLEY**
Produced & directed **Jonathan Miller**
BBC2 Broadcast 23 October 1980

TEACH YOURSELF HEATH

An ultra-rare flexidisc, given away as a free gift with the December 1972 issue of *Zigzag* magazine and included with initial pressings of *Monty Python's Previous Record*. Introduced by Michael Palin, it unsubtly satirised the Prime Minister at the time Edward Heath with soundbites from Eric Idle interrupting the instructions.

THAT WAS THE WEEK THAT WAS

John Cleese became involved in this ground-breaking show via his friendship with David Frost during their Footlight days – Frost wisely recruited talented folk from his university including Bill Oddie and John Cleese. Despite only having three sketches used, this was a major breakthrough for Cleese, introducing him to BBC television while still studying. In the show's final year, Odeon released an album of the best moments (Odeon PMC 1197 PCS 3040), put together by George Martin at the very start of Beatlemania. It featured one of John Cleese's contributions – Regella – exposing the stupidity of outlandish statistics in an incomprehensible astronomy lecture. Regella was originally used in the 1962 Footlights show *Double Take*, and Cleese sent it to Frost who bought it for TW3. Several others weren't used.

That Was The Week That Was
DAVID FROST, MILLICENT MARTIN, LANCE PERCIVAL, ROY KINNEAR, WILLIAM RUSHTON, KENNETH COPE & DAVID KERNAN
With **BERNARD LEVIN, JOHN WELLS, JOHN BIRD, ELEANOR BRON, ROY HUDD & FRANKIE HOWERD**
Written by **Christopher Booker, Caryl Brahms, John Cleese, Quentin Crewe, Peter Dobreiner, David Frost, Ron Grainer, Willis Hall, Richard Ingrams, Dave Lee, Peter Lewis, Leslie Mallory, Bill Oddie, Ned Sherrin, Steven Vinaver & Keith Waterson**
Additional writers – **Anthony Jay, David Nobbs, Dennis Potter**

Director/Producer **Ned Sherrin**
Special 29 September 1962 (150 mins) 1st series 24 November 1962–27 April 1963 (23 x 50 mins) 2nd series 28 September–21 December 1963 (13 x 50 mins) That Was The Year That Was 28 December 1963 (100 mins)

THEIR FINEST HOURS

A double bill of comedy plays from Michael Palin and Terry Jones which, although already written, were brought together when the writers were approached by the Crucible Theatre, Sheffield, for any production projects. It was staged from 20 May 1976. The cleverest of the two, *Buchanan's Finest Hour*, was an inspired experiment on the part of Jones and Palin, trying to create an hour of theatre with the actors invisible to the audience – the principals are in fact trapped in two large crates, which is all the audience have to look at on stage.
The second piece, *Underwood's Finest Hour*, was more conventionally *Python*esque, with a cricket-mad doctor refusing to deliver his patient's baby until England finished batting in the test match – with the gallant Derek Underwood coming in as last bat. The piece was received fairly well but failed to transfer.
Suitably, their experimental effort, *Buchanan's Finest Hour*, has had the longest life, being made into a film, *The Box: Buchanan's Finest Hour*, under the direction of ex-Monkee Mickey Dolenz and starring Richard Vernon as Sir Clive Henshaw, Terry Jones as Mr. Harrington, Michael Palin as the French escapologist Dobre Elapso and Charles McKeown as an Italian chap. Years later, in October 1990, the play was staged at Chicago's Second City under the direction of *Python* historian Kim 'Howard' Johnson, which featured an additional tantalising ploy from Jones, with a foot and a fist emerging from the boxes to give the audience both renewed interest in the piece and confirm the fact that these dedicated actors really did perform from within their crates rather than off-stage.

Minimalism – Beckett with the common man touch.

THREE MEN IN A BOAT

For a straight filming of Jerome K. Jerome's masterpiece, the cast enjoyed a glorious summer location filming on the Thames and had to postsync the entire show in the studio. Scriptwriter Stoppard later worked on *Brazil* but here he is happy to capture the spirit of the novel with three fine performances from the stars – Palin in particular being a wonderful extension of David Tomlinson's persona from the 1956 film version.

MICHAEL PALIN
TIM CURRY
STEPHEN MOORE
Screenplay by **Tom Stoppard**
Based on the story by **Jerome K. Jerome**
Producer **Rosemary Hill**
Director **Stephen Frears**
BBC2, 31 December 1975

THREE PIECE SUITE

A series of three half-hour programmes starring Diana Rigg, one of which, *Every Day in Every Way*, starred John Cleese.

Written by **Alan Coren**
Producer **Michael Mills**
BBC2 12 April 1977

TIME BANDITS

Terry Gilliam's lavish, nightmarish fantasy is perhaps the most successful attempt at capturing the wild, adventurous, exciting imaginations and dreams of childhood. A rip-roaring journey through time, space and historical characters. The contrast is between little Kevin's obsession with books and his parents' disinterest, with total commitment to modern gadgets and a tedious life revolving round television game shows. This heralds Gilliam's celebration of the imagination with

the boy's bedroom suddenly invaded by the spirits of adventure. The powerful sequence as a knight on horseback bursts through his wardrobe is the start of almost two hours of flights of fancy, clearly embracing the childhood memories of *The Lion, the Witch and the Wardrobe*, with the land of fantasy obtainable through your own room, while capturing the essence of imagination perfectly on film. Although overshadowed and over-billed by the starry array of impressive cameos, the real stars of the film are David Rappaport and his gang, crusading through holes in the universe, using and abusing their stolen information and clearly enjoying some major acting opportunities in roles playing like a Roald Dahl reworking of the seven dwarfs. Rappaport's performance (complete with Biggles-style hat) is a wonderfully cynical, streetwise creation, bumbling and mumbling his way through the cosmos with his bossed-about but beloved band of companions following his every word. A stunning comic performance, gaining great contrast with the charming performance of Warneck as Kevin (in this world the little boy who is ignored at home is the tallest guy in the group and thus initially a threat and then a hero in Rappaport's eyes) leads to a multi-faceted, touching piece of work. However the height of the six map-pinchers is only used in the narrative during the first historical interlude, during Napoleon's day, with Ian Holm's childish, paranoid leader clutching the gang to his heart as they are even smaller than him. Holm is a delight, bickering with his minions, relishing the mini scenes of violence included in the Punch and Judy show (completed with more than a touch of the *Python*esque macabre with the murder of the puppeteer) and playing the stunned, straight-faced amazement of the gang's reworking of *Me and My Shadow* with utter perfection. It's one of the highlights of the entire film, and Holm's skilful under-playing is the icing on the cake. Of course, it's all a trick to find favour with the great man, enter his

luxurious abode and pinch all his valuables, with the deed being done as Holm drunkenly mumbles on about the various heights of world dictators. That's the beauty of the plan, stealing stuff and then making a quick, untraceable exit through the mists of time. The resulting skip through the decades results in a crash landing into a romantic interlude between Michael Palin and Shelley Duvall, allowing the Python to turn on the British nervousness and girl-shy ramblings.

Palin was originally up for the choice role of Robin Hood and was intended as the only on-screen link with *Monty Python*'s past. In the end, of course, *Time Bandits* rounded up half the old squad, for executive producer Denis O'Brien was very keen to include major draw John Cleese in the cast and project a *Python*-edged feel to the whole project. As it happened Cleese was perfect casting for the ever-so-frightfully polite and well spoken Hood, charmingly greeting his unexpected guests and relieving them of their booty with supercilious grins and warm handshakes. This is, naturally, the definitive moment of *Monty Python*-type comedy in the film – with Cleese and his landed gentry pleasantries alongside the ultimate combination of Gilliam's dark, grime-ridden observational humour and Palin's lighter, more irreverent social parody. The setting is wonderful Middle Ages, following on from the overall feeling of dour atmosphere and filth from *Monty Python and the Holy Grail*, populated by half-chewed, half-brained forest bandits and shabby peasants. Gilliam's direction brilliantly contrasts the reality of the age with Cleese's Hood, straight out of *Kays* catalogue of historical rogues, resplendent in Lincoln green, smothered with niceties and television convention, sporting an over-sized, symbolically comic hat and overflowing with delicious, sarcastic lines. Like Basil Fawlty in full ingratiating mode, Cleese does his stuff brilliantly, relishing the pure genius of the line concerning his flock of poor followers – 'They haven't got two pennies to rub together, but that's because they're poor!' Cleese is the only actor around who could have added such bite to that line, so thank heavens for Mr. O'Brien. Besides, Palin has a choice couple of vignettes along the way, and during this journey through Sherwood Forest, finally finds himself tied to a tree, discovering the onset of his old, unmentionable problem and finally screaming 'I must have fruit!' – it never fails to crack me up and I still can't quite work out why it is so funny but, yes, this is the stuff we want. Gilliam's original hope to fully emerge from the *Python* myth was futile from the beginning, but there are many wonderfully spectacular sequences which highlight his unique cinematic vision and expertise (notably the Grecian feast scene, the chillingly tense sequence with the lads captured in a cage dangling above a bottomless pit of black nothingness and the final, all-for-one battle between the evil genius and tons of fantasy good guys employing westerns heroes, Sherman tanks and community people power).

In the casting too, Gilliam successfully rounded up some huge star names to take centre stage, none more so than Sean Connery, injecting his experience into the project and giving it pretty cool status throughout the industry. In a much quoted script annotation, the writers commented that King Agamemnon, having defeated the bull-headed beastie, removes his helmet to reveal himself as none other than Sean Connery or some equally impressive but cheaper actor! Although he was only available for two weeks, Connery helped launch the film (due to Gilliam's notion of getting the hardest part, the Morocco-based material, out of the way first), eased the tension from both novice child star and novice solo director, gave a majestic, powerful sweep to the contemporary burning house climax and enhanced the film with just a major dose of star, star, star quality. Thankfully, O'Brien had the foresight simply to send Connery the script, which he accepted. Besides, no-one but Sean the man could make such a spellbinding, super dude entrance.

In the less comically oriented section of the film, Gilliam's talent for historical dramatics is well illustrated before the roving gang of time bandits finally track down the happy as Larry Kevin and drag him back into play. As a sort of counterbalance to the muscles and sandals antics of the Connery segment, the film incorporates a moment of pure comedy (Palin's second failed attempt at courting Duvall) and one of those moments of hindsight when the audience comprehend the historical context of the show within the narrative which the main actors don't. Rappaport's ordering of more champagne, 'with plenty of ice!' is followed by a camera pan onto the ship's ring bearing the legend S.S. *Titanic*. It's these little *Dr. Who*-like elements of shared audience knowledge which gives *Time Bandits* that magical, family entertainment fantasy power. Later, Peter Vaughan's groaning Ogre with back pains and Katherine Helmond's sickly sweet wife add to the great roll-call of thespians (enhanced by the impressive Gilliam moment when the giant emerging from the sea with the Ogre's ship nestled atop his head – brilliantly done on the cheap by elongated camera angles and model making), but nothing is quite as impressive as the casting for *Time Bandits'* embodiments of pure evil and pure good. David Warner's charming Devil, full of dark one-liners, fiery temper and (in comparison with Kevin's parents) an obsession with the power of modern technology for the development of evil, is an immaculate picture of anger, furiously hitting out at any point against him and, memorably, in considering one ill-fated follower's idea he mutters 'Good question'. Smooth, fiendish and sophisticated, Warner's nemesis is a very brief bit of ancient bewilderment from Sir Ralph Richardson, playing God like a smart-suited businessman, calm, cool and collected, with a fine line in 'told you so' observations and acts of life-giving miracles. In a brilliant, throw-away mutter to himself Richardson comments, 'Well, I am the nice one!' It's a moment of class acting that will

sent shivers down the spine of any devotee of pure class. If *Brazil* is undoubtedly Gilliam's masterpiece *Time Bandits* has to be his most fun picture.

Did you know? Following major fame with *Bandits*, Rappaport struggled on through other less satisfactory roles before taking his own life. A teacher before trying his hand at acting, he explained that it was God's greatest gift to be 30 and look into the eyes of a child. Sadly, typecast as cute characters and elves, Rappaport threw in the towel. Gilliam enhances this sense of magical, shared experience between his mature heroes and child centre point with a cartoon-like viewpoint, structured around old *Tom and Jerry* shorts and filmed at a level of four feet above the ground to emphasise this. Gilliam made the film for a minuscule £5 million, using his limited budget wisely and allowing the finished product to look grand beyond belief. There's an essence of *Thief of Baghdad* about his fantasy and the small budget really impressed Hollywood backers – a sense of awe quickly dissipated following the major overspend for *Baron Munchausen*! Gilliam bitterly regrets losing one scene from the final cut of *Time Bandits* involving two Edwardian-style knitting ladies who are in fact spiders, capturing knights and devouring them later. Bandit Og is captured and helped to freedom by the rest of the gang with Gilliam constructing a stunning set in lace. Sadly he couldn't afford to film the linking scenes either side of the completed spider sequence and, much to the director's chagrin, it was scrapped. Although the basic plotline was Gilliam's he felt a lighter touch of comedy was needed and recruited *Python* pal Palin to collaborate on the dialogue – basically Gilliam's gags are all rat-eating and arm ripping, while Palin's is more traditional absurdist stuff. The deed was finished in February 1980 and by May they were filming with Connery! Although analysing the dysfunctional sense of modern British family values Gilliam says that his film's message is that 'God is British and evil is American!' with the commercial monster of the States infesting the UK. Even so, evil is perfectly brought to life by the very British David Warner.

Time Bandits had a budget of £5 million and reaped in £80 million but Gilliam, asked to remove more surreal elements such as the eating of rats, threatened to burn the negative if any changes were made. George Harrison described him as 'eccentric bordering on genius'.

Time Bandits
HandMade Films
Robin Hood **JOHN CLEESE**
King Agamemnon **SEAN CONNERY**
Pansy **SHELLEY DUVALL**
Mrs. Ogre **KATHERINE HELMOND**
Napoleon **IAN HOLM**
Vincent **MICHAEL PALIN**
Supreme Being **RALPH RICHARDSON**
Ogre **PETER VAUGHAN**
Evil Genius **DAVID WARNER**
Randall **DAVID RAPPAPORT**
Fidgit **KENNY BAKER**
Wally **JACK PURVIS**
Og **MIKE EDMONDS**
Strutter **MALCOLM DIXON**
Vermin **TINY ROSS**
Kevin **CRAIG WARNOCK**
Kevin's Father **DAVID DAKER**
Kevin's Mother **SHEILA FEARN**
Compere **JIM BROADBENT**
Reginald **JOHN YOUNG**
Beryl **MYRTLE DEVENISH**
Stunt Knight/Hussar **BRIAN BOWES**
1st Refugee **LEON LISSEK**
Lucien **TERENCE BAYLER**
Neguy **PRESTON LOCKWOOD**
Theatre Manager **CHARLES McKEOWN**
Puppeteer **DAVID LELAND**
The Great Rumbozo **JOHN HUGHMAN**
Robber Leader **DERRICK O'CONNOR**
Robbers **NEIL McCARTHY & DECLAN MULHOLLAND**
Arm Wrestler **PETER JONFIELD**
Robert **DEREK DEADMAN**
Benson **JEROLD WELLS**
Cartwright **ROGER FROST**
Baxi Brazilia III **MARTIN CARROLL**
Horseflesh **MARCUS POWELL**
Bull-headed Warrior **WINSTON DENNIS**
Greek Fighting Warrior **DEL BAKER**
Greek Queen **JULIETTE JAMES**
Giant **IAN MUIR**

Troll Father **MARK HOLMES**
Fireman **ANDREW MacLACHLAN**
Voice of TV Announcer **CHRIS GRANT**
Voice of Supreme Being **TONY JAY**
Supreme Being's Face **EDWIN FINN**
Screenplay by **Michael Palin & Terry Gilliam**
Music **Mike Moran**
Songs & additional material **George Harrison**
Me and My Shadow arranged by **Trevor Jones**
Music producer **Ray Cooper**
Production designer **Milly Burns**
Art director **Norman Garwood**
Hairdressing & make-up **Maggie Weston & Elaine Carew**
Production manager **Graham Ford**
Camera operator **David Garfath**
Assistant director **Simon Hinkly**
Casting director **Irene Lamb**
Costumes **Jim Acheson** in association with **Hazel Cote**
Photography **Peter Biziou**
Special effects senior technician **John Bunker**
Editor & 2nd unit director **Julian Doyle**
Associate producer **Neville C. Thompson**
Executive producers **George Harrison & Denis O'Brien**
Produced & directed by **Terry Gilliam**
Filmed at Lee International Studios and on location in England, Wales & Morocco
1981, 110 mins

TO NORWAY, HOME OF GIANTS

Made by the Norwegian Broadcasting Company as their entry for the 1979 Montreux Television Awards. John Cleese hosts this hilarious mock travelogue as the unconvincingly named Norman Fearless. With two and a half days filming and a brief to stick to the scripted dialogue Cleese did his bit in Oslo and returned home. The film won two prizes at the festival although, ironically, the BBC's *Fawlty Towers* – a late replacement for a *Goodies* show – won nothing!

BBC2 screened – May 1979
Nrk-Norwegian Broadcasting Company

THE TOM MACHINE

A short film concerning a robot maid (voiced by John Cleese) and his human master who gradually sees his grasp on life drift over to his mechanical invention.

British National Film School
Written & directed by **Paul Bamborough**
47 mins, 1980

TOO MUCH SUN

Lame, dubious and poorly scripted inheritance comedy which wastes Eric Idle in the lead role, playing a homosexual who has to have a child in order to get his hands on the family wealth. In his defence, Idle admits he only took on the film in order to work with comedian Jon Lovitz, who was subsequently sued by the studio for backing out of the project. Nevertheless, Idle still maintained an interest in the film's concept, believing there were parallels with Shakespearean comedy – yeah right!

Cinetel Films/Columbia
Sonny Rivers **ERIC IDLE**
Bitsy Rivers **ANDREA MARTIN**
Father Seamus **KELLY JIM HAYNIE**
Susan Connor **LAURA ERNST**
George Bianco **LEO ROSSI**
Old Man Rivers **HOWARD DUFF**
Reed Richmond **ROBERT DOWNEY Jr**
Screenplay by **Robert Downey Sr, Laura Ernst & Al Schwartz**
Photography **Robert Yeoman**
Editor **Joseph D'Augustine**
Producer **Lisa M. Hansen**
Director **Robert Downey Sr**
100 mins, 1991

THE TRANSFORMERS: THE MOVIE

Nutty animated feature film based on the popular Transformer toy range and cartoon series. Involving a couple of days recording in New York, Idle plays the part of Robot Wreck-Gar alongside an impressive array of guest voices including *Star Trek* icon

Leonard Nimoy and even Orson Welles, finding money for his own projects in any way he could. The characters certainly seemed more at home at Toys 'R Us than on the big screen and the whole thing looks like a drug induced reaction to the *Star Wars* explosion. The mighty, scrolled narrated legend at the beginning is a pure pinch from 'In a galaxy far, far away', while even the female Transformer adopts a pseudo-Princess Leia hairdo.

Overrun with dodgy transforming robots and, much worse, a retro backlash of heavy rock muzak on the soundtrack, this is pretty mindless all round despite scoring a big hit with its youthful market. Tackling the defence of the American dream or something like that – with lines like 'I've got better things to do tonight than die!' yeah right! – the makers toss in everything including jet-powered skateboards, gravel-voiced evil figures and talking, metal eating insect-like robots – an everyday story of simple folk really. There's an endearing buddy, buddy relationship with the good guy robots, the violence is well orchestrated while the fire-breathing dinosaur robots and weird shark-like things pad out the plot with throwaway one-liners and collapsing metal teeth. Orson Welles is pretty damn impressive as the ultimate figure of evil meeting his match in a climatic scene which crosses elements from *King Kong* and *The Night on Bald Mountain* section from *Fantasia*, but even his majestic cinematic genius clout can't stop this being a load of old guff. Certainly, Eric Idle doesn't help very much, vastly under-used and grabbing some fairly uninspired lines late on in the picture – he's not heard until 50 minutes in – his cynical comic robot creation, spouting television-influenced dialogue, talking in rhyming greeting cards language while even injecting a *Python*esque burst of tongue in cheek advertising jargon and American-styled quiz master banter, crops up on and off while much of his garbled material is totally unintelligible. Still it's Eric so he always raises a smile, although he's wasted and even the most die-

hard *Python* completist probably wouldn't go out of his way to catch this one.

De Laurentiis Entertainment Group
Featuring the voices of **ORSON WELLES as** Unicron
Ultra Magnus **ROBERT STACK**
Galratron **LEONARD NIMOY**
Wreck-Gar **ERIC IDLE**
Hot Rod, Rodmus Prime **JUDD NELSON**
Jazz **SCATMAN CROTHERS**
Producers **Joe Bacal & Tom Griffin**
Screenplay by **Ron Friedman**
Music **Vince DiCola**
Supervising editor **Steven C. Brown**
Director **Nelson Shin**
86 mins, 1986

TWELVE MONKEYS

This is Terry Gilliam playing the game of Hollywood and most definitely on his own unique terms. Following his own rule-breaking work on *The Fisher King* by directing a screenplay which he didn't write, Gilliam was tempted back to the comparative ease of just working as a studio director for this wondrous blast of futuristic mindbending. Proof, if indeed proof were needed, that Gilliam is the most original film-maker of his generation. Inspired by Chris Marker's film *La Jetée*, a montage of still images which details an unfortunate time-travelling man witnessing his own death, *Twelve Monkeys* grabs the basic premise and creates a surreal, disturbing, emotive and totally engrossing film entertainment. Cinematic clichés, from likeable hero to wholesome romance and cartoon violence to stereotyped authority figures, are enriched with a sincerity sadly lacking in most big budget Hollywood fests.

Embracing the quick return trick of employing huge star names, Gilliam again twists convention by allowing Bruce Willis to move away from wise-cracking macho man to embittered, confused and vicious character. His adult past is obviously one of crime (after all, we meet him in a criminal commune like a Fritz Lang set) while his disturbed mind is fuelled even

more by continual time-travel, misunderstanding people from the 1990s and facing hair-curling experiences within a mental institution.

On a grand scale this is a *Hamlet* for the new millennium, towering through a corrupt civilisation, struggling to eke out an existence with his own animal resources while lapsing between thoughts of his own, and other people's, insanity. Even more compellingly, we know he is sane but for a brief moment he doubts even his own belief – but once he violently removes his own tooth we know the mission is well and truly back on. The performance of Bruce Willis is an awe-inspiring one, building on his hard-bitten persona from Tarantino's *Pulp Fiction* to create an even darker, more mysterious side of his blueprint action hero.

Brad Pitt, on the other hand, signed up just before ballistic super-stardom with *Interview with the Vampire* and *Legends of the Fall*, but giving the film a major publicity buzz on release, completely overthrows his glam hunk characterisations to give a stunning portrayal of madness, injecting manic hand-movements, garbled but sensible flights of fancy and cold understanding of his own insanity – enhanced by the cartoon sound effects from the television reflecting his animated, surreal mannerisms. Even more terrifying, with traits from his 1990 performance still in evidence in the respectability of 1996's evening wear, Pitt's staring eyes and ever mobile features (apart from often looking amazingly like Gilliam himself circa the Spanish Inquisition sketch) signals pure driven action against the human race. Pitt was justly honoured with an Oscar nomination for an outstanding performance and won the Golden Globe for Best Supporting Actor. Madeleine Stowe, the female romantic lead in anybody else's movie, really symbolises the warm face of science, with an understanding of mental problems and ultimately getting drawn into Cole's fight to discover the truth. Usually within five minutes the

Which one is really crazy? Bruce Willis and Brad Pitt in *Twelve Monkeys*

principal leads would be at it like knifes but this is Gilliam cinema, where characters are realistic and touching. The hostage situation between the two is played with sheer conviction, with Gilliam coaxing performances of true depth from his players. The one sign of love at the airport, after more than an age of life and death perils, is all the more moving for the built-up tension it releases. Willis, yearning for just one more brush of her lips is denied and accepting of the fact. This is cinema with style. The story, of course, is all things to all men, spanning a time zone of 40 years and allowing Gilliam plenty of scope in contrasting the future with our present/recent past – Willis's well distant past. Willis, a sane man trapped in an unfamiliar world who see him as mad, reacts against their injustice like a caged beast, but this is modern America where no man is taken to heart. The scenes set in 2035, complete with familiar *Python* project actor Simon Jones (as part of the cold, nameless band of scientists merely billed as their occupation rather than

characterisation), follow on from Gilliam's brilliant *Brazil* vision, with the 21st century reverting to the glories of early industrial procedure. It is a world of pulleys and steam valves, clocks and pumps, all twisted to embrace the new age with a world-weary longing for the past. The film's most moving moment and, for me, arguably the high mark of Willis's performance, comes with Cole's eye-dampening, pure undiluted love for Fats Domino's *Blueberry Hill* on the radio. A remnant from the past that symbolises the best of the disease-free 20th century. This is intellectual cinematic skating around deep logic with enough high powered, energetic detective work to operate on a purely entertainment-based level. The Cassandra theory of time-travelling prophets predicting the correct future because they have already lived it sets up a stunning train of events and Gilliam's visual genius creates a spell-binding few minutes of hell in the First World War trenches. His ability to lace major Hollywood names into his demented, off-centre universe allows the best of both worlds – with

the studio more than happy to open a big new Willis movie while Gilliam effortlessly vindicates his own ideals by not compromising the subject matter. The initial isolated walk through deserted 21st century American is brilliantly achieved, with breathtaking, Oscar-nominated, condom-like costume design from Julie Weiss, a bleak midwinter setting with shock appearances from various wild animals and a subdued anti-heroic performance from Willis, at ease with fear and self-protection. The snatch of *Silent Night*, the recurring hazy childhood nightmare and Willis regressing as Stowe buys disguise clothes all signpost this film as a triumph of independence over the Hollywood factory.

An obsession with old movies and, as with *Brazil*, The Marx Brothers, helps to balance the stark insanity of 1990 with throwaway references to *Monkey Business* (which Pitt loves and seizes the day with) – while allowing Gilliam the film connoisseur to comment on the annoyance factor and disrespect of commercials within televised film as well as a barely audible but priceless Chicoism. Animation plays an important visual part as well, with extracts from Tex Avery and Woody Woodpecker time-travelling lightening the tone of uncontrolled, visual madness, while Buckmaster's score and the gloriously disjointed recurring theme – *Suite Punta Del Este* by Astor Piazzolla – captures the strangeness of the tale with an upbeat sense of destiny. However, the most poignant filmic link is connected to *Vertigo*, with the Willis allegory about movies running parallel with his experiences, the very notion of his disguised persona embracing the artificial creation sub-text of the movie, the obsession with eyes at the start and close of both *Twelve Monkeys* and *Vertigo*, and, at the end of the day, a few seconds excuse to enjoy some class material from James Stewart and Kim Novak. The shocked reaction to the Tippi Hedren attack in *The Birds*, the character allegiance with the audience involved in the cinema experience and the very Hitchcockian style of much of the film – untrusted and incarcerated falsely (*The Wrong Man*), a sense of danger that only a couple know about and frantic race to save the day (*The Man Who Knew Too Much*), the all powerful McGuffin is potent.

It's a film that latches onto the cinematic glories of the past as a link to the future, a warped, fascinating and beautiful piece of art and an adventure film with enough twists and turns for a score of serials. A less personal piece of film-making than *Brazil* or *Time Bandits* but a movie with Terry Gilliam's name running all the way through it. Finally, with a major big budget and star name blockbusting success, the director has been taken to the heart of Hollywood. And totally without compromise.

Twelve Monkeys
Polygram Filmed Entertainment & Universal Pictures Present
An Atlas Entertainment Production
James Cole **BRUCE WILLIS**
Doctor Kathryn Railly **MADELEINE STOWE**
Jeffrey Goines **BRAD PITT**
Dr. Goines **CHRISTOPHER PLUMMER**
Dr. Fletcher **FRANK GORSHIN**
Jose **JON SEDA**
Engineer **ERNEST ABUBA**
Microbiologist **BILL RAYMOND**
Zoologist **SIMON JONES**
Geologist **BOB ADRIAN**
Astrophysicist **CAROL FLORENCE**
Botanist **H. MICHAEL WALLS**
Young Cole **JOSEPH MELITO**
Scarface **MICHAEL CHANCE**
Tiny **VERNON CAMPBELL**
Poet **IRMA ST. PAULE**
Detective Franid **JOEY PERILLO**
Policemen **BRUCE KIRKPATRICK & WILFRED WILLIAMS**
Billings **ROZWILL YOUNG**
Ward Nurse **NELL JOHNSON**
L.J. Washington **FRED STROTHER**
Dr. Casey **RICK WARNER**
Dr. Goodin **ANTHONY 'CHIP' BRENZA**
Harassed Mother **JOLET HARRIS**
Waltzing Woman Patient **DRUCIE McDANIEL**
Old Man Patient **JOHN BLASSE**
Patient at Gate **LOUIS LIPPA**
X-Ray Doctor **STAN KANG**
WW1 Captain **PAT DIASS**
WW1 Sergeant **AARON MICHAEL LACEY**

Dr. Peters **DAVID MORSE**
Professor **CHARLES TECHMAN**
Marilou **JANN ELLIS**
Officer No. 1 **JOHNNIE HOBBS JR**
Anchorwoman **JANET L. ZAPPALA**
Evangelist **THOMAS ROY**
Louie/Rasping Voice **HARRY O'TOOLE**
Thugs **KORCHENKO & CHUCK JEFFREYS**
Teddy **LISA GAY HAMILTON**
Fale **FELIX A. PIRE**
Bee **MATTHEW ROSS**
Agents **BARRY PRICE & JOHN PANZARELLA**
Detective Dalva **PAUL MESHEJAN**
Kweskin **KEVIN THIGPEN**
Hotel Clerk **LEE GOLDEN**
Wallace **JOSEPH McKENNA**
Plain Clothes Cop **JEFF TANNER**
Store Clerk **FAITH POTTS**
Weller **MICHAEL RYAN SEGAL**
Woman Cabbie **ANNIE GOLDEN**
Ticket Agent **LISA TALERICO**
Airport Detective **STEPHEN BRIDGEWATER**
Plump Businessman **FRANKLIN HUFFMAN**
Gift Store Clerk **JOANN S. DAWSON**
Airport Security **JACK DOUGHERTY, LENNY DANIELS & HERBERT C. HAULS JR**
Impatient Traveller **CHARLEY SCALES**
Terrified Traveller **CAROLYN WALKER**
Stunt co-ordinator **Phil Neilson**
Stunt double for Mr. Willis **Terry Jackson**
Stunt agent **John Copeman**
Stunt guest **Cynthia Neilson**
Stunt waiter **Sean Kelly**
Stunts **Doug Crosby, George Agular, Ronald Jaynes, Paul Couch, Michael Walter, Phil Nelson, E.J. Evans, Chuck Jeffreys, Billy Anagnos, Elliot Santiago, Brian Smyj, Steve Earl Martin, Sandy Alexander, David Lomax & Steve Santosusso**
Interrogation Room set inspired by the work of **Lebbeus Woods**
Screenplay by **David Peoples & Janet Peoples**
Music **Paul Buckmaster**
Costume designer **Julie Weiss**
1st Assistant director **Mark Egerton**
Art director **William Lado Skinner**
Set decorator **Crispian Sallis**
Camera operator **Craig Haagensen**
Casting **Margery Simkin**
Editor **Mick Audsley**
Production designer **Jeffrey Beecroft**

Photography **Roger Pratt**
Associate producers **Kelley Smith-Wait & Mark Egerton**
Executive producers **Robert Cavallo, Gary Levinson & Robert Kosberg**
Co-producer **Lloyd Phillips**
Producer **Charles Roven**
Director **Terry Gilliam**
1995, 127 mins

TWICE A FORTNIGHT

Following their rather redundant positions as script-editors for *A Series of Birds*, Terry Jones and Michael Palin found themselves filling the same roles for this comedy show headlining Graeme Garden – with Jonathan Lynn & Dilys Watling. Contrary to some reference books, Tim Brooke-Taylor did not appear. A ten-week run which debuted on 21 October 1967 under the direction of Tony Palmer, it was ostensibly a live show which featured filmed inserts written and performed by Jones and Palin. Thankfully, owning to Jones and his obsession in retaining his penned material, these invaluable inserts survive – the only elements of the show to remain in archive, capturing the superb surreal quality of their early work with sketches like The Door (featuring Jones and Palin as two chaps carrying a disconnected door and discovering a fantasy work behind it) and The Battle of Hastings, which would later re-manifest itself in their hugely important, pre-*Python* series *The Complete and Utter History of Britain*. Springing from a clutch of old *I'm Sorry I'll Read That Again* gags and attracting the same hearty audience involvement, the comedy was interspersed with class rock performances from Cream, Cat Stevens, Small Faces and The Who, but ultimately the programme was marred by disagreements between Bill Oddie and Tony Palmer – Oddie didn't like the filmed interludes, considering them 'so-what' moments, pieces which looked great but weren't instantly funny. Mind you, these certainly influenced his fresh approach in *The Goodies*, when visual comedy was the key.

A second series was planned but quickly abandoned, although *Twice A Fortnight* itself was popular enough to warrant a further series for Garden (this time with Brooke-Taylor), *Broaden Your Mind*, broadcast from 28 October – 2 December 1968. Terry Jones and Michael Palin again contributed sketches, alongside John Cleese, Graham Chapman and Eric Idle.

Introduced by **Ronald Fletcher**
Produced & directed by **Tony Palmer**
21 October–23 December 1967 BBC1

VIDEO ARTS

This hugely influential outfit started in 1975 when Cleese was offered the chance to invest in training films for business management. The market at that time was small and predictable, utilising old American footage and dry lectures. Cleese, writing and performing many of the films, studied effective business skills and drew on his teaching experience, injecting humour into the message for an entertaining, informative package. With five major informative points and loads of non-verbal pointers, Cleese rounded up many old colleagues, like Tim Brooke-Taylor, Graeme Garden and Jonathan Lynn, plus fellow *Doctor in the House* survivor Angharad Rees and pros like June Whitfield, Bill Owen and Bernard Cribbins, to orchestrate a string of nearly 100 films, 90 percent of which had a heavy comedy slant. Although Cleese was not involved in all of these, his films have proved the most popular, usually latching onto his *Fawlty/Python* persona of pompous, aggressive chap who makes bombastic mistakes, while presenting him with the worldly wise, ongoing characterisation of St. Peter, dishing out good advice while surrounded by the swirling, atmospheric mists of eternal peace. Cleese has since sold his shares in the company, despite still writing and acting in the new films (including one with Prince Charles no less), happy in the knowledge that his scheme livened up a tried filmic niche proving healthy competition and comedy geared material from other firms.

Eight of these films were broadcast on BBC2 between 6 October and 24 November 1975 as:
The Selling Line – Who Sold You This, Then?
It's Alright, It's Only a Customer
The Competitive Spirit
In Two Minds
Awkward Customers
More Awkward Customers
I'll Think About It
How Not to Exhibit Yourself.
Two more series, Company Accident and The Office Line, followed in 1979.

Cleese summed up his success in the field thus – 'I find it rather easy to portray a businessman. Being bland, rather cruel and incompetent comes naturally to me.'

Awkward Customers – Starring **JOHN CLEESE** as the angry Mr. Tiger, the pompous Mrs. Camel and the suspicious Mrs. Ferret.
Written by **Antony Jay & John Cleese**
Director **Peter Robinson**
24 mins.
The Balance Sheet Barrier – Starring **JOHN CLEESE** as Julian Carruthers, the manager. With **RONNIE CORBETT** as Ron Scroggs, thrifty small businessman. Written by **Antony Jay**
Director **Peter Robinson**
30 mins.
Budgeting – Starring **JOHN CLEESE** as Julian Carruthers.
With **JOHN BIRD** as Scroggs.
Written by **Graeme Garden.**
Director **Peter Robinson**
30 mins.
Can We Please Have That the Right Way Round? – Starring **JOHN CLEESE** explaining the importance of equipment familiarity. With **JAMES COSSINS.**
Written by **Denis Norden**
Director **Peter Robinson**

The Cold Call – Starring **JOHN CLEESE** as an inexperienced telephone salesman. With **JONATHAN LYNN & LINDA JAMES.**
Written by **Jonathan Lynn & Antony Jay**
Director **Peter Robinson**
24 mins.
The Control of Working Capital – Starring **JOHN CLEESE** as Julian Carruthers.
With **RONNIE CORBETT** as Ron Scroggs
Written by **Antony Jay**
Director **Peter Robinson**
26 mins.
Cost, Profit and Break-Even – Starring **JOHN CLEESE** as Julian Carruthers.
With **JOHN BIRD** as Scroggs.
Written by **Antony Jay**
Director **Peter Robinson**
23 mins.
Depreciation and Inflation – Starring **JOHN CLEESE** as Julian Carruthers.
With **JOHN BIRD** as Scroggs.
Written by **Antony Jay**
Director **Peter Robinson**
17 mins.
Decisions, Decisions – Starring **JOHN CLEESE** as the manager, finding solutions to his organisation problems via visitations from such historical figures as Queen Elizabeth I, Churchill and Field Marshal Montgomery. With **PRUNELLA SCALES & NIGEL HAWTHORNE.**
Written by **Jonathan Lynn**
Director **Peter Robinson**
28 mins.
How Am I Doing? – Starring **JOHN CLEESE** as Ethelred the Unready, Ivan the Terrible and William the Silent.
Written by **Jonathan Lynn.**
Director **Peter Robinson.**
26 mins.
I'd Like a Word With You – Starring **JOHN CLEESE** in the final part of the Ethelred the Unready, Ivan the Terrible and William the Silent trilogy.
Written by **Jonathan Lynn**
Director **Peter Robinson**
27 mins.
The Importance of Mistakes – A lecture by **JOHN CLEESE**
33 mins.
In Two Minds – Starring **JOHN CLEESE** examining the problems between customer and assistant. With **TIM BROOKE-TAYLOR & CONNIE BOOTH.**
Written by **John Cleese & Antony Jay.**

Director **Peter Robinson**
18 mins.
Man Hunt – Starring **JOHN CLEESE** as three extremes of incorrect Managerial interviewers, thelred the Unready, the overbearing Ivan the Terrible and the unclear William the Silent.
Written by **John Cleese & Antony Jay**
Director **Peter Robinson**
31 mins.
The Meeting of Minds – Starring **JOHN CLEESE** in a sequel to In Two Minds. With **TIM BROOKE-TAYLOR & CONNIE BOOTH**
Written by **John Cleese & Antony Jay**
Director **Peter Robinson**
15 mins.
Meetings, Bloody Meetings – Starring **JOHN CLEESE** as the Manager on trial for bad organisation. With **GEORGE A. COOPER & TIMOTHY WEST** as The Judge
Written by **John Cleese & Antony Jay**
Director **Peter Robinson**
30 mins.
More Awkward Customers – Starring **JOHN CLEESE.**
Written by **Antony Jay & John Cleese**
Director **Peter Robinson**
31 mins.
More Bloody Meetings – Starring **JOHN CLEESE** as the Manager. With **GRAEME GARDEN & DAVE PROWSE** as Bonzo the Nurse
Written by **Antony Jay**
Director **Charles Crichton**
Return on Investment – Starring **JOHN CLEESE** as Julian Carruthers. With **JOHN BIRD** as Scroggs.
Written by **Graeme Garden**
Director **Peter Robinson**
20 mins.
The Unorganised Manager – A four-part serial starring **JOHN CLEESE** as St. Peter With **JAMES BOLAM** as Richard Lewis. Part 1, Damnation 24 mins. Part 2, Salvation 26 mins. Part 3, Lamentations 20 mins. Part 4, Revelations 29 mins. Parts 1 & 2 written by **Jonathan Lynn**, Parts 3 & 4 written by **Andrew Marshall & David Renwick**.
Director **Charles Crichton**.
Who Sold You This, Then? – Starring **JOHN CLEESE** as Charlie Jenkins. With **JONATHAN LYNN**.
Written by **Antony Jay & John Cleese**.
Director **Peter Robinson**
23 mins.

Working Capital – Starring **JOHN CLEESE**
With **RONNIE CORBETT**

WE HAVE WAYS OF MAKING YOU LAUGH

Or, as Eric Idle remembers it, they didn't! Importantly this was the first programme ever broadcast by the newly formed London Weekend Television and highlighted producer Humphrey Barclay's keenness to embrace every fledging avenue for his comedy projects. Thus, following the first series of Do Not Adjust Your Set and before he took that show over to the new network, Barclay recruited Eric Idle and Terry Gilliam to launch this series. Basically it was an old-fashioned chat show format, with witty one-liners provided from seasoned witty one-liner providers like series regulars Dick Vosburgh and Dennis Greene. The host was witty one-liner master Frank Muir, while Eric Idle provided the fresh blood with on-screen appearances and written contributions.
The talk show format would rely on contrived jokes and be interspersed with sketches from Idle, while poor old Terry Gilliam, plonked on the sidelines, was instructed to draw amusing caricatures of the performers in action. The camera would look over his shoulder to see his progress while the show lumbered on. The first programme, performed live in front of an audience, was a huge success, but teething problems and a technician's strike resulted in the plugs being pulled and the transmission was scuppered. The show's greatest legacy was Gilliam's first attempts at cut-out animation. Dick Vosburgh had collected scores of dubious linking gags and puns peddled by the flamboyant disc jockey Jimmy Young. With only a £400 budget and two weeks to get the animated film completed, Gilliam used the quicker, cheaper option of cut-outs, broke boundaries and created a sensation. Gilliam followed up with a spellbinding history of the Whoopee cushion before submitting the truly revolutionary, immortal and Python-signposting Beware the Elephant. With limited money and limited knowledge in traditional animation, Gilliam delighted in the relative ease of cut-outs, allowing his imagination full flight with the materials at hand – the Python style was born.

Presented by **Frank Muir**
Producer **Humphrey Barclay**
Director **Bill Turner**
London Weekend Television broadcast 23 August 1968 – 18 October 1968

THE WEEKEND

A Michael Palin play which ran for a limited time at the Strand Theatre in 1991. Based on reaction to his own childhood and the underlying tension between his parents, Palin constructed a one-set, suburban comedy with a darker side. It traced his father's life with a past aching for lost business success in the 1920s, a Cambridge education and a mixture of depression, war and children culminating in bitter regret. Originally written in 1980, Palin included major elements of expected straight farce via 'I don't believe it!' scenarios of incontinent dogs and nutty granddaughters, but this is poignantly contrasted with the later developments reflecting suicide, maternal struggles, pent-up misery, alcoholism and adultery. Richard Wilson and Angela Thorne starred as the retired couple Stephen and Virginia in a work which played like East of Ipswich meets One Foot in the Grave via Joe Orton.

Stephen **RICHARD WILSON**
Virginia **ANGELA THORNE**
Mrs Finlay **YVONNE D'ALPRA**
Duff Gardner **JOHN RINGHAM**
Charlotte **JOANNA FOREST**

Diana **JULIE PEASGOOD**
Alan **JONATHAN COY**
Bridget Gardner **MARCIA WARREN**
Hugh Bedales **MICHAEL MEDWIN**
Director **Robin Lefevre**

WHOOPS APOCALYPSE

Ambitious and expensive satire of
world politics leading up to World
War III and nuclear destruction which
saw John Cleese team up with old
Cambridge pal Humphrey Barclay for
the first time since *Doctor At Large*
in 1971. Moving totally away from
the sophisticated authority figure that
made him a star, Cleese was delighted
to play six, strongly defined, quickly
completed (each took just one day),
gloriously eccentric characters,
embracing a Swede, an Indian, a
Frenchmen, a West Country yokel, a
wild-haired zoo keeper and, best of
all, a South American terrorist with
Cleese almost unrecognisable behind
the make-up. Sadly Cleese was not
involved in the more widely available
movie version which starred Peter
Cook, Alexei Sayle and Rik Mayall.

Whoops Apocalypse
President **JOHNNY CYCLOPS
BARRY MORSE**
The Deacon **JOHN BARRON**
Premier Dubienkin **RICHARD
GRIFFITHS**
Commissar Solzhenitsyn **ALEXEI SAYLE**
Jay Garrick **ED BISHOP**
Shah Mashiq Rassim **BRUCE
MONTAGUE**
Abdad **DAVID KELLY**
French Foreign Minister **CHARLES KAY**
Kevin Pork **PETER JONES**
Foreign Secretary **GEOFFREY PALMER**
Lacrobat **JOHN CLEESE**
Screenplay by **Andrew Marshall &
David Renwick**
Producer **Humphrey Barclay**
Director **John Reardon**
London Weekend Television December
1981

THE WIND IN THE WILLOWS

Animated version of Kenneth
Grahame's classic tale from the same
studio that made *The Snowman* and

Yellow Submarine. A year in the
making and employing a staff of 300
people, this is a charming, faithful
retelling of the classic tale with Palin
turning on the dignified, sniffing
attitude for Ratty (the following year
Eric Idle was to do the honours for
Terry Jones). A sequel, *Winter In The
Willows*, followed, again with the
vocal talents of Palin, Mayall and
Bennett.

Grandmother/Narrator **VANESSA
REDGRAVE**
Toad **RIK MAYALL**
Rat **MICHAEL PALIN**
Mole **ALAN BENNETT**
Badger **MICHAEL GAMBON**
Magistrate **JAMES VILLIERS**
Gaoler's Daughter **EMMA CHAMBERS**
Barge Woman **JUDY CORNWELL**
Boatman **BARRY FOSTER**
Other Voices **ENN REITEL, DAVID
SINCLAIR & MARK LOCYER**
Director **Dave Unwin**
Producer **John Coates**
Broadcast Christmas Day, 5-05pm–6-
30pm, ITV, 1995

THE WIND IN THE WILLOWS

The first major *Monty Python*
reunion since Chapman's death, while
Terry Jones (in his multi-capacity as
actor, writer and director) tries to
spice up the action, in terms of
narrative this is still a fairly faithful
retelling of Kenneth Grahame's
classic riverbank tale. Jones brings a
sense of corrupted modernity to the
long since gone halcyon days of
idyllic country life while still
retaining the basic evil-versus-good
battle of the animal community. The
weasels are transformed from black
hat baddies to money-obsessed
'Thatcherite Children', destroying
their own environment in order to
built a dog food factory and
threatening our hapless heroes with a
crunching machine straight out of the
world of Terry Gilliam – brilliantly
realised by Jones within a meagre
budget of £10 million. Cynical, witty,
darkly sarcastic and humanised as
unscrupulous property developers,
eager to stab each other in the back
as the glorious Town Hall collapses

about them, the weasels are led by a
snarling central turn from Anthony
Sher, the most human of the
creatures with business suit, bowler
hat, piercing eyes behind John
Lennon glasses and a deliciously
modulated voice of evil. He heads the
only copper-bottom surreal
*Python*esque moment in the film,
with the brainstorming, dismem-
bered-limb, grotesquely dark song.
Lightening the horrific tendencies of
the weasel with a fine sense of Three
Stooges-like knockabout physical
comedy, Jones contrasts Sher's
distinguished baddie with a
distinguished thespian goodie in the
shape of Nicol Williamson's Badger.
The old school guru, played like a
grumpy but fine-minded Headmaster,
Williamson injects Scottish pearls of
wisdom and ponderous planning into
the slapstick, family values of Jones's
concept. The guest stars are all good
value, notably Nigel Planer's slimy
car salesman, Stephen Fry's aged
Judge and an all too brief Northern
tea-lady from Victoria Wood, while
up against two seasoned actors and
two seasoned Pythons, Steve Coogan
does a superb job as Mole, capturing
the self-doubt, self-pity and
endearingly sympathetic elements of
the original text.
However, by far the biggest treat
within the cast is the chance to enjoy
four *Monty Python* members joining
forces, albeit not all in the same
scene, blessing this delightful, family
entertainment with a happy wallow
in the comedy from a legendary team
but wisely without totally embracing
the ethos of the movement. Terry
Jones is simply perfect as Toad,
bloated, all green make-up and
perfectly timed 'Poop Poop's. As
director, Jones also allows himself a
wonderful, eye-catching entrance,
enjoying a character build-up
between Rat and Mole, a long
sweeping camera pan across his
luxurious grounds, nestling on a
close-up of a huge newspaper from
behind which Toad peers. A brilliant
piece of cinema. Eric Idle gives
arguably his finest film performance
as a frightfully well-mannered and
endearing Ratty, equipped with the
oft-repeated sight gag of pranged

whiskers, delighting in a wistful delivery of the fondly remembered 'Messing about in boats' diatribe and waxing lyrical on the contained, self-sufficient lifestyle of the riverbank. His sympathetic shake of the head and raised eyebrows at Toad's latest hare-brained scheme is perfect and, naturally, the film really kicks into classic mode when the two Pythons battle each other with false promises, false modesty and false pity. The various escapades are brilliantly played in children's fantasy terms with an understanding of bleak, embittered comedy tradition as Toad cunningly tries to out-fox his 'for your own good' captor.

Jones and Idle carry the movie with two outstanding leads but there is a lot of help from another couple of ex-Pythons with cameos from John Cleese and Michael Palin. Sadly, Palin is all but wasted as the friendly, all-knowing Sun, looking down on Jones's perils with told-you-so advice, while Cleese, in, if anything, an even smaller role, is quite brilliant as a typically irascible lawyer, happily condemning his charge to imprisonment with a string of archetypal Cleesian observations delivered with so much legal conviction that his two minutes on screen remain one of the strongest memories. You would have thought that Terry Gilliam could have been tossed in for a word or two. Sorry, but I love nostalgic reunion appearances and any film that welcomes four ex-Pythons should really go for broke – we should really have had Graham Chapman singing a snatch of *Free As A Bird* as well!! Anyway, back to reality: Jones's whimsical-cum-corrupted vision of a beloved childhood treasure is a pleasing and effective romp.

Did you know? Indeed, on the object of *Python* reunions, Terry Jones had, in fact, written a cameo role for the River, which was to advise Toad and the gang while interacting with Palin's Sun role. The part was earmarked for Terry Gilliam but was subsequently cut out of the script. Pity... A European law of authorship allowed Kenneth Grahame's work to

pass into public domain for a very short time and thus, when Terry Jones was commissioned to write *The Wind in the Willows* there were as many as six rival productions in the offing, including the much praised Alan Bennett adaptation over at Paramount. In the end, Jones' was the only version to make it into production, and several critics, besotted by the Bennett National Theatre version, took an instant dislike to the Jones film merely because it had curtailed the filming of Bennett's screenplay. Jones was approached about the project in January 1995, during Syrian location work on *Crusades*, and having never read the Kenneth Grahame book as a child, having only fair memories of A.A. Milne's *Toad of Toad Hall* and, himself, professing great affection for the Bennett stage version, found it a challenge to adapt the vintage classic for a modern generation, developing Bennett's naughty weasels into 'greed is good' baddies. Steve Coogan was such a huge fan of *Python* that he was almost in shock appearing in the same movie as Jones, Idle, Cleese and Palin – he would often fete Terry Jones and politely ask him to do 25-year-old sketches that the young pretender had learnt by heart as a kid. Jones himself was greatly impressed by Coogan's comic ability and predicted he would be the next Peter Sellers.

The Wind In The Willows
Allied Filmmakers
Toad **TERRY JONES**
Rat **ERIC IDLE**
Mole **STEVE COOGAN**
Badger **NICOL WILLIAMSON**
Tea Lady **VICTORIA WOOD**
Chief Weasel **ANTONY SHER**
Judge **STEPHEN FRY**
Defence Counsel **JOHN CLEESE**
Engine Driver **BERNARD HILL**
The Sun **MICHAEL PALIN**
Car Salesman **NIGEL PLANER**
Gaoler's Daughter **JULIA SAWALHA**
St. John Weasel **ROBERT BATHURST**
Sentry **DON HENDERSON**
Geoffrey Weasel **RICHARD JAMES**
Clarence Weasel & Clock **KEITH-LEE CASTLE** with
ROGER ASHTON-GRIFFITHS

HUGO BLICK
JOHN BOSWALL
SARAH CROWDEN
DAVID HATTON
WILLIAM LAWRANCE
JOHN LEVITT
GRAHAM McTAVISH
BERNARD PADDEN
RICHARD RIDINGS
PETER WHITFIELD
Written & directed by **Terry Jones**
Based on the book by **Kenneth Grahame**
Original songs & music by **Terry Jones, John Du Prez, Andre Jacquemin & Dave Howman**
Photography **David Tattersall**
Editor **Julian Doyle**
Production & costume design **James Acheson**
Producers **John Goldstone & Jake Eberts**
cert. U, 88 mins – opened October 1996

YELLOWBEARD

Graham Chapman's long standing ambition to film a comic pirate romp ended up many years after its first conception as this rambling, badly written load of old rot. Originally stemming from a suggestion by Keith Moon to organise a really corking adventure comedy yarn, Chapman envisaged Moon himself as a wide-eyed, Robert Newtonesque pirate. Although in the end, Chapman's continual plans to get Moon into film acting (*The Odd Job/Brian*) were curtailed by his early death in 1978 – the Moon connection made it to the film via Peter Boyle's character name – while owing to cold feet and lack of interest, production companies were hardly falling over themselves to sign up the rights. Even legendary *Python* saviours HandMade declined to make it. In fact, along with Bernard

McKenna, Chapman had fleshed out a *Treasure Island* spoof which was discussed with Moon in hospital – although as he was suffering from severe DTs and near death, he was hardly at his best to judge.

Chapman's favourite movie as a boy had been the Burt Lancaster classic *The Crimson Pirate* and while researching the essence of film pirate history he revelled in everything from Errol Flynn in *Captain Blood* to *Abbott and Costello Meet Captain Kidd* with the deliciously over-the-top Charles Laughton. Ultimately, Chapman and McKenna decided to finish the pirate comedy if only for Moon's memory and peace of mind, although the character of Yellowbeard was a historical element and hadn't as yet fully been included. McKenna took a back seat as Chapman embraced the chance to write with 'one of the funniest people in the world', Peter Cook, for a solid month. Much of the film's best moments, including the early Chapman/Feldman banter, came about via this happy collaboration. The final process was one of crafting the final script, losing some of the more outlandish elements and shaping the story to explore the pirate mythology fully. Chapman worked with David Sherlock on this final leg of the journey. In the end, this was an ambitious, but ultimately, unsuccessful attempt at merging film parody with historical fact – the convincing and cinematically interesting use of smoking gunpowder strains in Chapman's beard and hair was historically accurate and captured on film for the first time, but this struggle for detail and the ideal of creating a good pirate movie rather than a cliché-ridden pirate farce was probably Chapman's downfall.

For, despite a glorious array of great British comedy actors, a fascinating, distinguished cast of thespians, a reasonably sized budget and even cinematic heritage in the use of the ship set from *Mutiny on the Bounty*, there is an overall feel of desperation, smut, bad taste for bad taste's sake and reams of pretty dubious gung-ho action. Very much like the anti-pleasures of *Carry On Columbus*, this amalgam of *Python*, Mel Brooks and American comedy circuit is a glorious array of wasted opportunities, over-acting and dreadfully timed obvious gags. Kenneth Mars, in two roles, seriously over-plays his hand with absurd accents and face-pulling, while the sequences dedicated to Cheech and Chong take the film to new depths of mind-numbing over-acting (although tongue-in-cheekily pinpointed in the script) and unaffectionate sending up of the material without the endearing trait of likability. Despite a rather leaden and easy ploy of injecting nubile topless bimbos whenever possible, the stuff is still fairly unwatchable. Chapman, fast losing the total control of the project he desired, didn't know the work of the dope-induced comedians but Orion, who had financed their equally dubious Corsian Brothers picture suggested the casting. Chapman's original notion was to ask Marty Feldman to play one of the Spaniards, but Feldman, having read the script, begged for the role of Peter Boyle's bumbling henchman – Marty being wise to the end. Chapman was also keen to rope in some of his old high-profile friends, but several potential stars didn't make it into the final cast. Robin Williams, later to became part of Terry Gilliam's pool of talent, was mentioned, as was Olivia Newton-John for the part of Betty (subsequently played by Kahn). Adam Ant and Sting both longed to play the handsome hero son of Chapman which was rather muffed by the uninteresting delivery of Hewitt – an American actor incorporating a dubious English accent and losing the touch of experience and intriguing familiarity of the Rock names considered. Also Oliver Reed, whose controlled energy would have been perfect for this full-blooded pirate romp, was considered briefly. Chapman's friend Harry Nilsson, who hung out during some of the shooting, penned and recorded a song, *Black Sails in the Sunset* to accompany a long montage sequence of life on board ship but this dramatic interlude was cut. In any case, Chapman didn't really feel the song blended with the movie and, ultimately, the compromise of using the material for the closing credit sequence was dropped in favour of stirring seafaring music. The romantic leads are under-written and over-played, with the obsession with treasure dictating the course of untrue love and contrasting with the flowery declarations of passion and understanding with the cold reality of greed. Madeline Kahn, with the most dubious cockney accent since Dick Van Dyke, just about gets away it, thanks to some wonderful mugging opposite Chapman. Her energetic bodice squeezing, the priceless reasons why she's against book-reading and a sense that she's going through this torture for the fun rather than the money help. But she still doesn't stop great chunks of this movie drifting away into boredom and incomprehension.

However, it's not all bad news as, like *Columbus*, this little pirate yarn does have some effective moments in the first half hour despite its sudden total dive into disaster as the comedy ebbs away giving in to nonsensical guff once our heroes take to the high seas. Still, one glance at the cast list must surely highlight that the talent on display is formidable and even in a script as dodgy as this one can't keep so many good men down. Naturally, Graham Chapman, roars, rants and rapes his way through the mire of old gags, hidden behind a crop of yellow hair, snarling his dialogue with hidden passions and enlivening the movie with a bloodthirsty, uncontrollable sense of deliciousness, having a grand time of evil. There are subtle references to Al Capone (the pirate is finally imprisoned due to tax evasion), manic scenes of demonic anger, a hilarious scene as a suitable alias is hurriedly thought up with Chapman's suggestions of Professor Death and Professor Rape, continual cries of 'bugger 'im' and various unseemly plundering activities. A unique starring turn from Chapman this is quite unlike anything else he did. Patchy is hardly the word for the film as a whole, but Chapman's totally committed performance of sheer mayhem is enough to satisfy any comedy buff.

Long after Keith Moon's suggestion *Yellowbeard* finally went before the cameras when Orion forked out the dosh but only on the condition that a couple of other *Monty Python* stars were written into the proceedings. Like Harpo Marx's failed attempt at going solo in *Love Happy* (with Chico and Groucho eventually recruited in), *Yellowbeard* could only set sail once Cleese and Idle had jumped aboard the sinking ship. And thank heaven for them, for although only Chapman and Idle are about the place intermittently in the second half of the picture, the three ex-*Python*s are continually staggering about, swaggering and serving regal nobs in the first portion.

There are a couple of memorable scenes between Cleese and Idle (swamped by tried old routines and obvious jokes – the money on the end of the string ploy et all, which Cleese hastily wrote into his part much to the pleasure and hilarity of Chapman – effortlessly being pulled off via the power of comic genius and some knowing facial expressions). The classic highlight comes with Cleese's blind old bumbler as authority informant, creating some wonderful *Python* quality from some pretty dreadful jokes (a cute hearing/jewellery etc) and presenting Idle with at least one masterpiece in his condemnation of Cleese as 'cloth-eyes!' – well, it makes *me* laugh. Cleese is short-lived but unforgettable, eagerly listening out for the remotest noise, delivering full character details by mere smell and incorporating one charming bit of sight humour as he mysteriously wanders around the docklands, stopping by some children skipping and joining in their innocence play by jumping over the rope. It's a lovely touch. Although naturally happy to support his old writing partner, Cleese had persistently turned down the offer to appear in *Yellowbeard*, only agreeing following another nice but earnest request from Chapman and when he discovered the classic cameo of Pew's scenes were out of the way in a matter of days and entirely filmed in England. Idle took on the film under the agreement that all his sequences

(dotted throughout the picture) were filmed first and thus allowed him time to relax on location without pressures. Idle was certainly not going to turn down a part in *Yellowbeard*, whatever its quality, if it meant that his old *Python* cohort would see his pet project flounder, even if his first laugh comes from treading in some horse crap and the entire role is basically just pontificating about naval clap-trap. But at least Idle was in the movie, joining forces with his old workmates to drag this unseaworthy wreck home to port. Besides, he has a good bit of visual humour with some telescopes, a bit of bemused reaction opposite Peter Bull, a class scene in prison with Chapman (Mr. Yellowbeard!/Captain Yellowbeard, you scum!) and, anyway, nobody can get away with some seriously duff snuff-snorting foppish dialogue like Eric Idle. Believe me, it's a man of rare skill who can make some of this stuff funny.

Apart from the three Pythons, the old clan of inventive and influential post-war British comedians were out in force and enjoying a happy, final reunion on the film. Peter Cook, co-writing and supporting as the slightly drunken Lord Lambourn, is shamefully wasted, although Cook

can always be relied upon to drag some class comic moments out of the most feebly under-written role, memorably waffling on about the fact that 'I only drink while I'm working' and creating screen magic out of the worst comic situations imaginable. Surviving some dreadful stuff with a street urchin and some mindless babbling with his wife, Beryl Reid, there's an air of disrespectful respectability about Cook's performance, staggering through the muddle of pirates, piffle and puerile gags with dignity. His final embracing of the pirate ethos with a quick snarl is worth waiting the whole movie for. Marty Feldman, ferreting around like a demented cairn terrier, nestles up to authority, desperately tries to discover the secrets of Yellowbeard's treasure and basically turns in bucketloads of Uriah Heep-like mannerisms. His loud horn blowing (lapsing into the death march) during Cleese's last scene is good fun while the early sequences in prison with Chapman are arguably the best the film has to offer. Incarcerated in a typically *Python*esque prison for naughty people, Chapman's blood and thunder, sea-wise fighter exchanges memorable banter with the weedy Feldman, with unnoticed physical

abuse, obvious trick questions and a bit of old-fashioned anarchy.
And finally, added to the impressive roster of Chapman, Cleese, Feldman, Cook and Idle, is the main man of surreal British comedy himself, Spike Milligan, strolling in, dark-eyed and insane, with announcements of incoherent absurdity, raspberry blowing and social slips. It's only a very minor bit of reheated Goonery but, who cares; this is Spike, for God's sake. Treasure it. Amazingly, this rather corny old project also managed to attract some fine old thespians, including Nigel Stock, Michael Hordern and, in his penultimate role, a crusty, rusty and lusty old James Mason, embellishing his weary sea-dog mutterings with the sincerity of Shakespearean verse. Susannah York turns in a lip-licking cameo of sexual awareness, Peter Bull struggles through as the old Queen and even David Bowie crops up as a crafty sailor masquerading as a shark! – well, what did you expect but the unexpected. The mixture, of course, doesn't work, the old British school of comedians throw themselves into this low-brow feast of rubbish with total abandon; the Americans seem to be waiting for the lunch break. The screenplay desperately tries to combine good old innuendo with something approaching *Python*esque macabre, but the dismembered hand, blood spouting and nailed feet just don't gell in the surroundings. Take a deep breath, think of England and celebrate this major post-*Python* film role for Chapman by having an open mind and a forgiving nature – the likes of Cleese, Idle, Feldman and Cook are worth their weight in gold. Sadly, with his usual comic elegance, Feldman died of a massive heart attack on the very last day of shooting the film in Mexico. The film is respectfully dedicated 'For Marty'. A flawed memorial but an affectionate one nevertheless.

Did you know? Chapman, Cleese and Idle were interviewed in June 1983 for a special making of documentary – *Group Madness: The Making of Yellowbeard.*

Yellowbeard
A Seagoat Production/Orion Pictures release A Hemdale Film
Yellowbeard **GRAHAM CHAPMAN**
Bosun Moon **PETER BOYLE**
El Segundo **RICHARD 'CHEECH' MARIN**
El Nebuloso **TOMMY CHONG**
Lord Percy Lambourn **PETER COOK**
Gilbert **MARTY FELDMAN**
Dan **MARTIN HEWITT**
Dr. Ebenezer Gilpin **MICHAEL HORDERN**
Commander Clement **ERIC IDLE**
Betty **MADELINE KAHN**
Captain Hughes **JAMES MASON**
Blind Pew **JOHN CLEESE**
Mr. Crisp/Verdugo **KENNETH MARS**
Flunkie **SPIKE MILLIGAN**
Triola **STACEY NELKIN**
Mansell **NIGEL PLANER**
Lady Churchill **SUSANNAH YORK**
Lady Lambourn **BERYL REID**
Mr. Beamish **FERDINARD MAYNE**
Chaplain **JOHN FRANCIS**
Queen Anne **PETER BULL**
Tarbuck **BERNARD FOX**
Man with Parrot **RONALD LACEY**
Mr. Prostitute **GRETA BLACKBURN**
Admiral **NIGEL STOCK**
Mr. Martin **KENNETH DANZIGER**
Prison guard **MONTE LANDIS**
Pirate **RICHARD WREN**
Rosie **GILLIAN EATON**
Askey **BERNARD McKENNA**
Big John **JOHN DAIR**
Priest **CARLOS ROMANO**
Beggar **ALVARO CARCANO**
Helmsman **LEOPOLDO FRANCES**
Flower Girl **AVA HARELA**
Sergeant of the Marines **GARRY O'NEILL**
Stuntmen **BUDDY VAN HORN, TERRY WALSH, WALT ROBLES, CHUCK WATERS, MIKE CASSIDY, GEORGE WILBUR & LOREN JANES**
Screenplay by **Graham Chapman, Peter Cook & Bernard McKenna**
Editor **William Reynolds**
Photography **Gerry Fisher**
Music **John Morris**
Casting **Michael McLean & Nancy Foy**
Costume designer **T. Stephen Miles**
Production managers **Brad H. Aronson, Tony Rubio, Miguel Lima, David Ball & Dennis Holt**
Assistant directors **Mario Cisneros, Clive Reed & Ted Morley**
Art director **Jack Shampan**
Production designer **Joseph R.**

Jennings
Executive producer **John Daly**
Producer **Carter De Haven**
Director **Mel Damski**
Filmed on location in England & Mexico
DeLuxe, 1983, 97 mins
For Marty...

THE YOUNG INDIANA JONES CHRONICLES: Spain 1917

The tenth episode in the series, Terry Jones was approached by George Lucas and asked to tackle one of his ambitious spin-offs from the Harrison Ford movies. Jones was reluctant at first, preferring to write or direct in the cinema, but eventually he took on the assignment and worked with the writer on the idea. Filmed in Spain and Czechoslovakia in July 1991 the *Boy's Own* adventure embraced a smattering of vague World War I history, spying, ballets russes in Spain and loads of action. Enjoying a month's shoot, Jones latched onto the semi-historical/education tool of this icon of popular culture and shaped an enjoyable programme.

Indiana Jones **SEAN PATRICK FLANERY**
Screenplay by **Gavin Scott**
Producers **Rick McCallum & George Lucas**
Director **Terry Jones**
ABC-TV 1992

THE YOUNG ONES: Nasty

What Milligan was to the fifties, Ben Elton was to the eighties, structuring the hip style of a comic generation, ushering in a whole cluster of new faces for major exposure for the first time and touching a raw, youth culture nerve that needed touching. *The Young Ones* was basically about university students mucking around, cracking nob gags and shouting a lot, but it spoke for the nation, made stars of its cast and wallowed in a glorious anarchic tradition of surrealist humour – even resurrecting the Goonish ideal of a musical interlude (with some pretty damn cool bands guesting in the students' kitchen). The

Young Ones themselves over-acted, purloined *Python*esque silly captions (like the dangers of getting into fridges), reshaped the language (wriggle etc), broke up form (again the *Python* trick of wandering into framed pictures on the wall – with the ship sequence in this episode), *Not the Nine O'Clock*-like *Python* parody (the Sayle/Mayall cheeseshop-cum-silly walk in *Oil*), parodied classic movies (the bugger-it chess game with death – the lighter side of Bergman's *The Seventh Seal*), embraced anarchy (Edmondson pushing the wall closer rather than moving the video plug nearer), deconstructed performance (showing the scruffy students as the refined actors) and addressed the very nature of comedy (the bit part postman with the Olivier fixation). This second series show is widely considered to be *The Young Ones*' masterpiece, brilliantly incorporating spine-tingling chords from the Cliff hit in its spooky, thunder-cracking title theme, presenting the lads as ghoulish horror icons and spraying dripping red title credits as in *Carry On Screaming*! This is the one with Sayle as the wonderfully obvious South African vampire (aka Harry the Bastard – 'What a bastard!' – they don't end shows like that anymore), Damaris Hayman (familiar from Pertwee's *The Deamons Who* classic) doing the almighty 'dig graves' dialogue with Planer and the glorious nervous panic when virgins are on the blood menu.

However, the major treat is a very special guest appearance from Terry Jones – the young lads were all *Python* nuts and Elton and Mayall in particular were chuffed to welcome the star. In the event Jones does very little, acting to perfection as the drunken vicar grabbing copious amounts of booze from his robes, helpfully reminding them to inject the stiffy joke in case they had forgotten and gaze around, hair akimbo, with a look of dazed amazement. But then again, he need only to be in the scene with very little to do except endorse the new generation of comic greats. It's more than enough. To select the three most important collectives of post-war British comedy it must be

The Goons, *Python* and *The Young Ones*. With *Tales of a Men's Shirts* Spike handed the rally baton over to Cleese, here Jones does the same for the *Python* student generation. To the unenlightened it's hardly anything, to fans it's all. Check it out.

Vyvyan **ADRIAN EDMONDSON**
Rick **RIK MAYALL**
Neil **NIGEL PLANER**
Mike **CHRISTOPHER RYAN**
The Balowski Family **ALEXEI SAYLE**
DAWN FRENCH
NORMAN HALE
GARETH PACE
HELEN ATKINSON WOOD
MARK ADEN
DANNY PEACOCK
Vicar **TERRY JONES**
Written by **Ben Elton, Rik Mayall & Lise Mayer**
Producer **Paul Jackson**
Broadcast 29 May 1984, BBC2

The Monty Python Chronology

1939
27 October – John Cleese born

1940
22 November – Terry Gilliam born

1941
8 January – Graham Chapman born

1942
1 February – Terry Jones born

1943
29 March – Eric Idle born
5 May – Michael Palin born

1962
John Cleese and Graham Chapman team up together for the Cambridge revue *Double Take*.
24 November – 27 April – First series of *That Was The Week That Was* with written contributions from John Cleese.

1963
August, Edinburgh Festival boasts Eric Idle (in *Footlights '63*) and Terry Jones (in ****). Jones and Palin write Slapstick for *Loitering Within Tent*.

28 September – 21 December – Second series of *That Was The Week That Was* with written contributions from John Cleese, *That Was The Year That Was* followed 28 December.
Cleese/Chapman appear in *Cambridge Circus*.

1964
Cleese/Chapman take *Cambridge Circus* to New Zealand and America, which includes an appearance on *The Ed Sullivan Show* – an all British celebration, fellow guests are Joan Greenwood and The Animals.
Cleese writes for BBC radio *Emery At Large* (14 May edition) and *Not to Worry* (5 July).
Idle, appearing in Footlights Revue, meets Palin and Jones (in The Oxford Revue) at Edinburgh Palin and Jones appear in *Hang Down Your Head and Die*. Pilot launch for *I'm Sorry I'll Read That Again*.

1965
Chapman, Jones and Palin contribute material to the Roy Hudd series *The Illustrated Weekly Hudd*. Jones writes for *The Ken Dodd Show* and *The Billy Cotton Bandshow* while Chapman tows the mainstream television line with work on *The Petula Clark Show*. Idle performs *My Girl Herbert*, various cabaret dates and gains rep. theatre experience. Cleese stays in America, features in *Half A Sixpence*, *The Establishment* and in September enjoys a radio spot with Jack Palance.
Fun and Games by Harvey Kurtzman, published by Gold Medal Books – Terry Gilliam, the new guy in town on *Help!* magazine, assisted in the compilation of this book of brain-teasers.
Cambridge Circus record (Odeon PCS 3046) released.

1966
10 March – 28 April – First series of *The Frost Report*, BBC1, featuring appearances and written contributions from John Cleese. Also written by Graham Chapman, Michael Palin, Eric Idle and Terry Jones.
Cleese is interviewed on *Late Night Extra* (Light programme – 1 April)
The Frost Report on Britain with David Frost, John Cleese, Jean Hart and Colin Frechter released by Parlophone (PMC

7005) with written contributions from Graham Chapman, John Cleese and Terry Jones. Produced by James Gilbert, Cleese features on Matter of Taste, Schoolmaster, Just Four Just Men, Top of the Form, Unknown Soldier, Scrapbook, Adventure, Bulletin and Zookeeper. The disc was re-issued on *Starline* (MRS 5084)

Now! Hosted by Michael Palin (TWW) John Cleese performs in and contributes material to the BBC Light Programme *David Frost at the Phonograph* – the three editions he worked on are broadcast on 12 September, 8 October and 29 October

22 September – *Isadora: The Biggest Dancer in the World*, BBC1, featuring Michael Palin and Eric Idle.

15 October – First episode of *The Late Show*, featuring Michael Palin and Terry Jones.

19 October – First *The Frost Programme* (Rediffusion Network) Programme editors included John Cleese

28 December – *Alice in Wonderland*, BBC1, featuring Eric Idle.

1967

26 January, John Cleese guests on the BBC light programme *Call My Bluff*

At Last The 1948 Show, series one broadcast from 15 Feb – 22 March 1967 – Chapman & Cleese.

Single release of *The Ferret Song/The Rhubarb Tart Song* (Pye 7N 17336) credited to John Cleese and the *1948 Show* Choir – special studio recordings of the classic songs that close series one and two. An album, *At Last The 1948 Show* (Pye NPL 18198) includes highlights from series one – Bookshop, Sheepdog Trials, Where Were You?, The Wonderful World of the Ant, Gentleman Farmer, Witch, Top Of the Form, Someone Has Stolen the News, One Man Battalion, Doctor and Man with Skinny Legs, Ministerial Breakdown, Job Description, Engine Driver, The Four Sydney Lotterbys, Beekeeping, The Ferret Song – studio version, Vox Pop. Series two broadcast 26 September – 7 November

26 March – *Frost Over England* broadcast BBC1 – Compilation of *The Frost Report* for the Montreux Festival.

6 April – 18 May – Second series of *The Frost Report*, BBC1.

The Frost Report On Everything record

released by Janus (JLS-3005) with written contributions by Graham Chapman, John Cleese, Eric Idle, Terry Jones and Michael Palin. Cleese appeared in Theatre Critic, Three Classes of People, Narcissus Complex, The Secretary and Three Classes. *Interlude* featuring John Cleese. Compilation album of classic moments from *I'm Sorry, I'll Read That Again* (EMI M-11634) featured John Cleese on The Doctor, John and Mary (both with Bill Oddie) and Robin Hood (with Graeme Garden).

3 October – 21 November – *A Series of Birds* Written by John Bird and John Fortune. Producer Dennis Main Wilson. Additional material and script editing Michael Palin & Terry Jones.

21 October – 23 December – *Twice a Fortnight* featuring Michael Palin & Terry Jones

14 November – 19 December – *No – That's Me Over There* featuring scripts from Eric Idle and later Graham Chapman. Idle featured as actor in one episode.

17 December, John Cleese appears in the BBC radio show *Down Your Way* John Cleese attends David Frost's Christmas party dressed as Santa.

26 December – *Frost Over Christmas*

1968

4 January – 28 March First series of *Do Not Adjust Your Set*, written & performed by Michael Palin, Terry Jones & Eric Idle.

In February, *The Frost Report On Everything* (Pye NPL 18199) was released. A compilation album of highlights from the first series of *The Frost Report*, featured David Frost, Ronnie Barker, Ronnie Corbett, Sheila Steafel and John Cleese. An extract from this record would later crop up on Pye's *The Golden Hour of Comedy* (GH 530).

Albert Carter Q.O.S.O. short film starring Roy Kinnear as a London roadsweeper who rescues the Queen's corgi. Written by Eric Idle and Ian Brims, produced by Malcolm Heyworth and directed by Brims for Dormar Productions (27 mins).

Marty broadcast on BBC2 29 April – 3 June. Last show screened 13 Jan 1969 – Montreux best of edition screened 17 March. The two series would consist of

12 shows featuring additional material written by Palin, Jones, Cleese, Chapman and Idle. The five would be simply credited as 'writers' for the second series which began 9 December Jones and Palin would also play minor supporting bits on screen. Producer Dennis Main Wilson. Director Roger Race

6 July, Cleese features in radio's *Galaxy*.

4 August, Michael Palin starts his run on *Frost On Sunday*.

8 August, John Cleese presents the televised version of that classic Goon adventure *Tales of Men's Shirts,* Thames

23 August – 18 October *We Have Ways of Making You Laugh*, LWT, with Eric Idle and Terry Gilliam.

John Cleese appears in *Interlude, The Bliss of Mrs. Blossom, The Best House in London* and *The Avengers.* 11 November he talks about his film roles on *Movie-Go Round*

14 September, Cleese guests opposite Pete 'n' Dud in *Goodbye Again.* 28 October – 2 December – *Broaden Your Mind* Additional material and appearances by Terry Jones, Michael Palin and Graham Chapman also written by John Cleese and Eric Idle.

How to Irritate People written and performed by John Cleese and Graham Chapman with appearances by Michael Palin

26 December – *Do Not Adjust Your Stocking*

1969

12 January – 16 February *The Complete and Utter History of Britain* Written and performed by Terry Jones and Michael Palin.

19 February – 14 May – Second series of *Do Not Adjust Your Set* featuring the work of Jones, Idle, Gilliam and Palin.

8 April – 3 June, John Cleese appears in Radio 4's *What's So Funny...?*

The Magic Christian, co-written by and featuring John Cleese and Graham Chapman.

The Rise and Rise of Michael Rimmer, co-written and featuring John Cleese and Graham Chapman

11 May – Graham Chapman and John Cleese introduced to Michael Palin, Terry Jones, Eric Idle and Terry Gilliam following the recording of a *Do Not Adjust Your Set* show, the lads enjoy a

curry meal at Light of Kashmir, Fleet Road, Hampstead and adjourn to Cleese's Basil Street flat. 23 May, BBC meeting of the six, discussing possible ideas for their allotted 13-part television series together with a budget of £3,500 per episode

12 July – First episode of *Doctor in the House* written by John Cleese and Graham Chapman.

5 October – 18 January 1970 – *Monty Python's Flying Circus* series 1.

Fred Friendly writes a glowing report for *The Washington Post* urging America to embrace *Python* years before the actual invasion of the team.

1970

12 January – *Late Night Line Up*, BBC2, presented by Joan Bakewell, Michael Dean, Tony Bilbow and Sheridan Morley. Editor Rowan Ayers. Producer Mike Fentiman. Guests – John Cleese, Graham Chapman, Terry Gilliam, Eric Idle & Carol Cleveland discuss *Monty Python's Flying Circus* series one.

Monty Python's Flying Circus record released, special compilation episode of *Python* wins a Silver Rose at the Montreux Festival.

4 July, Cleese guests on Radio 4's *The Clever Stupid Game*

22 July – Premiere of the Vincent Price horror film *Cry of the Banshee* featuring Terry Gilliam's title sequence.

Doctor In Trouble featuring Graham Chapman.

The Statue featuring John Cleese.

August – BBC1 repeat five *Python* series one, 'super zany comedy' shows. The *Radio Times* explains that 'apart from John Cleese (the tall one) none of the cast is exactly a household face – yet' – hardly! The Pythons perform a live show of sketches at Belgrade Theatre, Coventry.

John Cleese and Michael Palin perform a television commercial for Hunky-Chunks dog food.

An unsuccessful attempt at breaking the American market includes a subdued Canadian tour taking in Montreal, Ottawa, Winnipeg, Edmonton, Calgary and Vancouver, culminating with an appearance on US television's *Tonight Show*. Cleese had returned home but guest host Joey Bishop (standing in for Johnny Carson) introduced the other members with 'Now here are five lads

from England. I'm told they're very funny!' – clips were shown and the whole thing was a disaster. Subsequently successful broadcasts in Japan come with 20-page booklets explaining every location, joke and comment! Telecast Japan broadcast of the dead parrot proves unpopular because the Japanese wouldn't argue so much if a product were unsatisfactory! However, the broadcasts proved so popular that within weeks material like the Ministry of Silly Walks was attracting bigger audiences than golf. Even though the translation at times put the lads' material under the catchy title of *The Gay Boy's Dragon Show*!

1 September, John Cleese is interviewed by Ed Boyle on Radio 4's *Today*. Donald Zee of *The Daily Mirror* organises an interview/meeting with the 'three funniest people in Britain' – Ronnie Corbett, Peter Cook and John Cleese. Cleese returned to Oxford to support charity for Biafra but refuses to 'do' the silly walk – the event coincides with the first and only meeting of the University's *Monty Python Fan Club* with every club suggestion voted out for not being silly enough!

15 September – 22 December – *Monty Python's Flying Circus* series 2. On the final day of *Python 2*, John Cleese is interviewed on *Woman's Hour*, Radio 4. The following day, 23 December, he selects his favourite funny books for the Radio 4 literary programme *Now Read On*.

1971

The radio 4 comedy series *Lines From My Grandfather's Forehead* starring Ronnie Barker, Terence Brady and Pauline Yates starts on 15 February. This first series runs until 5 April and a seasonal special, *Lines From My Grandfather's Christmas's Forehead* is broadcast on Christmas Eve. The second series of eight runs from 21 July to 8 September and boasted humorous contributions from the likes of Spike Milligan, Harold Pinter and Michael Palin.

John Cleese makes regular appearances on the Radio 4 panel game *Right Or Wrong*

The team make 20-minute comic sales film for Bird's Eye Frozen Food detailing the wondrous practice of picking peas

early for maximum tenderness. A typical inclusion of multiple Alan Whickers would be resurrected for the first show of series three.

John Cleese, Graham Chapman, Terry Jones, Michael Palin and Carol Cleveland star in *Who's There?*, a short instructional film commissioned by the Labour Party.

5 March – John Cleese guests on *Woman's Hour*.

Chapman co-writes a segment of the compendium comedy film *The Magnificent Seven Deadly Sins*.

Monty Python's Big Red Bok published by Eyre Methuen. *Another Monty Python Record* released

10 April – the first episode of *The Two Ronnies* broadcast on BBC1. Although there would be script contributions by Eric Idle, Michael Palin, Terry Jones, Graham Chapman and John Cleese, the majority would be re-working of previously aired *Frost Report* and *1948 Show* material. Cleese would guest star in his old guise as upper-class man for the renewed Three Classes material from *The Frost Report*.

16 April – Special *Monty Python* compilation wins the Silver Rose at Montreux Festival.

21 April John Cleese awarded the annual honorary position of Rector of St. Andrew's University giving a Pythonesque edged lecture proclaiming cowardice as a suitable way of life. Later in the day, a Cleese interview discussing the honour is broadcast on Radio 4's *News Desk*

17 July – Castaway number 1082 John Cleese selects his choice of records and luxury items on Roy Plumley's *Desert Island Discs*

October – *And Now For Something Completely Different* released.

October 8 – first episode of *The Marty Feldman Comedy Machine* with titles by Terry Gilliam. Ran until 14 January 1972. Director John Robins. Producer Larry Gilbert. Executive producer Colin Clews.

20 November – John Cleese is interviewed on Radio 4's *Film Time*.

The Pythons write and perform a series of in-house promotional films for the likes of Guinness, Gibbs Shampoo and Harmony Hair Spray. Terry Jones directs.

1972

Eric Idle (who else?) promotes the new chocolate sweetmeat, The Nudge Bar. Performed in his immortal Nudge, Nudge persona, the ads travelled to Australia and were so successful that more were commissioned. Reluctant to go back, Idle declined, so John Cleese, appearing as the Nudge, Nudge man's brother, took over the assignment.

July – Cleese judges the Modern Venus Bathing Beauty contest in Weston – awarding the prize to Deirdre Greenland of Machen

Graham Chapman interviewed by Richard Adams for issue four of *Gay Times*.

Jones and Palin record *Funny Game, Football*.

Terry Gilliam produces a couple of Fairground-geared animated adverts for The Great Gas Gala of British Gas Board.

Monty Python's Previous Record released.

29 April – John Cleese interviewed on *Sports Report*

Monty Python's Flying Circus received a BAFTA for Best Comedy series. *The Love Ban* featuring John Cleese.

19 October – 18 January 1973 – *Monty Python's Flying Circus* series 3

1973

3 January – *The After-School Special: William* (an introduction to the work of William Shakespeare), broadcast on ABC TV, featuring titles by Terry Gilliam.

18 January – As the last episode of series three of *Python* airs, John Cleese was starring as Sherlock Holmes in the BBC1 Comedy Playhouse, *Elementary, My Dear Watson*. Cleese reveals in interview that *Python* will be rested for a year but doesn't say he's leaving the group, while all six travel to Dallas for a weekend fund-raising for the Public Broadcasting System, KERA.

May – *Monty Python's First Farewell Tour* plays to packed houses across Britain for a three-week stint.

In a *Playboy* interview Cleese reveals he encountered his first groupie following a *Python* performance at Bristol's Hippodrome Theatre.

5 July – John Cleese guests on *Weekend Woman's Hour*

14 August – *Secrets* by Michael Palin & Terry Jones, BBC2.

18 August – Terry Gilliam provides an illustration for Oliver Trimble and the Jelly Hound – the 1st prize winner in the adult section of *The Times*/Jonathan Cape Children's Story Competition, published in *The Times*

The Brand New Monty Python Bok published by Eyre Methuen. Later appears in paperback format as *The Brand New Monty Python Papperbok* in 1974.

Monty Python's Matching Tie and Handkerchief released.

The team resurrected their best sketches from the television series for a stage version which was performed (with the added difficulty of dodgy radio mikes) in Sunderland, Glasgow and Leeds. A Summer tour of Canada embraces an appearance on *The Johnny Carson Show* which Cleese opts out of.

6 October – *Monty Pythons fliegende Zirkus*, BBC2. November – the final series of *I'm Sorry I'll Read That Again*.

24 December – Cleese guest stars in *The Goodies and the Beanstalk*, BBC1.

1974

The Terry Jones and Michael Palin book *Bert Fegg's Nasty Book For Boys and Girls*, published by Eyre Methuen.

Monty Python and the Holy Grail released. At the launch party Cleese, the reluctant Python, eagerly suggests a US tour to promote all things *Monty*, much to the other members' raised eyebrows.

February – Drury Lane shows, record released, Cleese makes first appearance with Les Dawson on *Sez Les*.

1974 Royal premiere, Python want to take along their cardboard cut-out of Princess Margaret who had appeared in the royal box during their Drury Lane shows – EMI curtail the idea. Cowards!

22 April – Following his time as Rector of St. Andrew's University (1971-1974) Cleese makes a Thames programme *A Place In History*, ITV.

5 May – Terry Gilliam is the guest in *The Do-It-Yourself Film Animation Show*, part three: Table top and cut-out animation, BBC1, presented by Bob Godfrey. Director Anna Jackson. Producer David Hargreaves.

John Cleese interviewed by Hunter Davies (*Daily Telegraph*, 21 June)

Romance with a Double Bass co-written by and starring John Cleese.

6 June – John Cleese contributes material to Radio 4's *Sheila Hancock's Sketchbook*.

31 October-5 December – *Monty Python* (series 4). American Public Service TV station took on the first, second and third series of *Monty Python's Flying Circus* and secured a massive cult audience.

6 December – William Hardcastle talks to Graham Chapman, Terry Gilliam, Terry Jones and Michael Palin about five years of *Python* for *In Vision*, BBC2. Producer Peter Foges. Editor Will Wyatt – clips and chat.

1975

Eric Idle guests on Barry Norman's *Film '75*, mimicking the presenter's laid back, cross-legged delivery and setting up next year's series, *Film '77* which, as its title would suggest would be a year early.

Jasper Carrott Rabbits On and On... (DJM DJLPS 462), album release culminating with the comedian's priceless homage to *Python*, Eric Idle My Idol, incorporating bits of Nudge, Nudge and wild Package Holiday outburst. *The Album of the Soundtrack of the Trailer of the Film of Monty Python and the Holy Grail* released

John Cleese appears on the ITV impressionist show *Who Do You Do?*

Terry Jones & Michael Palin interviewed by Sheridan Morley (*The Times*, 29 March) for The Complete and Utter Palin and Jones in a Two Man Python Team.

Hello Sailor by Eric Idle, published by Futura.

11 April – Pete Murray interviews John Cleese on Radio 2's *Open House*

12 May–16 June, *Rutland Weekend Television* – First series, written and performed by Eric Idle.

July, *Esquire* Magazine publishes Monty Python's American Diary (notes on our country by an all-wise visitor from utter space) – Palin's account of *Python*'s US experiences.

25 August – Cleese guests on Radio 4's *The Summer Show*.

19 September-24 October – First series of *Fawlty Towers* co-written and starring John Cleese. Wins BAFTA.

21 September – Cleese contributes to *Celebration*: 'The Art of Musical Parody'

on Radio 4.
American Federal Court oversees a complaint from the Pythons aimed at Time Life – the US distribution arm for the BBC – and ABC who had brought the rights to screen *Monty Python* series four in their Wide World of Entertainment slot. Michael Palin, having tuned into a broadcast from the fourth series on 3 October, was disgusted to see that three episodes had been edited together into a 70-minute special, with huge, damaging chunks removed and no explanation that the material had been cut. A second programme, utilising the remaining three shows, was scheduled and both Palin and Terry Gilliam appeared in court to explain the essence of *Python* humour and protect their interests. Judge Lasker decreed that an announcement should be broadcast before the second show on 26 December explaining that the programme was an edited highlights show which the Pythons disassociated themselves from. In the event, ABC got away with very minor apologies, although the compilations were never screened again and the BBC allowed the Python team as a unit to secure rights to their work.
6 October – 24 November eight Video Arts films written and performed by John Cleese broadcast on BBC2 as *The Selling Line*.
14 November, Cleese takes place in a book discussion – *Read All About It*, BBC1
Boxing Day – *Christmas with Rutland Weekend Television*, written & performed by Eric Idle.
31 December – *Three Men in a Boat*, BBC1, starring Michael Palin.

1976

7 January – *Tomkinson's Schooldays*, BBC2, written and performed by Michael Palin and Terry Jones.
10 January – *Out of the Trees*, BBC2 sketch show co-written by and starring Graham Chapman.
A double album re-release of the American versions of *Another Monty Python Record* and *Monty Python's Previous Record* appears in the States only as *The Worst* (crossed out) *Best of... Monty Python* (Kama Sutra KSBS 2611-2/Buddah BDS 5656-2).
Buddah release a promotional EP under

the title *The Least Bizarre* (CMP-EP).
20 February – Cleese guests on *Newsbeat* and is profiled on BBC1's *Tonight*.
14 April – 2 May New York's City Centre pays host to the *Monty Python* stage show, with a pop concert atmosphere; the familiar sketches are cheered uproariously on their starts and ending while for one show an almost unrecognisable George Harrison joins the team for the lumberjack chorus. Record version released.
April – during the Python's stint in New York Terry Gilliam is a guest contestant on the NBC game show *To Tell the Truth*. Gilliam illustrates the book – *Sporting Relations*.
Bert Fegg's Nasty Book is published in America as *Dr. Fegg's Nasty Book of Knowledge*.
The Two Ronnies BBC Records (REB 257) features the *1948 Show's* Grublian.
20 May – *Their Finest Hours* by Jones & Palin opens in Sheffield.
Eric Idle directs pop videos for *Crackerbox Palace* and *True Love* from George Harrison's *Thirty Three and a Third*, Cleese makes his first advert for General Accident car insurance.
A Poke In the Eye (With A Sharp Stick), the first Amnesty International Concert (April 1-3), featuring sketches written and performed by John Cleese, Graham Chapman, Terry Gilliam, Terry Jones and Michael Palin. A BBC film record, *Pleasure At Her Majesty's* and Transatlantic album (LP TRA 331) preserved the laughter for future generations. An unofficial American re-edit of the filmed footage surfaced as *Monty Python Meets Beyond the Fringe*. All six Pythons reunite on television for a special Festival 40 episode (16 August). Chapman remembers *Python* with an interview with David Gillard. Ian MacNaughton returns as producer.
29 October – John Cleese talks about his favourite childhood book on *First Impression* – Radio 4.
November – *Esquire* Magazine publishes *Monty Python's Regards to Broadway* and *The Wacky Adventures of Seven Men and a Girl on a British Airways Three Week 'Make-U-A-Star' Bargain Holiday* by Michael Palin. During the planning stages of *Brian*, Mary Whitehouse files a private prosecution

against *Gays News* editor Denis Leman for publishing a poem suggesting Christ was homosexual – the Pythons donate £1,000 for the unsuccessful fight fund
12 November – 24 December *Rutland Weekend Television* series 2 written & performed by Eric Idle.
BBC Records release *The Rutland Weekend Songbook* (REB 233), featuring studio remakes of Eric Idle sketches and Neil Innes songs from the television show: L'Amour Perdu, Gibberish, Wash With Mother, Say Sorry Again, The Rutles in Rutles For Sale, Twenty-four Hours in Tunbridge Wells, The Fabulous Bingo Brothers, In Concrete, The Children of Rock 'n' Roll, Startime, The Song O' The Insurance Men, Closedown, Testing, I Give Myself to You, Communist Cooking, Johnny Cash Live at Mrs. Fletchers, The Old Gay Whistle Test, Accountancy Shanty, Football, Boring, Goodafternoon, Disco, Closedown.
The Rutland Dirty Weekend Book published by Methuen. Written by Eric Idle with one contribution from Michael Palin.
The November issue of *Playboy* features Idle's Rutland piece The Vatican Sex Manuel. Eric Idle tours Canada on a book promotion, vowing it will be his last ever – he spends Christmas in Barbados with *Saturday Night Live* producer Lorne Michaels and hatches plans for a Rutles special.

1977

4 January-15 February – BBC2's *The Punch Review* presents material from the magazine's many contributors, including pieces by Michael Palin and Terry Jones.
28 January – Helen Reddy hosts the fourth anniversary episode of NBC's *Midnight Special* with guests Eric Idle, Terry Jones and Terry Gilliam.
February – Idle begins writing the script for *The Rutles: All You Need Is Cash*. Finished by July the filming begins almost immediately.
20 February – The final Python link with the *Doctor* television series when Chapman's final contribution (For Your Own Good for *Doctor On the Go*) is broadcast.
March – *Jabberwocky* released – Directed by Terry Gilliam and starring Michael Palin with Terry Jones and Terry

Gilliam. Some screenings support an X-rated musical of *Alice in Wonderland*! Promoting *Jabberwocky*, Gilliam is interviewed by George Parry (*Sunday Times*, 27 March). Terry Gilliam defends the critics of his filth obsession with 'There's nothing in the film you won't find in a Brueghel painting' – 6 April, *The Guardian*.

12 April – John Cleese stars opposite Diana Rigg in Every Day In Every Way, part of the *Three Piece Suite* series. The sculptor Nicholas Monro plans to immortalise Cleese in silly walk mode for an exhibition 'Genius of Britain' but a strong solicitor's letter refuses permission and Max Wall's comic walk is used instead.

1 May – Gilliam interviewed about *Jabberwocky* – A Python Comes To Grips with Lewis Carrol by Leticia Kent – for The New York *Times*. *The Mermaid Frolics*, Amnesty concert performed at the Mermaid Theatre on 8 May under the direction of Terry Jones. John Cleese joined his Python co-star in the show. The record, released by Polydor (LP 2384 101) featured a mix of comic and musical pieces from the show. *Monty Python and the Holy Grail* (aka *Monty Python Ik Den Holie Gralien*), edited by Terry Jones, designed by Derek Birdsall, published by Eyre Methuen, features the complete screenplay, photographs by Drew Mara, colour stills from the film, letters detailing the required and negotiated censoring of the script, story boards, Gilliam animation, production cost details and, above all, the Almighty buying an ant sketch which didn't make the final film. It also includes the legendary photograph of Graham Chapman's lowest, alcohol-induced ebb, sitting in the grass with a funny hat on and an expression of sheer despair. The screening rights for *Grail* are sold to CBS by mistake and the corporation show the film twice, cutting out violence and language. It is also immediately re-screened on PBS, intact and proud. The compilation collection, *The Instant Monty Python Record Collection*, released.

Jabberwocky by Ralph Hoover published by Pan Books. A novelisation of the Terry Gilliam/Charles Alverson screenplay.

4 August – Terry Gilliam and Michael Palin are interviewed about *Jabberwocky* for James Delson's article, Jabberwocky On the Loose, for *Circus Magazine*.

September 18 – John Cleese stars in and co-writes The Strange Case of the End of Civilisation As We Know It for London Weekend Television. *The Strange Case of the End of Civilisation As We Know It* by John Cleese, Jack Hobbs and Joseph McGrath published by Star Books Ltd. Available in two editions, one a movie tie-in with photograph of Cleese and Lowe astride bike and the other with a more novel-like feel with artistic impression cover. Both books are exactly the same.

20 September – 25 October First series of *Ripping Yarns* starring Michael Palin, written by Palin and Jones.

21 October – John Cleese guest stars on *The Muppet Show*.

Fawlty Towers by John Cleese and Connie Booth, is published by Futura, including extensive photos from the shows and the scripts for The Builders, The Hotel Inspectors and Gourmet Night.

14 December Cleese interviewed by Donny Macleod on *Pebble Mill*, BBC1. John Cleese begins his long association, until 1980, with Sony, writing and performing scores of television and radio ads, ranging from the sublime voice-over arch lamp campaign to the cute antics with Tiddles the cat for C6 telly/video.

The Two Ronnies Vol. 2 (REB 300) released by BBC records featuring Barker, Corbett and Moray Watson performing Cricket Commentators by Palin and Jones.

1978

After a three-month editing session *The Rutles* appears in March – Written, performed and co-directed by Eric Idle featuring Michael Palin. Original 'Stig' David Battley is replaced. Officially George is in it, John loves it, Ringo likes it after 1968 and Paul doesn't comment.

The Two Ronnies Sketchbook, edited by Peter Vincent for Star Books, features scripts by Palin and Jones.

20 May, Cleese is interviewed by Joan Bakewell on *Away From It All* – Radio 4. John Cleese performs a series of television adverts for the General Accident Insurance Company, getting into various scrapes but remaining uncharacteristically calm because of his superb insurance cover.

Ripping Yarns by Terry Jones & Michael Palin, published by Methuen, features the six scripts from the first series with photos from the shows. International Editions of *Penthouse* publish Stiff Upper Lips and Surgical Goods: How Michael Palin Revived the British Empire by Mich Brown.

24 October – Gilliam interviewed by Bevis Hillier (*Sunday Telegraph* Supplement).

25 Years of Recorded Comedy (Warner Brothers Records) features The Argument Sketch while other Python compilation appearances include *One More Chance* (Charisma Class 3) featuring Eric the Half a Bee and *Supertracks* (Vertigo Sport 1) with *The Money Song*.

Animations of Mortality by Terry Gilliam with Lucinda Cowell published by Methuen (0-413-39370-4) Hardback (0-413-39380-1) Paperback.

Kim 'Howard' Johnson publishes the first of a three-volume Python fanzine, featuring an interview with Michael Palin.

The Odd Job released – Graham Chapman starred, co-wrote and co-produced.

The Odd Job by Bernard McKenna & Colin Bostock-Smith published by Arrow Books (0-09-918950-X) – novelization of the Chapman film.

16 September – filming begins on the one and only *Monty Python's Life of Brian* in Tunisia.

John Cleese plugs the Postal Service with a string of stating the bleeding obvious commercials, parodying by Peter Cook in the Derek & Clive album *Ad Nauseam*

17 December – John Cleese appears in Rory McGrath & Clive Anderson's Radio 2 pantomime *Black Cinderella Two Goes East*, produced by Douglas Adams and featuring Peter Cook, Graeme Garden, Tim Brooke-Taylor, David Hatch, Jo Kendall, Bill Oddie, Richard Murdoch and Richard Baker. One hour.

BBC Records release a compilation of *I'm Sorry, I'll Read That Again* (REH 342) with John Cleese featured on Quickie (with David Hatch), Home This Afternoon (with Hatch, Oddie, Garden and the David Lee Group) and Opening (with Hatch and the David Lee Group).

1979

1 January, John Cleese appears on *Grandstand*, BBC1.
10 January – John Cleese talks with Alex Hamilton about the writing of *Fawlty Towers*, series two (*Guardian*).
January – The first cut of *Brian* is screened to a selected audience in London.
16 February, Cleese talks about the second series of *Fawlty Towers* on *Around Midnight* – Radio 2. 26 March, Michael Palin interviewed by Sally A. Lodge in *Publishers Weekly*
27 March – Cleese is interviewed about his celebrated training films on *PM* – BBC Radio.
From 18 March Cleese and Ronnie Corbett star in a series of five films on BBC1, *Company Account*: The Balance Sheet Barrier, from 14 September Cleese presents a further eight Video Arts films – *The Office Line*: The Secretary and Her Boss.
April – The Festival of Light condemns *Brian*.
May – *Feature* runs the article Monty Python's Chapman: Jesus Is Just All Right by R. Lacayo which features an interview with the Python that is Brian.
11 May – Michael Palin interviewed on *Good Morning America*.
22 June – Cleese is interviewed about the Police Ball, *Tonight In Town*, BBC1.
26 June – Cleese talks about *The Secret Policeman's Ball* on Radio 4's *Today* and following the first night, on 28 June – he is interviewed on *Kaleidoscope*. June 27 – June 30 The Amnesty International Comedy Gala at Her Majesty's Theatre, directed by John Cleese, showcased vintage sketches written and performed by Cleese, Terry Jones and Michael Palin. *The Secret Policeman's Ball* album (Island ILPS 9601) featured highlights from The Amnesty International Comedy Gala (with thanks to Terry Gilliam) and complemented a video release of best moments and a second album of musical items.
2 July – John Cleese interviewed about Basil 'Funny Fawlties of British TV' in *The Washington Post*.
20 July – *The Pythons*, a BBC1 documentary celebrates the tenth

anniversary of the 'best known British comedy group in the world'. Produced & narrated by Iain Johnstone. It also marks the filming of *Brian* with great informal team moments and Spike holding court. Michael Palin's It's Man graces the cover of the *Radio Times*.
Fawlty Towers 2 by John Cleese and Connie Booth published by Weidenfeld & Nicolson, includes the scripts for The Wedding Party, A Touch of Class and The Germans.
More Ripping Yarns by Terry Jones & Michael Palin, published by Methuen, features scripts for the three shows from series two, with art direction and design by Kate Hepburn – our heroes are depicted in brilliantly detailed cigarette card form on the cover. (0-413 47530 1).
Monty Python's Life of Brian. November – each of the Pythons invites someone (Gilliam's mum, Idle's wife, Palin's dentist) to record a radio advert for the film and John Cleese's 80-year-old mum, explains that she is, in fact, 102, imprisoned in a nursing home and about to be thrown into the street if the film doesn't make much money. It wins the best radio entertainment commercial award for the year. John Cleese puts together *Away From It All* to support *Brian*.
Religious uproar started by Rev. Patrick J. Sullivan – director of the Catholic Conference's Office for Film and Broadcasting.
Autumn – *Brian* is banned in two states in America.
Widespread banning causing religious debate and huge box office takings – in Milford Haven a gang go on the rampage spraying the church meeting place and town hall with '*Brian* Lives On!'
Monty Python's Life of Brian/MONTYPYTHONSCRAPBOOK, edited by Eric Idle, designed by Basil Pao, published by Eyre Methuen, the Brian record is released by Warners at the same time. Ace Books publish *The Life of Brian* – a paperback reissue of the Methuen book but removing the *Montypythonscrapbook* material and keeping just the script/photos from the film.
14 September – Cleese and Jones are among *Peter Cook and Co* (ITV).
John Cleese interviewed by *Rolling Stone* (18 October). Cleese gets a name

check in the last ever *Sykes* episode, with Hugh Burden's dithering Head of Light Entertainment believing him to be a weatherman!
20 October – Cleese guests in *Doctor Who*.
28 October – Chapman discusses *Life of Brian* on NBC Television's *Sunday Spectacular*
29 October – *People Weekly* features Sue Reilly's article, Monty Python's Graham Chapman Doesn't Walk On Water, and the Devout Call His Brian Spoof All Wet.
5 November – Chapman makes his first appearance on *Hollywood Squares* and Cleese discusses *Brian* on *Kaleidoscope* (Radio 4).
7 November – Cleese again defends *Python*'s finest hour on *Today*. He praises the dead parrot on *The Dick Cavett Show*.
8 November – British cinemas première *Monty Python's Life of Brian* uncut and proud.
9 November – *Friday Night, Saturday Morning*, BBC2, presented by Tim Rice. A debate concerning *Monty Python's Life of Brian* with John Cleese and Michael Palin speaking in defence and Malcolm Muggeridge and Dr. Mervyn Stockwood again considered the film blasphemous and, even worse, second rate. Director John Burrowes. Producer is Iain Johnstone, later mercilessly ridiculed in the *Not the Nine O'Clock News* sketch – General Synod's Life of Christ.
22 November – The New York *Times* publishes *Scraps from History's Table* by Michael Palin – in the form of excerpts from Puritan Gordon Ottershaw's diary recounting the 1st Thanksgiving Day.
31 December – Cleese reveals his hopes for the 1980s on *Today*.
BBC Records release *Fawlty Towers* (REB 377) which boasts a few words from John Howard Davies and features the original soundtracks of Hotel Inspectors and Mrs. Richards, with added musical links. The BBC Audio Collection *Fawlty* re-releases employ Andrew Sachs to provide new linking narration. *Fawlty* second series picks up a BAFTA. Terry Jones stood in as Harpo for one performance only of Dick Vosburgh's classic Marx Brothers homage *A Day In Hollywood/A Night In the Ukraine*.

1980

Not The Nine 'Clock Album (BBC REB 400) released in October, features *General Synod's Life of Python*, subsequently re-released on Music For Pleasure label (MFB 5810).

Monty Python's Contractual Obligation Album released.

4 March – NBC headline Chapman in their new variety programme *The Big Show*.

Graham Chapman interviewed by Roger Baker for *Gay Times* no. 201.

A Liar's Autobiography by Graham Chapman published by Eyre Methuen.

16 August – John Cleese talks about his interest in squash on BBC radio's *Sport On 4* and return to Clifton's College for a charity cricket match.

September – Chapman, Jones and Palin are interviewed on the *Dr. Demento* radio show promoting their forthcoming Hollywood Bowl performances.

22 October – Cleese promotes his forthcoming Shakespearean bash on *Parkinson*, BBC1.

23 October – *The Taming of the Shrew*, BBC2, starring John Cleese.

27 November – *Great Railway Journeys of the World* – episode four hosted by Michael Palin, BBC2.

Profiles of Terry Jones appear in *The New Standard* (28 November) and *The Guardian* (18 January, 1981) illustrating the historian behind the comedian in readiness for the publication of *Chaucer's Knight: The Portrait of a Medieval Mercenary*, published by Weidenfeld & Nicholson.

The Pythons perform four live shows at The Hollywood Bowl – their first US appearance in four years.

Rolling Stone publishes an interview with the Pythons (13 November) December, *Dark Star Magazine* publishes A Pepperpot Speaks: The Terry Jones Interview by Cliff Ash.

1981

2 January – *Publishers Weekly* includes PW Forecasts: A Liar's Autobiography by Genevieve Stuffaford – a Chapman Review.

24 February – Idle guests a Chapman review in *Laverne and Shirley* (ABC).

2 March – *An Evening with Graham Chapman* is formed from a personal appearance at Facets Multimedia, Chicago. The lecture would keep the ex-

Python busy for the rest of his life.

18 March – Chapman interviewed on PBS by Dick Cavett.

22 March – *Marital Tips for Charles* by Michael Palin published in The New York *Times*.

May – Cassette re-release of *The Secret Policeman's Ball* (ICT 9601 Z).

Not's Hedgehog Sandwich (BBC REB) album released, features Not the Parrot Sketch. The definitive record release from the *Not* gang, it also includes Constable Savage and the decidedly *Python*esque Gift Shop.

The Monty Python Instant Record Collection (Vol. II) released.

The Complete Works of William Shakespeare and Monty Python: Volume One – Monty Python, published by Eyre Methuen – a re-issue of both *Monty Python's Big Red Book* and *The Brand New Monty Python Bok*.

Time Bandits – Directed and co-written by Terry Gilliam. Starring John Cleese. Featured actor and co-writer Michael Palin.

The Great Muppet Caper featuring John Cleese.

Promoting *Time Bandits* Gilliam is interviewed by Michael Watts (*The Times*, 16 July), Anne Thompson (*Film Comment* November/December issue). The gang interviewed by Jean Rock, *Daily Express*.

6 August – Palin and Gilliam interviewed about *Time Bandits* by John Walker (*Sunday Express Magazine*, 12 July).

Time Bandits by Terry Gilliam and Michael Palin published by Hutchinson Books – included the screenplay and photos from the film, plus deleted material from the final cut.

Time Bandits by Charles Alverson published by Arrow Books – novelisation of the Gilliam film.

Time Bandits, adapted by S.J. Parkhouse with artwork by David Lloyd and John Stokes published by Marvel – a Comic Book version of the Gilliam film.

3 June – first of seven *Paperbacks* hosted by Terry Jones, BBC1.

17 June – *Live From Two*, Thames, features a piece on Michael Palin.

31 July – Graham Chapman interviewed from London on *Good Morning America*.

Fairy Tales by Terry Jones, published by Pavilion Books. *Cambridge Review Magazine* publishes The Myth of Progress by Terry Jones.

BBC Records release *Fawlty Towers: Second Sitting* (REB 405) featuring the original soundtracks of The Builders and Basil the Rat. Links are newly recorded by Andrew Sachs.

John Cleese interviewed by Chris Greenwood (*Daily Mail,* 17 August). Charisma release The Prince's Trust charity double record compilation *'We Are Most Amused' – The Very Best of British Comedy* (RTD 2067) with, alongside The Goons, Tony Hancock and Benny Hill, the *Fawlty Towers* team in an extract from The Health Inspector and Python represented by Massage From the Swedish Prime Minister (with a fabulous Hancock interjection), Yangtse Kiang and, of course, the parrot.

From the 9–12 of September, the Amnesty International Comedy Gala held residency at the Theatre Royal, Drury Lane, co-directed by John Cleese with written and performed contributions from Cleese and Graham Chapman.

The Secret Policeman's Other Ball album (Springtime HAHA 6003), released in November, included comic highlights from the show (with thanks to Palin and Jones) while a further release showcased the rock performances. The Julian Temple film featured concert footage of Cleese and Chapman as well as Palin's merchandising plug and caretaker cameo at the close. A book, *The Secret Policeman's Other Ball*, was published by Methuen and featured scripts, lyrics, photographs from the show, an introduction by John Cleese and production notes from Michael Palin and Terry Jones.

28 September – Michael Palin guest stars in *The Innes Book of Records*, BBC2.

10 October – Geoffrey Strachan of Methuen celebrates a decade of *Python* books with an article, Ten Years of Silly Publishing, in *The Bookseller*.

3 November – Eric Idle's *Pass the Butler* opens in Coventry.

6 November – Terry Jones hosts the first of a new series of *Friday Night...Saturday Morning*, BBC2.

15 November – *Terry Gilliam: On the Trail of Time Bandits* by Gary Arnold, published in *The Washington Post*.

19 November – Palin interviewed on *Dick Cavett*, PBS.

25 November – Eric Idle guest stars on *Steve Martin's Best Show Ever*, NBC.

21 December, *The Only Yank in Monty Python Stares Down Critics as His Time Bandits Steals $24 Million* by Jetrene Jones published in *People Weekly*.

1982
26 January – the first West End performance of *Pass the Butler* by Idle, Globe Theatre. The play is later published.
3 February – Terry Gilliam promotes *Time Bandits* on *Late Night with David Letterman*.
The Laughing Stock of the BBC album (BBC LAF 1) features material from *Monty Python's Flying Circus*, as well as The Goons, *Hancock's Half Hour*, *Round the Horne*, *Yes Minister*, *The Two Ronnies* and the *Not the Nine O'Clock News* classic the General Synod's Life of Python.
Fawlty Towers: At Your Service (REB 449) released by BBC records with Sachs introducing The Germans and The Kipper & the Corpse, followed later in the year by *Fawlty Towers: A La Carte* (REB 484) with Waldorf Salad and Gourmet Night.
May – *Twilight Zone Magazine* publishes Terry Gilliam: Finding Comedy on 'the Dark Side of the Coin' by James Verniere.
12 July – filming begins on *Monty Python's The Meaning of Life*.
24 July – Graham Chapman and Terry Gilliam promote *Monty Python Live at the Hollywood Bowl* on *Late Night With David Letterman*.
Eric Idle directs, writes and narrates *Faerie Tale Theatre: The Tale of the Frog Prince*.
Cleese attends a St. Peter's reunion at Dragonara Hall, Bristol – the guest speaker is fellow old boy Roald Dahl.
John Cleese co-wrote and performs a series of six radio ads for the British sweet manufacturer Callard & Bowser, aimed at the American market and produced by Lord, Geller, Federico, Einstein of New York.
No More Curried Eggs For Me (compiled by Roger Wilmut) and published by Methuen featured the script for *1948 Show*'s Bookshop. The script of Eric Idle's play *Pass the Butler* published by Methuen.
2 November – Palin promotes *The Missionary* on *Good Morning America* and two days later chats about his latest film on *Late Night with David Letterman*.
17 November – Palin guests on Merv Griffin, CBS.
3 December – Terry Jones guests on *Good Morning New York*, ABC Television, and later promotes *Fairee Tales* on *Late Night with David Letterman*, NBC.
9 December – Terry Jones' *The Rupert Bear Story* broadcast on Channel 4.
12 December, John Cleese talks to Barry Norman about *Privates on Parade*. *Film '82*, BBC1.

1983
Britain at the Pictures, David Robinson's celebration of 50 years since the establishment of the British Film Institute featured a clip from *Monty Python and the Holy Grail*. Produced by Colin Luke, Richard Attenborough narrated.
The Jones and Palin *Fegg's* book is re-issued in America as *Dr. Fegg's Encyclopaedia of All World Knowledge* which included specially written additional material – Peter Bedrick Books, Harper & Row.
21 January – John Cleese appeared in a charity revue at the Theatre Royal, Drury Lane, *An Evening at Court*, organised (by Adrian Slade and directed by Humphrey Barclay). Featuring Rowan Atkinson, David Frost, Eleanor Bron, Julian Slade, Dawn French, Jennifer Saunders and even, gasp, a mind-blowing reunion of Brooke-Taylor, Garden and Oddie, the highlight was Cleese performing Inalienable Rights with Peter Cook.
The script of Michael Palin's first *Great Railway Journeys of the World*, *Confessions of a Train-Spotter*, appears in the BBC book along with copious photographs from the show.
29 January – Cleese promotes *Privates on Parade* on *Wogan*, BBC1 and on 31 January does a similiar deed on *Nationwide*. Earlier he appears on *The John Dunne Show*, Radio 2, and crops up again on the station chatting to Gloria Hunniford on 2 February.
Cleese is hired by Jones, Lang & Wootton to promote a Covent Garden office block for sale, creating a typically irreverent audio tape for over 100 prospective clients.
1 February – John Cleese, in pyjamas and *Privates* promotion at the ready,
chats with Robert Kee, Anna Ford and David Frost on *Good Morning Britain*.
5 February – Cleese appears on *Sunday, Sunday* (ITV).
7 February – Barry Norman's *Film 83* includes a location report for *Yellowbeard*.
16 February – Palin promotes *The Missionary* on the first episode of a new seven part chat show with Tim Rice, BBC1.
24 February – Cleese on *Privates on Parade* for Star Sound Extra (Radio 2)
28 February, Barry Norman's *Film 83* interviews Palin on *The Missionary*.
3 March – Iain Johnstone's *Strictly Private* – a look behind the scenes of *Privates on Parade* – is shown on ITV.
14 March – Cleese promotes *Monty Python's The Meaning of Life* on *Late Night with David Letterman*, NBC 22 March, Eric Idle also plugs Python's latest big screen offering with Letterman.
30 March – *Life* is finally released, with the album version and the colour illustrated scriptbook by Methuen quick on its heels. Gilliam's *The Crimson Permanent Assurance* is the support picture.
The Missionary written by & starring Michael Palin.
The Missionary by Michael Palin published by Methuen (Hardback 0-413-51010-7)/(Paperback – 0-1413-51390-4), includes the complete screenplay for the film, photographs, and, most interestingly, a newly written prologue and Palin's *After the Story* follow-up biographies for the principal characters.
30 March – Graham Chapman is guest video disc jockey on MTV.
The first of John Cleese's hilarious American Express adverts, usually featuring him as a pompous, upper class chap whose butler is able to get a card while he is not!
While still at Sheffield University, Eddie Izzard interviews Michael Palin. Fourteen years later Izzard would conduct his second interview – with John Cleese. Both Palin and Cleese attended a performance of David Mamet's *The Cryptogram*, featuring Izzard, years later and joined Terry Jones for a comic performance in front of 35,000 Rock fans which instilled an understanding of Hitler's rallies in the Pythons.

1 April – Michael Palin plugs *The Meaning of Life* on *Late Night with David Letterman*.

13 April – Graham Chapman, Terry Gilliam and Terry Jones discuss *Monty Python's The Meaning of Life* with Merv Griffin on CBS Television, while on NBS a wee bit later, Chapman goes it alone on *Late Night with David Letterman*.

15 June – Michael Palin guest stars on the first programme in the short lived political satire show *The New Is The News*, NBC television, delivering a mock report from 10 Downing Street. Regular *Python* project actor and friend of Palin's, Simon Jones, was a regular contributor to the show.

20 June – *Good Morning Britain* hosted by Anne Diamond and Terry Jones.

11 July – *People Weekly* includes Screen: *Yellowbeard* and in November Chapman is interviewed by Ed Naha for *Heavy Metal*.

Frank Muir's tribute to BBC's situation comedy heritage, the two-part *Best of British Comedy*, included *Python*'s parrot and a bit of Gourmet Night magic from *Fawlty Towers*.

12 August – Michael Palin is featured in the first of four *Comic Roots* for BBC (the others in this fascinating insight in great comedians' early years were Irene Handl, Les Dawson and the sublime episode on Kenneth Williams).

Prevue Magazine publishes *The Confessions of Terry Jones* by Kim 'Howard' Johnson.

Palin interviewed for *Radio Times* (6-12 August) and *Film Review* (August) looks at *Meaning of Life* in the article Monty Python Splashes Out!

28 September – Cleese is interviewed about *Families & How to Survive Them* on *Woman's Hour* and, a mere two days later, on Gloria Hunniford's radio show.

Son of Curried Eggs, again complied by Roger Wilmut for Methuen books, featured the script for *1948 Show*'s Sheepdog Trials.

14 November – Terry Jones plugs *The Saga of Erik the Viking* on *Live at Five*, NBC and discusses the book with Dennis Wholey on the late talk show *Latenight America*, PBS.

19 December – the *Erik* book is promoted by Jones again on *Take 30*, CBS.

1984

A compilation of the first four Amnesty concerts is released on video in America as *The Secret Policeman's Private Parts*. Chapman, Cleese, Gilliam, Jones and Palin all appear along with Carol Cleveland, Connie Booth and Neil Innes in such classics as The Parrot, Slapstick, Bookshop and *The Lumberjack Song*.

John Cleese wins a Clio Award for his American Express adverts, produced by Ogilvy & Mather of New York.

3 April – Cleese plugs *Private's on Parade* on *Late Night With Letterman* and records four American radio ads for Kronenbourg, struggling with their 'Better, not bitter' soundbite – produced by Levine, Huntley, Schmidt & Beaver of New York. On television he played an inefficient executive who buys all the wrong equipment in a series of Ogilvy & Mather ads for Compaq Computers.

The Golden Skits of Wing Commander Muriel Volestrangler FRHS and Bar by John Cleese, with Graham Chapman, Michael Palin, Tim Brooke-Taylor, Marty Feldman and David Hatch.

A priceless Methuen collection of sketches from *Monty Python's Flying Circus*, *The Monty Python Matching Tie and Handkerchief*, *Monty Python's The Meaning of Life*, *At Last the 1948 Show*, *The Frost Report*, *Double Take*, *Cambridge Circus* and *I'm Sorry I'll Read That Again*: Architect, Shirt Shop, Goat, Sheep, Top of the Form, World Association Football, Bookshop, Arthur 'Two Sheds' Jackson, The Last Supper, Merchant Banker, Cricket Commentators, Fairly Silly Court Skit, Crunchy Frog, Regella, Hearing Aid, Argument, The Good Old Days, Lucky Gypsy, Mrs. Beulah Premise & Mrs. Wanda Conclusion Visit Mr. & Mrs. J. P. Sartre, Undertaker, Railway Carriage, Cheese Shop, String, Chapel, 'Ones', Army Protection Racket, Slightly Less Silly Than the Other Court Skit Court Skit, Courier, Ethel the Frog, Dead Parrot.

April – Cleese is interviewed about *Privates on Parade* on *Entertainment Tonight*, NBC Television

John Cleese writes the foreword for *Freaky Fables* by J.B. Handelsman, published by Methuen.

Michael Palin records a series of front-cloth commercials for WXRT, 93 FM

radio, including a classic one with him in a Beatles wig. Palin stars in *The Dress*.

29 May – Terry Jones guests in *The Young Ones* episode, Nasty. Terry Jones writes the foreword for *The Eliza Stories* by Brian Pain, classic turn-of-the-century comic stories repackaged by Pavilion.

A Private Function starring Michael Palin.

A Private Function by Alan Bennett, novel published by Faber & Faber.

13 September – Cleese on *Familes and How to Survive Them* (*Round Midnight*, Radio 2).

17 September – Cleese interviewed about his ads for Sony CD player on *Today* (Radio 4)

3 October – Cleese and Skinner plug the *Familes* series with Miriam Stoppard on *Where There's Life* (ITV), while Cleese returns yet again to *David Letterman*'s show with book promotion in mind on 27 November.

The Courage to Change by Dennis Wholey, published by Houghton Miffin – a collection of interviews with alcoholics in the public eye includes a chapter on Graham Chapman who, as a medic, could see the effects and knew what was in store for if he didn't stop.

16 November – Chapman ponders on the problem of worrying about your neighbours in Channel Four's *Opinions*

18 November, David Frost interviews Michael Palin and Terry Jones on *Good Morning Britain* and later in the day, Palin promotes *A Private Function* with Gloria Hunniford for *Sunday, Sunday*.

Brazil Directed & co-written by Terry Gilliam. Featuring Michael Palin. Hailed as a masterpiece by audiences and critics, the film is released across the world apart from America, where Twentieth Century-Fox handed the rights over to Universal. The studio refused to release Gilliam's bleak cut and US critics, hailing it as a classic, were flown out of the country in order to review it! A Christmas 1984 release was put back. Enthused test audiences who completely got the film's message left their reaction forms blank save for thickly scrawled defiant messages – 'No more paperwork!' Aptly enough, the narrow-minded studio execs discounted all such responses!!

1985

1 January, Cleese and Skinner plug the *Familes* book with Merv Griffin, CBS,

marking its release in America. *Silverado* starring John Cleese. Eric Idle stars in *Faerie Tale Theatre: The Pied Piper of Hamelin*.

January – Terry Gilliam presents his final cut of *Brazil* to Universal – they insist on a 17-minute cut of the massive 148-minute running time, so he delivers the new version one month later (complete with over-dubbed sequences, new optical effects and a lighter ending). Universal,still insist the length is too long and unhappy about the ending, request more cuts before release – it was fast becoming Terry Gilliam's nightmarish version of Orson Welles and *The Magnificent Ambersons*.

The Easter release in America for *Brazil* is cancelled. October, Gilliam and producer Arnon Milchan begin promoting the film via independent interviews and place a full-length ad in *Daily Variety* reading – 'Dear Sid Sheinberg; When are you going to release my film, *Brazil*? Terry Gilliam'. The film is greeted with high praise at the Deauville Film Festival in France and after a massive struggle Gilliam finally sees his film receive a limited run of one week from 18 December, subsequently running for a week in Las Vegas. This made it eligible for the 1986 Oscars (24 March), just, but despite nominations for Best Original Screenplay and Best Art Direction, it didn't win. The L.A. Film Critics voted it Best Picture – even before official release in the city!! Universal were still unhappy and pulled all the plugs on promotion for *Brazil*, clutching the print and re-arranging the content for a happy ending and action-based thrills.

27 February, – a special morning edition of *Late Night with David Letterman* features Michael Palin talking about *A Private Function*.

March – Palin promotes the pig comedy in New York on *Hot Properties*, *Live at Five* and, on 22 March, on CBS's *Merv Griffin*.

The BBC release *Monty Python's Flying Circus* on Video for the first time and the lads (with designer Nicky Downes) allow anarchic comedy to spread to the covers with menu design, newspaper articles, book club offers and, best of all, film celebration 'by arrangement with Fast Forward Films and You Can Always Wipe It Productions'.

1 April – Terry Jones hosts the April Fool's Day edition of *Woman's Hour* on Radio 4 – the first time the programme is ever presented by a man! *Chaucer's Knight* by Terry Jones published by Weidenfeld & Nicolson.

18 April – Michael Palin plugs *A Private Function* with Johnny Carson on *The Tonight Show* April, John Cleese talks about *Silverado* on *Wogan*, returning to Terry's sofa for some more promotion on 9 December.

24 May – John Cleese interviewed about his Volestrangler collection of sketches on the aptly named *Book Plug*, Radio 4.

July – *Starlog Magazine* features the Kim 'Howard' Johnson interview with John Cleese – 'Why Is *Starlog* Interviewing Me?'

13 September – *Newsnight* report on Charles Crichton's collaboration on Cleese's Video Arts films.

3 December – John Cleese uses his unique mix of laughter and education for a Party Political Broadcast on behalf of the Social Democratic Party and talks about the broadcast the following day on *Breakfast Time*.

20 December – Michael Palin appears on *Pebble Mill at One*. The John Cleese puppet mixes *Fawlty* and SDP on *Spitting Image*.

1986

Universal released Gilliam's watered-down but approved version of *Brazil* nationally throughout America.

31 January – *The South Bank Show* profiles Cleese. In March John Cleese wrote and starred in the BBC's greatest self-promotional ad when he resurrected the classic Romans speech from *Monty Python's Life of Brian* as What Have the BBC Ever Done For Us? Starring Cleese as a pub bore condemning the old corporation for its charge of £58 for a licence the likes of barman Michael Hordern, Barry Norman, David Jason, the two Ronnies, mega Cleese fan Steve Davis, Patrick Moore, Terry Wogan, Alan Whicker and Bob Geldof, fresh from Live Aid, highlight, via their own specialities, exactly what the BBC *do* do for us. Directed by Alan Parker who, as with all contributors, gave his services free of charge, it is a well deserved pat on the back for the old corporation. Cleese, a picture of comedy timing,

does a superb, irascible job, coughing up a bit of spare change for Geldof's collecting tin, listing the momentous array of entertainment on offer, finally moaning about the lack of commercials before muttering 'except this one!' and heralding the major message of the promotion: The BBC. Is 16p a day really too much to ask? This three-minute John Cleese masterpiece alone made it worthwhile.

12 March – David Frost hosts the *1985 BAFTA Craft Awards* (broadcast on Channel 4) with Terry Jones among those discussing the works of the winning entries.

17 March – Palin guests on *Wogan* and makes such an impact that he's back on 23 April in conversation with super-sub Kenneth Williams. Discussing *East of Ipswich* and his vintage *Great Train Journey*, Palin, nervously reads some of his own limericks, one by Kenny Everett and one by a youngster trying to win a signed copy of his book. Williams reasd a selection brilliantly, castigates Palin's hasty delivery and really turns the knife by spinning off another three crackers from memory – Williams wrote in his diary: 'We started OK and the thing went fine till I bade him goodnight too early and then asked him to fill in with more limericks. Had to say goodbye again to him, and go centre for closing speech.'

19 March – Cleese talks about his post-*Python* film career on *Pebble Mill at One*.

20 March – Cleese talks about *Clockwise* with Gloria Hunniford, Radio 2.

22 March – John Cleese appears on *Aspel and Co* (ITV).

24 March – Terry Gilliam guests on *Wogan* (BBC1).

27 March – Michael Palin reads his book, *Small Harry and the Toothache Pills*, for *Jackanory*.

4-6 April – Comic Relief takes the stage for the first time with everybody from Ben Elton to Billy Connolly doing their bit at the Shaftesbury Theatre – Graham Chapman and Michael Palin give the venture their blessing and experience.

May – The Comic Relief Presents Utterly Utterly Live features extensive Rowan Atkinson gems, while the cassette version (WX 51C) includes a bonus track – Michael Palin's Biggles. Search it out! *Python* also endorsed *The Utterly, Utterly Merry Comic Relief Christmas*

Book, published by Fontana, with Palin committing his Biggles and the Groupies to print (complete with an introduction by George Harrison), Terry Jones and Douglas Adams teaming up for *A Christmas Fairly Story* and Adams reuniting with Graham Chapman for a reworking of their *Out of the Woods* piece The Private Life of Genghis Khan.
May – Chapman was back for Bob Geldof's Sports Aid, helping raise money via a sponsored dangerous sport.
Labyrinth scripted by Terry Jones.
The Goblins of the Labyrinth by Brian Froud and Terry Jones, published by Pavilion Books (Hardback – 0-85145-058-0). Far more than just the book of the film and more like the book of the film that should have been.
Palin writes *Cyril and the Dinner Party* and *Cyril and the House of Commons*, published by Pavilion.
21 June – Cleese guests on Brian Johnston's Radio 3 programme *A View From the Boundary Town* and *Country Planning Magazine* publishes Public Transport – Indignation, Despair and Hope by Michael Palin.
The Transformers: The Movie featuring the voice of Eric Idle.
That's T.V. Entertainment – The First 50 Years of BBC Television, a mammoth three-hour salute to the wonders of BBC television started with Helen MacKay's ground-breaking broadcast and a spine-tingling arrangement of fave themes through the ages. Cleese from *Fawlty Towers* cropped up in the opening credits and the Python *Blue Peter* parody accompanied the burst of *Blue Peter* music on the score. Specially filmed interviews saw John Cleese remember Hancock and *Maigret* as the family favourites, provocatively waxing lyrical about the atmospheric qualities of the show and emulating the spine-tingling Rupert Davies match striking introduction. Michael Palin recalls with affection the Pete 'n' Dud Bloody Betty Grable sketch and sings a snatch of the *Muffin the Mule* theme, while Terry Jones makes the link between Spike Milligan and *Python*. With a seamless flow into the fish slapping dance, nudge nudge, a bit of Peter Davison doing nudge nudge and the lumberjack sketch, the best bit of all is Cleese remembering his first night nerves before recording *Python* with the dread that the audience

might sit in complete silence. They didn't, of course!
The compilation cassette (ARB 001), *Panama Comedy Greats*, exclusively available via a deal with Panama Cigars, includes the Cleese/Jones/Palin/Atkinson version of Four Yorkshiremen from *The Secret Policeman's Ball*.
18 September – Jonathan Miller's version of *The Mikado* opens at the London Coliseum starring Eric Idle as Ko-Ko, and continues until November.
7 October – BBC's *Breakfast Time* feature a piece on Idle's operatic debut.
6 October – Cleese promotes *Clockwise* on *Today* (NBC) and the following day talks to CBS *Morning News* and David Letterman.
From 12 October, eight 45-minute compilations *20 Years of the Two Ronnies* celebrated the duo's partnership from *The Frost Report* and included several *Python*-related sketches.
6 November – Michael Palin guests on *Breakfast Time*.
11 November – Terry Jones introduces a new season of *The Film Club*, BBC2, celebrating the work of comedy writer/director Preston Sturges.
3 December – Palin promotes the video release of *Ripping Yarns* with David Brenner on *Nightlife* and does the same thing the following day with Jay Leno on *The Tonight Show*.
22 December – Palin talks about the *Yarns* and his Russian trip on *Late Night with David Letterman*.

1987

25 January – for his performance in *Clockwise* John Cleese receives the Peter Sellers Award for Comedy at The London *Evening Standard* Film Awards.
28 January – Michael Palin appears on *Wogan*. The first major television blowout for Comic Relief included liberal sprinklings of *Python* and *Fawlty* footage. In the Radio One poll-of-polls to discover Britain's favourite comedy sketch, The Barber Shop/Lumberjack Song with Palin and Jones came in at number three, while the clear winner was, of course, Cleese, Palin and a certain deceased parrot. Michael Palin also made an appearance in one of the newly filmed sketches for the evening.
1 February – *East of Ipswich* by Michael Palin screened on BBC1.
February – April, Idle takes on another

stint in *The Mikado*.
18 February – Terry Gilliam is Sue MacGregor's guest of the week on *Woman's Hour*, Radio 4.
20 February – Eric Idle talks about *The Mikado* on *Wogan*. 4 March – Gilliam is interviewed about *Munchausen* on *Hershey's Hollywood* (WSBK-Boston Radio).
5 March – John Cleese appears in *Cheers*: Simon Says. Michael Palin Spins His Yarn by Maury Z. Levy published in *Video Magazine*.
20 March – Terry Jones talks about *Personal Services* with David Brenner on TV's *Nightlife*.
5 April – Chapman stars in *Still Crazy Like A Fox* for CBS Television.
12 April – *The Sunday Times* publishes Mark Brennan's Whipping Up a Poster Storm – an interview with Terry Jones about censorship.
16 April – Chapman talks to David Brenner about life, comedy and The Dangerous Sports Club on *Nightlife*.
Spring – *The Mikado* is revived in London before Idle plays the piece in Houston.
TV Times (13-19 June) publishes the Katie Ekberg interview with John Cleese, primarily to promote the British television premiere of his *Cheers* episode on Channel 4. Surprise, surprise... *Python*, *Wanda*, *Fawlty* and Video Arts are also covered.
19 June – John Cleese and Michael Palin muck about for *The Grand Knockout Tournament*. Cleese lends his voice to *In the Beginning*.
8 July – Palin discusses *Wanda* with Cheryl Washington in New York for the CNN show *Showbiz Today*.
19 July – Palin appears on *Late Night with David Letterman*.
August – Chapman hosts the first *The Dangerous Film Club*.
4 August – Chapman introduces film clips of *The Dangerous Sports Club* on NBC's *The Tonight Show* with Johnny Carson.
8 August – Cleese is interviewed by Steve Kroft on his training films, *West 57th Street*, CBS.
From 18 September a further eight compilation shows heralded *21 Years of the Two Ronnies*.
20 September – Cleese wins an Emmy for Outstanding Guest Performer in a Comedy Series for *Cheers*.

The video, of *The Secret Policeman's Private Parts* released, featuring highlights from the first four Amnesty International concerts. *Python* material included was Dead Parrot, The Courtroom Sketch, The Last Supper, College of Advanced Slapstick, *Silly Song* and The Lumberjack from *A Poke In the Eye*, Bookshop and Forgive Me from *Mermaid Frolics* and The Name's the Game from *The Secret Policeman's Ball*. Simon Mayo starts to use *Always Look On The Bright Side Of Life* as his Radio One jingle.

Brazil is screened on television, in a severely edited version reinstating the totally happy ending approved of by Universal. Terry Gilliam threatens legal action against the studio.

The Battle of Brazil by Jack Mathews, published by Crown Books gives the full account of Gilliam's struggle with the studio as well as featuring the Gilliam, Stoppard and McKeown screenplay for the film, complete with annotations.

11 October – *The Sunday Times Magazine* publishes extracts from the NSPCC book *Once Upon A Time When I Was Young* including the contribution from Terry Jones.

11, 12 October – Eric Idle records his part as Ko-Ko at Abbey Road Studios for the MCA Record (MCAD-6215) of *The Mikado*.

27 October – Graham Chapman returns to MTV as guest host.

30 October – Chapman discusses *Python*, Dangerous Sports and his involvement with the diabetes aid concert, Comedy Crusade, with host Mariette Hartley on the CBS show *The Morning Programme*.

31 October – Chapman makes a hasty reappearance on MTV in their Halloween Costume Party in the guise of a mouse.

2 November – Graham Chapman performs in *The First Annual Comedy Crusade*, Warner Theater, Washington DC.

7 November – *TV Guide* features Insider: The Life of Chapman by Paul Francis.

12 December – John Cleese interviewed by Bryan Appleyard – 'Funny How People Change' – for *The Times*.

30 December – ITV screen a 1986 recording of *The Mikado* starring Eric Idle, directed for television by John

Michael Phillips.

Personal Services directed by Terry Jones. *Personal Services* by David Leland, published by Pavilion Books, including the screenplay and photos from the film and an introduction written by Terry Jones.

The Secret Policeman's Third Ball, performed in March, featured John Cleese who appears in the video, *The Secret Policeman's Third Ball – The Comedy* (Virgin VVD 271). A record was released under the same name but didn't include any Cleese material, while Sidgwick & Jackson published the book *The Secret Policeman's Third Ball* including script extracts, song lyrics and photos from the shows.

Ben Elton's first record, *Motormouth*, listed all *Monty Python* albums as essential comedy vinyl, illustrated with the TV encased foot cover for the BBC release. *The Dandy and The Beano Fifty Golden Years* published by D.C. Thompson & Co. features a contribution from John Cleese (citing the legendary comics as 'the only two trustworthy journals in the United Kingdom'), while vintage hero Danny Longlegs tries a *Python*esque silly walk.

1988

A Fish Called Wanda. Written, co-produced and starred John Cleese with Michael Palin. For publicity Cleese was interviewed for American television by Viscount Linley and heavily endorsed the making of the documentary *John Cleese's First Farewell Performance* featuring an extensive interview with Michael Palin and a bit of *Python* banter. Cleese is voted 'The Funniest Man in Britain' in Steve Wright's Radio One poll. He beats Lenny Henry, Michael Barrymore, Ben Elton and Rik Mayall. During the publicity tour for *A Fish Called Wanda* John Cleese takes time out to record the *Talking Book of The Screwtape Letters*, the classic 1941 religious novel by C.S. Lewis. Released by Audio Literature Inc – 0-944993-15-X. *A Fish Called Wanda* by John Cleese and Charles Crichton, published by Methuen, features the screenplay and photographs from the film – Paperback 0-413-19550-3.

Python's The Final Rip-Off released *The Monty Python Gift Boks* published – a repackaging of both the *Big Red Book*

and the *New Bok* with bonus poster. John Cleese appears regularly on the syndicated show *Business This Morning* (WBBM-Chicago) spreading his business training knowledge across the American populace.

16 May – *Forbes Magazine* publishes extracts from Cleese's The Importance of Mistakes speech.

17 May – Cleese crops up briefly at the start of ABC's televised presentation of *The Second Annual American Comedy Awards*.

Graham Chapman works on the pilot of his unrealised CBS series project *Jake's Journey* and Jim Yoakum addresses the programme in the November *Rolling Stone* magazine (Graham Chapman's Journey).

25 April – Graham Chapman's lecture at Student Center Ballroom, Georgia Tech University is recorded for posterity. Years later this priceless 70 minutes resurfaced as *A Six Pack of Lies* (CDVBOO1).

The Complete Fawlty Towers by John Cleese and Connie Booth published by Methuen and, as the title suggests, includes all 12 scripts for the series.

June – *The Illustrated London News* magazine publishes A Place in the Pillory featuring interviews with Palin and Jones. The release of *Consuming Passions*, based on a Jones/Palin script.

Curse of the Vampire Socks by Terry Jones, published by Pavilion.

July – *Starlog* magazine publishes Kim 'Howard' Johnson's *Those Notorious Norsemen in Their Luxurious Long Ships* and Lynne Stephens talks to Erik's creator, Terry Jones, for *Confessions of the World's Greatest Liar*.

Cleese promotes *A Fish Called Wanda* on *Larry King Live* (CNN), CBS *News Nightwatch*, *Macneil-Lehrer Report* (PBS) and joins Michael Palin on HBO *Entertainment News*.

6 July – Cleese discusses *Wanda* on *Late Night with Letterman*.

7 July – Cleese interviewed by Chris Connelly on MTV's *The Big Picture*.

8 July – Cleese talks about *Wanda* and his life in Iain Blair's article A Wandaful Life for The *Chicago Tribune*.

13 July – he appears on *Entertainment Tonight*.

18 July – he talks to host Jay Leno on *The Tonight Show* and on 26 is interviewed by Dennis Michael on

Showbiz Today.

21 July – John Cleese is the guest disc jockey on *Elliott Forrest* (WNCN-FM Radio, New York), while Michael Palin plugs *Wanda* on *Paul W. Smith and Company* (WMCA-AM Radio, New York).

27 July – Cleese, Palin and Jamie Lee Curtis are interviewed via satellite on *Crook and Chase* (TNN – The Nashville Network). Cleese crops up on the channel again, 2 September.

28 July – *The Boston Globe* newspaper publishes A Proud Father of *A Fish Called Wanda* which includes extracts taken from the Parker House Cleese interview and later in the day, Cleese is interviewed by Jane Pauley in New York for NBC's *Today The Day*. The following day both Cleese and Palin appear on *Good Morning America.*

2 August – the *Wanda* cast are interviewed on *Phil Donahue* (NBC), Palin and Kline are in the studio, Cleese and Jamie Lee appear via satellite.

6 August – Cleese and Palin are interviewed on *Hersey's Hollywood*. Surprise, surprise, from 2 September another eight compilation shows showcased *22 Years of the Two Ronnies*.

September – Cleese interviewed for *PM Magazine.*

6 September – Cleese interviewed via satellite from Venice on *Today.*

27 September – Michael Palin hosts *Half Hour Comedy Hour*, showcasing new stand-up comedians on MTV.

Attacks of Opinion by Terry Jones, published by Penguin Books, with illustrations by Gerald Scarfe.

August – *Cinemax, Beyond the Screen*, takes a look at the making of *A Fish Called Wanda*.

3 August – *Funny People*, NBC Television, profiles John Cleese.

8 September – interest in the pre-Fab Four is maintained with the *Goldmine* newspaper article 'The Rutles: It Was Ten and a Third Years Ago Today' by Jeff Tamarkin.

8 October – Cleese is on *Aspel and Co.*

9 October – Channel 4's *The Media Show*, presented by Muriel Gray, includes an interview with Terry Gilliam.

18 October – *John Cleese's First Farewell Performance*, BBC1, donates £100,000 to Sussex University for a three-year research programme into 'psychological phenomenon of projection and denial'.

23 October – *Number 27* Written by Michael Palin screened on BBC1.

November – '20 Questions' with John Cleese published in *Playboy.*

25 December – major interview with John – 'Cleese Up Close' – appears in The New York *Times* Magazine.

1989

9 January – *Today* (NBC) features a piece on the making of *Erik the Viking* and includes interviews with Terry Jones and John Cleese. Vicki Woods' piece for *Sharp* includes an interview with John Cleese from Holland Park, London – photos by Max Vadukul.

15 January – Michael Palin wins an ACE award at the 10th annual ceremony in the category of Writing for a Movie/Miniseries for *East of Ipswich* – the play having just been broadcast on the Arts and Entertainment Cable channel in America.

28 January – Cleese, Jamie Lee and *Wanda* are nominated for Golden Globe Awards at the 46th Annual Award ceremony, screened on TBS. Michael Palin appears on *Don't Just Sit There*, Nickelodeon.

28 February – Terry Gilliam plugs *Munchausen* on NBC's *Late Night with David Letterman.*

The Radio 2 series celebrating comedy film, *Make 'Em Laugh*, tackled great team work with the working class uprising speech from *Monty Python and the Holy Grail*. Host Bernard Cribbins offered it as the finest piece of film comedy of its decade.

March – *Beyond the Screen*'s look at *Munchausen* includes interview contributions from Terry Gilliam and Eric Idle.

8 March – Gilliam discusses the *Baron* on *Crook and Chase* (TNN – The Nashville Network) and *Showbiz Today* (CNN). 10 March – Gilliam plugs the *Baron* again on *Good Morning America* (ABC Television).

12 March – *Entertainment Tonight* looks at the Gilliam/Idle *Munchausen* movie.

14 March – Cleese awarded the Jack Benny Award – the following day *Showbiz Today* (CNN) and *Entertainment Tonight* report.

17 March – *Entertainment Today* runs a piece on Cleese's British TV ads and includes a comment from the man himself taken from the earlier Jack Benny award interview.

During March, Michael Palin asks viewers to donate to the PBS Television fundraising campaign.

Graham Chapman is interviewed by Matthew Bullen for Birmingham University's *Redbrick* magazine. Later an edited version was printed in the May 1996 issue of *Comedy Review.*

The BBC Radio Collection release the double cassette *I'm Sorry, I'll Read That Again* with John Cleese starring in complete episodes originally broadcast on 9 June 1968, 5 April 1970 and 23 December 1973, plus the 22 March 1970 one in which Cleese didn't appear.

29 March – *Wanda*'s three Oscar nominations result in just the one win for Kevin Kline's supporting performance.

In Barry Norman's Barry Awards for Comic Relief, John Cleese was named top film comedian, his skills illustrated via clips from *Monty Python's Life of Brian* and *A Fish Called Wanda*. He was up against very stiff opposition – Groucho Marx, Bob Hope, W.C. Fields, Steve Martin, Woody Allen and Peter Sellers – all of whom were more film-oriented comedy players. Still, the winner out of the hat became the lucky owner of Cleese's underpants from the Russian strip sequence from *Wanda*. Penguin Books supports the charity with the publication of *The Utterly, Utterly Amusing and Pretty Damn Definitive Comic Relief Revue Book*, featuring Cleesian references to Volestrangler, the (ancient) history of the dead parrot and several *Python* penned pieces – The Last Supper (Cleese from *A Poke In The Eye*), Hendon (Palin/Jones from *The Frost Report*), John & Mary (Cleese/Oddie from *Cambridge Circus*), The Good Old Days (Cleese/Chapman/Brooke-Taylor/Feldman from *At Last the 1948 Show*) and Horace, an original poem by Terry Jones concerning a boy who eats himself.

Monty Python's Flying Circus: Just the Words (aka *The Complete Monty Python's Flying Circus: All the Words*) published in two volumes, Methuen.

6 April – Idle interviewed by Dennis Michael on *Showbiz Today.*

10 April – first episode of Eric Idle's *Nearly Departed* broadcast, NBC

13 April-17 April – four daily reports on the set of *Around the World in Eighty*

Days with Eric Idle, broadcast in *Entertainment Today.* The new version of Verne's classic is screened over three nights, 16, 17, 18 April, on NBC.
19 April – Michael Palin hosts The Prince's Trust: A Rock and Royal Gala benefit concert at The London Palladium. 24 April – Puzzling Out His Post-*Python* Life Leaves Eric Idle with Hands Full by Susan Schindehette & Michael Alexander in *People Weekly Magazine.*
May – the Social Democratic Party broadcast features old footage from John Cleese's 1987 lecture.
25 May – MTV's *The Big Picture* looks at *Nuns on the Run* – Idle is interviewed on TV's *Public People/Private Lives.*
The video release of *A Fish Called Wanda* is overshadowed by John Cleese's hilarious Schweppes ad which accompanies it, featuring him as his own twin brother giving a lecture on subliminal advertising and posing as a beach boy macho man. The tape becomes the number one rental in America. Cleese guests on *The Big Picture* and *Bullseye!*
Terry Gilliam directed an ambitious commercial for Orangina, featuring a plane-load of folk finding unique ways of shaking their drinks. Provided useful grounding in blue-screen effects (later employed on *Munchausen*) it featured *Brian*'s Charles McKeown and Terry Baylor. The director took on the assignment with the coda that the only country that could show it was France!
March – Over looked by the Oscars, *A Fish Called Wanda*'s Python connection are honoured by The British Academy Film Awards with Cleese receiving Best Actor and Michael Palin grabbing Best Supporting Actor. Cleese picks up an *Evening Standard* award, brilliantly mocks acceptance speech convention by thanking everyone from Agatha Christie to Herb Alpert & His Tijuna Brass and ultimately dropping the prized item. John Cleese wins damages in a libel case resulting from *The Daily Mirror* report detailing Fawlty-like manic attacks on cast and crew during the making of *A Fish Called Wanda.* Cleese donates the money to the charity Families at Risk, of which he's a trustee. *The Sunday Times* publishes 'Who's Reading Whom: Michael Palin' – featuring the Python's current choice of reading matter.

A long running association between John Cleese and *Yellow Pages* begins – notably featuring the classic ad with Cleese desperately searching for a ring for his beloved princess and the middle-aged mummy's boy who plays around, phones for help following his parents' breakdown and utters the immortal, *Python*-influenced – 'I'm 52 years old and a High Court Judge!' – it would run for years. Cleese films a BT advert about a man whose water pipes burst on a Bank Holiday and his phone comes to the rescue.
The Adventures of Baron Munchausen. Directed and co-written by Terry Gilliam. Starring Eric Idle. Both Idle and Gilliam contribute interview material to David Castell's 'Making of...' documentary, *Hot Air and Fantasy*, while Gilliam braved the live telephone audience on the BBC morning show *Open Air* for discussion about the problematic filming experience. *The Adventures of Baron Munchausen* by Charles McKeown and Terry Gilliam, published by Methuen/ Mandarin Books – (0-7493-0017-50 – a novel of the film. *The Adventures of Baron Munchausen* by Charles McKeown and Terry Gilliam published by Applause Theatre Books (1-55783-041-X) – Screenplay, photographs and unfilmed sequences from the film. *The Adventures of Baron Munchausen*, soundtrack of the Terry Gilliam film released by Warner Brothers Records (925826) featuring additional Eric Idle lyrics for *The Torturer's Apprentice*, *A Eunuch's Life Is Hard* and *Play Up and Win the Game.* The film's opening is heralded in *The Times* with Anne Billson's Gilliam interview (Money, magic and mischief), the film's failure is the final nail in David Puttnam's coffin and Gilliam's unjustified erratic reputation is at its peak. Despite this, Gilliam announces his new project as *Watchmen*, a fantasy about disillusioned superheros with *Die Hard/Lethal Weapon* producer Joel Silver. The intriguing logo, a happy face badge dripping blood, was, alas, the only result.
John Cleese makes two Party Political Broadcasts for SDP by invitation of David Steel. The most famous example, a classic, thought-provoking, hilarious and powerful argument for the use of proportional representation was

subsequently cited as the most successful programme ever made in its field, changing people's opinions with the political claptrap stripped away to reveal the common sense reality underneath. Although having got through the SDP/Liberal division, Cleese donated to the Green party explaining that 'My politics are those of bewilderment.' Graham Chapman, John Cleese, Terry Gilliam, Eric Idle and Michael Palin contribute interview footage to HandMade's tenth anniversary celebration documentary *The Movie Life of George.*
The Secret Policeman's Biggest Ball, performed in September, included appearances from John Cleese and Michael Palin, captured on video.
Eric Idle appears in a television advert for Metro Motors with Nigel Mansel.
22 September – Idle interviewed for *Showbiz Today* during rehearsals for a *Saturday Night Live* Special
Erik the Viking Written, directed and starring Terry Jones with John Cleese. Jones is dismayed when his final cut remains unreleased and some 300 copies have been printed of a ten-minute longer version of the film which received general release in England and American. Elements from the start and end of the film are shortened in the Jones-approved version and this cut subsequently makes the English video release, although in the US the longer version is used.
Erik the Viking by Terry Jones published by Applause Theatre Books (1-55783-054-1), featuring the screenplay and photographs from the film. *Erik the Viking* by Terry Jones published by Robson Books (0-86051-631-8), the comic book version of the film with illustrations by Graham Thompson. Sonet Records release the *Erik the Viking* soundtrack (SNTF 1023) narrated by Freddie Jones.
1 October – Terry Jones appears on *Sunday, Sunday* (LWT) with Gloria Hunniford.
4 October – Graham Chapman dies.
5 October – It was 20 years ago today and the BBC pay special tribute to the *Python* legacy while the Museum of Broadcasting in New York hosts a special retrospective. At the same time, Paramount begin releasing *Python* on video in the States for the first time.

8 October – Iain Johnstone pays tribute to Graham with Missing That Talent to Amuse (*The Sunday Times*).

11 October – First episode of *Around the World In 80 Days*, written and presented by Michael Palin, broadcast, BBC1 while earlier the same evening Palin was interviewed about the programme by Terry Wogan stand-in Joanna Lumley. Palin's best-selling book of his journey is published by the BBC (0-563-20826-0) the following Thursday, featuring extended extracts from his journals and photographs from the epic trip. For its American broadcast on the Arts & Entertainment Network the title read *Around the World in 80 Days?* – which kept that audience guessing! In the *Radio Times* (from October 7–13 issue) Palin's travel diary is printed, while the man himself endorses the journal's competition offering a hot air balloon trip over the Scottish Highlands!

27 October – Terry Jones is interviewed in Hollywood by Bella Shaw about *Erik the Viking* for *Showbiz Today* and takes time to pay special tribute to Graham Chapman.

28 October – ITV screen edited highlights of Cleese and Palin in *The Secret Policeman's Biggest Ball*. The grand but short-lived ITV film show *Saturday Night at the Movies* with Tony Slattery includes Terry Gilliam selecting the best of the Bristol Animation Festival.

30 October – *People Weekly*'s Susan Schindehette and Janine Di Giovanni put together an affectionate farewell – Mourning Monty Python Lays to Rest Silly, Brave, Unique, Graham Chapman. Still reluctant to silly walk, John Cleese attends the SDP conference in Blackpool and upon leaving a lift heralds a rousing chorus of the *Liberty Bell* from Deal servicemen. In the wake of the IRA bombing and emotion over Graham's death Cleese obilges with a few silly steps before going on his way.

Radio Times (November 18-24) salutes *Python*, with ex-*Late Night Line-up* link Tony Bilbow chatting to the lads, including Chapman's last interview, alongside Paul Fox's memoirs of the birth of the *Flying Circus*.

Michael Palin was one of 26 hosts for *The A-Z of T.V.* – a mammoth Channel 4 celebration from Illuminations

Productions (producer – Linda Zuck, director – Phil McDonald). Brylcreamed and relaxed, Palin presented the letter A in a glorious, self-contained, seven-minute section detailing the importance of Ally Pally, showcasing a host of priceless novelty TV turns, chatting with intercut interview footage with John Logie Baird and Benny Hill (the 'queer places' laughter reaction is spot on) and heralding the beginning of Angelia. Stunning, Palin's contribution stole the show from other notable hosts including Beryl Reid, Michael Hordern and Rodney Bewes.

Thanks to its use in *Punch* magazine television ads, *Always Look On The Bright Side Of Life* hits the singles chart at number 8 – Idle is approached by *Top of the Pops* to see if he can round up the surviving four fellow Pythons for an appearance. The album, *Monty Python Sings*, is released in memory of Graham The *Not the Nine O'Clock News* album Hedgehog Sandwich (featuring Not the Parrot Sketch) re-released as half of *Not the Nine O'Clock News* (BBC ZBBC 1009) in March 1989, coupled with 1984's *Not the Double Album* – itself a re-issue of the studio material from the 1982 classic *The Memory Kinda Lingers*

7–15 November – Palin appears in the BBC2 series, *The Art of Travel*.

6 December – John Cleese debates against the Broadcasting Bill on Network, BBC1.

December – Graham Chapman memorial service with Pythons (Idle performed *Always Look On The Bright Side Of Life*), Neil Innes wearing duck hat, Douglas Adams, Tim Brooke-Taylor and The Fred Tomlinson Singers who led a Chinese version of *Jerusalem* – the team drank to his memory in sherry. The delayed *Python* anniversary party followed.

John Cleese guests on *Wogan*.

11 December – Michael Palin promotes *Around the World in 80 Days* on TV's *Regis and Kathie Lee* and appears on Johnny Carson's *The Tonight Show* on 14 December.

22 December – Eric Idle features on Muriel Grey's Channel 4 chat show, *Walkie Talkie*. Directed by Hamish Barbour for Skyline and Gallus Besom productions, Idle wandered aimlessly around his childhood stomping ground of

Stratford-upon-Avon and, eventually, irritated by the waste of time, commented that the money for the show would be better spend on comedy!

25 December – John Cleese joins in another reunion for the 25th anniversary comeback of *I'm Sorry I'll Read That Again* on Radio 2

27 December – Terry Jones stars in the *Woman's Hour* play *Shivering Peaks*, written by Sue Limb – the rest of the cast includes Monica Dickens, Sarah Greene and Jeremy Hardy.

The first issue of *Empire* boasts John Cleese on its cover with the eye-catching legend, Sex God!

1990

January – Memorial held for Graham Chapman by the British Academy of Film and Television Arts in Los Angeles. David Sherlock and Harry Nilsson are among those who attend.

30 January – Cleese appears on *This Morning* (ITV)

Michael Palin joins Terry Wogan and Arthur Smith to discuss experiences while filming *Pole to Pole* (including the shock of being recognised in far-flung places, the skilfully employed technique of closing a door while naked but still not exposing himself – complete with 'didn't see anything!' line and amused audience reaction, and the refined, BBC attitude of ferreting out a witch doctor chappie for an interview.

17–24 May – Cleese is still heard defending *Life of Brian* against the blasphemy misconception on *How Far Can You Go?* (Radio 4). The spot also allowed Palin to plug his supporting role in Tracey Ullman's *A Class Act* playing a strict father and a aregressive hippie. Palin invests £40,000 in the documentary *Benjamin Huntsman – Man of Steel* and writes the foreword for the Railway Department Society's *Rail For The Future*.

The Complete Ripping Yarns by Terry Jones and Michael Palin published by Methuen. *Monty Python's Flying Circus – Just the Words*, reprinted as one volume.

11 June – Michael Palin struggles with a satirical political speech for the Nelson Mandela 70th Birthday Concert, Wembley. Filmed by Elephant House Productions (director Ken O'Neill/executive producer Neville Bolt),

a revised repeat appears on Christmas Day, 1990.

13 August – John Cleese is the special guest on Barry Cryer's excellent series, *Funny That Way*, allowing great funny people to select soundbites of their favourite funny people (Radio 4).

17 September – Cleese is interviewed at the Liberal Democrats' Party Conference for *Today* (Radio 4).

The Adventures of Baron Munchausen released on laser disc with the approval of Terry Gilliam who provides audio commentary and reinstates one classic missing scene featuring soldiers refusing to shoot people because it's Wednesday and half-day closing – thus explaining continual references to the dubious fact that it's Wednesday in the final cut. Laser, it's the only way to see the film...

Radio Times (3–9 November) publishes Michael Palin's article 'My Kind of Day'.

6 December – Cleese appears on the Radio 4 programme *Bookshelf*. *A Fish Called Wanda* is voted Best British Video of the Year and Best Comedy by the British Videogram Association.

From 12 December – John Cleese and Robin Skynner (interviewed by Carol Price in *Radio Times* (8–14 December) present the six-part Radio 4 version of their book *Families and How to Survive Them*, guest on *Wogan* and then head off for Tibet to make a film with the Dalai Lama.

In the dying embers of her power, Margaret Thatcher at the Bournemouth conference delivers the notorious 'This is an ex-parrot' speech concerning the SDP bird logo.

The fledgling BSB screen a season of *Python*-related films – *A Fish Called Wanda*, *Privates on Parade*, *Time Bandits* and *The Missionary*.

David Frost released his 1968 comedy classic *How To Irritate People* on video. Initially he requested John Cleese to oversee the project (he refused due to lack of time); in the end Michael Palin took time out to watch the old tape again, make a few minor cuts of weak material and see the show available on tape for the first time. Cleese does find time to pose for the lenses of Annie Leibovitz for a couple of American Express newspaper ads: dressed as a bat hanging from a tree in Windsor Great Park and posing in high-class

drag, complete with a couple of dogs, with the legend 'John Cleese, Card member since 1971'. He only took on the assignment provided the shots be as silly as possible and discarded ideas including hanging from the goalposts at Wimbledon Football Club, sitting naked in a refined gentleman's club and dressed in a chicken suit. Cleese was so familiar in the industry that a joke suggestion developed about awarding a prize for the best use of John Cleese with overseas endorsements including beer, pretzels and fish fingers in Australia, Lowney's Peanut Butter Cups in Canada, the Danish Shoes Council, Norwegian mayonnaise and the Dutch Post Office. Cleese admits, 'I've done commercials I would pay for you not to see!'

25 December – John Cleese is interviewed by Phil Easton on Orchard FM, Taunton Radio.

1991

Following the success of *The A-Z of T.V.* Illuminations producer Linda Zuck put together a Channel 4 semi-sequel called *1001 Nights Of Television* (director Steve Connelly). Clearly Palin's earlier hosting sessions had impressed as he fronted the entire three hours of television nostalgia, clocking up the exact number of nights of television viewing that this compilation provides. His downbeat, glittering suited, Northern working men's type host popped up throughout, alongside various incarnations from the flawless Alison Steadman and guest section presenters like Adam Faith and Rory Bremner – Graham Chapman and John Cleese crop up in vintage clips.

Michael Palin narrates the story of *Jack and the Beanstalk* for the Rabbit Ears series of *We All Have Tales* videos (REV 10260). Recorded at Pinewood Studios with music by Dave Stewart and illustrations from Edward Sorel.

30 January – Cleese interviewed on *This Morning*.

The Fisher King Directed by Terry Gilliam.

The Fisher King by Richard LaGravenese published by Applause Theatre Books, featured the screenplay of the film with extra deleted sequences and photographs from the film. Introduction written by Terry Gilliam.

The Fisher King by Leonore Fleischer published by Signet Ae (0-451-17222-1), the novel of the Terry Gilliam film. Following British football fans singing *Always Look On the Bright Side Of Life* in defeat, Virgin released a CD single (PYTHD 1 664740). It also featured *I'm So Worried*, *I Bet You They Won't Play This Song on the Radio* and *Holzfaller Song*, the rare German version of *Lumberjack Song*. It hit No. 1 in Ireland, stayed at No. 6 for three weeks in Germany and boosted the healthy sales of the album, *Monty Python Sings*.

On television Cleese appears in a series of promotions for Panasonic as well as a further endorsement of Schweppes, including the delicious *Python*esque test of the fizziness in drinks as a race.

May – Cleese attends a two-day reunion at Clifton College while Palin and Jones take part in a hay-on-Way comedy writing debate. Cleese provides voice characterisation for *An American Tail: Fievel Goes West*, Palin's *American Friends* released.

Losing the Light, Terry Gilliam and the Munchausen Saga by Andrew Yule published by Applause Theatre Books (1-55783-060-6).

Although an important part of his character development in *A Fish Called Wanda*, and played by Michael Palin with respect to his stammering father, some Stutterers Groups in the USA took severe offence at Palin's performance. Much to the disgust of the makers, ABC edited out portions of Kline's abuse of Palin when the film was screened on television. Amazing! At the same time, Palin embraced the cause and opened The Michael Palin Centre For Stammering Children at the Finsbury Health Centre, London. Established by the Association for Research into Stammering in Childhood and the Local National Health Service Trust, its chief therapist, Robert Spence, explained that limited resources dictated only five children could be assessed per week.

September – *The Very Best of Rowan Atkinson Live* cassette (Laughing Stock LAFFC1) includes the Jones, Cleese, Palin version of Four Yorkshiremen from *The Secret Policeman's Ball*. Laughing Stock also released the old 1979 *Secret Policeman's Ball* album as LAFFC2.

To mark the 15th anniversary of the A

Poke In the Eye concerts, Castle released a double CD and cassette (ESDCD/MC 153) The Complete Poke In The Eye (With A Sharp Stick), utilising Gilliam's original cover art and the 1976 record line-up with a totally new collection of unreleased material featuring Python gems, Pet Shop with Cleese and Palin, Argument Clinic and Crunchy Frog. Other fresh delights included Barry Humphreys, Eleanor Bron and three *Goodies* tracks (including the sublime beyond words Sick Man Blues).
October – *The Complete Secret Policeman's Other Ball* (Island ESDMC/CD 152) ultilises the original album with an extra hour of newly released comedy, none of which features *Python*-related material.
An episode of *Neighbours* crosses culture with an embrace of *At Last's* 'looxury' tagline from the Four Yorkshiremen.
Spike Milligan complains that the Pythons stole his act in Channel Four's *The Obituary Show.*
Terry Gilliam designs the poster for the 35th London Film Festival (6-21 November), a huge wave about to crash down on the spirit on film floating on a wooden raft. Joyous.
Monty Python's The Meaning of Life starts Channel four retrospective of great British comedy movies, *Beyond Ealing*, while the Gilliamesque hand pointing through the pearly gates accompanied the commercial breaks for all movies in the season.
G.B.H. starring Michael Palin, the Elvis Costello music is made available on CD, record and cassette.
John Cleese makes a brief contribution to Central television's *Amnesty's Big 30* programme. The video, A*mnesty International's Big 30 – The Comedy Concert* included Cleese's contribution plus a vintage piece with Hugh Laurie and Stephen Fry from *The Secret Policeman's Third Ball.*
7 December – Terry Jones writes and hosts the BBC history one-off special *So This is Progress.* The rumoured series in celebration of history was not forthcoming. Breaking into a *Mikado* set-up, Eric Idle performs the clean version of *Always Look On The Bright Side Of Life* at the Royal Command Performance – it is later included alongside Frankie Howerd, Sid James and Tommy Cooper

in Denis Norden's clip show celebration *Laughter By Royal Command.*

1992

Virgin re-release the classic *Monty Python's The Meaning of Life* track *The Galaxy Song* as a CD single. Two versions are made available: one coupled with *Christmas In Heaven* and *Always Look On the Bright Side of Life,* while the other is joined by *I Like Chinese* and *Brian Song.*
The Fisher King released on laser disc complete with audio commentary from Terry Gilliam and deleted sequences.
The Holy Grail book re-issued by Mandarin paperbacks. *Fantastic Stories* by Terry Jones published by Pavilion.
Pole to Pole Written and presented by Michael Palin and *Pole to Pole* by Michael Palin published by BBC Books. He resisted temptations to call it *Jules Verne's Pole to Pole* seeing he had pinched the idea for his first trip! *Pole to Pole With Palin* appears in the December issue of *BBC World Magazine,* an account of the Africa leg of the journey.
Terry Gilliam reviews *Delicatessen* for BBC's *Moving Pictures.*
The BBC examination of comedy in four parts *Funny Business,* ranged from the sublime comic lecture of Rowan Atkinson to the standard heartaches and trials of the double act – Cleese's work in *Fawlty Towers* was used alongside the likes of Buster Keaton and Peter Sellers to highlight the best in *Visual Comedy* and Cleese make a special appearance in the most ambitious series entry *A Question of Taste* (written by director Mark Chapman and producer Sarah Williams, Tiger Television for the BBC) – a mock (note the *Dr. Who* geared researcher), fly-on-the-wall, documentary beginning with the idea of the question of offensive comedy from a John Cleese Sunday Supplement. There's an inspirational quote 'No one has the right not to be offended', clips of *Meaning of Life* and finally a tracking down of Cleese to his home for a comment. Cleese is seen with Goofy mask over his privates, bandaged wearing a fur hat; two lush girls are seductively draped around him; a bishop is in there somewhere; the great man shoots a blind woman's guide dog and moans about women,

interviewers and nig-nogs before disgruntedly muttering – 'Now, F*** off!' with a two-finger salute and a slammed door. It's every taboo know to man and the series highlight by a mile...

1993

Python and *Fawlty* were again predominant during the Comic Relief fund raising while Terry Wogan struggled through the *Lumberjack Song* in the BBC Banned Audition Tapes section!
Lumiere's compilation programme *Make 'Em Laugh!*: School Daze features a bit of John Cleese ranting from *Clockwise.*
5 November – Michael Palin contributes to BBC2's Poetry Week with a reading on *Poets on the Box* (producer: Tim May).
20 March – Michael Palin appeared in BBC2's *Bore of the Year Awards* with Angus Deayton, Ian Hislop, Harry Enfield, Richard Ingrams and Peter Cook, who hosted the show and cropped up as Robert Maxwell. Directed by Janet Fraser Cook and produced by Hislop and Harry Thompson. One hour.
John Cleese stars in a series of American TV ads for Magnavox, *The Penguin Book of Comedy Sketches* – collected by Frank Muir and Simon Brett and features several *Python*-related pieces. Palin takes his second *Great Railway Journey* for BBC television.
Plans for a BBC animated series of the exploits of Greyfriar's favourite son, Billy Bunter, are shelved in the heated politically correct atmosphere – John Cleese and Michael Palin were to provide the voices.
27 December – Compilation show *The Best of Rutland Weekend Television* written and performed by Eric Idle. Originally aimed as a taster for a proposed video release which was later shelved. *Rutland Weekend Television* – 1993 going to New Year's Eve Parties; 1994 – nothing!! Regent Street's Liberties store features Cleese's silly walk in its laugh-in window display.

1994

Monty Python's 25th anniversary is suitably marked by a myriad of events, programmes and merchandising. The team are given the full cultural treatment on Radio 2's two-hour *Arts Programme* (10pm, Sunday 18

September), but only two Pythons (Michael Palin and Terry Jones) joined host Barry Took to discuss the show's vast legacy. *Python*'s 25th saw a huge marketing outburst, with Virgin's re-release of all the records on CD (available in the mega-bucks *Instant Monty Python* CD Collection) which contained eight *Python* albums on 6 CDs. Instantly, you could own *Another Monty Python Record*, *Monty Python's Previous Record*, *Monty Python's Matching Tie and Handkerchief*, *Monty Python Live at Drury Lane*, *Monty Python and the Holy Grail*, *Monty Python's Contractual Obligation Album* and *Meaning of Life*, although the pristine formats rather perversely saw albums lumped together and generally mucked about with. Virgin released *The Ultimate Monty Python Rip Off* (CDV 2748) as a taster for the set, while the albums were also available separately on compact discs and cassette in their Chattering Classics series – *Another*, *Previous*, *Handkerchief*, *Drury Lane*, *Grail*, *Contractual* and, for the first time even on CD, *Brian* and *Meaning of Life*. Philips released three CD-i titles, *Life Without Monty Python*, *Invasion From the Planet Skyron* and *More Naughty Bits*.

Sunday evenings on BBC2 during August and September paid host to the first series of *Monty Python's Flying Circus*, while the biggest celebration was held at The National Film Theatre. A huge foot cake was cut with four of the surviving team members – John Cleese, Terry Gilliam, Terry Jones and Michael Palin – in attendance. The foot leads the punter round MOMI.

12 January – John Cleese received The Jack Oakie Award for comedy from the Screen Actors Guild, presented by *Wanda* co-star Jamie Lee Curtis. The only other actor to have received the award was Walter Matthau, and in discussion afterwards Cleese announces that two sequels to *Wanda* are on the way – with *Death Fish II* still in the running as one of the titles.

Long overdue release of Marty Feldman material on BBC video; *It's Marty*, featured Python penned sketches and on-screen cameos from Palin and Jones in World Cup 1966.

March – *Starlog Magazine* publishes The Fantastic Realist: Terry Gilliam Lives in the Real World Or Maybe He's Just Imagining That by Kim 'Howard' Johnson.

Sunday 17 April – An Evening with Michael Palin is presented at the Cambridge Theatre at 8pm in aid of the Michael Palin Centre For Stammering Children – tickets start at £15.

The original Rutles soundtrack enjoyed a re-release with extra tracks. *Python* enlivened mugs, greetings cards, calendars, a diary…

The Simpsons episode, *Homer Goes To College*, features the title couch sequence gag with Home, Lisa and the gang squashed by a huge *Monty Python* foot. The homage is continued when the three computer nerds boast of knowing every *Python* piece off by heart and demonstrating with a bit of Ni Knights from *Grail,* while the sofa gag was repeated with *Lisa v. Malibu Stacy* and *Another Simpsons Clipshow* and *The Simpsons* 138th episode spectacular *A Fish Called Selma* twisted the title of Cleese's biggest film success for the Springfield community. Check out the Gilliamesque Mount Rushmore stage antics in *I Love Lisa* – Fab…

Life Before and After Monty Python: The Solo Flights of the Flying Circus by Kim 'Howard' Johnson with an introduction by Harry Nilsson published by St. Martin's Press, New York – all *Python* members royalties going to Rainforest Action Network, San Francisco.

Methuen reprint the *Holy Grail* book in all its hardback glory.

Omnibus, Quentin Tarantino: Hollywood's Boy Wonder, BBC1, marks the British release of *Pulp Fiction*. Cinematic guru Terry Gilliam is interviewed, praises Tarantino's skill and advises him to stop making movies about movies. Gilliam's support in the early days is acknowledged in the final credits for 1992's *Reservoir Dogs*.

Michael Palin, with his 'president of pressure group Transport 2000' cap on, presents the *Open Space Special*, Car Sick (BBC2), about the threat of too much traffic on our roads – he was tongue-in-cheekily concerned that dissenters would mercilessly bring up his own beloved Mercedes 190!

Palin's Column hits Channel 4 and *Radio Times* (4-10 June) features an edited extract of Mike's handiwork under the title, The Wight Side of Palin.

The two-part *South Bank Show* special on comedy includes Harry Enfield maintaining that *Monty Python* was always elitistly popular and *Dick Emery* was far more important.

Michael Palin's play *The Weekend* opens with Richard Wilson heading the cast. It is later published.

In August John Cleese makes a citizen's arrest on a 14-year-old boy who snatched a woman's handbag near the Python's home in Notting Hill, West London.

Michael Palin gives support to an impoverished drama student who appeals to famous actors for help – Timothy West, Sir Anthony Hopkins, Nigel Hawthorne, John Thaw and Kenneth Branagh are also among those who cough up.

Dead Parrot Society (Springtime/Rhino R2 71049) utilised material from the Amnesty shows *A Poke In the Eye* (*With A Sharp Stick*) and *The Secret Policeman's Ball*, featuring Cleese, Chapman, Gilliam, Jones and Palin in The Dead Parrot, The Courtroom, Crunchy Frog, Top of the Form, The Penultimate Supper, The Argument Clinic and The Lumberjack Song. Laughing Stock released the double CD set Amnesty International – *Best Of the Balls* (LAF CD 15), featuring highlights from five concert – *Python* material included Cleese on The Penultimate Supper and Parrot Sketch from *A Poke In the Eye*, Cleese, Palin and Jones with Atkinson on Four Yorkshiremen, Cleese and Cook's Interesting Facts and Palin and Jones performing How Do You Do It from *The Secret Policeman's Ball* and Cleese and Palin with the Parrot from the *Biggest Ball*.

The mugs, issued by The Ink Group, were released in exclusive 25 and a half anniversary packaging with designing featuring Gilliam's bespectacled man, Conquistador Coffee and the How to Spot a Royal game. Cornerstone Communications release a *Monty Python* Trading Card set with everything from Palin's Lumberjack being Okay to a rather dead-looking parrot. All cards were backed with a patriotic Union Jack. The Ink Group throw all the 25th anniversary card designs into one classic 1995 calendar, promising to 'prolong your life' thanks to an extra free month.

1995

Terry Gilliam hosts the centenary of film drama-documentary *The Last Machine*, BBC2 from 7 January. A BBC Education booklet is published.

From 10 January, *Crusades* broadcast on BBC2, written and presented by Terry Jones.

Radio Times (7–13 January) features Jones interviewed by Brian James ('Richard the Lionheart was a thug!') and a BBC book, *Crusades* by Terry Jones and Alan Ereira, is published.

March – BBC2 announce that in honour of the 20th anniversary of the first *Fawlty Towers* all 12 episodes will get another, much welcome, airing. And in May they do, with the Fab Four *Radio Times* cover stars ('Basil's Back!') and rumours that John Sachs, son of Andrew, has almost got plans for a Manuel spin-off series off the ground. Cleese has allegedly given full support to the project, and will even sit in on several development conferences to point the writer in the right direction – really!

April – The Health Education Authority drop John Cleese from a £13-million anti-smoking campaign due to the ads failing to make a dent in the problem. Mixing hilarious comedy and cold facts, these messages enlivened and educated for two years, with stunning moments of cigarette pack shooting, discussing the problem from within a rabbit hutch or a dustbin and, most powerfully of all, showing Cleese as a corpse in a morgue reflecting on the habit. One ad, featuring Cleese wedged inside the bonnet of a mini and instructing parents to smoke somewhere that wouldn't harm the kids – 'like Peru' was, believe it or not, condemned by the Peruvian embassy and the Foreign Office because Peru is an anti-smoking country and found Cleese's comment offensive. The ad hit the dust in January and may have led to Cleese's complete phase-out of these brilliantly constructed public health soundbites.

The tones of John Cleese blasting 'And Now For Something Completely Different!' welcomed our nation hero and his American colleagues during their space mission in February. Cleese, in vintage Fawlty form, cropped up in *Paul Merton's World of Comedy* and in *Interesting Facts/The End of the World*

(with Palin and Jones) on the Laughing Stock release *Peter Cook Anthology* (LAFFC 39).

18 April – Michael Palin discusses the myths of madness for the Radio 4 documentary *Don't Fence Me In* (producer Clare McGinn), part of the BBC Radio and Television *States of Mind* season. Palin is interviewed about his hosting of the programme, his sister's suicide and the madness of Goon/Python comedy by Andrew Duncan for the *Radio Times* (15–21 April).

29 April – *The Times Saturday Magazine* unveils the top 25 cult television favourites with the 'incandescent' Fawlty Towers coming in at no. 7 with *Monty Python's Flying Circus* bounding above *Dr. Who* and *Dad's Army* to position 4. Fittingly, Phil Silvers came out on top. BBC Radio Collection release *I'm Sorry I'll Read That Again* 3, featuring episodes from 26 May 1968, 22 February 1970, 3 May 1970 and 11 November 1973.

1 May – Peter Cook's memorial service at Hampstead is attended by Michael Palin, Terry Jones and John Cleese who read a touching tribute and later commented that, 'He was extraordinarily free of ambition and envy and rancour.' Eric Idle attended a tribute in America and, during Stephen Fry's escape from the British press in Barbados, dined with him and shared Cook stories.

May – two drunken men (Nicholas O'Connell & Glen Hilliard) tried unsuccessfully to break into Michael Palin's Belsize Park home before the Python contacted the police and saw the couple arrested.

In support of National Poetry Day prominent people were asked for their favourite verse – John Cleese chose *Essex Everyman* by Roger Woodis, while Michael Palin picked *Futility* by Wilfred Owen.

The old, old clips were yet again dragged out for Comic Relief's *Two's Company* compilation of BBC2 hits while, more interesting, Michael Palin joined the distinguished cast of the big film for the evening – *Oliver 2: Let's Twist Again*. Resurrecting glorious *Python* style with his flamboyantly moustachioed salesman with ever more bizarre and outrageous designs, the show was stolen by two returning faces

from the Carol Reed original – Oliver Reed as a manic wildman and Ron Moody, repeating his role as Fagin, effortlessly injecting some class.

John Cleese tackles British politics with the same Video Arts mix of fact and humour for *Look At The State We're In!* on BBC1 – discusses the implications with *The Times*' Lucy Bailey and is interviewed by Andrew Duncan for *Radio Times* (20–26 May).

Denis Norden's *40 Years of ITV Laughter* feature clips of Cleese and Chapman from *At Last the 1948 Show*. Eric Idle appears in *Casper*.

In his attack on modern television, So Why Can't Television Entertain Us Any More?, Roy Hattersley (29 July) comments '*Black Adder*, *Monty Python* and *Fawlty Towers* were all, in their time, regarded as both daring and dangerous... they made viewers happy'. Terry Gilliam's *Brazil* is screened as part of the BBC 100 series, celebrating the best in a century of cinema.

Christmas Day – (ITV, 5.05pm) Michael Palin features as Rat in an animated version of *The Wind in the Willows*.

October – Mandarin publish *The Fairly Incomplete and Rather Badly Illustrated Monty Python Song Book*, with bonus CD, coupling those great names of song Chapman, Cleese, Gilliam, Idle, Jones, Palin, Presley and Sinatra for the first time.

1996

Twelve Monkeys, directed by Terry Gilliam. Major publicity included a memorable interview on *Steve Wright's Saturday Show*, BBC Radio 2. For its opening American weekend the film makes $14.2 million – setting a new record for the year, while opening at the number one spot in every country in which it is released. By the end of the year *Twelve Monkeys* would make $160 million. *The Hamster Factor and Other Tales of Twelve Monkeys* documents the film's production.

Twelve Monkeys soundtrack – music by Paul Buckmaster MCA Records (MCD 11392) but unfortunately no soundbites from the film itself – not even Bruce Willis introducing Fats Domino's *Blueberry Hill* with the priceless 'I love the music of the 20th century'.

Puffin re-issue Kenneth Grahame's *The Wind in the Willows* in a Terry Jones film tie-in version.

John Cleese joined newsreader Jon Snow to be amazed by the bizarre trickery of *The Unpleasant World of Penn and Teller* – director Peter Orton, producer Alan Marke.

During nationwide press outrage at the pros and cons of releasing David Cronenberg's film version of the controversial J.G. Ballard novel *Crash*, a petition was signed by many leading players in the film industry urging its release. The signatories included Terry Gilliam, Terry Jones and Michael Palin. *Hemingway's Chair* by Michael Palin published. Press interviews included a major, enlightening one with Valerie Grove for *The Times* (5 April). 'John Cleese's silly walk' is included in Nick Hornby's novel *Fever Pitch* as representing suburban, post-war, middle-class English culture, alongside Jeffrey Archer, Adrian Mole and Evita. The Rutles launched their comeback album, *Archaeology*, although Eric Idle's Dirk McQuickly's reluctance to return resulted in the group becoming a three-man band. He received a prominent credit – The Rutles were conceived and created by Eric Idle – and headed the list of special thanks in the album booklet, a list which also included Terry Jones, Terry Gilliam and Michael Palin. Amidst anthology fever, *Magical Mystery Tour* is re-released on video and George Harrison tells VH-1 that The Rutles *Tragical History Tour* got it about right! There is a 21st anniversary video re-release and laser disc debut for *Monty Python and the Holy Grail*. Even almost 30 years after their first teaming, the Pythons were still bucking the system – pointing out the growing trend for extra material available on sell-through tapes with their generous inclusion of the 'missing 24 seconds!' The disc also includes the organ play-out music unheard since original cinema screenings.

September – John Bowis, The Road Safety Minister, unveils his 'It's good to walk' campaign, detailing the nation's walking habits and desperately trying to avoid any comparison with John Cleese. Only in this glorious country!

18 October – opening of *The Wind In The Willows*, Terry Jones's directorial/writing assignment updating Kenneth Grahame's classic headlines

four Pythons in the cast – Jones and Eric Idle in lead roles and helpful cameos from Michael Palin and John Cleese. Promotional interviews include a fine piece by Sue Sommers in *The Times* (14 October): 'We take genuine delight in one another's failures!' Eric Idle.

The Wind In The Willows by Terry Jones, published by Mandarin, includes the complete script, a wealth of colour photographs by Keith Mamshere and an unassuming introduction by Jones himself. Jones is interviewed by Simon Braund ('The Full Monty') in *Empire*'s Comedy Special.

In the top comedy pics of all-time poll, *Meaning of Life* comes in at no. 20, *Wanda* at 13, *Brian* at 9 and *Grail* at 5.

14 November – The 40th London Film Festival features *The Guardian* interview with Terry Gilliam at The National Film Theatre.

Monty Python is up for the best sketch comedy series in *The Auntie Awards* (celebrating 60 years of BBC television) but loses to *Victoria Wood – As Seen on TV*, while *Men Behaving Badly* beats the likes of *Dad's Army*, *Steptoe & Son* and *Fawlty Towers* to best situation comedy. However, the spectre of *Python* is used to sum up the whole anniversary with the Kipper Williams cartoon (*Radio Times* 2–8 November) featuring Cleese's Ministry man and the caption 'And now, a silly walk down memory lane'.

Methuen publish an affectionate collection of tributes to Peter Cook – *Something Like Fire Peter Cook Remembered*, including three Python contributions: Peter Amadeus Cook by John Cleese, The Funniest Man in the World by Eric Idle and I Had That Peter Cook in the Back of My Car by Michael Palin.

3 December – Channel 4 screen *Lumberjacks OK!* (director/producer Des Bradley), a mind-blowing test of skill and strength. During his third major travelogue, Michael Palin, with obvious *Python*esque lumberjack connections, dropped in on the famous Squamish Day as celebrity judge. The Ink Group publish *The Nearly New Monty Python Datebook* featuring everything from the lyrics to *Decomposing Composers* to Terry Jones as the nude organist. Both *The Swan Princess* (*The Swan Princess and the Secret of the Castle*) and *Casper* (*Casper A Spirited Beginning*) spawn

direct-to-video sequels although neither Cleese nor Idle reprise their original roles.

1997

New Year's Day sees a celebration of Ronnie Barker, who was awarded a special award at the BBC Sixty Years Awards. Michael Palin is among the interviewees.

Terry Gilliam announces his next project as *The Defective Detective*, although after only a few months at the planning stages this idea is dropped despite interest in the leading role from Nicholas Cage. Gilliam's replacement, a science-fiction Western called *The Trial*, gets initial backing from Warner Brothers and the cast is cited to include *Twelve Monkeys* main man Bruce Willis. John Cleese was the first castaway of the New Year on *Desert Island Discs* (9-05am 5 January, Radio 4, repeated 12-3pm 10 January) discussing *Python*, *Fawlty* and his new film with Sue Lawley. His chosen book was Tammy Wynette's autobiography because he wouldn't mind losing it and his object was Michael Palin, amended to Palin stuffed when he was forbidden another living human being.

On 15th January, John Cleese appeared on *Des O'Connor Tonight* plugging *Fierce Creatures* with a lemur in tow. His walk-on music was a rather dodgy arrangement of the *Fawlty Towers* theme and he happily repeated the much discussed real-life Fawlty, culminating with an absolutely priceless recreation of his first work performed on television, The Courier sketch. Cleese's relentless publicity tour continued with an interview spot on *Live and Kicking*, an in-depth discussion with Andrew Collins for *Empire* magazine and even a *National Lottery* appearance with Dale Winton.

Fierce Creatures, co-written by John Cleese who starred alongside Michael Palin, receives its European gala premiere at the Empire, Leicester Square on 28 January in aid of the Project Lemur Release. Both Cleese and Palin are in attendance, with cut-out figures of Jamie Lee Curtis and Kevin Kline. On the same day Cleese reveals that late the previous year he had had a cancer prostate scare – 'God's little practical joke'. The film goes on general release, 31 January.

Fierce Creatures, a novelisation of the film by Iain Johnstone, published by Arrow paperbacks.

John Cleese is interviewed by *Python* fan Eddie Izzard for *The Guardian* (31 January) expressing *Fierce Creatures* fatigue – with scores of interviews across the world, a feeling of drifting quietly into comic twilight and a major ambition to play Claudius as an energetic businessman who considers Hamlet a big disappointment.

Andrew Collins interviews Cleese for *Empire* under the heading 'Ullo John, Got A New Ending?'

Michael Palin, ostensibly plugging *Fierce Creatures* (on release nationwide from Valentine's Day), appeared on *The Frank Skinner Show* with discussion about his role as BBC travelogue favourite and, more importantly, tons of *Python.* Skinner, in hero-worship overdrive, was chuffed when Palin revealed he watched *Fantasy Football,* promoted a bit of lumberjack chewing and enjoyed Palin's Elvis Presley enjoying *Monty Python and the Holy Grail* impression. The most precious moment, of course, was a rare resurrection of the lumberjack song with Skinner doubling for Connie Booth and Palin going through the motions with sheer class. The rumours that John Cleese was considering a *Monty Python* reunion for a live show in Las Vegas was news to Palin and considered rather redundant since Graham Chapman would be absent. Over the weekend of 1/2 February, Michael Palin cropped up on *Steve Wright's Saturday Show* and John Cleese enlivened *Michael Parkinson's Sunday Supplement. Fierce Creatures* again took a back seat in favour of *Python,* Peter Cook, cricket and world travel.

Meanwhile, the four stars did the entire plug circuit, appearing on everything from The Movie Channel to UK Living. John Cleese narrates the Jersey Zoo documentary *Fierce and Gentle Creatures.* From February the BBC would present 25 Years of *the Two Ronnies,* moving the goalposts and dismissing *The Frost Report* work in order to celebrate the first broadcast of *The Two Ronnies* in April 1971.

After a mere 18 years, Swansea Borough Council finally lift their ban on screening *Monty Python's Life of Brian.*

5 March – London, Park Lane Hotel, Terry Gilliam wins the Best Director award at The Empire Awards for *Twelve Monkeys,* although he expresses surprise at not being mentioned in the Best British Director section – Ian Drury presents Gilliam with the prize while the main event of the day is a special honour for the entire *Monty Python* team with The Empire inspirational award. Elton John presents the prize to attendees Michael Palin, Terry Jones and Terry Gilliam while John Cleese and Eric Idle expressed tongue-in-cheek gratitude via a satellite link-up with Los Angeles. Idle, sitting outside Universal Studios, explained that he had Alzheimer's while Cleese, worrying about Palin's dubious X-ray, explained that Gilliam had died and that the Empire attendee was his brother Rodriguez; Jones had a few evenings left having dragged himself from a massive heart operation and Chapman was 'dead for several years now, which is sad. He may have been a silly old queen but we were fond of him.' Thank heavens for the never diminishing genius of pure *Python.*

16 April – John Cleese contributes a few words of praise to Channel Four's *Heroes of Comedy* celebration of Les Dawson and he would appear in clip form (Misleading Cases) for the Alastair Sim tribute.

7 May – Cleese would return, along with Michael Palin, to celebrate the genius of The Goons – with Palin describing Milligan's comic undertones by explaining that after a while you have to become desperate about the human condition; you can't always laugh at it.

17 April – *Ken Hom's Hot Wok* cookery show welcomes John Cleese as its guest, filmed on the last day's shoot for *Fierce Creatures* with its star tucking into vegetarian snacks alongside children on the set. Explaining that *Death Fish 2* couldn't stay as the title because it had absolutely no connection to the plot, Cleese got a further, belated plug for his classic film.

Following the huge success of *Twelve Monkeys,* Terry Gilliam is considered Hollywood-friendly after years in independent struggle. With director Alex Cox having a clash of personalities with Johnny Depp on the set of *Love and Drugs in Las Vegas* Terry Gilliam was approached as a quick directing sub.

Updated news of Joe Dante's big screen version of the classic Bill Bixby television series *My Favourite Martian* reveals that John Cleese is being considered for the friendly alien part (after the short-listed Martin Short had been shorted). Rumours abound that John Lithgow wants Cleese to play his brother in *Third Rock from the Sun.*

29 April – at the Royal Albert Hall Lenny Henry introduces 'the very funny indeed' Michael Palin to present the BAFTA award for Best Comedy series to *Only Fools & Horses* and Woody Allen, accepting a BAFTA fellowship, expresses honour at being associated with such greats of British comedy as Alastair Sim, Alec Guinness, Peter Sellers and the '*Monty Python* guys'.

Jim Carrey, interviewed about *Liar, Liar* by Richard Jobson on The Movie Channel, reveals that when he acts suppressed tension he thinks of John Cleese – illustrated via a clip of *Python*'s manic dirty fork chef.

Sky Movies run a series of thematic trailers and one based around headwear features a brief clip of Michael Palin from *And Now For Something Completely Different* – proclaiming 'I've got a hat!' Palin attends the David Bowie launch for *Blimey!* – a book in celebration of new British artists, appears with Chris Evans on *TFI Friday* and prematurely plugged *Full Circle* on Michael Parkinson's Radio 2 show (22 June).

Libby Purves interviews Palin for *Radio Times* (23-29 August) and kickstarts their, by now, expected series of extracts from his travel book in the following issue. The show itself is finally aired from 7 September.

The ultimate laser disc for *Python* fans – *Life of Brian* – is released in a special edition featuring the original trailer, deleted scenes (including 'Sheep' and Otto) and, best of all, audio commentary from Cleese, Gilliam, Idle, Jones and Palin.

12 May – Terry Jones appears on the first ever Ruby Wax discussion programme, *Ruby* (BBC2), talking about the difference in comedy across Europe alongside Eddie Izzard and a clutch of Euro-clowns. Jones wallowed in memories of filming *Python* in German, recalls the 30-year-old classic Slapstick and seems genuinely embarrassed to be

feted by almost every other guest on the show. The Holland chappie expresses nervousness simply to be sitting next to him, while familiar Pythonphile Izzard continues to use Python as a benchmark for everything. The Paramount Comedy Channel headline every Python show as one of their flagship presentations with bizarre Burt Kwouk commercials, Tilly Vosburgh's sex-obsessed, John Cleese besotted viewer and an entire Python day on 24 May with television rarities, screenings of Life, Bowl, Jabberwocky and more Python episodes than you can shake a stick at. At Cannes it is announced that, 15 years after the original, plans are afoot for Time Bandits II. John Cleese and Sean Connery have expressed interest in reprising their roles and Danny DeVito is keen to jump aboard. Best of all, Terry Gilliam was up for writing and directing duties. Cleese began filming Michael Winner's comedy blood fest Parting Shots with Joanna Lumley.

June – Cleese, Gilliam, Idle, Jones and Palin meet at the Cliveden Hotel in Berkshire to discuss serious plans for a Monty Python reunion. With overnight discussion and talking towards lunchtime the team survivors considered a stage show, performance in Las Vegas and even another film, but all plans are on ice in light of the five's heavy work load and it looks likely than the long-awaited reunion may only come about for Python's 30th anniversary in 1999.

10 August – Michael Palin talks about his favourite children's book on The Bookworm, BBC1.

Loaded features an excellent Michael Holden interview with John Cleese detailing his minute irritations with Fawlty's Germans, an affectionate memory of Peter Cook and a fascinating insight into Peter Sellers.

Palin plugs Full Circle with a sense of unease on Channel 5's The Jack Docherty Show and This Morning.

The Pythons invade Saturday Night Live for the first time in ages when John Cleese and Michael Palin forgetfully stumble through the almighty Dead Parrot sketch. Palin's Full Circle promotions takes in GLR and Johnnie Walker's Radio 2 show (17 September, complete with Milliganesque voices and

thoughts on George Harrison's un-broadcastable version of Guantanamera). 16 September – Brian Hall dies of cancer at the age of 59. Although his career encompassed co-writing Made It Ma for the Royal Court, film work opposite Bob Hoskins in The Long Good Friday and character work on television (Softly, Softly/Emmerdale Farm/Crocodile Shoes) his most celebrated work remains as Terry the chef in Fawlty Towers, series 2. A good friend of Cleese, Hall wrote wondering when his Rolls Royce from royalties was arriving – Cleese send him a model car by return of post.

John Cleese is featured on a set of stamps celebrating great comedians - others in the set include Jackie Gleason and Sid James. Terry Jones contributes to the surreal Omnibus celebration of Vic Reeves and Bob Mortimer (21 Sept). Michael Palin writes the foreword for Dad's Army – A Celebration by Richard Webber (Virgin).

1 October – Python's camping it up soldiers appear briefly alongside chunks of Williams, Howerd, Grayson and Everett in Bob Monkhouse's salute to camp comedy, What A Performance! ITV. 2 October – Michael Palin guests on Clive Anderson – All Talk (BBC1) plugging Full Circle, injecting Peter Cookian insight into Fierce Creatures and delighting in Monty Python memories – pretty much dismissing any truth in the reunion rumours.

The Knight and the Squire by Terry Jones, published by Pavilion. John Cleese's cameo crops up in The Last of the Summer Wine Selection Box and a vintage interview appears in The Wogan Years.

Royal Mail unveil plans to release a set of six British comedian stamps. Graham Chapman is on the shortlist but Michael Palin spoke for everyone: 'Hancock would have to be one of them, but beyond him it's difficult to say.'

Everyman kickstarts their new series on 16 November with Divine Comedy, a look at religion in humour, devoting a huge chunk to Monty Python's Life of Brian. Clips from Monty Python's Flying Circus are joined by everyone from Dick Emery to Rowan Atkinson. John Cleese is rumoured to have nailed his flag to Girl Power with a cameo role in The Spice Girls' big screen venture Spice

World: The Movie, although in the end he didn't join in the fun underthe direction of Fawlty series two's Bob Spiers. However, Cleese does provide the voice of the Ape in Disney's George of the Jungle. A laser disc special edition of Time Bandits is compiled for a January 1998 release. Terry Gilliam, Michael Palin and John Cleese record an audio commentary. A one-off edition of the BBC Scotland arts show Ex-S – Palin on Redpath – sees Michael on another journey, this time taking in the French Riviera and Glasgow in search of Anne Redpath's inspiration for a painting which hangs on his own wall (Broadcast 15 December, director Eleanor Yule/Producer Richard Downes). Michael Palin takes part in a BBC Internet interview and, amid much discussion of Full Circle, addresses the oft asked question concerning a Python reunion. Convinced it will happen very soon, the get-together is almost certainly planned to take place in America.

We're not satirical at all; the only intention of the show is to be funny, to make people laugh!
MONTY PYTHON   December 1969

VIDEOS

The Adventures of Baron Munchausen (Cinema Club CC7144)
American Friends (VV1081)
And Now For Something Completely Different (Cinema Club CC 7149)
Around the World in 80 Days with Michael Palin (BBCV4376)
The Big Picture (20-20 Vision NVT 11456)
Brazil (SO35636)
Clockwise (SO38003)
Consuming Passions (Vestron VA17251)
Doctor In Trouble (VC3458)
Doctor Who – City of Death (BBCV4492)
East Of The Moon (Based on Fairy Tales By Terry Jones) – The Island of the Purple Fruit, Some Day, Boodle-Dum-Dee, The Fly-By-Night Virgin VVC 533
East Of The Moon – An Old Fashioned Day In The Country, Think Before You Speak, The Witch and the Rainbow Cat, The Sea Tiger Virgin VCC 534
Erik the Viking (2201)
Fawlty Towers: The Germans (BBCV4000) (Also features The Builders and Wedding Party)

Fawlty Towers: The Psychiatrist (BBCV4001)
Fawlty Towers: The Kipper and the Corpse (BBCV4002) also featuring Waldorf Salad and The Gourmet Night
Fawlty Towers: Basil the Rat (BBCV4003) also featuring Communication Problems and The Anniversary
A Fish Called Wanda (MGM/UA SO51247)
The Fisher King (Cinema Club CC 7263)
G.B.H. – Episodes 1-3 (VVD854)
G.B.H. – Episodes 4-7 (VVD855)
The Goodies and the Beanstalk (also features The End & Bunfight at the O.K. Tea Rooms) BBCV 5370
Great Railway Journeys – Michael Palin (BBCV5223)
How To Irritate People (CVI1143)
It's Marty (BBCV 5360)
Jabberwocky (4270)
John Cleese's First Farewell Performance (SO51684)
Mary Shelley's Frankenstein (Columbia Tristar CVR 31976)
Missing Pieces (Columbia Tristar CVT 19770)
Monty Python's Flying Circus – Series 1 episodes 1-4 (BMG 74321 19332 3)
Monty Python's Flying Circus – Series 1 episodes 5-7 (BMG 74321 19333 3)
Monty Python's Flying Circus – Series 1 episodes 8-10 (BMG 74321 19334 3)
Monty Python's Flying Circus – Series 1 episodes 11-13 (BMG 74321 19335 3)
Monty Python's Flying Circus – Series 2 episodes 1-4 (BBCV 4145)

Monty Python's Flying Circus – Series 2 episodes 5-7 (BBCV 4146)
Monty Python's Flying Circus – Series 2 episodes 8-10 (BBCV 4147)
Monty Python's Flying Circus – Series 2 episodes 11-13 (BBCV 4148)
Monty Python's Flying Circus – Series 3 episodes 1-4 (BMG 74321 20543 3)
Monty Python's Flying Circus – Series 3 episodes 5-7 (BMG 74321 20544 3)
Monty Python's Flying Circus – Series 3 episodes 8-10 (BMG 74321 20545 3)
Monty Python's Flying Circus – Series 3 episodes 11-13 (BMG 74321 20546 3)
Monty Python – Episodes 1-3 (BMG 74321 20547 3)
Monty Python – Episodes 4-6 (BMG 74321 20548 3)
Monty Python's Life of Brian (CBS Fox 2101)
Monty Python's The Meaning of Life/The Crimson Permanent Assurance (CIC VHR 1093)
National Lampoon's European Vacation (SO11521)
Nuns On The Run (CBS Fox 1830)
The Odd Job (MIA V3293)
Parrot Sketch Not Included (2940)
Personal Services (0837803)
Pole to Pole with Michael Palin (BBCV4880)
A Private Function (Lumiere LUM2146)
The Rutles – All You Need Is Cash (Telstar TVE 6003)
The Secret Policeman's Ball (CVR16920)
The Secret Policeman's Biggest Ball (CVR16921)
The Secret Policeman's Early Bits

(Columbia Tristar CVR 21432)
The Secret Policeman's Other Ball (CVR16917)
The Secret Policeman's Third Ball – The Comedy (VVD271)
Silverado (Cinema Club CC7129)
Spies Like Us (SO11533)
Time Bandits (CBS Fox 2102)
Tracey Ullman – A Class Act (VC6295)
Twelve Monkeys/The Hamster Factor & Other Tales of Twelve Monkeys (Polygram 0544183)
Yellowbeard (Virgin VVD 566)
The Young Ones – Nasty (also features Bambi and Time) BBCV 4426

ADDRESSES

The Monty Python Fan Club – P.O. Box 365, University Station, Syracuse, New York 13210, United States of America

Monty Python Office
Python (Monty) Pictures Ltd
The Linen Hall
Room 537–538
162–168 Regent Street
London
W1R 5TB

BOOKS

And Now For Something Completely Trivial: The Monty Python Trivia and Quiz Book by Kim 'Howard' Johnson
Cleese Encounters by Jonathan Margolis, Chapman Publishers Ltd, 1992
The First 200 Years of Monty Python by Kim 'Howard' Johnson
From Fringe to Flying Circus by Roger Wilmut, London, 1980
The Laughtermakers by David Nathan (chapter 10 – Monty Python's Flying Breakthrough), Peter Owen Ltd, 1971
Life Before and After Monty Python; The Solo Flights of the Flying Circus by Kim 'Howard' Johnson, 1993
Life of Python by George Perry, 1983, Pavilion Books
Monty Python: The Case Against by Robert Hewison, London, 1981
Monty Python: A Chronological Listing of the Troupe's Creative Output and Articles and Reviews about Them, 1969-1989 by Douglas L. McCall, 1992
Monty Python: Complete and Utter Theory of the Grotesque edited by John O. Thompson, BFI, 1982